Readin; 0
*tle

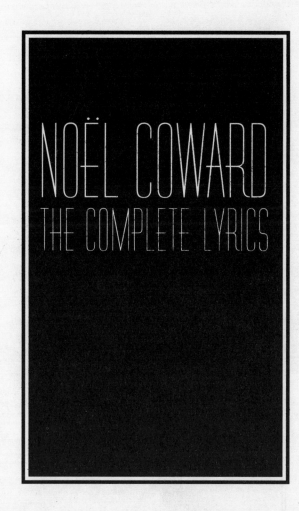

NOËL COWARD
THE COMPLETE LYRICS

NOËL COWARD
THE COMPLETE LYRICS

EDITED AND ANNOTATED BY BARRY DAY

DESIGNED BY BERNARD SCHLEIFER

methuen

For Graham

The Keeper of the Flame

Published by Methuen 1998

1 3 5 7 9 10 8 6 4 2

First published in the United Kingdom in 1998
by Methuen Publishing Limited
20 Vauxhall Bridge Road, London SW1V 2SA

Random House Australia (Pty) Limited
20 Alfred Street, Milsons Point, Sydney, New South Wales 2061, Australia
Random House New Zealand Limited
18 Poland Road, Glenfield, Auckland 10, New Zealand
Random House South Africa (Pty) Limited
Endulini, 5A Jubilee Rd, Parktown 2193, South Africa

Methuen Publishing Limited Reg. No. 3543167

A CIP catalogue record for this book is available
from the British Library

ISBN 0 413 73230 4

Printed and bound in Great Britain by
Butler & Tanner Ltd, Frome and London

CONTENTS

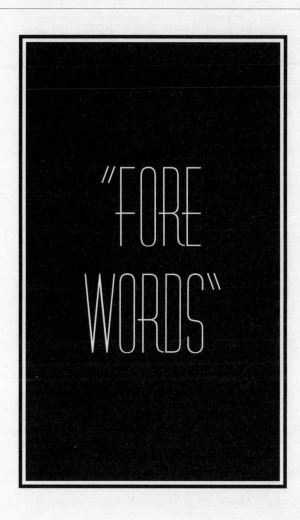

"FORE WORDS"

"The best of his kind since W. S. Gilbert."   —TERENCE RATTIGAN

". . . the songs we sang to our girls driving back in the red MG from the Thames pub on a summer night in 1936."   —JOHN WHITING

"He wrote with style, sang with style, painted with style, and even smoked a cigarette with a style that belonged exclusively to him . . . Even one of his lesser operettas . . . contains more charm, skill and originality than fifty musical plays put together by men specializing in particular fields."   —RICHARD RODGERS

"His ballads were literate, graceful, and glistened with the polish of Coward's readily identifiable language. His comedy lyrics were the funniest of anyone to come down the lyrical pike, be they witty, silly in the best sense, outrageous or glibly cynical. Of Noël, the pure and simple fact is that he was the most original composer/lyricist to emerge in England during the post-war years . . . IBM cannot create another Noël Coward."   —ALAN JAY LERNER

"Noël Coward was not an influence on my adolescence. He *was* my adolescence . . . I combed our Alabama Public Library for every scrap I could find on him, then tried to write like him, sing like him, dress like him; maybe I was trying to *be* Noël Coward! I never succeeded but he made my life funnier, warmer, richer in every way."   —HUGH MARTIN

"With grace, wit, talent and elegance, Noël Coward has impeccably defined his own era."   —CY COLEMAN

"The wit and wisdom of Noël Coward's lyrics will be as lively and contemporary in 100 years' time as they are today."   —TIM RICE

When Jerome Kern was told by fellow songwriter, Arthur Schwartz that a tune he was composing—"Who's Complaining?"—was a direct lift from "Mad Dogs and Englishmen," he replied—"I know. But I'm not stealing. I'm just quoting."

"Sarcastic or sentimental, bitchy or sweet, there has never been anyone quite like him!"
—JOHN KANDER

"When I first met Noël I was surprised to find he had a rhyming dictionary. 'If it's good enough for Cole,' he said, 'it's good enough for me.' Later he gave me one as a present. Inside he had written: *Do not let this aid to rhyming/Bitch your talent or your timing.*"
It's advice I've always tried to follow. . ."
—LIONEL BART

"There will never be another Noël Coward. But every lyric writer worthy of the name should read, mark, learn, and inwardly digest the legacy he left us . . . Noël gave me one lesson: 'Once you have the melody, let it lead the words. Do it the other way around and you're in trouble." He was, as usual, dead right!"
—SANDY WILSON

"'Parisian Pierrot' was the signature tune of the late 1920s."
—CECIL BEATON

"Was anyone ever more romantic, witty, and charming than Noël Coward? His was more than 'just a talent to amuse'."
—JERRY HERMAN

"He was always ready to help young songwriters but he was prepared to criticise as well as praise. When he came round to see me after *Salad Days*, the first thing he said was—'Well done, dear boy. Tunes! Tunes! Tunes!' Coming from him I was very flattered."
—JULIAN SLADE

"I adored Noël Coward. He was unique. Not a word he wrote was without charm, wit, sophistication, and romanticism."
—ADOLPH GREEN

INTRODUCTION

THE GREAT POPULAR LYRICISTS OF THE TWENTIETH CENTURY CAN BE COUNTED ON THE fingers of one hand—Lorenz Hart, Ira Gershwin, Cole Porter, Oscar Hammerstein and Noël Coward. Anyone anxious to argue the case for Irving Berlin, Stephen Sondheim, or anyone else for that matter, needs to open another hand . . .

The first five commanded a range of styles that enabled them to change mental key between literate sophistication and emotional simplicity and to do so apparently at will. With that as a qualification, if you really must now swap Hammerstein for Sondheim— feel free! But, in more ways than one, nobody touches Coward. Terence Rattigan called him "the best of his kind since W. S. Gilbert."

Of the other four, the one he resembles most closely is Porter in that he wrote the words *and* the music. Their sensibilities were close, too, and there was a friendly rivalry between "Noël and Cole" that often led them to make reference to each other's work in their songs. In *The Man Who Came to Dinner* Porter introduced a parody Coward number called "What Am I To Do?" sung by a Noël clone, Beverly Carlton and credited to "Noël Porter." When chronicling the doings of the wayward Nina, who "refused to begin the beguine when they besought her to," Noël in return had her "curse the man who taught her to"—and for good measure "she cursed Cole Porter too." In the cabaret phase of his career, of course, Noël was to actually "borrow" Cole's "Let's Do It," which he paraphrased with great success.

Noël was a great believer in the conditioning power of context and considered himself fortunate to have made his entrance when he did:

"I was born into a generation that still took light music seriously. The lyrics and melodies of operetta, musical comedy, Gilbert and Sullivan were hummed and strummed into my consciousness at an early age. My father sang them, my mother played them, my nurse, Emma breathed them through her teeth while she was washing me, undressing me and putting me to bed . . . I couldn't help composing tunes even if I wished to, and ever since I was a little boy they have dropped into my mind unbidden—and often in the most unlikely of circumstances!"

"I can only suppose that the compulsion to make rhymes was born in me," he wrote towards the end of his life. "There is no time I can remember when I was not fascinated by words "going together"; Lewis Carroll, Edward Lear, Beatrix Potter, all fed my childish passion, in addition to all the usual nursery rhymes that the flesh is heir to . . ."

Some early attempts at verse, "when I was rushing headlong towards puberty" he found generally discouraging. "Even my own memory, which is retentive to an extraordinary degree, has refused to hold on to them." He confessed that the competition provided by "the feverish industry" of his childhood friend and fellow child actor, Esmé Wynne, might also have had something to do with his early retirement from realms poetic. Instead he tried his hand at writing songs:

"I had the edge on her because, being a natural musician, I found it easier to write to tunes jangling in my head than to devote myself to mastering iambics, trochees, anapaests, or dactyls. If a tune came first I would set words to it. If the words came first I would set them to music at the piano.

"This latter process almost invariably necessitated changing the verse to fit the tune. If you happen to be born with a built-in sense of rhythm, any verse you write is apt to fall into a set pattern and remain within its set pattern until it is completed. This is perfectly satisfactory from the point of view of reading or reciting, but when you attempt to set your pattern to a tune, either the tune gives in and allows itself to be inhibited by the rigidity of your original scansion or it rebels, refuses to be dominated and displays some ideas of its own, usually in the form of unequal lines and unexpected accents. This is why I very seldom write a lyric first and set it to music later."

It was a philosophy he was to maintain throughout his career. The young Sandy Wilson was given the advice: "Don't write all the lyric before the music. The lyric imprisons the melody. Let the music be free."

The exceptions, presumably, were the comic songs, where the density of word play tended to dictate a set pattern that became almost formulaic.

Noël could say this with the benefit of the hindsight of a complete career to review, for much of which he did precisely as he said. But to begin with he was only too glad to collaborate with anyone who would help him write a song that someone might sing. While he was still in his teens his precocious promise secured him a contract with Darewski Music, where Max Darewski or Doris Joel put music to several of his lyrics. In one of his early plays, *I'll Leave It To You* (1919) we find him providing the music only to a song written by—the ubiquitous Esmé Wynne. However, in that same World War I period he had also written his first complete song, "It's the Peach" (later "Forbidden Fruit") and after the 1920s collaboration was rare, unless circumstances forced it on him. He was to find that "the best lyrics I have written are those which have developed more or less at the same time as the music" and he was determined to give himself as much of the freedom to work that way as possible.

For the greater part of his working life he was to enjoy a professional cameraderie that existed between songwriters who—though professional competitors—also constituted an instinctive mutual admiration society that surely spurred them on to greater individual effort. In the 1920s and 30s the work of Jerome Kern, Cole Porter, Rodgers and Hart, and the Gershwins was as well known on Shaftesbury Avenue as it was on

Noël and Esmé, 1915.

Broadway and it was by no means unusual for one of their shows to start life there. Accident of birthplace was no barrier to membership of this international community. Porter could parody Coward, Coward would paraphrase Porter. Kern and Hammerstein would dedicate "The Last Time I Saw Paris" to Coward, who would write "We Are Living In A Changing World" for Kern. Porter would ask Coward for help when frozen on a lyric for "Siberia." Not since the Elizabethan and Jacobean playwrights poured out their plays has there been such a renaissance of popular entertainment.

There was to be one rather sad coda. On vacation in Haiti, Noël was thrilled to find that fellow guests at his hotel were Mr. and Mrs. Irving Berlin. One evening he plucked up courage to sit down at the hotel piano and—in Berlin's presence—played a selection of his idol's work. A delighted but ageing Berlin asked him who had written a particular song he was playing. "Why, *you* did, sir," replied a saddened Noël. The song was "White Christmas"—and an era was over.

As one by one they left the stage, there proved to be no qualified new candidates for this particular "club." Talented songwriters, yes, but—just as the demise of the Hollywood studio system had changed the nature of making movies—so the economics of putting on a show curtailed the opportunities to stage a "book" musical. The rise of television as a medium with its emphasis on appealing to largely illiterate youth changed the emphasis of popular song. The "sound" took over from the words and music and only now—at the end of the century—are there signs of a balance being re-established. Ironically, one of those signs was an album of Coward songs re-interpreted by contemporary "pop" artistes who now hail him as the first British "global" talent in popular music. Neil Tennant of The Pet Shop Boys said: "Before the Beatles there was Noël Coward . . . He is such an icon of English style that people forget what a good songwriter he was—our Cole Porter." He has been called "the first English rapper"— a tribute which would undoubtedly have inspired the raising of a quizzical Coward eyebrow.

For almost fifty years the words and music would find each other—sometimes dropping into his mind unbidden, ("Suddenly a new and lovely tune appeared"), more often by sitting down and applying himself like the professional he was. Throughout his career his output was consistently varied. There were songs for revues—for the thirty or so years the form remained popular. There were musicals and here Noël publicly aligned himself with Hammerstein's view that "the perfect lyric for a musical should be inspired directly by the story and the characters contained in it. In fact, ideally, a song in a musical should carry on whenever the dialogue leaves off. Apart from one or two rare exceptions I concur with him entirely . . . any young lyric writer should learn early that if he wishes to write a successful 'book show' he must eschew irrelevance and stick to the script."

And, of course, there were the songs that just popped up, inspired by a particular event, place or person. Many of them would eventually find their home in a show, particularly during the heyday of revue. Noël tended to believe that there was some sort of natural balance to these things and, like many of his fellow lyricists and composers, would frequently try a number more than once in different contexts until he found the right fit. "Sail Away," for instance, he considered too good a song to lose in *Ace of Clubs* so he eventually wrote a whole show around it. Other numbers that he felt had received less than their just desserts would find their way into his own night club act and take on a whole new life of their own. There were many professional performers who felt

Irving Berlin

12

Frank Sinatra and Noël Coward backstage at The Desert Inn, 1955.

that Noël became by far the best interpreter of his own material. During his 1955 Las Vegas engagement Sammy Davis would exhort his own audience at the end of his act to go across the street "and see The Master at work," while Frank Sinatra went on radio to tell the world that, if they wanted "to hear how songs should be sung, get the hell over to the Desert Inn!"

During his lifetime Noël was nervous about committing his lyrics to print, feeling that—divorced from the context of performance—something was inevitably lost. Since his plays were written to be performed, Shakespeare may well have shared the concern, had he lived to see them published. In both cases the concern would have been misplaced. Without taking the comparison any further, in the case of Coward, interest in his work has only increased since his death in 1973. Perhaps, intuitively, he sensed that it would: "After I am dead, it is quite another matter. If at that time some yet unborn biographer should feel that he might acquire a more psychologically accurate knowledge of my character by reading them, he is welcome to if he can find them."

Well, the purpose of *The Complete Lyrics* is not to be Dr. Freud's Casebook. If the reader glimpses more of the man through the words, all well and good. What I have tried to do is to set at least some of the songs in the context of their time, to piece together at least some of the clues as to how they were written and performed and with what result. Many of the words will spring from the page and into the ear, complete with music, proving once again that it is, indeed, "Extraordinary how potent cheap music is." Others will show where an idea was born that would be developed later. All of them, I trust, will bring to life one aspect or another of the professional and persistent development of a man who was arguably the greatest writer of songs Britain has yet produced, and certainly a man with infinitely more than just "a talent to amuse."

BARRY DAY

MUM'S SUITCASE

1916-1919

Mum—Violet Coward.

VIOLET COWARD—WHOM POSTERITY PRAISE!—WAS A hoarder and, fortunately, she passed the trait on to her son, Noël. Without "Mum's Suitcase," now safely stowed away in the attic at Les Avants, we should have little or no record of his apprenticeship as a lyricist.

In the suitcase are two notebooks filled with Noël's distinctive and occasionally indecipherable handwriting. Read one way, the first contains part of an unfinished novel, *Sleuth Hounds*, while the second has a play, *The Unattainable*, which is notable for the first mention of a character called Elvira; a comedy scene about taking drugs, which reads like a cross between *The Vortex* and *Private Lives* and some early epigrams in the process of polishing . . .

—Man always sighs after the unattainable.
—What about Woman?
—Oh, Woman never admits even to herself that anything is unattainable

The date on that particular piece is May 15th, 1918.

Turn the notebooks upside down and on the reverse side you are in the world of the early lyrics. Many of them are clearly "fair copies," others show later corrections and there are a number of "dummy lyrics." Even some of those not specifically marked as such may well fall into this category. Every lyricist whose work has been seriously analysed can be seen to have used this method to fix the metre and

emphases in his mind. For Noël, who never learned to write music, this would have been an early and permanent necessity.

According to the dating, the thin grey notebook would appear to cover the period from 1916 to 1917 and the fat black one from c.1918 to 1919 but it would be as rash to base conclusions on the running order as it would to have assumed that the First Folio represented the order in which Shakespeare wrote his plays, since he certainly didn't start with *The Tempest*. There are, in any case, other extant songs from the period that *don't* appear in the notebooks. ("Mum's songs" are marked #)

What the songs *en masse* do reveal, though, are some of the influences the tyro songwriter was struggling to master or assimilate, as he developed a style of his own.

The predominant influence in the early years was undoubtedly his friend and fellow child actor, Esmé Wynne. The two became inseparable, inventing an emotional universe of their own, a flavour of which can be gleaned from the nicknames they gave each other. He teased her about being stodgy (Stoj), while she called him podgy (Poj).

Esmé (Noël recalled in *Present Indicative*) was "determined to be a writer, an ambition which filled me with competitive fervour. She wrote poems. Reams and reams of them . . . alive with elves, mermaids, leafy glades and Pan (a good deal of Pan). Not to be outdone in artistic endeavour, I set many

of the poems to music." Despite his ambitions, he was not particularly pleased with his output: "My actual achievements up to date amounted to very little. I had written quite a lot in spare moments . . . plays, singly and in collaboration with Stoj, short stories and verses and one meretricious full-length novel." In this he attempted to out-Pan her by writing *Cherry Pan*, the story of Peter Pan's daughter, which "contrived to be arch, and elfin, and altogether nauseating, for nearly thirty thousand words."

The notebooks reflect the influence of Esmé's, shall we say, ethereal sensibility, as Noël dutifully copied out several of her lyrics. There are titles like "Faith," "Temptation" and a love duet beginning . .

Through the tumbled flowers
Of dead years . . .

. . . a song called "Love's Lily Garden" and a whole sequence called "Songs of the Sea" (which includes songs of the "Shells," the "Seagull" and the "Merman"). Reading them reminds one of P.G. Wodehouse's immortal character, Madeline Bassett who (Bertie Wooster always recalled) thought "the stars were God's daisy chain."

It's encouraging to find Noël casting what would become the quizzical Coward gaze on the elfin universe in a slightly later lyric, the title of which, admittedly, does not augur well . . .

16

*THERE'S A PIXIE IN MY GARDEN(#)

There's a Pixie in the garden
And he's dancing in the Sun,
While a thrush sings lonely music in the tree.
He'll go dancing through the meadows
Till his little life be done—
A butterfly existence, you'll agree!
He never has a worry,
He never has a care,
He's happy all the while
Because he's free.
Oh, Pixie, as I watch you
Flitting gaily here and there,
How I wish that I were you and you were me!

Esmé Wynne.

Now that Pixie in the garden
Is a lazy little thing,
There's really lots of work for him to do.
He ought to get some mushrooms
And make a Fairy ring
And straighten out the Flower
Petals, too.
He's so very idle,
He goes darting all about
And lets the others do the work, it's true.
Oh, Pixie, as I watch you
Darting swiftly in and out,
I wish that you were me and I was you!

The pantheistic irreverence seemed to do the relationship no permanent harm and there was at least one major collaboration waiting to happen.

*   *   *

Meanwhile, the summer of 1917 brought a turning point for Noël as a lyricist in his own right. While playing in *Wild Heather* at the Gaiety Theatre, Manchester, he ran into Ivor Novello, who was also appearing in the city.

"... I tried to adjust my mind to the shock" (he wrote in *Present Indicative*) "My illusion of this romantic handsome youth who had composed "Keep the Home Fires Burning" drooped and died and lay in the gutter between the tram lines and the kerb ... I had caught him in a completely "off" moment. He was not sitting at a grand piano. He was not in naval uniform. The eager Galahad expression which distinguished every photograph of him was lacking. His face was yellow and he had omitted to shave owing to a morning rehearsal. He was wearing an odd overcoat with an Astrakhan collar and a degraded brown hat, and if he had suddenly produced a violin from somewhere and played the "Barcarole" from *The Tales of Hoffman*, I should have given him threepence from sheer pity."

Nonetheless, acquaintance ripened into "a friendship which has lasted hilariously ... and shows every indication of enduring through any worlds which may lie beyond us, always providing those worlds be as redundant of theatrical jokes and humours as this one is." As early as October of that year Noël is dedicating a song "To I." ...

*AS LONG AS YOU LOVE ME A LITTLE(#)

As long as you love me a little,
As long as I feel you care,
It's all that I ask of life, dear
All through this World of Strife, dear
The Sorrows and Cares
Of a hundred years
Contentedly I would bear.,
If only you'd think of me
Sometimes.
Tho' your love is not all for me,
When we're miles apart
In your dear big heart
Keep just a corner for me.

... and shortly afterwards the two of them are collaborating. The notebook entry reads: "Music by Ivor Novello. Words by Noël Coward" ...

(Novello was to use the music later in *Tails Up!* [1918] with a lyric by Ronald Jeans and Davy Burnaby.)

*ISN'T THERE ANY LITTLE THING?(#)

Music by Ivor Novello

VERSE I   If dear, you but realised
           How you are idealised,
           You've set me the lesson of love to learn.
           If you'd only care for me,
           Life's day would be fair for me,
           Shadows all would vanish away never to return.

REFRAIN   Isn't there any little thing
           That I can do for you?
           Isn't there any little thing
           To show I care?
           Can't you see I love you
           Madly?
           Cupid's dart has got me
           Badly.

           All life with you I'd like to share,
           Isn't there any little thing

That I can say to you?
Isn't there any little way
To prove I'm true?
And whenever you may go away,
I shall always be nearby to say—
Is there any thing that I can do for you!

But before that Manchester had revealed another surprise. He met the composer and impresario, Max Darewski and in August 1917 is writing to tell his mother the outcome of that meeting . . .

"My Darling,
At the moment I am nearly mad with excitement . . . I am collaborating with Max Darewski in a new song. I wrote the lyric yesterday after breakfast, I hummed it to him in the Midland lounge at 12 oc, we at once rushed up to his private room and he put harmonies to it, there were some other people there, when they had sung it over once or twice, Max leapt off the piano stool and danced for joy and said it was going to take London by storm! We are putting the verse to music this morning, it is to be published next week and probably sung by Lee White or Phyllis Dare! . . . I shall probably make a lot of money out of it, it is called When You Come Home on Leave, written and composed by Noël Coward and Max Darewski. You see, he is one of the most influential men in town, he owns three theatres . . ."

In writing this particular song Noël was consciously seeking—not for the last time—to emulate Ivor Novello. In 1914 Ivor had written the definitive patriotic song of World War I in "Keep The Home Fires Burning." Noël's ambition, however, would have to wait until the next war with "London Pride." "When You Come Home" was never published and on the manuscript he had scribbled: "Good old pot-boiling words, but what of it?" as if in recognition that the talent was still to match the ambition . . .

*WHEN YOU COME HOME ON LEAVE (1917)

Dear one, I want you just to know
That I am carrying on
Tho' life's at best a dreary show
Now that you have gone.
I'd like you just to realise
That tho' we're far apart
Where ere you go on land or sea
You have with you my heart.
Tho' days are dull and drear
You need not have the slightest fear
For—

When you come home on leave
I'll still be waiting
Waiting to greet you with a smile
To charm away your pain
And make you feel again
That life is going to be worthwhile.
I love you so my heart is simply yearning
And this is what I want you to believe
That tho' sorrows there may be
There'll be one glad day for me
On the day you come home on leave.

I dream of you the whole night through
I think of you all day
I'm weary for the sight of you
You've been so long away
The weeks for me are very sad
And happy days are few
Remember when you're feeling bad
That I am lonely too.
I dream of you the whole night through
I think of you all day
I'm weary for the sight of you
You've been so long away
The weeks for me are very sad
And happy days are few
Remember when you're feeling bad
That I am lonely too.
But as I gaze across the sea
I know that you'll return to me
And—
When you come home on leave . . . etc.

He went on to tell his mother that another song, "Bertha from Balham" was to be placed with one of his favourite singers, Margaret Cooper and a later profile in *Talk of the Town* (23 January 1918) noted that Miss Cooper was, indeed, "singing one of his songs, many of which have been published."

*BERTHA FROM BALHAM (1917)

Bertha lived at Balham,
She was always most refined
And like Caesar's wife was quite
Above suspicion.
She assisted in a Draper's shop
And often friends unkind

18

Said it wasn't quite a ladylike position!
But, mind you, Bertha didn't care
'Cos she never found the business very puzzling.
For she'd but to wink her eye
And deluded men would buy
Yards of *crêpe de chine* instead of butter muslin.

Bertha from Balham was wonderful,
Bertha from Balham was *great*
And when behind the counter she served
She looked like a Fashion-Plate.
When passionate males gave a scorching look
And cried—"Darling, come be mine!"
She coyly opened her order book
And said—"Sign, please, sign!"

Bertha lived at Balham
Bertha was a peach.
Now and then her beauty quite bereft the men
Of speech
As a little worker
Bertha did her bit
Selling dainty underwear to forms it didn't fit.
She was just a working girl
Struggling to earn her pay
Tho' men came wooing
And found nothing doing,
They never went empty away.

Bertha from Balham was sweet,
Bertha from Balham was neat.
Tho' frequently her customers
Attempted monkey tricks,
She managed to protect herself
From nine o'clock to six.
Flirting was all very fine
But the moment fellows overstepped the line
With an old fashioned look
She'd just open her book
And say—"Sign, please, sign!"

Bertha had a hobby
And on early closing day
She'd attire herself according to the Fashion
Then she'd dally forth enraptured to
Some London matinée,
Because autograph collecting was her passion.
Then she would pay a half a crown
And rush into the front row of a pit
And she quite forgot her cares
In watching Owen Nares
Though she didn't worship Doris Keane a bit!

Bertha from Balham was quite sublime
And when the performance was o'er
She waited long on the dusty kerb

Till her idol would come out of the door.
She would say—"I love your wavy hair,
It sends thrills all down my spine."
Then she'd open her little autograph book
And say—"Sign, please, sign!"

Bertha, growing older, found existence rather
    tame
She decided it was time that she should marry.
She fixed upon a super-knut, Lord Gumpot was
    his name,
Who in her department often used to tarry.
At him she gazed with loving eyes
While behind her hand a giggle she would smother.
He proposed to her one day
In a very ardent way
While she helped him choose a night dress for his
    mother!

Bertha from Balham obtained a ring
And married him right away
And in after life, if she wanted a thing
She'd only got to say—
"I've just seen the sweetest hat, old kid,
It'll make me look divine."
Then she'd scribble a cheque for a
Hundred quid
And say—"Sign, Duck, sign!"

(Alternative ending)
Bertha left the drapers
Under several clouds
Said she couldn't bear the heat
And simply loathed the crowds.
Offers of assistance
She would not accept
She could well afford to wait
Tho' she was never kept.
Soon she got a Government job
Well protected by the Crown
Keeping men standing
For hours on a landing
While she took particulars down.

Bertha from Balham was bright,
Bertha from Balham was right.
She made it clearly understood
Her views were anti-waste
But nobody could possibly deny
That she was chased.
Business and Beauty divine
She managed to combine
When officials got warm
She just flaunted her form
And said—"Sign, please, sign!"

His recollection in greater tranquility was that during this post-1917 period he had "composed a good many songs, and written lyrics for some tunes of Max Darewski's and Doris Joel's." In fact, through Max's good offices he was given a three year contract with a music publishing company owned by Max's brother, Herman, "for lyrics only."

His collaboration with Doris Joel—who preferred to publish under the name "Doris Doris"—was to result in his first program credit in a London theatre.

On June 1st, 1918 André Charlot presented "a musical entertainment in two acts by John Hastings Turner. Music by Philip Braham" at the Comedy Theatre. It was called *Tails Up*. The song was "Peter Pan"—later published by Herman Darewski Music as "The Story of Peter Pan."

The subject was one which—Esmé apart—provided an early thread through Noël's career. As a young actor he had played Slightly opposite Madge Titheradge's Peter. As critic Kenneth Tynan was later to remark: "Noël started as Slightly in *Peter Pan*—and has been wholly in it ever since . . ."

The first night program credited the lyric to "Noël Farque." This was soon amended!

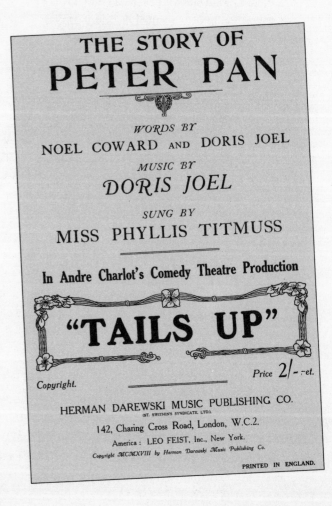

THE STORY OF
PETER PAN

WORDS BY
NOEL COWARD AND DORIS JOEL

MUSIC BY
DORIS JOEL

SUNG BY
MISS PHYLLIS TITMUSS

In Andre Charlot's Comedy Theatre Production

"TAILS UP"

Copyright.   Price 2/- net.

HERMAN DAREWSKI MUSIC PUBLISHING CO.
(ST. SWITHIN'S SYNDICATE, LTD.)
142, Charing Cross Road, London, W.C.2.
America : LEO FEIST, Inc., New York.
Copyright *MCMXVIII* by Herman Darewski Music Publishing Co.

PRINTED IN ENGLAND.

*THE STORY OF PETER PAN (1918)

(Phyllis Titmuss)

If you believe in Fairies, they say,
All thro' your lifetime happy you'll be,
Peter and Wendy both know the way,
That's why they're always children, you see,
Even the Fairies, so I've been told,
Follow the fashions too,
Once they get started, nothing can hold
Them back from a dance that is new.

Peter Pan has learned to do the latest dance,
Wendy too, thought she would like to take a
chance,
Captain Hook was really most disgusted,
Smee and Starky seemed to look quite
flustered
And pretty Tinker Bell,
Said to Peter Pan,
"Clap your hands if you believe in Fairies,
And come and dance as well!"

Even the mermaids in the lagoon,
Tho' they had only tails to wag,
Danced with the pirates under the moon,
Each time they heard that wonderful Rag,
Sometimes at night when ev'rything's still,
They try to sleep in vain,
Peter comes tripping up the hill,
Then off they go dancing again

Peter Pan has learnt to do the latest dance,
Wendy too, thought she would like to take a
chance
J.M. Barrie fainted when he knew it,
Cried, "You really must not do it," Peter Pan,
Said, "If it's wrong for boys to dance
It is most unkind,
And although I said I'd never grow up
I think I'll change my mind."

*   *   *

While J. M. Barrie was an obvious point of reference in the light of Noël's juvenile acting career, A.A. Milne and his saccharine verses about the infant Christopher Robin is less so. One would prefer to think that, in mining for a commercial vein Noël was attracted to Milne's current popular success—and he was dosing *his* saccharine with an ironic pinch of salt . . .

*MEMORIES (1917)

I can remember when I was a little tiny kid
A lot of very mischievous and naughty things I
did.
I recollect that teasing Nurse gave me great
delight
But I remember best my Mummy kissing me
"Goodnight".
She used to creep into the room
And kneel beside the bed
And all the time I said my prayers
She'd softly stroke my head.
I s'pose it's 'cos I'm growing up but anyhow
No one ever comes to kiss me goodnight now.

*   *   *

The first time Noël actually saw his name on the cover of sheet music was for "The Baseball Rag" in 1919 ("Words by Noël Coward, Music by Doris Doris") Noël admitted later that, despite the design of red and blue baseballs flying hither and thither, the song was "not as All-American" as they had both thought at the time . . .

*THE BASEBALL RAG(#)

VERSE 1   I've got a ripping new sensation
There's just no need for hesitation
Baseball's the game that
Makes the world go round.
It gets your heart a-palpitating
You can't sit still.
You'll go mad, you'll go bad, because you'll
never be contented
Until . . .

You do that Raggy Rag
It's just a baseball tune.
And it gets you syncopated mad

Like any old coon
You simply glide along, dear
You never want to lag
It's a cinch, it's a go,
It's a jazz, tally-ho
For that Baseball Rag.
You Rag.

VERSE 2   First do a kind of slashing single,
It sets your hands and feet a-tingle.
There's never been a strut like this before.
Farewell to hesitation waltzes,
Foxtrots goodbye.
Take a chance for a dance that makes you
want to shout

(Spoken) It's a pike, kill the umpire, Hi!
You do that raggy rag,
It's just a baseball tune.
And it gets you syncopated mad like any
old coon.
You simply glide along dear,
You never want to lag.
It's a joy, it's a dream,
It's a yell, it's a scream,
Gee! That Baseball Rag.
You Rag

The notebooks provide an interesting footnote to the song. In addition to an "extra verse" that clearly didn't fit the final form of the song and may well have been a dummy lyric . . .

(Extra Verse)
VERSE   Smiling, you've always got to keep on
Smiling, you've always got to keep on
Laughing, 'cos laughter
Makes the world go
Round.
Smiling, you've always got to keep on
Smiling all day.
It's the best way to keep
Yourself and everybody
Happy all day

Noël compiled a list of these "foreign" American phrases he had to come to terms with . . . He was not, after all, to pay his first visit to the US until 1921.

Texas leaguer
Stealing a single
Nipped it at second
In-field fly
Close at first
Kill the umpire
It's Pike

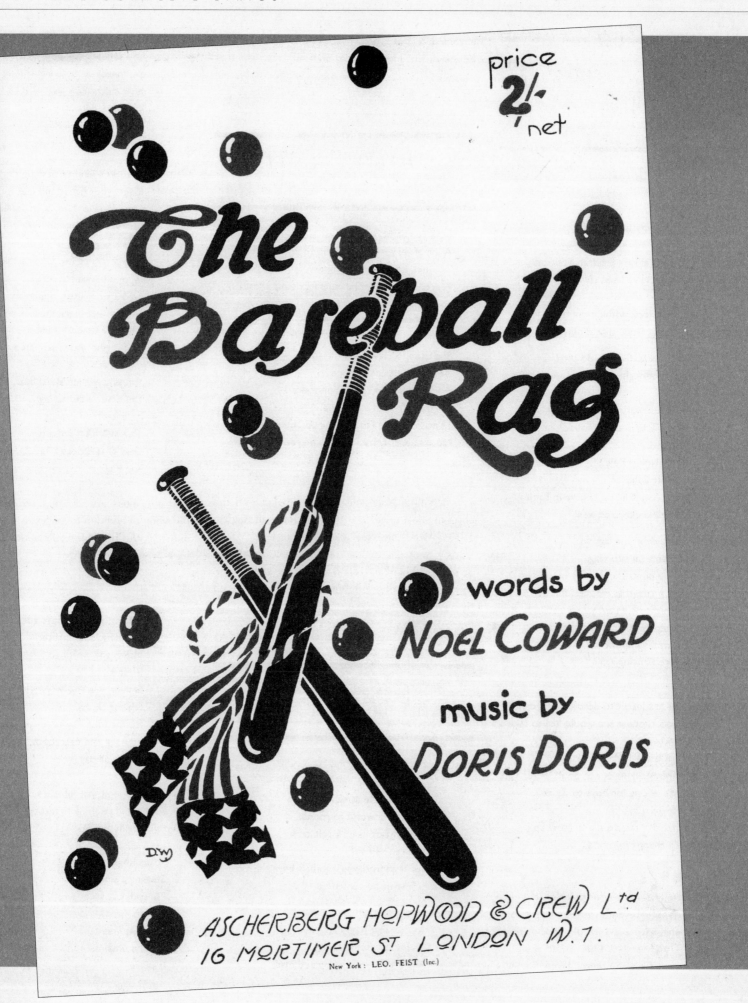

Shake a leg, you old son of a gun

Wind up

Smoke (name for nigger)

The Ball Game

Baseball fans (people who watch)

*   *   *

"Peter Pan" may have been performed first and "The Baseball Rag" published first but . . .

"The first complete lyric I ever wrote," (he records) "was 'Forbidden Fruit' (1916). The perceptive reader will, I am sure, detect, even in this very youthful effort, that unfortunate taint of worldly cynicism which, I am so frequently told, degrades much of my later work . . ." Another title for the song was "Every Little Peach," and when it was first performed in 1924 in a revue called *Yoicks!*, it was called "It's the Peach." By the time it was finally published, it had become—rather more grandly— "Forbidden Fruit," a title it had been given when it was being considered for *London Calling!* (1923)—and even earlier, when a character was meant to sing it in a play, *The Unattainable* (1918), which was never completed and, therefore, never performed.

It was included in *The Noël Coward Song Book* (1953) more as a curiosity than anything else. Another fourteen years later it was in the 1968 Robert Wise film, *Star!*, in a scene where Daniel Massey (Noël's real life godson) re-creates the audition Noël gave for impresario André Charlot. The reality was slightly less glamorous than the Hollywood version.

Bea Lillie recalls in her autobiography, *Every Other Inch a Lady*:

"We were in the middle of a production number involving chorus and singers when Noël walked in, pale and a little bit twitchy. The piano stopped for a short break. Charlot gave me a filthy look when I introduced this very nervous young man and said, "I just want him to play you this song he's written. It's called 'Forbidden Fruit'. You'll *love* it.

"The expression on Uncle André's quizzical face said, 'Want to bet?'

"Noël sat himself at the piano and played 'Every Peach, Out of Reach' . . .

"Though listening politely, Charlot could scarcely wait for him to finish. He grabbed his hand, shook it vigorously and walked him towards the door, murmuring, 'Very kind of you. Thank you very much.' Out went Noël, nudged by a very subtle cold shoulder. Charlot just stopped short of slamming the door behind him.

"'How dare you,' said Dada, turning on me, 'bring people here with no talent *whatsoever*?'"

FORBIDDEN FRUIT (1916)

VERSE 1   Ordinary man invariably sights
Vainly for what cannot be,
If he's in an orchard he will cast his eyes

Below, sheet music of "Forbidden Fruit" the first complete lyric from Noël Coward. Right, the young Noël.

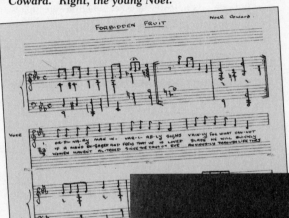

Up into the highest tree,
There may be a lot of windfalls
Lying all around,
But you'll never see a man enjoy the fruit
that's on the ground

REFRAIN 1   Every peach out of reach is attractive
'Cos it's just a little bit too high,
And you'll find that every man
Will try to pluck it if he can
As he passes by.
For the brute loves the fruit that's forbidden
And I'll bet you half a crown
He'll appreciate the flavour of it much
much more
If he has to climb a bit to shake it down.

VERSE 2   If a man's engaged and feels that he is loved,
Blasé he will quickly be,
Often on one side his ladylove is shoved
While he goes upon the spree.
Then perhaps she'll marry,

22

And you can bet your life
He'll want her very badly when she's
        someone else's wife.

REFRAIN 2 Every peach out of reach is attractive
'Cos it's just a little bit too high,
Though it isn't very sane
To make the things you can't attain,
Still you always try.
If you find that you're blind with devotion
For delightful Mrs. Brown,
You'll appreciate eloping with her much
        much more
If her husband comes along and knocks
        you down.

VERSE 3 Women haven't altered since the days of Eve,
Anxiously through life they prowl,
Always trying to better what their friends
        achieve,
Either by fair means or foul
A girl may be quite careful
Of the sort of life she picks,
But to be a real success she's got to know
        a lot of tricks.

REFRAIN 3 Every peach out of reach is attractive
'Cos it's just a little bit too high,
Even well-brought-up young girls
Will look at other women's pearls
With a yearning eye.
If they fight day and night persevering
And a small string they collect,
They'll appreciate the colour of them much
        much more
If they've sacrificed a little self-respect.

In later years Noël professed himself less than satisfied with at least one phrase in the original lyric: ". . . the suggested wager of half a crown rather lets down the tone. One cannot help feeling that a bet of fifty pounds, or at least a fiver, would be more in keeping with the general urbanity of the theme; for a brief moment the veneer is scratched and Boodle's, White's and Buck's are elbowed aside by the Clapham Tennis Club, but this perhaps is hyper-criticism and it must be remembered that to the author half a crown in 1916 was the equivalent of five pounds in 1926. Also, it rhymes with 'down' . . ."

*   *   *

The relationship with Darewski and Joel was rather more productive, although it wouldn't appear so from Noël's account in *Present Indicative*:

"I was to be paid fifty pounds the first year, seventy-five pounds the second year, and one hundred pounds the third year. I appeared dutifully every week or so, for the first few months, armed with verses, and ideas for songs. I waited many hours in the outer office, and sometimes even penetrated into the next-to-the-outer office, but seldom, if ever, clapped eyes on Herman Darewski, and nobody seemed at all interested in my lyrics."

One of the first of the lyrics Mr. Darewski showed no apparent interest in was entitled "Anna the Auctioneer." Is it stretching the imagination to find in it a foretaste of "Alice is At It Again"?

*ANNA THE AUCTIONEER (1917)(#)

VERSE   Annabel Devigne
Had a flat at Golder's Green
And her ways were really most endearing
She desired to learn a bit
And she thought she'd make a hit
If she did a little auctioneering
On a box she'd take her stand
With a hammer in her hand
And a firm resolve to keep from skidding
But don't think that she fell,
She went most awfully well
With the men who came to do her bidding.

REFRAIN   Anna was an Auctioneer
Tho' what she sold is not quite clear
And as a business woman she
May never quite have shone
She discovered young men's choice was
To hear how nice her voice was—
Going, Going, GONE!

Noël's account of his dealings with the Darewski Music Company makes amusing reading and certainly he would have hoped to emulate Tin Pan Alley with the constant sound of his songs being played all over town. In point of fact, the notebooks reveal that, even if they were not eventually published, he and Max Darewski produced a number of complete songs for which Max wrote the music. At least three specify the credit . . .

*HOME AGAIN(#)

(Music by Max Darewski)

VERSION 1
REFRAIN   Honey dear, I'm feeling lonely,
Honey dear, I want you only.
I want your kisses,
I want your kisses,
I want your loving always.

I want your hugging most every day,
I'm simply longing to hear you say—
"Oh, you honey baby".
When you're away from me.

One very good reason why Noël may have decided to revise the opening of this particular song was that it had distinct echoes of a recent Sophie Tucker success—the 1914 "Some of These Days"—with its reference to her "honey" being about to miss her "huggin" and "kissin." So, on mature reflection . . .

VERSION 2
REFRAIN   Home again to firesides gleaming,
Home again to dear ones dreaming.
How they've been yearning
For my returning,
The happy days they're scheming,
Loving arms stretching forth to
Greet me,
Loving hearts are there to meet me.
I'm longing only to hear you say
That you were lonely with me away.
How my heart is aching
To get back home again.

VERSE 1   When you are far away from home
It doesn't take you long to find
However far you chance to roam
You sigh for those you've left behind.
You see new faces, meet new friends
And wander 'neath the bluest skies
But always 'till the journey ends
Your soul in memory cries—

VERSE 2   Now that the war is left behind
And all the cruel fighting o'er,
The home for which you often pined
You realise you'll see once more.
There's no more sadness, no more tears,

Master Coward, 1912.

*Gertrude Lawrence as she looked
when Noël first met her, 1913.*

*Noël Coward with Philip Tonge, 1911
in* Where the Rainbow Ends. *Tonge would
appear in Coward plays televised in America
into the mid-1950s.*

24

The dark clouds are all swept away.
You look with gladness down the years
And with a smile you will say—

HOME AGAIN (REVISED)

VERSE 1   When you are far away from home
And wandering 'neath greyest skies,
How ever far you chance to roam
Your soul in memory cries—

VERSE 2   Now that the War is left behind
There's no more sadness, no more pain,
The home for which you often pined
You know you'll see once again—

*FAIRYLAND (#)

Lyric by Noël Coward and Max Darewski
Music by Doris Joel

VERSE 1   When the world is dark
And Poppies are asleep
Snuggle into bed and close your eyes.
Softly through the window
Midnight fairies creep
And fly with you away
To where the fairy kingdom lies.
I'll be there to greet you
By the open gate,
Hand in hand we'll
Wander 'neath the moon.
We shall be so happy,
Do not hesitate,
Say that you will
Come quite soon.

CHORUS   Fairyland, where little fairy
Lanterns shine.
You and I will have a
Really topping time.
Underneath a fairy tree,
Cuddled up where none
Can see us.

Up and down the Fairy dancers
Start to stray,
While the Fairy orchestra
Begins to play.
Then we two
Will bill and coo
In Fairyland
Like true lovers do.

VERSE 2   We will climb a Rainbow,
Chase a star or two.
Sailing in a gossamer
Balloon.
Then, as it's considered
Quite the thing to do,
We will go and look
For buried treasures on the moon.
When the silver dawn
Comes creeping up the sky
All the Fairy clocks
Begin to chime.
You and I together
Swiftly we will fly
And come again another time.

*DREAM GIRL (#)

VERSE 1   There's nothing left to live for
Now I have lost you,
There is no joy in life,
No birds have song.
I try hard to forget you,
Forget I've ever met you
But still you haunt my dreams the whole
       night long.
I've searched the whole wide world
To find a girl to take your place—
But everywhere I go
I only see your smiling face.
If you'll not come to life, dear
To drive away my fears,
I'm so afraid my life, dear
I'll drown in absinthe tears,
Till I find you again.

REFRAIN   I long for night time
And the stars above,
I long for dreamland
And the vision of one I love.

Of all the real girls I have met,
Dream girl, here's to thoughts of you!

VERSE 2   And through the misty clouds
I seem to wander
In search of you
Who only I loved so, dear.
Where comes to me this singing
Of dreaming voices saying?
I seem to hear your footsteps drawing near
I seem to feel your arms
Come stealing around me, soft and white
I hear you say you
Love me in the silence of the night.
Oh, say you will return, dear,
My wounded heart to heal,
My absinthe dreams are passing.
I want you to be real.

REFRAIN   I long for night time
And the king of dreams
Who lets me wander
Where the star of oblivion gleams
But all my dreams so swiftly fly
'Tis you that I adore, dear.
Dream girl, come to
My heart once more.

*   *   *

The world of dreams was as much a convention for the popular songwriter of those rather depressing times as poems of courtly love were for medieval poets. Gritty was transformed into pretty . . .

*I LIVE IN A WORLD OF MY OWN (1918)

I've been existing of late
In a most sublimely satisfied state
The ordinary trifles that used to annoy
I have banished away with the greatest of joy
And the irritating folk who for years
Have almost unceasingly bored me to tears
They no longer worry or flurry me now.
I'm living in peace, I'll just explain how—

I live in a world of my own.
It's a perfectly charming idea
The people one hates

Are debarred from its gates
And one's friends are conveniently known
The everyday trials of life
I consign to a more torrid zone.
No hideous hag
Very much on the make
Who says—"*Do* buy a flag
Just for Charity's sake",
When I gaze on these harpies
No more shall I quake—
'Cos I live in a world of my own!

One suspects that his internal universe was Noël's safe haven for the rest of his life—though it did nothing to prevent him from peering out and observing the day to day world in which he had his physical being. Memories of Teddington and Clapham loomed large . . .

*SUBURBIA

VERSE 1   If you tire of London or the country
And feel you want to settle down,
Don't take a house at Harrogate or Brighton
Or a maisonette in Camden Town.
Quite a lot of charming little suburbs
Are lying very close at hand,
Each has a Boot's Cash Chemist
And a cinema and a band.
So grab your hat and stick
And travel down here quick.

VERSE 2   Sometimes as a very special honour
The Vicar's wife will come to tea.
She will bring the Parish Magazine
And gossip most amazingly.
All the latest scandals she will tell you,
What the curate's wife had said,
What Mr. Mud was divorced for
And why Mrs. Mud's nose was red.
And though her tales are queer,
It's lovely living here.

REFRAIN 1   Come along to Suburbia and mingle with the
Très élite
You can rent a little villa
With an imitation pillar
And a Pretty Stucco Porch complete
People down in Suburbia
Play bridge and go to matinées a lot.

The Vicar's keen on Botany
And money—if you've got any
Our Suburbia is a *charming* spot!

REFRAIN 2   Come along to Suburbia and be among the
Smarter Set.
If you like a little shooting
With your swagger friends at Tooting
It's a thing the Parish won't forget.
People down in Suburbia
Are rather apt to criticise a lot.
If you have been a little fast,
They're sure to ferret out your past—
Our Surburbia's a *delightful* spot!

*   *   *

The early part of the period included the end of the War to End Wars, so it's not surprising to find the young Noël referring to it, if not always in the jingoistic vein of "When You Come Home on Leave." The aftermath would bring a more wistful and reflective tone . . .

*"IT'S ONLY ME!"(#)

Once I knew a kid
She used to live down Poplar way,
She 'adn't got the lingo of a Swell.
She used to work 'er 'eart out for about two
bob a day
And keep her ailing Grandfather as well.
She 'adn't got no Mother
And she 'adn't got no Dad
And she ain't the sort
That walks out much with men.
I reckon I was just about the only friend she 'ad,
I realised the honour
Even then.
Sometimes when I was lonely
And my 'eart was feeling sad
I'd 'ear 'er voice a-calling,
Then she'd whisper thro' the door—
"It's only me, it's only me,
I've brough yer in a bit of cake,
You 'ave it wiv yer tea,"
She wasn't really pretty,
Yet you couldn't call 'er plain,
There was something in 'er eyes
That made you want to look again,
I seem to 'ear that kidding

Voice a-ringing in my brain—
"It's only me, it's only me."

When the War just started, I enlisted like
a shot,
I looked upon it as a bit of fun,
I didn't stop to think if I'd come back all right
or not,
I just desired to bash the 'omely 'un
They send me out to Flanders
And I stood it for a bit
'Till a dirty bit of shrapnel done me down
And, do you know, I never realised that I'd
been 'it
'Till I woke up in an 'ospital in town.
One night me wound was painful
And I felt distinctly bored
When I 'eard some well known footsteps
Creeping soft like down the ward.

"It's only me, dear. It's only me.
I've just dropped in to talk a bit and keep yer
company."
You wouldn't call 'er pretty,
Yet you couldn't call 'er plain,
You've no idea how glad I was to see that kid
again.
When she was bending over me
I quite forgot my pain.
"It's only me, it's only me."

"It's only me, it's only me,
I've just dropped in to 'ave a talk
And keep you company."
When this War is over and they end up all this
strife,
I'm going to ask that little kid to come and be
my wife.
I think that tender voice of 'ers
Will brighten up my life.
"It's only me, dear—it's only me."

*   *   *

Noël was brought up during the era of the Victorian and Edwardian music hall. He never missed an opportunity to parody it affectionately in his later work and to the end of his life he could sit at the piano and sing many of its classic songs with total recall. Among his personal effects were several albums of post cards featuring music hall stars.

"Elizabeth May" was a lady he toyed with but never quite made up his mind about . . . only fragments remain.

*ELIZABETH MAY (1918?)(#)

VERSE

Once I knew a man
Who adored a very smart
And charming little chorus lady.
She was quite prepared
To take him to her heart
Tho' his past had been a trifle shady.
From the theatre he would
Fetch her every night
And drive her in his
Motor through the bright
Moon light.
As they drove along,
He would whisper loving words.

(Extra Verse)

Elizabeth said
She would rather be dead
Than live with her mother at home
She decided to go
In some nice West End show
At the Empire or Hippodrome.
So she tripped up to Town
In a ravishing gown
To visit an agent called Vickers.
He said—"You'll just do
For my latest revue
But you'll have to wear
Transparent —
Stockings!"

VERSE 3 *(revised)*

Elizabeth danced and
Elizabeth pranced
In the chorus for nearly three years
But she quickly tired at being admired
By rather degenerate peers.
They said—"Come away
To the briny today,
The sea air's a wonderful
Tonic"
Then she'd say—"If I go,
I should like you to know
That my friendships are always
Platonic!"

(New) CHORUS

My name's Elizabeth May
And no one takes liberties with me.
I wasn't born yesterday
And I know a thing or two, you see
Your love making really upsets me a lot
If you don't stop it soon,
I shall go off my dot!
And all I say is—"Well,
You can all go to—!"
'Cos no one takes liberties,
No one takes liberties,
No one takes liberties with me.

*LITTLE GIRL

REFRAIN

HE: I'd like to take you out to luncheon or tea

SHE: Kindly leave me in peace, sir,
    Or I shall call the police, sir.

HE: I'd like to hold you for a
    While on my knee.

SHE: But your likes and my likes
    Are different, you see!

VERSE 1

HE: Little girl, I'm feeling lonely.
    May I take a stroll with you?

SHE: I dislike your forward tone, sir.
    I'd prefer to walk alone, sir.

HE: Little girl, I rather hoped
    That you were feeling lonely, too.

SHE: I object to your persistence—
    Will you kindly keep your distance!

VERSE 2

HE: You would never think that
    I was something by the look of me

SHE: Your appearance is deceiving.
    What amusement are you receiving?

ALTERNATIVE

HE: I'd like to help you, little girl, if I may

SHE: I don't require assistance.
    Please will you keep your distance?

*MADELINE(#)

Madeline, I want to see
More of you.
Madeline, I want to see
More of you.
When your husband
Hits you with his big
Sam Browne,
Really thought that
One had won the case
Hands down.

Madeline, who was
That good friend of yours
Who raised your salary?
If your husband doesn't
Want to go and live with you,
You'd better come and live with
Better come and live with
Better come and live with
Me.

*(AND) THAT GIRL'S YOU(#)

HE: You've got lovely eyes, dear
    Of such a wonderful blue

SHE: I would be telling lies, dear
    If I said you had them, too

HE: Don't be catty,
    You've got hair like gold dust

SHE: And yours is stinking of glue

HE: Just one little girl's
    Set my head in a whirl—
    And that girl's you

Everyone composes
The same old love songs each day—
Broken hearts and roses
Are just the only things
That pay
And they bore me.
I had quite determined
That I would write something
New.

Of your eyes I'm dreaming
And for your kisses I pine
All day long I'm scheming
'Cos I want to make you mine
Very badly.
I'll make love demanding
If you'll but give me
The cue.
There's one little girl
Sets my head in a whirl—
And that girl's you.

---

*SUSIE SUNSHINE(#)

VERSE 1   A lady in society
Desiring notoriety
Decided she would go upon the land.
Her income wasn't very large
And as a sort of camouflage
She thought she'd change her name,
          you understand.
Each morning with the dawn she rose
And put some powder on her nose,
Of coyness or shirking she could never be
          accused.
The work did not progress apace
But still she brightened up the place
By tying bows of ribbon on the implements
          she used.
She'd work like anything
And as she plied her rake, she'd sing—

REFRAIN   I'm Susie Sunshine
And I live along at Sunshine Farm
And the men just love to have me round,
Because I never do the cattle any harm.
They just adore me
And they worry me as lovers do.
They generally fight
And try with all their might
To cuddle up to Sunshine Sue.

VERSE 2   Her wonderful vivacity
Was coupled with audacity,
She didn't care a rap what people said.
She'd milk the cow at break of day
And drink the milk without delay
Then walk home with the pail on her head.
One morning by the roadside

She met a journalist who cried—
"You're Lady Jane Plantagenet,
I've seen you up at Court."
His words filled her with great alarm
But she remained quite cool and calm
And cried—"Sir, you imagine it,
I'm nothing of the sort.
Your eyesight is to blame.
If you desire to know my name . . .

REFRAIN   I'm Susie Sunshine
And I live along at Sunshine Farm
And the men just love to have me around
Because I have such personality and charm.
Don't be mistaken,
Tho' you think I'm someone else, 'tis true
That if you linger here,
I very sadly fear
You'll fall in love with Sunshine Sue!

Verse 3   Tho' he was a nonentity,
He found out her identity
And said he'd tell and leave her in the lurch.
She sang out what she thought of him,
It wasn't quite the sort of Hymn
That folk are used to warbling in Church.
A millionaire was passing near
And happened just to overhear
Some swear words the constabulary would
          never quite permit
He hopped across the hedge and cried—
"Say, kiddo, you must be my bride,
I worship your vocabulary, it's absolutely it."

She arrested him that day
And when people asked her why, she'd
          say . . .

REFRAIN   I'm Susie Sunshine
And I want to live in gay New York.
I just love Americans, you see,
Because they get me with their fascinating
          talk.
I'm so excited,
There'll be such a lot of things to do.
And when I'm over there
I'll warn my millionaire
To keep his eye on Sunshine Sue.

---

*(UNTITLED)(#)

You are not the cutest kid
I've ever seen
Nor should I describe you as
A baby queen.
Infant puppets I detest,
Great big eyes and all the rest
Make me feel so depressed
I should like to murder
Anyone who said you were a honey lamb.

Noël and Betty Chester, 1919.

28 Several of the attempts are clearly unfinished and were probably discarded but "Bertha from Balham," "Elizabeth May," "That Girl's You" and "Susie Sunshine" sound as though they would have been well worth performing at a local Palace of Varieties with the audience joining in the chorus.

*   *   *

In the world of art these were years when there was a widespread interest in all things oriental, from poetry to art to furniture, Noël—not one to look a gift trend in the face—left Fairyland behind and produced two song "cycles" to suit the times . . .

*CHINESE CYCLE(#)
BLUE LANTERNS

Through this purple night
Amid the almond trees
Blue lanterns spilling light
Wave upon the breeze.

Perfumed in the air,
Trembling as a dove,
Songs are heard, oh everywhere
Telling of our love.

The pale moon on high,
Oh surely you must know,
Beloved, and draw nigh
Where the lanterns blow.

THE SILKEN CORD
(THE DREAM OF DEATH)

When the citron moon sails high
O'er the green rice glimmering,
Wilt thou be unkind,
Wilt thou bring me anything?

The Earth has ceased to be,
There is no joy for me,
One thing left, happily—
The Silken Cord.

Death closed her almond eyes,
So tender and so wise.
She may not hear my cries—
The Silken Cord.

Her tiny hands and feet,
Like flowers at rest are
Sweet.
How gladly I shall greet—
The Silken Cord.

SONG OF THE RICE GROVE

All day the sunlit rice
Waves in the arms of the Wind
Which caresses a world entire
But to be unkind, unkind.

*JAPANESE CYCLE(#)
SATSAIMA

The big red Sun is setting,
Satsiama.
The lotus leaves are floating down the stream.
I seek the lonely orchard,
Satsiama,
And there beneath the cherry
Boughs I dream of long ago,
The drowsy sunlit garden
Where you and I together
Used to play
And at the shrine of Happiness and Laughter
The drooping flowers of
Memory I lay.

THE WATER LILY POND

By the water lily pond
Where the goldfish play

I will wait until you come
At the close of day
And the nightingale will trill
A love song gay
By the water lily pond
Where the goldfish play.

By the water lily pond
Where the goldfish play
When the happy hours of youth
Have passed away
In the twilight of our lives
We'll kneel and pray
By the water lily pond
Where the goldfish play.

PRETTY WHITE DOVE
(ORIGINALLY LITTLE WHITE DOVE)

Pretty white dove at my window
Leave your warm nest in the trees
Wing your way over the Willows
That sway to and fro in the breeze.
Fly to a sweet scented garden
And leave there a message of love
And if there's an answer, return to me.
Fly away, pretty white dove.
Pretty white dove, I am waiting,
Waiting for you to fly home.
I shall be ready to greet you
To stroke your tired wings
When you come.
Lonely I kneel in my Shoji
And pray that dear Buddha above
In his compassion may guide you safe
Back to my heart, Pretty Dove.

LITTLE LACQUER LADY

Little Lacquer Lady
With your charming smile,
Let me be your lover
For a little while.

Talented,
Optimistic . . . but
Unemployed, 1916.

Laughing eyes that haunt me
When I am alone
Little Lacquer Lady,
Take me for your own.

Little Lacquer Lady
Smiling down no more
You are lying broken,
Shattered on the floor.
See, I kiss your hand shaped
Like a little shell,
Hear your lonely call
Bidding you farewell

*   *   *

No young songwriter worth his rhyming dictionary could afford to seem happy all the time and Noël was no exception. He duly yearned for love lost, pined, roamed in the lonely twilight and dreamed a great deal . . .

*NO MORE (#)

REFRAIN 1 No more I'm going gay,
No more I'll stay away,
I've found my one ideal in you
I'll stop the man from stealin' you.
No more I'll sigh in vain,
My love will never wane,
You've found a home, dear
In my heart
No more we'll part again

REFRAIN 2 No more I'll hesitate,
No more I'll stay out late.
Let other fellows have their fun,
For me those wild oat days are done.
No more you'll find me shy
Until the day I die.
I'll never let you go again,
No more we'll say goodbye.

VERSE 1 People say that love is just a bubble
Bursting at the slightest sign
I have found without a lot of trouble
That this is a great big lie.
Other fellows searching hard for Cupid
May have thought him hard to find,
That's because they're blundering and
        stupid

And they think that love is blind.
    That's true maybe
        But we can see
Enough to make you fond of me . . .

VERSE 2 I've had quite a lot of dissipation
And a slightly lurid past,
Gay days seem to lose their fascination
Now I've found the girl at last.
No more binges at the Piccadilly,
Café Royal and Ritz, goodbye,
Those things now seem
Meaningless and silly,
I leave them without a sigh.
        Life starts anew
        For I love you
And love has made you love me too . . .

*TWILIGHT (#)

When the Summer day is over
And the Poppies are all sleeping
Through the deep grey mist of
Twilight
Shadows from the past come creeping.
Faces that are long forgotten,
Sorrows that I thought were ending.
It were vain to hope for
Happiness.
Broken hearts can ne'er
Be mended.

*FOR YOU I'M PINING (#)

Tho' you do not, dear
Possess a lot, dear,
Thank God you've got, dear
Such a loving heart.

VERSE 1 I'm feeling lonely
With none to cheer me
And wishing only
That you were near me.
You are so charming
It's quite alarming
The way you make me feel.

VERSE 2 It may be fate, dear
Or accidental
That I'm not bright, dear
But sentimental.
The writers write wrong,
I want a light song,
I'm sick to death of long.

REFRAIN 1 I'm rather lonely
With just my dreams, dear
If life were only
What it sometimes seems,
There'd be no more pain.
I'd be so glad, dear
I'd never sigh
But it makes me sad, dear
When illusions die.
Tho' broken hearted
The day we parted,
I thought you loved me
When we said goodbye.

And then for the first—but by no means the last—time he took to parodying his own creation . . .

REFRAIN 2 I'm so tired of dreaming
And I will not sit and pine
I'm so sick of scheming
And I should hate to
Make you mine.
You get plainer
Every time I see you
And if you fell down a well,
I'd laugh up my sleeve
'Cos I firmly believe
You'd go to da-da-da-da!

*BYGONE DAYS (#)

REFRAIN Appetising. Tantalizing.
Bygone days.
Ever taunting. Ever haunting
Bygone ways.
When the dancing firelight gleams
I surrender to my dreams.
How long ago it seems
When we used to wander
Hand in had through
That dear land
Of heart's content.

For the joys gone by
One always pays—
Satisfying dreams are dying
Mem'ry flying, leaving us sighing.
Oh, I fain would like
Again those
Bygone days.

VERSE 1   When Cupid's left you alone
And love you never have known,
You'll go through life
All uncaring
Until your youth has flown
And then you may realise
How quickly happiness dies
When you've had no one
To love you
Or just to sympathise.
Tho' memory may pain,
It lets one love again.

*LET MY DREAMS RETURN (#)

Shine out, thou Stars,
And let thy shining light my way
To that far golden land
Where with my love at close of day
I wandered hand in hand.
Within that Slumberland
The light of Happiness doth burn.
Oh, shine into my soul tonight
And let my dreams return.

In an unfinished play, *Copy Katt*, in the same note-book Noël indicates that a scene is to be set at a "tea party in a London house" during which the waltz "Dream Your Dreams" is to be played . . .

*DREAM YOUR DREAM AGAIN (#)

When life seems wrong
Everything's gray,
Laughter and song
Vanish away
Welcome the lady with

Hands full of sleep
For into your heart
She'll creep.

REFRAIN   Memories haunting,
Memories taunting
Fly to your heart on the wing
Of Dawn,
Making you only
Saddened and lonely
Weary of life, but let
Weeping and sorrow
Keep for tomorrow.
Laugh in the face of pain.
Tears may be falling
But slumber is calling
So dream all your dreams
Again.

VERSE 1   Waiting is sad,
Time is so slow
But I am glad
Now that you know
To that fair garden
Where silver light gleams
I will return, dear, in
Dreams.

*DREAMS (APRIL 20, 1919) (#)

VERSE 1   Dreams—what are dreams
But just the embers
Glowing from a love long dead?
Ah, how one sorrowfully
Remembers
The angry words that once
Were said
Pray God there be
No other tears to shed.

VERSE 2   Dreams—what are dreams
But idle fancies
Flitting through a weary brain
Recalling dead and gone romances,
Renewing long forgotten pain?
Thank God that we awake
And live again.

*   *   *

Having paid his lyrical dues to *angst*, it was never long before irreverence broke through. Even when

superficially following an existing form, a touch of anarchy was often close to the surface.

So this was the Jazz Age? Well, if "The Baseball Rag" hadn't been totally authentic, perhaps the fact that you were singing in an alien tongue should be made part of the point?

*EVERYBODY'S JAZZING MAD (#)

VERSE 1   Everybody's gay,
Dancing all the day,
No one knows exactly why but
Still you hear them say—
"Go on, Mr. Coon,
Play another tune".
If I get appendicitis soon,
I shan't give a damn.
Come, my honey lamb
Feel about as frisky as
A baby in a pram.
Once I'm on the hop,
Never want to stop—
This has got me going till
I drop.

REFRAIN   Jazz away, it gets you mad for a start,
Jazz away, it gets a hold on your heart.
Something new has crept across the
Herring pond,
Done by every actor, duke and
Demi-mond.
Never mind if you are tired
Of the band
Or if you're feeling sad,
When you hear this syncopation,
You will understand
Why everybody's jazzing,
Everybody's jazzing,
Everybody's jazzing mad.

Verse 2   Do a little slide,
Jerks you up inside
Like a frisky horse, when you are
Learning how to ride.
Tie yourself in bows,
Rock upon your toes,
Even if your sock suspender goes.
If you are a "she",
Take a tip from me,
Leave your little corsets

On the table with your tea.
Never mind the crowd,
Pushing is allowed—
Kick 'em on the shins
'Till they are cowed.

And what was wrong with taking that ballad beloved of concert party tenors, "The Girl With the Nut Brown Hair," and having a little fun with it. . .?

*THE GIRL WITH THE DULL BROWN EYE (#)

Give me a girl with a dull brown eye
And I know just where I am
I don't care a damn
For the grey eyes and the green eyes
And the just what might-have-been eyes
People may rave over Kirchner Girls
But I can pass them by
It's the shyness that entrances
And the slightly frowning glances
Of the Girl with the Dull Brown Eye.

There were early attempts at the duet form, which he would later adapt to the song-integrated-with-a-sketch that set up the characters. The attempts of Jack and Phyllis to conduct a romance, despite the demands of office life, is moving in that direction.

*OFFICE HOURS (#)

JACK: I'm so darn fed up with these long
           office hours

PHYLLIS: I just long to see a meadow full of flowers.

J: I know just the spot you'd like
           Couldn't we both go out on strike?
           I've got a motor bike
           With the cutest side car.

P: I've got fifty pages more to type out twice

J: Can't you leave them to another day, say

I've some cash—let's go and blue it.

P: It is awfully wrong to do it.

J: No one's looking, come along,
           Dear, let's go gay.

VERSE 1
P: We used to lunch every day
           At Princes over the way.

J: We used to earn
           Quite a lot, dear
           And people used to say—
           'There go that talented pair,
           The tall young man with wavy hair
           Is quite the cleverest dancer
           You could see anywhere".

P: It makes me want to cry
           When I think of days gone by—

J: One more hour will do the trick, dear
           We'll go mad, so we'd better be getting
               slick, dear.

P: Snatch your little hat and stick, dear
           And let's go gay.

VERSE 2
P: I think you're rather absurd
           If anyone overheard
           There'd be a horrible row, dear
           And we should get the bird.

J: I wouldn't mind what they said,
           I think I'd rather be dead
           Than go on pushing this pen, dear.
           I'm absolutely fed,
           I'd rather like to tell
           Them all to go to —
           At work!

In many of his later writings Noël would smile at his early attempts to strike the note of sophisticated cynicism for which he was to become famous. 1918 saw two other examples . . .

*I'M NOT A FOOL AS A RULE (#)

When I was a child
I drove my parents wild
I used to ask them questions all the day,
Father used to frown

And put his paper down
"The kid's a bally lunatic," he'd say.
Then Mother used to smile and cry "The Darling,
He really has the most abnormal brain."
But I'm never certain quite
As to which of them was right:
I've tried to make up my mind, but in vain . . .

Mother used to say that I was clever
Father always told me I was not
And between them both
I give my solemn oath
I knew not which was which or what was what.
How often I have tried to solve the puzzle
And sometimes I'm afraid I never will.
When I was quite a child I had the colic
And they said the thing to cure it was a pill
It's bad to hesitate
So I swallowed seven or eight.
I'm not a fool as a rule, but still . . .!

*LITTLE FRENCH LADY (1918) (#)

Once in a corner of England
There lived a good little maid
She soon grew horribly weary
Of being so prim and so staid.
And then there came to the village
A Frenchman dapper and gay,
He took her driving just once or twice
And smiled on hearing her say . . .

"I'd like to be a little French lady
I'd like to live in a little French town
I'd like to have a lovely ring
And a beautiful evening gown
I'd like to have a little French sweetheart
And he must love me night and day
And I would like to spend a week end
In the sweet Parisienne's way!"

He found her manners delightful
He found her kisses so sweet
He said "You're *toute à fait charmante*"
And knelt at her tiny feet.
She gazed at him in compassion
And as the weather was hot
She wasn't sure of the French for "No"
So had to say "Oui" on the spot . . .

Young Actor
Available . . .
Drawing Room
Comedy Wanted."

*   *   *

In 1919 there was optimistic talk at Darewski Music of a two act opera. Noël and Esmé were to collaborate on *Crissa*, set in exotic Sicily, with a view to its being produced in the US. *The Sketch* carried the report. While the project never saw a stage, fragments remain in the notebook. There is also mention of the involvement of Doris Joel in the libretto, while the music was to be composed by Max Darewski. As the excerpts progress, Crissa mutates into Chrissa. A symbolic religious overtone is perhaps pitching it high—but then the hero *is* called Buonamici (Good Friend) . . . According to Darewski's widow, actress Ruby Miller, he was too busy to complete the music.

CRISSA (CHRISSA) (#)

(An Opera by Noël Coward and Esmé Wynne)
Music by Max Darewski

CHRISSA'S ENTRANCE

> Some day my lover will come to me,
> Some day no longer a dream he'll be,
> Fairies will fly like leaves on the wind,
> True love I surely will find,
> If Fate be only kind.
> Doubts and fears—unwanted,
> Shadows from my sight will go creeping,
> Nightingales will sing above
> The City when it is sleeping.
> Happiness is waiting,
> The call I'll gladly obey
> And cast all sorrow away
> When true love comes some day.

ARIA: I am Crissa, singing maid of Sicily,

> My lips are scarlet blossom stained with wine.
> The mountains rise into the skies of Sicily,
> Shading the air with purple of the vine.
> Long ago some Wizards snared a nightingale
> And laid it bound and
> Fettered in my heart.
> This melody within my breast
> I must set free before I rest.
> I'm Crissa, Crissa, singing
> Maid of Sicily.

PRELUDE TO BUONAMICI'S ARIA

(End of Act 1)

Ah, see the sun once more shines down into the
    valley,
Weaving into rainbows tinted
The mournful rising mist
Dispelling gloom and sadness
And turning into jewels
The raindrops glistening on the vine leaves.
But stay—I see Onssas, the Storm God, in
The hurry of his flight
Has dropped some priceless gems from heaven's
    fair casket.
Hasten, hasten, lest the spirits and Woodland things
Hide it away from Buonamici's sight.

(Kneeling beside Crissa)
A wondrous thing the Gods
This day have sent
So that my weary eyes
At last may see
Some glimpse of Heaven's
Magic wonderment.
Turn not this vision into
Fantasy.

DUET: CRISSA AND BUONAMICI

BOTH:
Love brings to us the message of Spring,
Life proves to be a wonderful thing.
No more the skies will weep with sadness
For now the world is full of melody and song.

For I am yours and you are mine,
Now and ever after,
Come sorrow and come laughter.

I love you, Crissa
I love you, Buonamici

BUONAMICI:
Ah, see the hills and flowers
Awake
And from our love their happiness
Take

CRISSA:
Ah, how the hills have echoed our joy,
Not even death this love can destroy.

BOTH:
No more the skies . . . .

*   *   *

Thus ended Noël's contract with the Darewski company. Looking back on it twenty years later, Noël felt obliged to be somewhat dismissive. He recalls:

"During the third year of my contract I was too busy with other affairs to go near the office until the last day, when I called to receive my cheque for a hundred pounds. Herman Darewski's third or fourth secretary handed it to me with a charming smile and, after a brief exchange of social amenities, I had a cup of tea in the outer office and went home. Some while after this, the Herman Darewski publishing firm went bust, a fact that has never altogether astonished me."

Published or not, the Darewski years provided the young Noël with the incentive to learn the rudiments of his craft with a degree of professional privacy. By the end of the decade he was ready to venture forth. At that point the notebooks end . . .

. . . and Mrs. Coward quietly snared a couple of them for her suitcase.

*   *   *

Noël listed the songs he intended to write under "Unfinished Songs." Some would appear in the next decade, though many were to remain somewhere in the back of his mind.

> I Dreamed of You
> What a Wonderful Tune
> Floradora
> I Wouldn't Mind
> Marriage Is the Game for Me
> Strong and Silent
> It Isn't What You Do
> Why Not Leave Me Alone?
> You've Gone Away
> Love a Little
> Tell Me If You Knew
> This Year, Next Year
> Bunch
> It Was All Very Pretty
> Hungarian Tune
> Andalusia
> Ladybird
> Louise

THE 1920s

THE CO-OPTIMISTS

A PIERROTIC ENTERTAINMENT

1921-1930

38

The Co-Optimists were a kind of "repertory revue" troupe. They based their format loosely on the end of the pier groups of entertainers then popular during summer seasons, down to the distinctive pierrot costumes. The core members were Melville Gideon, Davy Burnaby, Laddie Cliff, Stanley Holloway, Phyllis Monkman and Betty Chester.

Their first "entertainment" was produced at the Royalty Theatre, London on June 24, 1921 and later transferred to the Palace Theatre that October. The third program of the opening season (May 1922) contained two Coward songs with music by Melville Gideon:

DOWN WITH THE WHOLE DARN LOT! (1922)

(A Democratic Quartet)
(Stanley Holloway and others)

VERSE 1   We're men of democratic thought
And independent means,
We're full of plans of every sort
To give old England beans.
Conscription made us go and fight
Our country's cause to win,
And now that we've got back all right
We're going to 'do her in'!

Stanley Holloway.

CHORUS   Down with the idle rich!
The bloated upper classes.
They drive to Lord's
In expensive Fords
With their jewelled op'ra glasses.
Down with the London P'lice!
We'll quickly have them shot.
We'll spread destruction everywhere.
Burn things up in a fine old flare.
What about the lions in Trafalgar Square?
Down with the whole darn lot!

REPEAT CHORUS
Down with the Courts of Law!
With flaming swords we'll raid 'em,
And slay the blokes
Who have laughed at jokes
Just because the judges made 'em.
We'll have the murder trials
Arranged by Malcolm Scott,
And as each one to death is sent
The court will rock with merriment.
What about the people who are innocent?
Down with the whole darn lot!

VERSE 2   We're really men of sterling worth.
Democracy's our aim.
We're going to Bolshevize the earth,
Protected by that name.
To outrage any sacred law
We'd give our dying breath,
And if we started Civil War
We'd laugh ourselves to death!

CHORUS 2   Down with the working man!
We'll starve his wives and sisters,
For any sin
Can be fitted in
With our 'Democratic vistas'.
Down with the London stage!
We'll let them have it hot.
If Laurillard or Sachs resists
We'll kill them both as Royalists.
What about the frolicking Co-Optimists?
Down with the whole darn lot!

REPEAT CHORUS
Down with the daily Press!
We'll wipe it out completely.
I'd hate the lives
Of my murdered wives
To be published indiscreetly.
Editors and their staffs

Shall languish till they rot.
We'll stop the London *Mail* each week.
On every side our spite we'll wreak.
What about the paragraphs of Pip and
    Squeak?
Down with the whole darn lot!

VERSE 3   With Ireland we're offended quite,
We trusted her for years.
She's now infringed our copyright
And stolen our ideas.
We're holding back our hand to strike
And bash her well and good.
We'll show her what the feeling's like
To be "Misunderstood".

CHORUS 3   Down with the bold Sinn Fein!
We'll rout them willy-nilly.
They flaunt their crimes
In the *Belfast Times*,
Which makes us look so silly.
Down with the Ulster men!
They don't know which from what.
If Ireland sunk beneath the sea
How peaceful everyone would be!
You haven't said a word about the R.I.C?
Down with the whole darn lot!

REPEAT CHORUS
Down with the modern dance!
That craze we'll quickly smother.
It looks all right
If your coat's on tight
And you really love each other.
Down with the Shimmie Shake
That makes poor Auntie hot!
We'll see that every dance club fails,
And slap Pavlova till she wails.
What about Salomé and her seven veils?
Down with the whole darn lot!

EXTRA CHORUS
Down with the Garrick Club,
And Kensington Museum!
The Albert Hall
Must abruptly fall,
And the London Coliseum.
Down with the Marble Arch!
It's always been a blot.
England in its blood shall souse,
Mother, father, husband, spouse.
You haven't said a word about the 'Corner
    House'!
Down with the whole darn lot!

Noël's notes unearth a further unused chorus:

*BOLSHEVIST CHORUSES

Down with the telephone
With all its charges doubled.
We'll just remark
As we stab each clerk
That we're sorry she's been troubled.
When we are asked to put
Three pennies in the slot,
To be stone deaf we'll all pretend
And every coin we'll carefully bend—
What about the person on the other end?
Down with the whole darn lot!

A few years later, when moral standards had relaxed somewhat, "Darn" became "Damn"!
. . . and a subversive Quartette . . .

*THE CO-COMMUNISTS

(QUARTETTE)
(*Laddie Cliff, Davy Burnaby, Gilbert Childs
and Stanley Holloway*)

We're four representative men of today,
The state of the country is critical
We don't wish to loot or to burn
Or to slay—
Our object is purely political.
Like Old Roman Emperors
We're full of ideas
In those days they knew what a
Gala meant
We're vulgar self-centered
Illiterate DEARS
And all of us standing for Parliament,
With a hey ho and nonny no
And a whack fol mi dol
Poll, Pretty Poll, Pretty Poll.

GILBERT

I'm standing as a member
For Rudeworth-on-Ooze
I'm out to get everything free—
Free living, free thinking, free love and free booze
Is the state in which England should be.
When any small trifle you wish to obtain
Is brought free of charge to your door in a train
And the Government doles out your weekly
        cocaine,
You'll know that they've voted for me!

LADDIE

I'm standing as a member
For Fuddlehoe Bay
I'm filled with aesthetic desires
I'll make all our prisons
Quite pretty and gay
With fairy lamps hanging from wire.
I've got lots of plans for the Old Bailey too
So when you observe that the hangings are new
And the Judge's black cap is an art shade of blue!
You'll know they've voted for me!

STANLEY

I'm standing as a member
For Berwick-on-Tweed,
I'll hatch revolutions with glee
I feel that as England is running to seed,
I ought to be running to see.
So when you watch masses rise up in a flood—
The Albert Memorial fall with a thud
And Lancaster Gate simply running with blood—
You'll know that they've voted for me.

DAVY

I'm standing as a member
For Newington Butts,
A power in the land I shall be—
I'll build quite eight hundred huts
And wipe out the whole LCC
So when all the Council are lured from their
        haunts
And driven to jail amid mockings and taunts
And finally shot in the Palais de Dance
You'll know that they've voted for me.

ALL

We mean to start quite a new
Foreign campaign
And run the near east diplomatically
We'll give some smart lunches
With lots of champagne
And speak to the Turks most emphatically—
Of course, if you choose to dispute

Our ideas
And start being rude and correcting us
We'll tax you so hugely you'll burst into tears
And serve you all right for electing us
With a hey ho and nonny no
And a whack fol mi dol
Poll, Pretty Poll, Pretty Poll.

EXTRA VERSES

I'm standing as member
For Moosley-in-Marsh,
I'm sporting enough, Heaven knows
I think coloured contests exceedingly harsh
But men will be men, I suppose
So when in Hyde Park you see natives in hordes
And black aborigines driving in Fords
And Chinese and Eskimaux playing at Lord's
You'll know that they've voted for me.

I'm standing as a member
For Ochburn-on-Clyde,
I'm full of inventive ideas.
I mean to get thoroughly into my stride
In twenty or twenty-five years
So if on a vicious career you begin
And when you're committing original sin
And you find that her husband is in
You'll know that they've voted for me.

I'm standing as member
For Burton-on-Trent,
No Government money I'll spend.
I'll make author's royalties 90 percent
And write novels every weekend.
I mean to cut all the expenditure down
So when taxi drivers who drive you to town
Are REALLY content if you tip half a crown,
You'll know that they've voted for me.

The seventh program of the third season (January 1924) at the Prince of Wales Theatre included another—also with music by Gideon:

*THERE MAY BE DAYS (1923)

My advice,
If you want to find Paradise,

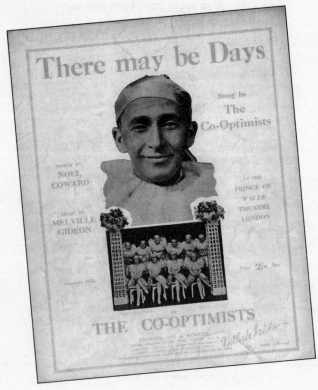

Just make up your mind
Don't say die,
Never mope or sigh,
Wait until the clouds roll by.

There may be days when things look bright for you
There may be days as black as night for you
Whether joys or sadness are blending,
There is sure to be a happy ending.

There may be days when you can jump the moon,
There may be days you wish were over soon.
You must keep on persevering
Till the happy days have come to stay.

In *Collected Lyrics* Noël also attributes "Back to Nature" to *The Co-Optimists* but there is no evidence of their ever performing it. Presumably he wrote it with them in mind. It was later considered for *This Year of Grace* (1928)—and even included in the published score, but once again never used.

BACK TO NATURE (1928)

(TRIO)

VERSE 1

ALL: We're here to make confession,
        We're forming a triple alliance.
        Our years of drab repression
        Have burst into open defiance.
        We've bid goodbye to faces dear
        And mother-in-laws and wives.
        We now intend to disappear
        And reconstruct our lives.

REFRAIN

ALL: We're over-civilized,
        That's the trouble with us.
        Our hearts of pickled oak
        Are casting off the yoke.
        Though we are undersized
        We're not giving a cuss,
        We're striking off the chains today.

1ST: We find that the town
        Is keeping us down,
        We're yearning to expand

2ND: For life in a bank
        Is dingy and dank,
        It's more that we can stand.

3RD: We mean to abscond
        Into the beyond
        And roll in blood and sand.

ALL: We're going back to nature right away!

VERSE 2

ALL: The climate rules the nation,
        The temperature's rapidly falling,
        With over-population
        The squalor of life is appalling.
        We're tired of trying year by year
        To imitate plaster saints,
        We mean to change our atmosphere
        And lose our self-restraints.

REFRAIN 2

ALL: We're too respectable,
        That's what's holding us back,
        We lie and dream at nights
        Of primitive delights.

        Think how delectable
        Life would be in a shack
        With nobody to say us nay.

3RD: I'll jump on my horse,
        Side saddle of course,
        And ride across the green,

1ST: I'll gallop and shoot
        And plunder and loot
        With none to intervene.

2ND: As quick as a wink
        I'll carelessly drink
        A pail of Ovaltine.

ALL: We're going back to nature right away!

VERSE 3

ALL: We must admit the movies
        Have helped to complete our damnation.
        Now what we want to prove is
        Our utter demoralization.
        We don't intend to waste our time
        With celibacy and such,
        We'll lead a life of social crime
        And like it very much.

REFRAIN 3

ALL: We're too adaptable,
        That's what's wrong with us now,
        There must be hidden charms
        In North Canadian farms.
        We've never slapped a bull,
        Never sworn at a cow,
        We can't distinguish straw from hay,

2ND: But nevertheless,
        I'm bound to confess,
        I'm full of do and dare.

3RD: If life is a bore
        I'll hire a squaw,
        With charming *savoir faire*,

1ST: Where women are bold
        And quite uncontrolled
        All in the open air.

ALL: We're going back to nature right away!

*   *   *

Noël clearly wrote other material for *The Co-Optimists* but there is no evidence of its having been performed.

There was a surrealistic solo number for Laddie Cliff . . .

*CYCLING HOME

(Laddie Cliff)

I'm feeling mighty lonesome
And I'm feeling mighty blue
I'm going to pump my tires up right away
The chain is rather twisted
And the pedal's missing too
But I've quite made up my mind to start today.
Cycling home, cycling home, cycling home
To the old plantation
My folks are there, I know
I shall hear when I'm near
Mum and Dad
Crooning sad
Melodies on Uncle Fred's banjo.
I'm weary and I'm homesick and I'm drunk
So I'm packing my crocodile trunk

REFRAIN

Cycling home
To the old plantation,
My folks are there, I know
Mum and Dad
Crooning sad
Melodies on Uncle Bob's banjo
I can smell the Glaxo burning
There's a pink blancmange, I know
On my cycle I'm returning
Where the custard apples grow.

. . . an ensemble number poking gentle fun at the troupe's longevity . . .

*CO-OCTOGENERIANS

(The Company)

MELVILLE: Hello, everybody
We've been here for forty years
We've been so optimistic
We've moved audiences to tears.
The younger generation's fairly banging
at the door

But I shall be a juvenile until I'm eighty-four.

ALL: Bow wow! Goodness gracious!

PHYLLIS: I'm Phyllis Monkman, age
At last has turned me grey
I've had a bitter fight to keep the enemy
at bay
I must admit I find it hard to kick my legs
about
I suffer so acutely from sciatica and gout.

ALL: Bow wow! Poor old thing!

DAVY: I'm Davy Burnaby,
Renowned for being plump,
With fearful jocularity I used to skip and
jump
Your kind appreciation of my humour I shall
prize
But the strain of being funny
Made me shrink to half my size.

ALL: Bow wow! Bow wow!

BETTY: I'm Betty Chester. I am now a little tired
But once my deep contralto voice was
very much admired
I used to sing "Sea Fever" till
It weighed upon my brain.
I know I'll get brain fever if I see the sea
again.

ALL: Bow wow! Bow wow!

STANLEY: I am Stanley Holloway, my repertoire isn't
large
I sing of rolling roysterers or coaling in a
barge
I have a great success because my baritone
is rich
I often sing such hearty songs
I give myself the stitch.

ALL: Bow wow! Bow wow!

LADDIE: I am Laddie Cliff and still maddeningly
bright
My voice has lost its cunning but my feet
are still all right
I finish up the programme
In the finest place, you bet
With a damn sight better number than the
others ever get.

ALL: Bow wow! Bow wow!
Bow wow! We're so chockful of verve
Bow wow! that we strain every nerve
Sere and yellow leaves may fall

That will make no difference at all
We love having fun there's no doubt
We shove one another about
We're so gay we're ill all day
But we're bright quite alright at night.

. . . and a duet . . .

*LITTLE BUNDLE OF DREAMS

(Melville Gideon and Phyllis Monkman)

MELLVILLE: Some girls love me,
Some girls don't

PHYLLIS: Some men woo me,
Some men won't

MELLVILLE: Therefore you're the maid for me

PHYLLIS: I'm the one you prayed for, see.

MELLVILLE: You're my bundle of dreams

PHYLLIS: Tell me more, tell me more

MELLVILLE: When the fire light gleams

PHYLLIS: Aren't you just such a flirt?

MELLVILLE: When you're near me life just seems,
dear . . .

PHYLLIS: What?

MELLVILLE: Just a winsome, yearning, beautiful bundle
of dreams!

1921: THE FIRST NEW YORK VISIT

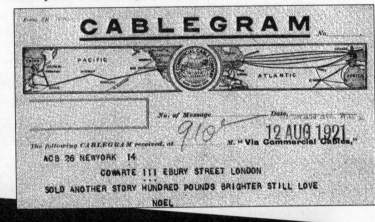

Below, Good news from Broadway to Ebury Street. (Noël Cowarte doesn't have quite the same ring!)

CABLEGRAM

New York, 1921. Top, Times Square looking North. Below, the Flatiron Building.

Alfred Lunt and Lynn Fontanne, the first and closest of Noël's American friends.

1923

Like many other lyricists, Noël would frequently "recycle" a song, often changing it significantly in the process—not simply for the sake of updating references that might have dated but usually to simplify it to its core meaning.

An early example of this was the duet "Touring Days." Originally written as the pay-off to a 1923 (unproduced) sketch called "Customs House, Dover" in which the Customs Official (Joe Bush) meets a lady called Lulu Higgins in the line of duty, only to discover that Lulu, now a show girl at the *Folies Bergères*, is none other than his old partner from touring days. It was initially pencilled in for the 1923 revue that became *London Calling!* To begin with the characters were called Marty and Desirée and would have been played by Noël and Gertie—an interesting anticipation of The Red Peppers of thirteen years later.

*TOURING DAYS (1923)

DIALOGUE:

JOE: 'Ow many years is it since we first met—it was in Leeds, wasn't it?

LULU: Yes, Wilson Barret opened on the Monday at the Grand with *The Sign of the Cross* and we were in *Hey, Diddle Diddle* at the Empire.

JOE: Lulu

LULU: Joe

SONG:

JOE: It's many years ago
Since we took the British drama by the throat

LULU: How time flies!

JOE: You've increased in weight and size.

LULU: I feel thinner since I left the beastly boat.

JOE: I can remember
Late in November
Opening in Ashton-under-Lyne.

LULU: Your suit was sweet
With a patch in the seat
For the sake of Auld Lang Syne.

BOTH: Touring days, touring days
What ages it seems to be,

JOE: Since the landlady at Norwich
Served a mouse up in the porridge,
And a beetle in the morning tea.

BOTH: Touring days, touring days,
Far back into the past we gaze.

JOE: They battered in your luggage once in
Miller's Dale,

LULU: I had to wrap my washing in the *Daily Mail*,

JOE: The platform looked exactly like a jumble sale,

BOTH: Those wonderful touring days!
Touring days, touring days.

LULU: I frequently call to mind
What you said to Mrs. Bluett
When you broke her silver cruet
And she made you leave your watch behind.

BOTH: Touring days, alluring days
Far back into the past we gaze.

JOE: The landlady was always drunk at Aberdeen,
She used to keep her money in the soup
tureen,

LULU: One night you swallowed half a crown and
turned pea-green.

BOTH: Those wonderful touring days.

BOTH: Touring days, touring days,
What glorious lives we led.

JOE: Was it *Caste* or *Julius Caesar*
When you blew up with the geyser.
And I dragged you from the bath half dead?

BOTH: Touring days, touring days
Far back into the past we gaze.

JOE: Do you remember playing in *The Shulamite*?
Your understudy greased your rubber heels
for spite

LULU: I fell and broke me contract on the Friday
night,

BOTH: Those wonderful touring days.

Joe and Lulu were to be reincarnated as George and Lily Pepper, the "Red Peppers" in *Tonight at 8:30* (1935) and the joys of third-rate music hall came flooding back . . .

"Touring Days" had to wait until *Cowardy Custard*—"an entertainment featuring the words and music of Noël Coward"—was staged at The Mermaid on July 10, 1972 for its revival. Alan Strachan, who devised the show with Wendy Toye and Gerald Frow, recalls how the song turned up:

"We found it at the bottom of a trunk in the flat

Noël Coward and Betty Chester from their "touring days," Birmingham, 1919.

44

of his then London representative who had hoarded over the years scrapbooks, cuttings—all the things he hadn't bothered to take out to Switzerland or Jamaica. There was this rather ragged piece of sheet music. I think he'd written it when he was something like nineteen . . . The memory of it had totally left him. I mean, he didn't deny that he had written it but he'd actually forgotten . . . It's a very affectionate number about the joys and miseries of life on the road, obviously written out of personal experience."

Strachan used it in a slightly changed and abbreviated form in which it was eventually published . . .

GIRL: I've often wondered if it's possible to recapture
The magic of bygone days.
I feel one couldn't quite resuscitate
All the rapture and joy of a youthful phase.
But still, it's nice to remember
The things we used to do,

BOY: When you were on tour with me, my dear,
And I was on tour with you.

BOTH: Touring days, touring days,
What ages it seems to be,

GIRL: Since the landlady at Norwich
Served a mouse up in the porridge,

BOY: And a beetle in the morning tea.

BOTH: Touring days, alluring days,
Far back into the past we gaze.

GIRL: We used to tip the dressers every Friday night,

BOY: And pass it over lightly when they came in tight.

BOTH: But somehow to us it seemed all right,
Those wonderful touring days . . .

Wendy Toye, in fact, hated the title of the show. She wanted to call it *Master Pieces*. As usual, the Master had the last word. Since he'd thought of *Cowardy Custard*, it was hardly surprising.

Many of Noël's plays contain a song—sometimes several. *Fallen Angels* had a song sung by one of the "angels" (Julia) to pass one of her many idle moments—and to show off her French, while she awaits the arrival of her French lover. Noël himself spoke more than passable French and once played Garry Essendine in the Paris version of *Present Laughter* (*Joyeux Chagrins*), though not, he later admitted, with great success . . .

*MÊME LES ANGES (1923)

Même les Anges succombent à l'amour,
C'est pourquoi donc je vous en prie—
Dieu qui arrange les jours et les séjours
Laisse moi encore une heure de paradis.
Tous mes amours me semblent comme des fleurs,
Leurs parfums restent douce quand même
Donne moi tes lèvres, ton ame, et ton coeur,
Parce que follement je t'aime—je t'aime—je t'aime.

Above: Opening lines from "Même Les Anges." Left, Tallulah Bankhead as Julia Sterroll and Edna Best as Jane Banbury.

Hermione Gingold and Hermione Baddeley (upside down) in the 1949 revival. The play was also to become a vehicle for such actresses as Nancy Walker, Dorothy Lamour, Joan Greenwood and Constance Cummings.

Tallulah Bankhead.

46

(Working title: HELTER SKELTER)

Written in 1922 and 1923 in collaboration with Ronald Jeans. First presented by André Charlot at the Duke of York's Theatre, London on September 4, 1923. (316 performances).

Book by Ronald Jeans and Noël Coward. Lyrics and music by Noël Coward. Additional numbers by Philip Braham and Sissel and Blake.

Cast included: Noël Coward, Gertrude Lawrence, Maisie Gay, Tubby Edlin, Eileen Molyneux.

Noël renewed the professional relationship with Charlot that had tentatively begun five years earlier with his contribution to Tails Up. Now he was to contribute half of the twenty-six numbers in this revue named after the call sign of the new radio station, 2LO London. He wrote to his mother:

". . . it will be gorgeous to do, specially with people like Maisie (Gay) and Gertie, I have written Maisie a divine burlesque song ('There's Life in the Old Girl Yet'). She is to

wear a fair wig and very 'bitty' clothes and look *quite* 55, she does a parasol dance after the song with a male chorus, falling over once or twice on her fanny—it's one of the *wittiest* burlesques I've ever done . . . I'm writing her a male impersonator burlesque, 'I'm Bertie from the Bath Club, But I've *Never* Learned to Swim.' Gertie will sing 'Prenez Garde, Lisette' (new and excellent), 'Tamarisk Town'—'Carrie Was a Careful Girl' with full chorus in lovely Victorian dresses, all very demure—I am to give myself a new song to open with then 'Russian Blues' . . ."

The opening number celebrated a theatre new to revue . . .

---

*DUKE OF YORK'S

PRINCIPALS:

The Duke of York's
The Duke of York's
Is not the kind of theatre that one talks about the least

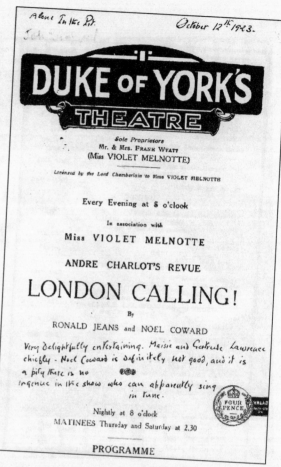

John Gielgud's personal annotated program.

Neglectfully.
We must treat it respectfully.
We're rather scared,
We're rather scared
Because we feel the Management should not have dared
To do here
Intimate Revue here.
It's all wrong.
You must excuse us if the chorus just exhibit a few legs,
We've introduced them slowly so that you can get your
Revue legs
We're feeling shy,
We're feeling shy
And that is why we hope we shan't be cursed
Because we have to burst
Into dance and song.

Producer André Charlot.

*GINGER UP

ALL   Ginger up your Mother
      And your Father and your Brother
      And your Sister and the folks next door.
      Ginger up your cousins
      And your relatives in dozens
      'Till they positively leave the floor.
      Life can be a very dreary thing
      If you give in and never begin to sing.
      Every life is like a bubble,
      Some are single, some are double,
      Lighter than the salt sea foam.
      If your life's a double bubble,
      You will find a lot of trouble.
      If a drink is standing still the sediment will
          drop
      Always keep your sense of humour floating
          on the top
      And take the opportunity to ginger up your
          'Home Sweet Home'

TAMARISK TOWN (1917?)

(Gertrude Lawrence)

VERSE 1
      On an island far across the sea,
      A maid sat dreaming,
      While above the Tamarisks,
      The moon was softly gleaming,
      And as the perfumed Southern breeze
          caressed her,
      She dreamed of how her lover's arms had
          pressed her.
      And she was sighing, sighing.

REFRAIN 1
      Come to Tamarisk Town,
      When the birds in Spring are mating,
      I'm tired of waiting
      I love you so.
      The honey-wind is blowing o'er the bay,
      It calls to mind the day you went away.

From the look in your eyes
I can tell your heart is yearning
To be returning to me
In Tamarisk Town again.

VERSE 2
      Softly o'er the skies the silver dawn came creeping,
      Weary were her eyes and sad her heart, with
          weeping.
      Then suddenly she saw a sail appearing,
      And then a graceful schooner swiftly nearing.
      With joy bells ringing,
      She's gaily singing, singing.

REFRAIN 2
      Come to Tamarisk Town,
      When the birds in Spring are mating,
      I'm tired of waiting
      I love you so.
      The honey-wind is blowing o'er the bay,
      It calls to mind the day you went away.
      From the look in your eyes
      I can tell your heart is yearning
      To be returning to me
      In Tamarisk Town again.

Gertrude Lawrence in "Tamarisk Town."

Noël Coward and the "Other Girls."

OTHER GIRLS

(Noël and Chorus)

VERSE 1   I've always longed to see
Myself at twenty-three
In some dramatic situation,
A slightly cruel man,
With some fair courtesan,
Serenely driving in the Bois,
Though when you're young it's nice
To dream of gilded vice
With all its lurid fascination,
I've learnt to see beyond
The flaunting *femme-du-monde*
And hitch my wagon to a star.

REFRAIN 1   She hasn't rings and sables and things,
Like other girls I know,
She hasn't stockings,
Openwork clockings,
Other girls would show,
Her eyes would never cause a stir,
She's such a simple character,

I don't know why,
But I'd say goodbye
To other girls for her.

VERSE 2   When young men leave their schools,
They make a lot of rules,
They feel their destiny is calling,
They want to burn their boats
And sow the wildest oats
And lead a life of scarlet sin,
I had such smart ideas
But now around my ears
My youthful dreams are gently falling,
My plans have all gone wrong,
Since this girl came along
I've never wanted to begin.

REFRAIN 2   She hasn't guiles and feminine wiles,
Like other girls I've seen,
She never races
Or goes to places
Other girls have been,
She has such sweet simplicity,
So full of domesticity,
I don't know why,
But I'd say goodbye
To other girls for her.

WHEN MY SHIP COMES HOME

(Winifred Satchell)

VERSE 1   Sometimes when I'm weary
And the world seems grey
And the firelight flickers blue,
Somewhere in the future,
Maybe far away,
There are dreams that may come true.
Cinderella's story is so lovely, to pretend,
Some day soon my story too
May have a happy end.

REFRAIN 1   When my ship comes home,
When my ship comes home,
Silks and velvets and cloth of gold,
Caskets bursting with wealth untold,
When my ship comes home.
Through the world I'll roam,
Open skies above me,
Someone dear to love me,
When my ship comes home.

VERSE 2 Life is nothing but a game of make-believe
Until true love comes your way,
Such a dreary pattern
Through the years you weave.
You can't afford to pay
Fate is sometimes cruel,
And a new dawn soon my break,
Every single jewel
I'll be wearing for your sake.

REFRAIN 2 When my ship comes home,
When my ship comes home,
No more waiting through empty years,
Pearls and diamonds in place of tears,
When my ship comes home.
Through the world I'll roam,
Open skies above me,
Someone dear to love me,
When my ship comes home.

CARRIE WAS A CAREFUL GIRL

(Gertrude Lawrence)

VERSE 1 Carrie as a baby was a darling little pet,
And everybody loved her from the Vicar to the
Vet.

Her manners when at school were most
ingenuous and quaint,
She had the reputation of a little plaster saint.

REFRAIN 1 Carrie was a careful girl,
Such a very careful girl,
Nobody imagined from the day that she was
weaned,
That underneath her sweetness was the
temper of a fiend,
Carrie was a careful girl,
Quite a little cultured pearl,
The teachers all adored her and the pupils
did the same,
At every sort of girlish sport she quickly
made a name
And nobody suspected that she played a
double game,
Carrie was a careful girl.

REFRAIN 2 Carrie was a careful girl,
Such a very careful girl,
She stole out on the landing while the others
were at Prayers,
And rubbed a lot of grease upon the dormitory
stairs,
Carrie was a careful girl,
In her little cot she'd curl,
The teacher fell down half a flight and landed
on her head,
And naturally to Carrie not a single word was
said
'Cos they found a pat of butter in her little
sister's bed,
Carrie was a careful girl.

VERSE 2 Carrie had a father with a rather mottled past,
And evils of heredity are bound to show at last,
But Carrie always realized the danger from the
start,
So she stole dear father's diary and learnt it
off by heart.

REFRAIN 3 Carrie was a careful girl,
Such a very careful girl,
When papa departed to the angels meek and
mild,
He left a lot of souvenirs and maxims to his child,
Carrie was a careful girl,
And when in the social whirl,

Though she wasn't tempted by the usual forms
of vice,
She said she thought that games of chance were
really awfully nice
But still she never played a game without her
father's dice,
Carrie was a careful girl.

REFRAIN 4 Carrie was a careful girl,
Such a very careful girl,
So far and no further she was quite prepared
to go,
But still she took precautions 'cos of course you
never know,
Carrie was a careful girl,
Once she met a noble Earl,
He thought that Carrie lived alone and so she let
him think,
She asked him to her flat one night to have a little
drink
But she had her Auntie Jessie underneath the
kitchen sink,
Carrie was a careful girl.

And an unused alternative . . .

Carrie was a careful girl
Once she met a noble earl,
He wasn't very good at psychological research,
He never met her family until they left the
church,
Carrie was a very careful girl.

RUSSIAN BLUES

(Noël)

VERSE I'm just a Russian Refugee,
There's nothing left in all the world for me,
But within my brain
I seem to hear those lovely melodies again
That made my Motherland what she used to be,
I'm weary and my heart is sore
For, even though I do return once more,
Skies are overcast
And I'll have nothing but my memories
of the past
To make me weep for days that have
gone before.

REFRAIN All day long I've got those Russian Blues,
The blues I'll never lose
Until I die.
For while I'm sleeping,
The lovely melodies come creeping,
Just to remind me of days gone by.
Fairy tales
That I learnt at my mother's knee,
And the echo of nightingales
In a magical tree.
Then I find I'm waking with a sigh,
That's the reason why
I've got those Russian Blues.

PATTER Bowled over, bowled over,
Morning noon and night
I'm simply longing for the sight
Of dear old Petrograd and Moscow gay
And the jolly little tinkle of a bell upon
a sleigh!
The Northern lights gleaming,
Samovars steaming,
Maybe I'll return some day.
It may be hysteria
But even if it means Siberia
Start your locomotive, rock your little boat,
I shall feel so happy when I know that
I'm afloat,
I've been too long away.

THERE'S LIFE IN THE OLD GIRL YET (SOUBRETTE)

(Maisie Gay)

Lady Kitty enters laughing girlishly and carrying a basket of roses in one hand and a very fluffy parasol in the other. She is rather fat with metallic golden hair, her dress is extremely 'bitty' with rosebuds and small bows wherever they are humanly possible.

VERSE 1 I'm a naughty little lady,
Full of winsome girlish tricks;
Though I'm rather past my heyday,
I began with Seymour Hicks:
With the chorus boys behind me
i'm a sight you can't forget,
Though the years have rather lined me
I am still a firm soubrette.

CHORUS: Tell us why, tell us which,
Tell us what, tell us how;

BOYS: Tell us when, tell us soon,
Tell us now.

REFRAIN 1
LADY KITTY: They call me Kitty,

CHORUS: Why?

KITTY: Because I'm pretty,

CHORUS: Ah!

KITTY: And because I have a dainty curl

CHORUS: Naughty girl!

KITTY: Men pursue me and woo me, and ask me
to dine
But I'm always in bed by a quarter past nine:
I'm awfully sporty
And I'll be forty

CHORUS: When?

KITTY: On October the twenty-third:

CHORUS: *(Derisively)*
What a bird!

KITTY: Though there may be one or two notes that
I can't quite get,

CHORUS: Well—
There's life in the old girl yet.

VERSE 2
KITTY: I'm as playful as a kitten,
Love has seldom passed me by;
I have more than once been bitten,
Though I'm hardly ever shy,
Though if Winter came, my style would
Be a little undermined;
Still the Spring of second childhood
Can't be very far behind.

CHORUS: Pretty soon, pretty near,
Pretty quaint, pretty queer;
Pretty poll, pretty pet,
Pretty dear.

REFRAIN 2
KITTY: They call me Flossie,

CHORUS: Why?

KITTY: Because I'm mossy,

CHORUS: *(Firmly)* Yes

Kitty: And because I always go the pace;

CHORUS: *(Rudely)* Shut yer face!

KITTY: *(Coyly)*
I show traces of laces, and silk underneath,
I'm as old as my tongue but much
older than my teeth:
My goodness gracious

CHORUS: Well?

KITTY: I'm so vivacious,

CHORUS: Hell!

KITTY: Always ready for a kiss or two:

CHORUS: Fancy you!

KITTY: Though at one time people always called
me "Gladstone's Pet",
Still, there's life in the old girl yet.

Maisie Gay had been a boyhood idol of Noël's and he did for her something he was to do for few others—he crafted her own personalised version of the song.

*You're a versatile old party
Time will never dim your star
And your laughs are just as hearty
In the theatre or the bar
With the bottles ranged behind you
You're a sight I won't forget
In whatever age I find you
You're my favourite soubrette

CHORUS BOYS:
Mine's a port, mine's a splash,
Mine's a gin with a dash,
Mine's a beer,
Bring it here,
Maisie dear.

REFRAIN: They call you Maisie
Though years are hazy
I can see you with your old brown jug

CHORUS: What a mug

You're a pro, dear, and so, dear, you'll
never give in
You're the bitters in beer and the tonic in gin.
Your wit is clearer
Than old Madeira
I salute you with a phrase, "Here's how"

CHORUS: What a cow

But I know whatever happens when the
last act's set
There'll be life in the old girl yet

PRENEZ GARDE, LISETTE

(Maisie Gay)

VERSE 1   Lisette was witty and naughty and pretty,
          She started flirting when she was ten,
          And she intended
          When schooldays were ended
          To grow up a *soignée* Parisienne.
          Young men would sigh
          As she passed by,
          And all her anxious relatives
          Would rush at her and cry:

REFRAIN 1 Prenez Garde, Lisette,
          You are rather young as yet,
          Though of soldiers and of sailors you
          May be extremely fond,
          We don't wish you to turn into
          A flaming demi-monde,
          Prenez Garde, Lisette,
          You seem to be a born coquette,
          But when the Poilus come marching right
              up to your door,
          They'll love you and leave you but wiser
              than before,
          Allons enfants de la Patrie,
          Mais Prenez Garde, Lisette.

VERSE 2   Lisette was charming, alluring, disarming,
          Desiring, acquiring experience.
          Military honour
          Was showered upon her,
          Her love for her country was so intense,
          Soldiers adored,
          Raved and implored,
          But when she only laughed at them they
              cried with one accord:

REFRAIN 2 Prenez Garde, Lisette,
          You have caught us in your net,
          Though where ignorance is bliss they say
              'tis folly to be wise,
          We never knew
          An ingénue
          With quite your kind of eyes,
          Prenez Garde, Lisette,
          But she had made her plans you bet,
          And when the Generals came marching
              right up to her door,
          They'd love her and leave her but richer
              than before,
          Allons enfants de la Patrie,
          Mais Prenez Garde, Lisette.

And an unused alternative couplet . . .

          When sailors came marching right up to
              her door
          They felt quite at sea when they left her
              on the shore.

(In the original mss. 'Lisette' was spelled 'Lissette')

WHAT LOVE MEANS TO GIRLS LIKE ME

(Maisie Gay)

VERSE 1   A little word, four letters only,
          And yet it means a lot you must admit.
          It seems absurd,
          But when I'm lonely
          I lose my sense of values just a bit.
          If men are really willing,
          I must say I find it thrilling
          Just to listen to the charming things they
              say.

          Though I'm not exactly fickle,
          I enjoy a slap and tickle
          In a quiet unassuming sort of way.

REFRAIN 1 It isn't that I'm naughty or capricious,
          It isn't that I single out my prey,
          I'm sure that I've a mind
          To flaunt my girlish charms in any way
          I sometimes think that Eve was very
              thoughtless
          To wrench the fruit of knowledge from
              the tree,
          More abstemious she'd have been,
          Could she only have foreseen
          What love means to girls like me.

VERSE 2   If love is blind and people say so,
          I'm certain that that statement's incorrect.
          I shouldn't mind,
          If he would stay so,
          It's when he starts to see things I object.
          To say that Cupid hates me,
          And deliberately baits me,
          Would really not exaggerate the case.
          You could wheel away in barrows
          All the bleeding blunted arrows
          That from time to time he's fired in my
              face.

REFRAIN 2 It isn't that I'm thoroughly degraded,
          It isn't that I go from bad to worse,
          It isn't that I pine
          For Roses, Love and Wine,
          I'm a victim of a temperamental curse.
          I often try to suffocate my passion,
          Though all the time I yearn to set it free,
          Cleopatra at her best
          Would have shuddered if she'd guessed
          What love means to girls like me.

REFRAIN 3 It isn't that I'm consciously alluring,
          It isn't that I'm altogether bad.
          A girl may have her dreams
          Without going to extremes,
          Though I shouldn't like to mention some
              I've had.
          It isn't that I take all and give nothing,
          I'm sure I'm generous-hearted as can be,
          But poor Mary, Queen of Scots,
          Would have tied herself in knots
          For what love means to girls like me.

*FOLLOW A STAR

(Gertrude Lawrence and Company)

Follow a star,
You'll see wherever you are
It's always there in the blue.
Make for the best
And never falter or rest
Until your dreams come true.
Strike out a line
And fix a definite shrine,
No matter how the cruel fates conspire
Things may look far from mending
But when your journey's ending,
Then you will find your heart's desire.

VERSE 1   Never be depressed or blue,
Here's the reason why—
Somewhere there's a star for you
Shining in the sky
Pay no heed to little things
Doubts and shadows all have wings,
Welcome what the future brings
And as the years roll by . . .

VERSE 2   If you're weary, never mind,
I always travel light
Such a lot of peace you'll find
Any starry night
Keep your heart sincere and real
Hopeless you will never feel
If you have a true ideal
And keep it well in sight.

*   *   *

Comedian Tubby Edlin was given the comic song, "Devon." Written in 1920, it was Noël's subversive version of all the hymns to bucolic bliss favoured by concert party tenors up and down the country of the "Devon, Glorious Devon" variety . . .

DEVON

VERSE 1   You men may quaff your frothing ale,
From tankards, mugs and pots,
But Devonshire's the only place

To find forget-me-knots.
The earth is red,
The beer is red,
The girls are redder still,
The sun looks down with a roguish eye,
So up your glasses fill,
Fill up, fill up, fill up, fill up, fill up.

REFRAIN   Oh! Some may go to Clacton
And some may care for Bude,
You may laugh Ho! Ho! at Felixstowe,
Though as a resort it's rather rude.
Oh! Some may go to Bognor,
Or Ashton-under-Lyne,
But Francis Drake cried Todaloodaloo,
In Devon by the Brine.

VERSE 2   But when life's sky is overcast
And death is in the vale,
Though we may go to rest at last,
Thank God we've got our ale.
For Devon men are red throughout
In April, May and June,
So let your sturdy voices shout,
For Drake and Lorna Doon,
Hey Doon, Fie Doon, Fie Doon, Fie Doon,
Fie Doon.

REFRAIN   Oh! Wigan men are hearty
And Bolton men are bold,
There's something coy in a Blackpool boy,
And the Bedford lads have hearts of gold,
But the chaps that live on Dartmoor
Are breezy, bright and gay,
Singing a tra la la
With a hey ho ha
And a whack fol do
And a nin noni no
And a down derry down, sing hey,
Down derry down, sing hey,
Ha ha, ha ha, ha ha, ha ha,
Ha ha.

Thirty years later for his cabaret act, Noël dusted off Devon, so to speak . . . (He also learned the correct spelling of Lorna Doone!) The second version is rhythmically quite different and is virtually a complete reworking . . .

DEVON (1951)

VERSE 1   Both near and far
I've followed my star
Wherever that star has led me,
From Zanzibar
To Leamington Spa
My vagabond feet have sped me,
But in my dreams
It always seems
I'm on some Devonshire hill
Where the earth is red
And the beer is red
And the girls are redder still,
Fill up—fill up—the girls are redder still.

REFRAIN 1   It's mighty fine to rattle home
To Tiverton or Torquay,
And Babbacombe Bay
The wise men say
Is just the only place to be,
Let others call the cattle home
Across the sands of Dee
For Francis Drake cried 'Toodle-oodle-oo'
In Devon by the sea.

VERSE 2   But when life's sky is overcast
And death is in the vale
Though we may go to rest at last
Thank God we've got our ale,
For Devon men are red throughout
In April, May and June,
So let your sturdy voices shout
For Drake and Lorna Doone,
Fie Doone—Fie Doone—Fie Doone,
     Fie Doone,
Fie Doone.

REFRAIN 2   For Wigan men are hearty
And Bolton men are bold,
There's something coy in a Blackpool boy
And the Bedford lads have hearts of gold,
But the chaps that live on Dartmoor
Are breezy, bright and gay,
Singing Hey ha ha with a fa la la and a
     hey nonny
And whack folly o,
Ha ha ha ha ha ha ha ha ha ha ha ha
     HA HA HA
HA!

* * *

The only song to survive *London Calling!* which became, according to Cecil Beaton, "the signature tune of the late 1920s" was "Parisian Pierrot." Noël wrote it for Gertie during a holiday in Germany:

> "The idea of it came to me in a nightclub in Berlin in 1922. A frowsy blonde, wearing a sequin chest-protector and a divided skirt, appeared in the course of the cabaret with a rag pierrot doll dressed in black velvet. She placed it on a cushion where it sprawled in pathetic abandon while she pranced around it emitting guttural noises. Her performance was unimpressive but the doll fascinated me. The title 'Parisian Pierrot' slipped into my mind, and in the taxi on the way back to the hotel the song began."

Noël reported that Gertie wearing yellow and green pantaloons and a tulle ruff, sang the song "exquisitely" and that Edward Molyneux, who designed the costumes, "made it one of the loveliest stage pictures I have ever seen." He was a little less enchanted by her singing in rehearsal. Her voice he always found a little—idiosyncratic: "If you would sing a little *more* out of tune, darling, you would find yourself singing in thirds, which would be a great improvement."

Seventy years later the song remains in the top ten among Coward's royalties.

1920's audiences would have been very familiar with the pantomime character of Pierrot (and his feminine equivalent, Pierrette) with his whitened face, loose white clothing and soft conical hat. Descended—like Harlequin, Columbine and Pantaloon—from the 17th century *commedia dell'arte*—Pierrot came to embody the lyrical and sentimental. Around the turn of the century concert parties, particularly those performing on seaside piers, took to dressing in Pierrot costumes and by the mid-20's it was all the rage. Noël himself used the characters frequently in his early unpublished poems. Best known of the troupes was probably *The Co-Optimists* (see p. 37), who even called their revue "a Pierrotic Entertainment." Like all vogues, it passed and when Joan Littlewood ironically dressed the cast of her anti-war revue, *Oh, What a Lovely War* (1963) in the costumes, few of the audience even understood the reference.

Gertrude Lawrence performing "Parisian Pierrot."

54

PARISIAN PIERROT

VERSE 1   Fantasy in olden days
In varying and different ways
Was very much in vogue,
Columbine and Pantaloon,
A wistful Pierrot 'neath the moon,
And Harlequin a rogue.
Nowadays Parisians of leisure
Wake the echo of an old refrain,
Each some ragged effigy will treasure
For his pleasure,
Till the shadows of their story live again.

VERSE 2   Mournfulness has always been
The keynote of a Pierrot scene,
When passion plays a part,
Pierrot in a tragic pose
Will kiss a faded silver rose
With sadness in his heart.
Some day soon he'll leave his tears behind
    him,
Comedy comes laughing down the street,
Columbine will fly to him
Admiring and desiring,
Laying love and adoration at his feet.

REFRAIN   Parisian Pierrot,
Society's hero,
The Lord of a day,
The Rue de la Paix
Is under your sway,
The world may flatter
But what does that matter,
They'll never shatter
Your gloom profound,
Parisian Pierrot,
Your spirit's at zero,
Divinely forlorn,
With exquisite scorn
From sunset to dawn,
The limbo is calling,
Your star will be falling,
As soon as the clock goes round.

*   *   *

Noël had less success with a song he'd written for himself, even though he'd had Fred Astaire stage it for him. He would bound on stage,

"immaculately dressed in tails, with a silk hat and cane. I sang every couplet with perfect dic-

Noël Coward and Gertrude
Lawrence share a moment
in "You Were Meant For Me"
a non-Coward number choreographed by Fred Astaire.

tion and a wealth of implication which sent the lines winging out into the dark auditorium, where they fell wetly like pennies into mud. Unfortunately, the number could not be taken out, owing to the running order of the revue, and so nightly the audience and I were forced to endure it."

SENTIMENT

(Music by Philip Braham)

VERSE 1 People have said sentiment's dead
But it's a lie!
Listen to what I say—
It has remained firmly ingrained
Never will die
Look at the world today.

REFRAIN 1 Sentiment, it's simply sentiment
That makes the world go round at all,
It keeps the undiscerning
Home fires burning
Though the skies may fall,
Many a loving couple have their motives
    misconstrued,
For there's a fundamental code with which
    we're all imbued,
If they're alone together after half past ten
    it's rude,
Sentiment that's all!

REFRAIN 2 Sentiment, it's simply sentiment
That makes the world go round at all,
The British as a race
Just hate to face
The faintest moral squall,
Foreigners' immorality may make us look
    askance,
Though we are not above it if we get the
    slightest chance.
What is it makes an Englishman enjoy
    himself in France?
Sentiment, that's all!

VERSE 2 People may laugh, people may chaff,
Brush it away!
Thinking the time is ripe,
Nevertheless you must confess
Here it will stay,
We are so true to type.

REFRAIN 3 Sentiment, it's simply sentiment
That makes the world go round at all,
Though people deprecate it,
Say they hate it,
All the same they fall,
What is it makes a magistrate when some
    divorce is filed,
Lecture the woman sternly on the wrongs
    of running wild?
Then give the husband custody of someone
    else's child?
Sentiment that's all!

REFRAIN 4 Sentiment, it's simply sentiment
That makes the world go round at all,
You'll find the Public Taste
Is fiercely chaste
No matter what befall,
When some poor girl falls victim to the
    local ne'er-do-well,
When it's too late to wonder as to
    "should a woman tell",
What is it makes her marry him though
    hating him like hell?
Sentiment that's all!

Noël's notes indicate some alternative lines for Refrains 3 and 4:

For the meek and undiscerning
It will keep the home fires burning,
Magistrates and country candidates
Beneath the spell will fall . . .

. . . .

Mothers with unruly daughters
Pour it thick on troubled waters,
It will aid the weak and much afraid
To answer honour's call . . .

*   *   *

A year later Charlot decided to try his luck on Broadway by taking the best items from his previous revues and putting them into a compilation called *André Charlot's London Revue of 1924*. The show was to star Beatrice Lillie, Gertrude Lawrence and Jack Buchanan. Much of the material was Noël's, including "Sentiment":

"I experienced the mixed pain and pleasure of seeing Jack Buchanan bring the house down in top hat, white tie and tails . . . watching to see why he should succeed so triumphantly where I had failed, and finding at first no adequate reason, except perhaps that it was because he made no effort at all. It wasn't until much later that I acknowledged to myself in secret that the truth of the matter was that his whole technique was superior to mine."

The Times reviewer reported that: "The piece received a very enthusiastic reception after its first performance . . ." and that "Mr. Noël Coward is the Pooh-Bah of the production. He takes a leading part in it, and acts, dances and sings with credit . . . it was his handiwork that gave the others many of their opportunities of shining." The *Manchester Dispatch*, however, found that his voice, though "pleasing" was "at present not extremely powerful."

An early professional critic was the young John Gielgud, who attended the opening performance and scribbled on his program: "When pruned of three or four poor items, it will be a really excellent show. Maisie Gay is magnificent—and Gertrude Lawrence very good—Coward will be better when he is less nervous but he's a little ineffectual and amateurish at present. Edlin quite funny—some very good scenes—but it all suffered from the nervous slowness of the players today and the inordinate length of the program, which will, of course, be cut." He clearly enjoyed himself enough to pay a return visit a month later, when he concluded: "Noël Coward is definitely not good, and it is a pity there is no ingénue in the show who can apparently sing in tune."

As with most revues, there were several other numbers written and even rehearsed. Noël's handwritten running lists even indicate where they would have been placed in the show. In several his continued ambivalence towards American popular song forms is apparent. At this stage he seemed to find it hard to understand that it is difficult to satirise something that is a parody in itself.

*PARK YOUR FANNY

An item he considered adding to the show later in the run was a parody of "an American Song and Dance Show"—a surrealistic abbreviation of the kind of musical where the plot makes no sense and is, in any case, constantly being interrupted for an irrelevant song.

The heroine is Miss Cherry Ripe, "the famous American ingénue," who plays the leading part of Pegeen, "a hotel maidservant with no particular talents outside her profession, who has just received offers of

marriage from 5 millionaires and a Chinaman . . . She is discovered standing in the centre of the stage, exquisitely pretty, exquisitely dressed and exquisitely stupid." Her suitors surround her. Suddenly Jake ("in Bowery clothes") bursts in and sings—

> I've got those 'Park Your Fanny Blues',
> My toes are peeping through my shoes.
> In Alabama
> We have got the greatest panarama
> But it wearies me so.
> Back in Kentucky
> I can see my gal if I am lucky,
> Tho' plain and quite a dullard
> She's more than twopence coloured.
> Virginia always makes me frown,
> Chicago's really a most disgusting town.
> I've let down my basket and the well's run dry
> That's why I'm sighing.
> I've got the Park Your Fanny Blues—
> Which means I want to sit down.
>
> I've got those Park Your Fanny Blues,
> I guess my lights are going to fuse,
> In Carolina
> It would really be a lot diviner
> If it weren't for the coona
> Louisiana
> Echoes to the banjo and the piana,
> They simply drive me silly.
> There's a place in Piccadilly
> Compared with that Ohio shore
> It makes this poor guy sigh, "Oh my, oh lor!"
> I feel like the engine with the tender behind,
> That's what I'm minding.
> I've got the Park Your Fanny Blues—
> Which means I want to sit down.

A Policeman enters, arrests Pegeen and then sings an updated version of "Everybody's Jazzing Mad" . . .

*THE SAGGIE BOO

> Say, folks, if you like pep
> You're simply going dippy on the "Saggie Boo" step.
> Roll your eyes and slap your thighs,
> I guess you'll give the Vanderbilts a horrible
>   surprise
>   Can you do the Saggie Boo?
>   It's a step that's really new.

> You commence by merely bleating like a goat,
> Heaving like a boat,
> Tie your sock suspenders to the lapels of your
>   coat.
> Take a tip from me
> If you get water on the knee,
> Then North, South, West you prance
> Saving up the East for a supper dance.
> When you're black and blue
> You'll have done the Saggie Boo.

> ALL: Can you do the Saggie Boo?
> It's a step that's really new,
> All you do is take your partner in your grip
> Then you make her trip
> Swing her round the room until you dislocate her
>   hip
> If she makes a sound,
> You simply fell her to the ground.
> Then North, East, West you fight,
> Saving up the South for a Gala night.
> Then you've got a clue
> How to do the Saggie Boo.

Jake reappears and sings to Pegeen—

> There's a look in your eyes,
> Which is quite a surprise
> 'Cos it brings back my old Uncle Bob.
> Your expression's so sad
> It reminds me of Dad
> When he'd just been kicked out of his job.
> You've a kink in your nose
> Like my poor Auntie Rose
> Who was recently stung by a bee
> But I think most of all
> It's your ears that recall
> My old-fashioned Mother to me.

Noël was to have played Jake, Gertie Pegeen, Tubby Edlin the Policeman and a part was inked in for Maisie Gay.

*MRS 'ARRIS

> It was all very pretty,
> Very, very pretty
> But we never went much faster than a crawl
> The engine blew up early
> Just outside a pub at Purley

58

So I don't think I liked it after all.

It was all very pretty,
Very, very pretty
But it seemed to me to be a trifle small
Tho' the line was quite *de rigeur*
It showed rather too much—figure
So I don't think I liked it after all.

It was all very pretty,
Very, very pretty
And we lingered till the night began to fall
But the small green chair we sat on
Left a most peculiar pattern
So I don't think I liked it after all.

At one point he considered including the "Customs House, Dover" sketch, which would have meant that he and Gertie would have introduced "Touring Days" (see p. 43).

*   *   *

When Charlot took Gertie out of the show for his New York production, she was replaced by Joyce Barbour for the second edition, which opened on December 1, 1923. Noël provided two new songs.

"I Prefer To Be On The Safe Side" was a solo for Joyce, while the second appears to have suffered the fate of many a marginal revue number. On the night it turned up as a solo for "Noël and Chorus" but at some point he had experimented with it as a duet, presumably for himself and Joyce Barbour. Only that version remains . . .

---

*TEMPERAMENTAL HONEYMOON

VERSE

HE: Now you and I are wed, dear,
        Our cares will all be over,

SHE: When all is done and said, dear,
        We'll live our lives in clover.

BOTH: We'll be happy as two clams, you'll see
        (*Aside*) Once I've made you the person
        That I want you to be . . .

REFRAIN I

SHE: Darling, could I make a small suggestion?

HE: Of course, dear

SHE: *Must the toothpaste be without its top?*

HE: And if I could also raise a question . . .

SHE: Yes, darling?

HE: *Must the gin be drained to the last drop?*

BOTH: Just a thought
        And hardly worth the mention
        And I'm sure
        You don't doubt my good intention?

        (*Spoken*) Oh no, darling . . . Absolutely not!
        (*Sung*) If we're to make some changes
        We should make them soon
        And what better time
        Than on our honeymoon?

REFRAIN 2

HE: If I say something, please don't be
        offended . . .

SHE: Oh, don't be silly!

HE: Must you take up *every* hanger for your
        clothes?

SHE: And just one tiny thought, quite
        open-ended . . .

HE: And what's that?

SHE: Cigar smoke is one thing I really loathe!

BOTH: Don't think in any way
        We're in contention—
        They say
        Necessity's the mother of invention.

        (*Spoken*) Certainly . . . No question about it,

        (*Sung*) If we're to make some changes,
        We should make them soon
        And what better time than on our
        honeymoon?

REFRAIN 3

SHE: There's just one thing you mustn't mind
        my raising . . .

HE: Fire away, old thing!

SHE: Your laugh sounds just a little like a horse . . .

HE: And the things that you call hats are quite
        amazing.
        You'd like me to speak honestly?

SHE: (*grimly*) Of course!

BOTH: And what better time to speak your mind,
        To tell the truth,
        Though it sounds unkind,
        Than on the one occasion

    They say love is blind,
    On our very sentimental—
    Just slightly temperamental—
    Honeymoon?

*   *   *

A third edition followed on February 20th 1924. Of the original stars only Maisie Gay remained. Noël added further numbers:

WHEN WE WERE GIRLS TOGETHER

(*Maisie Gay and A. W. Baskcomb*)

VERSE I

    Once we were maidens of bashful fifteen,
        Ah fal la la
        Whack folly olly O,
    Though we were not what we ought to have been,
        Hey lack-a-day
        Nin nonny nonny no,
    I used to bloom like a flowering shrub,
    I was the toast of the Ham and Bone Club,
    People would cycle for miles and miles
    To bask in the light of our radiant smiles.

REFRAIN I

    When we were girls together,
    Ready to do and dare,
    Roguish and winsome and naughty and gay,
    Bold at our lessons and
    Rascals at play,
    Don't give a jot for weather,
    Spiced with devil-may-care,
    Dreams of romance we would never dismiss,
    Life was a frolic of virginal bliss
    Wanting the magic of somebody's kiss,
    That was our maiden's prayer.

VERSE 2

    Oh how the gallants of Battersea Rise,
        Ah fal la la
        Whack folly olly O,
    Followed us round with lascivious eyes,
        Hey lack-a-day
        Nin nonny nonny no,
    Medical students besieged me in mobs,

I was a riot at Arding and Hobbs,
Roués would tempt us to amorous sin,
Their patience gave out
But we never gave in.

REFRAIN 2

When we were girls together,
Brushing our golden hair
Over the fire when daytime was done,
Whispering fragments of naughtiest fun,
Fresh as the wind-blown heather,
Laying our secrets bare,
Biblical stories we'd always believe,
All kinds of knowledge we tried to achieve,
And oh for the apple the Serpent gave Eve,
That was our maiden's prayer.

VERSE 3

One Sunday evening we met a young man,
    Ah fal la la
    Whack folly olly O,
Though it was rash we fell in with his plan,
    Hey lack-a-day
    Hi nonny nonny no,
I had misgivings I'm bound to confess,
I kept myself to myself more or less,
Maybe we did go a little too far
But we didn't get tired as he'd such a nice car.

REFRAIN 3

When we were girls together,
Oh what an elfin pair,
As we grew older
We're bound to admit
Our maidenly fancies
Developed a bit,
Often our thoughts we'd tether,
Though we were well aware
We'd done naughty things that we oughtn't to do,
We wanted no longer to bill and to coo
But marriage with someone
We didn't care who,
That was our maiden's prayer

SPANISH GRANDEE

(Teddie Gerard)

VERSE

Spain with its mountains and streams

Is a country of dreams
Where romance always seems
To be found
There in the coolness of night
When the stars are alight
And the moonlight is bright
On the ground,
Spain sunshine and rain
Deep in my brain
Calling ever,
Spain must I remain
See you again
Never, never.

REFRAIN

Somewhere there's a Spanish Grandee
Waiting for a lover like me
And while he whispers my name
My heart he'll claim
Under a flaming tangerine moon.
Swept off my feet
By kisses sweet
I hope I'll meet
Him terribly soon.
Some day we'll assuredly be
Lovers by the warm southern sea
With passion flowers swaying
And mandolins playing
My thoughts ever straying
To my Spanish Grandee.

*   *   *

He also registered three other numbers with the
Lord Chamberlain's Office that were never used . . .

*SHAKE YOUR FEET

Everybody, everybody, listen to me,
I can not help but enthuse
I just heard a happy snappy melody
So put on your dancing shoes.
Come along, and join the throng and gather
    around.
I dug up something that's new
Don't you hesitate, don't proversinate,
Here's what I want you to do.

CHORUS: Shake your feet, just hear that beat
        Oh boy! That's sweet, let's stop
        You can't help dancing

You start in a-prancing
    Just hear that rhythm
You can't help go with 'em
    Loosen up a little
Do your stuff but not too rough
But just enough. Be neat!
Start stepping to that dancing meter
    What could be sweeter
Swing along, swing along, swing along
    Shake your feet

"The Baseball Rag" strikes again . . . !

*LADY

(Presumably intended for Gertrude Lawrence)

BOYS: We don't know you,
          Pretty Lady, but we'd like to show you
          Just a bit of gratitude, if you'd
          Now, give us a chance for one little dance.

CHIQUETTE: Oh, I don't know you
          Gentlemen, but I would like to show you
          What you'll say is nothing new to me.

BOYS: But we don't agree.

CHIQUETTE: Here's what it will be . . .

CHORUS BOYS:
          Lady, we'd like to know you,
          Lady, we'd like to show you
          Maybe you'll listen to our plea
          You see, we're sort of lonely
          You'll be the one and only
          Lady, on whom we could agree.
          On this a pleasant meeting
          One kiss is just a greeting
          So we are just entreating you.
          Tonight, as we are dancing
          You're quite the most entrancing
          Lady, we really ever knew.

PATTER
CHORUS BOYS:
          We believe you'd like to tell us
          We are just the kind of fellows
          You would like to have around you,
          Such is our vanity, touch of insanity, too.

CHIQUETTE: I like you all the same,
          Perhaps the weather is to blame.

60

BOYS: You are such a darling ducky
          This is our happy-go-lucky day, we'll say
          You're a nugget, and we'd like to hug it
               right away.

CHIQUETTE: For one I cannot fall
            I'll be a sister after all.

BOYS: You would make a peach of a teacher,
               wouldn't you?
          You could make us do quite a few things,
               couldn't you?
          Try us and see what you can do.

CHIQUETTE: That isn't easy to, for I am just an
            ingénue.

BOYS: You will find that we are kind
          And, if you wouldn't mind we'd like a
               souvenir, my dear,
          Have pity on a city bunch of boys who
          Want it to remember you.

*   *   *

The song Noël refers to in his letter to his mother—
the solo he intended for Maisie Gay—did not survive
into any edition of the show. Perhaps on reflection
he found it too close to the classic music hall song,
"Burlington Bertie."

*BERTIE FROM THE BATH CLUB

I'm Bertie from the Bath Club
From girl to girl I skim
There's Frowsy Fanny
And Prancing Prue
And Bowlegged Beryl from the Bakerloo.
God bless the ladies,
They tear me limb from limb
I'm Bertie from the Bath Club
But I've never learned to swim

Is it stretching to find in it an early draft of "Men
About Town"? Noël was ever loath to throw anything
away . . .

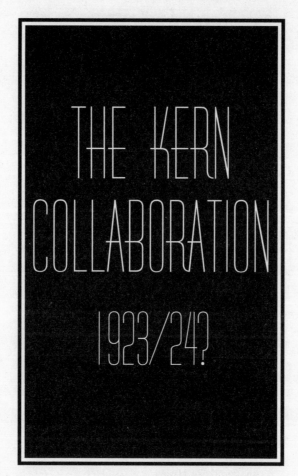

Surprisingly for one who documented his life so
carefully, in none of his published writings does
Noël make any reference to his collaboration with
Jerome Kern. It was only when two Kern/Coward
manuscripts turned up in the Secaucus warehouse
treasure trove of 1986 that questions began to be
asked.

The first clue came in lyricist Howard Dietz's
1974 autobiography, *Dancing In The Dark*. Dietz
recalls being summoned to Kern's Bronxville home
to collaborate on a show called *Vanity Fair* (eventually *Dear Sir*). At this time Kern—who wrote several
musicals a year in the 1910s and 1920s, many of
them with collaborators P. G. Wodehouse and Guy
Bolton—was experimenting with new young partners. In the course of his career he was to work with
over seventy different lyricists.

Arriving at Kern's house, Dietz had a sheet
music manuscript thrust at him by the great man
with the instruction to "do a twist on these lyrics." At
the top of the lead sheet was the name "Noël
Coward" and the title Kern had scribbled—"If You
Will Be My Morganatic Wife." A second song was
entitled "Tamaran."

A few days later Dietz duly returned with the
lyrical 'twist'—"If We Could Lead a Merry Mormon

Life." Kern appeared pleased with his efforts,
although the number didn't survive rehearsals. The
second song became "Gypsy Caravan" and did. *Dear
Sir* was not destined to be a Kern success and ran for
only 15 performances.

How, why and when the Coward/Kern collaboration took place at all—and why it never came to
fruition—is unlikely to be totally explained but
there are clues. Lee Davis in his book, *Bolton and
Wodehouse and Kern* (1993) claims that Noël visited
Kern while he was in New York in late 1925 during
the Broadway run of *The Vortex* and "wrote two lyrics
for two songs Jerry was writing for *Vanity Fair* . . .
They were apparently the only lyrics he would ever
write for music not composed by himself."

Davis is wrong on both scores. Noël was to write
lyrics to music by Melville Gideon for *The Co-
Optimists* and Philip Braham in 1920s revues, not to
mention Max Darewski. In addition, he could hardly
have written lyrics in 1925 for a show that enjoyed
its brief life in September 1924.

The fact of the matter seems to be that Noël
wrote an entire musical comedy called *Tamaran* with
Kern specifically in mind and Kern was sufficiently
interested to put music to two of his songs.

Noël's fascination with the highly successful
Kern is not hard to understand. On his first impov-
erished visit to New York in 1921 . . . "We went to the
New Amsterdam Theatre to see Marilyn Miller in
Sally, and came away cheerfully enchanted." In
1923 both men were working in London, where
Kern was just as popular as he was on Broadway.
London Calling! opened on September 4th and
Kern's *The Beauty Prize* a day later. It is inconceiv-
able that the two of them did not meet at this time
and very likely that the collaboration—such as it
turned out to be—took place then.

Noël's papers contain an almost complete libretto for *Tamaran* and, although it is undated, the edi-
torial references seem to confirm a 1923/4 date of
writing. The second act is set in the British Empire
Exhibition at Wembley, which opened in 1924 and
continued through 1925.

(We know Noël went to and was impressed by
this event. Gladys Cooper recounts that she and
Noël attended the opening: "We got there very
early in quite old clothes, determined to enjoy ourselves at all the side shows and so on before the
place became packed out." They also ran into
impressario, C. B. Cochran who insisted they join
his party which included a host of movie stars,
including Mary Pickford and Douglas Fairbanks—
which presumably gave Noël the idea for the Act 3
Finale.)

The manuscript contains various interruptions where songs are to be placed with "Note to Mr. Kern" and Noël attempts to indicate to Kern the kind of song he has in mind by referring to specific earlier Kern numbers from shows such as *Sally* (1920), *The Cabaret Girl* (1921), *The Beauty Prize* (1923) and *Stepping Stones* (1923).

Kern was notoriously difficult to work with and it must be assumed that he lost interest in the project and moved on to other things. Perhaps the young Noël was so disappointed that his first "book" musical petered out that he developed some sort of mental bloc about mentioning it. Certainly Kern's departure wasn't the end of *Tamaran*. Noël went on to write lyrics for at least two of the other planned songs but in the end he, too, must have felt that the time for this kind of musical comedy was probably past.

CHARACTERS
(The following names are subject to alteration)

ATLAS BLUBB (Sometimes BUBB): Wigmaker and costumier; a very precious personage with supreme contempt for chorus girls and a veneration for the titled class especially Royalty. (*Leslie Henson* was pencilled in for this part.)

TONI CARARA (Sometimes GUIDO): An Argentine adventurer, reputed to have unlimited wealth; a complete Don Juan; overdresses.

COUNT PETER: The hereditary Prince of Tamaran, exiled and unknown in London; under the name of Count Peter he is working as a dress designer with Atlas.

WINTHROP: A young actor.

HEREFORD: General factotum and greasy assistant to Atlas Blubb.

BORAILIC: A Tamarani. The father of Fayra; Bolshevik tendency (Small part).

FAYRA: A humble assistant at Blubb's shop; daughter of a Tamaran father and English mother who thinks always of a dream Prince who will regenerate her Country of which she has heard so much from her father.

ZAZA DOLMONDLEY: A brainless, beautiful English movie star. (The English counterpart of Constance Talmadge). She preaches Hollywood in London and is full of plans for her own career; followed always by a retinue of young men—changes her costume for every occasion.

LADY TIARA POOTER: (Sometimes LADY HYACINTHE) A society dancing girl, reeking of the Embassy Club and vaguely attached to Toni/Guido.

In one of the versions . . .

JENKINS, POTTER, MAUDIE and SNOOKS:
    Assistants at Blubb's

THE MARCHIONESS, LADY ANGELA, LADY UCKFIELD and THE HON. MOIRA:
    Society Clients of Blubb's

YASHA and TINA: Tamarani Girls at the Wembley Pavilion (YASHA is the Village Beauty)

RATZI and PAULUS: Borailic's Henchmen

The main idea of the play is founded on the standing advertisement of Albania, which is advertising in the papers for a KING—"English Country Gentleman preferred." Albania—in this case, TAMARAN is a country with no resources but of infinite beauty.

*   *   *

The following plot summary is taken from fragments of two complementary scripts.

ACT 1

Atlas Blubb's London salon. Atlas enters, an active, rather vulgar little man who has trouble with his aspirates. We see some of the typical activity as Blubb roundly insults several distinguished patrons, who seem to enjoy it hugely. Winthrop, a young actor, is fitted for a Shakespearean role. Several Society matrons enter, one of whom is called Lady Uckfield (the beginning of Noël's fascination with the *sound* of the place). Blubb reveals he lives there, too—"Nice little place—chicken farm. Queen Anne with trellis work over the stucco." He leaves with the ladies and Peter, his new assistant, enters, causing havoc among the girls in the salon.

The notes for this first act are incomplete but at some early point we are introduced to Fayra. Sitting with the other girls, all dressing wigs, she has a number which Noël says in his "Note to Mr. Kern" . . . "should be on the lines of 'Joan of Arc' in *Sally* and tell the story of the Prince who will one day come back and, perhaps, take her with him."

We then meet Zaza, the movie star, and Toni/Guido, the Argentinian millionaire who is pursuing her. The two of them have a duet. ("This should be a typical Kern semi-love duet—'What Would You Do For Me?' in which he undertakes to do anything and she promises very little in return.")

Count Peter, as he calls himself, has a solo number. ("This should be the equivalent of 'Sally In Our Alley.' Men's voices only might be used in refrain, but the tall girls dressed in the costumes of his new designs parade through the second verse.")

Later in the act Atlas is looking at the racing form in the daily paper when he spots an advertisement. "King wanted. Tamaran, at present without ruler, in urgent need of Monarch—English Country Gentleman preferred; bachelor essential; write or wire Box Z International News Agency." He immediately drafts his acceptance. Up to this point Atlas had been vying with Toni for Zaza's affections but the 'bachelor essential' qualification puts something of a damper on that. When Zaza and Toni ask him what he has read in the paper that interests him so much, he prevaricates. ("I was looking at 'so' and 'so', referring to some topic in another part of the paper. This topic should form the subject of the trio which should be a topical trio.")

Meanwhile, Peter and Fayra are becoming attracted to one another and they have a duet. ("This should be a 'Silver Lining' number; not, of course, a definite love theme, as they are only just attracted to each other and promise to be very good friends.")

Noël did write the lyric for this duet, even though Kern didn't put it to music . . .

*ONE FINE DAY

REFRAIN

PETER: One fine day
We shall find a meaning
For the way
That our lives unfold.
Come what may,
We'll banish tears and sorrow
And we'll borrow
Joy and sunshine from tomorrow.

FAYRA: One fine day
All the intervening
Clouds of grey
Will change into gold.
If our Faith is strong,
We shan't have to wait long,
They will fade away
One fine day.

BOTH: All our doubts and fears
And the sadness of years
Will have flown away
One fine day.

VERSE 1

PETER: Tho' I scarcely know you,
I've a keen desire
Tenderly to show you
How you can acquire
Laughter tho' hope seems dying—
You'll wonder after why you were crying.
Tho' things you care for
May seem departed,
They're always there for
The happy hearted.

VERSE 2

FAYRA: I don't mind confessing
All you say is true,
Things seem less depressing
Since I've talked to you.

Waiting may soon be ended,
It's comforting to be befriended.
We'll try to smother
All cares and sadness
And help each other
To search for gladness.

As the act ends Toni suggests that, if Atlas is serious about becoming King of Tamaran, he had better meet some Tamaranis. As it happens, there is a real Tamaran village at the Wembley Exhibition. They should all go there that very evening.

Finale. General entrance followed by the re-entry of the show girls in their costumes with a reprise of Peter's number; then entrance of ladies and young men who think she is some great personage, surround her in admiration. Atlas enters and orders her to take off the dress at once. ('Mixing with my customers like this'.) He explains to the ladies, she is only one of his little work girls. Before he leaves on an important mission—to file his reply—he orders Fayra to mind the shop.

Peter whispers that he will rescue her later and they reprise their duet. He leaves and she reprises her 'Fairy Prince' number.

ACT 2

The Amusement Park, the British Empire Exhibition, Wembley. "On one side of the stage is a floral archway leading into the Tamaran village, outside of which is the Tamaran café advertising the special delicacies, drinks, etc., with waiter and waitress in Tamaran costume; on the other side is the entrance to the switchbacks and some other side show and at the back are seen the mountain railway, electric lights and the minarets, etc. of the Exhibition."

General opening chorus with specialty native dance by Tamaran native girl. ("Half of the chorus obviously foreigners. This might perhaps form part of theme of chorus—Girl from America, Girl from Spain, etc., etc. Musically one should hear the cacophony of the Exhibition; that is to say distant sounds and music of the other side shows.")

Winthrop enters with a group of Society people and sings "Out For The Night."

Borailic, the Bolshevik Tamarani, enters and introduces his troupe—Yasha (the Village Beauty), The Fat Lady, the Juggler, etc., etc., as well as his henchmen, Paulus and Ratzi. He discusses his plans to return to Tamaran and make himself Dictator.

The three of them sing a native song—which happened to be one of the two Kern compositions.

*TAMARAN

VERSE 1 Hooska bolly wolly,
Hooska bolly wolly,
Hooska bolly wolly boo
That's the Tamarani phrase for
"How d' you do?"
Tishka toodle oodle
Tishka toodle oodle
Tishka toodle oodle oo
That's the Tamarani phrase for
"I love you"

When I hear them calling me
It almost seems
Like all my dreams
Come true.

REFRAIN 1 Tam, Tam, Tam Tam, Tamaran,
Skies are always fair
Poet and prince and courtesan
Will find their heart's desire right there.
Tam, Tam, Tam, Tam, Tamaran
Journey's end comes soon
I'd like to steer my caravan
Neath a Tamaran moon

VERSE 2 Hoyo calabala
Hoyo calabala
Hoyo calabala boo
That's the Tamarani way to book a date
Blasko wagger wagger,
Blasko wagger wagger,
Blasko wagger wagger woo
That's the Tamarani phrase I can't translate

When in Tamaran once more
I set my feet
I'm sure to meet
My fate.

REFRAIN 2 Tam, Tam, Tam, Tam, Tamaran
Skies are always fair
Poet and prince and courtesan
Will find their heart's desire right there.
Tam, Tam, Tam, Tam, Tamaran
Life's a lazy tune
Someday I'll rest my caravan
Neath a Tamaran moon

(On the back of the manuscript—in Kern's expansive handwriting—is the notation "Weeping Willow Tree—Hitch Your Wagon To A Star—What's The Use . . ./House Boat/Handy Andy," while on the front sheet "Tamaran" is crossed out and "Gypsy Caravan" substituted. The others were clearly songs Kern intended to write for *Dear Sir*. "Weeping Willow Tree" did, in fact, make it to the final show.)

Fayra and Peter enter and sit at a table in the nearby café. During their conversation they hear men's voices from the Tamarani village singing a Tamarani song—possibly a reprise of the previous number. (NOTE for Mr. Kern: Possibly "Tan Tan Tamaran" would be better here and some perfectly unmelodious War song in the previous position.") Instinctively, they both rise. There is some indication that Fayra joins in the song. In a moment the men have arrived and recognised Fayra from the old days. Yes, she admits to Peter, she is a Tamarani herself. Peter is not ready to admit his own origins and makes an excuse to leave for a moment.

Fayra and the Tamarani men sing the "Wild Rose" number.

Toni and Zaza enter and also sit in the café. He begins to make verbal love to her, though she is distracted by thoughts of what has happened to Atlas. In full flight Toni spots an attractive native girl and—Harpo-like—follows her off stage. Atlas enters and

joins Zaza. They begin to discuss what he will do as King. Zaza clearly has her thoughts on becoming his Queen but the best Atlas can come up with is that she can become his morganatic wife. Zaza is initially insulted until she realises that in history mistresses have better parts than wives . . .

ZAZA: Mary Pickford's face would be a study!
ATLAS: Mrs. Talmadge would'ave another daughter out of sheer pique!

Zaza sings the song—"Publicity." She then graciously accepts his offer.

They sing the duet "Morganatic Love"—the other Kern composition.

*MORGANATIC LOVE (IF YOU WILL BE MY MORGANATIC WIFE)

ATLAS: Any King
 May have his fling
 But when it comes to love
 A bitter sacrifice
 He always has to make . . .

ZAZA: Royalties
 Have loyalties,
 Which have to be considered
 When the morale
 Of the country is at stake.

ATLAS: I'd like to take you for my own
 And plant you firmly on the throne
 But, as I'm King,
 You'll understand
 We'll have to be
 More underhand . . .

BOTH: We'll have a spree,
 Morganatically

ZAZA: For we agree
 Love is free,
 Most emphatically,

ATLAS: We'll manage things
 Diplomatically . . .

ZAZA: And as we can't be good,
 We'll lead a careful life.

ATLAS: If you will only be
 My morganatic wife.

ZAZA: I shall pit
 My polished wit
 Against the bold ambassadors
 Who've tried to win my heart
 And been refused . . .

ATLAS: Any folk
 Who make a joke
 Against your reputation
 I shall quell by saying—
 "We are not amused!"

ZAZA: And when I have to meet the Queen

ATLAS: (Oh, dear!)

ZAZA: There'll be a most dramatic scene
 She'll cloak her hate beneath a sneer
 And I shall say—
 "Look here, old dear . . ."

BOTH: We'll have a spree,
 Morganatically

ZAZA: I've got the King
 On a string
 Systematically.
 I rule the roost
 Automatically.

ATLAS: And we will lead them all
 The devil of a life
 When you're my cosy little
 Morganatic wife.

BOTH: And we will lead them all
 The devil of a life

ATLAS: When you're my

ZAZA: When I'm your

BOTH: Cosy little
 Morganatic wife!

Lady Hyacinthe, a Society butterfly, enters expecting to meet Toni. Catching sight of Peter, who has just returned, she insists that he join her at the table. (At this point Noël slips in a very 'in' joke. Hyacinthe tells Peter: "Everything's gone wrong tonight. I promised to meet Flo Lancaster and Nicky at the Embassy"—a reference to the lead characters in his recent play, *The Vortex* written in 1923, though not performed until November 1924). Fayra sees them together, misreads the situ-

64

ation and feels she can never compete with such sophistication.

Soon Atlas returns and Peter is able to slip away, leaving Atlas to bore Lady Hyacinthe with his plans as King. At the height of his enthusiasm he sings with full Chorus the "Sneitza Komiski" number. (Note to Mr. Kern: "Song preferably not about country, as we have had this before. The position is open to any subject. A song like "Non-Stop Dancing Craze" from *The Beauty Prize* could easily be introduced.") Atlas is then borne away by his high-spirited Tamarani "subjects."

Zaza and Fayra enter and discuss Fayra's love for "Count" Peter—in reality Prince Peter of Tamaran. Zaza tells her new friend how she made the ascent from Gladys Bluggins to Zaza Dolmondeley. If things with Peter don't work out, why doesn't Fayra do the same? She must practice her charms and here's the very man to practice on—as Toni enters.

Automatically Toni goes into his Latin lover routine and soon he is singing "The Argentine Way" . . . (Note to Mr. Kern: "I would like a note of originality introduced into this number. The little girl sitting at the table sipping her lemon squash and Toni singing a song on the lines of Yvonne George. Partly dramatic—partly comic—partly Spanish—singing of love, conquests, dancing and death. "Whenever I get into a great crisis in my life—I dance out of it.")

Atlas enters, followed by Borailic and Tatzi, who have learned of his regal aspirations and have other, more revolutionary ideas. As they begin to threaten him, the script for the act ends.

There are various partial drafts that indicate Noël was not sure of the construction to follow.

For example . . . There was to be a scene with Peter and a group of Society girls. He has momentarily forgotten Fayra and is telling the girls that he is giving up his old social ways and sticking to work. "You'll never get away from us."

In another sequence Atlas, Toni and Zaza consider what might happen should they get to Tamaran and their plans misfire in a song called "I'll Take the High Road" . . .

---

*I TAKE THE HIGH ROAD

ATLAS: I take the High Road

Toni: And I take the low road

ZAZA: And I take the one in between.

ATLAS: I am resourceful,
           Violent and forceful

ZAZA: While others forge away
           I choose the Borgia way

TONI: I've not followed tradition—
           I've got girlish ambitions!

ATLAS: I take the High Road . . .

TONI: And I take the low road . . .

ZAZA: And I take the one in between.

ATLAS: I take the High Road . . .

TONI: And I take the low Road . . .

ZAZA: And I take the one in between
           All revolutions
           Love executions

TONI: Once they have seen us all,
           They'll guillotine us all.

ATLAS: When we find out their habits,
           We'll be running like rabbits—
           Me on the High Road . . .

TONI: And me on the low road . . .

ZAZA: And me on the one in between!

In another version it is Peter who is now in despair at the loss of Fayra. He sings a song of his lost hopes and is then discovered by Zaza. He tells her his dreams for his native Tamaran are never to be fulfilled. The country has no resources but its incredible natural beauty and eternal sunshine. This gives Zaza an idea. Why not turn Tamaran into the Hollywood of Europe? "But the money to start it with?" Peter asks. Toni enters and solves that problem.

Atlas enters and discovers that his assistant has yet to send off the fateful telegram of acceptance. Peter snatches it, signs it himself and dispatches it. He sings a short reprise of "Goodbye, Girls" with the new lyrics about his return to "his own dear land." This is overheard by Fayra and Lady Hyacinthe entering from opposite sides.

Short chorus: "What Is This Strange News?" Lady Hyacinthe congratulates "Your Royal Highness" and Fayra faints. Peter takes her in his arms but her father, Borailic snatches her away and denounces Peter as one of the hated Bomanoff family.

Fayra rejects Peter and reproaches him in song for having deceived her. She will return to the shop. "If he is going to be a king, you're going to be a movie

Queen," says Zaza and takes her off. There is general chaos as the curtain falls.

ACT 3

Two years later. We are now in the film city of Tamaran, "the Hollywood of Europe." The backdrop shows American built studios, while on the distant hills are the picturesque villas of movie stars.

(N.B. "Most of this short act is production work as with *Sally*, *The Cabaret Girl* and *The Beauty Prize*.")

Opening Chorus and ballet introducing famous film stars—Mary Pickford, Constance and Norma Talmadge, Charlie Chaplin, Harold Lloyd, Tom Mix, etc.

Atlas is now the president of Tamar Filmco Inc. and "the local D. W. Griffith." Borailic is his Manager as well as Mayor of Tamaru, the capital of Tamaran. The commercial imperative has triumphed again. In the opening scene these plot developments are explained to a visiting journalist.

Enter Hereford, formerly Blubb's assistant and now his cameraman. He hs just finished filming "Zaza Dolmondley—star comic series No. 5—*Jiggedy Jane*." He exits as Zaza and the Girls enter to sing "Jiggedy Jane." ("This is just to indicate the type of song—'Raggedy Ann' from *Stepping Stones*—To make a contrast to her former appearances, Zaza should now appear in comic get-up with girls ditto. Type of Clown song.")

Winthrop enters with the Society matrons we met in Act 1. They are here for the Coronation. With them is Lady Hyacinthe. Toni enters. The two of them are now engaged but, provoked by Atlas, they begin a violent quarrel, which turns out to have been for the benefit of Hereford's camera. One more movie is in the can!

Hyacinthe leaves and Atlas and Toni sing a duet—"or some 'Plum' (P.G. Wodehouse) number."

Peter enters with Zaza. He thanks her for all she has done for Tamaran and congratulates her on her engagement to Atlas. Who is this protégée she has been talking about? At that moment Fayra (the protégée) enters. Peter doesn't quite recognise her but when she has left with Zaza, he sings the refrain of "One Fine Day." She takes up the refrain off stage and Peter, now knowing the voice, calls her name as the curtain falls.

Scene 2 takes place in the Throne Room of the Old Palace of Tamaru. There is an open terrace beyond which we can see the hills of Tamaran and a winding stone staircase down which the principal characters enter. On a low dais is the ancient throne of Tamaran. Once all the courtiers are assembled,

Prince Peter mounts the throne and the Movie Coronation procession begins.

Down the steps come famous movie stars playing the characters they are best known for . . .

Nazimova
Pauline Frederick
Betty Balfour (in *Squibbs*)
Norma Talmadge (*Smilin' Thru'*—1922)
Mae Marsh (*Birth of a Nation*—1915)
Followed by a nigger
Constance Talmadge (as Mountain Girl in *Intolerance*—1916)
Anna Christie
Charlie Chaplin & Harold Lloyd (arm in arm)
Mary Pickford (*Daddy Longlegs*—1919)
Douglas Fairbanks (Terry Kendall, who does Feature dance)
Valentino (Heather Thatcher) in *The Four Horsemen Of the Apocalypse*—1921)

The last to enter is Fayra in queenly robes to the Tamarani March. Everyone greets her but it is Peter who breaks through the crowd, leads her to his throne and places his crown on her head. "My Queen!" Fanfare of trumpets and general huzzas.

CURTAIN.

*   *   *

The link to Kern remained unbroken until Kern's death in 1945. 1941 finds Noël dedicating a song to him . . .

*WE ARE LIVING IN A CHANGING WORLD

(*To Jerome Kern*)

Wake up, forget your dreams,
For it seems
We're living in a changing world
We know the past is dead
Far ahead
Our challenge to the Gods is hurled.

Trumpets blow
There's always a star beyond a star,
Courage travels far.
And your heart is where you are.
Don't cry—"Love never dies"
Realise we're living in a changing world.

The world was young
So many million years ago,
The passage of time must show
Some traces of change.
Love songs once sung,
Much laughter, many tears,
Have echo'd down the years.
The past is old and strange.
Each waning moon
All days that dawn, all suns that set
Change like the tides that flow across the sands
Each little tune
That fills our hearts with vague regret
Each little love duet
Fades in our hands.
Don't stray among
The moments that have fled
New days are just ahead
New words are still unsaid.
Live life in terms of "Now"
Anyhow
We're living in a changing world.

Don't keep your eager mind too refined
And permanently waved and curled,
Think of it—this strange, unexplainable parade
Dreams are doomed to fade
In a world we never made.
Farewell to "Flaming Youth"
Face the truth.
We're living in a changing world.

There was to be one further semi-"collaboration" at long distance. Just as he was to "borrow" material from Cole Porter, Noël asked permission to record "his" version of the 1942 Jerome Kern/Johnny Mercer song, "I'm Old Fashioned." The final lyric (recorded in 1943) is a Mercer-Coward combination with Noël's lines italicized . . .

*I'M OLD FASHIONED

REFRAIN I I'm old fashioned,
I love the moonlight,
I love the old fashioned things;
The sound of rain
Upon a window pane,
The daffodils that April brings.
This year's fancies
Are passing fancies,
But sighing sighs, holding hands,
These my heart understands.
I'm old fashioned, but I don't mind it,
That's how I'll always be,
If only you'll agree
To stay old fashioned with me.

VERSE I am not such a clever one
About the latest fads;
I'll admit I was never one
Of those sophisticated lads;
Not that I ever try to be a saint,
I'm the type that they classify as quaint.

REFRAIN 2 *I'm old fashioned,*
I love cheap music,
The feel of Spring in the air;
Moons and Junes,
Those sentimental tunes,
Those nightingales in Berkeley Square.

66

Things are rationed,
I don't require them.
When high white clouds sail above
Dreams are dreams,
Love is love

I'm old fashioned,
We'd better face it,
That's how I'll always be,
If only you'll agree
To stay old fashioned with me.

In many ways it was his way of saying thank you for the fact that a couple of years earlier Kern and Oscar Hammerstein had dedicated their song—"The Last Time I Saw Paris"—to him.

*　　*　　*

Noël had another notion for a musical in these early 1920s. Among his notes is a fairly full synopsis and a few early scenes for *Dream a Little*. Set in a fairground, it concerned a God-like impresario called Mr. Heavenly Smith, who takes three of the fairground people—one of them Esmeralda, a lady who performs a snake act—and grants each of them their most fantastic wish. In the three acts of the play we would have followed each of them in turn. The lady, for instance, would have taken us to Tamaran. (Noël threw nothing away!)

At the end Mr. Heavenly Smith brings them back, gives them money and returns them to their normal lives with no memory of their recent adventures.

Nothing more appears to have been done with the idea and no songs were written, although Noël listed four that he intended to write . . .

> Just As You Are
> Sleeping Beauty
> Anywhere
> Mad About You

There wasn't to be a full-scale "book" musical until 1929 and *Bitter Sweet* and, in any case, by 1923 revue was calling . . . specifically *London Calling!*

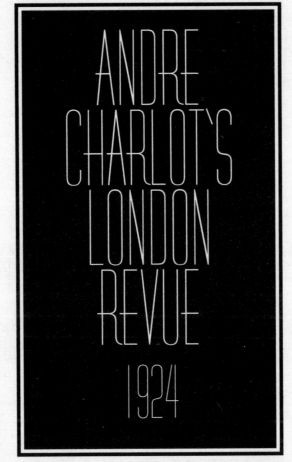

ANDRE CHARLOT'S LONDON REVUE 1924

The revue, mainly compiled from previous successes, was tried out at Golders Green Hippodrome, London on December 3, 1923 prior to its production at the Times Square Theatre, New York on January 9, 1924.

The show included three Coward songs from *London Calling!* "Parisian Pierrot" was included as a matter of course. In the chorus and understudying Gertie for the number was the young Jessie Matthews:

"In my room at the Martha Washington Hotel I'd scrape my hair under a tight handkerchief and pretend it was the little black skull cap Gertie wore. I'd pull the pillows from the bed and lie on the floor like she did and sing 'Parisian Pierrot.' Every gesture Gertie had made I practised, every movement I copied. By the time opening night arrived I was a little, under-sized, immature carbon copy of Gertrude Lawrence."

Later in the run, Gertie handed the number over to her.

In addition to Jack Buchanan's version of "Sentiment," Beatrice Lillie performed Maisie Gay's original number, "There's Life in the Old Girl Yet."

Top: Jack Buchanan.
Bottom: Jessie Matthews as "Parisian Pierrot."

The SELWYNS present
CHARLOT'S REVUE
OF 1924

Left: Beatrice Lillie as Britannia in "March With Me."

Right: Gertrude Lawrence, André Charlot, Beatrice Lillie and Jack Buchanan sail to America.

Below: André Charlot (the tall man by the box office) with the entire company in Atlantic City.

68

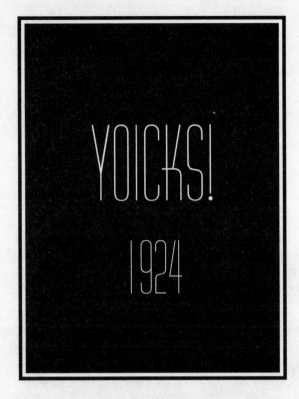

A revue presented at the Kingsway Theatre, London on June 11, 1924. (271 performances.) It contained two items by Noël. One was "It's the Peach." The other was "I'd Like To See You Try."

As with the earlier "Touring Days," the song emerges from a sketch, which establishes the context and the characters. The sketch was originally called "Palm Sunday" and pencilled in for Gertie and Clifton Webb, although there is no indication of the show it was intended to appear in . . .

*FORTUNE TELLING DUET (I'D LIKE TO SEE YOU TRY)

(*Mary Leigh and Richard Dolman*)

(*Scene is a Park. She is seated on a round wooden seat under a tree reading. He enters.*)

HE:	(*Raising his hat*) Good afternoon.
SHE:	Frightfully (*There is a moment's pause. She goes on reading*)
HE:	Look out, there's a spider just near you.
SHE:	(*Not looking up*) It's all right, I put it there.
HE:	(*After another pause*) I say—

SHE:	(*Sweetly*) Yes?
HE:	Don't you see that I want to talk to you most awfully?
SHE:	Yes.
HE:	Well, why don't we start?
SHE:	Because I'm reading.
HE:	What is it? (*He takes the book from her and reads the title*) "First Steps to Palmistry" Humph!
SHE:	Why not?
HE:	A lot of rubbish.
SHE:	Don't you believe in Palmistry?
HE:	(*Sitting beside her*) I need convincing.
SHE:	You need smacking. (*She snatches the book out of his hand and begins to read again.*)
HE:	I say, don't be cross.
SHE:	Well, it's so silly to jeer at things just because you don't understand them.
HE:	I wasn't jeering.
SHE:	Yes, you were, and as long as you do that, nothing nice will ever happen to you.
HE:	Won't you forgive me?
SHE:	(*Loftily*) I don't mind one way or another.
HE:	Will you read my hand?
SHE:	I'm afraid I'm not practised enough.
HE:	I'm not so sure.
SHE:	(*Turning*) Are you going to be insulting?
HE:	(*Holding out his hand*) Perhaps—Tell me.
SHE:	If the future you would see,
HE:	The past's enough for me.
SHE:	I can read it in your hand. (*She takes his hand*)
HE:	(*Nestling closer*) Go on, dear, this is grand.
SHE:	Don't begin to laugh and sneer Try to concentrate. By the lines imprinted here I can tell your fate.

REFRAIN

SHE:	I see a faithful heart
HE:	That's a splendid start.
SHE:	I see a brilliant brain,
HE:	Better look again.
SHE:	I see a day in June, Two hearts in tune.
HE:	Say how did you get it right so soon?
SHE:	I see some shady trees
HE:	Be a lady, please!
SHE:	I seem to hear a lover's sigh.
HE:	I'd like to kiss you to bliss in my arms, dear. (*He takes her in his arms—she smacks his face and breaks away*)
SHE:	I'd like to see you try!
SHE:	(*Spoken*) I told you you needed smacking.
HE:	You are a bit of a dragon for your age.

VERSE II

HE:	I can tell your future too, At quite a careless glance.
SHE:	You'd romance till all was blue, If I gave you the chance. (*He takes her hand*)
HE:	See how soon your heart's desire In your hand appears.
SHE:	You're the most unblushing liar I have met for years!

REFRAIN 2

HE:	I see a punt or two.
SHE:	Typical of you
HE:	I see a tiny flat
SHE:	That's enough of that.
HE:	I see a day in June, A honeymoon.
SHE:	(*Pinching him*) I'm sorry to wake you up so soon!
HE:	(*Furious*) I see a quick divorce
SHE:	(*Hotly*) Blaming me, of course.
HE:	I see a hundred reasons why
SHE:	Do you suppose Pulling your nose Would annoy you?
HE:	(*Dodging her*) I'd like to see you try

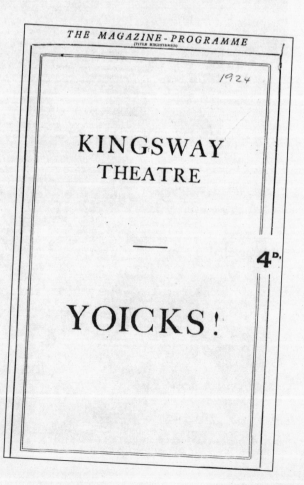

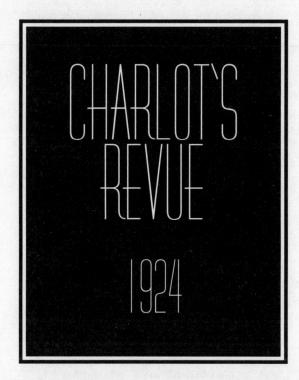

CHARLOT'S REVUE 1924

First presented at the Prince of Wales Theatre, London on September 23, 1924. During the run of 518 performances, the cast and material changed frequently.

The original company included Phyllis Monkman, Maisie Gay, Henry Kendall, Hugh Sinclair and Leonard Henry.

Noël contributed the following songs:

*THAT'LL BE VERY USEFUL LATER ON

(Phyllis Monkman)

Mary was a miser in an unassuming way,
Always hoarding trifles for a future rainy day.
Though she was material
She managed fairly well,
Her life was like a serial
Controlled by Ethel Dell.

REFRAIN

That'll be a comfort one day,
That'll come in handy some day.
Tho' young men gave her presents quite
    regardless of expense
Her promises were always in the strictly future
    tense.

She said—"I don't let passion overrule my
    Common Sense.
And that'll be very useful later on."

Mary as a debutante was quite a 'succès fou',
She pranced about at parties with the Gentile
    and the Jew,
Eventually a husband she decided to obtain
Whose income more than compensated for his
    lack of brain.

REFRAIN

That'll be a comfort one day,
That'll come in handy some day.
He dressed her up in diamonds from her
    eyebrows to her toes,
He always let his little wife have everything
    she chose
Her son-and-heir, though rather fair, had got his
    father's nose.
That'll be very useful later on

Mary growing older found existence rather tame,
Thought that being married was a rather dreary
    game,
Then she gave her principles a rather sudden
    shove,
And said that having married money she would
    live for love.

REFRAIN

That'll be a comfort later on,
That'll come in handy later on.
In the matrimonial clay her thoughts began to
    bud,
And later when they blossomed all her clay had
    turned to mud.

Phyllis Monkman.

She said—"I may look quiet but I've lots of
    southern blood
And
That'll be very useful later on."

EXTRA REFRAIN

That'll be a comfort later on,
That'll come in handy later on.
Husband had a flutter with a Midnight Follies Queen
And Mary had them watched from Charing Cross
    to Golders Green.
She smiled at a Detective when he told her what
    he'd seen.
That'll be very useful later on.

JESSIE HOOPER

(Morris Harvey)

VERSE

Have ye heard of Jessie Hooper?
On the banks of Loch MacRae.
Stepping lightly from her truckle,
To salute the coming day.
All the sheep and cows adored her,
She was sonsie, braw and gay,
As she rocked with girlish laughter
On the banks of Loch MacRae.

REFRAIN I

Where are ye now, Jessie, where are ye now?
Never a sheep will say, nary a cow,
For Jessie she hangs to the willow tree bough.
Where are ye now, Jessie? Where are ye now?

VERSE 2

Do not weep for Jessie Hooper,
She whose eyes with death are closed
For even though she is a corpse,
She isn't decomposed.
You could hear the haggis wailing
Over bonny loch and brae
When the soul of Jessie Hooper
So completely passed away.

REFRAIN 2

Where are ye now, Jessie, where are ye now?
Swinging about on the willow tree bough.
Was it the laird who brought ye so low?
Where are ye now, Jessie? Where are ye now?

HENRY
KENDALL
AND
PHYLLIS
MONKMAN

*SPECIALLY FOR YOU

(Phyllis Monkman and Henry Kendall)

(Alternative intro)

VERSE 1

The time is past when girls require a chaperone,
They've reached at last an independence
    of their own.
Emancipation made the Nation what it is today
But all the same free life's a game that one can
    overplay.
To use a potion at the minimum expense
Just blend emotion with a word of commonsense.
A hectic life demands a very heavy price
So please take my advice.

VERSE 1

HE: I've been adoring you, imploring you for ages
To melt divinely and supinely in my arms;
I've been a victim to the jealousies and rages
Which all the sages describe as Love's
    endearing charms
Tho' I've a notion my devotion's not
    returned, dear,
In the palpitating way it ought to be,
For ever since a child you've always yearned, dear,
To be a *Belle Dame Sans Merci.*

REFRAIN 1

HE: Specially for you,
    I gave up flirting.

SHE: How disconcerting!

HE: Specially for you,
    I gave up smoking.

SHE: That's most provoking!

HE: I'd cast aside all trace of pride,
    Won't you decide?
    I'm on my knees, dear.
    Please, dear
    Specially for you
    I left my mother!

SHE: Tell me another!

HE: Specially for you
    I changed my vices
    To sacrifices
    If you only knew how I've been craving,
    Saving
    All my life, all my love,
    Specially for you.

VERSE 2

SHE: You feel persistence my resistance
      undermining
    Will make me tenderly surrender to your
      plea.
    You feel in spite of love the light of love is
      shining,
    And that I'm pining to nestle coyly on your
      knee.
    Now let me tell you it's as well you aren't a
      shy man;
    I've been crushing you unblushingly for days.
    You seem to be the sort of "do or die" man
    Who treats a snub as fulsome praise.

REFRAIN 2

HE: Specially for you
    I've been to Night Clubs
    That weren't the right clubs!
    Specially for you
    I'd fight and win, dear.

SHE: Go on—begin, dear!

HE: For you I'd play a soldier's part

SHE: Take him away!

HE: I love sincerely.

SHE: Really!

HE: Specially for you
    I've saved my money

SHE: That's very funny!

HE: Think of what I'd do to make you love me

SHE: You needn't shove me;
    I've a husband who is contemplating
    Waiting,
    Six foot one, with a gun,
    Specially for you.

Soon after the show closed—Henry Kendall
recalls— he and Phyllis Monkman were asked to
film it as one of the first sound "shorts" or program
fillers. It preceded the first sound feature film by several years.

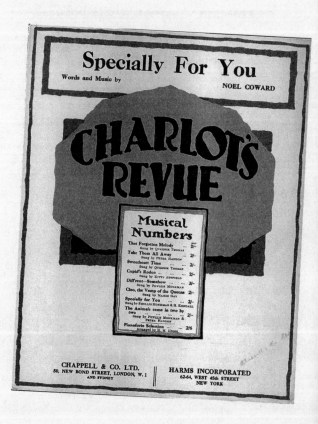

LOVE, LIFE AND LAUGHTER

(Maisie Gay and Morris Harvey)

Paris 1890. The setting—La Chatte Vierge, a café in Montmartre. The characters—Rupert Shufflebotham ("an elegant Englishman") and La Flamme, a night club queen (so called "because I make men mad"). From which it may reasonably be deduced that their eventual duet is not entirely serious . . .

LA FLAMME: Hark to the music enthralling, appalling,
　　　　　It dies away, and then—

RUPERT: Women like you, so inviting, exciting,
　　　　Play fast and loose with men.
　　　　Fate has smiled on our meeting,
　　　　Feel my pulse madly beating.

LA FLAMME: Call for more drinks,
　　　　　This is what the world thinks
　　　　　Is La Vie Parisienne.

BOTH: Love, life and laughter,
　　　To the devil with what comes after.

RUPERT: Hearts are on fire
　　　　With the flame of desire.

LA FLAMME: Lovers surrender
　　　　　Regardless of gender.
　　　　　Away care and sorrow,
　　　　　Never worry about tomorrow.

BOTH: We will rule passion's kingdom for a day.
　　　For that's just the Bohemian way.

RUPERT: Teach me the bliss of profanity's kiss
　　　　As we sway beneath the moon.

LA FLAMME: Lovers may sip
　　　　　Passion's wine from my lip
　　　　　To a gay romantic tune.

RUPERT: Cupid's dart has impaled me,
　　　　All my breeding has failed me,
　　　　I want to smite you and beat you and bite you
　　　　And swoon and swoon and swoon.

BOTH: Love, life and laughter,
　　　To the devil with what comes after.

RUPERT: Here is my heart, you can tear it apart,
　　　　Nothing suffices but decadent vices.

BOTH: And mirth, folly, madness,

Never giving a thought to sadness.

LA FLAMME: If you told me to die I should obey.

BOTH: For that's just the Bohemian way.

AFTER-DINNER MUSIC

(A Sketch with Songs)
(Maisie Gay)

The sketch, described in the program as "Miss Fancy Robinson in Selections from Her Repertoire. At the piano Mr. Edgar Stoope. N.B. Miss Robinson only sings the works of Mr. Noël Coward," consisted of three songs: "A Little Slut of Six," "The Roses Have Made Me Remember" and "The Girl I am Leaving in England Today." They were sung to the accompaniment of a piano on stage by Maisie Gay and later by Beatrice Lillie in the New York production (*Charlot's Revue of 1926*).

Left: Maisie Gay as "Miss Fancy Robinson" with Mr. Edgar Stoope at the piano.
Above: portion of program.

72

In her autobiography, *Laughing Through Life* (1931) Maisie Gay writes about the initial problems she had with the material:

"He (Noël) has written three amusing ballads; one for a child, another for an "adenoidy" amateur, and the last for a professional singer. He wanted me to sing these at the piano, playing my own accompaniment, but my technique was much too wobbly to do that . . .

"For several days I thought about the group of songs, and didn't see how I was going to do anything with them. Then one night I woke up in a bath of perspiration as the result of a sudden brain-wave. I would have a male accompanist on the stage, a grand piano, a bunch of property flowers, and a gold chair, and I would work like a third-rate music hall act.

"Then I happened to drop in at the Palladium one afternoon, where I saw that brilliant American artiste, Nora Bayes. I loved her performance, and was fascinated by the way she used a chair on the stage, always making as if just about to sit down, yet never actually doing so. The clever way in which she manipulated a huge feather fan also gave me food for thought.

"I sang my first two songs in the way I had originally thought of, but in the last number I gave a slightly exaggerated impression of Nora Bayes.

"I appeared on the programme as 'Miss Fancy Robinson,' and was told it was rather amusing to hear people, when they had looked at their programmes, say: 'Who is this woman? I don't think much of her.' Before I got to the Bayes number they were 'wise' to me."

When Bea Lillie came to perform the material, her interpretation was even broader:

"After Dinner Music is a sketch involving an aging *prima donna* in a garish red wig, a green velour court gown and a mangy feathered fan, who sings a few songs for her guests—her repartee is expensive, she says—while having a mishap or two along the way . . . My *prima's* bedraggled fan was waggled so grandly that it shed feathers all over stage. When she picked up her evening cloak, an end of a tablecloth got caught up, too, and a tableful of china and silverware crashed to the floor. She reached for a high note and a floor lamp that was part of the sketch lost its shade. She tried again, and the same thing happened. Ever resourceful, she seized the shade and held it fast while she made a final, successful struggle to reach her high 'C,' at which point, naturally, the light bulb exploded."

*AFTER DINNER MUSIC A LITTLE SLUT OF SIX

My nurse is often cross wiv me
Becos I'se naughty bold
And if I'm ever late for tea
Good gwacious how she'll scold.
She says I'm awfully mischievous
And up to Monkey Tricks
Be bad I must
Becos I'se just
A little slut of six.

At bye-bye time my mumsie comes
And kisses me goodnight
And oh, I'm defful frightened
When she switches out the light
But she says Dod is looking down
On all his tiny chicks.
I hope He's got good eye-sight
Cos I'm just a slut of six.
When I'm a gwown up lady
I'll be full of 'do and dare'
And hiccup just like Mummy does
And smoke and spit and swear.
And when I'm safely married
I'll learn lots of lovely tricks
To save myself from having
Any little sluts of six.

The last three lines, not surprisingly, set off a heated correspondence with the Lord Chamberlain's Office, resulting in their ironic replacement with . . .

I shall count my little chicks
And maybe, if I'm lucky,
I'll have lots of sluts of six

THE ROSES HAVE MADE ME REMEMBER

REFRAIN
The memories of love in my garden
Like flowers in an altar I group
You kissed me without asking pardon
And bowled me about like a hoop.
One evening in early September

The grass was exceedingly wet
The roses have made me remember
What any nice girl should forget.

VERSE
A quaint old world garden I'm calling to mind
With rude rustic pathway and roses entwined
An old-fashioned girl in an old-fashioned gown
With old-fashioned stockings about to come down.

Many in the audience laughing at the pastiche may not have realised what Noël knew perfectly well—that the title of the song had actually been used by his old colleague, Herman Darewski in a 1916 tearjerker—"The Roses Have Made Me Remember (All That I Tried to Forget) with lyrics by Lilian Grey that ran (in part) . . .

Roses of June, once more in bloom,
Whisper their message divine.
They seem to say love lives always,
Happiness yet may be mine . . .

THE GIRL I AM LEAVING IN ENGLAND TODAY

All my life I've been a constant lover,
But a wife I never could discover
No just right girl anywhere could I find
Oh baby!
Till last year I came across the Ocean
Someone here has given me the notion,
Oh gee!
She has made me alter my mind.

REFRAIN
I have left the girl of my dreams in Arizona,
I have left the love of my life in Ohio
Here I go! Here I go!
And strictly entre nous
I have left a girl or two
In old Virginia
The place where the cotton blossoms grow.
I've left the cutest brunette in Carolina,
I've left the craziest blonde down Texas way
Hear them say! Hear them say!
There's one for whom I'll fall
I love her best of all
And that's the girl I'm leaving in England today.

Note: This should be sung with a decided English syncopation, jerky movements, generally off the beat.

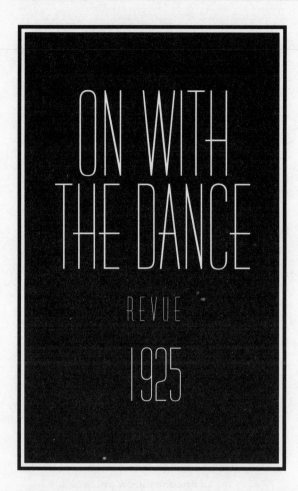

ON WITH THE DANCE

REVUE

1925

First presented by Charles B. Cochran at the Palace Theatre, Manchester on March 17, 1925 before transferring to the London Pavilion on April 30, 1925. (229 performances.) Book and lyrics by Noël Coward. Music by Philip Braham and Noël Coward.

The cast included Alice Delysia, Hermione Baddeley, Douglas Byng, Lance Lister, Ernest Thesiger, Florence Desmond and Nigel Bruce.

The first of nine collaborations with Charlot's great rival, Charles B. Cochran ("Cockie"), *On With the Dance* started with an argument over the size of respective egos: "The show was labeled 'Charles B. Cochran's Revue,' which, since I had done three-quarters of the score, all the lyrics, all the book, and directed all the dialogue, scenes, and several of the numbers, seemed to be a slight overstatement."

Their other battle—in what was to be a generally pacific working relationship—was over one of the songs in the show. Cochran considered "Poor Little Rich Girl" to be "too dreary" and wished to take it out of the show. "I fought like a steer, backed up by Delysia (the French star who introduced the song), and fortunately for all concerned we won, as it turned out to be the big song hit of the revue."

The song was sung by Alice Delysia to and about Hermione Baddeley, who recalled:

"Delysia played a lady's maid preparing her young mistress for yet another party. I was the wild girl whose life had become a mess of drink and drugs and men. Alice sang the song to me and then we did it together . . . These poor little rich girls were part of the scene in 1925 and there were always some, with their doomed and mournful eyes, in the society of the Bright Young Things. I had seen many of them . . ."

Noël recalls Ms. Baddeley herself standing about "in evening dress looking far from healthy."

POOR LITTLE RICH GIRL

VERSE

You're only
A baby,
You're lonely,
And maybe
Some day soon you'll know
The tears
You are tasting

Are years
You are wasting,
Life's a bitter foe,
With Fate it's no use competing,
Youth is so terribly fleeting;
By dancing
Much faster,
You're chancing
Disaster,
Time alone will show.

REFRAIN

Poor little rich girl,
You're a bewitched girl,
Better beware!
Laughing at danger,
Virtue a stranger,
Better take care!
The life you lead sets all your nerves a-jangle,
Your love affairs are in a hopeless tangle,
Though you're a child, dear,
Your life's a wild typhoon,
In lives of leisure
The craze for pleasure
Steadily grows.
Cocktails and laughter,
But what comes after?
Nobody knows.
You're weaving love into a mad jazz pattern,
Ruled by Pantaloon.
Poor little rich girl, don't drop a stitch too soon.

"Oh, Cockie," Noël said, "I've just seen my name in lights."

74

VERSE 2

The role you are acting,
The toll is exacting,
Soon you'll have to pay.
The music of living,
You lose in the giving,
False things soon decay.
These words from me may surprise you,
I've got no right to advise you,
I've known Life too well, dear,
Your own Life must tell, dear,
Please don't turn away.

There were at least two other introductions to the song, according to Noël's notes. In the first—used in Manchester—Daisy (Delysia) is walking alone in the park at night and finds herself at Fred's coffee stall. They are old friends and, as they chat, the Girl enters with her married boyfriend. They argue and he leaves her in tears. Daisy comforts her. She has been there herself:

Alice Delysia as the "Cosmopolitan Lady."

GIRL: No, no—you don't understand.

DAISY: Yes, I do. I understand only too well. You're dancing too much and drinking too much and living too much. I've watched so many girls like you—drifting along, never knowing where to stop—until suddenly it's too late.

GIRL: What do you mean?

After the number Daisy takes the Girl's arm and leads her away:

DAISY: Silly baby. Come with me and we'll find a taxi.

In another version the Girl (Anne) is in her boyfriend's apartment. She refuses his advances and he leaves in a huff. His former lover (Coral Bennett), an older woman, arrives and the song is her advice to her rival.

When she thought that he might be considering letting Gertie use the song in New York, Miss Delysia temporarily lost her *sang froid*. Noël, she declared, was "a sheet and a bougairr."

Controversy seemed destined to accompany the song. To begin with, the title was not a million miles from "Poor Little Ritz Girl," a song that had given its name to the successful Rodgers and Hart show of 1920 and someone who was an admirer of their output—as Noël undoubtedly was—could hardly have failed to know that. His title was presumably, therefore, by way of an *hommage* . . .

Then when Gertie eventually did perform the number in New York in the second Charlot revue, she decided to do it dressed as a streetwalker, lecturing a society girl (Constance Carpenter) who also "stood about in evening dress, looking drained and far from healthy." Noël objected heatedly but had to admit that Gertie's treatment gave the song a new and valid meaning which made it a hit all over again.

COSMOPOLITAN LADY

(*Alice Delysia*)

VERSE   When I was quite a little mite of seven,
I secretly decided on my course;
Though maybe I'm not heading straight
    for heaven,

I have never put the cart before the horse.

CHORUS She wouldn't do that of course!

VERSE   It's seldom that my "joie de vivre" forsakes
    me,
I frequently succeed where others fail,
And when the day of judgment overtakes
    me,
I shall make a very firm appeal for bail!

CHORUS She seems successfully to dominate
And utterly control her fate,
We'll try to follow firmly on her trail!

REFRAIN I'm a cosmopolitan lady,
With a cosmopolitan soul,
Every dashing blonde
Of the demi-monde
Starts to quake when I take a stroll
As my past's incredibly shady,
And my future grows more doubtful every
    day,
Though determined to be pleasant,
I shall utilize the present
In a cosmopolitan way.

VERSE   The world to me will always be a gamble,
I don't care if I win or if I lose;
The straight and narrow path is such a
    scramble,
And is such an unattractive life to choose.

CHORUS We'd like to be in your shoes!

VERSE   I much prefer a flutter at the tables,
I treat my whole existence as a game,
And if I end in sackcloth or in sables
I shall not have lived for nothing, all the
    same!

CHORUS We're really quite impatient to begin
A life of unassuming sin,
And try to reach your pinnacle of fame!

REFRAIN I'm a cosmopolitan lady,
With a cosmopolitan heart,
And I've lived so long
Between right and wrong,
That I can't tell the two apart,
Though my past's incredibly shady,
And my future grows more doubtful
    every day;
Though my methods may be breezy,
I find virtue very easy,
In the cosmopolitan way.

(I'M) SO IN LOVE

(Pat and Terry Kendall)

HE: Ever since I met you,
I've been absolutely crazy, dear;
Just why I can't explain,
Even though your character
Is languid, loose and lazy, dear,
My love will still remain,
Look down and say my pleading and my
    prayers are not in vain.

REFRAIN 1 I'm so in love with you,
Sort of a cross between a habit and a vice,
You thrill me through and through
Though you behave exactly like a block of ice.
Beneath the spell of your endearing young
    charms,
I'd break the Ten Commandments,
And jazz up the Psalms,
I'm so in love with you,
And if I have to keep proposing till I'm blue,
I'll override your dignity,
I'll grab you tight and shake you,
Until I make you say that you're in love with me.

SHE: Ever since we met that night,
You take delight in shattering
My perfect peace of mind;
All my winsome girlish dreams
You make a point of scattering
Like leaves upon the wind.
You have such perfect charm and fearful
    selfishness combined.

REFRAIN 2 I'm so in love with you,
Sort of passion Mister Plato wouldn't pass;
I don't know what to do,
When I'm away from you I feel as bold as
    brass,
But when I gaze into your wonderful eyes
I find them undermining
My enterprise.
I'm so in love with you,
If you could only understand my point of
    view,
Just think how happy we could be,
I'd never once divorce you,
Unless of course you started in divorcing me!

*   *   *

A form that Coward was developing at this time was that of the "sketch-song." As with "Touring Days" in "Customs House, Dover," the song would resolve the sketch and lead into the "blackout." Noël found it a convenient way to resolve arguments with his early producers as to how much of a show's material he should be allowed to contribute, since it was virtually impossible for someone else to interpolate a song into his sketch!

A good example in *On With the Dance* is "First Love." The sketch is set in a schoolroom where an adolescent brother and sister tease each other until the young man contrives to get their young French teacher alone:

Dialogue:
MLLE: Do you know your verbs?
RUPERT: Only one.
MLLE: Which one?
RUPERT: *(Looking up)* Je t'aime.
MLLE: I thought that was it.
RUPERT: You knew all the time?
MLLE: I guessed, silly boy.
Rupert: It's not silly; it's the most wonderful thing
    in the world . . . love!
MLLE: First love.

FIRST LOVE

(Alice Delysia and Lance Lister)

VERSE 1
HE: If you could only realise
And know how I idealise
The very slightest thing
You say or do.

SHE: I've guessed and felt a little bit
Depressed because I know that it
Leads to complications,
Think of your relations'
Point of view.

REFRAIN 1
HE: First love,
Completely unrehearsed love,
Has all the spontaneity of youth.

SHE: Well, to tell the truth,
I'm quite unversed, love,
In treating suitably
These adolescent scenes.
You're indisputably
The victim of your teens.

New love
Must always seem the true love,
Experience will teach you as you go,
Till you really know
Just the way to woo, love.

HE: I wish you'd show me how my passion
    should be nursed,

SHE: Your papa must raise my wages first, love.

HE: I've burned to kiss your darling hand,
And yearned to make you understand
That you're the only one
In life for me!

SHE: I fear I can't reciprocate,
But, dear, I do appreciate
Having made you suffer,
Darling little duffer,
You'll soon see.

REFRAIN 2
SHE: First love
Is generally the worst love.

HE: I'm trying to restrain it all the time.
I've a feeling I'm
Really going to burst, love.

SHE: I fully realize
Your true romantic soul,
But you must utilize
A little self-control.

HE: Calf love
Is never half and half love,
To me you're just the fairest of your sex.
How I love you.

Lance Lister and Alice Delysia.

SHE: Excuse me if I laugh, love.

HE: Let's plunge in passion till we're totally
          immersed.

SHE: I shall have to ask my husband first, love.

COULDN'T WE KEEP ON DANCING?

(Music by Philip Braham)
(Company)

REFRAIN 1   If we try, you and I,
            Couldn't we keep on dancing?
            Man and wife, what a life!
            Wouldn't it be entrancing?
            Never mind if we find
            People a bore,
            Never blue,
            Follow through
            Every encore.
            Couldn't we, couldn't we,
            Couldn't we keep on dancing?

VERSE 1   With our fingers interlacing,
            We'll go rapturously pacing,
            Hand in hand, dear,
            Fairyland, dear.
            Couldn't be more grand, dear,
            I should welcome growing older
            With your head upon my shoulder.
            Lights are gleaming
            While we're scheming,
            What a lovely dream!

Verse 2   Absent-minded syncopation
            So improves the circulation,
            Law-abiding
            Love is hiding
            As we're gently gliding;
            In my dreams I've contemplated
            Being rhythmically mated.
            Never leave me,
            That would grieve me,
            Let us make believe!

REFRAIN 2   If we try, you and I,

Couldn't we keep on dancing?
Man and wife, what a life!
Wouldn't it be entrancing?
Never mind if we find
People a bore,
Never blue,
Follow through
Every encore.
Couldn't we, couldn't we,
Couldn't we keep on dancing?

INTERLUDE:
          Drifting through the world to some
              sweet tune,
          What a fascinating honeymoon!
          Happiness acquiring,
          Never tiring,
          Don't let's wake too soon.

REFRAIN 3   If we try, you and I,
            Couldn't we keep on dancing?
            Man and wife, what a life!
            Wouldn't it be entrancing?
            Never mind if we find
            People a bore,
            Never blue,
            Follow through
            Every encore.
            Couldn't we, couldn't we,
            Couldn't we keep on dancing?

---

*LADYBIRD

(Terry Kendall)

VERSE 1
          There isn't much a fellow can do
          When he feels his true ideals are falling;
          Love is such a brittle game to play,
          Women seem to whittle it away.
          I've cherished dreams that never come true,
          Now I find my state of mind appalling;
          Ev'ry girl I thought romantic,
          Leaves me flat and drives me frantic;
          What am I to do?
          What am I to do?
          Must I be forever calling.

Refrain:
          Ladybird,

Ladybird,
You've flown away with never a word
Free as air, you don't care;
Unthinking, unheeding,
Tho' love lies bleeding.
Ladybird,
Ladybird,
Your moral sense is rather absurd,
Just admit, you're a bit
Shady,
Ladybird.

VERSE 2
          I'm disillusioned each time I try
          To explore the world for more romances,
          Whether in the country or the town,
          Ev'ry girl I meet just turns me down.
          I think I'd feel much better if I'd
          Really tried to curb my idle fancies;
          All my love affairs I'll wind up,
          And my broken heart I'll bind up,
          Let it go at that,
          Let it go at that,
          I shall take no further chances.

REFRAIN
          Ladybird,
          Ladybird,
          You've flown away with never a word
          Free as air, you don't care;
          Unthinking, unheeding.
          Ladybird,
          Ladybird,
          Your moral sense is rather absurd,
          Just admit, you're a bit
          Shady,
          Ladybird.

COME A LITTLE CLOSER

(Music by Philip Braham)
(Greta Fayne and Richard Dolman)

HE: Sometimes you whisper
          After a kiss,
          How much I mean to you.

She   You're so persistent,
          Just think of this.

What is a girl to do?
When you are pleading
Close by my side,
Gaily unheeding
Time and tide.
If you have meant the nice things you say,
I might relent
And look your way.

REFRAIN   Come a little closer, closer dear to me;
If you answer, "No, Sir," how annoyed I'll be.
Why do you crush me and try to rush me,
Each single word I say?
Come a little closer, please don't turn away.
Sometimes you're sweet and adorably small,
Then you're so grand I can't reach you at all.
Come a little closer, closer dear to me.

HE: Think of the rapture
When we're at last
Lost in our love intense.

SHE: Try to recapture
Out of the past
One little shred of sense.
You're so tenacious
With your desire;
If you were gracious
You'd soon tire.

HE: That isn't fair, dear,
Doubting me so,
I couldn't bear
To let you go.

CODA
I'll never falter, take me on trust!
If at the altar you would just
Come a little closer, closer dear to me.

*   *   *

Once again Noël tried his hand at a French song. In a sketch called "The Café de la Paix" a group of the characters sitting in the café are approached by a "drab woman selling violets. She is singing gustily."

*VIOLET SELLER'S SONG

Nous avons fait un beau voyage,
Nous avons fait un beau voyage,
Nous arrêtant à tous les pas,
Nous arrêtant à tous les pas,

Buvant du cidre à chaque village,
Cueillant dans les clos des lilas
Cueillant dans les clos des lilas

Noël was secretly quite proud of his French and there were several songs in the language that were never to find a place in one of his shows . . .

*JOURNÉE HEUREUSE

Journée heureuse,
Journée heureuse.
Papillons parmi les fleurs
Remplissent de joie mon coeur
Matin plein de tendre ivresse
Vent leger qui caresse
D'ou vient cette charmante
Melodie tremblante
M'apportant ce doux bonheur
Ah—jour d'été
Mes pensées
Legères et gaies
Comme enchantées
S'envolent au loin par cieux ensorcelés
Revant parmi les jardins entournés
Journée heureuse,
Journée heureuse,
Belle journée

*   *   *

In a sketch called "Fête Galante"—a vicarage garden party at Runcorn—there were a series of numbers credited to Coward and Braham:

"RASPBERRY TIME IN RUNCORN"

OPENING CHORUS
The Scoutmaster (Ernest Lindsay) and Company

When it's raspberry time in Runcorn,
In Runcorn, in Runcorn,
The air is like a draught of wine,

The undertaker cleans his sign,
The Hull express goes off the line,
When it's raspberry time in Runcorn.

SOLO: The happy-hearted Rural Dean—

CHORUS: In Runcorn, in Runcorn—

SOLO: Plays cricket on the village green—

CHORUS: In Runcorn, in Runcorn—

SOLO: And as before the vestry door
With cricket bat he poises,
From far and near you always hear
The most peculiar noises.

CHORUS: For it's raspberry time, raspberry time,
raspberry time in Runcorn

THE SPINSTERS QUARTETE

We're little Parish workers,
With indefinite desires,
Determined to improve the shining hour
Through years of firm repression
May have quenched our inward fires,
Undoubtedly we've turned a trifle sour.
We're busy little beavers,
And we decorate the Church.
Our moral standard's very, very high.
The flower of English manhood
May have left us in the lurch
But we know we'll go to Heaven when
we die.

There is evidence of another lyric with the same title but whether it was intended as part of the same song or as an alternative version is not clear.

*SPINSTER QUARTETTE

Chorus 1: We never did that when we were girls,
We shouldn't have made so free.
Our lives were calm
And well arranged
We hate to see how things

78

Hermione Baddeley with the Company in "Fête Galante."

Have changed
We never were lax
And showed our backs
For all the world to see.
We never wore our frocks to there
But when at night we brushed our hair
We laid our girlish secrets bare—
Victorian girls were we.

CHORUS 2: We never did that when we were girls.
It wouldn't have been refined
When tired of reading Ethel Dell
We overlook the Grand Hotel
And nevertheless
We must confess
A curious turn of mind
A smart young lady dressed in white
Before retiring for the night
Just ties a hanky round the light
And then she pulls down the blind

THE VICARAGE DANCE

Nellie (Hermione Baddeley) and Company

I'm just seventeen and a rogue of a girl;
My heart is a-throbbing with carnival's whirl.
Lovers in plenty I'll have before dawn,
As I dance in my semi of mercerized lawn!

REFRAIN   Come with me, come to the vicarage dance.
Quick to the ball we must hasten.
Those who have gout are allowed to sit out
Under the lavatory basin.
Several old deans behind Japanese screens
Give naughty cupid a chance,
Though I get cramp
I'm no end of a scamp
Down at the vicarage dance.

The "scamp" was the result of the Lord Chamberlain's intervention. His Lordship clearly felt that the original couplet—

Although I can stitch
I'm no end of a —

though discreetly incomplete, was inappropriate in a spiritual context.

THE CHOIRBOYS' SONG

SEXTET

We're six dirty little choir boys
With really frightful minds,
We scream and shout and rush about
And pinch our friends' behinds.
Nobody could admire boys
With dirty hands and knees,
But the countryside rejoices
At our sweet soprano voices,
So we do what we damn well please.

EVEN CLERGYMEN ARE NAUGHTY NOW AND THEN

Vicar and Curate (Douglas Byng and Ernest Thesiger)

VERSE I   People have a wrong idea of Members
of the Cloth;
It's really an enjoyable profession.
And though we don't indulge in much
frivolity and froth
We really haven't cause for much depression.
Our lives are full of jollity and gaeity and fun,
With christenings and funerals and such,
There's not a week goes by
In which someone doesn't die,
So we really mustn't grumble very much.

REFRAIN I   When we wake up in the morning and
the birds are trilling
There is something thrilling
In the air:

CURATE: I can feel my pulses starting
As I struggle with my parting,

And my thoughts go gaily darting
Here and there.
When we visit village invalids on New
    Year's Day
We're really just as gay
As other men;

VICAR: Mrs. Jones whom I was chaffing
           Had a fit and died from laughing.

BOTH: Even clergymen are naughty
           Now and then.

VERSE 2
VICAR: The villagers will never disregard a
               festive cause
           To join in any jumble sale or raffle,
           And every Christmas evening I appear as
               Santa Claus,
           A good disguise which never fails to baffle.
           A whist drive in the Parish Room
           Could only be described
           As a positively brilliant affair.
           And when old Mrs. Meyer
           Gives a picnic for the choir
           It's really almost more than we can bear.

REFRAIN 2
BOTH: When we wake up in the morning and the
               weather's bad
           We're really always glad
           To be alive.

VICAR: With a faithful repetition
           Of our family tradition
           Every year a new addition will arrive.

BOTH: Though we fill the cup of duty to the very brim
           Ideas may sometimes swim
           Into our ken.

CURATE: When our thoughts are most volcanic
           We remember in our panic
           Even clergymen are naughty
           Now and then.

FINALE: "CHURCH PARADE"

The Vicar's Wife (Betty Shale) and Full Company

VERSE   On every Sunday morning
           See the righteous leave their houses,
           With perching hats adorning,

Feather boas and dressy blouses,
Their souls devoid of base emotions,
They're on their way to their devotions.

REFRAIN 1 Church parade, church parade,
           See the different types displayed.
           Tall ones, short ones, thin and stout,
           Everyone looking quite aggressively devout.
           Church parade, church parade,
           Truculent and undismayed,
           There's Mrs. Bowls in grey sateen,
           Her hat's the queerest shape I can
               remember having seen,
           It makes me quite suspicious as to what it
               might have been
           On Church parade.

REFRAIN 2 Church parade, church parade,
           See the different types portrayed.
           Christian women, large and small,
           With nothing in their faces to distinguish
               them at all.
           Church parade, church parade,
           Truculent and undismayed,
           Those young ladies don't read Freud,
           Their virginal mentalities are otherwise
               employed;
           Maybe that's the reason that they look
               so unenjoyed
           On Church parade.

*   *   *

Noël wrote three other songs for the show for which
Philip Braham provided the music—none of which
were eventually used.

*ELDORADO

REFRAIN 1 Eldorado, Eldorado,
           How near you seem.
           Years of sorrow
           With tomorrow
           Fade like a dream.
           Eldorado, Eldorado,
           Troubles are past,
           In your olden
           Legend Golden
           Fold me at last.

VERSE 1   Before the day is born
           Within the hush of Dawn
           Where sea and sky are faintest blue
           I see a mirage shining through.
           Alluring vision false or true
           I call—to you.

There was a song earmarked for Hermione Baddeley
to sing (in Cockney), which has alternative refrains
and appears unfinished . . .

*CINDERELLA SONG

REFRAIN   I've read that sweet Cinderella song,
           Nothing like that ever comes my way.
           Nobody wants to enfold me
           And close within their arms they would hold me.
           Heigh Ho,
           I know
           'Twas ever thus on the Underground.

           You used to say such wonderful things
           That thrilled me more than diamonds and rings
           But now I don't mean much to you . . .

REFRAIN   I don't aspire to a dashing Guardsman,
           I couldn't manage a gay hussar.
           I've got the simplest taste
           I don't intend to marry in haste
           Some day
           I may
           Be wooed and won in an 'igh class way
           And I don't suppose it will be a policeman,
           I'd be afraid if he came to tea.
           A thousand kids are born every day
           And somehow somewhere hiding away
           There must be just a commonplace boy for me.

The third Coward/Braham collaboration poses a
problem, since it's quite unlike anything else they
produced together and is much nearer to the Music
Hall pastiches Noël produced in his teens—although
a lot less genteel. It is indicated as a "Trio" and all we
have is a "dummy" lyric—a device used by all song
writers to "fix" the musical rhythm to which they
would have to fit the final words. (Lyricist Irving
Caesar claimed his words for "Tea for Two" were
written that way . . . and then *stayed* that way.)

80

*CORSETS

REFRAIN I met her when she had her corsets on.
Oh dear, oh dear
I don't suppose she ever realised
I met her when she had her corsets on.

VERSE One Sunday night when I was tight
I met a charming girl.
She said—"Good evening, dear,
You're rather drunk, I fear."

First I detached her from her blouse
And kissed her on the spot
Oh, for the bliss of that sweet kiss
It thrilled me through and through

What happened then we shall never know . . .

*   *   *

Since credit is meticulously given to Braham in Noël's notes for supplying music, its absence on this next song suggests Noël wrote both words and music . . .

*I'M NOT THAT KIND OF GIRL!

(*Dancing Duet*)

VERSE

HE: I want you—you want me
False or true—love is free

SHE: Don't try to fashion with infinite pains
A cage for passion with fetters and chains.

REFRAIN

HE: I can't define a parallel line
Or add up two by two,
My brain is so incredibly slow.
Whene'er I talk to you
I feel my sense flying away
And all the things I'm dying to say
Won't do.

SHE: Little boy, you needn't look so blue.

HE: I don't suppose anyone knows
The anguish of my soul

SHE: Please realise it wouldn't be wise
To lose your self control.

HE: I long to make you quickly forsake
This simply social whirl.

SHE: You'd very soon find
I'm not that kind of girl

*   *   *

The original script submitted to the Lord Chamberlain's Office contains other material not used in the show. "Caballero" eventually turned up in *This Year of Grace* (see p. 97); "(Take It From Me) I Was A Good Girl Then" became " She Was A Good Girl Then" (see p. 82) and "The Touch Of A Woman's Hand" never did find a home. Perhaps it was too predictive of *the* woman politician with its reference to the way a woman's hand . . .

" . . . is improving the Motherland
For the woman politicians have a nasty gift
Of detecting shifting sand."

*THE TOUCH OF A WOMAN'S HAND (1925)

VERSE I Ever since the world began
Woman's been the slave of man;
Years of hard experience have taught her
To be led quite meekly to the slaughter.
But , in quite a subtle way,
She has learnt the game to play.
Gently persevering through the ages,
She has left her mark on history's pages.

REFRAIN I Just the touch of a woman's hand
Was ignored when the world was planned,
Why the Tree of Good and Evil should be
firmly shunned,
Eve could never understand.
So she fell for the serpent's hiss,
And surrendered to love's first kiss,
Thus the primitive emotions to a blaze
were fanned
By the touch of a woman's hand.

VERSE 2 Since that early marriage scene,
Centuries have rolled between;
Husbands of remarkable complacence
Flourished in the days of the Renaissance.
People never tried divorce
When their love had run its course.
If a husband bored his wife completely
She'd prepare his supper very neatly.

REFRAIN 2 Just the touch of a woman's hand,
Lent a charm to each costly viand,
With the very blissful knowledge that
she'd bribed her cook,
She'd contrive to look quite bland.
If with some little charming speech
She would help him to half a peach,
He'd be painfully transported to a better land
By the touch of a woman's hand.

VERSE 3 Girls of the domestic kind,
Nowadays are hard to find,
Hearths and homes are violently changing,
Women have a craze for re-arranging.
Happy little homes are few,
Politics have claimed their due,
Wives who try to regulate the nations
Devastate their conjugal relations.

No show would be complete without Mr. Cochran's Young Ladies, this time a group of eccentric and character dancers: the Faun, the Russian, the Huzzars, the Modernist and the Charleston blend themselves into another rhythmic ensemble.

REFRAIN 3 Just the touch of a woman's hand
Is improving the Motherland,
For the woman politicians have a nasty gift
Of detecting shifting sand.
It would shatter the Empire's hopes
If we listened to Marie Stopes.
All the crèches in the country would at
once disband
By the touch of a woman's hand.

1924/1925

Noël would occasionally write a number for a favourite artiste. Nora Bayes, the American comedienne and singer who had so impressed Maisie Gay, was one. When Miss Bayes appeared in a variety season at the New Oxford Theatre, London in September 1924, Noël contributed . . .

*ONE FINE DAY

VERSE 1 Tho' I scarcely know you, I've a keen desire
Tenderly, to show you how you can acquire
Laughter, tho' hope seems dying,
You'll wonder after why you were crying,
Tho' things you care for may seem departed
They're always there for the happy hearted.

REFRAIN One fine day, anyway, troubles may fade away
Leaving skies serenely blue,
Doubts and fears,
Weary years,
Need for tears
Disappears
When you find your dreams come true.
When life's a difficult game
And seems to lose its meaning,

Remember stars shine the same
Tho' clouds are intervening, above you
One fine day, anyway, someone sweet may
say
"I love you".

VERSE 2 I don't mind confessing all you say is true,
Things seem less depressing since I've talk'd
to you.
Waiting may soon be ended,
It's comforting to be befriended,
We'll try to smother all cares and sadness
And help each other to search for gladness.

Miss Bayes was not to know that it was a minor revision to a number intended for *Tamaran*.

HE NEVER DID THAT TO ME

VERSE 1 I have been a Movie fan
Since the cinemas first began;
My young brother's a cameraman,
And when I start
Meeting heroes of romance,
I shall firmly take my chance.
Though I find the hero charming,
I prefer the more alarming
Man who plays the villain's part.
The things he does to nice young girls
Aren't easy to forget;
He never minces matters,
When he traps them in his net.

REFRAIN 1 He never did that to me;
He never did that to me;
Though I must admit
He wasn't a bit
Like what I'd supposed he'd be.
The way that he uses
Ingénues is
Really a sight to see;
He binds them across his saddle tight,
Regardless of all their shrieks of fright,
And carries them upside down all night,
He never did that to me.

REFRAIN 2 He never did that to me;
He never did that to me;
Though I must admit

He wasn't a bit
Like what I'd supposed he'd be.
I once saw him save
A Christian slave,
And gallantly set her free.
She knelt at his feet with downcast head;
"God will reward you, sir", she said.
He gave her a look and shot her dead
He never did that to me.

VERSE 2 Though my disappointment's great,
I shall never procrastinate,
I'm determined to watch and wait,
And then you'll see;
He'll revert to type, perhaps,
Have a violent moral lapse,
When the moment's quite propitious,
He'll do something really vicious.
Think how lovely that will be.
His reputation's terrible,
Which comforts me a lot;
If any girl is seen with him,
She's branded on the spot.

REFRAIN 3 He never did that to me;
He never did that to me;
Though I must admit
He wasn't a bit
Like what I'd supposed he'd be.
He went in his car

*Nora Bayes from
the sheet music of
"One Fine Day."*

But not too far,
Some mutual friends to see;
The car gave a lurch and then a skid,
We didn't turn over—God forbid!
Whatever you may have *thought* he did,
He never did that to me.

REFRAIN 4 He never did that to me;
He never did that to me;
Though I must admit
He wasn't a bit
Like what I'd supposed he'd be.
I once saw him fish
The Sisters Gish
From out of a stormy sea;
He locked them in his refined Rolls Royce,
And said in a most determined voice,
"It's death or dishonour—take your choice!"
He never did that to me.

Clearly, the nature of feminine morality continued
to give him pause . . .

SHE WAS A GOOD GIRL THEN (1926)

Verse 1

I remember Mary at a very early age,
She was sweet, sweet, sweet as pie,
She was like a fairy who has fallen on Life's stage
And forgotten how to fly.
She was full of charming and alluring little ways,
Her modesty would leave you quite aghast.
Innocence to her was like a cosy little cage,
But alas! Those days are past.

REFRAIN 1

Take it from me she was a good girl then,
She was as fragrant as the blooming cyclamen.
If a schoolboy
Brought her a bunch of flowers
She'd weep with joy for hours,
She was never misled
And was always in bed
By ten;
Take it from me
That child could do no wrong
Though lots of horrible temptations came along.
One occasion

When her watch was stolen by her sister Nell,
Mary promptly offered her the chain as well.
Take it from me she was a good girl then.

VERSE 2

Mary growing older was extremely *comme-il-faut*
And her ignorance was bliss.
No one ever told her all the things a girl should
know,
And the reason why was this.
She was unsophisticated, dancing to and fro
She didn't know the value of her charms,
Dwelling in such innocence it only goes to show
That she seldom suffered qualms.

REFRAIN 2

Take it from me she was a good girl then,
Above her bed was hung "The Monarch of the
Glen",
In the morning
She never pulled the blind up
Till she had made her mind up,
And she finished her prayers with a very devout
"Ah-men",
Take it from me she never went too far.
One day a young man took her driving in his car
And I must say
Though he drove her straight to a barbed wire
fence
She had never fallen in the stricter sense.
Take it from me she was a good girl then.

REFRAIN 3

Take it from me she was a good girl then,
She really hadn't much experience of men.
She would always blush with surprise if teased
much,
Give piercing cries if squeezed much,
And she looked on the world as a sort of lions'
den,
Take it from me she was as pure as snow,
She seemed to know by instinct just how far to
go.
In the morning
When she took her cousin Jack his early tea
Neither of them had their lunch till half past
three.
Take it from me she was a good girl then.

REFRAIN 4

Take it from me she was a good girl then,
Peculiar thoughts had never crept into her ken.
She was never really depressed or humpy,
Maybe her nerves were jumpy,
But she left it at that—

And took lots of Sanat-ogen.
Take it from me she was a bit run down,
The doctor looked at her with quite a worried
frown,
Then he told her
Tactfully and firmly that she needed care,
So she went to Canada and had it there.
Take it from me she was a good girl then.

But whatever the subject—say the familial obligations of domestic life—the Coward tongue was never
far from the cheek . . .

WE MUST ALL BE VERY KIND TO AUNT JESSIE (C. 1924)

VERSE 1 I remember clearly when a tiny little child
My Auntie came to stay with us.
Maybe as a family we were a trifle wild,
Our spirits ran away with us.
Every single day
When we were at play
Mother used to creep into the nursery
and say:

REFRAIN 1 We must all be very kind to Auntie Jessie,
For she's never been a Mother or a Wife,
You mustn't throw your toys at her
Or make a vulgar noise at her,
She hasn't led a very happy life.
You must never lock her playfully in the
bathroom
Or play tunes on her enamelled Spanish
comb.
Though unpleasant to behold
She's a heart of purest gold
And Charity you know begins at home.

VERSE 2 Relatives who come to stay are generally
inclined
To fray the children's nerves a bit,
Something in a maiden aunt just stupefies
the mind,
From Virtue's path one swerves a bit,
Though our childish joys
May have made a noise
Mother used to murmur though *I know*,
Boys will be Boys.

REFRAIN 2 We must all be very kind to Auntie Jessie,
And do everything we can to keep her bright.
If when you're in the Underground
You hear her make a funny sound
It's very rude to laugh at her outright.
You must never fill her nightdress case with
    beetles
Or beat up her Horlick's Malted Milk to foam,
Though her kiss is worse than death
It's unkind to hold your breath
For Charity you know begins at home.

REFRAIN 3 We must all be very kind to Auntie Jessie,
And encourage her to see the sunny side,
It isn't kind to rush at her
And hurl the blacking brush at her,
It's things like this that trample on her pride,
Don't molest her with a pail of *Icy* water,
If when wandering at night she chanced to roam,
Though the attic stairs are steep
Death comes peacefully in sleep
And Charity *we hope* begins at home.

Another prescient feminist tract from around the same time . . .

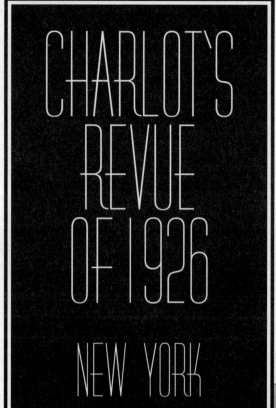

CHARLOT'S
REVUE
OF 1926

NEW YORK

Charlot repeated his compilation experiment for New York. Once again, the show was tried out at the Golders Green Hippodrome on October 5, 1925 and opened at the Selwyn Theatre, New York on November 10, 1925.

Coward contributed "Russian Blues" and "Carrie" from *London Calling!* "Poor Little Rich Girl" from *On With the Dance* and "After-Dinner Music" from the earlier Charlot revue.

Jessie Matthews sang "Carrie Was a Careful Girl" and found she had to take care of herself in a way the London stage had not prepared her for. The staging of the number required her to use a catwalk: "As I sang, round me swept the show girls, bare bosoms gleaming, long legs teetering on the highest of heels, feathers, spangles, just a breath away from the bumps and grinds of burlesque. As I floated back along the catwalk, a young man leaned over and pinched me where it hurt." After that Carrie was rather more careful . . .

*WHEN WOMEN COME INTO THEIR OWN

When women come into their own
You'll notice a difference in tone.
The present iniquitous laws of divorce
Will alter at once as a matter of course.
If tired of your husband you've grown
And wish to be free and alone,
Without restricting your conjugal right
Or blazing your name in publicity's light
You can just have him shot if he coughs in the
    night!
When women come into their own.

Right: Nelson Keys, flanked by Beatrice Lillie and Gertrude Lawrence, replaced Jack Buchanan during the run of the show.

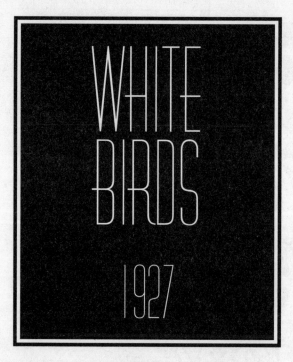

The revue presented at His Majesty's Theatre on May 31, 1927 contained one Coward song.

"What is to Become of the Children?" was sung by Maisie Gay and was used for only part of the run.

WHAT IS TO BECOME OF THE CHILDREN?

I've a message for the women of the Empire,
A message to the women great and small,
A definite appeal to those who still can feel
That a life of shallow pleasure isn't all.
I've a message for the housemaid and the duchess
Whose feet are drawing nearer the abyss,
You may bow your heads in shame
But you can't escape the blame
For the question I am asking you is this.

What's going to happen to the children, when
          there aren't
Any more grown-ups?
The hand that rocks the cradle will no longer
          rule the world
When silver threads amongst the gold are
          permanently curled.
Who's going to hear their prayers at twilight
And tuck the little darlings in their cots?
If comfort, warmth and nourishment cannot be
          guaranteed

It's very very hard for any child to overfeed,
If Mother's in the bathroom being massaged by a
          Swede
What's going to happen to the tots?

I've a message for the mothers who are married,
I've a message for the mothers who are not,
I have a message too for the many and the few
Who always strike the iron—when it's hot.,
I've a message for the ingenue of forty
Who multiplies her love affairs by ten,
Who although she looks a fool,
Still she proves the ancient rule
That the chicken should look older than the hen

What's going to happen to the children, when
          there aren't
Any more grown-ups?
The stately homes of England will look desolate
          and cold
When Grandpa's so athletic that's he's painful to
          behold.
Who's going to telephone the doctor
When the baby's little face breaks out in spots?
If Auntie's girlish figure is encased in rubber bands
And Father screams with passion when his
          diaphragm expands
And Mother is injected with the most peculiar glands,
What's going to happen to the tots?

What's going to happen to the children, when
          there aren't any
Any more grown-ups?
It's very had on nature when she's made a lot of
          plans
To have them all frustrated by a lot of Peter Pans.
Who has the baby got to turn to
When his underclothes get tangled up in knots?
One contemplates with nervousness, with horror
          and dismay
The juvenile behaviour of the parents of today.
When Mother's face is lifted till it's almost
          whisked away
What's going to happen to the tots?

The manuscript contains another partial Refrain . . .

  *If Father in an effort to be captain of his soul
  Collapses with excitement when he flukes the
            second hole
  And Mother's giving lectures on the use of birth
            control—
  What's going to happen to the tots?

Nearly thirty years later in *Together With Music* (1955) Noël was to re-visit the theme of growing old disgracefully. It's interesting to see how little had

Maisie Gay.

changed in the human condition, except for the addition of a few brand names and the ubiquitous mid-century psychiatrist . . .

WHAT'S GOING TO HAPPEN TO THE TOTS? (1955)

(American Version)

VERSE 1   Life today is hectic
           Our world is running away,
           Only the wise
           Can recognize
           The process of decay,

Unhappily all our dialectic
Is quite unable to say
Whether we're on the beam or not
Whether we'll rise supreme or not
Whether this new regime or not
Is leading us astray.
We all have Frigidaires, radios,
Television and movie shows
To shield us from the ultimate abyss,
We have our daily bread neatly cut,
Every modern convenience, but
The question that confronts us all is this:

REFRAIN 1 What's going to happen to the children
When there aren't any more grown-ups?
Having been injected with some rather
    peculiar glands
Darling Mum's gone platinum and dances to
    all the rhumba bands,
The songs that she sings at twilight
Would certainly be the highlight
For some of those claques
That Elsa Maxwell takes around in yachts.
Rock-a-bye, rock-a-bye, rock-a-bye, my darlings,
Mother requires a few more shots,
Does it amuse the tiny mites
To see their parents high as kites?
What's, what's, what's going to happen to
    the tots?

VERSE 2 Life today's neurotic
A ceaseless battle we wage,
Millions are spent
To circumvent
The march of middle-age,
The fact that we grab each new narcotic
Can only prove in the end
Whether our hormones jell or not
Whether our cells rebel or not
Whether we're blown to hell or not
We'll all be round the bend
From taking Benzedrine, Dexamil,
Every possible sleeping pill
To knock us out or knock us into shape,
We all have shots for this, shots for that,
Shots for making us thin or fat,
But there's one problem that we can't escape:

REFRAIN 2 What's going to happen to the children
When there aren't any more grown-ups?
Thanks to plastic surgery and Uncle's abrupt
    demise
Dear Aunt Rose has changed her nose but
    doesn't appear to realize
The pleasures that once were heaven
Look silly at sixty-seven

And youthful allure you can't procure
In terms of perms and pots—so
Lullaby, lullaby, lullaby, my darlings,
Try not to scratch those large red spots.
Think of the shock when Mummy's face
Is lifted from its proper place.
What's, what's, what's going to happen to
    the tots?

REFRAIN 3 What's going to happen to the children
When there aren't any more grown-ups?
It's bizarre when Grandmamma, without
    getting out of breath,
Starts to jive at eighty-five
And frightens the little ones to death,
The police had to send a squad car
When Daddy got fried on Vodka
And tied a tweed coat round Mummy's throat
In several sailor's knots.
Hush-a-bye, hush-a-bye, hush-a-bye, my darlings,
Try not to fret and wet your cots,
One day you'll clench your tiny fists
And murder your psychiatrists,
What's, what's, what's going to happen to
    the tots?

If Noël's memory was correct concerning the genesis of the song "A Room With a View," he relates in *Present Indicative* that it came to him on a beach in Hawaii in 1927. It was used the following year in his revue, *This Year of Grace* and became an immediate and lasting hit (see p. 89).

What he nowhere records is that it was originally intended for a "book" musical to be called *Star Dust*.

The story was the "show-within-a-show" formula, which he would eventually attempt with *Operette* (1938). Set on the stage of the Spinet Theatre, the

cast rehearsed for the musical, *Mary Make Believe*. According to the "wish list" casting Noël was in the habit of using at the beginning of any draft, Irene Browne was intended to play Sue Gordon (Mary Maine in the show), while Maisie Gay would be Ada Jackson (her mother, Mrs. Maine).

The story of the "show" is typical for a twenties musical romance but by putting it inside the main structure—rather as Cole Porter was to do with *The Taming of the Shrew* in *Kiss Me, Kate*—Noël could gently satirise the form.

Mary and her mother are living comfortably in the South of France. At the casino she meets a charming young man. In an attempt to see her, he climbs into the garden, where he is surprised by the maid, Leonore, who smuggles him out. Later, Prince Beloff, who is generally regarded as the catch of the social season, arrives for dinner. Mary is initially reluctant to meet him, until she recognises him as her young man from the casino. We, however, recognise him as the young man from the garden who was flirting with Leonore.

In the Second Act at Prince Beloff's reception the Prince maintains his deception, pretending that his secretary, Philip Radnor, is Beloff. Philip is by now wildly in love with Mary, while Beloff is in love with Leonore (didn't I say this was a typical 20s plot!). Finally, Mrs. Maine uncovers the deception, which Philip has to admit to. Mary is distraught. "After dancing more and more wildly, she falls swooning into the arms of the real Prince Beloff."

Act Three finds Philip trying to forget his sorrows in the Gambling Room at the casino. Mary arrives on the terrace, laments her woes, then also enters the casino. To fill in time Beloff and Leonore have a "comedy scene," before Mary emerges, having lost everything. Philip follows, having won heavily. A reprise of their theme song soon makes up their quarrel.

All that Noël actually wrote was part of the first scene in which some of the actors are being coached in their lines for *Mary* by Billy, the Assistant Stage Manager. We are allowed to see the Maisie Gay character enter, complete with her small dog, Bogey before the mss. stops.

In his "Tentative List of Numbers" Noël only sketches out the first act in any detail . . .

OPENING CHORUS

Number with Girls	-	Prince Beloff
"Mary Make Believe"	-	Mary
Duet	-	Lenore and Beloff
Number with Men	-	Philip
Duet "Room With a View"	-	Philip and Mary

FINALE

In his cast list Noël indicates some forty actors as well as "Photographers, stage hands, musicians, etc." and even with doubling up, this would have made the show an expensive proposition to mount—a fact which may well have proved decisive in the final analysis.

Fortunately, he soon had a new home for the two numbers he had written, though knowing their intended parody context adds a new dimension to hearing their familiar sounds again.

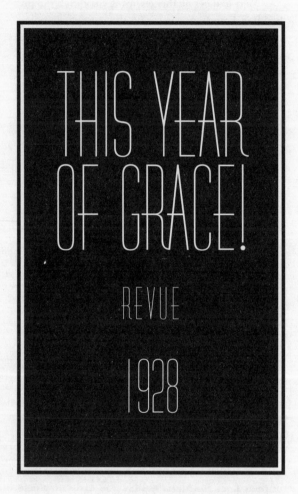

First presented by Charles B. Cochran at the Palace Theatre, Manchester on February 28, 1928 as Charles B. Cochran's 1928 Revue. Trans-ferred to the London Pavilion on March 22, 1928 as This Year of Grace! (316 performances). Book, lyrics and music by Noël Coward.

Cast included Maisie Gay, Sonnie Hale, Jessie Matthews, Tilly Losch, Douglas Byng, Lance Lister, Moya Nugent, Lauri Devine.

Noël was to call this "the best of all my revues." Another collaboration with Cochran and this time there were no arguments over who did what . . . "the whole show was to be mine: music, book, lyrics, and

supervision of production. . . I remember leaving his office much cheered and with a new tune whirling round in my head, a tune to which the words 'Dance, Dance, Dance, Little Lady' had resolutely set themselves even before I got home to the piano."

DANCE, LITTLE LADY

(Sonnie Hale)

VERSE 1

Though you're only seventeen
Far too much of life you've seen,
Syncopated child.
Maybe if you only knew
Where your path was leading to
You'd become less wild.
But I know it's vain
Trying to explain
While there's this insane
Music in your brain.

REFRAIN

Dance, dance, dance little lady,
Youth is fleeting—to the rhythm beating
In your mind.
Dance, dance, dance little lady,
So obsessed with second best,
No rest you'll ever find,
Time and tide and trouble
Never, never wait,
Let the cauldron bubble
Justify your fate.
Dance, dance, dance little lady
Leave tomorrow behind.

PATTER

When the saxophone
Gives a wicked moan,
Charleston hey hey,
Rhythms fall and rise,
Start dancing to the tune,
The band's crooning—
For soon
The night will be gone,
Start swaying like a reed
Without heeding
The speed
That hurries you on.
Nigger melodies
Syncopate your nerves
Till your body curves

Drooping—stooping,
Laughter some day dies
And when the lights are starting to gutter
Dawn through the shutter
Shows you're living in a world of lies.

Noël records that on opening night Sonnie Hale "brought down the house" with the song "which he did with Lauri Devine against a group of glittering, macabre figures wearing Oliver Messel masks." Ms. Devine "wore evening dress and looked drained and far from healthy"—a condition that seemed to be de rigeur for leading female characters in Coward revues.

In his Observer review St. John Ervine praised the number's "Hogarthian humour. In this scene a clever dancer, Miss Lauri Devine, mimes the part of a modern girl dancing in that lifeless, exhausted, unsmiling fashion that is common among the young who were reared on food-tickets and were bombed into neurosis. Mr. Oliver Messel has designed masks for this scene which faithfully reproduce the mirthless, vacuous expression which one may see for oneself any night in smart restaurants and clubs, where empty-looking youths dance with empty-looking maidens in an empty shuffle. The scene is almost cruel in its veracity, but it is a genuine satire on our time, and it confirms me in my belief that Mr. Coward's talents are growing . . ." Noël agreed and noted with straight face that "The high tone of moral indignation implicit in the lyric impressed a number of people, notably the late Aimée Semple Macpherson."

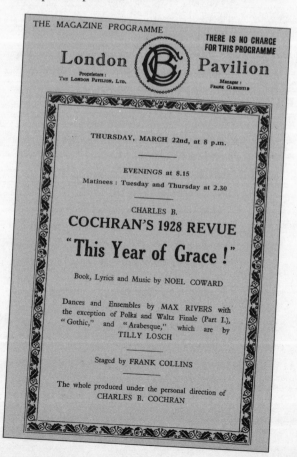

There were a few questioning voices, even though one was that of a friend. Beverley Nichols pointed out that "the first eight bars revealed themselves as identical with a charming Edwardian ballad." Noël had to admit that he had accidentally plagiarised, "but I didn't realise this when it came into my head and now it's too late to do anything about it." Another was that of critic, A. G. MacDonnell, who found the lyrics "innocuously neat and harmless, except for one tiresome mannerism. Mr. Coward has apparently just discovered the internal rhyme and uses it *ad nauseam*."

Hale and Jessie Matthews, Noël felt, were "charming" in "A Room With a View" and "Try to Learn to Love"—advice they took soon after the show, when Hale left his wife, Evelyn Laye, for Matthews and created a problem for Noël when he came to cast his next show, *Bitter Sweet* . . . In her autobiography, *Over My Shoulder*, Jessie Matthews records: "At the end of our song, Sonnie whispered, 'Let's make it come true' . . . Who was to blame? Could we blame Noël Coward for writing his sweet song that we had made our own? For I defy any young couple to sing that song together every night without a strong bond growing between them."

Lauri Devine and the Masked Chorus in "Dance, Little Lady."
Masks were designed by Oliver Messel.

A ROOM WITH A VIEW

VERSE 1

HE:
I've been cherishing
Through the perishing
Winter nights and days
A funny little phrase
That means
Such a lot to me
That you've got to be
With me heart and soul
For on you the whole
Thing leans.

SHE:
Won't you kindly tell me what you're
    driving at,
What conclusion you're arriving at?

HE:
Please don't turn away
Or my dream will stay
Hidden out of sight
Among a lot of might-
Have-Beens!

REFRAIN 1
A room with a view—and you,
And no one to worry us,
No one to hurry us—through
This dream we've found,
We'll gaze at the sky—and try
To guess what it's all about,
Then we will figure out—why
The world is round.

SHE:
We'll be as happy and contented
As birds upon a tree,
High above the mountains and the sea.

BOTH:
We'll bill and we'll coo-oo-oo
And sorrow will never come,
Oh, will it ever come—true,
Our room with a view.

VERSE 2
SHE:
I'm so practical
I'd make tactical
Errors as your wife,
I'd try to set your life
To rights.
I'm upset a bit
For I get a bit
Dizzy now and then
Following your mental flights.

HE:
Come with me and leave behind the noisy
    crowds,
Sunlight shines for us above the clouds.

SHE:
My eyes glistened too
While I listened to
All the things you said,
I'm glad I've got a head
For heights

REFRAIN 2
SHE:
A room with a view—and you,
And no one to give advice,
That sounds a paradise—few
Could fail to choose,
With fingers entwined we'll find
Relief from the preachers who
Always beseech us to—mind
Our P's and Q's.

HE:
We'll watch the whole world pass before us
While we are sitting still
Leaning on our own window-sill.

BOTH:
We'll bill and we'll coo-oo-oo
And maybe a stork will bring
This, that and t'other thing—to
Our room with a view.

"A Room With a View" was one of a handful of songs which seemed to come to Noël fully-formed during his career. This one "came tumbling into his mind one day while dozing in the sun" in Hawaii where he was convalescing in 1927 from a nervous breakdown caused by the failure of his latest play, *Sirocco*. The recovery began on that "lonely beach in Honolulu." The title of the song, Noël admitted was "unblushingly pinched from E. M. Forster's novel" and it "came into my mind together with a musical phrase to fit it." *Sirocco* was literally gone with the wind as "I splashed up and down in the shallows, searching for shells and rhymes at the same time."

Matthews also introduced "Mary Make-Believe" and found herself with a different kind of problem. She started out by being very nervous: "I got through the verse and the chorus. I could hear the girls coming on behind me. The theme of the number was that the chorus girls seduce me away from my ballet movements with their rhythmic dancing. The cue for my dance came. I couldn't stop trembling, my arms shook, my legs shook . . . ready—now! I raised my right foot for the high sweeping kick I had made my own . . . Oh God! Down I went on my bottom!"

Counter Melody sung by Chorus

She's just a girl who's always blowing mental bubbles
   Till she's quite out of breath—quite out of breath,
She seems to have the knack of magnifying troubles
   Till they crush her to death—crush her to death.
   She's just a duffer
   Of the ineffective kind,
   She's bound to suffer
   From her introspective mind,
Her indecisions
Quite prevent her visions
Coming true.
   Imagination
   Is a form of flagellation,
   If a sensitive child
   Lets it run wild
It dims the firmament
Till all the world is permanently blue.
She's simply bound
To make a bloomer
Until she's found
Her sense of humour,
If love should touch her ever
   She'll never, never see it through.

REFRAIN   Waiting in a queue
Waiting in a queue
Everybody's always waiting in a queue,
Fat and thin
They all begin
To take their stand—it's grand—queueing it.
Everywhere you go
Everywhere you go
Everybody's always standing in a row,
Short and tall
And one and all
The same as sheep—just keep—doing it.

No one says why
No one says how
No one says what is this for,
No one says no
No one says go
No one says this is a bore,
If you want to do
Anything that's new,
If you're feeling happy, furious or blue,
Wet or fine
You get in line
For everybody's waiting in a queue.

MARY MAKE-BELIEVE

VERSE   I have been reading in this book of mine
About a foolish maiden's prayer
And every gesture, word and look of mine
Seems to be mirrored there.
She had such terribly pedantic dreams
That her romantic schemes
Went all awry,
Her thoughts were such
She claimed too much
And true love passed her by.

REFRAIN   Mary make-believe
Dreamed the whole day through,
Foolish fancies,
Love romances,
How could they come true?
Mary make-believe
Sighed a little up her sleeve,
Nobody claimed her,
They only named her
Mary make-believe.

Facing page: Sonnie Hale and Jessie Matthews in "A Room With A View."

WAITING IN A QUEUE

(Sonnie Hale)

VERSE   In a rut
In a rut
In a rut
We go along,
Nothing but
Nothing but
Nothing but
The same old song,
To those who view us

light]y

We must seem slightly
Absurd,
We never break the ritual,
One habitual
Herd.

Miss Jessie Matthews and ladies of the chorus in "Mary Make-Believe."

LORELEI

(Sonnie Hale and Adrienne Brune)

VERSE 1   When the day
Fades away,
Twilight dies,
Sirens rise
Combing their hair with cool green fingers,
Crooning out their song,
Let him beware who loves and lingers
Over-long.

REFRAIN 1   Lorelei, Lorelei,
Call to sailors drifting by,
Cooo, cooo, come hither,
While they're sailing
A voice is wailing
A beckoning tune.
No use praying,
They'll all be paying
A reckoning soon.
Under the moon.

Lorelei, Lorelei,
Silver voices fade and die
Smiling with glee
Into the sea,
They slither
Down in the depths profound,
Where passionate joys are drowned,
There lie the lovers wooed by the Lorelei.

VERSE 2   All that is past
And now at last
Everything's altered and changed about,
Progress goes on,
Glamour has gone
From where the schooners once ranged
about.
Speed and power,
Hour by hour,
Liners tower high,
Onward churning,
Never turning
For a yearning cry,
Coal dust and grime,
No one has time
For any simple romance at all,
Beckon and coo
Till you are blue,
Mermaids have got no damned chance
at all.

REFRAIN 2   Lorelei, Lorelei,
Sit around and weep and cry,
Days are so long,
Everything's wrong
Completely.
All the sirens
In these environs
Are sorry they spoke,
Coaling steamers
Are belching streamers
Of horrible smoke
Making them choke.

Lorelei, Lorelei,
Sadly sigh
And wonder why
Every new ship,
Gives them the slip
So neatly.
What could be more obscene
Than vamping a submarine?
Pity the languid left-alone Lorelei.

(I'M) MAD ABOUT YOU

(Sheilah Graham and William Cavanagh)

VERSE

HE: Dear, your personality
Is bad for my morality,
It's more than I can bear.

SHE: Though I surmise it isn't wise
To set my cap at you,
I've lost all control and on the whole
I can't live through a single minute,
Dear, without your image in it.

HE: When you are inclined to be
Encouraging and kind to me
I simply walk on air,
Maybe I'll wake up soon and break my heart
To find that you—aren't there.

REFRAIN

HE: I'd like to tell you that I'm mad about—
Mad about you—mad about you.

SHE: But there is one thing that I'm sad about—
Sad about—sad about too.

HE: When you met me you swore
You were essentially nice
But I wasn't so sure
When we had kissed once or twice.

SHE: For all I know you're just a gadabout—
Gadabout—gadabout who
Is always eager to exchange old love for new.

BOTH: I've a feeling—you've been concealing
A thousand or two
Mad about, mad about, mad about you!

Eight of Mr. Cochran's Young Ladies in "Mad About You."

IT DOESN'T MATTER HOW OLD YOU ARE

(Maisie Gay)

VERSE 1   Life is just a gamble
And without preamble
I should like to state my case.
I'm no Messalina,
I've a slightly cleaner
Outlook on the human race.
Don't imagine that I'm hewn from
Marble or stone,
I'm not utterly immune from
Pangs of my own.
Though I'm over forty
I can still be naughty
In an unassuming way.
Beauty doesn't always win the day
I say.

REFRAIN 1   It doesn't matter how old you are
If the joys of life are sweet.
It doesn't matter how cold you are
If you've still got central heat.
I've seen raddled wrecks
With false pearls hung round their necks
Get away with lots of sex appeal
And though I may have been through the mill
I'm a creature of passion still,
It doesn't matter how old you are,
It's just how young you feel.

VERSE 2   Though I'm not a gay girl
I'm a 'come-what-may' girl,
Nothing in my life is planned.
Men with love get blinded
But I'm so broad-minded
I just smile and understand,
Men don't always want to marry,
They're not to blame,
I'm quite certain that Dubarry
Felt just the same.
Too much love is nauseous,
One can't be too cautious,
Cupid's such a wily foe,
Though I never let myself quite go,
I know.

REFRAIN 2   It doesn't matter how old you are
If your heart can still beat fast,
It doesn't matter how bold you are
When the dangerous age is past,
Though my face is lined
And my outlook too refined
I shall never let my mind congeal,
Pompadour found her love a curse
But I'll go further and fare much worse,
It doesn't matter how old you are,
It's just how young you feel.

REFRAIN 3   It doesn't matter how old you are
If you've still the strength to care,
However naughty you're told you are
It's entirely your affair.
Though I come a smack
And go rolling off the track
It will never be from lack of zeal.
You may laugh when you look at me
But watch the papers and wait and see!
It doesn't matter how old you are,
It's just how young you feel.

TEACH ME TO DANCE LIKE GRANDMA

(Jessie Matthews)

VERSE   I'm getting tired of jazz tunes
Monotonous,
They've gotten us

"Teach Me To Dance Like Grandma."
From left: Jack Holland, Jean Barry, Sonnie Hale,
Tilly Losch, Maisie Gay, Douglas Byng, Joan Clarkson,
and Lance Lister.

Crazy now.
Though they're amusing as tunes
Music has gone somehow.
I hear the moaning
Groaning
Of a saxophone band,
It simply shakes me,
Makes me
Want to play a
Lone hand.
Please understand
I want an age that has tunes
Simple and slow,
I'm feeling so
Lazy now.

REFRAIN   Teach me to dance like Grandma used to
dance,
I refuse to dance—Blues.
Black Bottoms, Charlestons, what wind
blew them in,
Monkeys do them in zoos.
Back in the past the dancing signified
Just a dignified glow.
They didn't have to be so strong
Though they revolved the whole night
long.
Teach me to dance like Grandma used to
dance
Sixty summers ago!

LITTLE WOMEN

*(Jessie Matthews, Sheilah Graham,
Madge Aubrey and Moya Nugent)*

VERSE 1

ALL: We're little girls of certain ages
Fresh from London town,
Like an instalment plan of Drage's
We want so much down.
We have discovered years ago
That flesh is often clay
We're not a new sin,
We're on the loose in
Quite the nicest way.
We have renounced domestic cares
For ever and for aye,
We're not so vicious,
Merely ambitious,
If there must be love
Let it be free love.

REFRAIN   We're little women,
Alluring little women,
Cute but cold fish
Just like goldfish
Looking for a bowl to swim in.
We lead ornamental
But uncreative lives,
We may be little women
But we're not good wives.

VIOLET: I am just an ingénue
And shall be till I'm eighty-two,
At any rude remark my spirit winces,
I've a keen religious sense
But in girlish self-defence
I always have to put my faith in princes.

ALL: Do not trust them, gentle maiden,
They will kick you in the pants.

RUTH: I'm not a type that is frequently seen,
I wear my hair in a narrow bang,
I have remained at the age of eighteen
Since I left home in a charabanc,
Though men all pursue me
When they woo me
They construe me as innocent,
But when I hear things suggestively phrased
I'm not unduly amazed.

ALL: It takes far more than that to wake
Sweet wonder in her eyes.

JANE: I waste no time on things
That other girls are arch about,
I much prefer to march about
Alone.
I am a baby vamp,
I'd take a postage stamp,
I just believe in grabbing
Anything that's offered me.
If Mother Hubbard proffered me
A bone
I should not be upset,
Have the darned thing re-set.

ALL: Much further than the Swanee River
She keep her old folks at home.

IVY: I am a girl whose soul with domesticity
    abounds,
I know a man of six foot three who's worth
    a million pounds,
Though he is like a brother
I haven't told my mother
He's given me a lovely house and grounds!

ALL: Be it ever so humbug
There's no place like home.

SECOND REFRAIN

ALL: We're little women,
Alluring little women,
Cute but cold fish
Just like goldfish
Looking for a bowl to swim in.
Though we're very clinging
Our independence thrives,
We may be little women
But we're not good wives.

THE LIDO BEACH

ALL: A narrow strip of sand
Where Byron used to ride about,
While stately ships would glide about
The sea on either hand.
But now the times have changed,
For civilized society
With infinite variety
Has had it rearranged.
No more the moon
On the still Lagoon
Can please the young enchanted,

They must have this
And they must have that
And they take it all for granted.
They hitch their star
To a cocktail bar
Which is all they really wanted,
That narrow strip of sand
Now reeks with asininity
With in the near vicinity "
A syncopated band
That plays the blues—all the day long—
And all the old Venetians say
They'd like a nice torpedo
To blow the Lido away.

WIVES: Beneath the blue skies
Of sunny Italy
We lie on the sand
But please understand
We're terribly grand.
We firmly married
The old nobility,
But we can spend happy days here,
Take off our stays here,
Tarnish our laurels,
Loosen our morals.
Oh! you'll never know
The great relief it is
To let our feelings go,
We're *comme-il-faut*
You see and so
It doesn't matter what vulgarity
We show!

HUSBANDS: Ladies of abundant means
And less abundant minds,
Although we're not romantic
We crossed the cold Atlantic
To choose a few commercial queens
Of different sorts and kinds.
Returning with a cargo
Of girlhood from Chicago,
Though we regret it more from day to day
We think it only fair to you to say:
It wasn't for your beauty that we married
    you,
It wasn't for your culture or your wit,
It wasn't for the quality that Mrs Glyn
    describes
As 'It', just it.
It wasn't your position in society
That led us on to making such a fuss.

Forgive us being frank,
But your balance in the bank
Made you just the only wives for us.

ALL: This narrow strip of sand
Makes something seem to burst in us,
Brings out the very worst in us,
But kindly understand
We've got the blues all the day long
And every year we always say
We'd like a nice torpedo
To blow the Lido away!

MOTHER'S COMPLAINT

*(Ann Codrington, Joan Clarkson, Madge
Aubrey, Betty Shale)*

We're all of us mothers,
We're all of us wives,
The whole depressing crowd of us,
With our kind assistance
The Motherland thrives.
We hope the nation's proud of us.
For one dreary fortnight
In each dreary year
We bring our obstreperous families here.
We paddle and bathe while it hails and it rains,
In spite of anaemia and varicose veins,
Hey nonny, ho nonny, no no no!

Our lodgings are frowsy,
Expensive and damp,
The food is indigestible.
We sit on the beach
Till we're tortured with cramp
And life is quite detestable.

The children go out with a bucket and spade
And injure themselves on the asphalt parade,
There's sand in the porridge and sand in the bed,
And if this is pleasure, we'd rather be dead,
Hey nonny, ho nonny, no no no!

ENGLISH LIDO

Opening Chorus

ALL: Hurray, hurray, hurray!
The holidays!
The jolly days
When laughter, fun and folly days
Appear
Hurray, hurray, hurray
The laity
With gaiety
And charming spontaneity
Must cheer.

MR. HARRIS: I've left my bowler hat and rubber collar
far behind.

MRS. HARRIS: I wish to God you'd left that awful
Panama behind,
It looks gaga behind.

ALL: But never mind
Because the holidays are here,
Our tastes are very far from Oriental,
We have a very fixed idea of fun,
The thought of anything experimental
Or Continental
We shun.
We take to innovations very badly,
We'd rather be uncomfortable than not,
In fighting any new suggestion madly
We'd gladly
Be shot!
We much prefer to take our pleasures
sadly
Because we're thoroughly contented with
our lot.

BRITANNIA RULES THE WAVES

(Maisie Gay)

CHORUS: Hail, Neptune's daughter,
The pride of Finsbury Park,
Behold a modest clerk
Is goddess of the water.
Hail, pioneer girl,
Though rain and wind have come
You've swum and swum and swum,
You really are a dear girl.

DAISY: Kind friends, I thank you one and all
For your delightful greetings.
I merely heard my country's call
At patriotic meetings.

CHORUS: Just think of that,
Just think of that,
She got her inspiration at
A patriotic meeting.
Oh, tell us more,
Oh, tell us more,
Oh, tell us what you do it for,
It must be overheating.

DAISY: Kind friends, I thank you all again
And since you ask me to
I will explain.

VERSE
DAISY: Like other chaste stenographers
I simply hate photographers,
I also hate publicity.

CHORUS: She lives for sheer simplicity.

DAISY: For any woman more or less
A photo in the daily press
Is horribly embarrassing.

CHORUS: It must be dreadfully harassing.

DAISY: The British male
May often fail,
Our faith in sport is shaken,
So English girls awaken
And save the nation's bacon.

REFRAIN I
Up girls and at 'em
And play the game to win,
The men must all give in
Before the feminine.
Bowl 'em and bat 'em
And put them on the run,
Defeat them every one,
Old Caspar's work is done.
We'll do our bit till our muscles crack,
We'll put a frill on the Union Jack,
If Russia has planned
To conquer us and
America misbehaves,
Up girls and at 'em,
Britannia rules the waves!

REFRAIN 2
DAISY: Up girls and at 'em,
Go out and win your spurs
For England much prefers
Applauding amateurs.
Man is an atom
So break your silly necks
In order to annex

Supremacy of sex.
Valiantly over the world we'll roam,
Husbands must wait till the cows come
    home.
The men of today
Who get in our way
Are digging their early graves.
Up girls and at 'em,
Britannia rules the waves!

REFRAIN

DAISY AND CHORUS:

Up girls and at 'em
And play the game to win,
 The men must all give in
Before the feminine.
Bowl 'em and bat 'em
And put them on the run,
Defeat them every one,
Old Caspar's work is done.
We'll do our bit
Till our muscles crack,
We'll put a frill On the Union Jack.

DAISY: Here's to the maid
Who isn't afraid,
Who shingles and shoots and shaves.

CHORUS: Up girls and at 'em,
Britannia rules the waves!

CHAUVE-SOURIS
(A RUSSIAN BURLESQUE)

*(Maisie Gay, Sonnie Hale, Douglas Byng,
Fred Groves and Robert Algar)*

QUINTETTE: Ish con broshka
Whoops dad illoshka
Whoops dad illoshka
Inkle drob vaard.

Ish con broshka
Whoops dad illoshka
Whoops dad illoshka
Inkle drob vaard.

Wheeshka eeglee
Wheeshka bombolom
Wheeshka weedlewee
Chock chock wish laa.

Wheeshka eeglee
Wheeshka bombolom
Wheeshka weedlewee
Inkle drob vaard.

TRY TO LEARN TO LOVE

(Jessie Matthews and Sonnie Hale

VERSE 1

HE: In kindergartens
In country or town
Our education begins,
Like little Spartans
We're taught to crush down
The inclination to sin.
When we change to gentle adolescence
Things get rather strained,
There's a strange, peculiar effervescence
No one has explained.

REFRAIN 1

First you learn to spell
A little bit,
Then, if you excel
A little bit,

Other things as well
A little bit
Come your way;
Though the process may be slow to you
Knowledge of the world will flow to you,
Steadily you grow a little bit,
Day by day;
Though you're too gentle, sentimental,
In fact, quite a dreary bore,
Though you're aesthetic, apathetic
To all men but Bernard Shaw,
Use the velvet glove
A little bit,
Emulate the dove
A little bit,
Try to learn to love a little bit more.

VERSE 2

SHE: The art of wooing,
I'm firmly resolved,
For men is terribly crude.
To be pursuing
Is not so involved
As having to be pursued.
Doubts and fears
Make women work much faster
Though they're frail and weak,
Taking years
Successfully to master
Feminine technique.

REFRAIN 2

First you droop your eyes
A little bit,
Then if you are wise
A little bit
Register surprise
A little bit,
If he's bold,
Stamp your foot with some celerity,
Murmur with intense sincerity
That his immature temerity
Leaves you cold.
But when you get him
You must let him
Have the joy he's yearning for
And whisper sweetly,
Indiscreetly,
He's the boy that you adore.
Use the moon above
A little bit,
Emulate the dove
A little bit,
Try to learn to love—a little bit more.

The Entire Company assembles for the "Finale."

CABALLERO
(LATER RETITLED A SPANISH FANTASY)

(Adrienne Brune)

VERSE 1   Night falls, love calls tender and sweet,
　　　　　　just there in the street below,
Teach me, reach me,
Wooing with song an echo of long ago.
Though all my dreams are in your serenade,
I'm afraid dreams must fade.

REFRAIN   Caballero,
You've simply swept me off my feet,
I love to listen to you sweetly
Serenading in the street

Outside.
Caballero,
I haven't got a heart of stone,
I'm waiting here for you alone,
You're sure to win me, if you only
Tried;
The southern night is soft and tender,
I'm simply burning to surrender,
Caballero.
The creamy passion flowers swoon,
Beneath a honey-coloured moon
I'm only praying to be soon
Your bride.

VERSE 2   Star shine, carmine life for the asking,
　　　　　　passion unmasking soon,
Hold me, fold me,
Blossoms are fragrant, wooed by your
　　　　　　vagrant tune;
I hear the echo of romance gone by;
That is why now I sigh

FINALE

(Parody version of "A Room With a View")

Scene:　　*Stage door.*
　　　　　Eight stage hands enter singing:

We're eight stage hands,
Weary and winsome,
Embassy Club be blowed.
We've got wives and a nice drop of gin
Somewhere in the Old Kent Road.
Good night! Good night!

　　　　　Eight Chorus Girls enter. They come down
　　　　　to the footlights and sing:

One, two, three, four,
Five, six, seven, eight

All going home to bed.
Nobody's asked us to supper,
We wish we were dead.
Tho' we know quite
Well if we are late
Mother will leave the light,
We're feeling depressed
'Cos no one wants us;

They exit singing last two lines.

So it would be best
For us to say good night.

Eight Show Girls enter—

You'll never know girls
Nicer than show girls,
For our behaviour
Reeks of Belgravia,
We're so restrained that
Men have complained that

They exit singing last two lines.

We've nothing left to show,
Good night, good night, good night.

Small parts enter—

Tho' we hardly speak parts
We support the weak parts
In our unpretentious way.
Now that you have seen us
Kindly choose between us
We shall all be stars some day.

They exit singing last two lines.

Good night and in the next revue that
    Cochran produces
We'll see our talents have more definite uses.

All Principals enter

Now you know our
Personalities
What is it all about?
We're most surprised to discover
You haven't walked out.
We've exhausted
Our vitalities,
Sorry we've been so bright,
Just hurry and go
And put your coats on
We've come to the moment
When we say good night,
Good night, good night, good night.
Black out

All the Company are discovered in motor-cars.

We are the cause
Of all the traffic jam in Piccadilly,
Motoring laws
We disregard because they are so silly,
Toot-toot—toot-toot,
Toot-toot—toot-toot—toot-toot.
We're driving home in our
Driving home in our
High-powered cars,
You'd better hurry and take cover
For our knowledge of driving is slight,
Toot-toot—toot-toot,
Toot-toot—toot-toot—toot-toot,
So good goody good good night.

You've seen the Revue
Right through.
We hope you're applauding too
For it's according to
You—the money speaks.
We hope you can rouse
Keith Prowse
To something sensational,
Their approbation'll
House us here for weeks.
We thought it best to have a try-out,
We're not allowed to shirk.
Please don't let us fly out
Of work.
The best we can do
It's true
May not make you yearn again
Soon to return again to
This dreary Revue.

(At some point the words "dreary" and "Cochran"
were interchanged!)

ALTERNATE FINALE

(Used in New York production)

ANNOUNCEMENT:
Ladies and Gentlemen, Mr. Cochran has suddenly
arrived, rather tardily I fear, at the realisation that
our Revue is completely lacking in the two essentials
of American musical entertainment—pep and speed
—so therefore we propose to remedy these deficiencies as best we can in the short time left to us.

*OPENING CHORUS (PLAYING THE GAME)

Playing the game
You have to biff the ball
And bang the ball
In playing the game
You have to whiff the ball
And whang the ball
And rah rah—rah rah—rah rah—rah rah—
    rah rah—
We're so Collegiate—so Collegiate—
You are to blame
For all the speed of it
Your need of it
Is really a terrible shame
Rah rah—rah rah—rah rah—rah rah—rah rah—
Everybody plays the game.

*   *   *

Later in the run a new number was introduced—
"Lilac Time," performed by Maisie Gay and Sonnie
Hale.

LILAC TIME

HE: Oh tell me, little maiden, pray
           Why should you choose to hide away
           On such a lovely summer's day?

SHE: *(aside)* He does not know that I am the Princess,
               disguised as a beggar maid. Ah me!
           (To him)
           Kind sir, I know not who you are
           But if you should presume too far
           I shall seek refuge with mamma.

HE: *(aside)* She does not know that I am the Crown
           Prince disguised as a Gardener—Ah me!

SHE: Spring is the time for folly—Ah ah—ah ah—

HE: Fly away melancholy—ah ah—ah ah—

SHE: Spring is the time

HE: Spring is the time

SHE: Spring is the time

HE: Spring is the time

SHE: For folly,

HE: So melancholy fly away—
For it is Spring and life is gay and jolly.

REFRAIN 1

BOTH: Lilac time, lilac time
Blossoms are o'er the lea.

HE: Birds are chirruping love's sweet song

SHE: Church bells ring-a-ding-ding-ding-dong!

HE: Steal a kiss,
Just like this,
(He kisses her.)

SHE: You are too bold and free
(She slaps him roguishly.)

BOTH: That is why it's lilac time
Under the chestnut tree.

VERSE 2

SHE: (holding up book)
I am engrossed as you can see
In reading some philosophy.

HE: Literature this year must be
So very much in vogue,
Why should you bury that dainty nose
In so much dry and dusty prose?

SHE: You're making love to me, I suppose,

HE: You charming little rogue,

SHE: A charming little rogue,

BOTH: A charming, charming, charming little rogue.

REFRAIN 2

BOTH: Lilac time, lilac time
Blossoms are o'er the lea.

HE: Birds are mating near and far

SHE: Tra-la-lalala—la, la, la.

HE: Steal a kiss
Just like this.

SHE: You are too bold and free.

BOTH: That is why it's lilac time
Under the chestnut tree,
Ah ah—ah ah—
Ah ah—ah ah—ah ah ah ah ah ah,
Heigho nin nonny no,
Heigho wack jolly-o,

Heigho nin nonny no,
Heigho lackaday do,
That is why it's lilac time,
That is why it's lilac time,
Ha ha ha ha ha ha ha ha ha ha ha ha ha ha ha!

Two other songs were written but never performed.
One was for Maisie Gay . . .

*I LOVE MY BABIES BEST

VERSE 1 Sin and pleasure are brothers,
Pay no heed to their call.
Wives and sisters and mothers,
What's the use of it all?
Sad, weary souls everywhere I see,
Lost in the longing for luxury.

VERSE 2 I spend hours in the nursery
Crooning over the cots.
I give more than a cursory
Glance at my tiny tots.
Of all the perfumes I love the best
Give me the fragrance of babies at rest.

REFRAIN 1 There are diamonds that gleam and glitter,
There are rubies as red as fire,
Take a sapphire of blue,
Or a turquoise or two,
If it gratifies your heart's desire.
There are emeralds that seem to beckon
From some winsome woman's breast
There are pearls and to spare
For a devil-may-care—
I love my babies best.

REFRAIN 2 There are perfumes that reek of Egypt
And aromas that breathe of flowers.
In the sinister dusk
A suggestion of musk
Will facilitate the passing hours.
There are perfumes that just spell passion
When two hearts are fondly pressed
But I long when I roam
For the odour of home—
I love my babies best.

. . . the other for Sonnie Hale . . .

*MEXICO

(Sonnie Hale)

VERSE I'm what you'd call romantic,
Dull people drive me frantic,
I get tired of false connections everywhere
I go.
I feel I have remained too
Long with the things I'm chained to,
I really feel constrained to go to Mexico.
That's where the joy of the massacre
Never quite abates,
They have great fun,
And it's definitely one
Of the less United States.

REFRAIN 1 Mexico—I want to go to Mexico,
Because my sweetie says it's grand there
And there
Isn't any reason why not!
Skies are blue the winter through—
extremely blue
And I've a feeling I'd adore it
For it
Sounds a most salubrious spot.
Out on some verandah, shady and cool
All that a man requires
That's where I can pander—just like a fool
To all my worst desires.
That's the place where folk of every gender
Long to spend a honeymoon.
Mexico—I want to go to Mexico
Soon.

REFRAIN 2 Mexico—I want to go to Mexico
Tho' people say that for a stranger
Danger
Lurks around each Tropical Tree.
Dirty tricks in politics—disgusting tricks
I wouldn't mind because it's hot there,
What they're
Fighting for would not worry me.
Something in the climate—flowers a-swoon
After the noonday heat
Whispering to my mate under the moon
God, I'll be indiscreet
Tho' there are a lot of murders and it's
Full of Bandits anyhow!
Mexico—I want to go to Mexico
Now!

*   *   *

The show was to create one unlikely new and temporary fan for Noël. Virginia Woolf wrote to him telling him how some of his songs "struck me on the forehead like a bullet. And what's more I remember them and see them enveloped in atmosphere—works of art in short." Letters of mutual admiration were exchanged for several years but by 1934 and *Conversation Piece* Miss Woolf's ardour had somewhat cooled, perhaps encouraged by an evening they both attended a party given by society hostess, Sybil Colefax, at which Noël inevitably performed: "Then he played his new opera," Woolf wrote to her nephew, Quentin Bell, "and sang like a tipsy crow—quite without self consciousness."

Beatrice Lillie and Noël Coward
as sketched by "wah."
(William Auerbach Levy)

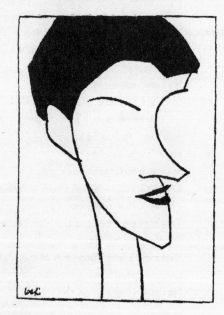

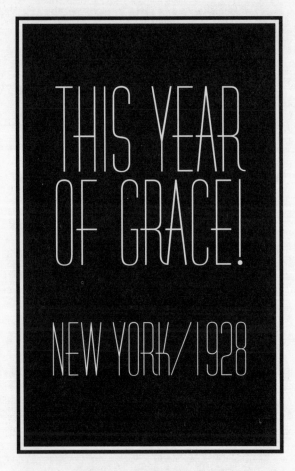

THIS YEAR OF GRACE!
NEW YORK/1928

The revue was presented at the Selwyn Theatre, New York on November 7, 1928, the leads being played by Noël Coward and Beatrice Lillie.

"The show was unchanged except for the interpolation of two single numbers for Beattie, 'World Weary' and 'I Can't Think' (an imitation of Gertrude Lawrence); two duets which we did together: 'Lilac Time,' an *opera bouffe* burlesque, and 'Love, Life and Laughter,' a sketch and song of Paris night life in the eighties, which had originally been created by Maisie Gay in one of the Charlot revues." (1924)

WORLD WEARY

VERSE 1 When I'm feeling dreary and blue,
I'm only too
Glad to be left alone,
Dreaming of a place in the sun.
When day is done,
Far from a telephone;
Bustle and the weary crowd
Make me want to cry out loud,

Give me something peaceful and grand
Where all the land
Slumbers in monotone.

REFRAIN 1 I'm world weary, world weary,
Living in a great big town,
I find it so dreary, so dreary,
Everything looks grey or brown,
I want an ocean blue,
Great big trees,
A bird's eye view
Of the Pyrenees,
I want to watch the moon rise up
And see the great red sun go down,
Watching clouds go by
Through a Winter sky
Fascinates me
But if I do it in the street,
Every cop I meet
Simply hates me,
Because I'm world weary, world weary,
I could kiss the railroad tracks,
I want to get right back to nature and relax.

VERSE 2 Get up in the morning at eight,
Relentless Fate,
Drives me to work at nine;
Toiling like a bee in a hive
From four to five
Whether it's wet or fine,
Hardly ever see the sky,
Buildings seem to grow so high.
Maybe in the future I will
Perhaps fulfil
This little dream of mine.

REFRAIN 2 I'm world weary, world weary,
Living in a great big town,
I find it so dreary, so dreary,
Everything looks grey or brown,
I want a horse and plough,
Chickens too,
Just one cow
With a wistful moo,
A country where the verb to work
Becomes a most improper noun;
I can hardly wait
Till I see the great
Open spaces,
My loving friends will not be there,
I'm so sick of their
God-damned faces,
Because I'm world weary, world weary,
Tired of all these jumping jacks,
I want to get right back to nature and relax.

ARCH SELWYN *presents*

BEATRICE NOEL

LILLIE AND COWARD

IN

CHARLES B. COCHRAN'S LONDON REVUE

THIS YEAR OF GRACE

with *Moss and Fontana*

Book, Music, Lyrics by *Noel Coward*

"Swiftest and smartest merry-maker of its sort in town".
—*Gilbert Gabriel*, New York American.

SELWYN THEATRE

42nd St., West of Broadway — Matinees Thursday and Saturday 2:30
Telephone: Wisconsin 7840

Evenings 8:30

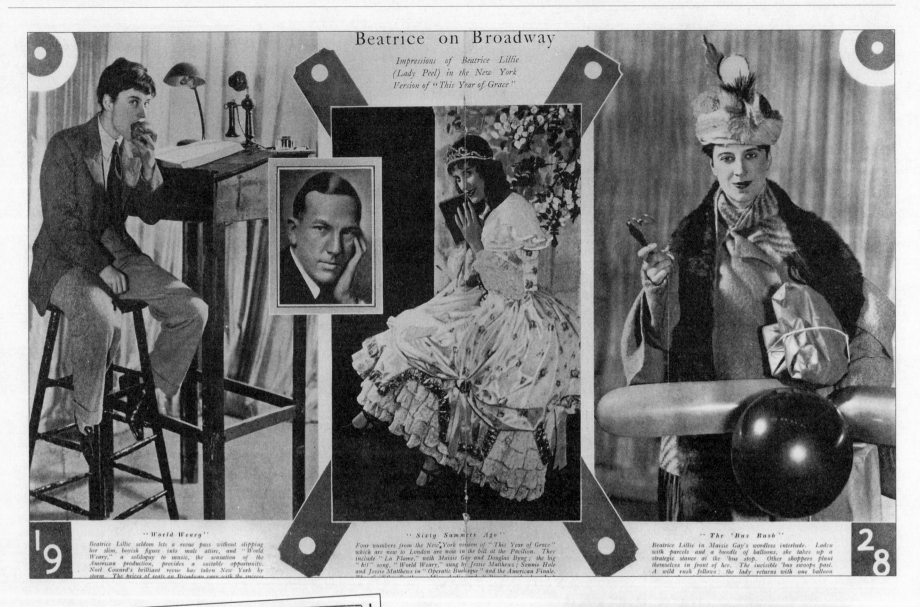

Beatrice on Broadway

Impressions of Beatrice Lillie (Lady Peel) in the New York Version of "This Year of Grace"

19

"World Weary"

Beatrice Lillie seldom lets a revue pass without slipping her slim, boyish figure into male attire, and "World Weary," a soliloquy to music, the sensation of the American production, provides a suitable opportunity. Noël Coward's brilliant revue has taken New York by storm. The prices of seats on Broadway vary with the success

"Sixty Summers Ago"

Four numbers from the New York version of "This Year of Grace" which are new to London are now in the bill at the Pavilion. They include "La Flame," with Maisie Gay and Douglas Byng ; the big "hit" song, "World Weary," sung by Jessie Matthews; Sonnie Hale and Jessie Matthews in "Operatic Burlesque" and the American Finale.

"The 'Bus Rush"

Beatrice Lillie in Maisie Gay's wordless interlude. Laden with parcels and a bundle of balloons, she takes up a strategic stance at the 'bus stop. Other shoppers plant themselves in front of her. The invisible 'bus swoops past. A wild rush follows : the lady returns with one balloon

28

THE THEATERS
By PERCY HAMMOND

Beatrice Lillie

"This Year of Grace," a revue by Noël Coward, presented at the Selwyn Theater under the direction of Arch Selwyn, with a cast containing the author, composer and Miss Beatrice Lillie.

AS THE author and composer of "This Year of Grace" Mr. Noël Coward last night was a benefaction. His songs and satires were of an upper class, ranging from competent to superlative, and the fleet manner in which they sped along made Mr. Cochran's London revue one of the merriest of its closet type. Mr. Coward was not, however, so brilliant as a musical comedian. Unendowed with the impish attributes of a clown, his efforts were slightly laborious, and he sang in a weedy voice and danced with small facility. But when he grew dramatic in a tragic number reminiscent of his famous "Poor Little Rich Girl" he stirred his audience to transports similar to those he used to arouse in "The Vortex." Entitled "Dance, Little Lady," it was quite a grisly warning to the black-bottomers.

It wasn't really necessary for Mr. Coward to be comic last evening. Miss Beatrice Lillie was at his elbow, funnier, to my mind, than she has been heretofore. Her subtle rowdiness was quieter than its custom when it visits Broadway, and, although she indulged in numerous neck-falls, they seemed less frequent than usual.

In "This Year of Grace"

tacle, not to be compared to the Broadway durbars of Mr. White and Mr. Carroll, and plumes and rosettes are absent from what Mr. Woollcott used to term the decor.

Noël Coward tries his hand in "Dance, Little Lady."

"World Weary"—Noël's considered verdict at the age of 28—sounds as though it should have been sung by one of his "drained and far from healthy" *mondaines*. Instead, it was sung by Bea as a little office boy perched on a high chair while munching an apple. She recalled that Noël had felt she sang it with "infinite pathos." His recollection is that she ate the apple "realistically, sometimes at the expense of the lyric." When he used the number subsequently in his cabaret appearances at the Café de Paris, he sang it "wearing an alpaca jacket and not munching an apple." And when (later still) he used it in his TV debut with Mary Martin in 1955 he took note of the changing times by prefacing it with the ironic hope that "its strong moral nature will not unduly depress you . . ."

A problem occurred when the song came to be published and broadcast. The line "I'm so sick of their God-damned faces" had to be changed to "Gosh-darned" (or in some versions "damn-fool") "This compromise, while soothing outraged public opinion, weakened the song considerably."

"I Can't Think" found Bea Lillie recalling an embarrassing encounter with a handsome stranger at whose feet she literally fell:

"I felt as he had not the strength to raise me,
He might at least have joined me on the ground."

Audiences who had seen *André Charlot's Revue of 1924* immediately recognized this pastiche of "I Don't Know," in which Gertie had described a rather more successful flirtation . . .

I CAN'T THINK

VERSE 1   It was early in September
That we met each other first,
And my entrance, I remember,
Was distinctly unrehearsed.
I had been to buy some butter
And some raspberries and some eggs,
When I slipped up in the gutter
And clasped him round the legs.

REFRAIN 1   I can't think why he looked at me so queerly,
I can't think why he scowled and walked away,
I feel, as I apologized sincerely,

He might have—well, perhaps I shouldn't say.
I can't think how he managed to resist me,
Perhaps the wish was father to the thought,
I can't think why he didn't even kiss me,
But I do think he did nothing of the sort.

VERSE 2   It was later in October
When we met—heigho!—once more,
I believe that I was sober,
But I couldn't be quite sure.
It was early in the morning
And the air was pure and sweet,
When I staggered without warning
And fell prostrate at his feet.

REFRAIN 2   I can't think why my balance so betrayed me,
I can't think why he hiccoughed and then
frowned,
I feel as he had not the strength to raise me,
He might at least have joined me on the
ground.
I can't think why his manners so depressed me,
Perhaps he was too social and refined,
If you think he attempted to molest me,
I *do* think he did nothing of the kind.

In the finale he also included a "burlesque of an American musical"—"The Sun, the Moon and You."

THE SUN, THE MOON AND YOU

VERSE 1   Little Girlie,
Late or early,
I just dream of you.
Since that happy Tuesday when we met,
If you only knew,
One and one are two,
That's a thing you never should forget.

REFRAIN   I want the sun, the moon and you,
They simply thrill me through and through,
The little stars that shine above
Just fill me full of thoughts of love
My heart is throbbing,
For you're robbing

Me of all my pride,
So listen, baby
Don't say maybe,
You will be my bride.
Sweetheart, I could never be blue
With just the sun, the moon and you.

"Lilac Time" was to haunt him for some time to come:

"From then onwards Beattie and I co-starred not only theatrically but socially in all directions . . . At large Charity Balls where we sang 'Lilac Time,' at fashionable night clubs where our entrance was the signal for an immediate flood of requests for us to sing 'Lilac Time,' and at small convivial theatrical parties to which we were invited on the strict understanding that in no circumstances would we sing 'Lilac Time.'"

Noël also performed "Dance, Little Lady" with Florence Desmond and the Oliver Messel masks. In this "and in most of the other things I had to do in the show I felt myself to be only adequate." In "A Room With a View" he felt he was "not nearly as effective as Sonnie Hale," which is perhaps why after a while he refused to sing "those terribly slushy words" and handed the part over to Billy Milton.

The Gay Victorian: Miss Maisie Gay in the London production in The Sketch as drawn by Wells.

BITTER
SWEET

AN OPERETTE

1929

(Originally entitled SARI LINDEN on the original mss. and inscribed "S.S. Berengaria—1928.")

First presented by Charles B. Cochran at the Palace Theatre, Manchester on July 2, 1929 before transferring to His Majesty's Theatre, London on July 12, 1929. (697 performances.)

The cast included Peggy Wood, George Metaxa, Ivy St. Helier, Austin Trevor, Robert Newton.

"The idea of *Bitter Sweet* was born in the early summer of 1928. It appeared quite unexpectedly and with no other motivation beyond the fact that I had vaguely discussed with Gladys (Calthrop—his designer) the possibilities of writing a romantic Operette." Noël was well aware that "there had been little or no sentiment on the London musical stage for a long while" and during a weekend with some friends of Gladys's, he happened to find himself listening to a new German orchestral recording of *Die Fledermaus* . . . "Immediately a confused picture of uniforms, bustles, chandeliers, and gas-lit cafés formed in my mind, and later, when we were driving over Wimbledon Common, we drew the car to a standstill by the roadside, and in the shade of a giant horse-chestnut tree mapped out roughly the story of Sari Linden."

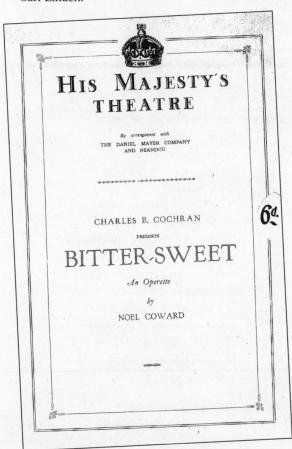

HIS MAJESTY'S
THEATRE

By arrangement with
THE DANIEL MAYER COMPANY
AND REANDCO

CHARLES B. COCHRAN
PRESENTS

BITTER-SWEET

An Operette
by
NOEL COWARD

6ᵈ·

Opposite: Peggy Wood and George Mextaxa, "I'll See You Again."

Noël wrote the part of Sari with Gertie in mind "but when the score was almost done, she and I both realised that her voice, though light and charming, was not strong enough to carry such a heavy singing role." (Kurt Weill once observed that "she has the best range between C and C sharp of any singer I know.") The obvious choice was Evelyn Laye but she was not best pleased with Cochran, since his teaming of her husband, Sonnie Hale with Jessie Matthews in *This Year of Grace!* would lead to their divorce. "I'd rather scrub floors," she told Noël, "than work for him again."

The part went to American actress Peggy Wood.

In early 1929 the final piece fell into place: "The book had been completed long since, but the score had been causing me trouble, until one day, when I was in a taxi on my way back to the apartment after a matinée, the 'I'll See You Again' waltz dropped into my mind, whole and complete, during a twenty minutes' traffic block."

I'LL SEE YOU AGAIN

(Peggy Wood and George Metaxa)

CARL: Now Miss Sarah, if you please,
Sing a scale for me.

SARAH: Ah—Ah—Ah—

CARL: Take a breath and then reprise
In a different key.

SARAH: Ah—Ah—Ah——

CARL: All my life I shall remember knowing you,
All the pleasure I have found in showing you
The different ways
That one may phrase
The changing light, and changing shade;
Happiness that must die,
Melodies that must fly,
Memories that must fade,
Dusty and forgotten by and by.

SARAH: Learning scales will never seem so sweet again
Till our Destiny shall let us meet again.

CARL: The will of Fate
May come too late.

SARAH: When I'm recalling these hours we've had
Why will the foolish tears
Tremble across the years,
Why shall I feel so sad,
Treasuring the memory of these days
Always?

CARL: I'll see you again,
Whenever Spring breaks through again;
Time may lie heavy between,
But what has been
Is past forgetting.

SARAH: This sweet memory,
Across the years will come to me;
Though my world may go awry,
In my heart will ever lie
Just the echo of a sigh,
Goodbye.

The song turned out to be one of the greatest hits Noël was ever to have: "Brass bands have blared it, string orchestras have swooned it, Palm Court quartets have murdered it, barrel organs have ground it out in London squares and swing bands have tortured it beyond recognition . . . and I am still very fond of it and very proud of it."

ACT 1

It's 1929 and the elderly Marchioness of Shayne is holding a dance at her Grosvenor Square home. The singer with the band is crooning a banal song typical of the period.

*THAT WONDERFUL MELODY

Play something romantic
Play me a romantic tune
I'm weary of frantic
Syncopation jazz sensations
Played by a coon.

Play something romantic
As sweet as can be
Cares will not dismay me
If you'll just sit down and play me
A romantic memory

Supper is announced and everyone moves into the room beyond, leaving only the pianist, Vincent Howard, improvising to amuse himself. Dolly

106

Chamberlain and Henry Jekyll enter. They are engaged but clearly ill-suited. Dolly speculates about what the future will hold and the conversation turns to their hostess. She must have had a thrilling life. The pompous Henry expresses the view that with such a chequered past, she was very lucky to get back into society by marrying the late Lord Shayne. His remarks annoy Dolly, who tells him to go away. She is left alone with Vincent. Before long he is confessing his own love for her. As he takes her in his arms, Lady Shayne enters. Vincent assures her that his intentions are strictly honourable. What does *Dolly* intend to do, Lady Shayne asks? She must make her mind up. Indecision is the worst mistake one can make in life.

Some of the guests begin to drift back from supper and Vincent strikes up a jazz tune for them—only to be stopped by Lady Shayne. None of them knows or wants anything beyond noise and speed, she tells them. She will teach them something more. She sings . . .

THE CALL OF LIFE

(Peggy Wood)

LADY S.: Your romance could not live the length of a day,
You hesitate and analyse,
Betray your love with compromise,
Till glamour fades away;
And all too soon you realize
That there is nothing left to say.

CHORUS: Hey, hey—hey, hey,
How does she get that way?
She'd be more light-hearted
If she started—to Charleston;
She's never danced it,
She's never chanced it;
Perhaps her muscles are disinclined,
Perhaps she hasn't the strength of mind.

LADY S.: Love that's true can mean naught to you but a name,
A thing that isn't part of you;
Can never touch the heart of you;
It's nothing but a game,
A fire without a flame.

MEN: We find it difficult to grasp your meaning.

LADY S.: Maybe the past is intervening.

CHORUS: We very much regret that times have changed so,
Life is more speedily arranged so.

LADY S.: In your world of swiftly turning wheels
Life must be extremely grey.

CHORUS: We've no time to waste on Love Ideals,
That which to our senses most appeals
Is all we can obey.

LADY S.: No—no. Not so:
There must be something further on,
A vision you can count upon,
To help you to acquire
A memory when Youth is gone
Of what was once your heart's desire.

There is a call that echoes sweetly
When it is Spring and Love is in the air;
Whate'er befall, respond to it completely,
Though it may bring you sadness and despair;
Fling far behind you
The chains that bind you,
That love may find you
In joy or strife;
Though Fate may cheat you,
And defeat you,
Your Youth must answer to the Call of Life.

As she sings, the lights fade and somehow her voice seems to grow younger . . .

As the lights come up, we see her younger self in Victorian dress. The year is now 1875 and the sixteen year old Sarah Millick is singing for her music teacher, Carl Linden. At the end of the song he tells her he wrote it many years ago for his ideal woman—someone just like her. He describes the beauties of his native Austria. If only he could show it to her.

IF YOU COULD ONLY COME WITH ME

(George Metaxa)

Though there may be beauty in this land of yours,
Skies are very often dull and grey;
If I could but take that little hand of yours,
Just to lead you secretly away.
We would watch the Danube as it gently flows,

Like a silver ribbon winding free;
Even as I speak of it my longing grows,
Once again my own dear land to see.
If you could only come with me,
If you could only come with me.

He then tells her that he won't be able to play at her forthcoming wedding; he has to go away. The news clearly disappoints her. To cover their feelings, they launch into a singing exercise that is transparently a love duet—"I'll See You Again"—which is interrupted by the arrival of Sarah's fiancé, Hugh Devon, and her mother. It is time for Sarah to be fitted for her wedding dress. Carl bows and takes his leave. Deeply upset, Sarah argues with her fiancé and bursts into tears.

Mrs. Millick is giving a ball attended by all Sarah's friends and their titled admirers. Sarah herself is behaving unpredictably, to the annoyance of Hugh. Carl is leading the orchestra—having found it impossible to leave after all—and Sarah demands he play "something gay." She waltzes around the stage on her own and is soon joined by the rest of the young people.

TELL ME, WHAT IS LOVE?

(Peggy Wood)

SARAH: Play something gay for me,
Play for me, play for me;
Set me free,
I'm in a trance tonight,
Can't you see
How I want to dance tonight?
Madly my heart is beating,
Some insane melody possessing me,
In my brain thrilling and obsessing me;
How can I leave it to call in vain?
Is it joy or pain?
Live your life, for time is fleeting,
Some insistent voice repeating;
Hear me—hear me,
How can I leave it to call in vain?
Is it joy or pain?

REFRAIN Tell me—tell me—tell me, what is love?
Is it some consuming flame;
Part of the moon, part of the sun,
Part of a dream barely begun?
When is the moment of breaking—waking?
Skies change, nothing is the same,

Some strange magic is to blame;
Voices that seem to echo round me and
     above,
Tell me, what is love, love, love?

Play something gay for me,
Play for me—play for me;
Tell me why
Spring has so enchanted me;
Why this shy
Passion has been granted me;
Am I awake or dreaming?
Far and near
Every lover follows you,
Swift and clear,
Flying as the swallows do;
Leave me no longer to call in vain,
Are you joy or pain? Leave me not by
     love forsaken,
If I sleep, then let me waken;
Hear me—hear me,
Leave me no longer to call in vain
Are you joy or pain?

The party begins to break up. Sarah is somewhat repentant but Hugh stands on his dignity. With the older guests out of the way, the young people steal back and sing their own number.

THE LAST DANCE

MEN: They've all gone now—have no fear—

GIRLS: Sarah's mother may be near,
          If she should hear

ALL: She might be rather cross with us,
          Elderly people make too much fuss.

MEN: Always insist on a chaperone,
          Never leave love alone.

GIRLS: We feel frightened, if you please
          Don't flirt or tease.

MEN: Gentle and sweet in your purity,
          We give our hearts as security.

GIRLS: We shall be scolded a lot for this.

MEN: You won't miss just one kiss.
          (They all kiss)

GIRLS: Think of the consequences, please, you
             haven't realized

They are too excited to go to bed and decide to play "Blind Man's Buff". Peggy Wood, center, as Sarah goes first, "Eeny Meeny Miny Mo."

          What an appalling thing for us to be so
             compromised,
          So dreadfully, dreadfully, dreadfully
             compromised.

MEN: Everything's ending,
          The moon is descending,
          Behind the tall trees in the park.

GIRLS: Silence falls,
          Slumber calls.

MEN: We men together
          Were wondering whether
          We might have a bit of a lark.

GIRLS: No jokes in the dark, please,
          What sort of a lark, please?

ALL: Just a slight dance,
          One more dream-of-delight dance,
          Just a sort of good-night dance
          Would be glorious fun.

MEN: Won't you let us, please let us, just stay for
             a while,
          Won't you, please won't you, be gay for
             a while?
          All we desire is to play for a while
          Now the party's done.

GIRLS: Just a fast waltz,
          Till the world seems a vast waltz,
          Very often the last waltz
          Is the birth of romance.

ALL: It's a June night,
          There's a thrill in the moonlight;
          Let's give way to the tender surrender
          Of one last dance.

. . . after which the men depart, leaving the girls to await their chaperones. They are too excited to go to bed and decide to play "Blind Man's Buff".

EENY MEENY MINY MO

GLORIA: Eeny meeny miny mo

HARRIET: Catch a nigger by his toe

VICTORIA: If he hollers let him go

ALL: O.U.T. spells out and so

GLORIA: Out goes she. (She points to Effie)

EFFIE: Out goes me. (Skipping about) This is the
          loveliest, loveliest part of the party.

GLORIA: Eeny meeny miny mo

HARRIET: Catch a nigger by his toe

VICTORIA: If he hollers let him go

ALL: O.U.T. spells out and so

GLORIA: Out goes she. (She points to Harriet)

HARRIET: Out goes me. (She and Effie take hands
and twirl around)

HARRIET/EFFIE: Now we're free to know who'll be he!

GLORIA: Eeeny meeny miny mo

VICTORIA: Catch a nigger by his toe

SARAH: If he hollers let him go

ALL: O.U.T. spells out and so

VICTORIA: Out goes she. (She points to Gloria)

GLORIA: Out goes me. (She joins Effie and Harriet)

HARRIET/EFFIE/GLORIA:
This is the loveliest, loveliest part of the party.

VICTORIA: Eeny meeny miny mo

SARAH: Catch a nigger by his toe

JANE: If he hollers let him go

JANE: Out goes she. (Points to Victoria)

VICTORIA: Out goes me. (She joins Effie, Harriet and
Gloria)

ALL: This is the loveliest, loveliest part of the
party.

EFFIE/HARRIET:
Only three of them left now, we're excited
to see

GLORIA/VICTORIA:
Who is going to be blind man, who's it going
to be?

SARAH: I have a strange presentiment it's me.

JANE: Eeny meeny miny mo
Out goes she. (She points to Honor, who
joins the others)

SARAH: Eeny meeny miny mo
Out goes she. (She points to Jane)
I'm HE—it's me,
It's me—I'm HE.

GIRLS: Just get a handkerchief and bind it around
her eyes.

SARAH: Not too tight, not too tight.
(They blindfold her)

GIRLS: She mustn't see a thing no matter how
much she tries.

SARAH: That's all right—that's all right.

GIRLS: She will cheat if she can,
That corner's raised a bit,
Turn her round till she's dazed a bit,

Are you ready now.
One, two, three!

SARAH: Since the party began,
Something's been taunting me,
Some presentiment haunting me,
What can it be?

GIRLS: Start now—start now,
She can see the ground,
She can see the ground.

SARAH: Somehow, somehow,
Some forgotten sound,
Some forgotten sound,
Echoes deep in my heart,
Strangely enthralling me,
Someone secretly calling me,
Like a melody far away.

GIRLS: Oh, for Heaven's sake start,
Here go along with you,
We can see nothing wrong with you,
We want to play.

SARAH: Should happiness forsake me,
And disillusion break me,
Come what may,
Lead the way,
Take me, take me.
Although I may discover
Love crucifies the lover,
Whate'er Fate has in store,
My heart is yours evermore.

Sarah is the first to be blindfolded. Carl comes in to collect his music and Sarah bumps into him, throwing her arms around him. Unable to restrain himself, Carl kisses her passionately. Tearing off the blindfold, she stands there gazing at him, while the girls watch open mouthed. "It's you I love," she tells him, "now and always . . ."

CARL: Oh, Lady, you are far above me,
And yet you whisper that you love me,
Can this be true or is it just some foolish
dream?

SARAH: (speaking) You know it's true, look in my
eyes—can't you see?

CARL: (speaking softly) Oh, my dear, dear love.
(singing) Now though your fears are sleeping,
Look well before the leaping.
Love of me
May be repaid
By weeping.
Life can be bitter learning,

When there is no returning,
Whate'er Fate has in store,
My heart is yours for evermore,
I love you—I love you—I love you.

GLORIA: You cannot realize the things you say.
You quite forget yourself, please go away.

HARRIET: Now leave all this to me, my dear,
It's really too absurd.

EFFIE: It's quite the most romantic thing that I have
ever heard!

The girls are trying to talk sense into her when they hear footmen approaching to tidy the room. Everyone hides. As the footmen attend to their duties, they sing . . .

FOOTMEN QUARTETTE

Now the party's really ended,
And our betters have ascended,
All with throbbing heads,
To their welcome beds,
Pity us, who have to be up,
Sadly clearing the debris up,
Getting for our pains
Most of the remains.

Though the Major-Domo is a trifle tight,
Though the mistress hiccoughed when she said
good night,
We in our secluded garret,
Mean to finish up the claret
Cup all right.

When we've doused the final candles,
We'll discuss the latest scandals
We have overheard,
Pleasure long deferred.
When the Duke of So-and So stares
At his wife, we know below stairs,
While she smirks and struts,
That he hates her guts.
Though we all disguise our feelings pretty
well,
What we mean by 'Very good' is 'Go to hell'.
Though they're all so grand and pompous,
Most of them are now non compos,
Serve them right,
Good night.

After they leave, everyone re-emerges. Sarah tells them she has made up her mind. She is going with Carl. One of the girls finds her hat and cloak and the lovers go out through the open French windows.

*   *   *

Act II opens in Schlick's Café in Vienna. It is now 1880. Carl is rehearsing with the orchestra, while waiters and cleaners are busy getting the cafe ready for its customers. They sing as they work . . .

LIFE IN THE MORNING

WAITERS: Life in the morning isn't too bright,
When you've had to hurry round and carry plates all night;
And the evening isn't too gay,
When you know you've got to rise and be at work all day.
This café merely caters
For a horde of drunken satyrs,
Why, oh why, we're waiters
Nobody can say.

CLEANERS: Oh dear, it's clear to see that cleaners lead a worse life,
Every day we curse life;
More and more
The muscles on our brawny arms like iron bands are
Scrubbing till our hands are
Sore;
We scour and polish till our fingers ache.

WAITERS: *(humming)* Hum—hum—!

CLEANERS: Each hour we feel as though our backs would break,

WAITERS: Hum—hum—!

CLEANERS: We weep and keep our growing families as well,
Why we're here at all nobody can tell.

WAITERS: Life in the morning isn't too bright,
When you've had to hurry round and carry plates all night.

CLEANERS: Oh dear, it's clear to see that cleaners lead a worse life.

WAITERS: And the evening isn't too gay
When you know you've got to rise and be at work all day.

CLEANERS: You see the reason why each day we want to curse life.

WAITERS: For this café merely caters

CLEANERS: Weary

WAITERS: For a horde of drunken satyrs;

CLEANERS: Dreary

WAITERS: Why, oh why, we're waiters nobody can say.

CLEANERS: Every day.

WAITERS: Ah—Ah—Ah——

Cleaners: Ah—Ah—Ah——

Four regular customers are seated at a table, their night's work over . . .

LADIES OF THE TOWN

(Millie Sim, Betty Huntley-Wright, Marjorie Rogers, Norah Howard)

Though we're often accused of excessively plastic, drastic sins,
When we're asked to decide on the wrong or the right life,
Night life wins,
We know that destiny will never bring

A wedding ring about.
Our moral sense may really not be quite the thing
To fling about,
Sing about;
We'll achieve independence before it's too late, and
Wait and see.
What care, what care we?

REFRAIN
Ladies of the town, ladies of the town,
Though we've not a confessional air,
We have quite a professional flair,
Strolling up and down, strolling up and down,
We employ quite an amiable system
Of achieving renown,
Though the church and state abuses us,
For as long as it amuses us,
We'll remain, no matter how they frown,
Haughty, naughty ladies of the town.

We can often behave in a very disarming, charming way,
Which can frequently add to the money we lay by,
Day by day.
If we are told of something on the Stock Exchange
We pry a bit,
And if it's safe we get some kindly banker
To supply a bit, buy a bit,

"Ladies of the Town": Freda (Betty Huntley-Wright), Hansi (Marjorie Rogers), Lotte (Millie Sim), and Gussi (Norah Howard).

And if later our helpers may wish to forget us,
Set us free,
What care, what care we?

REFRAIN

Ladies of the town, ladies of the town,
Though we're socially under a cloud,
Please forgive us for laughing aloud,
Strolling up and down, strolling up and down,
Disapproval may sometimes submerge us,
But we none of us drown,
We have known in great variety
Members of the best society,
And should we decide to settle down,
We'll be wealthy ladies of the town.

The café singer, Manon la Crevette, starts to rehearse with Carl but acts very temperamentally. She was in love with Carl before he married Sari (as Sarah is now called) and admits to being jealous. Feeling sorry for herself, she sings her song . . .

IF LOVE WERE ALL

(Ivy St. Helier)

Life is a very rough and tumble,
For a humble
Diseuse,
One can betray one's troubles never,
Whatever
Occurs,
Night after night,
Have to look bright,
Whether you're well or ill
People must laugh their fill.
You mustn't sleep
Till dawn comes creeping.
Though I never really grumble
Life's a jumble.
Indeed——
And in my efforts to succeed
I've had to formulate a creed——

REFRAIN

I believe in doing what I can,
In crying when I must,
In laughing when I choose.
Heigho, if love were all

I should be lonely,
I believe the more you love a man,
The more you give your trust,
The more you're bound to lose.
Although when shadows fall
I think if only——
Somebody splendid really needed me,
Someone affectionate and dear,
Cares would be ended if I knew that he
Wanted to have me near.
But I believe that since my life began
The most I've had is just
A talent to amuse.
Heigho, if love were all!

Though life buffets me obscenely,
It serenely
Goes on.
Although I question its conclusion,
Illusion
Is gone.
Frequently I
Put a bit by
Safe for a rainy day.
Nobody here can say
To what, indeed,
The years are leading.
Fate may often treat me meanly,
But I keenly
Pursue
A little mirage in the blue.
Determination helps me through.

(In the handwritten mss. the first line reads:
     I believe in *working* all I can
—but his revision works much better.)

*   *   *

This became something of a personal theme song for Noël in later years, despite the fact that it was written to be performed by a woman. The sentiments transcended the song's original context and it became "a hymn for what might have been." It was the last song he ever sang in public at the dinner given in his honour at Claridge's in November 1972 and the line "A Talent to Amuse" was engraved on his memorial tablet in Westminster Abbey.

*   *   *

Sari and Carl sing a duet, "Evermore And A Day," which was cut from the London production but used in the New York version.

EVERMORE AND A DAY (PEACE ENFOLD YOU)

(Peggy Wood and George Metaxa)

VERSE
CARL: Why are you weeping, dear?
        What shadow haunted you in sleeping, dear?
        Though portents and fears your courage may
            be plundering.
        Your faith in my love should leave no time
            for wondering.
        Even your dreams are in my keeping, dear.

SARI: Ah, no! my sweet,
        Fate knows our happiness is too complete.
        Though now in our love's security we live
            awhile
        A little of heart's content the gods may give
            awhile,
        Time's on the wing, my love, and time is fleet.

REFRAIN
CARL: Peace enfold you;
        Here in my arms I will hold you,
        Fears receding further and further away.

SARI: Peace enfold me;
        Here in your arms you will hold me,
        Fears receding further and further away.

CARL: Though the world may divide us,
        And ill-fortune betide us,
        Yet our love is a token
        That cannot be broken
        Or stolen away.
        There's a passionate glory
        In the heart of our story;
        We have something to guide us
        Evermore and a day.

CARL/SARI: Though the world may divide us,
        And ill-fortune betide us,
        Yet our love is a token
        That cannot be broken
        Or stolen away.
        There's a passionate glory
        In the heart of our story;
        We have something to guide us,
        We have something to guide us,
        Evermore and a day,
        Evermore and a day.

SARI: Peace enfold me,
          Here in your arms you will hold me.

CARL: Peace enfold you,
          Here in my arms I will hold you.

BOTH: Fears receding further and further away.
          Fears receding further and further away.

*   *   *

Captain August Lutte enters the café. Handsome
and arrogant, he has his eye on the cafe's new dancer
(Sari) but complains to Herr Schlick that she is an
"iceberg." Schlick must arrange a private dinner for
the two of them. As he is about to leave, Sari enters
and enrages him by refusing his invitation. Carl
returns and Sari begs him to leave the cafe. She has
a premonition that something terrible will happen.
He calms her by telling her that they will leave very
soon. A few more weeks and they will have saved
enough to buy that little cafe they have set their
hearts on.

Peggy Wood and George Metaxa, "Little Café."

LITTLE CAFE
(DEAR LITTLE CAFE)

(Peggy Wood and George Metaxa)

CARL: We share a mutual ambition
          Which naught can disarrange,

SARI: Based on the hopeful supposition
          That soon our luck will change.

CARL: Though we very often wonder whether
          Poverty will win the day,

SARI: Just as long as we remain together
          Troubles seem to fade away.

BOTH: However hard the bed one lies on
          The same old dreams begin,
          We're always scanning the horizon
          For when our ship comes in.

REFRAIN
CARL: We'll have a sweet little café
          In a neat little square,

SARI: We'll find our fortune
          And our happiness there.

CARL: We shall thrive on the vain and
          resplendent

SARI: And contrive to remain independent.

CARL: We'll have a meek reputation
          And a chic clientèle,

SARI: Kings will fall under our spell.

BOTH: We'll be so jealous
          That the world will be zealous
          Of our sweet little café in a square.

SARI: Can you imagine our sensations
          When we've security?

CARL: And all our dreary deprivations
          Are just a memory.

SARI: Though we're very often driven frantic,
          Peace is very hard to find.

CARL: All these dreadful days will seem romantic
          When we've left them far behind.

BOTH: Fate needn't be quite such a dragon,
          He knows how tired we are.

          We'll hitch our hopeful little wagon
          Onto a lucky star.

REFRAIN
CARL: We'll have a sweet little café
          In a neat little square,

SARI: We'll find our fortune
          And our happiness there.

CARL: We shall thrive on the vain and resplendent

SARI: And contrive to remain independent.

CARL: We'll have a meek reputation
          And a chic clientèle,

SARI: Kings will fall under our spell.

BOTH: We'll be so zealous
          That the world will be jealous
          Of our sweet little café in a square.

Sari is reassured for the moment . . .
     It is 2:00 a.m. and the café is crowded. A group
of officers comes in and sings with the girls.

OFFICERS' CHORUS

OFFICERS: We wish to order wine, please,
Expressly from the Rhine, please,
The year we really don't much care.

LADIES: Oh dear,
Now that you're here
Think of the wear and tear.

Ivy St. Helier as Manon, with Sari in Herr Schlick's Café.

OFFICERS: We hope without insistence
To overcome resistance
In all you little ladies fair.

LADIES: Oh well,
How can we tell
Whether you'd really dare?

OFFICERS: We sincerely hope it's really not a thankless
task
Amusing us,
Won't you please agree?

LADIES: Ah me!

OFFICERS: You could quickly break our hearts by
everything we ask
Refusing us;
Cruel that would be,
Ladies, can't you see!

We're officers and gentlemen,
Reliable and true,
Considerate and chivalrous
In everything we do.

Though we're gay and drunk a trifle,
All our laughter we should stifle,
Were we summoned by a bugle call.
We're amorous and passionate,
But dignified and stern,
Which if you play us false you'll quickly learn.
Do not let our presence grieve you,
When we've loved you we shall leave you,
For we're officers and gentlemen, that's all!

Captain August enters and sings, accompanied by
the officers . . .

TOKAY

(Gerald Nodin)

OFFICERS: Tokay!

CAPTAIN A.: When we're thoroughly wined and dined,
And the barracks are left behind,
We come down to the town to find
Some relief from the daily grind.
Love is kind,
Love is blind.

OFFICERS: Tokay!

CAPTAIN A.: When the thoughts of a man incline
To the grapes of a sunlit vine,
On the banks of the golden Rhine,

Slowly ripening pure and fine,
Sweet divine,
Lovers' wine.
Lift your voices till the rafters ring,
Fill your glasses to the brim and sing:

REFRAIN Tokay!
The golden sunshine of a summer day,
Tokay!
Will bear the burden of your cares away,
Here's to the love in you,
The hate in you,
Desire in you.

OFFICERS: Wine of the sun that will waft you along,
Lifting you high on the wings of a song.

CAPTAIN A.: Dreams in you,
The flame in you,
The fire in you,
Tokay—Tokay.

OFFICERS: So while forgetfulness we borrow,
Never minding what tomorrow has to say,

CAPTAIN A.: Tokay!

ALL: The only call we all obey,
Tokay—Tokay—Tokay!

They then settle down to the serious business of
drinking. Sari has been sitting with Manon, who is
then whisked away to dance with August's companion, leaving her to the Captain. Carl manages to
head him off for the moment and whispers to Sari
that this will be their last night at the café. Not to be
put off, the Captain invites her to dance. When she
refuses, Herr Schlick reminds her that she is being
paid to do just that. Unless she performs her duties,
he will withold her salary and Carl's.

He then announces the evening's entertainment, which opens with six dancing girls. They are
followed by Manon . . .

BONNE NUIT, MERCI!

(Ivy St. Helier)

MANON: *Lorsque j'étais petite fille*
En marchant parmi les prés
J'entendis la voix d'ma tante
Qui murmura à côté,
'N'oublie pas la politesse
Lorsque viendra un amant
Car tout le bonheur réside là dedans.'

REFRAIN *C'est pourquoi dans mes affaires*
Soit de coeur ou soit d'esprit,
C'est pourquoi je tâche de plaire
Toute la foule de mes amis,
Soit qu'ils m'offrent pied-à-terre
Ou me montrent une bonne affaire
J'leur réponds, 'Vas-y. Bonne nuit,
Merçi!'

Lorsque je suis v'nue à Paris
J'étais bien sage de nature,
Mais que faire dans la vie
Étant trop jeune pour rester pure!
Quand ma politesse m'obligea
Lorsqu' je suivais par hasard
Une aventure dans les bôites des boulevards.

REFRAIN *Et j'ai rencontré en ville*
Un monsieur bien comme-il-faut,
Il m'a dit, Ma petite fille,
Veux-tu faire un p'tit do-do?'
Lorsqu' j'arrive chez lui toute de suite
Il m'dit 'Deshabilles-toi vite!'
J'me suis dit, 'Vas'y. Bonne nuit,
Merçi!'

Manon then sings an encore in which she invites the
audience to join her . . .

KISS ME

(Ivy St. Helier)

MANON: 'Tis time that we were parted,
You and I,
However broken-hearted,
'Tis goodbye!
Although our love has ended
And darkness has descended,
I call to you with one last cry:

Kiss me
Before you go away!
Miss me
Through every night and day,
Though clouds are grey above you,
You'll hear me say I love you!
Kiss me
Before you go away!

Parmi les chansons tristes
De l'amour,
Joies et chagrins existent
Tour à tour,

Et presqu'avec contrainte
On risque la douce étreinte
Qui nous sépare enfin toujours.

REFRAIN *Je t'aime,*
Tes baisers m'ont grisés,
Même
A l'heure de t'en aller,
La volupté troublante
Brise mes lèvres brulantes,
Je t'aime,
A l'heure de t'en aller.

The show over, the dancing starts again. The
Captain claims his waltz with Sari. Drunk by now, he
becomes increasingly amorous and kisses her. Carl
stops the music, leaps to the dance floor and strikes
the Captain. A duel ensues but, of course, Carl is no
match for the professional soldier. He is mortally
wounded and dies in Sari's arms.

ACT III

It's fifteen years later. Lord Shayne, a distinguished
elderly man, is giving a party. Among the guests are
the girls we saw earlier—now established society
matrons. As they enter, to be greeted by Lord
Shayne, they sing the opening chorus . . .

TA-RA-RA-BOOM-DE-AY

ALL: Tarara boom-de-ay,
Tarara boom-de-ay,
We are the most effectual,
Intellectual
Movement of the day.
Our moral standards sway
Like Mrs Tanqueray,
And we are theoretically
Most aesthetically
Eager to display
The fact that we're aggressively
And excessively
Anxious to destroy
All the snobbery
And hob-nobbery
Of the hoi-polloi.
Tarara boom-de-ay,
It's mental washing day,
And come what may
We'll scrub until the nation's morals shrink
away.
Tarara boom-de-ay.

EXQUISITES: Though we are languid in appearance
We're in the vanguard,
We feel we can guard
The cause of Art.
We shall ignore all interference,
For our complaisance
With this renaissance
Is frightfully smart.
Please do not think us unrelenting,
Our charming frolic
With the symbolic
Is meek and mild.
We merely spend our time preventing
Some earnest stripling
From liking Kipling
Instead of Wilde.

Now that we find the dreary nineteenth
century is closing,
We mean to start the twentieth in ecstasies
of posing.

ALL: Tarara boom-de-ay,
It's mental washing day,
And come what may
We'll scrub until the tiresome bourgeois
shrink away.
Tarara boom-de-ay.

The ladies then sing a sextette . . .

ALAS, THE TIME IS PAST

SEXTETTE: Alas the time is past when we
Could frolic with impunity.
Secure in our virginity,
We sometimes look aghast
Adown the lanes of memory,
Alas the time is past.
Ah, then the world was at our feet,
When we were sweet and twenty,
We never guessed that what we'd got,
Though not a lot—was plenty.
We gaily sought some Abélard
To cherish, guard and own us,
But all we know of storm and strife
Our married life—has shown us.
Alas, the time is past when we
Could frolic with impunity.
Secure in our virginity,
We sometimes look aghast
Adown the lanes of memory.
Alas, the time is past.
Alack-a-day me—alack-a-day-me!
Ah, then the world was at our feet,
Alas, the time is past.

They begin to speculate on the evening's special guest, the famous European singer, Madame Sari Linden, whom their host describes as "one of the few really beautiful people in the world." When she arrives, they are amazed to see that she is their old friend, whom they had all thought was dead. Lord Shayne takes her in to supper and the others follow, except four exquisitely-dressed young men who proceed to sing a quartet.

*   *   *

A number that proved surprisingly uncontroversial, given the times, was Coward's satire on the aesthetes of the 1890s—and particularly on the floral affectations of Oscar Wilde and his lover, Lord Alfred Douglas, who liked to draw attention to themselves by wearing carnations in their buttonholes dyed a vivid shade of green. A poet, a playwright, a painter and a dilettante extol the delights of the period that celebrated the concept of "camp" long before the phrase was invented . . .

(WE ALL WORE A) GREEN CARNATION

QUARTETTE: Blasé boys are we,
Exquisitely free
From the dreary and quite absurd
Moral views of the common herd.
We like porphyry bowls,
Chandeliers and stoles,
We're most spirited,
Carefully filleted 'souls'.

REFRAIN
Pretty boys, witty boys, too, too, too
Lazy to fight stagnation,
Haughty boys, naughty boys, all we do
Is to pursue sensation.
The portals of society
Are always opened wide,
The world our eccentricity condones,
A note of quaint variety
We're certain to provide,
We dress in very decorative tones.
Faded boys, jaded boys, womankind's
Gift to a bulldog nation,
In order to distinguish us from less enlightened
minds,
We all wear a green carnation.

We believe in Art,
Though we're poles apart
From the fools who are thrilled by Greuze.
We like Beardsley and Green Chartreuse.
Women say we're too
Bored to bill and coo,
We smile wearily,
It's so drearily true!

REFRAIN
Pretty boys, witty boys, you may sneer
At our disintegration,
Haughty boys, naughty boys, dear, dear, dear!
Swooning with affectation.
Our figures sleek and willowy,
Our lips incarnadine,
May worry the majority a bit.
But matrons rich and billowy
Invite us out to dine,
And revel in our phosphorescent wit,
Faded boys, jaded boys, come what may,
Art is our inspiration,

And as we are the reason for the 'Nineties'
being gay,
We all wear a green carnation.

REFRAIN
Pretty boys, witty boys, yearning for
Permanent adulation,
Haughty boys, naughty boys, every pore
Bursting with self-inflation.
We feel we're rather Grecian,
As our manners indicate,
Our sense of moral values isn't strong.
For ultimate completion
We shall really have to wait
Until the Day of Judgment comes along.
Faded boys, jaded boys, each one craves
Some sort of soul salvation,
But when we rise reluctantly but gracefully from
our graves,
We'll all wear a green carnation.

After dinner Lord Shayne enters with Sari and proposes—not for the first time. She promises to "think it over" this time. The others return and clamour to hear the famous singer. She sings one of Carl's songs, the story of a princess who loved a gypsy . . .

ZIGEUNER

(Peggy Wood)

VERSE 1   Once upon a time,
Many years ago,
Lived a fair Princess,
Hating to confess
Loneliness was torturing her so.
Then a gipsy came,
Called to her by name,
Woo'd her with a song,
Sensuous and strong,
All the summer long;
Her passion seemed to tremble like a
living flame.

REFRAIN   Play to me beneath the summer moon,
Zigeuner!—Zigeuner!—Zigeuner!
All I ask of life is just to listen
To the songs that you sing,
My spirit like a bird on the wing
Your melodies adoring—soaring,
Call to me with some barbaric tune,

Zigeuner!—Zigeuner!—Zigeuner!
Now you hold me in your power,
Play to me for just an hour,
Zigeuner!

VERSE 2 Bid my weeping cease,
Melody that brings
Merciful release,
Promises of peace,
Through the gentle throbbing of the strings.
Music of the plain,
Music of the wild,
Come to me again,
Hear me not in vain,
Soothe a heart in pain,
And let me to my happiness be reconciled.

As she sings the refrain of "I'll See You Again," the lights fade once more . . .

REPRISE I'll see you again,
I live each moment through again.
Time has lain heavy between,
But what has been
Can leave me never;
Your dear memory
Throughout my life has guided me.
Though my world has gone awry,
Though the years my tears may dry
I shall love you till I die,
Goodbye!

When they rise, we are back in the first scene with the young people listening to the old Lady Shayne. Overcome by the emotion, Dolly rushes over to Vincent and flings her arms around him, as if in emulation of Sarah and Carl. He begins to play "I'll See You Again" as a foxtrot and everyone goes off dancing. Left alone, Lady Shayne reprises . . .

Though my world has gone awry,
Though the end is drawing nigh,
I shall love you till I die
Goodbye!

THE CURTAIN FALLS.

*   *   *

The place that *Bitter Sweet* would take in the history of popular music was not immediately recognised by the London critics: "The Press notices . . . were remarkable for their tone of rather grudging patronage. It seemed as though the critics were ashamed of their recent outburst of enthusiasm over *This Year of Grace!* and wished to retrench themselves behind a barricade of noncommittal clichés. . . Some praised the book, but dismissed the music as being reminiscent and of no consequence. Some liked the music, but were horrified by the commonplace sentimentality of the book. The lyrics were hardly mentioned . . . It was generally agreed that the show would run for about three months; in fact, it ran for over eighteen and was seen, in all its initial productions, by about a million people."

Opened at the Ziegfeld Theatre, New York on November 5, 1929. (159 performances.)

In this production Evelyn Laye took over the part of Sari Linden, returning to London the following year to replace Peggy Wood for the last two months of the London production and the subsequent tour. Although there were problems with casting some of the other parts, the opening night was a triumph for the new star: "It was Evelyn's night from first to last. She played as though she were enchanted . . . Early in the ballroom scene she conquered the audience completely by singing the quick waltz song, "Tell Me, What is Love?" so brilliantly, and with such a quality of excitement, that the next few minutes of the play were entirely lost in one of the most prolonged outbursts of cheering I have ever heard in a theatre."

Evelyn Laye recalls the dedicated preparation that went into that performance in her 1958 autobiography, *Boo, to My Friends*:

"I tried to sing Noël's lovely melodies in three voices, making it a little breathless and sweet for the young girl, powerful for the woman of forty, and deeper and more resonant for the elderly woman.

I went to the theatre on the morning that Noël was going to hear me sing for the first time. Elsie April (Noël's musical amanuensis) was going to play for me. Noël was an isolated figure, sitting in the middle of the empty stalls. I was very nervous. Noël is such an enthusiast, with such a superb flair for knowing what is right that he can be a task-master with a whip, or a fiend if things are done badly.

'Well, I'm ready, dear,' he said in his clipped precise voice. 'Noël, before I start I want to ask you a favour?' I told him, 'please let me sing the whole score right through, and even if there are passages you don't like, please don't stop me until the end. If you stop me you won't see what I'm trying to do with it.'

Evelyn Laye conquered Broadway replacing Peggy Wood as Sari Linden for the New York production.

A "Bitter Sweet" reunion:
Noël with his three Saris.
Left to right, Evelyn Laye,
Anna Neagle (1933 film),
and Peggy Wood.

'Very well,' said the young man who was already dubbed 'The Master' by most of the people who worked for him.

I began to sing.

After a while Noël left his seat and started walking up and down the main aisle of the stalls. Elsie nodded at me encouragingly. This was a good sign. He was interested. As I went on his pace increased, till, at the last number, he was marching up and down very quickly, his hands clasped firmly behind his back.

As I finished he wheeled round to come up to the orchestra rail. 'Very exciting, very exciting,' he said. 'That's your personality, your interpretation. It's good, very good. Don't change it. Stay there.'

He came round to the stage. 'It's good, darling,' he repeated. He kissed me and said in a matter-of-fact voice, 'Now I'm going to get some lunch,' and vanished.

I looked at Elsie. 'There'd have been no lunch for him, or for you, if he hadn't liked it,' she observed . . ."

*   *   *

In the 1934 US revival that played in Washington a scene was cut before the production reached Broadway. It was set in Herr Schlick's cafe in Act 2 and took place immediately after Manon's "If Love Were All." Herr Schlick and his wife, Lizzie are teasing the waiter, Fritz . . .

SCHLICK: That's how you won me—by a trick.

LIZZIE: And when I won your hand, you were the easiest trick I ever took in. Begging your pardon, Fritz for slighting you.

FRITZ: I'm glad I found out that the woman I was running after was really chasing me.

SCHLICK: She may have been chasing you but she caught me, and how I was trapped.

LIZZIE: Ha, ha! You men think you are always the hunters but you're just the game.

*IT'S ALWAYS THE MAN THAT'S PURSUED

(*Schlick, Lizzie and Fritz*)

SCHLICK: Ever since the days of Eden
         Every woman has been needin'
         Someone to officiate—and act as mate.

FRITZ: Even wise old Aristotle
        Grasping women couldn't throttle
        "No's" the only word in Greek he couldn't speak.

LIZZIE: A woman overwhelms a man—the weaker sex is strong
         She holds her man until another woman comes along.

REFRAIN

SCHLICK: It's always the man who's pursued,

FRITZ: It's always the man who's wooed.

LIZZIE: He may think he's the hunter
         But he's really just the game,
         And any wild man is just a mild man
         When she's filed her claim.

FRITZ: It's always the man who has bragged
        That he can't be caught that she's tagged.

SCHLICK: Be he a devil or a prude
          The chase is on and then renewed

LIZZIE: Till he is caught and firmly glued

FRITZ: For his goose is cooked—

SCHLICK: His dish is stewed,
          It's a man—poor old man who's pursued.

After song all exit. Enter Carl from left. Sari from right . . .

There will inevitably be controversy as to whether this was a Coward song. He makes no reference to it and Mander & Mitchenson never picked it up. Nonetheless, there it was, typed on a carbon in a copy of the script filed in the Shubert Archive and laid out in the same way as his other typewritten manuscripts. Further in its favour it can be argued that Noël by this time had total control of his output and it is highly unlikely that anyone would have dared interpolate other material into one of his shows. That would have to wait until the mid-1950s, when Jeanette MacDonald, touring with *Bitter Sweet*, managed to incorporate "Mad About the Boy" into "If Love Were All" before Noël was made aware of this and other small "improvements" and forbade her to bring the production to Broadway.

No, the most likely explanation for the song is that Noël may have felt that the second act was emotionally extended and needed a little light relief at this point. Having tried it, he realised that it would be too difficult to rebuild the dramatic tension in time for the duel—and out came the blue pencil.

I include it as a curiosity, if nothing more . . .

*   *   *

Perhaps Max Beerbohm summed up the show's appeal when he concluded that "Sentiment is out of fashion. Yet *Bitter Sweet*, which is nothing if not sentimental, has not been a failure. Thus we see the things that are out of fashion do not cease to exist. Sentiment goes on unaffrighted by the roarings of the young lions and lionesses of Bloomsbury."

There were a number of other "Miscellaneous" songs from the 1920s, many from the immediate post-Darewski era. Suburban mores continued to amuse.

*I MUSTN'T SAY THAT (EVERYBODY SAYS THAT I'M A CHATTERBOX)

Everybody says that I'm a chatterbox
And that I grow more spiteful every day.
It isn't really spite
But morning, noon and night
My tongue just simply carries me away.
My cousin Freda came to stay last Friday
And told me about Roger and his wife
And if you could have heard
Her account of what occurred
You'd go into a Nunnery for life.

I must say—he was justified.
At least one can condone his point of view
And I must say—she was horrified
'Cos it really was a fearful thing to do.

I must say—if I'd been him
I'd have soon divorced the brazen little cat.
He came home, people said
And he found them both—
Oh, I mustn't say that!

But Romantic Love—usually the lack or loss of it—continued to be the theme of endless variations. One seems an early draft of "Try To Learn To Love" . . .

*LOVE A LITTLE

Dream a little,
Scheme a little,
Laugh a little,
Chaff a little.
Keep near the shore
You'll succeed
With tact and taste.
Work with speed
But don't show haste.
Play a little,
Say a little,
Cry a little,
Lie a little.
Don't overdraw.
Life's extremely brittle
So do everything a little—
But love a little bit more.

It can only encourage aspiring lyricists to know that in the margin of many of these songs—all of which were handwritten, the early ones in pencil—Noël had jotted down possible "more" rhymes . . . "galore/adore/bore/flaw/sure/gore/jaw/poor".

*YOU'VE GOT A LITTLE PIECE OF LOVE IN YOUR HEART

You've got a little piece of love in your heart,
I'm going to find it if I can.
Nothing'll stop me now I've made a start
'Cos I'm a very determined man.

*TELL ME IF YOU KNEW

VERSE 1   Do you remember the first
Quite unrehearsed
Kiss 'neath a lovely moon?
The stars were shining above,
In love with love
I felt a crazy coon.
What a wonderful thrill
The whole wide world
Just seemed to stand still.
I prayed I wouldn't wake too soon.

REFRAIN   Tell me if you knew
The day I fell in love with you
Just like a bolt from out of the blue,
Blue sky.
Tell me if you guessed
That fearful weight upon my chest
Made me so wretchedly depressed
And shy.
Could Cupid send—just for a lark—
That arrow unkind?
Did you intend that vital spark
To light up my mind?
Did you feel it too
When I went crazy over you?
Oh, lady, tell me if you knew
The reason why!

*WE'LL ALWAYS SIGH

Are we mistaken
In this remembering of little things
That made our first shy love awaken?
Should we not leave them with those other
    dreams
That Time and Tide have overtaken?

You're just a skittle in a game of the Gods
And you may be bowled out quite soon,
For Cupid isn't taking
Any risks when he is staking
All his odds on a honeymoon.

We can't live among our yesterdays
Nor let their light forever blind us
For with the mellowness of later years
Perhaps some wiser love may find us.
But still however much we try,
We'll always sigh.

*YOU'VE GONE AWAY

REFRAIN   You've gone away
And left me lonely,
The saddest day
I ever knew
But come what may
I'll love you only
Until our happy hearted
Dear departed
Dreams come true.

VERSE 1   Just because we're lovers
Don't let's laugh at Fate.
Often one discovers
When it is too late
Vows that have been spoken
While the tide was high
Lie around us broken
When the sands are dry.

VERSE 2   Things can't last forever
Time's relentless wand
Frequently must sever
Hearts however fond.
Passion is uncertain
Tho' it's been sublime.
Love rings down the curtain
Way before its time.

The song was slightly reworked and retitled:

THE DREAM IS OVER

VERSE 1   Just because we're lovers,
Don't let's laugh at fate;
Often one discovers
When it is too late
Vows that have been spoken

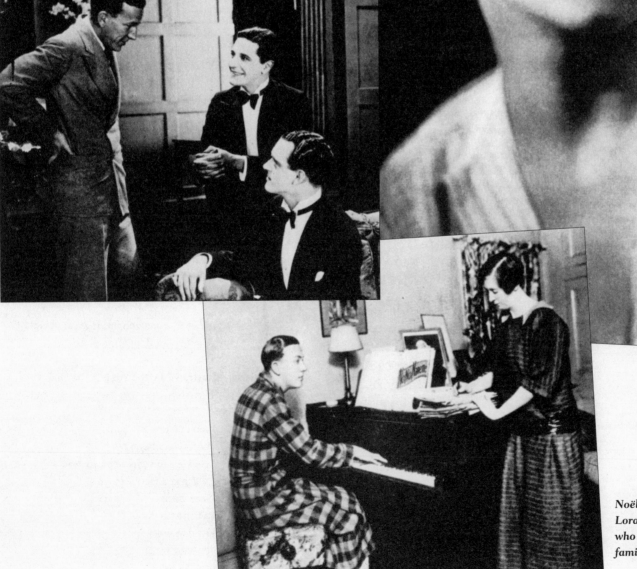

Ivor Novello, actor, playwright, composer, was a lifelong friend of Noël's.

Noël visiting Ivor Novello during the filming of Coward's "The Vortex" (1927).

Noël with Lorn ("Lornie") Loraine, his secretary, who became part of "the family."

When the tide is high
Lie around us broken
When the sands are dry.

REFRAIN   I love you so, but the dream is over,
Days come and go, but the dream is over
I've tried to fool myself,
School myself into believing
Our love could still go on,
But it's gone beyond retrieving,
My hopes were vain like a fool in clover,
Never again for the dream is over.

VERSE 2   Things can't last for ever,
Lover's hours are fleet,
Destiny may sever
Happiness complete,
Passion's so uncertain,
Some unfinished rhyme
May bring down the curtain
Long before it's time.

*Alternative Earlier Version

VERSE 1   Over now
The dream is over now
Maybe it wasn't so important anyhow.
To start over again
Believing it was true
If you should ask me to
I'd say—"To Hell with you!"

VERSE 2   Over now
The thrill is over now
Maybe it wasn't more than an illusion
anyhow.
What's been can't be again
Reluctantly I see
My heart is free again,
Belongs to me again.

VERSE 3   Over now
The dream is over now
Maybe is wasn't so important anyhow.
What's been can't be again
Reluctantly I see again
My heart is free again,
Belongs to me again
The brief illusion I lived for has gone,
No more confusion and tears from now on.

To start again,
To break my heart again.
If you should ask me to
I'd say—"To Hell with you!"

Increasingly, as the years went by, Romance became tinged with a little of the fashionable scepticism that became one of his trademarks . . .

*It Isn't What You Do

It isn't what you do
That makes the men run after you,
It's what you don't do—
That's true.
It isn't when you try
That you get kissed on the sly,
It's when you don't try—
That's why.
The peach that's out of reach
Is more attractive
Than the fruit that's lying on the ground.
It may not be such fun
But it's the things you leave undone
That make the whole wide world
Follow you around.

Mind when you strive
To get the honey in your love
It's when you don't strive
You thrive.
It isn't what you say
That makes success come your way,
It's words you don't say—
That pay.
It's always wise to guard your reputation
And keep your morals bloody but unbowed.
It's better to be cold
For it's the gifts that you withhold
That make the whole wide world
Follow you around.

If the lines about peaches out of reach being more attractive than fruit that's lying on the ground have a familiar ring, it's because Noël had used them earlier in his first song, "Every Peach." He presumably had no qualms about plagiarising himself!

As the decade progressed—along with many other song writers—he began to investigate the possibility that Moon/June/Honeymoon might end all too soon . . .

*Marriage Is a Fatal Curse

VERSE 1   Marriage is a fatal curse
Temperamental folks, beware.
Anticipation of your fate
Realisation dawns too late.
Maybe as the years roll by
You begin to think and sigh.
Poets of long ago were all wrong,.
Oh, just look at Shakespeare's song.
Every happy Wedding Day
Always ends the same old way.

VERSE 2   People won't believe a ring
Simply alters everything.
Hardened Romancers
Even jazz dancers
Take the same chances
All in a trance.
Up the aisle you see them go,
Poor deluded Belles and Beaux.

REFRAIN   First you murmur sweetly
That you're hers completely,
Linger indiscreetly long.
Men may ask you questions,
Make absurd suggestions,
Never pay the slightest heed

For the missing line—which Noël apparently never completed—he listed the following possible rhymes . . .

"strong/long/wrong/gong/prong/song/belong/
Hong Kong/ding-dong/ping-pong."

Perhaps frustrated by the subject, he then wrote an alternative version:

Don't be taken in by
People who begin by
Lending you some book to read.
Talking at a fearful speed
Many chaps
Bait their traps
Just that way
Speeding you,
Leading you

Well astray.
Some are awfully eager
Fresh from the bodega
More than half a league away

Then, to prove that a professional songwriter could espouse any point of view . . .

*MARRIAGE IS THE GAME FOR ME

A married lady
I mean to be,
Tho' people warn me
Marriage is a sort of bother,
I shall succeed in my mission,
Get a position
Nobody's going to stamp on
My ambition—
I know marriage is the game for me

*   *   *

There is a famous—though probably apochryphal—story about Noël attending a stand-up fork supper at the Dorchester and being the only person present to be given a knife. When asked why, he replied—"After all, I *did* write *Cavalcade*." Writing that one play would have been enough to create his lifetime reputation as a heart-on-the-sleeve patriot, which indeed he was. But a decade earlier, while the nostalgia was visible, so was a certain (unpublished) unease about days gone by.

*NINETEEN HUNDRED AND SIX

This is the year of comparative grace,
Nineteen hundred and six,
When insular prejudice
Found reward
And every thin edge of the wedge you disdained.
Englishmen still were ahead in the race
Of the nastiest political tricks.

Our national pride was completely secure
We felt that we really had nothing to fear.
In fact we were rather too smug in the year
Nineteen hundred and six.

*LADY FROM VIENNA

Lady from Vienna,
What are your memories?
Lady from Vienna,
We want to know,
Lady from Vienna,
Why gypsy melodies
Haunt you with a longing
For long ago.

Let them go,
Memories must die
In my heart I've buried deep
Those melodies of long ago.
Let them lie,
Memories must die—
It's better so.

Ah—ah—ah
My heart has travelled far.

Another in Noël's litany of ladies who were no better than they should be . . .

*MAUDIE GOLIGHTLY

Maudie Golightly
By dancing twice nightly
Drew all the young men of the town to her.
She was always most discreet,
Though she had a flat in Albermarle Street.
Highly wed mothers
And wives, and some others
Applied a most improper word to her
But she was way above their spleen
When she kicked her tambourine
And could hear people roaring

'Bravo' and encoring,
She would say—"What can they mean?
What have I got
That those ladies have not?"
And she'd laugh—Ho, ho
And cheerfully go
Into her next routine

Maudie was brought out of retirement for consideration in *After The Ball* (1954) but failed the audition.

*THIS YEAR, NEXT YEAR

This year, next year, never maybe
Virtue's prize will come to me.
Some strong man will take me on his knee
'Cos he likes my personality.
Tinker, tailor, sailor or coon,
Even quite a common dragoon
Would not be inopportune—
I've got to find a good man soon.

During the 1920s—in fact, until the movies found their voice—the music hall or what came to be called the "variety show" continued to be a powerful factor in Great Britain. No town of any size was without a theatre and the growth of radio created a desire to see in person the artistes you listened to every week. With Noël the interest went further back to the sentimental or robust songs he had heard in his Edwardian youth and he continued to parody them for the rest of his career.

*ALWAYS BE NICE TO FATHER

Always be nice to Father, children,
Always be nice to Father.
Be bright and gay
Both night and day
And drive his heavy cares away—
Always be nice to Father.

Tho' it annoys him rather, children,
Tho' it annoys him rather,
Be roguish quite
Both day and night
For youthful laughter keeps him bright.
Tho' it annoys him rather, children—
Always be nice to Father!

In 1916 Noël had a small part in *The Light Blues*, a musical comedy produced by impresario Robert Courtneidge—father of Cicely. During the next few years he became a friend and fan of one of Courtneidge's regular performers, light comedian Nelson ("Bunch") Keys (1886-1939). Cicely later described him as "small, highly strung, moody and quick on the uptake—a practical joker." Noël celebrated the *soigné* performer in song . . .

*BUNCH, BUNCH

VERSE I
BUNCH: In the morning I rise at ten,
Have a nice cup of tea and a bath and then—
I'm ready to receive . . .

GIRLS' CHORUS: Early to bed and early rising makes
one very wise, we believe—

BUNCH: Women all pursue me gaily,
Giving me no peace,
Burst into my bedroom daily—
When will their attentions cease . . .?

REFRAIN
GIRLS' CHORUS: Bunch, Bunch
Take us out to lunch,
Take us out to supper or to dine.
It's laughter we're after
With love thrown in.
As long as you're original
We can supply the sin.
Bunch, Bunch,
You're wittier than *Punch*
And we ask you on our bended knees,
Tho' your heart has many doors,
Do not shut them all because
We simply can't live without
The keys!

REFRAIN 2 Bunch, Bunch
Take us out to lunch,
We don't care where we go or what we do
Tho' we hate admirers to pass us by,
Just as long as you're about
Nobody need apply.
Bunch, Bunch,
You're wittier than *Punch*,
You always do your best to please.
If you took a little flat,
Why we'd go as far as that,
Because we can't live without
The keys.

If you don't do as we like,
We shall simply go on strike!

(Shades of P.G. Wodehouse and Bertie Wooster! Only Jeeves is missing—but then perhaps he drew the young master's bath . . .)

*   *   *

When Noël was a boy it was the Coward family habit to sing around the piano. He was clearly recalling those days in a song he left unfinished . . .

*MUSICAL MEMORIES

I've often watched my old Aunt Jane
Dissolve in wistful tears
On hearing some old song again
That charmed her maiden years.
I see her trembling smile and know
Her tears are mixed with gladness,
The songs of fifty years ago
Were filled with awful sadness.

The drawing rooms of yesterday
We'd like to fix your mind on,
The piano mother used to play
Blow, Blow, Thou Winter Wind on

The songs our father used to sing
Before our mother stopped them
Would set the chandeliers to ring—
No songs today can top them

And one of his frequent descents into pseudo-Cockney . . .

*I REMEMBER

I remember long ago
We used to sit and dream a bit
And wonder if our dreaming would come true
We used to sort of kid ourselves we'd money,
Quite a lot of it
And if we had—exactly what we'd do.
And you was always keen on a gramophone
To cheer you up when things was looking blue
You 'adn't much ambition
For an elegant position
But when you asked me wot I wanted too,
I'd always set me 'eart on a barrow
With perhaps a little moke to give a tone
And I'd feel so blooming proud
As I hollered to the crowd
And made an honest living on me own.

I'm sick of being mucked about and ordered
here and there
It's enough to try the patience of a saint
I'd make conditions easier
For blokes like you and me
If I 'ad pots of money—which I ain't!

*   *   *

Noël's notes frequently indicate numbers he was considering for one or other of the 20s revues. Here are a few that didn't survive to the actual show.

*I DREAMED YOU

REFRAIN   I dream'd you,
You dream'd me—
Love soon grew
Instantly
On waking life seem'd a dreary affair,
Heart breaking strife seem'd around us
Everywhere—
You dream'd me
I dream'd you—
Clouds broke free,
Sun shone through.
Now we'll try,
You and I
To make those dreams come true.

Noël, with Gladys
Calthrop, designer
and friend, 1924.

Coney Island, 1925: Left to right, Gladys Calthrop,
Noël, Robert Andrews, Henry Kendall and Alan Hollis.

Violet Coward surrounded by
Fred Astaire and his mother,
Atlantic City, 1925.

*CROSS YOUR HEART

REFRAIN Cross your heart
Before you say you love me truly,
Cross your heart
Or we must part.
I want more than half and half love
Are you sure it isn't calf love?
Cross your heart
Before our wedding day is over
And upon our honeymoon we start
When our passion's rags and tatters
There'll be nothing left that matters
So I think you'd better cross your heart.

*TAKING AFTER DEAR OLD DAD

PATTER: Nine o'clock or thereabouts
I advertise my whereabouts
By ringing for my butler and my valet and my cook
Then while I relay to them
The orders of the day to them
I idly scan the pages of a magazine or book.
Later on I meet a pal
And stroll with him along the Mall
Or canter for a while in Rotten Row.
Then I meet a girl or two
With whom I have a rendezvous
And blow
Breezily to Soho.
Later in the afternoon
I drop into the club saloon
And quaff a glass of bubbly with some lordly
      undergrad.
Home again in time to dress
For dinner with a Marchioness
Whose hubby's been behaving like a cad.
I order Chicken à la King and maybe caviar
But when I try to steal a kiss, she murmurs,
      "La-di-da,
You're taking after dear old Dad".

*LOUISE

VERSE: I have been a careless lover
Taking pleasure where I may
Ever trying to discover
Someone true from day to day
Tho' a heart like mine often seems
Mighty hard to please
I've a vision now in my dreams
And her name's Louise
And her home is in the opera
Not so very far away.

Louise, you've such wonderful charm about you
I don't mind much whether you're faithful or true
When you're with me I'm content
When you're not my hours are spent
Cursing you, hating you, loving you madly
Oh, my God, you treat me badly.

Louise, I love just every note that you sing
You're like a dove brushing my heart with your
      wing
I try to please you
And yet you always tease.
But I'll never let you go, Louise.

*VIOLETS

HE: Do you remember the very first time we met?
'Twas at a party among the smarter set.
You wore a pink silk sash that looked so cute
I wore a lanyard with my sailor suit
Tho' I was barely ten
I made my mind up then.

REFRAIN: Every morn I'd send you
Out of my garden just a tiny bunch of violets
Just to prove my love was true.
Tho' my voice was rather shrill, dear, still, dear
All my dreams were filled with thoughts of you.
Schoolboys may be
Fickle and stupid but the tiny darts of Cupid
Caused me quite a lot of pain
I'd scarcely met you
But I vowed I'd get you
And never never let you go again.

SHE: As we grew older
Your love for me remained
Tho' I grew colder
Your passion never waned
You used to irritate me quite a lot
I often longed to shoot you on the spot
But when you went away
I missed you more each day.

REFRAIN: Every day you'd send me
Out of your garden just a tiny bunch of violets
As to win my heart you tried
Tho' I laughed and said 't'was
Half love—calf love
All your evergreen affection never died.
Tho' at times I may have
Wanted to strike you
But I couldn't quite dislike you
And since first you looked my way
Tho' you adored me
You never bored me
I always knew I'd be your wife some day—
Today's the day!

*JAPANESE LOVE SONG

When the citron moon sails high
O'er the green rice glimmering
Through the purple night
'Mid the almond trees
If you gaze into the sky
There are fireflies shimmering.
Songs of love's delight
Float upon the breeze.

Come where Samisens are playing
'Neath a Japanese moon
Coloured lanterns softly swaying
To a Japanese tune.
Temple bells are ringing low
Slanting almond eyes aglow
Blossoms falling white as driven snow
Lovers—arms entwined—are sleeping
'Neath the cinnamon tree
'Till the eastern sun comes creeping
Slowly o'er the sea
Love like a sigh is passing by
Each maid and man—
That's the tale of spring in old Japan.

The first two lines, of course, are identical with his youthful "The Silken Cord" (See p. 28).

*LISTEN TO ME

Listen to me
What makes a birdie take
A mate and build a nest
When Spring is calling?
Listen to me
What makes the cats
Go on the tiles and make a row
When night is falling?
Listen to me
All you scientists and others,
Bring along your super-educated brothers …

(Incomplete)

*BUBBLES

REFRAIN: Every life is like a bubble
Some are simple, some are double.
Floating through the empty air
If your life's a double bubble
You will have a lot of trouble
Coming if you don't take care.

This is clearly a variant of part of "Ginger Up" (See p. 47).

*   *   *

Most of the other unused songs of the period fall into two distinct groups—the optimistic and the pessimistic—but since these were the two prevailing moods in which popular songs were tending to be written at a time when Noël was finding his professional voice, we probably shouldn't read too much of a personal nature into these mood swings.

The Bad News was . . .

*I ALWAYS WANTED TO BE TRUE TO YOU (1926)

REFRAIN: I've always wanted to be true to you
And when you came along
I made a vow to stick like glue to you
And then it all went wrong.
You were inclined to flirt a bit
But I didn't mind—I sighed awhile
Later, of course, it hurt a bit
I thought of divorce—and tried to smile
You never gave me what I most desired,
You seemed reserved and cold
Pretty soon I tired of remaining as good as
gold
Nothing you do can shame me now
It isn't for you to blame me now
For beating up the town
I always wanted to be true to you
Until you let me down.

*IT WAS HORRID

REFRAIN: It was horrid—
Everything was wrong
From A to Z.
Those boring days we knew,
Just you and me and you,
How gallantly we fought against the dread
Of going to bed.
We were dancing—and my shoe lace came
undone
While the crooner crooned that uninspiring
song.
Our love affair while active
Was certainly unattractive—
It was horrid and it lasted far too long.

The last line at least was to turn up in "The Parting Of The Ways" in his 1945 revue, *Sigh No More*.

*OLD STORY

A note, some flowers,
Some yearning, burning hours,
A honeymoon of thrills.
Some months elapse
A year or two perhaps
Then she starts to think a bit,
He starts to drink a bit. And
He makes a slip,
A Brighton business trip
With double hotel bills.
Very soon he's of course caught
They end in the Divorce Court
It's a story that's as old as the hills.

*THAT IS THE TIME TO GO

REFRAIN   When the hours
Cease to be enchanted,
When the flowers
Take the spring for granted,
When the skies look gray
That is the moment to ride away.
When the moon
Isn't so inviting,
When the tune
Isn't so exciting,
When the words aren't gay—
That is the moment to hide away.
Tho' romance may colour your story,
Harmonise your song.
Trailing clouds of passionate glory
Can't be kept up too long—so
When the sun
Ceases to be sunny,
When the fun
Isn't quite so funny,
When your secret heart says 'No'—
That is the time to go.

Seen in retrospect, it's an early expression of a theme he handled with more confidence in *Sail Away* (see p. 263).

126

*SOMETIMES WHEN I'M WEARY

VERSE 1 Sometimes when I'm weary and the world
seems grey
And the firelight flickers blue
Somewhere in the future, maybe far away
There's a dream that may come true
Hope may be a bubble that will vanish at a sigh
Joy may banish trouble e'er my youth has passed
me by.

VERSE 2 Life is just a silly game of make believe
Until true love comes your way,
Tho' a dreary pattern through the years you weave
There will always come a day
When your heart with happiness is bursting to be
free
Some time I may wake and find that day
Has dawned for me.

Then there was the Good News . . .

*SHE SHALL HAVE MUSIC

She shall have music
Wherever she goes,
Rings on her fingers
And bells on her toes
Wherever she goes—
She shall have music.

She shall have music
To help her to dream
Cartier bracelets
That glitter and gleam
Wherever she goes—
She shall have music.

She'll dance in only
Chinchilla and mink
Each time she's lonely
And feels her spirits sinking—
She shall have music.

*IS SHE HAPPY?

Is she happy? —I should say she was
She's as full of vim
As a funeral hymn
Never snappy—even when her man
Won't wear the socks she knits him
She just hits him—
Is she happy? —I should say she was
And the reason is because
Now she's married she is never bored,
She's got triplets and a baby Ford.
Is she happy?—I should say she was.

*THIS MOMENT

This moment, on the verge of life
No future shall betray
We'll hold it through a thousand dark
Decembers
Who cares, if in the surge of life
Some dreams are swept away?

Such dreams are what the sentimental heart
remembers
Sweeps other loves away
Here, as we planned, we will stand, hand
in hand
Just as close as we're standing today.

Noël was in the habit of tinkering with certain lyrics over time. He started his "Summertime" song as early as the 20s but was still playing with it as late as the 50s, when "peace" had become "rest," for instance. He never did find a home for it . . .

*HERE IN THE SUMMERTIME (1920s)

Here in the Summertime
Life is complete for us
Tender and sweet for us all.
Here in the Summertime
Each tired heart receives
Peace till the yellow leaves fall
Here like a flowing stream
Peace provides a theme
Fit for us to dream
Here in the Summertime

*HERE IN THE SUMMERTIME (1950s)

Here in the Summertime
Days gently come and go
Our happy world is so small.
Here in the Summertime
Each tired heart receives
Rest 'till the yellow leaves fall.
Here like a flowing stream
Peace provides a theme
Fit for us to dream.
Here in the Summertime
Life is complete for us
Tender and sweet for us all.

*COCKTAIL CHORUS

Cocktails, cocktails, we must have some
cocktails
Bring the ice and gin
We are just an alcoholic league, a
Parcel of meagre

Folk who are eager
To begin.

Mix them, mix them, hurry up and mix them,
Satisfy our lust
All our social fun will be spoiled
Unless we are oiled
So get a bit boiled
We simply must.

*TRAVEL IN A TRAIN WITH ME

It's simply wonderful
The places and the faces you'll see,
Travel in a train with me.
You can't imagine
The sensation and elation there'll be.
The Restaurant saloon
Is just the place for a honeymoon
And with you by my side
We'll whistle through the countryside—
Travel in a train with me.

*SATURDAY NIGHT

When the weary week has ended
Time ceases to be,
For a little while it seems
Life really is easy.
Through the dreary week we've wended,
All pleasure denied
But when he is by my side
Gay music will guide us.

Saturday night
My heart will be light,
I'll feel like Cinderella.
Now at last I can see
Stars are forecasting a dream for me.
He'll take my hand
And there we shall stand
Enchanted by a spell
Thanks to you
My dream may come true at first sight
On Saturday night.

*OH, BABY

Oh, Baby, with your roguish ways
And sympathetic smile
A sweet veneer which overlays
Such quantities of guile.
Your wistful yearning mother eyes
I watch with bated breath
Or when with little wifely cries
You fondle Charles to death.
I'll hitch my wagon to your star
From summer round to spring.
I know you just for what you are—
A winsome elfin thing!

What better way to end that irreverent decade than on an unfinished and slightly racous note? Scribbled on a scrap of paper is the "refrain" . . .

Any port in a storm, boys,
You can't afford to choose.
You take a look
And you drop your hook . . .

. . . and the rest he left to our imagination.

During the 1920s Noël kept up the habit of listing

the titles of songs he had in mind to write. Among those not destined to be heard were . . . .

Never Tell A Lie Unless You Have To
Love Can Make a Little Go a Long Long Way
If It's Done with Je Ne Sais Quoi
Cross Your T's and Dot Your I's (and Mind Your
    P's and Q's)
You Were a Very Good Baby (But You've Grown
    Into a Damn Bad Man)
What A Wonderful Time
I Wouldn't Mind
There Isn't Much a Fellow Can Do
Moyra
Victorian Girls
Why Not Leave Me Alone?
Andalusia
You Can't Go Wrong
If I Should Ever Travel
Give As Good As You Get
A Woman Always Knows
A Lady Lives and Learns
To Be Or Not To Be
I Am a Stranger Here

Looking back on the prolific decade, Noël's verdict was: "Everyone raves about the fabulous Twenties—I think the Thirties were much more exciting in the theatre."

THE 1930s

1930

February 1930 found Noël and Jeffrey Amherst, a regular travelling companion, wandering around the Far East. In the Imperial Hotel, Tokyo, Noël was awakened from sleep as "Gertie appeared in a white Molyneux dress on a terrace in the South of France and refused to leave until 4:00 A.M. by which time *Private Lives*, title and all, had constructed itself." A few weeks later in the Cathay Hotel, Shanghai, while recuperating from a bout of influenza, the play was written.

With that out of the way, they continued their voyage into Indo-China (now Vietnam). On the way from Hanoi to Tonkin a song popped into his head— "Mad Dogs and Englishmen."

"True the only white people to be seen were French, but one can't have everything . . . This drive took about a week and while jungles and river and mountain and rice fields were unrolling by the window of the car, I wrestled in my mind with the complicated rhythms and rhymes of the song until finally it was complete, without even the aid of pencil and paper. I sang it triumphantly and unaccompanied to my travelling companion on the verandah of a small jungle guest house. Not only Jeffrey, but the gekko lizards and the tree frogs gave every vocal indication of enthusiasm."

MAD DOGS AND ENGLISHMEN

In tropical climes there are certain times of day
When all the citizens retire
To tear their clothes off and perspire.
It's one of those rules that the greatest fools obey,
Because the sun is much too sultry
And one must avoid its ultry-violet ray.

Papalaka papalaka papalaka boo,
Papalaka papalaka papalaka boo,
Digariga digariga digariga doo,
Digariga digariga digariga doo.

The natives grieve when the white men leave
their huts,
Because they're obviously definitely nuts!

Mad dogs and Englishmen
Go out in the midday sun,
The Japanese don't care to.
The Chinese wouldn't dare to,
Hindoos and Argentines sleep firmly from twelve
to one.
But Englishmen detest a siesta.
In the Philippines
There are lovely screens
To protect you from the glare.
In the Malay States
There are hats like plates
Which the Britishers won't wear.
At twelve noon
The natives swoon
And no further work is done.
But mad dogs and Englishmen
Go out in the midday sun.

It's such a surprise for the Eastern eyes to see
That though the English are effete,
They're quite impervious to heat,
When the white man rides every native hides in
glee,
Because the simple creatures hope he
Will impale his solar topee on a tree.

Bolyboly bolyboly bolyboly baa,
Bolyboly bolyboly bolyboly baa,
Habaninny habaninny habaninny haa,
Habaninny habaninny habaninny haa.

It seems such a shame
When the English claim
The earth
That they give rise to such hilarity and mirth.

Below: Original lyrics in the Master's own hand.

Below left: Beatrice Lillie, "Mad Dogs and Englishmen" in Set To Music.

Mad dogs and Englishmen
Go out in the midday sun.
The toughest Burmese bandit
Can never understand it.
In Rangoon the heat of noon
Is just what the natives shun.
They put their Scotch or Rye down
And lie down.
In a jungle town
Where the sun beats down
To the rage of man and beast
The English garb
Of the English sahib
Merely gets a bit more creased.
In Bangkok
At twelve o'clock
They foam at the mouth and run,
But mad dogs and Englishmen
Go out in the midday sun.

Mad dogs and Englishmen
Go out in the midday sun.
The smallest Malay rabbit
Deplores this stupid habit.
In Hongkong
They strike a gong
And fire off a noonday gun
To reprimand each inmate
Who's in late.
In the mangrove swamps
Where the python romps
There is peace from twelve till two.
Even caribous
Lie around and snooze;
For there's nothing else to do.
In Bengal
To move at all
Is seldom, if ever done,
But mad dogs and Englishmen
Go out in the midday sun.

The song was first performed by Beatrice Lillie in the revue, *The Third Little Show* at the Music Box Theatre, New York on June 1, 1931 and subsequently in *Words and Music* by Romney Brent (who took the number over from John Mills after two out-of-town performances) "as a missionary in one of Britain's tropical colonies." After which Noël sang it himself in cabaret "*ad nauseam.*"

* * *

It once reached the level of an international incident—or rather, two. When Noël volunteered for service in World War II, he was told by Winston Churchill:

"'Get into a warship and see some action! Go and sing to them when the guns are firing—that's your job!' With, I think, commendable restraint, I bit back the retort that if the morale of the Royal Navy was at such low ebb that the troops were unable to go into action without my singing 'Mad Dogs and Englishmen' to them, we were in trouble at the outset and that, although theoretically 'Singing when the guns are firing' sounds extremely gallant, it is, in reality, impracticable, because during a naval battle all ship's companies are at action stations and the only place to sing would be in the ward-room by myself."

Churchill's answer was not one that pleased Noël—quite apart from the fact that his affection for the song—Noël said—"bordered on the pathological." Which led to the international incident.

Churchill hosted a dinner party in honour of President Roosevelt on board *H.M.S. Prince of Wales* on the evening following the signing of the Atlantic Charter. As the evening progressed the two men became involved in a heated argument, not over the future of civilisation as we know it but over whether "In Bangkok at twelve o'clock they foam at the mouth and run" came at the end of the first refrain or at the end of the second. Roosevelt adhered firmly to the latter view and remained unpersuaded by any amount of Churchillian rhetoric. When Noël later told Churchill that Roosevelt had been correct, Churchill was supposed to have muttered that "Britain can take it."

By way of a postscript, on a 90th birthday TV tribute to Winston that Noël compered Noël repeated the story and then proceeded to sing the "authorised" version to prove the point—except that he mixed up the second and third refrains *himself.* Churchill would have been perfectly entitled to ask for a recount . . .

* * *

Travel was a theme that threaded through the whole of Noël's life and work. A few years later—and with no specific show in mind—he was to write perhaps the most autobiographical of all his travel songs—"I Travel Alone." Although he usually took very good care to be accompanied on his trips, the sentiment foreshadows a remark he made in a late interview:

"I was born alone. I have lived my life more or less alone. And I expect I shall die alone." He was expressing a fear more than a fact and, luckily, it was not to come true. . .

I TRAVEL ALONE

VERSE
The world is wide, and when my day is done
I shall at least have travelled free,
Led by this wanderlust that turns my eyes to far
    horizons.
Though time and tide won't wait for anyone,
There's one illusion left for me
And that's the happiness I've known alone.

REFRAIN
I travel alone,
Sometimes I'm East,
Sometimes I'm West,
No chains can ever bind me;
No remembered love can ever find me;
I travel alone.
Fair though the faces and places I've known,
When the dream is ended and passion has flown
I travel alone.
Free from love's illusion, my heart is my own:
I travel alone.

The song was never in a show: "I wrote it and recorded it a trifle morosely and it sold, I believe, fairly well. I liked it at the time, but not to excess. It is one of the songs that people ask for at parties, not from any passionate desire to hear it but merely to prove their cleverness in remembering that I wrote it."

Noël composed and recorded the song in 1934. At that time jazz singer, Alberta Hunter was in cabaret at the Dorchester Hotel in London and Noël went along there frequently to hear her. Hunter was flattered when Noël asked her to make a demonstration recording of the song to take with him to the US. She was always convinced that he had written the song for her (she told her biographer), as the words applied as much to her life as to his.

PRIVATE LIVES

An Intimate Comedy in Three Acts

1930

First presented by Charles B. Cochran at the King's Theatre, Edinburgh on August 18, 1930. The production then toured Liverpool, Birmingham, Manchester and Southsea before opening at the Phoenix Theatre, London on September 24, 1930. (101 performances.)

The cast consisted of Noël Coward, Gertrude Lawrence, Laurence Olivier, Adrianne Allen and Everley Gregg.

Coward's "intimate comedy" saw the introduction of what many people consider his best love song. Elyot and Amanda have divorced and both of them have remarried. Fate decides to take a mischievous hand by placing the two new honeymoon couples not merely in the same hotel but in adjacent rooms. They meet on the balcony and the conversation is stilted to say the least, until the strains of the hotel orchestra reach them, playing a song that has a special meaning for each of them.

ELYOT: That orchestra seems to have a remarkably small repertoire.

AMANDA: Extraordinary how potent cheap music is.

Amanda begins to sing with the unseen orchestra . . .

SOMEDAY I'LL FIND YOU

VERSE 1   When one is lonely the days are long;
You seem so near
But never appear.
Each night I sing you a lover's song;
Please try, try to hear,
My dear, my dear.

VERSE 2   Can't you remember the fun we had?
Time is so fleet,
Why shouldn't we meet?
When you're away from me days are sad,
Life's not complete,
My sweet, my sweet.

REFRAIN   Some day I'll find you,
Moonlight behind you,
True to the dream I am dreaming

Gertrude Lawrence as Amanda and Noël Coward as Elyot across a balcony in Private Live.

As I draw near you
You'll smile a little smile;
For a little while
We shall stand
Hand in hand.
I'll leave you never,
Love you for ever,
All our past sorrow redeeming,
Try to make it true,
Say you love me too.
Someday I'll find you again.

ELYOT: You always had a sweet voice, Amanda.

AMANDA: Thank you.

"For me the memory of her standing on that moon-lit stage balcony in a dead-white Molyneux dress will never fade. She was the epitome of grace and charm and imperishable glamour . . . 'Someday I'll Find You,' among my sentimental songs, ranks next in popularity to 'I'll See You Again' and, now that Gertie is no longer alive, I find the nostalgia of it almost unbearable."

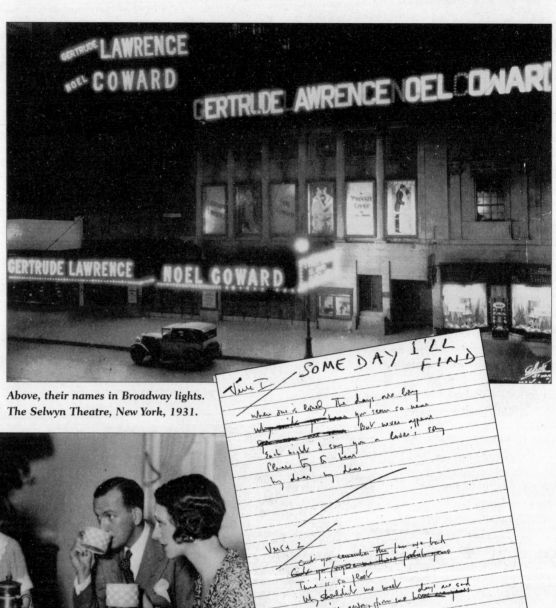

Above, their names in Broadway lights. The Selwyn Theatre, New York, 1931.

Left to right: Laurence Olivier, Adrianne Allen, Noël Coward and Gertrude Lawrence.

Someday I'll find you,
Moonlight behind you . . .

For everyone who swears that the quotation from Macbeth is "Lead on, Macduff," when it is, in fact, "*Lay* on, Macduff," you find a dozen Coward fans misquoting Amanda's line about "cheap music." For that we have Gertie to thank. The line in the *play* reads: "Extraordinary how potent cheap music is" but when Noël and Gertie recorded the scene, she managed to transform it to—"Strange how potent cheap music can be." Consequently, when the argument rages around—"Yes, but I heard her actually *say* "Strange," whoever says it will be right . . . but *she* was wrong.

*   *   *

Reflecting on the song in a 1970 interview, Noël hummed a few bars . . .

"Personally, from the point of view of lighting, I think I would always prefer the moonlight in front of me. It's not a lyric of high intellectual content, but it's a good opening phrase. I forget where I wrote it but it came very easily. Gertie Lawrence and I always liked a little sing occasionally, and as we were going to do a straight comedy, we thought we might have a song in it. You see, I was trained when I was very young as a show-off, and I've continued."

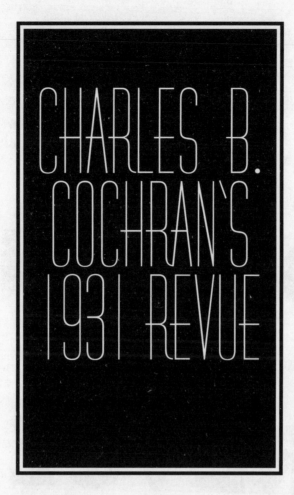

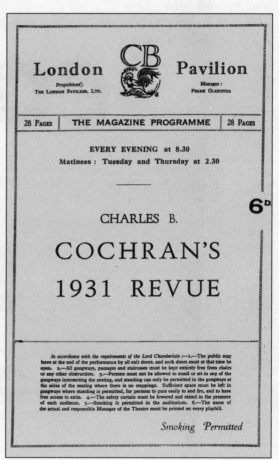

First presented at the Palace Theatre, Manchester on February 18, 1931 and subsequently at the London Pavilion on March 19, 1931. (27 performances.)

Although the program stated that the show had "Music by Noël Coward and others," this was in no sense a "Coward Revue." Apart from the Opening Chorus" featuring Mr. Cochran's Young Ladies *and* the John Tiller Girls, he contributed only four numbers . . .

1930: To mark the occasion of the continuing success of "Bitter Sweet." "Private Lives" was to open a month later in Edinburgh.

*OPENING CHORUS

Hooray, Hooray, Hooray,
Fling all your troubles away,
For this show will prove your wildest hopes,
For Mr. Cochran knows the ropes.
Hooroo, Hooroo, Hooroo.
Come here if you're feeling blue
And have a frolic of feast and fun

To cheer you up when work is done
At Mr. Cochran's 1931
Revue.

INTERLUDE

Ladies and Gentlemen,
We've come out here to warn you
If you're really expecting a lavish display
Far exceeding the price you've consented to pay
You had better retreat
And exchange your seats for *Bitter Sweet*
Or, failing this,
There's one thing that you shouldn't miss
If you're really requiring a cast of a million
And eighty-two changes of scene,
You'd better keep out of the London Pavilion

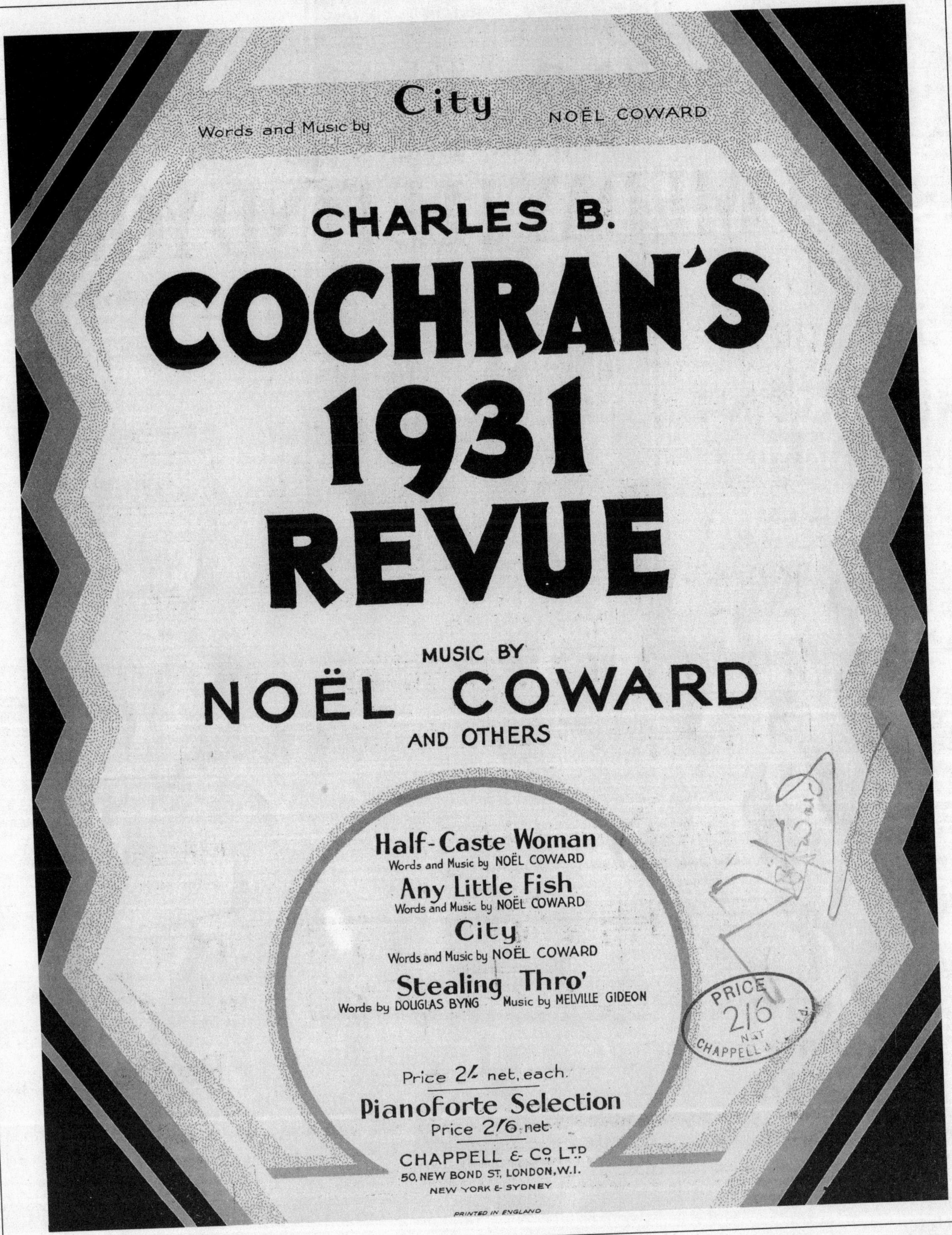
City
Words and Music by
NOËL COWARD
CHARLES B.
COCHRAN'S
1931
REVUE
MUSIC BY
NOËL COWARD
AND OTHERS
Half-Caste Woman
Words and Music by NOËL COWARD
Any Little Fish
Words and Music by NOËL COWARD
City
Words and Music by NOËL COWARD
Stealing Thro'
Words by DOUGLAS BYNG Music by MELVILLE GIDEON
PRICE 2/6 NET
Price 2/- net, each.
Pianoforte Selection
Price 2/6 net
CHAPPELL & Co. LTD
50, NEW BOND ST, LONDON, W.1.
NEW YORK & SYDNEY
PRINTED IN ENGLAND

And go to *Evergreen*.
Dear, dear, this is not so hot
What a cast we've got.

Ladies and Gentlemen,
From your dinner we've torn you
You will find that the score is excessively weak
And doubt if you'll think that the scenery's chic
You had much better go.
In us you've seen the best of it,
We're in the know
And tremble for the rest of it.
For you will find that the evening gets duller and
    duller
So listen to all we say
If you don't appreciate Clark and McCullough
Or care for Ada-May
For God's sake, keep away!

CITY

(Bernardi)

Only one among millions,
Life's a sad routine,
Striving for a goal that hasn't a meaning,
Lonely, living in shadow, part of a machine,
Rising from despair, the buildings are leaning,
Nearer, nearer each day, pressing life away.

REFRAIN 1
City, why are you casting this spell on me?
City, what if you crumbled and fell on me!
Unbelievably tiring,
Life passes by me;
Noise and speed are conspiring
To crucify me,
Ever making me crawl for my daily bread,
Never letting me rest till my dreams are dead.
Every weary prisoner
Some day must be free;
City, have pity on me!

INTERLUDE
Day in, day out,
Life will be soon over and done.
Where has it led and why?
Day in, day out,
Where is the moon?
Where is the sun?

Where is the open sky?
Ever seeking, and believing
There is hope for us all.

Sirens shrieking, progress weaving
Poor humanity's pall.
Iron, rot, steel, rust,
Speed, noise, death, dust,
Why should we work?
Why should we live?
Why should we even die?

REFRAIN 2
City, why are you casting this spell on me?
City, what if you crumbled and fell on me?
Unbelievably tiring,
Life passes by me;
Noise and speed are conspiring
To crucify me,
Ever making me crawl for my daily bread,
Never letting me rest till my dreams are dead.
Every weary prisoner
Some day must be free;
City, please have pity on me!

BRIGHT YOUNG PEOPLE

---

*(Queenie Leonard, Edward Cooper
and Effie Atherton)*

VERSE   Look at us three,
Representative we
Of a nation renowned for virility.
We've formed a cult of puerility
Just for fun.
You may deplore
The effects of war
Which are causing the world to decay a bit.
We've found our place and will play a bit
In the sun.
Though Waterloo was won upon the playing fields
    of Eton,
The next war will be photographed, and lost, by
    Cecil Beaton.

REFRAIN 1   Bright young people,
Ready to do and to dare
We casually strive
To keep London alive

From Chelsea to Bloomsbury Square.
We fondly imagine we're cynical elves,
In charity tableaux we pose upon shelves.
It's just an excuse to exhibit ourselves.
What could be duller than that?

REFRAIN 2   Bright young people,
Gay to the utmost degree
We play funny jokes
On more dignified folks
And laugh with extravagant glee.
We give lovely parties that last through the night,
I dress as a woman and scream with delight,
We wake up at lunch time and find we're still
    tight.
What could be duller than that?

VERSE 2   Things that we do
'Neath the Red, White and Blue,
Though they can't be called happy or glorious,
Certainly keep us notorious.
And it's grand.
We've made some chums
In the heart of the slums,
And we ask to our parties the rougher ones.
We find the low class and tougher ones,
    understand,
We know a darling Bolshevik
Who's taught us Dosvidanya
And he can sing 'God Save the King'
And lovely 'Rule Britannia'.

**Impresario Charles B. Cochran
by Max Beerbohm.**

140

REFRAIN 3 Bright young people,
Don't think our lives are not full.
I make little hats
From Victorian mats
And I work in tin-foil and wool.
Our critics are often excessively rude,
To one of my portraits they always allude:
It's me, worked in beads, upside down, in the
nude.
What could be duller than that?

REFRAIN 4 Bright young people,
Making the most of our youth.
They speak in the Press
Of our social success,
But quite the reverse is the truth.
Psychology experts we often perplex
And doctors have warned us we'll end up as
wrecks.
They take a degree if they find out our sex.
What could be duller than that?

Neither song survived in the hearts and minds of
Coward or his admirers but the next one did sneak in
and still holds a playful place of its own . . .

ANY LITTLE FISH
(I CAN'T DO ANYTHING AT
ALL BUT JUST LOVE YOU)

(Ada-May)

VERSE
I've fallen in love with you,
I'm taking it badly,
Freezing, burning,
Tossing, turning,
Never know when to laugh or cry,
Just look what our dumb friends do, they
welcome it gladly.
Passion in a dromedary doesn't go so deep,
Camels when they're mating never sob
themselves to sleep,
Buffaloes can revel in it, so can any sheep;
Why can't I?

REFRAIN 1
Any little fish can swim, any little bird can fly,
Any little dog and any little cat
Can do a bit of this and just a bit of that;
Any little horse can neigh, and any little cow
can moo,
But I can't do anything at all
But just love you.

REFRAIN 2
Any little cock can crow, any little fox can run,
Any little crab on any little shore
Can have a little dab and then a little more;
Any little owl can hoot, and any little dove can
coo,
But I can't do anything at all but just love you.

VERSE
You've pulled me across the brink,
You've chained me and bound me,
No escape now,
Buy the crepe now,
When is the funeral going to be?

Whenever I stop to think,
See nature all around me,
Then I see how stupidly monogamous I am,
A lion in the circumstances wouldn't give a damn,
For if there was no lioness he'd lie down with a
lamb;
Why can't I?

REFRAIN 3
Any little bug can bite, any little bee can
buzz,
Any little snail on any little oak
Can feel a little frail and have a little joke;
Any little frog can jump like any little kangaroo,
But I can't do anything at all but just love you.

REFRAIN 4
Any little duck can quack, any little worm
can crawl,
Any little mole can frolic in the sun
And make a little hole and have a little fun;
Any little snake can hiss in any little local zoo,
But I can't do anything at all but just love you.

Set design for "Half-Caste Woman."

It was to become a song Noël "always found very useful. It is bright and snappy and over quickly, and when sung with sufficient grimaces and innuendoes it can be tolerably suggestive."

He never felt, on the other hand, that "poor 'Half-Caste Woman' ever had a fair deal." Sung in the revue by Ada-May, performed later that same year by torch singer, Helen Morgan in *The Ziegfeld Follies of 1931*, the number in Noël's view was a "flop." Even his own recording of it "is only adequate." Perhaps what the song experienced was the first stirring of political correctness!

HALF-CASTE WOMAN

Drink a bit, laugh a bit, love a bit more,
I can supply your need,
Think a bit, chaff a bit, what's it all for?
That's my Eurasian creed.
Sailors with sentimental hearts who love and sail
    away,
When the dawn is grey
Look at me and say—

REFRAIN   Half-caste woman, living a life apart,
  Where did your story begin?
Half-caste woman, have you a secret heart
  Waiting for someone to win?
Were you born of some queer magic
In your shimmering gown?
Is there something strange and tragic
Deep, deep down?
Half-caste woman, what are your slanting eyes
Waiting and hoping to see?
Scanning the far horizon
Wondering what the end will be.

Down along the river
The sky is aquiver
For dawn is beginning to break;
Hear the sirens wailing,
Some big ship is sailing
And losing my dreams in its wake.
Why should I remember the things that are
    past,
Moments so swiftly gone;
Why worry, for the Lord knows time goes on.
Go to bed in daylight,

Try to sleep in vain,
Get up in the evening
Work begins again,
Tinker, tailor, soldier, sailor,
Rich man, poor man, beggar man, thief,
Questioning the same refrain.

A number that was used in Manchester but didn't survive the transfer to London was "Foolish Virgins." It turned up later in *Operette* (see p. 186) in a significantly altered form.

*FOOLISH VIRGINS

*(Effie Atherton, Queenie Leonard
and Jane Welsh)*

VERSE: We may be young,
  We may be gay,
  We may be brimming with the effervescent
  Fragrance of our adolescent status.
  We may be flung
  Some sunny day
  Into the arms of some embarrassed squire who
  Cherishes a rash desire to—mate us.
  As an exact
  Matter of fact
  We're quite prepared for the fray
  And as we have planned
  To honour, love and obey,
  We'll play the game
  But all the same
  Please understand we're a triumvirate who
  Need a most substantial bait to—bait us!

REFRAIN I
  We're young girls of more or less high degree,
  Our reputations not about yet,
  We haven't properly come out yet.
  So far we've played our lives in rather a minor
    key
  But while we adolescence
  We progress
  Later on you'll see.
  Tho' we prattle brightly in our girlish way,
  We shall alter slightly on our wedding day
  Who knows what our innermost thoughts
    may be
  Oh dear—ha ha—ha ha—Foolish Virgins we!

*Ada-May sings
"Half-Caste
Woman."*

REFRAIN 2 We're young girls of more or less high degree,
  Because we're winsome and alluring,
  Don't think our minds are not maturing,
  Tho' we appear to be such thoroughly 'jeune'
    'Jeunes Filles',
  We're merely marking time
  Till we climb
  Up the social tree.
  Tho' we giggle sweetly in our bridal veils,
  As we're led discreetly to the altar rails,
  God preserve our husbands that are to be
  Oh dear—ha ha—ha ha—Foolish Virgins we!

In the submission to the Lord Chamberlain's Office he also included "Mad Dogs" but must have decided to hold it back for his next "real" revue the following year.

CAVALCADE

1931

144 *First presented by Charles B. Cochran at the Theatre Royal, Drury Lane on October 13, 1931. (405 performances.)*

The cast included Mary Clare, Edward Sinclair, Una O'Connor, Fred Groves, Irene Browne, Alison Leggatt, John Mills, Arthur Macrae and Binnie Barnes.

Noël was to write in *Present Indicative* that "The emotional basis of *Cavalcade* was undoubtedly music. The whole story was threaded on to a string of popular melodies . . . Popular tunes probe the memory more swiftly than anything else, and *Cavalcade*, whatever else it did, certainly awakened many echoes."

During the run of *Private Lives* Noël and Cochran had discussed the idea of doing a big spectacular production at the Coliseum, at that time the home of such shows. After dismissing "a series of tremendous mob scenes," such as the storming of the Bastille or the massacre of the Huguenots—"I believe even the Decline and Fall of the Roman Empire flirted with me for a little"—he happened to find himself one day at Foyle's book shop in the Charing Cross Road, where "some ancient bound volumes of *Black and White* and the *Illustrated London News*" caught his eye. The first one he opened dealt with the Boer War. "I can't explain why it rang the bell so sharply, I only know that it did. The tunes came into my mind first, tunes belonging to my very earliest childhood: "'Dolly Gray,' 'The Absent-Minded Beggar,' 'Soldiers of the Queen' . . ."

"Events took precedence in my mind, and against them I moved a group of people . . ." It would not be enough to skate on the surface, as he had frequently managed to do in the past. "I had flogged the bright young people enough, my vehemence against them had congealed, they were now no more than damp squibs, my Poor Little Rich Girls and Dance, Little Ladies." The plot he finally constructed would follow the story of a family (the Marryots) and their upstairs/downstairs servants (the Bridges) from New Year's Eve 1899 to New Year's Eve 1930.

As well as the period songs that punctuated and underlined the plot, Noël introduced a few of his own. In the first instance he used a device that he would utilise more than once in the future—the show-within-a-show. Jane Marryot and a friend spend an evening at the musical comedy, *Mirabelle*. They sit in their box and watch a sextet in uniform sing "Girls of the C.I.V."

THE GIRLS OF THE C.I.V.

We're the girls of the C.I.V.
Form fours, get in line, one two three,
For our bravery is such
That the Boers won't like it much
When we chase them across the veldt and teach
    them Double Dutch
We're the girls of the C.I.V.
And we're out for a lark and a spree.
In our uniforms so stunning,
We shall soon have Kruger running
From the girls of the C.I.V.

Then Mirabelle herself (a princess disguised as a village maiden) sings with her suitor the Mirabelle Waltz, "Lover of My Dreams." . . .

"It was really written as a satire on the popular musical comedy waltzes of the period, i.e. 1900. The words are deliberately trite and so is the tune, but it has a certain charm, I think."

THE MIRABELLE WALTZ (LOVER OF MY DREAMS)

(Strella Wilson)

SHE: A simple country maid am I,
       As innocent as any flower.
       The great big world has passed me by,
       No lover comes my way to greet me shyly in
          my bower

HE: Oh, say not so!
       Such modesty enchants me:
       Could I but stay to while away with you a
          happy hour.

SHE: It must be Spring that fills my heart to
          overflowing,
       Ah, whither am I going?
       What is the voice that seems to say:
       Be kind to love, don't let him call to you
          unknowing.

HE: If true love comes to you don't turn your
          face away.

"The Marryots and the Bridges" in 1900: Left to right, Edward Sinclair, Mary Clare, Una O'Connor and Fred Groves.

SHE: Maybe 'tis something in the air:
For Spring is made for lovers only.

HE: Live for the moment and take care
Lest love should fly and leave us lonely.
Ah, if love should leave us lonely.

REFRAIN

SHE: All my life I have been waiting
Dreaming ages through;
Until today I suddenly discover
The form and face of he who is my lover.
No more tears and hesitating;
Fate has sent me you.
Time and tide can never sever
Those whom love has bound for ever,
Dear Lover of my Dreams come true.

Next comes the comedy number—Ada, the dairy-maid (really the Princess's lady-in-waiting) and Tom, the sailor, sing "Fun of the Farm."

ALL THE FUN OF THE FARM

VERSE

ADA: Though sailors are so brave and bold,
It really must be dreadfully cold
To sail across the sea

TOM: I quite agree
I quite agree,
I'm sick of the ocean wild and free,
Heigho, heigho, this is the place for me.

ADA: Now I am weary of the town
And feel inclined to settle down,
A milk pail on my arm.

TOM: I feel afraid
A London Maid
Would never know how the eggs are laid.

ADA: I'd find a cow
And milk til the pail was full

TOM: I'd shear the sow
And probably milk the bull.

BOTH: You must agree
That it would be
The height of true rusticity
If you and I should settle on a farm.

REFRAIN

BOTH: Oh, the Fun of the Farmyard,
The roosters are crowing,
The cattle are lowing,
The turkeys go gobbly gobbly goo,
This really is an alarm yard

ADA: Like Little Bo-Peep,
I lose my sheep
And cannot find them anywhere

TOM: I ought to be shot,
For I forgot
To coax the horse to meet the mare.

BOTH: Who left the canary
Locked up in the dairy?

ADA: Cheep, cheep, cheep, cheep,

TOM: Snort, snort, snort, snort

ADA: Moo, moo, moo, moo,

TOM: Cock a doodle doodle do!

BOTH: Oh, dear, far from being a calm yard,
Quack, quack, quack, quack,
All the fun of the farm.

Just as the "show" reaches its finale, the stage manager interrupts with the news—"Mafeking has been relieved!"

*   *   *

At the end of the show the principal members of the cast are in a night club on New Year's Eve 1930. At the piano Fanny (the Bridges' daughter) sings "Twentieth Century Blues," Noël's summation of the century so far. Looking back, he found it "ironic in theme and musically rather untidy. It is also exceedingly difficult to sing, but in the play it achieved its purpose. It struck the required note of harsh discordancy and typified, within its frame, the curious, hectic desperation I wished to convey."

TWENTIETH CENTURY BLUES

(Binnie Barnes)

VERSE Why is it that civilized humanity
Must make the world so wrong?
In this hurly-burly of insanity
Our dreams cannot last long.

We've reached a deadline—
The Press headline—every sorrow,
Blues value
Is News value
Tomorrow.

REFRAIN Blues,
Twentieth Century Blues,
Are getting me down.
Who's
Escaped those weary
Twentieth Century Blues?
Why,
If there's a God in the sky,
Why shouldn't he grin?
High
Above this dreary
Twentieth Century din,
In this strange illusion,
Chaos and confusion,
People seem to lose their way.
What is there to strive for,
Love or keep alive for?Say—
Hey, hey, call it a day.
Blues,
Nothing to win or to lose.
It's getting me down.
Blues,
I've got those weary Twentieth Century
Blues.

New Year's Eve, December 31, 1930, Binnie Barnes as Fanny Bridges sings "Twentieth Cenury Blues."

WORDS
AND MUSIC

REVUE

1932

First presented by Charles B. Cochran at the Opera House, Manchester on August 25, 1932 and subsequently at the Adelphi Theatre, London on September 16, 1932. (164 performances.)

Cast included Ivy St. Helier, Joyce Barbour, John Mills, Doris Hare, Edward Underdown, Romney Brent, Effie Atherton, Moya Nugent and Master Graham Payn.

This was the revue that included the English premiere of "Mad Dogs and Englishmen," a fact which tends to overshadow the many and varied other numbers Coward wrote for it.

It began with a song which supposedly revealed the inner thoughts of Mr. Cochran's fabled "young ladies." Like Ziegfeld, Cochran was inclined to solve every problem by putting on the girls to distract the audience—hence . . .

> We're Mr. Cochran's Young Invincibles,
> He much prefers us to the Principals,
> For every scene he cuts out
> He says, "Just send the Sluts out"
> And that's the reason why we have to work
>   our guts out.

OPENING CHORUS: MAGGIE

(Ivy St. Helier and Girls)

GIRLS: We shan't be on tonight,
We shan't be on tonight.
Because the overture is near
We're paralysed with fear.
The opening chorus
Is too complicated for us.
In this damned Revue
We've far too much to do,
We sing till our throats are aching,
Dance till our backs are breaking.
During the applause
We rush and change our drawers,
Tearing at ribbons while our hands are
    shaking,
Always getting dressed
Without a moment's rest,
We're worked to death,
Out of breath,
Nervous of every music cue,

Anxious the whole performance through.
Maggie!
Have you the scissors handy?
Maggie!
We want a port and brandy.
Maggie!
Our brassières don't set right.
Maggie!
We've upset all our wet-white.

MAGGIE: Oh my God, don't hurry me,
You'll miss your entrance if you worry me,
Flurry me.

GIRLS: Maggie!
These aren't our first-act stockings.
Maggie!
Our shoes are tight.
Maggie! Maggie!
Our trunks are far too baggy.
We shan't be on tonight.

MAGGIE: Now, Freda dear, you must
Do something with your bust.
You'd best tie a knot, dear,
You can't show them all you've got, dear.
Dorothy my duck,
Your eyelashes ain't stuck,
You can't look in every scene, dear,
Just like an Aberdeen, dear.
Rosie, hold this pin
And keep your stomach in
And don't do a pratfall in your first routine,
    dear.

Nora, there's a smear
Of eye-black on your ear.
You must look right
Every night,
You know until the show is through
I have to take the blame for you.

GIRLS: Maggie!
We want an orange stick, dear.
Maggie!
We're feeling rather sick, dear.
Maggie!
Our mirrors need adjusting.
Maggie!
Our make-ups look disgusting.

MAGGIE: Oh, my God, don't hurry me,
You'll miss your entrance if you worry me,
Flurry me.

GIRLS: Maggie!
Our shoulder straps are slipping.
Maggie!
There's nothing right.
Maggie! Maggie!
They've made our wigs too shaggy.
We shan't be on tonight.
Maggie! Maggie! Maggie! Maggie!
Maggie! Maggie!
Maggie! Maggie! Maggie! Maggie!
We shan't be on tonight.

CALLBOY: Overture Beginners!

GIRLS: La lalalalalala

Ivy St. Helier as Maggie and Mr. Cochran's Young Ladies.

Lalalalala la
La lalalalalalala
Lalalalala la.

CALLBOY: Overture Beginners!

MAGGIE: All right, all right.

GIRLS: La lalalala la la la
La lalalala la la la
La lalalala la la la
La lalalala la la la.
We shan't be on tonight,
We shan't be on tonight.

MAGGIE: They must look right
Every night.
Worked to death,
Out of breath,
I'll stay and tidy up a bit
And pray the blasted show's a hit!

GIRLS: Good evening, Ladies and Gentlemen,
You'll be tickled to death
To recognize the Chorus
And as we're opening the show
It's really comforting now and then
To discover for once
That you are here before us.
It may astonish you to know
We're Mr Cochran's Young Invincibles,
He much prefers us to the Principals,
For every scene he cuts out
He says, 'Just send the Sluts out'
And that's the reason why we have to work
our guts out.

GIRLS: Hallo!
We're always on the trigger.
Please note our girlish vigour.
Hallo!
We have to hop and bustle.
Hallo!
We're straining every muscle.
While we break our necks we feel
That so much animation wrecks appeal.
Sex appeal
Never
Can show when there's too much
Endeavour.
It lays us low,
We don't mind now,
We're really quite resigned now.
Hallo! Hallo! Hallo!

To demonstrate his even-handedness, Noël then turned his attention to . . .

THE DEBUTANTES (3 SEQUENCES)

(Phyllis Harding, Betty Hare, Moya Nugent)

1 Four little Debutantes are we,
Born of these restless, changing years,
Conscious of vague, unwilling fears,
What is our Destiny to be?
Shall we escape the strange 'Ennui'
Of civilized futility?
When we are old and wearied through
Shall we regret how wise we were?
Shall we at last have time to spare
Tears for the dreams we never knew?

2 The Gin is lasting out,
No matter whose,
We're merely casting out
The Blues,
For Gin, in cruel
Sober truth,
Supplies the fuel
For flaming youth.
A drink is known
To help a dream along,
A Saxophone
Provides our Theme Song,
Though we dishevel
Our girlish bloom
To the Devil
With Gloom!

The Gin is lasting out,
No matter whose,
We're merely casting out
The Blues,
For Gin, in cruel
Sober truth,
Supplies the fuel
For flaming youth,
We can't refuse,
The Gin is lasting out,
We're merely casting out
The Blues!

Prelude to Finale
Four little Debutantes, so tired.
Yearning to seek our virgin beds,

Longing to rest our aching heads,
Weary of all that we desired,
When in the morning we awake
Shall we be glad to undertake
Further exhausting hours among
Pleasures and joys so carefully planned,
Shall we continue to withstand
The heavy task of being young?

The Debutantes were to cause one of the few arguments between Noël and C.B.Cochran in their ten year association. In one of his several autobiographies, *Cock-A-Doodle-Do* (1941) Cockie recalled:

"What came in for the most unfavourable comment from audiences was the appearance from time to time of the three debutantes, 'bright young things' of Coward's earlier period, now burdened with depression and disillusionment.

While I saw what Coward the satirist was seriously driving at through these characters, I knew that they could never be popular in revue, which, like the Spanish matador, hangs bright streamers and flowers on its sharpest barbs. Their words and their musical theme were alike depressing, but Noël felt they were so much part of the whole pattern of the revue as he had planned it, that he could not consent to cut them."

Cochran also felt in retrospect that the whole concept of a revue "planned, written, composed and directed throughout by one brain" was fatally flawed . . . "in revue homogeneity may lead to monotony; the essence of revue is variety, rapidity, change of mood, and contrast of line and colour. Coward's scheme was an interesting experiment, but not sufficiently varied to be popular."

LET'S LIVE DANGEROUSLY

(John Mills and Doris Hare)

VERSE Life won't fool us,
Because we're out to lick it,
We've got its ticket
And we'll kick it
In the pants.
Fate will never catch us asleep,
We'll be ready to leap

*Joyce Barbour
and "Children
of the Ritz."*

When there's the slightest chance.
Life won't rule us,
Determined to subdue it
We'll give the raspberry to it,
Do it in the eye.
We believe in following through
All we're ready to do
Or die.

REFRAIN   Let's live dangerously dangerously
                 dangerously,
Let's grab every opportunity we can,
Let's swill
Each pill
Destiny has in store,
Absorbing life at every pore
We'll scream and yell for more.
Let's live turbulently turbulently turbulently,

Let's add something to the history of man,
Come what may
We'll be spectacular
And say, 'Hey! Hey!'
In the vernacular,
And so until we break beneath the strain
In various ways
We're going to be raising Cain.

REFRAIN 2 Let's live dangerously dangerously
                 dangerously,
Let's all glory in the bludgeonings of chance,
Let's win
Out in
Spite of the angry crowd,
And if the simile's allowed
Be bloody but unbowed.
Let's live boisterously boisterously

roisterously,
Let's lead moralists the devil of a dance,
Let's succumb
Completely to temptation,
Probe and plumb
To find a new sensation,
Where we'll end up
Nobody can tell,
So pardon the phrase,
We mean to be raising Hell!

*   *   *

The Ritz Hotel clearly loomed large in Noël's mytho-
logy. His unpublished play, *Semi-Monde* had originally
been called *Ritz Bar*, while his "Poor Little Ritz Girl"
grew up to become one of the "Children of the Ritz" …

CHILDREN OF THE RITZ

(Joyce Barbour and Company)

PART 1   Children of the Ritz,
Children of the Ritz,
Sleek and civilized—fretfully surprised,
Though Mr Molyneux has gowned us
The world is tumbling around us,
Without a sou
What can we do?
We'll soon be begging for a crust,
We can't survive
And keep alive
Without the darling Banker's Trust,
In the lovely gay
Years before the Crash
Mr Cartier
Never asked for cash,
Now shops we patronized are serving us
    with writs,
What's going to happen to the Children
    of the Ritz?
We owe Elizabeth Arden
Several thousand pounds,
Though we can't pay
We just blow in
If we're passing that way,
While we're going
On our rounds,
We'll persevere
Till our arteries harden,
Then we shan't much care
Whether our chins
Have a crinkle in them,
Whether our skins
Have a wrinkle here and there,
We shan't much mind
For we shall then have left our dreary lives
    behind.

Children of the Ritz,
Children of the Ritz,
Vaguely debonair,
Only half aware
That all we've counted on is breaking into bits,
What shall we do,
What's going to happen to
The foolish little Children of the Ritz?

PART 2   Children of the Ritz,
Children of the Ritz,
Mentally congealed
Lilies of the Field
We say just how we want our quails done,
And then we go and have our nails done,
Each single year
We all appear
At Monte Carlo or at Cannes,
We lie in flocks
Along the rocks
Because we have to get a Tan.
Though we never work,
Though we always play,
Though we always shirk
Things we ought to pay,
Whatever crimes the Proletariat commits
It can't be beastly to the Children of the Ritz.

We all economize madly
Now in every way,
Only one car,
An Isotta,
Though it doesn't go far
Still we potter
Through the day,
The times are changing—
We realize sadly
That we're near the brink.
Nothing to wear

We're in tatters
And we honestly swear
That it shatters us to think,
It's really grim
To wonder just how long we're going to sink or
    swim.

Children of the Ritz,
Children of the Ritz,
Though our day is past—
Gallant to the last—
Without the wherewithal to live upon our wits.
Please say a prayer
For all the frail and fair
And futile little Children of the Ritz.

In the London production—as opposed to the earlier New York performance—"Mad Dogs" was part of a sketch, which also included the lament of the Planters' Wives . . .

PLANTERS' WIVES

CHORUS

The Sun never sets on Government House
For English Might
Selected the site.

No matter how much the Communists grouse
The Sun never sets on Government House.

The Sun never sets on Government House,
The Nation smiles
O'er thousands of miles,
No matter how much we sozzle and souse
The Sun never sets on Government House.

PLANTER'S WIVES:

Our Husbands deal in Sugar and in Rubber,
Our Husbands deal in Coffee and in Tea,
Whenever we meet the Vicar's wife we snub her
To prove our vast superiority,
We're usually sour and apathetic
In tropical heat,
Nobody who's sweet survives,
We powder and primp
And try to be sympathetic,
Oh dear,
It's queer
That only with men
We're thoroughly energetic,
We're Planters' Wives

One of the romantic duets from the show was "Let's Say Goodbye," which in retrospect Noël classified as "the forerunner of several songs in the same genre: 'Thanks For the Memory,' 'Let's Call It a Day,' 'It Was Swell While It Lasted,' etc. Its emphasis is on the transience of physical passion . . . Wise advice indeed but not in strict accordance with the views of the Church of England."

LET'S SAY GOODBYE

(Rita Lyle and Edward Underdown)

VERSE   Now we've embarked on this foolish game
    Don't let's destroy it with tears.
    Once we begin

To let sentiment in
Happiness disappears.
Reason may sleep
For a moment in Spring
But please let us keep
This a casual thing,
Something that's sweet
To remember through the years.

REFRAIN   Let our affair be a gay thing
And when these hours have flown
Then, without forgetting
Happiness that has passed,
There'll be no regretting
Fun that didn't quite last.
Let's look on love as a plaything.
All these sweet moments we've known
Mustn't be degraded,
When the thrill of them has faded
Let's say, 'Good-bye' and leave it alone.

THREE WHITE FEATHERS

(Edward Underdown and Doris Hare)

VERSE 1   I can't help feeling
Fate's made a fool of me rather,
It placed me where I shouldn't be
And really couldn't be by rights;
We lived at Ealing,
Me and me mother and father;
I've scaled the social ladder
And I've never had a head for heights;
We had a pawnshop on the corner of
    the street,
And Father did a roaring trade.
I used to think those rings and necklaces
    were sweet,
Now I wouldn't give them to my maid.

REFRAIN 1   I've travelled a long long way
And the journey hasn't been all jam;
I must admit
The Rolls in which I sit
Is one up on the dear old tram;
I say to myself each day
In definitely Marble Halls,
Today it may be three white feathers,
But yesterday it was three brass balls.

VERSE 2   By easy stages
Though my beginnings were humble
I've studied each small movement
Of my self-improvement
From the start;
I've toured for ages,
I'll never falter or stumble;
I'll give an air of breeding
And a first-rate reading
Of the part;
You must forgive me if I kid myself a bit
In me tiara and me gown,
And though my accent may not altogether
    fit,
Don't be afraid I'll let you down.

REFRAIN 2   I've travelled a long long way
And had a lot of jolts and bumps;
I'll concentrate
And be ahead of fate,
Whichever way the old cat jumps;
I'll wink as I slyly drink
To the ancestors who line our halls,
Today it may be three white feathers,
But yesterday it was three brass balls.

REFRAIN 3   I've travelled a long long way
And now I've found the man I love;
I'll do my share, so long as he is there,
To help me with a gentle shove . . .

(She stops singing)
We're moving.

HALL OF FAME

ANNOUNCEMENT

Ladies and Gentlemen,
In this peculiar Era
Communal unity
Is daily drawing nearer,
We are indebted to the papers
For thus dispersing of the vapours
Which have hitherto concealed
A lot of simple lives that should have been
    revealed.
Think what Publicity
Means to the teeming masses,
Think what it signifies
To all those lads and lasses

Who, but for being advertised,
Might have lived all their days unrecognized,
So we and they together bless
The kindly efforts of the Press.

The Man who Caught the Biggest Shrimp

I'm the man who caught the biggest shrimp in
    the world
And the second biggest prawn as well,
I live at Ryde
And I take great pride
In the tale I have to tell.
The Reporters flock
To examine every rock
And to explore each stretch of sand,
Though why they choose
Me to figure in the News
I shall never understand.

The Oldest Postmistress in England

I'm the very oldest Postmistress in England
And probably the oldest on the Earth,
I've been asked by all the Papers for a statement
So I give you these few facts for what they're
    worth.
My appetite is absolutely splendid,
There's nothing in the world I can't digest,
I seldom feel uneasy or distended
And I'm never disagreeable or depressed,
I still deliver all the letters daily,
Though my memory is just as good as new
I've a hazy recollection of Disraeli
And I lived in Bray in Eighteen Forty-Two,
I think the Modern Girl is very pretty,
I've never smoked a single cigarette,
I think all this Divorcing is a pity
And I'm sorry that the Nation is upset,
I well recall in Eighteen Thirty-Seven
My parents lived in Weston-Super-Mare,
I'm actually one hundred and eleven
But I cannot see why anyone should care!

The Man who Rowed Across Lake Windermere
in an Indiarubber Bath

For years and years and years and years
I've burned to satisfy
A passionate desire in me
To catch the Public Eye,
When living in obscurity
In Station Road, Penarth,
I thought of crossing Windermere
In an indiarubber bath.

ALL: He rowed across Lake Windermere
In an indiarubber bath!

The Press responded to a man,
I'm known from coast to coast
And eighty lonely women
Have proposed to me by post,
I'm made a lifelong member
Of a most exclusive Club
For I rowed across Lake Windermere
In an indiarubber tub.

ALL: He rowed across Lake Windermere
In an indiarubber tub!

I'm grateful to the *Mirror*
And the *Sketch* for my success
And also to the *Telegraph*,
The *Mail*, and the *Express*.
It doesn't matter now to me
What shadows cross my path
For I rowed across Lake Windermere
In an indiarubber bath.

ALL: He rowed across Lake Windermere
In an indiarubber bath!

The Holiday Mermaid

I'm a Typist from Putney, and once every year
I stay with my aunt at Torquay
And last time I went there, as no one was near,
I decided to bathe in the sea,
I'd put on me costume and folded me frock
And was tying me 'air in a veil
When two men nipped out from behind a big
    rock
And gave me this kid with a pail,
Now me face wasn't powdered, me fringe wasn't
    curled,
And me parents are properly wild
'Cos me photo's been published all over the
    world
As a 'Holiday Mermaid with Child'!

The Clergyman Who's Never Been to London

I'm the Clergyman who's never been to
    London,
I'm the Clergyman who's never been to Town,
An enterprising journalist approached me
And every word I said he jotted down,
I had to face a battery of cameras
And hold an extra service in the snow
And all because I've never been to London
And haven't got the least desire to go!

My Life Story

I've been paid by kind Lord Rotherbrook
A very handsome sum
Though I'm stupid and illiterate
And practically dumb.
I cannot really count
How many choruses I've graced
But the story of my life
Is in the very best of taste.
I was on the stage at seventeen
And off at twenty-three
And living with a business man
At Birchington-on-Sea.
My appendix caused me trouble
And in order to survive
I had it taken out three times
In nineteen twenty-five.
In April nineteen twenty-eight
I married Lord St Lyne,
Divorcing him in January
Nineteen twenty-nine.
I've been photographed four hundred times
On foot, and in my car,
And that's the human story
Of how I became a Star!

Choral Finale

Long live the Press,
Long live the Press,
We're grateful for its subtlety,
Its power and its finesse,
It's brought us from obscurity
To well-deserved success,
Long live the Daily Press!

*   *   *

Not for the first time Noël had a run in with the Lord Chamberlain's Office, which acted as a censor of questionable material. They'd picked on and nearly banned *The Vortex* for being about drugs. "No," said Noël, "it's *against* drugs!" And luckily his argument prevailed. With "Something To Do With Spring" there *was* no argument. When the lines—

"I'd like to know what that stallion thinks—
It must be something to do with Spring"

were heard on the opening night, they were excised by the second night!

SOMETHING TO DO WITH SPRING

*(Joyce Barbour, John Mills, Mr. Cochran's Young
Ladies and the Dancing Boys)*

VERSE
HE: The Spring is here, dear,
    Oh dear, oh dear, dear,
    Can't you see
    The simply agonizing sheen
    On every angry little tree?

SHE: I must admit it's rather fun
    To think that every single thing
    That Nature ever does is overdone.

HE: I know exactly what you mean.
    It all looks far too clean—
    A badly painted scene,
    The grass is far too green.

SHE: Perhaps there's something we have missed.

HE: I never could have kissed
    A sentimentalist.

SHE: Still there's something in the atmosphere
    That makes me happy here.

HE: Don't make me giggle, dear.

REFRAIN I
SHE: The sun is shining where clouds have been—

HE: Maybe it's something to do with Spring.

SHE: I feel no older than seventeen—

HE: Maybe it's something to do with Spring.

SHE: A something I can't express,
    A sort of lilt in the air,
    A lyrical loveliness,
    Seems everywhere.

HE: That sheep's behaviour is most obscene.

BOTH: Maybe it's something to do with Spring.

REFRAIN 2
HE: The dewdrops glitter like diamond links—

SHE: Maybe it's something to do with Spring.

HE: They say that rabbits have minds like sinks—

SHE: Maybe it's something to do with Spring.

HE: The way that the sows behave
    May seem delightfully quaint.
    But why should the cows behave
    With no restraint?

SHE: I'd love to know what that stallion thinks—

HE: Maybe it's something to do with Spring.

Noël's main personal recollection from the show was having to step in one evening to conduct the orchestra, "never having done so before; the breathless agony on the faces of Joyce Barbour and John Mills when I took the tempo of 'Something To Do With Spring' so fast that they couldn't fit their very complicated dance to it and finally, staggered off the stage cursing and exhausted." He remembered and used the incident a few years later to end the much less accomplished routine performed by the "Red Peppers" . . .

Words and Music contained none of the world-weary numbers that had featured in earlier Coward revues. It was as though the next decade was being dedicated to a new generation . . .

THE YOUNGER GENERATION

(Phyllis Harding, Betty Hare, Moya Nugent)

VERSE

GIRLS: Mother, tell us, Mother,
Have you anything in your heart to tell the
four of us,
Are you perfectly sure of us,
We are eager to know?

MOTHER: I trust you everywhere you go.

GIRLS: Mother, tell us, Mother,
If the dreams that you dreamed in
Springtime have come true for you.
What love promised to do for you
Did it actually do?

MOTHER: With Love the whole wide world seems
new.

GIRLS: Teach us to understand this magic flame,
As you did when at first your lover came,
What did he bring to you?
What melodies did he sing to you?

MOTHER: The same . . .
Melodies that lovers sing
Whenever the heart is gay with Spring
And Youth is there.
I assure you the truth is there.
The years hurry for young love is brief,

Tears follow with the fall of the leaf,
Age may bring you sadly to grief
Unless you're wise and realize
That dignity is the greatest prize
To guard.

GIRLS: We'll try so hard.

MOTHER: Once on a time I was young and fair like you.

GIRLS: We know.

MOTHER: Happily dreaming my adolescence through.

GIRLS: Heigho.

MOTHER: Then I married your father,
Gay and handsome and frank,
But it shattered me rather
When I found he drank.

GIRLS: Oh what a shock,
That was really too too bad!

MOTHER: So sad,
Then I took stock
Of the assets that I had.

GIRLS: We're glad.

MOTHER: Ten long years I had sly love,
Then I whispered to my love,
Get thee behind me,
Life has resigned me,
I'd never stoop to buy love.

REFRAIN

Age calls the tune,
Youth's over soon,
That is the natural law.
There's a Younger Generation
Knock knock knocking at the door.
Why sit and fret?
Vainly regret
Things that have gone before?
There's a Younger Generation
Knock knock knocking at the door.
Though the world is well lost for love dreams
There's wisdom above dreams
To compensate mothers and wives,
When the days of youth have passed them,
This should last them
All their lives.
I've had my fun,
All that is done,
Why should I sigh for more?
There's a Younger Generation
Knock knock knocking at the door.

GIRLS: Dear dear Mamma,
Your wise advice to us
Has made us see that the doubts in our
hearts were vain.

MOTHER: Love comes
But once or twice to us,

Rita Lyle and The Dancing Boys: "It's the younger generation, knock, knock, knocking at the door."

If it is wise love, the memory will remain
Through the years,
Have no more fears,
For Age brings peace,
Sweet release
From all
The fetters that have bound you,
Call
Your memories around you,
All your troubled dreams will cease.

(spoken) Marie—Marie—MARIE!
Don't keep me waiting,
Can't you see how very late I am?

MARIE: May I venture to state, Madame,
            That I answered the bell.

MOTHER: (speaks) My dress quickly.
            (sings) So aggravating,
            Can't you see in what a nervous state I am?

MARIE: It's a quarter to eight, Madame.

MOTHER: (spoken) Very well, very well.
            I waste a lot of time on those damned girls,
            I think I'll wear the rubies and the pearls.

MARIE: They're in the jewel case,
            But hadn't you better do your face
            And hair?

MOTHER: All right then, there!
            La lala la la lalalala,
            Lalala lala lalala—lalala lala la.

MARIE: This wig must be sent to be dressed,
            And could I be allowed to suggest
            That before retiring to rest
            You lock the door
            And in this drawer
            Hide every garment that you wore
            From sight.

MOTHER: All right—all right.
            Who would suppose I was nearly forty-three.
            Ah me!
            I can knock spots off those simpering 'Jeunes
                Filles'.
            You see
            Virgin charms don't allure men,
            They need something beyond,
            All the wise and mature men
            Need a 'Femme du Monde',
            I can be tender
            And wise and witty too
            It's true
            I don't surrender.
            Before surrender's due.
            A few—

Lovers may have betrayed me
When my heart disobeyed me
But I've escaped now,
I have them taped now,
Life has indeed repaid me.

Age can be gay,
Age can betray
Destiny's foolish law,
Though the Younger Generation's
Knock knock knocking at the door,
Age is a joke
Planned to provoke
Dreams that the fools ignore,
When the Younger Generation's
Knock knock knocking at the door,
I shall still be gay and attractive,
As long as I'm active,
I'll savour each delicate sin,
Not until my footsteps stagger
And I'm 'Gaga'
I'll give in.
Give me a moon,
Give me a tune,
Give me a dancing floor.
There's a Younger Generation
Knock knock knocking at the door.

*   *   *

On a trip to Singapore in 1930 Noël had run into an amateur touring group called "The Quaints" in which one of the leading actors was the young John Mills. The group was about to stage R. C. Sherriff's famous anti-war play, *Journey's End* and the actor playing one of the leading characters, Stanhope, had just fallen ill. Noël was persuaded at virtually no notice to step in for three performances. Mills as Raleigh, Noël records, "gave the finest performance I have ever seen given of that part" but he was much less satisfied with his own:

"The elite of Singapore assembled in white ducks and flowered chiffons and politely watched me take a fine part in a fine play and throw it into the alley. The only cause for pride I had over the whole business was that I don't dry-up on any of the lines . . . Bob Sherriff's lines remained, on the whole, intact, although I spoke the majority of them with such over-emphasis that it might have been better if they hadn't."

In *Words and Music* Noël made amends in his own way. Two of The Quaints—John Mills and Betty Hare—were in the show, as they had been in *Calvalcade*, and Noël composed a special item

("with acknowledgments and apologies to R.C. Sherriff") . . .

The musical version of *Journey's End*, featuring such characters as Marie Françoise "in National Peasant costume singing a yodelling song," a Raleigh who turned out to be a girl in disguise, German prisoners of war who "execute a violent slapping dance, laughing merrily," six "saucily dressed nuns" and the Kaiser in a dreadnought. John Mills this time found himself cast as Harry Happy," a typical low comedian in comic Tyrolean costume." One way or another, Noël had much to apologize for . . .

JOURNEY'S END

(The Company)

ANNOUNCEMENT

Ladies and Gentlemen
Forgive my strange appearance
Our kindly author has
With splendid perseverance
Worked without stint for your enjoyment
And in this age of un-employment
He decided on a plan
To utilise as many aliens as he can
For, like Sir Oswald Stoll
He feels an obligation
To do his level best
To help the German Nation
And if Charell would condescend
To make a spectacle of *Journey's End*
It is our author's little scheme
To show this strange "Teutonic Dream!"

YODELLING SONG

(Marie Françoise)

MARIE: La dalaito
            La dalaito
            Swift mountain streams
            Play the music of dreams
            La dalaito
            La dalaito
            Morning sweet morning
            So happily gleams
            La dalaito—La dalaito—etc., etc.

KLEINE PUPCHEN

Kleine Pupchen
Boop oop adoop-chen
You are my own vis-a-vis
Kleine Pupchen
Boob oob adoob-chen
My sweetheart some day you'll be
So if you leave me
Don't go too far
Da da un dahda
This is my firm protocol
Hold me in your arms a bit
Display your charms a bit
There could be no harm in it
For you're my Baby Doll!

TE QUIERO

In an old Spanish Garden I found you
The hibiscus was shining all round you
The guitars in the distance were playing
All the love songs I longed to be saying
'Neath the stars that were gleaming above you
I laid my dreams at your feet
Tho' now I have lost you, I love you
"Te Quiero," my sweet Senorita.

DUET: A GONDOLA ON THE RHINE

BOTH: You and me in a Gondola
    Just a Gondola
    On the Rhine

SHE.: Gazing without ending
    In each other's eyes

HE: I shall catch you bending
    On your Bridge of Sighs

BOTH: We'll tour all round the Mond-ola
    We'll abscond-ola
    Pom, pom!
    And maybe

One day there will be three
In our Gondola on the Rhine.

LOVE AND WAR

Love and War
Those are the games worth playing
No man could ask any more
When the bugles and trumpets bray
Love and War
Open Adventure's door
All that men sigh for
Live, Laugh and Die for
Love and War!

In his autobiography, *Up in the Air, Gentlemen, Please!*, John Mills recalled The Master's words of theatrical wisdom that were imparted on this occasion:

"... the theatre is a place of entertainment and people pay to be entertained, and as long as they are paying customers and not complimentaries, they are entitled to (a) yawn, (b) go to sleep, (c) snore, (d) eat pounds of chocolates from crinkly brown wrappers, (e) describe the scene taking place in a loud voice to a deaf aunt with an ear trumpet, or (f) even knit!"

THE WIFE OF AN ACROBAT

(Ivy St. Helier)

VERSE Always travelling to and fro
    And always packing to go
    Is apt to derange one.
    I believe I should lose my head
    If once I slept in a bed
    That wasn't a strange one.
    Never topping the Bill at all
    In each Variety Hall
    We open or close them.
    Apart from waving my hand about
    When he's finished a trick
    I do nothing but stand about
    Feeling slightly sick.
    Even if I had lovely legs I'm not the type
      of girl

Who blatantly shows them.
When I look at the pair I've got
It seems a little bit hard
To have to expose them.
People say that a pride in tricks
Every animal feels.
I'd prefer to be one of six
Old performing seals.

REFRAIN 1 I'm the wife of an Acrobat
    And the world has passed me by.
    I'm dressed in tights
    To play the 'Twice a Nights'
    And only God knows why.
    What a life!
    For an Acrobat
    As he flies from hoop to hoop
    I have a sort of feeling, when our souls have
      passed away
    When giving shows in Heaven, three
      performances a day,
    I'll say what all the angels are expecting me
      to say,
    'Allez OOp—Allez OOp—Allez OOp!'

REFRAIN 2 I'm the wife of an Acrobat
    And our eldest boy's a scout.
    I hate the lad
    To come and see his dad
    Entirely inside out.
    Now the wives of the Acrobats
    Form a most exclusive group,
    You'll seldom see us riding 'Haute École'
      along the park
    And many of us look as if we'd come out
      of the Ark,
    Our conversation meagrely consists of
      one remark,
    'Allez OOp—Allez OOp—Allez OOp!'

REFRAIN 3 I'm the wife of an Acrobat,
    When my old man don't feel well—
    To hold each prop
    And wonder if he'll drop
    Is my idea of Hell.
    What a life for an Acrobat!
    When I watch him loop and loop
    I wonder what he's thinking upside down
      on the trapeze
    And if he's really happy with his head
      between his knees
    And then his face gets crimson
    And I know he's going to sneeze!
    'Allez OOp—Allez OOp—Allez OOp!'

156 REFRAIN 4 I'm the wife of an Acrobat,
When our kids are in their cots
It's kind of sad
To realize their Dad
Is tying himself in knots.
Now the wife of an Acrobat
Is the 'Dead Pan' of the troupe,
I've stood about for twenty years,
My hair is turning grey,
I hear my old man gasping as I watch him
    swing and sway
And if he broke his bloody neck I know I'd
    only say,
'Allez OOp—Allez OOp—Allez OOp!'

HOUSEMAID'S KNEES

*(Effie Atherton and Mr. Cochran's
Young Ladies)*

VERSE Pretty little housemaids proper and sedate,
Um um umum um um,
We seldom go to bed too early and we rise
    extremely late.
Um um umum um um um,
Pretty little housemaids eager to improve,
Each shining hour by slightly widening our
    small domestic groove.
We wish to help the Nation
To forget its pence and pounds,
Our little innovation
Is on patriotic grounds.

REFRAIN: Make England brighter
That's what we try to do,
Our clothes are lighter,
Our skirts are shorter too,
When there's the slightest breeze
You see these
Housemaids' knees.
When there's a crisis
Forget it while you can,
Our firm advice is
To every business man
Just take a look at these
Housemaids' knees
In our domestic and our personal
    relationships
You must forgive us if our consciousness
    of 'station' slips,

A little beauty
May stop you feeling blue,
We feel our duty
Is to enable you
To gaze at skittish,
Absolutely British,
Housemaids' knees!

The files contain other unused material . . . .
    *Get England going,
That's what we all intend,
There is no knowing
Where this idea will end.
In every social 'crise'
Think of these
Housemaids' knees.
We've got the saxes
To try to time it to.
Forget your taxes,
Forget the climate, too
The coldest night won't freeze
Housemaids' knees.
Altho' the Puritans may look at us with
    nausea,
We're growing haughtier and naughtier and
    saucier.
Civilisation would make a great advance
If all the world would only take a glance
At our exotic,
Fiercely patriotic
Housemaids' knees.

*   *   *

Never loath to satirise pretensions in the arts—
including, on occasion, his own—Noël chose as his
subject the modern ballet. The Announcer (Moya
Nugent) introduced a trio of short works "arranged
by the author."

*BALLET ANNOUNCEMENT

Ladies and Gentlemen,
The next scene needs explaining
And Mr. Cochran hopes
You'll find it entertaining.
It is his firm determination to make you use
    imagination
And to gather at a glance
The charm of ordinary life in terms of dance.

The scene is a mens' club smoking-room and the ballet is
danced by four elderly members of the club.

Think of an English Club
On lines of Russian Ballet,
Picture those dear old men
Cavorting musically;
What could be prettier to see
Than angry Colonels in captivity,
Pointing the light fantastic toe
As through their daily lives they go!

The scene is a boarding-house dining room, the dancers are
typical guests

See how the 'Dance' can bring to bloom
Even a boarding-house in Ilfracombe.
The Ballet Spirit as portrayed
At number five Marine Parade.

This is danced by the doctor, matron and nurse of a crèche,
the "babies" being large rubber balls with faces painted on
them.

Now for the sake of our Revue
You'll see a crèche of infants under two.
Note the effect of airy grace
In this clean sanitary place!

MIDNIGHT MATINEE

SPEECH IN VERSE

GIRLS:
(in masks—which makes speech incomprehensible)
Een arrarah ola brure
Taala caana effalure
Tar Apollo nuraling
Jupiter abalching.

Tanger weero avaloy
Burel ammalee to Troy
Baara weether dolaser
Mount Olympus bolaser.

Een arrarah ola brure
Taala caana effalure
Tar Apollo nuraling
Jupiter abalching.

Hola jaaga ammo purtain
Borrodah anula curtain.

Cleopatra's (Rita Lyle) entrance in the "Midnight Matinée."

OPENING CHORUS

We're going to do a Midnight Matinée!
We're going to do a Midnight Show!
We're not *quite* sure
What Charity it's for
But probably the Press will know,
We're going to have a talk on Saturday
To make a list of friends who'll go,
The Season's such a bore,
We haven't had much excitement since the War
And so . . .
We'll do a Midnight Show.

Last year we did a 'Feather Parade',
That was a great success.
But some got bent
And some would break
And a lot got sent
To Melton by mistake.
At Easter we went mad, I'm afraid,
We really must confess,
We gave a great—
Big 'Circus Ball'
But forgot the date
So no one came at all.

We're going to do a Midnight Matinée!
We're going to do a Midnight Show!
A sort of 'Masque'
Where everyone will ask
And nobody will *ever* know,

We're going to have a talk on Saturday
To make a list of friends who'll go,
God knows how much we'll fetch
But we shall have all our pictures in the *Sketch*
And so—
We'll do a Midnight Show.

PAGEANT OF BYGONE ENCHANTRESSES

Bygone Loves and bygone Lovers
Live again in History's pages,
As one turns them one discovers
Love's Romance across the Ages.
Diane de Poitiers.

Queen of every fascination,
This Enchantress lives again,
Siren of the Restoration,
Mistress Gwynn of Drury Lane.
Nell Gwynn.

Eastern Stars, your light grows less,
Oh Eastern Moon, your beauty pales
Before this sinister Princess
Salomé of the Seven Veils.
Salomé.

Tragic Queen of Tragic Story,
Memory that haunts us yet,
Here we see you in your glory,
Lovely Marie Antoinette.
Marie Antoinette.

Battle Queen of History
Gallant Memory, Brave Romance,

Welcome, Welcome, Hail to Thee,
Joan of Arc. The Maid of France!
Joan of Arc.

Beauty rare, and stately calm,
England holds your memory dear,
Queen of Fashion, Queen of Charm,
Lady Blessington is here.
Lady Blessington.

Lady sweet beyond compare,
Strange the legend, strange the deed,
Shielded by your flowing hair,
Riding on your snow-white steed.
Lady Godiva.

*   *   *

Apart from "Mad Dogs," the undoubted hit of the show was "Mad About the Boy." Frequently sung since as a torch song with the implication that it is the yearning of a mature woman for a younger man, the context in the show was quite different.

Noël describes the setting: "(It) was presented in a composite vocal scene. A society lady, a street-walker, a schoolgirl and a scullery maid in turn sang their impression of a famous film star. The singers were Joyce Barbour, Steffi Duna, Nora Howard and Doris Hare. The film star, who appeared briefly at the end was played by Edward Underdown. I have always been very attached to this number. The refrain remains constant, with different lyrics, but the verses vary and are, I think, musically interesting, particularly the "school-girl" verse which is begun against an accompaniment of five-finger exercises."

"Mad Dogs And Englishmen," left to right: Ivy St. Helier, Gerald Nodin and Romney Brent.

Graham Payn, who made his debut in the show and was to become Noël's lifelong companion after the war, had his own personal recollection of the way the number was staged in *My Life With Noël Coward* . . .

"There was not very much for me to do in *Words and Music*. Wearing a white jacket, shorts and top hat, I announced 'Mad Dogs.' I was also the beggar boy singing to a cinema queue as the lead-in to 'Mad About the Boy.' Never had a young busker given such full value to his audience . . . Pretty impressive stuff, I thought, until after a few rehearsals Noël came up and wagged his finger at me, the first of many thousand times.

"Graham," he said, "*we* know what a good little artiste you are, but this boy, the character you're playing, he wouldn't know what you know. He'd stand quite still and just *sing*."

"So stand still I did. Like a rock. Never let it be said we pros can't take direction. Unfortunately for me, the part of the stage where I had to stand was just over the brass section of the orchestra. While I was singing my little heart out with the buskers' anthem, 'I Hear You Calling Me,' nobody out front could hear a single plaintive note over the sound of trumpets blasting out 'Mad About the Boy.'"

MAD ABOUT THE BOY

(Joyce Barbour, Norah Howard,
Steffi Dunn. Doris Hare)

VERSE
SOCIETY WOMAN: I met him at a party just a couple of
    years ago,
    He was rather over-hearty and ridiculous
    But as I'd seen him on the Screen
    He cast a certain spell.
    I basked in his attraction for a couple of hours
      or so,
    His manners were a fraction too meticulous,
    If he was real or not I couldn't tell
    But like a silly fool, I fell.

REFRAIN
    Mad about the boy,
    I know it's stupid to be mad about the boy,
    I'm so ashamed of it
    But must admit
    The sleepless nights I've had about the boy.

On the Silver Screen
He melts my foolish heart in every single scene.
Although I'm quite aware
That here and there
Are traces of the cad about the boy,
Lord knows I'm not a fool girl,
I really shouldn't care,
Lord knows I'm not a schoolgirl
In the flurry of her first affair.
Will it ever cloy?
This odd diversity of misery and joy,
I'm feeling quite insane
And young again
And all because I'm mad about the boy.

VERSE
SCHOOLGIRL: Home work, home work,
    Every night there's home work,
    While Elsie practises the gas goes pop,
    I wish, I wish she'd stop,
    Oh dear, oh dear,
    Here it's always 'No, dear,
    You can't go out again, you must stay home,
    You waste your money on that common
        Picturedrome,
    Don't shirk—stay here and do your work.'

    Yearning, yearning,
    How my heart is burning.
    I'll see him Saturday in *Strong Man's Pain*
    And then on Monday and on Friday week again.
    To me he is the sole man
    Who can kiss as well as Colman,
    I could faint whenever there's a close-up of his
      lips,
    Though John Barrymore is larger
    When my hero's on his charger
    Even Douglas Fairbanks Junior hasn't smaller hips.
    If only he could know
    That I adore him so.

REFRAIN
    Mad about the boy,
    It's simply scrumptious to be mad about the boy,
    I know that quite sincerely
    Housman really
    Wrote *The Shropshire Lad* about the boy.
    In my English Prose
    I've done a tracing of his forehead and his nose
    And there is, honour bright,
    A certain slight
    Effect of Galahad about the boy.
    I've talked to Rosie Hooper,
    She feels the same as me,

She says that Gary Cooper
Doesn't thrill her to the same degree.
In *Can Love Destroy?*
When he meets Garbo in a suit of corduroy,
He gives a little frown
And knocks her down.
Oh dear, oh dear, I'm mad about the boy.

VERSE
COCKNEY: Every Wednesday afternoon
    I get a little time off from three to eleven,
    Then I go to the Picture House
    And taste a little of my particular heaven.
    He appears
    In a little while,
    Through a mist of tears
    I can see him smiling
    Above me.
    Every picture I see him in,
    Every lover's caress,
    Makes my wonderful dreams begin,
    Makes me long to confess
    That if ever he looked at me
    And thought perhaps it was worth the trouble to
    Love me,
    I'd give in and I wouldn't care
    However far from the path of virtue he'd
    Shove me,
    Just supposing our love was brief,
    If he treated me rough
    I'd be happy beyond belief,
    Once would be enough.

REFRAIN
    Mad about the boy,
    I know I'm potty but I'm mad about the boy.
    He sets me 'eart on fire
    With love's desire,
    In fact I've got it bad about the boy.
    When I do the rooms
    I see 'is face in all the brushes and the brooms.
    Last week I strained me back
    And got the sack,
    And 'ad a row with Dad about the boy.
    I'm finished with Navarro,
    I'm tired of Richard Dix,
    I'm pierced by Cupid's arrow
    Every Wednesday from four till six.
    'Ow I should enjoy
    To let 'im treat me like a plaything or a toy,
    I'd give my all to him
    And crawl to him,
    So 'elp me Gawd I'm mad about the boy.

VERSE

TART: It seems a little silly
For a girl of my age and weight
To walk down Piccadilly
In a haze of love.

It ought to take a good deal more to get a bad
girl down,
I should have been exempt, for
My particular kind of Fate
Has taught me such contempt for
Every phase of love,
And now I've been and spent my last half-crown
To weep about a painted clown.

"Mad About The Boy": Above, left to right, Steffi Dunn (Tart),
Doris Hare (Cockney) and Norah Howard (Schoolgirl). Also seen
below with Joyce Barbour (Society Woman) at The Cinema.

160 REFRAIN

Mad about the boy,
It's pretty funny but I'm mad about the boy,
He has a gay appeal
That makes me feel
There's maybe something sad about the boy.
Walking down the street,
His eyes look out at me from people that I meet,
I can't believe it's true
But when I'm blue
In some strange way I'm glad about the boy.
I'm hardly sentimental,
Love isn't so sublime,
I have to pay my rental
And I can't afford to waste much time,
If I could employ
A little magic that would finally destroy
This dream that pains me
And enchains me,
But I can't because I'm mad about the boy.

There has been speculation ever since about the identity of the "boy." On the textual evidence the specific comparisons with Ronald Colman, John Barrymore, Richard Dix, Ramon Navarro, Gary Cooper and Douglas Fairbanks, Jr. would appear to rule them out and Rudolph Valentino had been dead for some years when the song was introduced. Graham Payn is inclined to believe that Noël had a composite version of all these and other contemporaries in mind, rather than a specific star. The "boy," in fact, was whoever you wanted him to be, which is as it should be . . .

*   *   *

The show's Finale was a song Noël was to use himself in years to come to end his cabaret performances. It was, he said "a pleasant little song without being startlingly original."

THE PARTY'S OVER NOW

(The Company)

Though we hate
Abominate
Each party we're invited to
To stay out
And dance about
Because we've nothing else to do.
Though every night
We start out bright
And finish with a row
We've been so bored,
Thank the Lord
That the Party's over now!

VERSE
Night is over, dawn is breaking,
Everywhere the Town is waking
Just as we are on our way to sleep.
Lovers meet and dance
A little,
Snatching from romance
A little
Souvenir of happiness to keep.
The music of an hour ago
Was just a sort of 'Let's pretend',
The melodies that charmed us so
At last are ended.

REFRAIN
The Party's over now,
The dawn is drawing very nigh,
The candles gutter,
The starlight leaves the sky.
It's time for little boys and girls
To hurry home to bed
For there's a new day
Waiting just ahead.
Life is sweet
But time is fleet,
Beneath the magic of the moon,
Dancing time
May seem sublime
But it is ended all too soon,
The thrill has gone,
To linger on
Would spoil it anyhow,
Let's creep away from the day
For the Party's over now.

First presented by Charles B. Cochran at His Majesty's Theatre on February 16, 1934. (177 performances.)

Cast included Noël Coward, Yvonne Printemps, Louis Hayward, Heather Thatcher, Moya Nugent, Maidie Andrews, Irene Browne and George Sanders. (Printemps' husband, Pierre Fresnay, took over Noël's part for much of the London and all of the New York run.)

The operetta form—which Noël insisted on calling the *operette*—had always fascinated him and for the rest of his career he made intermittent attempts to write a successor to *Bitter Sweet*. In terms of equalling its impact he was not to succeed. *Conversation Piece* was a modest success, due largely to the presence of the French star, Yvonne Printemps, for whom it was "conceived, written and composed." Looking back, Noël remembered her as being a "fine actress in addition to having one of the loveliest voices it has ever been my privilege to hear . . . and in spite of the fact that her English began and ended with 'Good morning,' 'Yes' and 'No' . . . It is an undoubted tribute to her that, by the end of the London and New York runs, most of the company spoke French fluently."

One thing Noël and every composer of operetta knew was that the score, however melodic and witty it might otherwise be, is nothing without its romantic theme song. *Bitter Sweet* had revolved around "I'll See You Again" but in the case of *Conversation Piece*, that piece of the puzzle refused to fall into place for him: "I knew I could never complete the score without a main theme, and sat for ten days at the piano gloomily facing the fact that my talent had withered . . . I finally decided to give up, poured myself a stiff whisky, switched off the piano light and was about to go to bed in despair when 'I'll Follow My Secret Heart' suddenly emerged in G flat, a key I had never played before."

*   *   *

The piece was set in Regency Brighton c. 1811. Act 1 begins with a classic Prologue spoken in rhymed couplets—by two upperclass courtesans, Sophie Otford (Heather Thatcher) and Martha James (Moya Nugent) . . .

Gladys Calthrop, scenic and costume designer and lifelong friend of Noël Coward. Below her sketch for Yvonne Printemps' costume for the Ballroom scene.

PROLOGUE

SOPHIE: Ladies and Gentlemen,
          A prologue to a play is out of date,
          A leisurely technique of past decades.
          So please regard us as two friendly shades
          Returning down the years to indicate,
          More by our presence, than by what we say,
          The atmosphere and tempo of this play.

MARTHA: My friend has explained it most concisely,
          She always was one to put things nicely!

SOPHIE: We represent the fine but faded flower
          Of that old "Demi-Monde" that used to be
          At Vauxhall, and at Brighton by the sea
          Before the pure in heart came into power,
          Before the great, but sanctimonious Queen
          Firmly rang down the curtain on our scene.

MARTHA: Please don't suppose our flowers were faded,
          Others were pushed, we were persuaded!

SOPHIE: The interruptions of my friend are meant
          To clarify for you our "Status Quo",
          A social level neither high nor low
          With which we were entirely content
          And which provides the background, may I say,
          Of this polite, but faintly raffish play.

In 1951 Noël made an LP recording of the show with Lily Pons and recorded himself not only a version of the Prologue but narrative linkage between the songs . . .

*Ladies and Gentlemen
A Prologue to a play is out of date,
A leisurely technique of masquerade.
So please regard me as a friendly shade,
Returning down the years to indicate,
More by my presence than by what I say,
The atmosphere and setting of this play.

I must beware of this modern medium,
Long-playing records can spell tedium.
In any case, an overture is inevitable.

(MUSIC UNDER)

The scene is laid in Brighton by the sea.

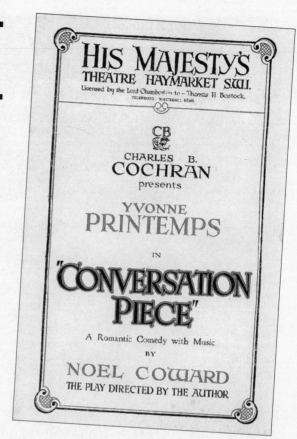

HIS MAJESTY'S
THEATRE HAYMARKET SW1.
Licensed by the Lord Chamberlain to ~ Thomas H. Bostock.
TELEPHONE WHITEHALL 6606

CHARLES B.
COCHRAN
presents
YVONNE
PRINTEMPS
IN
"CONVERSATION
PIECE"
A Romantic Comedy with Music
BY
NOEL COWARD
THE PLAY DIRECTED BY THE AUTHOR

Above: Noël Coward, Romney Brent (originally cast as Paul) and Yvonne Printemps.

Opening scene, "tableau vivant," depicting life in Regency Brighton, with the gay throng of bucks, ladies, children and soldiers of that fashionable town.

A fishing village which became
A social playground of enduring fame,
In the gay heyday of the Regency.

Presided over by the stout, absurd,
But rather charming son of George the Third.
What elegant language they discoursed in!
If you're in doubt, just read Jane Austen.
I'm sure you could imagine, if you tried,
During the burst of music that ensues
A most ingenuous of ingénues,
Who's been brought from Paris to reside
In a small, rented Georgian house,
In order to acquire a wealthy spouse.

The gentleman who has brought the lady,
Though a French Duke, is rather shady.
The man, the Duke de Chaucigny-Varennes,
Distinguished, elegant of middle age,
Has also had the forethought to engage
An English maid, a Cockney, Magdalene,
Whose job it is to earn her bed and board
By teaching English to his so-called ward.

Paul, the Duc de Chaucigny-Varennes, visits his ward, Melanie. He is annoyed to find she has been talking French with her maid. She must forget the humble background from which he took her and remember only the aristocratic "history" he has created for her. Melanie agrees—but she can still have her dreams. She sings "I'll Follow My Secret Heart." She goes to get ready for the visit of an admirer, the Marquis of Sheere (Louis Hayward).

I'LL FOLLOW MY SECRET HEART

(Yvonne Printemps)

MELANIE: A cloud has passed across the sun,
The morning seems no longer gay.
With so much business to be done,
Even the sea looks grey.
C'est vrai. C'est vrai.
It seems that all the joy has faded from the day
As though the foolish world no longer wants to play.

PAUL: *(Speaking)* Go and dress.

MELANIE: *(Speaking)* What shall I wear? A black crêpe with a little bonnet?

PAUL: What on earth is the matter with you this morning?

MELANIE: White, white for a bride. But the sun ought to shine on a bride.

PAUL: You're not a bride yet.

MELANIE: But I shall be soon, shall I not? A very quiet aristocratic bride with a discreet heart!

(Sings)
You ask me to have a discreet heart
Until marriage is out of the way
But what if I meet
With a sweetheart so sweet
That my wayward heart cannot obey
A single word that you may say?

PAUL: *(Speaking)* Then we shall have to go away.

MELANIE: *(Sings)*
No. For there is nowhere we could go
Where we could hide from what we know
Is true.
Don't be afraid I'll betray you
And destroy all the plans you have made,
But even your schemes
Must leave room for my dreams.
So when all I owe to you is paid

Yvonne Printemps as Melanie.

I'll still have something of my own,
A little prize that's mine alone.

I'll follow my secret heart
My whole life through,
I'll keep all my dreams apart
Till one comes true.
No matter what price is paid,
What stars may fade
Above,
I'll follow my secret heart
Till I find love.

The Marquis arrives and is surprised to find Paul, who chooses to act as though the Marquis is naturally here to propose marriage to his ward. Even though it was not his original intention, when Melanie appears, he does so. She is not prepared to give him her answer, telling him to return later. As she watches him leave, she reprises her song . . .

On the Parade four young men are taking the air.

(In *Bitter Sweet* the success of the male quartet singing "Green Carnation" encouraged Noël to try it again. The four aesthetes have now been transformed into the rather more robust Regency Rakes, led by "a tall, handsome young man who later achieved fame as a film star"—George Sanders.)

The Regent and his retinue
Contrived to make an atmosphere
Of raffishness and bawdiness,
In town or by the sea.

The gentlemen were dandified,
And often over-brandified.
The ladies were as modest
As it suited them to be.
The gentlemen allowed no sense of decency to interfere
With the pleasures of the table or the bottle or the bed.

This over-masculinity,
Which bored the whole vicinity,
Is summed up in a lyric
That is better sung than said:

REGENCY RAKES

(George Sanders, Pat Worsley, Antony Brian,
and Sydney Grammar)

VERSE   You may think
          Looking at the four of us
          Food and drink
          Constitute the core of us.
          That may be,
          But still you'll see
          Our names on posterity's page.
          You will read
          Histories galore of us
          Strutting England's stage.
          We represent

To a certain extent
The ineffable scent
Of our age.

REFRAIN 1 We're Regency Rakes
           And each of us takes
           A personal pride
           In the thickness of hide
           Which prevents us from seeing
           How vulgar we're being,
           Without making us wince,
           We're ruthless and rude
           And boast of a crude
           And lordly disdain
           Both for mind and for brain.
           Though obtuse and slow-witted,
           We're not to be pitied,
           For we follow the Prince,
           Every orgy
           With our Georgie
           Lasts till dawn without a lull.
           We can venture
           Without censure
           To be noisy, drunk and dull!
           We revel in Sport
           Madeira, and Port,
           And when we pass out
           With Sclerosis and Gout
           All our children will rue our mistakes,
           Roistering Regency Rakes,
           Ho! Ho!
           Roistering Regency Rakes.

REFRAIN 2 We're Regency Rakes
           And each of makes
           A personal issue
           Of adipose tissue
           But still notwithstanding,
           Our stomachs expanding,
           We all yearn for romance.
           We frequently start
           Affairs of the heart,
           Sublimely unheeding
           That long over-feeding
           Has made so disgusting
           Our loving or lusting
           That girls eye us askance,
           Though we wonder
           As we blunder
           Into this or that bordel,
           Whom we know there,
           Why we go there,
           But we're far too drunk to tell,
           Though over-jocose,

The Regency Rakes and Ladies of the Town enjoy an encounter in the streets of Brighton.

Unfunny and gross,
We don't lose a fraction
Of self-satisfaction.
Complacency never forsakes
Roistering Regency Rakes!
Ho! Ho!
Roistering Regency Rakes.

*   *   *

Two English Ladies with English names,
Sophie Otford and Martha James,
Devoured by curiosity, decided to call on Melanie.
Their hats were stylish, their clothes were chic.
Their nails were manicured twice a week.
Their reputation about the town
Was based upon a most improper noun.
Their favors were sought—and bought—and sold
In fact they were tarts—with hearts of gold.

Conversation between the ladies is difficult to begin with, due to Melanie's lack of English but they find a universal language in the admiration of clothes . . .

Moya Nugent, Betty Shale, Heather Thatcher, Maidie Andrews, and Yvonne Printemps are "Charming, Charming."

CHARMING, CHARMING

(Yvonne Printemps, Maidie Andrews, Heather Thatcher, Moya Nugent)

SOPHIE: Charming! Charming! Charming!

ROSE: This gown is for the morning,
            When Mademoiselle goes out,
            As Madame sees
            In the slightest breeze
            The feathers float about.

SOPHIE/MARTHA:
            Charming! Charming! Charming!

ROSE: This jacket is for driving,
            Or strolling beside the sea.

SOPHIE: Pretty as it seems to be
            It's a little too full in the sleeves for me.

ALL: Ah la la la—la la—la la.

SOPHIE: Pretty as it seems to be
            It's a trifle full in the sleeves for me.

MELANIE: This dress is for the evening,
            To wear when I meet my dear,

            Whenever that may chance to be.
            In the moment that he looks at me
            The skies will suddenly clear.
            I'll know him then for my destiny,
            And so through each changing year
            I shall leave him never, for evermore.

ROSE: Don't you think these pinks and blues are
            sweet?
            This stuff is sent especially from France.

MELANIE: Oh, please, please say you think these satin
            shoes are sweet,
            They make me feel I want to dance.

            Danser—danser—la Vie est gaie.
            Je me sens libre, abandonnée.
            Le chant trouble mon coeur
            Qui donc m'envoie ce doux bonheur,
            Mon corps, mes pieds, ensorcelés,
            Légers, ailés, vont s'envoler.
            Tra la la la la—la la la—la la la la la,
            Tra la la la la—la la la—lalalalalala—la la.

SOPHIE/MARTHA/ROSE/MELANIE:
            Look for a love that is gay and sweet.

SOPHIE/MARTHA/ROSE/MELANIE:
            Music to guide your dancing feet.

SOPHIE/MARTHA/ROSE:
            Follow your secret strain

            And you won t be living in vain,
            Treat your desire by word and deed
            Lightly—lightly—
            And if at first you don't succeed
            Try and try again.

MELANIE: *Mon corps, mes pieds, ensorcelés,*
            Légers, ailés, vont s'envoler.
            Tra la la la la—la la la—la la la—la,
            Tra la la la—la la la—

            (ALL rush to window to watch the soldiers go by)

DEAR LITTLE SOLDIERS

ROSE: When I see the soldiers marching by
            With fife and drum
            Beneath a summer sky,

SOPHIE/MARTHA:
            Little dears who love to do and die,

ROSE: My spirit sings
            And spreads its wings to fly,
            Think of all the battles they have won.

MELANIE: So brave and strong

166

They march along
Like little boys
Who play with toys
For fun.

SOPHIE/MARTHA:
Little boys who frolic in the sun.

ROSE: Right—right—right left right,

ALL: Right—right—right left right left—
March little soldiers, we all adore you,
We'd swoon before you
If we thought that you would care,
What e'er befalls you,
Where duty calls you,
We should love to be there
To share
All your troubles, but we'd never dare,
But we're quite prepared to cheer you to
    victory,
To joy or despair,
Joy or despair,
That's only fair.
Dear little soldiers,
Should you admire us
And feel desirous
On returning from the fray,
We'd soon surrender,
You'd find us tender
And sublimely unresisting
In assisting
You to spend
Your soldiers' pay pay pay.

There is a knock at the door . . .

The mother and father of dear Lord Sheere,
Suspecting their Edward of dalliance,
Arrive at the house with the clear idea
Of scotching all chance of misalliance.

Imagine the elderly Duchess' shame,
As into the salon she swoops,
And observes two young women of fairly ill-fame,
With a girl to whom Edward has offered his name,
Hysterically cheering the troops.

Poor Sophie and Martha,
Who sense
The tense
Embarrassment, beat
A retreat.
They snatch up their hats and their bags,
Like stags
And make a bee-line for the street.

In the silence that follows their giggles and squeaks,
The Duchess, with a rigid frigidity
Speaks:

Melanie must not associate further with their son.
If she will agree, they will even pay her. Far from
being outraged, Melanie finds the whole thing vastly
amusing . . .

*   *   *

Like any Englishman worth the name, Noël was
extremely suspicious—or publicly pretended to be—
of the foreigner. In World War II the Germans would
be a natural target. For now our age-old opposite
number, the French would have to do . . .

We British are an island race,
The sea lies all around us,
And visitors from other lands,
With different sets of different glands,
Bewilder and astound us.

Suspicious of the slightest trace of foreign intonation
Even our local lights of love,
Trained in the wrongs and rights of love,
Show signs of irritation
When gentlemen of alien grace,
French or Italiano,
Suggest a non-aggression pact.
The ladies, with consummate tact,
Say "Try it on your piano!"

THERE'S ALWAYS SOMETHING FISHY ABOUT THE FRENCH

(Heather Thatcher and Moya Nugent)

VERSE I

SOPHIE: A life of Love is curious
But not injurious
If you are wise.

MARTHA: For you get pleasure,
Leisure,
Knowledge to treasure
After the gay life dies;

SOPHIE: Though men we seldom bind to us
They're often kind to us,

MARTHA: And entre nous
English Gentlemen,
Spanish Noblemen,
Indian Merchantmen too,
Always play the game,
Never cause us shame.

Heather Thatcher and Moya Nugent
discover that "There's Always
Something Fishy About the French."

REFRAIN 1

BOTH: But there's always something fishy about
        the French!
    Whether Prince or Politician
    We've a sinister suspicion
    That behind their *savoir faire*
    They share
    A common contempt
    For every mother's son of us.
    Though they smile and smirk
    We know they're out for dirty work,
    We're most polite
    But don't put out the night-light!
    Every wise and thoroughly worldly wench
    Knows there's always something fishy about
        the French

REFRAIN 2

BOTH: Oh, there's always something fishy about
        the French!
    As a race, they're conscientious
    But undoubtedly licentious,
    Though the compliments they pay
    Are gay
    And ever so nice,
    We don't believe a word of them,
    They may kiss our hands
    And talk to us of foreign lands,
    We 'Toi' and 'Moi'
    And watch for 'Je ne sais quoi'—
    Every time their fingers begin to clench—
    Well, we know there's something fishy about
        the French!

*   *   *

Imagine a summer evening if you please,
Long ago in the nineteenth century.
Imagine the world of fashion passing by,
Laughing and gossiping beneath the trees.
For here in the public gardens,
The élite traditionally sniff the evening air.
Soldiers in scarlet coats,
Salute and stare,
As the Prince Regent passes with his sweet.

Ladies and gentlemen superbly clad,
Whose names sing through our island history,
Chatter, take snuff, and smiling raffishly,
Lightly discuss their monarch.
Who is mad.
Imagine this summer evening if you please,
With music playing underneath the trees.

Lord Sheere and his father pass by.
They seem to be arguing—heatedly.
Our friend, Sophie Otford,
In deep evening dress,

Appears with an exquisite dandy.
It would not require much clairvoyance to guess
That he's had a bash at the brandy.

Through the darkening trees
Comes a lady in green,
With her maid trotting meekly behind her.
Her wit, I admit, has a cynical sheen,
And she doesn't let sentiment blind her.
Lady Julia, dear listeners, believe it or not,
Is very integrally part of the plot.

Lord Sheere and his father, the Duke, reappear,
And they play a short scene,
Which, with luck, you will hear.

Vows are exchanged,
And later, when the Duke and Edward stroll away,
The Duke de Chaucigny-Varennes,
Who's searching for his protégée
Meets Lady Julia face to face.
She curtsies with ironic grace.

Julia (Irene Browne) and Paul have known each other many years ago but each had thought the other dead. When she is introduced to Melanie, Julia is puzzled. She knows Melanie cannot be who Paul claims her to be. At that moment an equerry arrives from the Prince Regent inviting Melanie to supper. Paul refuses on her behalf. He will be honoured to present his ward "on a more formal occasion."

*   *   *

Act 2 also begins with a Prologue, Sophie and Martha's commentary in verse . . .

PROLOGUE

(Heather Thatcher and Moya Nugent)

SOPHIE: This play, or let us say, this pantomime,
    Being too small in scope, too tenuous,
    Too personal to illustrate the strenuous
    And glittering excitements of the time,
    We feel it, in a sense, obligatory
    To hint at what goes on behind the story.

MARTHA: My friend, though a trifle too rhetorical,
    Means it should be more historical.

SOPHIE: We ask you to imagine, if you please,
    That just around the corner of the tale,
    Mrs Fitzherbert and the Prince inhale

    The selfsame air, the same urbane sea
        breeze.
    Imagine that this world is living still
    And passing just beneath the window-sill.

MARTHA: You've left out Brummell, the pert impostor,
    And what about Pitt? And the Duke of
        Gloucester?

SOPHIE: Picture a little further if you will
    The neat Pavilion Gardens, and the Steyne.
    The little band that orchestrates the scene.
    The Fireworks, the Races, the Quadrille
    And furthermore, the bawdy, merry Hell
    Created by our lordly clientele!

Once more the house, so modest, so discreet,
Once more a lazy summer afternoon.
A group of children sing a little tune
Beneath the windows in the sunny street.

The music, not unnaturally disturbs
Poor Melanie, who's wrestling in vain
To beat into her unresponsive brain
Some regular, but dreary, English verbs . . .

ENGLISH LESSON

(Yvonne Printemps)

VERSE 1   The tree is in the garden,
    The water is in the pot;
    The little sheep
    On the mountain sleep,
    The fire is very hot.

REFRAIN: *Oh! c'est dur*
    Tous ces mots obscurs
    Me rendent triste;
    Rien n'existe
    Que le malheur qui insiste;
    Dieu, je tâche d'apprendre, mais voilà
    Je ne peux pas.

VERSE 2   The fire is not in the garden,
    The tree is not in the pot,
    The silly sheep
    On the something sleep
    But whether they do or not,
    I do not care a jot;
    I don't care if they're cold
    Or if they're hot.

168

REFRAIN 2 *Oh! c'est dur,*
Tous ces mots obscurs
Me rendent triste;
Rien n'existe
Que le malheur qui insiste;
Dieu, je tâche d'apprendre, mais voilà
Je ne peux pas.

Melanie's lesson is interrupted by the arrival of Julia who, not believing the story of the "ward," has come to see what sort of mistress Paul has chosen. In the middle of the argument that ensues Paul arrives. He refuses Melanie's request to send Julia away and, while she leaves in tears, explains his problems to Julia. Since the Revolution he has been impoverished. His hope is that Melanie will make a rich marriage from which he will make a commission. If it's money he wants, says Julia, he had better marry her, since she has plenty. Alternatively, she will help launch Melanie into society and improve her prospects.

*   *   *

A quartet of fishermen bemoan the changes introduced into their quiet lives by so-called civilisation . . .

The melody that follows used to be presented on
The stage as quartet
Sung as it was, in closest harmony,
It very much enhanced this operette.
Alas, alas, Columbia* forgot
To pay the price for bass and baritone.
Therefore, as expert singers cost a lot,
I'll sing the number firmly and alone.
Now that you know how limited your choice is,
Please picture me as four resounding voices . . .

(*the recording company)

THERE WAS ONCE A LITTLE VILLAGE BY THE SEA

There was once a little village by the sea,
Where we lived our lives in amiable tranquillity.
We were humble in our ways
And we swam through all our days
As little fishes swim

In immobility;
We watched for gales
In the evening sky
And we trimmed our sails
Till the night went by,
No less, no more,
Than stones on an English shore.

Then whimsical Fate,
Resenting our state,
Decided to break us
And mould and re-make us;
Our sweet isolation
From civilization
Has all vanished away.
We're urban and proud
Supporting a crowd
Of Doxys and Dandys
And Regency Randys,
Who fiddle and faddle
And piddle and paddle
And turn night into day.
The Pavilion
Cost a million
As a monument to Art,
And the wits here
Say it sits here
Like an Oriental tart!
The dashing 'beau monde'
Has ruffled our pond
And even the turbot
Know Mrs Fitzherbert,
We're richer than ever before
But Brighton is Brighton no more,
No more
Brighton is Brighton no more.

*   *   *

An elegant party is taking place in Melanie's house. Melanie, Paul and Lady Julia are receiving their titled guests.

Please try to envisage a social occasion:
An elegant Regency rout.
The ladies are slim, in diaphanous gowns,
The gentlemen mainly in beiges and browns,
Are languidly standing about.

If only my words had sufficient persuasion
To color the scene for your ears.
To whisk you away from these dangerous days,
And carry you back on the wings of a phrase
One hundred and forty-odd years.

Lady Julia, whose blood is impeccable blue
And whose status is quite indisputable,
Is prepared to proclaim,
To the crème de la crème,
That Melanie is socially suitable.
She certainly does what she promised to do,
And with cynical glee, supervises
The sending of cards to distinguished diehards,
And all the old snobs she despises.

The Duke and Duchess of Benedon who,
Have been spoken to firmly by Julia.
Take a very dim view of the hullabaloo,
And consider the set-up peculiar.

Sophie and Martha arrive at Melanie's invitation and the other ladies make excuses to leave. When only the men are left, Melanie sings her aria of rejection . . .

MELANIE'S ARIA

(*Yvonne Printemps*)

MELANIE: Dear Friends,
Will you forgive me, pray.
If many of the words I say
In English may be wrong.

ALL: She hasn't been in England very long.

MELANIE: A stranger in a foreign land,
I beg that you will understand
How gratefully I find
The gentlemen so very kind,
So very kind.

(*to the Duke of Beneden*)
The offer of protection
That Monsieur le Duc has made
I set aside,
For my foolish pride
Would feel itself betrayed.

ALL: Charming! Charming! Charming!

MELANIE: (*to Lord St Marys*)
Monsieur, my Lord St Marys
Has made me an offer too.
Royal though his scheme may be,
It could never be part of a dream for me.

ALL: Ah la la la—la la—la la.

MELANIE: Handsome though your Prince may be
He is far too broad in the beam for me.

(to the Marquis of Sheere)
But there is one, one only,
Who honours me with his heart,
Although I'm not the wife for him
I shall cherish all my life for him
A feeling somehow apart.
I'd suffer sorrow and strife for him.
Though we may be lovers never,
We're friends for ever—for evermore.

MELANIE: *C'est assez de mensonge,*
Le secret qui me ronge,
Que tout au fond de moi
J'ai tendrement gardé.
Enfin avec franchise
Il faut que je le dise,
Avouant mon secret,
Que tu n'as pas compris
Plus de coeur discret,
C'est toi qui par l'amour,

Toi qui m'as delivrée,
Je suis à toi toujours.
Esclave de mon coeur,
Me rendras-tu la vie
Je t'en supplie, crois-moi,
Lorsque je dis c'est toi
Plus de coeur discret.

C'est toi qui par l'amour,
Toi qui m'as delivrée,
Je suis a toi toujours.
Esclave de mon coeur,
Me rendras-tu la vie.
Je t'en supplie, crois-moi,
Je t'en supplie, crois-moi,
C'est toi.
Parmi le monde entier c'est toi que j'aime.
Je t'en supplie,
Crois-le si même
Tu ne le veux.
Toi,
Parmi le monde entier c'est toi que j'aime,
Je suis à toi toujours.

For the benefit of listeners whose French is
    non-existent,
I will rather superciliously explain,
The aria they have listened to is perfectly
    consistent,
And we really can't go through it all again.

Poor Melanie, on finishing her vocal declaration,
And having thus betrayed her secret heart,
Bursts into tears which frankly doesn't help the
    situation,
While, silently, the noble guests depart.

Having declared at the end of her aria that Paul is
the only one she truly loves, Melanie faints. When
she comes to, everyone but Paul has left. He is angry
and accuses her of making a fool of him and ruining
his plans. She tells him that he is the stupid one—
doesn't he understand that feelings matter more
than plans?

The Marquis of Sheere (Louis Hayward)
hovers over Melanie (Yvonne Printemps)
after she faints, having admitted
her love for Paul (Noël Coward).

Noël was uncomfortable as Paul and soon allowed himself to be replaced by Mlle Printemps' husband, Pierre Fresnay, who completed the London run and took the the play to Broadway.

Left: Melanie's party in progress.

*   *   *

Act 3 opens with *le tout Brighton* once again promenading . . . This time the Ladies and the ladies have something to talk about—Melanie's party. They will never forgive her and as for that Duc, well—there certainly is something fishy about the French. This leads them into a consideration of their own lives in a song that was not used in the final production . . .

MOTHERS AND WIVES

Quartette

In an atmosphere of bawdy *jeu d'esprit*
We contrive to be tenaciously conventional,
Though intelligent, we hope,
Our imaginative scope
When all is said and done
Is one-dimensional.
Our appearance should be ample guarantee
Of our vigorous and rigorous morality,
We regard our husbands' gout
As a proper and devout
And Godly recompense
For sensuality.
But when we look at our greying hairs
We sometimes sigh as we say our prayers,
Dear Lord, we're bored,
Is virtue enough reward?

The ladies depart as Paul and Julia enter.

The following scene is the following day,
Lady Julia and Paul are alone.
In Julia's voice you quite possibly may
Discern a more predatory tone.

She admits she has loved him for years and he, touched by her admission, seems about to admit to a similar feeling.

We now return to Melanie's house . . .

And now for a rather charming scene,
Romantic, sweet, and gentle,
Adroitly planned for those who lean to the
sentimental.
Lord Sheere, whose loving heart is torn,
Finds Melanie, equally forlorn.

Melanie and Edward wish to play a trick on Paul. When he arrives, he will find them embracing. There are several false alarms. In song Melanie regrets the fact that neither of them, who have so much love to give, seem free to choose the objects of their love. . .

NEVERMORE

(Yvonne Printemps)

VERSE   Dear Friend,
If hearts could only be
Content with love and sympathy;
How sweetly we could live,
We both of us have so much love to give.
No matter how our minds conspire,
Imprisoned by our own desire,
We are not free to choose.
What love we gain,
What love we lose,
We cannot choose.

REFRAIN   Nevermore. Nevermore,
Can life be quite the same.
The lights and shadows change,
All the old familiar world is strange,
Evermore. Evermore,
Our hearts are in the flame.
Others may regain their freedom,
But for you and me,
Never-nevermore.

Finally, Paul arrives and the ploy works. He tell them that he is to marry Julia. Melanie appears to take the news well. Paul must bring Julia to a farewell supper with Edward and herself.

Walking alone in the gardens, Paul can think of nothing but Melanie.

In the final scene Melanie's house is being packed for departure. Edward arrives to be told by the maid that Melanie has left for France. When Lady Julia also arrives the maid says that Paul has gone too. They both leave. Enter Paul, to be given a farewell note from Melanie. As he reads it despairingly, a woman enters behind him. He is expecting the maid but it is, of course, Melanie. She sits at his feet as the curtain falls.

*   *   *

Conversation Piece was the last Coward/Cochran collaboration and all in all, Noël was pleased with its reception—"it is a pleasant entertainment, and I hope that one day, if we can ever find an artiste half as good as Yvonne Printemps, it may be revived." But they never did and it never was.

1936

The "theatrical mother" was a phenomenon Noël understood well—after all, he'd had one of his own! And since he'd been heavily involved in the production of his shows from early in his career, he'd become all too used to sitting through seemingly endless auditions involving variously talented tots.

To this day Graham Payn remembers his audition for *Words and Music* in early 1932 in "a cold and extremely cheerless Adelphi Theatre, London":

"In the front row of the 'audience' several apparently disinterested theatrical executives, including one elegantly poised man. (I remember thinking he was smoking his cigarette in a funny way.) On *our* side of the 'footlights' an upright piano with an elderly lady accompanist who'd seen it all before, and my mother, aggressively swathed in her best and only fur. And me.

"The words my mother had dinned into me before we entered the theatre rang in my ears: 'There can't be much scope for a boy soprano in a show like that . . . so sing and dance at the same time.' The moment the accompanist rattled the keys, I launched into an all-out display of my singing and dancing prowess . . . Undoubtedly these theatrical ladies and gentlemen had been exposed to more than their fair share of child prodigies. But, clearly, never to one singing 'Nearer My God To Thee,' while doing a tap dance.

"Visibly moved, the elegant man got to his feet, turned to his colleagues and declared in clipped tones, 'We have to have that kid in the show.'"

Thousands of other kids were not destined to be so lucky. Thousands of other mothers, however, continued to hope and contact "that nice Mr. Coward" who, after all, had been a child actor himself, had he not, and would therefore understand. In a song not intended for any show—until Noël used it in cabaret and the Coward "anthologies" began in the late 1960s—Noël tried to disabuse them of this idea in his "letter" to "Dear Mrs. Worthington" . . .

In a July 1943 entry in his *Middle East Diary* (1944) he records the inspiration for the song:

"The weather is still grey. I was very touched to realise that the ship (a P&O liner now converted to a troop ship) sailing along nearest to us is an old friend of mine . . . It was . . . in her that I sailed away from Singapore in 1936 and, during the voyage home, evolved the idea of *Tonight at Eight-Thirty*. . . . There, crowded now with khaki figures was the promenade deck round which I had been pursued by the over-anxious mother who ultimately inspired 'Don't Put Your Daughter on the Stage, Mrs. Worthington.'"

(DON'T PUT YOUR DAUGHTER ON THE STAGE,) MRS. WORTHINGTON

Regarding yours, dear Mrs Worthington,
Of Wednesday the 23rd,
Although your baby
May be,
Keen on a stage career,
How can I make it clear,
That this is not a good idea.
For her to hope,
Dear Mrs Worthington,
Is on the face of it absurd,
Her personality
Is not in reality
Inviting enough,
Exciting enough
For this particular sphere.

REFRAIN 1 Don't put your daughter on the stage,
    Mrs Worthington,
Don't put your daughter on the stage,
The profession is overcrowded
And the struggle's pretty tough
And admitting the fact
She's burning to act,
That isn't quite enough.
She has nice hands, to give the wretched
    girl her due,
But don't you think her bust is too
Developed for her age?

I repeat
Mrs Worthington,
Sweet
Mrs Worthington,
Don't put your daughter on the stage.

REFRAIN 2 Don't put your daughter on the stage,
    Mrs Worthington,
Don't put your daughter on the stage,
She's a bit of an ugly duckling
You must honestly confess,
And the width of her seat
Would surely defeat
Her chances of success,
It's a loud voice, and though it's not
    exactly flat,
She'll need a little more than that
To earn a living wage.
On my knees,
Mrs Worthington,
Please
Mrs Worthington,
Don't put your daughter on the stage.

REFRAIN 3 Don't put your daughter on the stage,
    Mrs Worthington,
Don't put your daughter on the stage,
Though they said at the school of acting
She was lovely as Peer Gynt,
I'm afraid on the whole
An ingénue role
Would emphasize her squint,
She's a big girl, and though her teeth are
    fairly good
She's not the type I ever would
Be eager to engage,
No more buts,
Mrs Worthington,
NUTS,
Mrs Worthington,
Don't put your daughter on the stage.

At which point the number normally ended. There was, however, one final verse which should leave the most insensitive "Mrs. Worthington" in no doubt . . .

REFRAIN 4 Don't put your daughter on the stage,
    Mrs Worthington,
Don't put your daughter on the stage,
One look at her bandy legs should prove
She hasn't got a chance,
In addition to which
The son of a bitch

Can neither sing nor dance,
She's a *vile* girl and uglier than mortal sin,
One look at her has put me in
A tearing bloody rage,
That sufficed,
Mrs Worthington,
Christ!
Mrs Worthington,
Don't put your daughter on the stage.

Sad to say, the song had quite the opposite effect from the one Noël intended, leading to the conclusion that "Mrs. Worthington" is always and invariably someone else. Noël took the outcome stoically: "The road of the social reformer," he said, "is paved with disillusion."

Noël's recollection of the song's origins makes for amusing reading but there is another, rather more mundane version told by a young actress who remembers Noël visiting her producer father. The father tossed aside a letter he had been reading and when asked what about the letter had clearly upset him, replied: "Oh, it's just a letter from some maddening woman called Mrs. Worthington, asking me if I can put her daughter on the stage."Noël, the lady recalled, went straight upstairs and wrote . . .

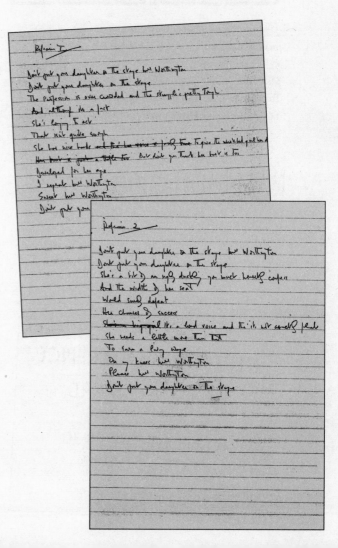

A series of nine (originally ten) one act plays performed three per evening, combined in various orders.

The first program presented by John C. Wilson as Tonight at 7.30 *and consisting of* We Were Dancing, The Astonished Heart *and* "Red Peppers" *was staged*

PHOENIX THEATRE
W.C.2

CHARING CROSS ROAD

Licensed by the Lord Chamberlain to   VICTOR LUXEMBURG

JOHN C. WILSON

presents

GERTRUDE LAWRENCE
NOEL COWARD

"TO-NIGHT AT 8.30"

THREE PLAYS by NOEL COWARD

at the Opera House, Manchester on October 15, 1935. Over the next several weeks, which included an extensive tour, the rest of the plays were added to the repertoire, some of them after the London opening. Presented at the opening of the Phoenix Theatre, London on January 6, 1936 as Tonight at 8.30 *with* Family Album, The Astonished Heart, *and* "Red Peppers." *(157 performances.)*

Noël described his intention in writing the plays, "upheld by my stubborn faith in the 'star system,'" as "acting, singing and dancing vehicles for Gertrude Lawrence and myself. The success we had had with *Private Lives* both in London and New York encouraged me to believe the public liked to see us playing together, and this belief, happily for us both and the managements concerned, turned out to be fully justified."

Four of the plays contained music.

WE WERE DANCING

· A COMEDY IN TWO SCENES

A couple fall in love instantly and irrationally as they find themselves in each other's arms on the dance floor . . . ("Gertie and I sang the number very quickly indeed with little vocal prowess but considerable abandon. Fortunately, the audiences appeared to enjoy it.")

WE WERE DANCING

VERSE 1   If you can
Imagine my embarrassment when you
    politely asked me to explain
Man to man,
I cannot help but feel conventional apologies
    are all in vain.
You must see

We've stepped into a dream that's set
    us free,
Don't think we planned it,
Please understand it.

REFRAIN 1   We were dancing
And the gods must have found it
    entrancing
For they smiled
On a moment undefiled
By the care and woe
That mortals know.
We were dancing
And the music and lights were enhancing
Our desire,
When the world caught on fire,
She and I were dancing.

VERSE 2   Love lay in wait for us,
Twisted our fate for us,
No one warned us,
Reason scorned us,
Time stood still.
In that first strange thrill.
Destiny knew of us,
Guided the two of us,
How could we
Refuse to see
That wrong seemed right,
On this lyrical enchanted night?
Logic supplies no laws for it,
Only one cause for it.

REFRAIN 2   We were dancing
And the gods must have found it
    entrancing
For they smiled
On a moment undefiled
By the care and woe
That mortals know.
We were dancing
And the music and lights were enhancing
Our desire,
When the world caught on fire,
She and I were dancing.

. . . in the cold light of morning, the music over, they come to their senses and go their separate ways.

HAS ANYBODY SEEN OUR SHIP?

Gertrude Lawrence and Noël Coward, We Were Dancing.

"RED PEPPERS"

AN INTERLUDE WITH MUSIC

Described by Noël as "a vaudeville sketch sandwiched in between two parodies of music hall songs."

In the pre-TV 1930s "music hall" was still a potent force in British entertainment with chains of theatres criss-crossing the country changing their bill on a weekly basis. Since every town had its Palace of Varieties(or the equivalent), many of them relics of grander Victorian times, the quality of bookings was variable indeed and if you were an act on the way down—as the "Red Peppers" indubitably was—you took what you could get and, in the case of George Pepper, remembered better times. The play finds George and his wife and partner, Lily, performing one of their principal numbers, dressed in sailor suits and curly red wigs. It tells of the mishaps of two sailors out on a spree . . .

VERSE I   What shall we do with the drunken sailor?
          So the saying goes.
          We're not tight but we're none too bright,
          Great Scott! I don't suppose!
          We've lost our way
          And we've lost our pay,
          And to make the thing complete,
          We've been and gone and lost the bloomin'
              fleet!

REFRAIN I Has anybody seen our ship?
          The *H.M.S. Peculiar.*
          We've been on shore
          For a month or more,
          And when we see the Captain we shall get
              'what for'.
          Heave ho, me hearties,
          Sing Glory Hallelujah,
          A lady bold as she could be
          Pinched our whistles at 'The Golden Key'.
          Now we're in between the devil and the
              deep blue sea.
          Has anybody seen our ship?

VERSE 2   What's to be done with the girls on shore
          Who lead our Tars astray?
          What's to be done with the drinks galore
          That make them pass away?
          We got wet ears
          From our first five beers—
          After that we lost control,
          And now we find we're up the blinking pole!

REFRAIN 2 Has anybody seen our ship?
          The *H.M.S. Disgusting.*
          We've three guns aft
          And another one fore
          And they've promised us a funnel for the
              next world war.
          Heave ho, me hearties,
          The quarterdeck needs dusting.
          We had a binge last Christmas year,
          Nice plum puddings and a round of beer,
          But the Captain pulled his cracker and we
              cried, 'Oh dear!'
          Has anybody seen our ship?

VERSE 3   Has anybody seen our ship?
          The *H.M.S. Suggestive.*
          She sailed away
          Across the bay,

The studio at Goldenhurst where Noël and Gertrude Lawrence (below) started rehearsing the one-act plays that would make up Tonight At 8.30.

The Goldenhurst visitors' book reads like a "Who's Who" of the theatre.

Noël in Tonight at 8.30.

And we haven't had a smell of her since
    New Year's Day.
Heave ho, me hearties,
We're getting rather restive.
We pooled our money, spent the lot,
The world forgetting by the world forgot,
Now we haven't got a penny for the you
    know what!
Has anybody seen our ship?

Lily ruins their exit by dropping her telescope and a row ensues in their dressing room. Various other members of the management and cast become involved before the call boy announces "Three minutes!" and the Red Peppers have to complete their quick change for their "toff" number. The show, however third rate, must go on . . .

The "Red Peppers" George and Lily, as played by Noël Coward and Gertrude Lawrence. Below, Graham Payn and Gertrude Lawrence in the 1948 New York production.

MEN ABOUT TOWN

VERSE   We're two chaps who
    Find it thrilling
    To do the killing,
    We're always willing
    To give the girls a treat.
    Just a drink at the Ritz,
    Call it double or quits,
    Then we feel the world is at our feet.
    Top hats, white spats
    Look divine on us,
    There's a shine on us,
    Get a line on us
    When we come your way.
    Gad! Eleven o'clock!
    Let's pop into the Troc.
    Ere we start the business of the day.

REFRAIN 1 As we stroll down Picc-Piccadilly
    In the bright morning air,
    All the girls turn and stare,
    We're so nonchalant and frightfully
      debonair.
    When we chat to Rose, Maud or Lily
    You should see the way their boy friends
      frown,
    For they know without a doubt
    That their luck's right out,
    Up against a couple of men about town.

REFRAIN 2 As we stroll down Picc-Piccadilly
    All the girls say, 'Who's here?
    Put your hat straight, my dear,
    For it's Marmaduke and Percy Vere de Vere.'
    As we doff hats, each pretty filly
    Gives a wink at us and then looks down
    For they long with all their might
    For a red-hot night
    When they see a couple of men about town

SHADOW PLAY

A PLAY WITH MUSIC

When the play opens Simon and Vicky Gayforth's four year old marriage appears to have broken down. Vicky has left yet another party, taken a heavy dose of sleeping pills and is preparing for bed when Simon arrives and during the conversation, asks for a divorce. "When did things begin to go wrong?" she asks, as the pills begin to work—"it was all so lovely in the beginning." From this point the play takes on the quality of her drowsy thoughts. There is a dreamlike quality to it with characters appearing and disappearing in spotlights, fade-outs and music coming from nowhere.

In the "dream" Vicky and Simon sing a duet . . .

belted it out in the teeth of the audience while the stage staff were changing the scene behind us.")

YOU WERE THERE

1

SIMON: Was it in the real world
Or was it in a dream?
Was it just a note from some eternal
theme?
Was it accidental
Or accurately planned?
How could I hesitate
Knowing that my fate
Led me by the hand?

REFRAIN You were there,
I saw you and my heart stopped beating,
You were there
And in that first enchanted meeting
Life changed its tune,
The stars, the moon
Came near to me.
Dreams that I dreamed,
Like magic seemed
To be clear to me, dear to me.
You were there.
Your eyes looked into mine and faltered.
Everywhere
The colour of the whole world altered.
False became true,
My universe tumbled in two,
The earth became heaven, for you
Were there.

THEN

SIMON: Here in the light of this unkind familiar now
Every gesture is clear and cold for us,
Every yesterday's growing old for us,
Everything changed somehow,
If some forgotten lover's vow
Could wake a memory in my heart again,
Perhaps the joys that we knew would start
again.
Can't we reclaim an hour or so?
The past is not so long ago.

VICKY: Then, love was complete for us,
Then, the days were sweet for us,
Life rose to its feet for us
And stepped aside
Before our pride.
Then, we knew the best of it,
Then, our hearts stood the test of it.
Now, the magic has flown,
We face the unknown,
Apart and alone.

Later, it seems that all may not be quite lost. Perhaps their first feelings are still there after all . . . ("We

PLAY, ORCHESTRA, PLAY

Listen to the strain
It plays once more for us,
There it is again,
The past in store for us.
Wake
In memory some forgotten song,
To break
The rhythm—driving us along
And make
Harmony again a last encore for us.

Play, orchestra, play,
Play something light and sweet and gay
For we must have music,
We must have music
To drive our fears away.
While our illusions
Swiftly fade for us,
Let's have an orchestra score
In the confusions
The years have made for us,
Serenade for us,
Just once more.
Life needn't be grey,
Although it's changing day by day,
Though a few old dreams may decay,
Play, orchestra, play.

Past and present intermingle in Vicky's brain. She remembers how she and Simon first met . . .

2

VICKY: How can we explain it,
The spark, and then the fire?
How add up the total
Of our hearts' desire?
Maybe some magician,
A thousand years ago—
Wove us a subtle spell
So that we could tell
So that we could know—

REFRAIN You were there,
I saw you and my heart stopped beating,
You were there
And in that first enchanted meeting
Life changed its tune,
The stars, the moon
Came near to me.
Dreams that I dreamed,
Like magic seemed

Gertrude Lawrence and Noël Coward as Vicky and Simon engage in "Shadow Play."

To be clear to me, dear to me.
You were there,
Your eyes looked into mine and faltered.
Everywhere
The colour of the whole world altered.
False became true,
My universe tumbled in two,
The earth became heaven, for you
Were there.

"'You Were There' we sang and danced more tran-
quilly in a moonlit garden. It was reprised by me later
in the show while Gertie was scrambling breathlessly
into a grey bouffant dress in the quick-change room
at the side of the stage. It is a pleasant, sentimental
little song and we both enjoyed doing it."

She comes round to find Simon still there.
Somehow he has shared her recollections. When she
asks him about the divorce, he has changed his mind.

FAMILY ALBUM

A VICTORIAN COMEDY WITH MUSIC

Noël described it as "a sly satire on Victorian
hypocrisy, adorned with an unobtrusive but agreeable musical score. It was stylised both in its *décor*
and its performance."

On an evening in 1860 the Featherways family
are gathered to read their late father's will and getting steadily tipsy in the process. Before they open
the box containing the will, they drink a toast—to
*themselve*s . . .

DRINKING SONG
(HERE'S A TOAST)

JASPER: Here's a toast to each of us
And all of us together.
Here's a toast to happiness
And reasonable pride.
May our touch on life be lighter
Than a seabird's feather;
May all sorrows as we pass
Politely step aside.

JANE: Jasper, my love,
You ask for too much, I fear,
What if your hopes
Should never come true, my dear?
Best be prepared for sorrow to stay
At least for a day,
At least for a day.
How can we find
The wisdom you dream for us?
There must be tears
In Destiny's scheme for us
But if at last we're able to smile
We'll prove it was all worth while!

JASPER: Now I drink to those of us who, happily united,
Ornament our family and share our joy
and pain.
Charles, my friend, and Edward, too,
connubially plighted,
Last, my dears, but always best, my own
beloved Jane.

JASPER: Harriet married a soldier,
A man of pleasant birth,
A man of sterling worth
And finely tempered steel,
Ready to die for the Empire,
The sun must never set
Upon this brave but yet
Ambiguous ideal.
So now, dear Charles, I am saluting you,
That never-setting sun
Shall call you blest,
If far-off natives take to shooting you
You will at least have done
Your level best.

ALL: Harriet married a soldier,
May life be bright for him;
May might be right for him
For ever and for aye.
Harriet married a soldier
And in the matrimonial fray,
Despite his glories in the field,
He'll have to honour and obey
And be defeated till Judgement day!

JASPER: Now we come to Emily whose progress
has been steady;
Only married two short years and three fat
sons already.

Emily married a doctor,
A mild and gentle man,
A sentimental man
Of scientific mind.
Doing his best for the nation,
For ever dutiful,
A really beautiful
Example for the rest of us,
A challenge for the rest of us,
The noblest and the best of us combined.

JASPER: Now then, for my dearest dear
I must ask your kind and grave indulgence for
How then, can I make it clear to you?

JANE: Sweet love, I appreciate
All these noble sentiments, but time is so
Fleet, love, what's this hesitating for—
Waiting for?

JASPER: You, love,
For ever a part of me,
True love,
Enshrined in the heart of me,
Who cares
What dreams we may lose?
For ever we choose
This lovely illusion.

JANE: After the difficult years have fled
Laughter will mock at the tears we've shed.

BOTH: We hold the future in store
Together for evermore.

ALL: Here's a toast for each of them
And both of them together.
Here's a toast to happiness
And reasonable pride.
May their touch on life be lighter
Than a seabird's feather;
May their sorrows as they pass
Politely step aside.

At first, they confuse boxes and open one that
was their "dressing-up box" when they were children. They used to play a game called "Princes and
Princesses" and for old times' sake they go through
the ritual again and sing the song that went with
it . . .

PRINCES AND PRINCESSES

Princes and Princesses,
Every rainy day,
In our party dresses
Made a trifle gay
With a rose and a shawl,
We would act a play
In the servants' hall.

Lavvy was the evil Queen
Wickeder than Nero,
Jasper, being just thirteen,
Always played the hero.
Crown and sceptre,
Rose and ring,
Magic charms for everything.
Death, destruction, fire and flame
Was our Sunday game.

Princes and Princesses,

Every rainy day,
In our party dresses
Made a trifle gay
With a rose and shawl,
We would act a play
In the servants' hall.

Inside the box they also find their old music box . . .

MUSIC BOX

ALL: Let's play a tune on the music box;
Let's play a tune on the music box.

BOYS: Let the angels guide you,
Be good and brave and true.
Let the angels guide you,
Oh do! Oh do! Oh do!

GIRLS: Let the angels guide you,
Be good and brave and true.
Let the angels guide you,
Oh do! Oh do! Oh do!

182

JANE: Spurn each vile temptation,
Avoid each evil lure.

JASPER: Keep your conversation
Inordinately pure.

EMILY: Lift your hearts to heaven
And pray for ultimate grace.

ALL: Be always virtuous just in case.

JANE: But of course in this vale of tears
Life may sometimes cheat a bit.
Hearts are prone to beat a bit
Causing great confusion.
When temptation to sin appears
Try to be discreet a bit,
Look well before the leaping,
Dream true awake or sleeping,
Love tears are waste of weeping.
Let reason over-ride you, guide you.

ALL: Look well before the leaping,
Dream true awake or sleeping,
Love tears are waste of weeping.
Let reason be your guiding star.

JASPER: Jane, I'm surprised, I'm ashamed of you;
Such a material point of view.
Keep your soul's endeavour
Sufficiently sincere.
Purity is ever
An excellent veneer.
Good may be rewarded
In some indefinite place.

ALL: Be always virtuous just in case.

JANE & JASPER: Death may have shaken us,
Gloom overtaken us,
Life may awaken us yet.
The sable plumes and cypresses
We might as well forget.

LAVINIA: Jasper, cry shame on you!
Decency's claim on you
Should at this moment prevent
Such bad, impertinent
Ungodly argument.

ALL: Let the angels guide you,
Be good and brave and true.
Let the angels guide you,
Oh do! Oh do! Oh do!
Spurn each vile temptation,
Avoid each evil lure.
Keep your conversation
Inordinately pure.
Good may be rewarded
In some indefinite place;
Be always virtuous just in case.

*Left and right: Noël Coward and
Gertrude Lawrence in Family Album.*

When the will is read, Lavinia, the unmarried daughter—now well in her cups—reveals that it is, in fact, an earlier will. The later one, which would have disinherited them all and given the money to their father's string of mistresses, was destroyed by her and Burrows, the old family retainer. The family wind up the music box again and dance around him as the curtain falls.

HEARTS AND FLOWERS

JANE: Hearts and Flowers,
Dreaming hours
Under skies of blue,
Two fond hearts so sweetly beat in tune
'Neath the midnight magic of the moon.
Petals falling,
Love-birds softly calling,
Life begins anew,
When Cupid's dart discloses
The secret of the roses,
Hearts and Flowers and You.

JANE & JASPER: Hearts and Flowers,
Bygone hours,
How the time has flown!

JASPER: You wore white camellias in your hair;

JANE: All you did was hold my hand and stare,

BOTH: Have we altered,
Have our footsteps faltered
Through the years we've known?
When all our days are done, love,
There'll still be only one love,
You and you alone.

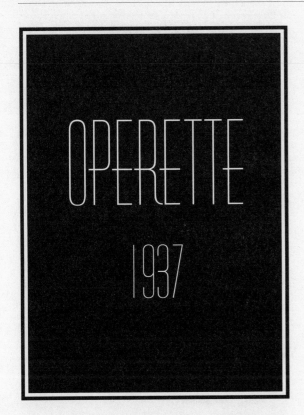

As with many of his shows, a title was used twice. *Operette* would not appear before the public until the following year but it had its genesis in 1937 when Noël was invited to pay a visit to Eleonora von Mendelssohn, the composer's granddaughter, at her imposing Schloss Kammer am Attersee, near Salzburg. His fellow guests were a mixed and exotic collection, not the least the distinguished conductor/pianist, Arturo Toscanini, with whom his hostess was besotted. Another guest was the Viennese singer, Fritzi Massary, whom Noël had first seen and admired in the early 1920s.

The result of the visit was the first act and a half of *Operette*, a play with music set in an Austrian schloss and reading like *Hay Fever* according to Chekhov. In the script as it exists there are, in fact, only two songs. A leading character, the famous singer, Liesl Haren (Massary) sings "Operette," while in the opening scene the servants (Frieda, Kathie, Kurt and Franzl sing a verse of what would become the "Opening Chorus."

> When we wake in the morning, the very first thing
> That we Austrians do is to sing and to sing.
> Tho' on every occasion our voices excel
> In a National crisis we yodel as well.
>
> We've discovered that music discourages gloom
> So we vocalise firmly on leaving the womb
> And when age and decay cause our final retreat
> We shall sing a few bars and expire on beat.

* * *

Although the verse was obviously never used in the context for which it was written, Noël did manage to find a later use for it in adapted form. In *Pacific 1860* (1946) the diva, Madame Salvador is telling her young admirer about the Austrians . . .

ELENA: . . . they are sweet people, but over-musical.

> (*Singing*)
> When you wake in the morning the very first thing
> The Austrians do is to sing and to sing:
> And when death overtakes them, in Heaven or Hell
> I'm perfectly certain they yodel as well!

He then adds a personal joke that would inevitably go over the heads of the audience, who had no reason to know anything about the origins, by having her say . . .

ELENA: I wrote that myself in an ornate little chalet near Salzburg. It made everyone very cross.

* * *

In an envelope lying next to the notes for this "Austrian Version" are the words and music for three completely unknown waltzes marked "German love." They also have page numbers for an unknown script. Whether they were intended for yet another uncompleted project or refer to a lost draft of this one there is no way of knowing. Since it would have been unthinkable for Noël to compose any "operette" without at least one waltz and since they are clearly of the period, I have included them here . . .

*I GAVE MY HEART AWAY (FIRST WALTZ)

> I gave my heart away
> How could it every stay,
> It was lost from the start
> Not a chance of escape,
> For my heart
> It is yours, and is glad to be
> Yours for eternity,
> And we know all our troubles are done
> Now our hearts are one.

VERSE
> Birds may sing, and sun may shine,
> My heart's yours, and yours is mine,
> While they share one single beat
> They know that life is sweet,
> Now my heart is not my own,
> It cannot live alone.

*JE T'AIME (SECOND WALTZ)

> There's no one to say what the future will show,
> Who can fortell what may happen tomorrow.
> One only can guess which direction to go,
> All is uncertain and yet there's one thing I know.
>
> For ever and ever I'll love you, for ever I know,
> I shall never forget you my whole life through,
> For ever and ever, it must be for ever,
> For nothing can sever the love that unites us two.

*THERE'S NO MORE TO SAY ABOUT LOVE (LAST WALTZ)

> There's no more to say about love,
> The poets have said it for ages,
> They rhyme it with "dove" and "above",
> And praise it for pages and pages,
> There isn't one passionate phrase that they miss,
> Yet lovers find new ones each time that they kiss.
> So what's a love poet to do
> When lovers are all poets too?
>
> There's no more to say about love
> Or rapture or feverish passion.
> Why can't we be gay about love
> And end this ridiculous fashion?
> Let love be a glad and delightful young thing,
> A happy sensation that blooms with the spring,
> Let's meet it with joy while you may,
> We must make the most of today.

VERSE How can words content a lover?
How can songs conceal his pain?
All the arts than men discover
Can not heal his heart again.
Yet still he sighs and he beseeches,
Still he tries his pretty speeches
Every time he finds a new love,
Never has there been such true love

Let's meet it with joy while you may,
We must make the most of today.

OPERETTE 1938

First presented by John C. Wilson at the Opera House, Manchester on February 17, 1938 and subsequently at His Majesty's Theatre, London on March 16, 1938. (132 performances.)

Cast included Fritzi Massary, Peggy Wood, Irene Vanbrugh, Griffith Jones, Phyllis Monkman, Hugh French, Kenneth Carten, John Gatrell, Ross Landon, John Laurie.

One more attempt to recapture the sweetness of *Bitter Sweet*—to the extent of appropriating the name of the genre and casting Peggy Wood (the original star of his earlier success), though this time not in the sole leading role. This she shared with European star Fritzi Massary.

PROLOGUE

Ladies and Gentlemen,
With your very kind permission
In accordance with tradition
We appear.
Unsentimental men
May declare us nauseating,
But by clear articulating
We are bent upon creating
Atmosphere.
We represent those carefree days
That still retained a bland hypocrisy
And looked upon Democracy
As quaint—
A certain transitory phase
Which every accurate historian
Has blamed upon Victorian
Restraint.
Our life was gay,
Champagne adorning it,
It passed away
And left us mourning it.
We've run our race
Time can't replace
These years of grace.
Non-temperamental men,
We implore you to surrender
To a mood of gay and tender
Sentiment. Ladies and Gentlemen,

Peggy Wood and Fritzi Massary

Though we wish our words were clearer,
If they've brought your memory nearer
To the light
Edwardian Era
We're content—
We've said our fill
Without much skill,
But thank you very very much for keeping still.

We meet the principal characters on the stage of the Jubilee Theatre, where they are playing the first act of the musical comedy, *The Model Maid . . .*

OPENING CHORUS

Hurray! Hurray!
We're ever so gay
And French as French can be,
We say 'Merci'
And 'This is the Vie'
Without exactly proving much.
We might as well be Russian or Dutch
Or Japanese,
Our sole intention is to please;
We're so vivacious
That we carry all before us
Prancing about beside the silver sea.
But goodness gracious
If it wasn't for the Chorus
Dancing about where would the Peerage be?
Hurray! Hurray!
We're ever so gay,
We smile and smirk and grin
Through thick and thin,
We'll never give in.
And though we tear ourselves to shreds
And wear these foolish hats on our heads
And do high kicks,
We all rehearsed with Seymour Hicks
In Trouville—Trouville Trouville—Nineteen-six.
On the Plage
Where the shady little ladies are at large,
It's Continental Hades
Where you sell your soul for this and that and
    those,
Spend your money
On milk and honey
And frills and furbelows.
If you're rich

You can take Yvette
To play roulette,
For which
She'll overcharge;
But nevertheless when day is done
A man must have a little fun
And fun is fun at Trouville on the Plage.

*　　*　　*

The famous hairdresser, Monsieur Pom-Pom arrives at the hotel in Trouville, where the scene is set . . .

POM-POM

Hurrah—Hurrah!
Wherever we are
We'll cheer until we're blue
The famous new
Couturier who
With velvet, crèpe de chine and lace,
Can help us in the horrible race
To commandeer
The nearest eligible Peer,
So lift your voices up and cheer
For Pom-Pom—Pom-Pom—Darling Pom-Pom's
　　here!

. . . only to find the place has been taken over by the Countess Mitzi, who introduces herself . . .

COUNTESS MITZI

(Fritzi Massary)

VERSE 1
MITZI:　My Father was Hungarian,
　　　　My Mother came from Spain,
　　　　I've several Aunts
　　　　In the South of France
　　　　And a Grandmamma—Maternal
　　　　　　Grandmamma
　　　　In the Ukraine.

CHORUS:　She went too far—poor Grandmamma,
　　　　For it's cold in the old Ukraine.

MITZI:　My Uncle is Bavarian,
　　　　I'm quite a pet of his,
　　　　So if I'm not
　　　　A Polyglot
　　　　I should like to know who is!

CHORUS:　If she's not a Polyglot we should like to
　　　　know who is.

Phyllis Monkham and Edward Cooper appear in "The Model Maid" as Pansy Brown and Monsieur Pom-Pom.

REFRAIN
MITZI:　They call me Countess Mitzi,
　　　　But I can't imagine why,
　　　　For my name is really Ludovika
　　　　Anastasie Frederika Isabel Rosa Mariposa
　　　　　　Nikinikolai.

CHORUS:　We can perfectly well see why
　　　　That to alter it people try;

MITZI:　For they'd rather say 'Countess Mitzi'
　　　　Just a teensy weensy bitsie,
　　　　Than a string of names like Ludovika
　　　　Anastasie Frederika Isabel Rosa Mariposa
　　　　　　Nikinikolai.

VERSE 2
MITZI:　My Grandpapa on Mother's side
　　　　Was far more East than West,
　　　　He spent his life
　　　　With a Chinese wife
　　　　In a mental home—half-Oriental home
　　　　In Bucharest.

CHORUS:　What cruel fate!
　　　　We'd simply hate
　　　　To be 'batty' in Bucharest.

The opening chorus of "The Model Maid," the play-within-the-play.

MITZI: My Grandma on the other side
          Was Russian to the core,
          She danced in Kiev
          But came to grief
          In a brawl in Singapore.

CHORUS: Ah, what a blow
          To sink so low
          As a brawl in Singapore.

REFRAIN

MITZI: Beware of Countess Mitzi,
          The world will tell you why,
          For my name is really
          Ludovika—Anastasie—Frederika
          Isabel—Rosa—Mariposa
          Nikinikolai.
          You can perfectly well see why
          People think I've a naughty eye
          For they'd rather say Countess Mitzi
          Just a teensy weensy bitsie
          Than a string of names like
          Ludovika—Anastasie—Frederika
          Isabel—Rosa—Mariposa
          Nikinikolai!

The hero and heroine of *The Model Maid* sing the
theme song duet from both plays . . .

DEAREST LOVE

(*Peggy Wood and Max Oldaker*)

JOHN: I saw your face,
          Shadows of the morning cleared,
          I knew that suddenly
          The world had dropped away.

MARY: Somewhere in space
          Some new lovely star appeared
          To rule our destiny
          For ever and a day.

JOHN: I knew, the moment that I touched your
              hand,
          The gods had planned
          Our meeting.

MARY: Now in this instant in the whole of Time
          Our lovers' rhyme
          Is near completing.

JOHN: I saw you turn away and for a while
          My poor heart drooped and faltered;
          And then I saw your strange elusive smile
          And all my life was altered.

BOTH: My dearest dear,
          For evermore
          The happiness we've waited for
          At last is here.

REFRAIN

JOHN: Dearest Love,
          Now that I've found you
          The stars change in the sky,
          Every song is new,
          Every note is true,
          Sorrows like the clouds go sailing by.

MARY: Here, my Love,
          Magic has bound you
          To me—ever to be
          In my heart supreme,
          Dearer than my dearest dream,
          The only love for me.

JOHN: Skies that were cloudy are clear again,
          All other people seem
          Like figures in a dream;

MARY: Every song that I loved I seem to hear again,
          Time goes by like a murmuring stream.

JOHN: Love has enchanted the two of us,
          A magic we can share,
          A something in the air,

MARY: Proving that Destiny knew of us
          Now Heaven is at our feet,
          This happiness complete
          Could not be merely chance,
          This exquisite romance

BOTH: For ever has us bound,
          For this that we have found
          No time or tide could sever—ever.

          Dearest Love,
          Now that I've found you
          The stars change in the sky,
          Every song is new,
          Every note is true,
          Sorrows like the clouds go sailing by.
          Here, my Love,
          Magic has bound you
          To me—ever to be
          In my heart supreme,
          Dearer than my dearest dream,
          The only love for me!

Noël's notes include an additional and final refrain . . .

          *Dear Love,
          Waking or sleeping
          I think only of you,
          Tho' our story's told,
          Tho' our world is cold,
          Tho' we have to build our lives anew,
          Here love lies in your keeping
          Till all memories die.
          Tho' we go our ways,
          Thank you for those lovely days,
          My only love, goodbye.

*   *   *

Noël then attempts a form rare for him in a "double
sextette," as six men and six girls sing about "Foolish
Virgins" . . .

FOOLISH VIRGINS

MEN: Here are ladies,
          Charming ladies,
          A fascinating flock of them—
          Our hearts are taking stock of them;
          No well-respected amorist

Could be expected to resist
This lovely group
Of femininity,
So we stoop
On bended knee.

GIRLS: Here are gentlemen,
Handsome gentlemen,
Though conscience may be muttering,
Our hearts insist on fluttering;
We feel today our luck is in
But can't betray our genuine
Relief to meet
So much virility
At our feet
In all humility,
None the less
Our gay fragility
They mustn't guess.

MEN: Dear little ladies, we beseech you
Not to be deaf to what we say,
If our romantic thoughts could reach you
Maybe you'd consent to stay
And not be too offended;
We should think it splendid
If you'd just consent to stay.

GIRLS: If we were offended
We'd go away,
But we must not appear too willing
Lest you should think us not quite nice,
Though we admit it might be thrilling
Just for once to sacrifice
Our sense of obligation
To our education,
Which was very strict and stern.

MEN: What is education
If not to learn?
Just a stroll beside the ocean
Might be a notion
More or less acceptable to moral views.

GIRLS: It really would be too ungracious to refuse,
MEN: After that delicious ramble
We might enjoy a little gamble:

GIRLS: Backing your luck may be a thrill
But we prefer a game of skill.

MEN: Later on with Moët Chandon
You might abandon
All disturbing fears of what Mamma would
think.

GIRLS: You surely don't suppose we'd ever take
to drink!

MEN: Later still we might persuade you
To take a swim as Nature made you.

GIRLS: Fie and for shame, you go too far,
Kindly remember that we are:

REFRAIN One little
Two little
Three little
Four little
Five little
Six little

*Right, The Jubilee Theatre
Sextette: left to right, Lisa
d'Esterre, Jean Barnes, Peggy
Wood, Pamela Randell, Hedli
Anderson and Linda Gray.*

*Below the "double sextette," sing
about "Foolish Virgins."*

Foolish Virgins
Eager to be some good man's wife
And learn the facts of life.
Neat little
Sweet little
Shy little
Sly little
Meek little
Chic little
Chicks emerging
Out of the shell that held them fast
At last—at last—at last.
Please excuse our artless prattling,
We're as green as nuts in May,
On the loose and almost rattling
For the matrimonial fray.
We've one little
Two little
Three little
Four little
Five little
Six little ego's urgin'
Any rich man we chance to see
To take us on a spree
With a substantial guarantee,
Foolish Virgins we.

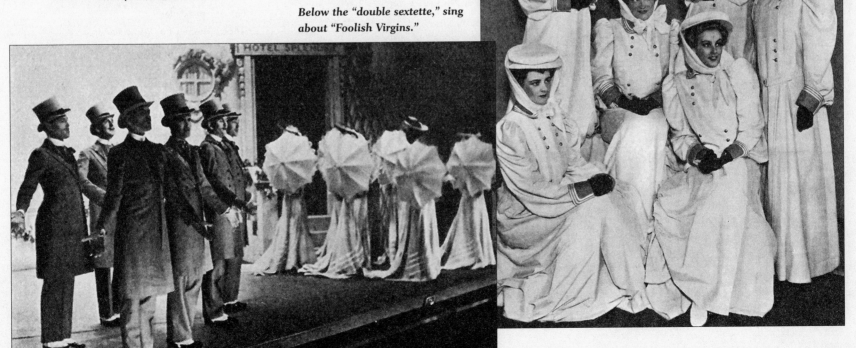

188 * * *

In what is essentially an interpolated number having little or nothing to do with the plot of either play, the quartet of Lord Elderley, Lord Borrowmere, Lord Sickert and Lord Camp chronicle the fate of "The Stately Homes of England."

THE STATELY HOMES OF ENGLAND

VERSE 1

Lord Elderley, Lord Borrowmere,
Lord Sickert and Lord Camp,
With every virtue, every grace,
Ah what avails the sceptred race,
Here you see—the four of us,
And there are so many more of us,
Eldest sons that must succeed.
We know how Caesar conquered Gaul
And how to whack a cricket ball;
Apart from this, our education lacks co-ordination.
Though we're young and tentative
And rather rip-representative,
Scions of a noble breed,
We are the products of those homes serene and
    stately
Which only lately
Seem to have run to seed!

REFRAIN 1

The Stately Homes of England,
How beautiful they stand,
To prove the upper classes
Have still the upper hand;
Though the fact that they have to be rebuilt
And frequently mortgaged to the hilt
Is inclined to take the gilt
Off the gingerbread,
And certainly damps the fun
Of the eldest son—
But still we won't be beaten,
We'll scrimp and scrape and save,
The playing fields of Eton
Have made us frightfully brave—
And though if the Van Dycks have to go
And we pawn the Bechstein Grand,
We'll stand
By the Stately Homes of England.

VERSE 2

Here you see
The pick of us,
You may be heartily sick of us,
Still with sense
We're all imbued.
Our homes command extensive views
And with assistance from the Jews
We have been able to dispose of
Rows and rows and rows of
Gainsboroughs and Lawrences,
Some sporting prints of Aunt Florence's,
Some of which were rather rude.
Although we sometimes flaunt our family
    conventions,
Our good intentions
Mustn't be misconstrued.

REFRAIN 2

The Stately Homes of England
We proudly represent,
We only keep them up for
Americans to rent,
Though the pipes that supply the bathroom
    burst
And the lavatory makes you fear the worst,
It was used by Charles the First
Quite informally,
And later by George the Fourth
On a journey north.
The State Apartments keep their
Historical renown,
It's wiser not to sleep there
In case they tumble down;
But still if they ever catch on fire
Which, with any luck, they might
We'll fight
For the Stately Homes of England

REFRAIN 3

The Stately Homes of England,
Though rather in the lurch,
Provide a lot of chances
For Psychical Research—
There's the ghost of a crazy younger son
Who murdered, in thirteen fifty-one,
An extremely rowdy Nun
Who resented it,
And people who come to call
Meet her in the hall.
The baby in the guest wing,
Who crouches by the grate,
Was walled up in the west wing
In fourteen twenty-eight.

If anyone spots
The Queen of Scots
In a hand-embroidered shroud
We're proud
Of the Stately Homes of England.

REPRISE—ACT II

VERSE 3

Lord Elderley, Lord Borrowmere,
Lord Sickert and Lord Camp,
Behold us in our hours of ease,
Uncertain, coy and hard to please.
Reading in *Debrett* of us,
This fine Patrician quartette of us,
We can feel extremely proud,
Our ancient lineage we trace
Back to the cradle of the Race
Before those beastly Roman bowmen
Bitched our local Yeomen.
Through the new democracy
May pain the old Aristocracy
We've not winced nor cried aloud,
Under the bludgeonings of chance what will be—
    will be.
Our heads will still be
Bloody but quite unbowed!

REFRAIN 4

The Stately Homes of England
In valley, dale and glen
Produce a race of charming,
Innocuous young men.
Though our mental equipment may be slight
And we barely distinguish left from right,
We are quite prepared to fight
For our principles,
Though none of us know so far
What they really are.
Our duty to the nation,
It's only fair to state,
Lies not in pro-creation
But what we pro-create;
And so we can cry
With kindling eye
As to married life we go,
What ho!
For the Stately Homes of England!

REFRAIN 5

The stately Homes of England,
Although a trifle bleak,
Historically speaking,
Are more or less unique.

"Lord Elderley, Lord Borrowmere, Lord Sickert and Lord Camp,"
extol the virtues of "The Stately Homes of England."

We've a cousin who won the Golden Fleece
And a very peculiar fowling-piece
Which was sent to Cromwell's niece,
Who detested it,
And rapidly sent it back
With a dirty crack.
A note we have from Chaucer
Contains a bawdy joke.
We also have a saucer
That Bloody Mary broke.
We've two pairs of tights
King Arthur's Knights
Had completely worn away.
Sing Hey!
For the Stately Homes of England.

The song, Noël recalled, "was what is colloquially known as a "show stopper." It was performed by Hugh French, John Gatrell, Angus Menzies and Ross Landon. They were all nice-looking, their diction was clear and they never went off without resounding applause. Since then I have recorded it and sung it all over the world and it has been popular with everyone with the exception of a Mayoress

in New Zealand, who said it let down the British Empire."

Noël's notes reveal some alternate couplets that didn't survive into the final version. In reference to their being in *Debrett* . . .

And every single bloody entry
Lands the landed gentry

. . . while Chaucer alternatively appeared . . .

We've got some notes of Chaucer's
And Boadecia's toque

And in defence of their lineage . . .

We're not exactly come what may
Which so emboldens us to say
We may have a chequered past
But still we seem to last

There is also one more complete refrain . . .

The Stately Homes of England,
Tho' rather on the blink
Provide a lot of reasons

For what we do and think.
Tho' we freely admit we may be wrong,
Our conviction that we are right is strong
Tho' it may not be for long,
We'll hold on to it
We might as well hold the bat
Till they knock us flat
Our dignity of race may
Retire into its shell
Our Minister of Grace may
Defend us none too well
But still if a child
Becomes too wild
And we're forced to use the rod,
Thank God
For the Stately Homes of England

*   *   *

Back in the play outside the play, the real lovers—Nigel and Roxanne—are dining tête-à-tête and telling each other the stories of their lives. Roxanne confides in him how she felt the first time she was in love . . .

WHERE ARE THE SONGS WE SUNG?

(Peggy Wood)

VERSE

Once in a lifetime
When we are very very young—and Love
Comes out to greet us for the first time,
We open wide our arms and say to him
This is the only, and the last time.
That young surrender
We can remember when some little tune
Recalls our hearts to vanished splendour
Like organ music in a sunny street
So sweetly flat—so sadly tender.
And so when Love again rides by
We sometimes sigh:

REFRAIN 1

Where are the songs we sung
When Love in our hearts was young?
Where, in the limbo of the swiftly passing
    years,
Lie all our hopes and dreams and fears?

Where have they gone—words that rang so true
When Love in our hearts was new?
Where in the shadows that we have to pass
    among,
Lie those songs that once we sung?

REFRAIN 2

Where are the songs we sung
When Love in our hearts was young?
Can you remember all the foolish things we said,
The plans we planned—the tears we shed?
Where is it now—that enchanted dawn
When Love in our hearts was born?
Where, in the shadows that we have to pass
    among,
Lie those songs that once we sung?

*VERSE 2

Are we mistaken
In this remembering of little things
That made our first story love awaken?
Should we not leave them with those other
    dreams
The passing years have overtaken?
Youth is behind us,
We cannot live among our yesterdays
Nor let their light forever blind us
For with the wisdom of our later days
Perhaps some deeper love may find us.
But still tho' life make us wise
An echo cries

Noël noted that the song was "melodic but depressing," although "musically speaking, the verse is unusual and offsets the conventionality of the refrain."

*   *   *

Back in the world of *The Model Maid* the leading comedian (Pom-Pom) sings his Wodehouseian comic song . . .

THE ISLAND OF BOLLAMAZOO

(Edward Cooper)

REFRAIN 1

ALL: On the Island of Bollamazoo
       Life is almost too good to be true.

POM-POM: You can fish on a reef
       Wearing pearls and a leaf
       Which at Brighton you never could do.
       For a few coloured beads from the Penny
         Bazaar
       You can buy luscious oysters wherever you are
       And you don't have to wait for a month with
         an R
       On the Island of Bollamazoo.

ALL: On the Island of Bollamazoo
       Life is almost too good to be true.

POM-POM: You don't have to care what your neighbours
         might think
       If a charming young lady should give you a wink
       You can buy her outright for the price of
         a drink
       On the Island of Bollamazoo.

REFRAIN 2

ALL: On the Island of Bollamazoo
       Life is almost too good to be true.

POM-POM: No one ever gets warm
       Over Tariff Reform
       And the thought of Home Rule is taboo.
       Unlike Campbell-Bannerman's dignified pose
       The local Prime Minister welcomes his foes
       With a club in one hand and a ring through
         his nose
       On the Island of Bollamazoo.

ALL: On the Island of Bollamazoo
       Life is almost too good to be true.

POM-POM: The ladies are dusky, domestic and fair,
       For the suffragette movement they wouldn't
         much care,
       And they'd think 'Votes for Women' were
         something to wear
       On the Island of Bollamazoo.

*   *   *

Act 2 opens with another sextette. This time the men and girls are paired off in hansom cabs . . .

PROLOGUE (ACT II)

Ladies and Gentlemen,
Though it wasn't our ambition
To succeed the intermission,

Here we are,
Ladies and Gentlemen,
Do not think us too ironic
If we hope you've quenched your chronic
Thirst for Scotch or Gin and Tonic
In the Bar.

We now begin the Second Act
Which we believe will be effectual
And not too intellectual
A bore—
But still we cannot blink the fact
That though you get a little wit through us
It's hard to have to sit through us
Once more.
The only vindication for us is
We're like those classical Greek Choruses
Who made the curse
Of laboured verse
A great deal worse.
Bluff Regimental men
Would—we feel—prefer a frolic
To this rather mock-symbolic
Rhymed refrain.
Ladies and Gentlemen,
Do not think the author cheated,
This effect has been repeated
Once again;
Although we lack
Charm and attack
We thank you very, very much for coming back.

Two more songs from *The Model Maid*. The heroine, Mary, is expecting to elope with her aristocratic suitor . . .

SING FOR JOY

(Peggy Wood)

MARY: Rhapsody—there is rhapsody
    In the atmosphere.

CHORUS: The lady is enchanted.
    The lady is enchanted.

MARY: My dearest wish is granted,
    My heart had found wings,
    Each moment brings
    My lover near.

CHORUS: Each fleeting moment brings him near.

MARY: Every note of my song he'll hear,

True and clear,
Love is here,
Love is here,
He'll answer.

Sing for joy
I will echo it,
Sing for Joy,
Let the music play,
Lifting us away
Beyond retreating,
Lyrically meeting
To the tune that our hearts are beating.
This moment is divine, love,
Yours and mine, love,
This melody enthralling,
Calling—calling .
Sing for Joy,
I will echo it,
Tra la la—tra la la, tra la la—tra la la,
Sing for the joy of love.
Ah ah ah ah
Ah ah ah ah

CHORUS: Let their heaven last,
    The future and the past
    Merging in the dream they're sharing.

MARY: Ah ah ah ah
    Ah ah ah ah.

CHORUS: Now no matter how the Gods conspire
    This moment is their hearts' desire.

MARY: Joy is the song I sing to you.
    Ever new,
    Ever true.

Sing for Joy,
I will echo it,
Sing for Joy,
Let the music play,
Lifting us away
Beyond retreating,
Lyrically meeting
To the tune that our hearts are beating.
This moment is divine, love,
Yours and mine, love,
This melody enthralling,
Calling—calling .
Sing for Joy,
I will echo it,
Tra la la—tra la la
Tra la la—tra la la,
Sing for the joy of love.

. . . when she receives a letter saying that he has changed his mind . . .

MY DEAR MISS DALE

(Peggy Wood)

'My dear Miss Dale,
When you receive this letter
I shall be far away,
And hope you will forgive me when I say
That it is better
For you and I
To say goodbye . . .'
Trust must prevail
And in our hearts' confusion
Whatever love we give
It's better far that we should learn to live
Without illusion . . .'

What have I done that you should treat me so?
What bitter Fate should wish to cheat me so?
Why should this hour of happiness supreme
Change to despair with the swiftness of a
    troubled dream?
I only know all my love I gave to you
With happy heart willingly a slave to you,
This foolish heart that you have so cruelly
    betrayed
I now withdraw from you,
For ever more from you,
For ever more!

*   *   *

Back in the "real" world the chorus girls are having tea with Liesl (Countess Mitzi), the experienced older actress. They ask her about her early career and she answers them in song . . .

OPERETTE

(Fritzi Massary)

GIRLS: Tell us, darling Liesl, please,
    How you became a star:
    Was it hard in the beginning?
    Were you sinned against?—Or were you
      sinning?

LIESL: In reconstructing my career for you
    I must make one thing clear for you,
    That's only fair.

GIRLS: We'll concentrate with all our might.

LIESL: Be under no misapprehension,
           I do not intend to mention
           Who my lovers were,

GIRLS: How disappointing, but how right!

LIESL: But all the same
           You will agree
           An artist's life can never be
           Quite free from blame.
           But don't forget
           And try to see
           That everything in life to me
           Is Operette.

           Ever since a child of tender age
           The world has been a stage
           For me to dance upon;
           Wedding bells could never ring for me,
           The only thing for me
           Was 'Getting On'.
           I made my start
           While other girls were having love affairs,
           I set my heart
           Upon a destiny above affairs
           Throughout my lonely youth

I knew too much reality,
So now my only truth
Is artificiality.
But if some light refrain
Can make me live again
Then you can really clearly see
All that I am or wish to be.

REFRAIN

Something remembered of joy and regret,
That's Operette—that's Operette!
Melodies that call to mind forgotten laughter
Songs that linger in the memory for ever after,
That was my start,
That is my heart,
Life for me is ever orchestrated,
Everywhere my scene is set,
Singers of songs have the world in their debt.
Memories that Time can never stop,

*   *   *

"*Operette,*" Noël was to write, "from my point of view, is the least successful musical play I have ever done . . . it is over-written and under-composed. The story of an imaginary 'Gaiety Girl' of the early nineteen-hundreds who achieves overnight stardom and then has to sacrifice her love-life to her career, while not fiercely original, is an agreeable enough background for gay music and lyrics and beguiling 'period' costumes. Unfortunately, however, the plot which should have been the background, became the foreground, and the music, which should have dominated the action, established the atmosphere, and whirled the play into a lilting success, was meagre and only at moments adequate."

Matters were not helped by Noël's inclusion of his favourite play-within-a-play device. *Cavalcade* had introduced the operetta, *Mirabelle* for two of the leading characters to visit but then the episodic structure of the play permitted it. In *Operette* it loomed too large and simply created "triumphant-confusion . . . in the minds of the audience . . . I remember peering from my box . . . and watching bewildered playgoers rustling their programmes and furtively striking matches in a frantic effort to discover where they were and what was going on."

Despite that experience, he did not remain deterred. The device was tried again in *Ace of Clubs* as well as *The Girl Who Came to Supper* and one of the original *Operette* numbers ("Countess Mitzi") was even recycled in the latter as "My Family Tree."

Fritzi Massary, as Liesl Haren, singing "Operrette."

First presented by John C. Wilson at the Shubert Theatre, Boston on December 26, 1938 and subsequently at the Music Box Theatre, New York on January 18, 1939. (129 performances).

Cast included Beatrice Lillie, Richard Haydn, Hugh French, Anna Jackson, Laura Duncan, Ruby Green, Eva Ortega, Kenneth Carten, Anthony Pélissier.

Noël described the show as a "rehash" of *Words and Music* and, indeed, many of the numbers were simply transposed and reinterpreted. He also added several numbers—including "The Stately Homes of England" (from *Operette*) and "A Fragonard Impression" . . .

*A FRAGONARD IMPRESSION

CHARACTERS

A Young Singer . . . . Eva Ortega
Lisette. . . . . Mary Ann Carr
Tiger Plon Plon . . . . Leonard Gibson
La Marquise de Sauriole (Maman) . . . . . .
                     Maidie Andrews
Monsieur L'Abbé . . . . Sanders Draper
Blanche . . . . Penelope Dudley
Germaine. . . . . Moya Nugent
Eugénie . . . . Rosemary Lomax
Marguerite. . . . . Sarah Burton
Giselle. . . . . Beatrice Lillie

The scene is a bedroom in Eighteenth Century France.

The Young Singer appears before the curtain rises and sings the following:

Now the dawn has put to flight
Fears and shadows of the night
Phoebus in the summer sky
Impatiently is riding high
Encouraging the clouds to hurry by.
Many years may lie between
Nowadays and what has been
Yet the mists shall roll away
Before a gentler sweeter day
When France the land of elegance and grace
Smiled at the summer's early morning face.

The curtains part disclosing a bedroom decorated in the Style of Fragonard. There are shuttered windows through which the sunlight is filtering. On the right there is a dressing table. On the left a clothes press and in the centre a large four-poster bed with the curtains drawn. Lisette and Tiger bustle on to music followed by the Marquise. Tiger is a litttle black page. He carries a tray of chocolate. The Marquise sings.

MARQUISE: Keep your voices low
And go tip toe—tip toe
The Princess is sleeping
Through dreamland her heart is creeping

(Lisette pulls up the blinds)

Let the sunlight in,
The brave new day begin
The morning is shining brightly
Don't wake her impolitely
Tiger, walk with care
And put the tray down there.
Don't let it rattle
Like the drums of battle.
Softly I entreat
For morning sleep is sweet
And dreams bring peace,
Light release
From all our sharp realities
Don't wake her too abruptly, please.

(Monsieur L'Abbé enters to music. The Marquise puts her finger to her lips and they converse in whispers. Blanche, Eugénie, Germaine and Marguerite enter. They curtsey to the Marquise and then dutifully kiss her. They also curtsey to the Abbé.)

GIRLS: *(Singing)*
Bon jour, Maman
We've put our ribbons on
To greet with joy our sister's betrothal morn.

MARQUISE: *Bien fait*
But whisper low, I pray
She yet is sleeping the sleep of a babe new
     born.
So be still,
Darlings, be still
For dreams bring peace,
Light release
From all our sharp realities.
Don't wake her too abruptly, please.

(The girls giggle and dance about a little, then they cluster round their mother.)

GIRLS: *(Singing)*
Mother, tell us, mother,
Have you anything in your heart to tell our
     sister dear?
Any words that we should not hear
That we're too young to know?

MARQUISE: *(Speaking)*
If that were so—I'd bid you go.

194

GIRLS: (Singing)
           Mother, tell us, mother
           If the dreams that you dreamed in Springtime
           Have come true for you
           What Love promised to do for you
           Did it actually do?

MARQUISE: (Singing)
           With Love the whole wide world seems new.

GIRLS: And will she understand the magic flame
           As you did when at first your lover came?
           What did he bring to you?
           What melodies did he sing to you?

MARQUISE: The same
           Melodies that lovers sing
           Whenever the heart is gay with Spring
           And youth is there.
           I assure you the truth is there
           The years hurry for young love is brief
           Tears follow with the fall of the leaf
           Age may bring you sadly to grief
           Unless you're wise
           And realise
           That dignity is the greatest prize
           To guard.

GIRLS: That's dreadfully hard!

MARQUISE: Once on a time I was young and fair like you.

GIRLS: We know.

MARQUISE: Happily dreaming my adolescence through.

GIRLS: Heigho.

MARQUISE: Then I married your father
           Gay and handsome and strong
           Kind love taught me my lessons as I went
              along.
           One must be tender
           And wise and witty, too.

GIRLS: How true!

MARQUISE: Never surrender
           Until surrender's due
           A few—thoughts may lead you astray, dears
           But recall what I say, dears.
           Life is for living
           Love is for giving,
           That is the only way, dears.

*(The girls who have been kneeling at her feet, rise
and stand round the bed. Everyone sings together.)*

           Awake—Awake—Princess, Awake.
           The happy day is waiting for your laughter
           Your love is near

You soon will start your life anew,
Awake and hear
The joyful melodies romance will gladly sing
   to you
Awake—Awake—Be proud to take
Your lover's hand in yours for ever after
The loveliest dream that you ever knew
Is coming true
Awake—Awake—Awake!

*(They pull the bed curtains aside disclosing Giselle
dressed as one of the Valkyrie carrying a spear, sitting
on a white horse, and singing at the top of her lungs.)*

BLACK OUT

RUG OF PERSIA

(Beatrice Lillie)

*(The scene is a Persian harem. MARSINAH is working at a
large tapestry held up by two Eunuchs. All the wives of the
Sultan are seated on cushions being waited on hand and foot
by a small black boy.)*

GIRLS: AH—AH AH AH

MARSINAH: Just a rug of Persia
           Less than the dust
           Yet it's a woman's art

GIRLS: Ah Ah Ah Ah.

MARSINAH: Tread upon it lightly
           If tread you must
           For in it lies my heart

GIRLS: Ah Ah Ah Ah

MARSINAH: Click clack—click clack
           Goes my needle sharp and bright
           From early dawn till late at night
           My busy fingers weave.

GIRLS: Click clack—click clack
           Goes the needle sharp and bright
           She's at her tricks from morn till night
           With nothing up her sleeve.

MARSINAH: Until my own true love appears
           I shall sit here for years and years
           Each stitch is watered by my tears
           When will he come to me
           When will he come to me
           This wondrous Prince I see?
           I weave my destiny
           Here on my tapestry

ALL: Ah Ah Ah Ah

MARSINAH: This is the forest of my girlish fancies,
           This is my world of dreams,
           This is the hero of my love romances
           Splashing through lakes and laughing
              streams
           Here on the right Is the moon of my
              delight
           This is a Persian horse
           This rather deft little object on the left
           Is the Star of the East, of course
           Tho' you may think that I'm far too faddy,
           My heart belongs to my old Bag-Daddy.
           Ah Ah Ah Ah
           Ah Ah Ah Ah
           Ah Ah Ah Ah

*(Singing madly she catches her foot in the thread
and, as she goes off, unfortunately unravels her dream
lover completely.)*

*   *   *

In addition to playing the Schoolgirl part in "Mad
About the Boy," Bea Lillie introduced two new songs.
The first, "Weary of it All" was the sad story of the
jaded socialite who has constantly to go and dine
with "this or that rich man about town" on "caviar
and grouse/In an overheated house/God, how it gets
me down!" In many respects it formed the companion piece to the earlier "World Weary" . . .

(I'M SO)
WEARY OF IT ALL

VERSE   People that I sing to
           Bring a breath of Spring to
           Envy me my gay career.
           No one in the city
           Has much time for pity,
           Nobody can be sincere;
           Thousands cheer me and applaud me,
           Every one stares.
           If they've wounded me and bored me
           Nobody cares;
           Women at the tables,
           Loosening their sables,
           Look at me with cruel eyes,
           Then a little something in me dies
           And cries.

REFRAIN Weary of it all,
This getting and spending,
This futile unending
Refrain,
It's driving me insane;
I'm so weary of it all.
Other voices call,
The cattle at twilight,
The birds in the sky light
Of dawn,
Yet here am I forlorn
And so weary of it all.
I miss the wild-wood
I wandered through in childhood
With a heart as light as air,
What would I give once again to be there
With my old, deaf mother!
Night begins to fall,
By memory tortured
I dream of an orchard
In Spring,
The songs I used to sing.
Now I have to swing,
I'm so weary of it all.

PATTER Wake up in the morning
'Round about noon,
A little lunch on a tray,
Shopping without stopping till my senses
swoon,
Or else some dreary matinée,
Home at five,
More dead then alive,
Another day nearly gone.
Cocktails to mix,
My face and hair to fix,
The weary round goes on.
Eight or nine,
I have to go and dine
With this or that rich man about town,
Caviar and grouse
In an overheated house,
God, how it gets me down!
Home I go defeated and depressed again,
Only time for just one hour of rest again.
Bright lights,
White lights,
Waiters leering,
Faces sneering,
Laughing, chaffing,
Shouting, cheering,
Weary of it all
This giving and giving,
This life that I'm living in hell.

With broken dreams to sell,
Just an empty shell,
Weary, weary, weary of it all!

But the undoubted hit of the revue was her rendering of "Marvellous Party"—variously sung later by both her and Noël as "I went to . . ." or "I've been to . . ." with identical effect . . .

"During the summer of 1937 or 1938, I forget which, Elsa Maxwell gave a party in the South of France. It was a 'Beach' party and when she invited Grace Moore, Beatrice Lillie and me she explained that we were to come as we were and that it would be 'just ourselves.' When we arrived (as we were) we discovered that 'just ourselves' meant about a hundred of us, all in the last stages of evening dress. We also discovered that one of the objects of the party was for us to entertain. As we were on holiday and had no accompanist and were not in any way prepared to perform, we refused. Elsa was perfectly understanding, but the other guests were a trifle disgruntled. I believe Beattie was persuaded to sing, but Grace and I held firm. The whole glittering episode was my original inspiration for 'I Went to a Marvellous Party.' Beattie eventually sang the song . . . wearing slacks, a fisherman's shirt, several ropes of pearls, a large sunhat and dark glasses. She has sung it a great deal since."

I WENT TO A MARVELLOUS PARTY

VERSE 1 Quite for no reason
I'm here for the Season
And high as a kite,
Living in error
With Maud at Cap Ferrat
Which couldn't be right.
Everyone's here and frightfully gay,
Nobody cares what people say,
Though the Riviera
Seems really much queerer
Than Rome at its height,
Yesterday night—

REFRAIN 1 I went to a marvellous party
With Nounou and Nada and Nell,
It was in the fresh air
And we went as we were
And we stayed as we were
Which was Hell.
Poor Grace started singing at midnight
And didn't stop singing till four;
We knew the excitement was bound to begin
When Laura got blind on Dubonnet and gin
And scratched her veneer with a Cartier pin,
I couldn't have liked it more.

REFRAIN 2 I went to a marvellous party,
I must say the fun was intense,
We all had to do
What the people we knew
Would be doing a hundred years hence.
Dear Cecil arrived wearing armour,
Some shells and a black feather boa,
Poor Millicent wore a surrealist comb
Made of bits of mosaic from St. Peter's
in Rome,
But the weight was so great that she had
to go home,
I couldn't have liked it more.

VERSE 2 People's behaviour
Away from Belgravia
Would make you aghast,
So much variety
Watching Society
Scampering past,
If you have any mind at all
Gibbon's divine *Decline and Fall*
Seems pretty flimsy,
No more than a whimsy,
By way of contrast
On Saturday last—

REFRAIN 3 I went to a marvellous party,
We didn't start dinner till ten
And young Bobbie Carr
Did a stunt at the bar
With a lot of extraordinary men;
Dear Baba arrived with a turtle
Which shattered us all to the core,
The Grand Duke was dancing a foxtrot
with me
When suddenly Cyril screamed "Fiddledidee"
And ripped off his trousers and jumped in
the sea,
I couldn't have liked it more.

196

Refrain 1

[handwritten lyrics, Refrain 1]

Refrain 2

[handwritten lyrics, Refrain 2]

Noël could never quite decide whether he'd "been to" or "went to" that marvellous party . . .

I Went To A Marvellous Party

Words and Music by
NOÉL COWARD

2/6
NET

Chappell

In rehearsal REFRAIN 5 had a different ending . . .

> We talked about politics madly
> And Niki was all for a war
> He said—"I give Russia her seven year plan
> And I give you that Hitler's a maddening man"
> Then Jane got the giggles and gave me Japan!
> I couldn't have liked it more!

Noël's notes show several small variations from the published lyric "Nounou and Nada" were originally "Tiger and Boo Boo," while Grace (presumably Grace Moore) was "Poor Claire." Instead of "The Grand Duke"—"The Duchess passed out at a quarter to three." In addition . . .

REFRAIN 4   I went to a marvellous party,
Elise made an entrance with May,
You'd never have guessed
From her fisherman's vest
That her bust had been whittled away.
Poor Lulu got fried on Chianti
And talked about *esprit de corps.*
Maurice made a couple of passes at Gus
And Freddie, who hates any kind of a fuss,
Did half the Big Apple and twisted his truss,
I couldn't have liked it more.

REFRAIN 5   I went to a marvellous party,
We played the most wonderful game,
Maureen disappeared
And came back in a beard
And we all had to guess at her name!
We talked about growing old gracefully
And Elsie who's seventy-four
Said, 'A, it's a question of being sincere,
And B, if you're supple you've nothing
    to fear."
Then she swung upside down from a glass
    chandelier,
I couldn't have liked it more.

Party Girl—Beatrice Lillie.

Daphne Pop Oliver got very tight,
Piggie and Jane had a hand to hand fight,
And Lulu struck Maud and went out like a light . .
.

****

Poor Leila was there looking frightful
And Michael arrived with a whore.
We knew the excitement was bound to begin
When Laura demolished a bottle of gin . . .

****

Poor Charles took against the spaghetti
And lay down and cried on the floor.
Old Daisy, who anyhow doesn't make sense,
Arrived in a rage and a Mercedes-Benz
And only referred to the King and the Kents.

****

I went to a marvellous party,
I only wish you had been there
Although the allure
Of the dear Côte d'Azur
May well not survive the *affaire*.
Dear Pru brought a guru from Goa
Who everyone thought was a bore.
Eduardo arrived with a small chimpanzee
Which insisted on sitting on everyone's knee
Till it bit Maisie's bosom—and shinned up a tree.
I couldn't have liked it more.

*　　*　　*

Bea Lillie was to repeat "Marvellous Party" and "Weary of It All" in the H. M. Tennent revue *All Clear* at the Queen's Theatre, London. Its title was no doubt ironically intended, since it opened a few weeks after war was declared but—162 performances later—it closed well before peace broke out.

*　　*　　*

"Mad About the Boy" very nearly had a very controversial verse added for the New York production. A soberly-suited businessman was supposed to have sung:

VERSE

'Referring to your letter of October the twenty-
first,
We very much regret our inability
To reconsider our decision of the twenty-third . . .'
I can't do any more, Miss Webb, my head is about
to burst,
I'm suffering from heartburn and debility,
I simply can't dictate another word,
I'm trembling like a frightened bird . . .

REFRAIN

Mad about the boy,
It's most peculiar but I'm mad about the boy.
No one but Doctor Freud
Could have enjoyed
The vexing dreams I've had about the boy.
When I told my wife
She said she'd never heard such nonsense in her
life.
Her lack of sympathy
Embarrassed me
And made me, frankly, glad about the boy!
My doctor can't advise me,
He'd help me if he could;
Three times he's tried to psychoanalyse me
But it's just no good.
People I employ
Have the impertinence to call me 'Myrna Loy',
I rise about it
Almost love it,
For I'm absolutely mad about the boy!

In the end, wiser councils prevailed. It was, after all, only 1938 . . .

*　　*　　*

The other new number in the show was "Never Again," sung by Eva Ortega. In his *New York Times* review Brooks Atkinson praised her "vibrant singing" but Noël's verdict was less generous. He refers to "a Spanish lady . . . who evaded the worldly cynicism implicit in the lyric by the cunning device of singing it quite unintelligibly" and goes on to note that "Much later, in 1945, it was sung, clearly, by Graham Payn in *Sigh No More*." It's also worth noting its origins in the 1920's "The Dream Is Over" . . .

NEVER AGAIN

(Eva Ortega)

Over now,
The dream is over now,
Maybe it really wasn't so important anyhow.
What's been can't be again
Reluctantly I see,
My heart is free again,
Belongs to me again,
The brief illusion I lived for has gone.

No more confusion and tears from now on;
To start again
And break my heart again
If you should ask me to,
I'd say, 'To hell with you!
Away with you!'

REFRAIN

No, never again,
Never the strange unthinking joy,
Never the pain;
Let me be wise,
Let me learn to doubt romance,
Try to live without romance,
Let me be sane.
Time changes the tune.
Changes the pale unwinking stars,
Even the moon,
Let me be soon
Strong enough to flout romance—
And say, 'You're out, romance,'
Never again!

*　　*　　*

Later in the show Beatrice Lillie has a sketch ("Secret Service") with Richard Haydn in which she plays a comic spy, The Countess. Noël wrote a song to fit the character, though it was never used.

*I'M A SPY

I'm a spy
And I can't imagine why,
As a job it couldn't be less glamorous.
I should like to be seductive, sly and amorous
And be cluttered up with loads
Of extremely secret codes.
Though some men
Ask me questions now and then,
Their demands are not exactly clamorous,
All I had to do in August Nineteen Thirty-Eight
Was take a rather common flat not far from
    Prince's Gate
And wait and wait and wait and wait and wait
    and wait and wait.
Oh why—am I a spy?

I'm a spy.
I can't tell you how I try

Beatrice Lillie and Richard Haydn.

But I really must admit I'm mystified,
I have never even seen a fort that's fortified
And I couldn't travel less
In the Orient Express.
In Lausanne
A peculiar looking man
One night offered me a glass of port if I'd
Give him information on the lighter life of
    Spain
And if it was more comfortable to go by car or
    train.
He pinched my knee, since when I've not clapped
    eyes on him again.
Oh, why—am I a spy?

*   *   *

Another number in the *Set To Music* file appears to
have been written for *Words and Music*. In the end it
was used in neither show. The characters are a
retired Colonel and his man servant, Waters . . .

*PUT OUT MY SHOOTING SUIT, WATERS

VERSE 1
SERVANT: You rang sir?

COLONEL: I did, yes, confound it!
        D'you think the dam' bell rang itself?
        Just get me a stiff double whiskey
        And a box of cigars off that shelf.
        I'm leaving at three for the country.

SERVANT: Indeed, sir?—I 'ope it won't rain

COLONEL: And—er—put out my shooting-suit, Waters,
        My daughter's in trouble again.

VERSE 2
SERVANT: Indeed, sir? —I'm sorry to 'ear it,
        I presume you refer to Miss Maude?

COLONEL: Yes, send in the usual notice
        To *The Times*—she will winter abroad.

SERVANT: If I might make bold to suggest, sir
        Some barbed wire across Lovers' Lane

COLONEL: Just put out my shooting-suit, Waters,
        My daughter's in trouble again

VERSE 3
COLONEL: I was due to play bridge with Carruthers
        At the club at a quarter-to-four

SERVANT: If that, sir, 'ad come to 'er knowledge
        Miss Maude would 'ave waited, I'm sure.

COLONEL: I'm dashed if I know how she does it,
        She's forty and cross-eyed and plain
        But—er—put out my shooting-suit, Waters
        The dam' girl's in trouble again

*   *   *

And finally, an attribution that is admittedly something of a gamble. The program for *Set To Music*
refers to a number called "Velasquez." In its review
of the show *The New Yorker* spoke of "a long song
(that) introduced a pretty but tedious dance."
On the lyric mss. of "Portrait of a Lady" Noël's
handwritten annotation says: "Solo building up to a
production number." Are they one and the same?
The song probably had its origins in a 1920's Charlot
revue but was never used.

*PORTRAIT OF A LADY

VERSE 1   Lady of the past in your tarnished frame
        You've set the world on fire
        Time quenched at last the very ardent flame
        Of your intense desire.
        Artists of the period have painted you
        And loved you and despaired.
        Gossips say the world had rather tainted
            you—
        I wonder if you care.

REFRAIN   Portrait of a lady—a pretty lady.
        A flower of yesterday,
        Painted in a pensive mood.
        Heroes of the past have loved and woo'd
            you,
        Reputation shady—a trifle shady
        And all the legends say
        You had a thousand lovers
        Over the hills and far away.
VERSE 1   Passionate and pale as any light of love,
        Elusive as a dream.
        Though you were so frail, you kept in spite
            of love
        Your dignity supreme.

Curtain call: Noël Coward and the cast of Set To Music.

History says your qualities were thrown
    away
On rather worthless things
If you'd been an angel you'd have flown away
But life had crushed your wings.

Noël would often add an extra verse or refrain as a parody of the original. It's impossible to tell whether the additional material was intended to be used or merely written for his own amusement.

EXTRA REFRAIN
Portrait of a lady—a perfect lady,
Born in the present day.
Gentle as a cooing dove,
Every man she meets just longs to love her,
Some of them succeeding
When she is needing
A bill or two to pay.
Then she rejoins her husband
Over the hills and far away.

200

MISCELLANEOUS THE 1930s

Many of Noël's songs predate the production in which they were first heard by the general public. Often they were written on the spur of the moment and included in a subsequent revue, since the format permitted that flexibility. Some were "discovered" much later when the vogue for the emotionally articulate cabaret-pianist fortunately returned in the 1980s. "Most of Every Day" is one of them . . .

MOST OF EVERY DAY (1934)

Time makes a mess of things,
Oh what a mess of things
Time makes!
Time breaks a lot of things,
Oh what a lot of things
Time breaks!
Now I'm apart from you
Remembering
Joys that we both of us knew
Time keeps on beating,
Repeating, repeating
My heartaches.

REFRAIN   Most of every day,
Most of every hour of every day
I'm thinking of you,
Lovely one;
When you turned away,
When you smiled that smile and turned away
I knew we were through,
Lovely one.

Still my foolish heart insists on aching,
No release
Asleep or waking,
Most of every day,
Most of every hour of every day
I'm thinking of you.

*WOMAN OF THE WORLD

REFRAIN 1   Woman of the world
What does it signify?
A phrase to dignify
A certain 'Chic'
Someone who has something still to give
    life
Someone who has certainly discovered
    how to live life
She's calm—she's wise
She keeps behind her eyes
The secrets of her past discreetly furled
And no one ever knows
How many hearts that ache
Have helped to make
A woman of the world.

REFRAIN 2   Woman of the world
What is her history?
What subtle mystery
Is in her smile?

No one has been able to discover
Whether Grand Duke So-and-So was,
    or was not, her lover.
She smokes—she drinks
You can't tell what she thinks
Her lip is rather cynically curled
Tho' far from the Ideal
A nice girl prays to be
It pays to be
A woman of the world.

REFRAIN 3   Woman of the world
Who pays her debts for her?
Goes out and gets for her
Those ropes of pearls
Some suspect the King of Ruritania
Everyone agrees it must be Love or
    Kleptomania
The Market rocks
She keeps her bonds and stocks
No matter to what depths they may
    be hurled
And if sometimes she falls
For landing on her feet
You cannot beat
The woman of the world.

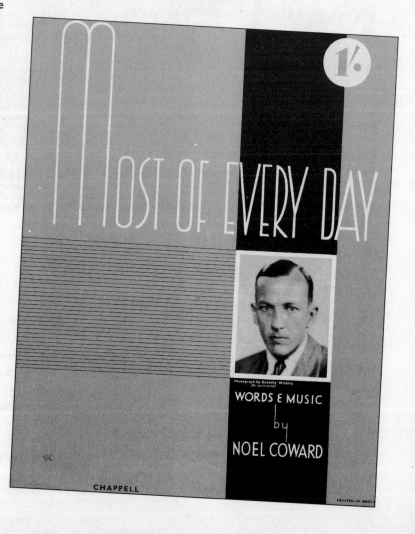

WORLD WAR II

During the First World War the teenage Noël had been moved—along with the rest of the nation—by Ivor Novello's hymn to patriotism, "Keep the Home Fires Burning," and tried to emulate it with his own "When You Come Home On Leave" (p. 17). His song was never published and was presumed lost until the indefatigable Mander and Mitchenson discovered the manuscript in 1966. They sent it to Noël, who wrote back: "I was absolutely fascinated that (it) should turn up after getting on for fifty years . . . Yes, certainly it is genuine, even the tune came back to me and I sang it all through to Coley when he brought me your letter."

His turn was to come in World War II with a very different type of song that perfectly caught the banked down emotion living though the Blitz brought out in Londoners . . .

"'London Pride' was written in the spring of 1941 . . . I was standing on the platform of a London railway station on the morning after a bad blitz. Most of the glass in the station roof had been blown out and there was dust in the air and the smell of burning. The train I was waiting to meet was running late and so I sat on a platform seat and watched the Londoners scurrying about in the thin spring sunshine. They all seemed to me to be gay and determined and wholly admirable and for a moment or two I was overwhelmed by a wave of sentimental pride. The song started in my head then and there and was finished in a couple of days The tune is based on the old traditional lavender-seller's song "Won't you buy my sweet blooming lavender, there are sixteen blue bunches one penny." This age-old melody was appropriated by the Germans and used as a foundation for "Deutschland Uber Alles," and I considered that the time had come for us to have it back in London where it belonged. I am proud of the words of this song. They express what I felt at the time and what I still feel, i.e. London Pride."

The song was introduced in the Firth Shephard revue, *Up and Doing* at the Saville Theatre. The show, which had opened in April 1940, was interrupted by the Blitz and reopened in May 1941 for a run of a further 322 performances. "London Pride" was introduced during the second part of the run and sung by Binnie Hale.

LONDON PRIDE (1941)

London Pride has been handed down to us.
London Pride is a flower that's free.
London Pride means our own dear town to us,
And our pride it for ever will be.
Woa, Liza,
See the coster barrows,
Vegetable marrows
And the fruit piled high.
Woa, Liza,
Little London sparrows,
Covent Garden Market where the costers cry.
Cockney feet
Mark the beat of history.
Every street
Pins a memory down.
Nothing ever can quite replace
The grace of London Town.

INTERLUDE   There's a little city flower every spring
                unfailing
Growing in the crevices by some London railing,
Though it has a Latin name, in town and country-
                side
We in England call it London Pride.

London Pride has been handed down to us.
London Pride is a flower that's free.
London Pride means our own dear town to us,
And our pride it for ever will be.
Hey, lady,
When the day is dawning
See the policeman yawning
On his lonely beat.
Gay lady,
Mayfair in the morning,
Hear your footsteps echo in the empty street.
Early rain
And the pavement's glistening.
All Park Lane

In a shimmering gown.
Nothing ever could break or harm
The charm of London Town.

INTERLUDE   In our city darkened now, street and
                square and crescent,
We can feel our living past in our shadowed
                present,
Ghosts beside our starlit Thames
Who lived and loved and died
Keep throughout the ages London Pride.

London Pride has been handed down to us.
London Pride is a flower that's free.
London Pride means our own dear town to us,
And our pride it for ever will be.
Grey city
Stubbornly implanted,
Taken so for granted
For a thousand years.
Stay, city,
Smokily enchanted,
Cradle of our memories and hopes and fears.
Every Blitz
Your resistance
Toughening,
From the Ritz
To the Anchor and Crown,
Nothing ever could override
The pride of London Town.

204 A sort of companion piece to "London Pride" was "There Have Been Songs in England" (1941), which on reflection Noël found "quite pleasant but a little pretentious. It is heavy and soggy and fares ill in comparison with 'London Pride'" . . .

THERE HAVE BEEN SONGS IN ENGLAND (1941)

A nation's music belongs to the Race
Through the slow time changes
And the rhythm of moving years.
Our nation's songs are its pride and its grace
Evermore and after,
Though the shape of the world may alter,
In our songs the laughter
Blends the tears.
From the past
We hear the echo of the songs that proved us
    free.
They are bequeathed to you and me
For ever and ever.

REFRAIN

There have been songs in England
Since our island rose from the seas,
As the dry land lay on that early English day
A sea wind rustled through the trees,
Very soon the birds appeared,
Later, lyric words appeared,
Later on the people sang,
Still they're singing free.
There have been songs in England
And songs there will always be.

In a later (1944) version of the song he followed the refrain with a "montage" of examples cleverly woven together (by Norman Hackforth) from sources as different as Shakespeare, Ben Jonson and traditional street songs . . .

*Oh mistress mine where art thou roaming?
O stay and hear your true love's coming,
That can sing both high and low.
Trip no further, pretty sweeting;
Journeys end in lovers meeting,
Every wise man's son doth know.

Here's a health unto His Majesty
With a fa la la, la la la la la la
La la la la la la la la la.

Drink to me only with thine eyes
And I will pledge with mine.
Or leave a kiss but in the cup
And I'll not ask for wine.
The Thirst that from the soul doth rise
Doth ask a drink divine.
Cherry ripe, cherry ripe
Cherry ripe, cherry ripe
Ripe, ripe, ripe,
Oh, fair one, come and bide.

Won't you buy my sweet blooming lavender?
There are sixteen bunches one penny.

Sigh no more ladies, sigh no more
Man, what is he but heaven?
With a hey, nonny nonny hey
Nonny nonny, hey nonny nonny
Nonny

There have been songs in England
And songs there will always be.
There have been songs in England
And songs there will always be.

*   *   *

Noël wrote other less sentimental war songs. One commented on the reverberations the new forced equality was having in the upper echelons. The stately homes of England may have been crumbling for years but not even the social structure was now sacrosanct . . .

IMAGINE THE DUCHESS'S FEELINGS (1941)

VERSE 1   The Duchess had manner
For dignity lurks
In the shadow of *Debrett*
But fate threw a spanner
Smack in the works
Tarnishing her coronet.
Three large sons were born to her
But one sad morn to her
There came a horrid moment of regret,

Said the Duchess,
'Well!
Something doesn't jell!'
Said the Duchess, 'Well—Hell!'

REFRAIN 1   Imagine the Duchess's feelings
When she had hatched out her brood
To find her first son was weak though well
    mannered,
Her second rather stupid and her third plain
    rude.
Her eldest son when in trouble went
    white,
Her second soon looked blue and hung his
    head,
But imagine the Duchess's feelings
When her youngest son went Red!

VERSE 2   She sent them to Eton,
Traditional youth
Was theirs whatever else they got,
But nothing could sweeten
The bitterest truth
That baby wasn't quite so hot
High life gave no joy to him,
The Hoi Polloi to him
Provided something that his peers did not,
Said her Grace, aghast,
'Is it going to last ?'
Said her Grace, aghast—'Blast!'

REFRAIN 2   Imagine the Duchess's feelings,
You could have pierced her with swords
When she discovered her pet lamb liked
    Lenin
And sold the *Daily Worker* near the House
    of Lords.
Her eldest son went to Boodle's and
    White's,
Her second joined the Blues his father led,
But imagine the Duchess's feelings
When her youngest son went Red!

REFRAIN 3   Imagine the Duchess's feelings,
Her overwhelming despair
To find her third son hobnobbed with the
    butler
And sang the 'Internationale' in Belgrave
    Square.
Her first son's debts bled the family white,
Her second son blued everything and fled,
But imagine the Duchess's feelings
When her youngest son went Red!

At the outbreak of hostilities men who were either too old to enlist, medically disqualified or employed in occupations contributing directly to the war effort signed up for the Home Guard, a rag tag and bobtail affair to begin with, affectionately remembered as "Dad's Army." In those early days it was quite common to have only part of a uniform and as for weapons . . . With typical British politeness Noël respectfully requests . . .

COULD YOU PLEASE OBLIGE US WITH A BREN GUN? (1941)

VERSE 1

Colonel Montmorency who
Was in Calcutta in ninety-two
Emerged from his retirement for the war.
He wasn't very pleased with what he heard and
    what he saw.
But whatever he felt
He tightened his belt—
And organized a corps.
Poor Colonel Montmorency thought,
Considering all the wars he'd fought,
The Home Guard was his job to do or die;
But after days and weeks and years
Bravely drying his manly tears
He wrote the following letter to the Minister of
    Supply:

REFRAIN 1

'Could you please oblige us with a Bren gun?
Or, failing that, a hand grenade would do.
We've got some ammunition
In a rather damp condition,
And Mayor Huss
Has an arquebus
That was used at Waterloo.
With the Vicar's stirrup pump, a pitch-fork and a
    spade
It's rather hard to guard an aerodrome;
So if you can't oblige us with a Bren gun—
The Home Guard might as well go home.'

VERSE 2

Colonel Montmorency planned
In case the enemy tried to land
To fling them back by skill and armoured force.
He realized his army should be mechanized, of
    course;
But somewhere inside
Experience cried:
'My kingdom for a horse'—
Poor Colonel Montmorency tried
At infinite cost of time and pride
To tackle his superiors again—
Having just one motor bike,
Fourteen swords and a marlinspike,
He couched the following letter in the following
    urgent strain:

REFRAIN 2

'Could you please oblige us with a Bren gun?
We're getting awfully tired of drawing lots.
Today we had a shipment
Of some curious equipment—
And just for a prank
They sent us a tank
That ties itself in knots.
On Sunday's mock invasion Captain Clarke was
    heard to say
He hadn't even got a brush and comb;
So if you can't oblige us with a Bren gun—
The Home Guard might as well go home.'

REFRAIN 3

'Could you please oblige us with a Bren gun?
We need it rather badly, I'm afraid.
Our local crossword-solver.
Has an excellent revolver;
But during a short
Attack on a fort
The trigger got mislaid.
In course of operations planned for Friday
    afternoon
Our Orders are to storm the Hippodrome;
So if you can't oblige us with a Bren gun—
The Home Guard might as well go home.'

REFRAIN 4

'Could you please oblige us with a Bren gun?
The lack of one is wounding to our pride.
Last night we found the cutest
Little German parachutist
Who looked at our kit
And giggled a bit,
Then laughed until he cried.

We'll have to hide that armoured car when
    marching to Berlin,
We'd almost be ashamed of it in Rome.
So if you can't oblige us with a Bren gun—
The Home Guard might as well go home.'

Noël considered that "as a period piece (it) is not without merit" and certainly it can still raise a smile for those who lived through those farcically tragic years. However, he rated it as inferior to his other topical song, which was "quite unwittingly, scathingly prophetic."

"When 'Don't Let's Be Beastly to the Germans' was written in the spring of 1943, Mr. Winston Churchill liked it so much that I had to sing it to him seven times in one evening. On the other hand certain rather obtuse members of the general public objected to it on the grounds that it was pro-German! This odd misconception flung both the BBC and His Master's Voice Gramophone Company into a panic. The former organisation refused to allow it to be broadcast and the latter suppressed for three months the record I had made of it. I was away at the time, entertaining troops in the Middle East, and knew nothing of this rumpus until my return. Later on, the song became absorbed into the public consciousness in its correct perspective and now 'Don't Let's Be Beastly . . .' has become a catch phrase. I shall never cease to be surprised at the sublime silliness of some of those protesting letters. After all, 'Let's help the dirty swine again to occupy the Rhine again' and 'Let's give them full air-parity and treat the rats with charity' are not, as phrases, exactly oozing with brotherly love. International circumstances have by now set the seal of irony on the whole thing. I must really be more careful what I write about in future."

The BBC did, in fact, allow the song to be broadcast once and Noël became the first person to use the word "bloody" over the air. He left the country the next day and didn't hear the BBC's hasty disclaimer. While it undoubtedly shocked some people, it amused many more. Wartime comedian, Tommy Handley, joked: "If I were Noël Coward, I would be able to tell you what I think of you!"

NOEL COWARD   MAKES HIS OWN   CONTRIBUTION

TO THE PROBLEM   OF HOW TO   TREAT GERMANY

MONDAY night at 9.20. Priestley is on the Home Service programme. He talks about a place called Bad Tolz in Bavaria. He makes us feel the magic of this place in spring, in peacetime. Now it is the training school for the Waffen Storm Troopers, "the very cream of Nazi thugs and butcherers." Priestley stresses the fact that these Storm Troopers are not only Germans but Dutchmen, Flemings, Swiss, Norwegians, Danes, Swedes, Finns, Estonians and Croats—anybody who will do the work of gangsterism. His point is that "Naziism is neither more nor less than a naked power system and not a truly national expression of anything at all." Of course, the Germans are a dangerous people, but they will be the ones to be shot down by these Waffen S.S. If we condemn them lock, stock and barrel, and leave it at that, it shows a superficial and unrealistic attitude of mind. "It is trying to solve the problems of 1943," he says—and as he draws near the end of his time we get ready to switch over, "with the ideas of 1843." On the forces wave-length, at this moment, Noël Coward is singing. And this is what he sings: "Don't let's be beastly to the Germans, when our victory is ultimately won. It's just those nasty Nazis who persuaded them to fight, etc., etc." Can it be that the song was written in reply to Priestley? Can it be that it was timed to reach the air at this moment in reply to Priestley? And can it be that Priestley made this report in advance when he referred to the ideas of 1843? Is this the B.B.C.'s way of 'giving both sides'? The idea opens up new vistas of radio controversy.

DON'T LET'S BE BEASTLY TO THE GERMANS (1943)

VERSE 1

We must be kind
And with an open mind
We must endeavour to find
A way—
To let the Germans know that when the war is
    over
They are not the ones who'll have to pay.
We must be sweet—
And tactful and discreet
And when they've suffered defeat
We mustn't let
Them feel upset
Or ever get
The feeling that we're cross with them or hate
    them,
Our future policy must be to reinstate them.

REFRAIN 1

Don't let's be beastly to the Germans
When our victory is ultimately won,
It was just those nasty Nazis who persuaded
    them to fight
And their Beethoven and Bach are really far
    worse than their bite
Let's be meek to them—
And turn the other cheek to them
And try to bring out their latent sense of fun.
Let's give them full air parity—
And treat the rats with charity,
But don't let's be beastly to the Hun.

VERSE 2

We must be just—
And win their love and trust
And in addition we must
Be wise
And ask the conquered lands to join our hands
    to aid them.
That would be a wonderful surprise.
For many years—
They've been in floods of tears
Because the poor little dears
Have been so wronged and only longed
To cheat the world,
Deplete the world
And beat

The world to blazes.
This is the moment when we ought to sing their
    praises.

REFRAIN 2

Don't let's be beastly to the Germans
When we've definitely got them on the run—
Let us treat them very kindly as we would a
    valued friend
We might send them out some Bishops as a form
    of lease and lend,
Let's be sweet to them—
And day by day repeat to them
That 'sterilization' simply isn't done.
Let's help the dirty swine again—
To occupy the Rhine again,
But don't let's be beastly to the Hun.

REFRAIN 3

Don't let's be beastly to the Germans
When the age of peace and plenty has begun.
We must send them steel and oil and coal and
    everything they need
For their peaceable intentions can be always
    guaranteed.
Let's employ with them a sort of 'strength
    through joy' with them,
They're better than us at honest manly fun.
Let's let them feel they're swell again and bomb us
    all to hell again,
But don't let's be beastly to the Hun.

REFRAIN 4

Don't let's be beastly to the Germans
For you can't deprive a gangster of his gun
Though they've been a little naughty to the
    Czechs and Poles and Dutch
But I don't suppose those countries really minded
    very much
Let's be free with them and share the B.B.C. with
    them.
We mustn't prevent them basking in the sun.
Let's soften their defeat again—and build their
    bloody fleet again,
But don't let's be beastly to the Hun

Once again, Noël's own handwritten notes contain
some other variations . . .

Let's be nice to them
And give our best advice to them
And try to remember all the good they've
    done.
We'll sweetly sympathise again
And help the rats to rise again . . .

* * * * * * * * * * * * * *

Don't let's be beastly to the Germans
For they're civilised when all is said and done
Tho' they gave us science, culture, art and
    music to excess,
They also gave us two world wars and Mr.
    Rudolph Hess

As an alternative to the last line he had experimented
with . . .

They gave us 1914, 1939 and Hess

By way of extra verses . . .

We must embrace
The splendid German race
And all defend them in case
They're blamed
For trying time and time again to kill and conquer
Never never let them feel ashamed.

* * * * * * * * * * * * * *

We must be sports
And send out loving thoughts
And think of various sorts
Of means and ways to help
To raise
Their spirits at a moment when their destiny has
    downed them
This is the time
They'll need their friends to rally around them.

(The song was supposed to have been sung by
Douglas Byng in the revue, *Flying Colours* at the
Lyric Theatre on August 26th 1943 and remained in
the program for several days. It was decided to drop
the number after the dress rehearsal—for reasons
which became clear later.)

In America they took a different view. On behalf
of the Writers' War Board in New York, the chair-
man, crime novelist, Rex Stout, approached Ira
Gershwin to write an extra refrain with an American
bite to it. In his letter of reply Gershwin said: "Not
knowing the tune, I may be all wrong on accents but
since it's a Coward topical I take it for granted it's in
6/8 . . . The first line of the chorus, by the way, can
be changed to:

Don't Make a Patsy of the Nazi

unless you pronounce Nazi the way Churchill does.
Me, obviously, I pronounce Nazi to rhyme with patsy."

*Don't let's be beastly to the Germans,
For it isn't cricket or Amerikun!
When we've got 'em yelling "Uncle", don't put
Fritzie on the fritz;

Lend them plenty so in twenty years they'll
Start another Blitz.
Let our policy
Be "Deutchland Uber Alles"-y;
We mustn't destroy the dreams that they have
    spun.
Don't treat them too ignobally—
They just were thinking globally
So why be provincial to the Hun?

The potency of the sentiment appears to be timeless, even now the old enemies are supposedly good united Europeans. During a recent period of *détente, The Times* could reproduce the original record label, replacing the His Master's Voice dog with a John Major version listening to a gramophone marked "Euro-Sceptics" and expect their readers to pick up the reference—over fifty years later!

*   *   *

And then, of course, there was the "enemy within." Just about every entertainer who wasn't serving in the armed forces was enlisted to entertain the armed forces at home or in the field of battle—most of them under the auspices of the Entertainment National Service Association (ENSA). So variable was the quality of that entertainment that the organization was jokingly (?) referred to as "Every Night

Something Awful." Quite unfairly—since many of the biggest stars of their day were involved as well as a host of untalented hopefuls—the joke went on to say that ENSA's great contribution to the war effort was to drive the troops back to the front line, where they could feel safe from a faded soprano warbling "Roses of Picardy."

Noël himself toured extensively, though not with ENSA. Nonetheless, he was well aware of its reputation and, though he was perfectly sympathetic to the conditions under which the performers had to work, he couldn't resist a target like this, particularly when it was run by a theatrical martinet like Basil Dean, a director with whom Noël had had differences of peacetime opinion . . .

In an unproduced sketch a fading theatrical *grande dame* is interviewed about her wartime experiences. When the reporter has left, she goes to her trunk, takes out her E.N.S.A. uniform and "begins, brokenly, to sing" . . .

*GOODBYE, OLD FRIEND

VERSE 1   We've had good times,
            You and I—you and I.
            Now comes the moment
            When we must say "Goodbye".
            The hour chimes
            From the East—From the West
            And so I know,
            That sadly I must lay you down to rest.

REFRAIN 1 Goodbye, old friend.
            We've had our fill of it
            We've known the thrill of it
            Undismayed
            For when the bugle sounded, we obeyed.
            Upheld by Rudyard Kipling, the *Express* and
                Cavalcade.
            To do or die, old friend.
            That was the best of it,
            We stood the test of it
            To the end,

            All set to play the final scene no matter what
                befell
            With Aspirin and Benzedrin and Mothersill as
                well.
            We pledged ourselves to Basil Dean and
                followed him through Hell!
            Goodbye, old friend.

VERSE 2:   We've played our part
            You and I—You and I
            Adventure beckoned
            Beneath the open sky
            With heavy heart
            I can tell—I can tell
            The hour has struck
            When I must whisper low 'Old Pal—Farewell'

REFRAIN 2 Goodbye, old friend.
            Though stormy weather blew,
            We've been together through
            Hail and snow.
            When sometimes men stampeded from our
                show,
            We didn't want to lose them but we knew
                they had to go.
            Morale was high, old friend
            We sort of heightened it
            Though we were frightened it
            Might descend.

Here, with Marlene Dietrich and children from Actors' Orphanage.
During the war he organized the evacuation of sixty children. In New York,
with his mother and aunt, he organized homes for the orphan evacuees.

Mrs. Coward in New York, 1942.

Coward made tours to different fronts, and here
with Norman Hackforth visits the Navy.

While driving through a coastal town in
   Southern Italy
Three stalwart groups of German troops
   emerged from the debris,
They saw the E.N.S.A. uniform and plunged
   into the sea!
Good-bye, old friend.

(While she is singing this refrain the lights dim. From
far away comes the sound of marching feet and also
the sound of voices singing. They grow louder and louder
and then, at the back, as though in a dream, she sees a
vision of the E.N.S.A. boys and girls marching to victory.)

CHORUS 1

March—March—March
Fighting for E.N.S.A
March—March—March
Fighting for Dean.
Though our jokes worry the censor
We try to keep the party clean
We firmly shall
Uphold morale
No matter if we flop
We'll never stop
Amusing the troops until they drop
With might and main
Singing a glad refrain
Fighting for E.N.S.A, Dean and Drury Lane.

CHORUS 2:

March—March—March
Fighting for E.N.S.A.
March—March—March
Follow the drum
Though the crowds might have been denser
Not all the troops are all that dumb
When all this ends

In Which We Serve (1942) was the first British war film of importance. Noël on the set with Gladys Calthrop and co-director, David Lean during filming.

And bitter friends
Say "Tell us furthermore
Apart from one encore
Just what did you do to win the war?"
With pride serene
We shall reply "We've been
Fighting for E.N.S.A., Drury Lane and Dean.

(The vision fades and once more she is alone with her memories.)

REFRAIN 3 Goodbye, old friend.
We've learned the trick of it
Right in the thick of it
Wet or fine
From Burma to the forests of the Rhine.
The men who heard us couldn't wait to get
    back to the line.
We'd bravely try, old friend
Ways of controlling them
Means of cajoling them
To attend
When during one performance someone
    hissed and threw a stone
I flung my N.A.A.F.I. sandwich down and
    seized the microphone
And shouted "God for Harry Roy—
    Geraldo—and St. Joan!"
Goodbye, old friend.

Alternative:
We had to try, old friend,
In each locality
We had vitality
To expend
While driving unescorted on the coast of Italy
We met three groups of German troops and as
    we tried to flee
They saw our E.N.S.A. uniforms and plunged
    into the sea.

*   *   *

When the war began, "I decided," Noël wrote, "with tight-lipped patriotism, to renounce all creative impulse for the duration and devote myself, hook, line and sinker to the service of my country. This gesture, admirable as it appeared to me at the time, turned out on more mature consideration to be a rather silly one."

In fact, he was to conclude later, those years, "apart from their more obvious disadvantages, were for me exceedingly productive." As soon as he began his overseas travels, "a spate of lyrics gushed out of me."

After a short and abortive period as a not very

secret agent, Noël finally did take Churchill's advice to sing "Mad Dogs" while the guns were firing—and while he was about it, sang the rest of his repertoire to servicemen and women in just about every theatre of the war.

Those travels took him from "Australia to South Africa, from the Gold Coast to the jungles of Assam and Burma, from the blazing heat of the Persian Gulf in August to Malta, Gibraltar, Scapa Flow, Cairo, Jerusalem, Mombasa and India's Coral Strand," and many of them were to provide inspiration for a song.

In India, for instance, he found—perhaps slightly to his surprise—that the Raj was far from dead and so were the crusty old soldiers. Although their memories weren't quite what they were . . . "(It) was written and firmly sung in Calcutta in 1944. Only a very few outraged 'Indian Colonels' protested."

I WONDER WHAT HAPPENED TO HIM (1944)

VERSE 1

The India that one read about
And may have been misled about
In one respect has kept itself intact.
Though 'Pukka Sahib' traditions may have cracked
And thinned
The good old Indian army's still a fact.
That famous monumental man
The Officer and Gentleman
Still lives and breathes and functions from Bombay
    to Katmandu
At any moment one can glimpse
Matured or embryonic 'Blimps'
Vivaciously speculating as to what became of
    who.
Though Eastern sounds may fascinate your ear
When West meets West you're always sure to
    hear—

REFRAIN 1

Whatever became of old Bagot?
I haven't seen him for a year.
Is it true that young Forbes had to marry that
    Faggot

He met in the Vale of Kashmir?
Have you had any news
Of that chap in the 'Blues',
Was it Prosser or Pyecroft or Pym?
He was stationed in Simla, or was it Bengal?
I know he got tight at a ball in Nepal
And wrote several four-letter words on the wall.
I wonder what happened to him!

REFRAIN 2

Whatever became of old Shelley?
Is it true that young Briggs was cashiered
For riding quite nude on a push-bike through
    Delhi
The day the new Viceroy appeared?
Have you had any word
Of that bloke in the 'Third',
Was it Southerby, Sedgwick or Sim?
They had him thrown out of the club in Bombay
For, apart from his mess bills exceeding his pay,
He took to pig-sticking in quite the wrong way.
I wonder what happened to him!

VERSE 2

One must admit that by and large
Upholders of the British Raj
Don't shine in conversation as a breed.
Though Indian army officers can read
A bit
Their verbal wit—has rather run to seed.
Their splendid insularity
And roguish jocularity
Was echoing through when Victoria was Queen.
In restaurants and dining-cars,
In messes, clubs and hotel bars
They try to maintain tradition in the way it's
    always been.
Though worlds may change and nations
    disappear
Above the shrieking chaos you will hear—

REFRAIN 3

Whatever became of old Tucker?
Have you heard any word of young Mills
Who ruptured himself at the end of a chukka
And had to be sent to the hills?
They say that young Lees
Had a go of 'D.T.s'
And his hopes of promotion are slim.
According to Stubbs, who's a bit of a louse,
The silly young blighter went out on a 'souse',
And took two old tarts into Government
    House.
I wonder what happened to him!

REFRAIN 4

Whatever became of old Keeling?
I hear that he got back from France
And frightened three nuns in a train in
    Darjeeling
By stripping and waving his lance!
D'you remember Munroe,
In the P.A.V.O?
He was tallish and mentally dim.
The talk of heredity can't be quite true,
He was dropped on his head by his ayah at
    two,
I presume that by now he'll have reached
    G. H. Q.
I'm sure that's what happened to him!

REFRAIN 5

Whatever became of old Archie?
I hear he departed this life
After rounding up ten sacred cows in Karachi
To welcome the Governor's wife.
D'you remember young Phipps
Who had *very* large hips
And whose waist was excessively slim?
Well, it seems that some doctor in Grosvenor
    Square
Gave him hormone injections for growing his
    hair
And he grew something here, and he grew
    something there.
I wonder what happened to her—him?

In an early version the lack of conversational skills of the "upholders of the British Raj" was replaced by—

Devote themselves to action and to deed.

*   *   *

It was during this period—in Jamaica in 1944—that he met Uncle Harry and "Uncle Harry" over the years provides a good example of the metamorphosis of a successful lyric.

Having used the number as a standby in his troop concerts, Noël was later to interpolate it after the opening night of his first post-war musical, *Pacific 1860*, when he decided another comedy number was required to liven up the proceedings. He later made it a part of his cabaret act in both London and Las Vegas.

The version he put into the *Lyrics* (1965) purports to be the one used in *Pacific 1860* (1946) . . .

UNCLE HARRY

VERSE 1

We all of us have relations,
Our crosses in life we bear,
A gloomy group of uncles, cousins and aunts,
We meet them in railway stations,
In Harrods or Chester Square,
And always on the Channel boat to France.
We have to be polite to them,
They sometimes send us pheasants,
We always have to write to them
To thank for Christmas presents.
These family obligations
Admittedly are a bore
But I possess one uncle that I positively adore.

REFRAIN 1

Poor Uncle Harry
Wanted to be a missionary
So he took a ship and sailed away.
This visionary,
Hotly pursued by dear Aunt Mary,
Found a South Sea Isle on which to stay.
The natives greeted them kindly and invited them
    to dine
On yams and clams and human hams and vintage
    coconut wine,
The taste of which was filthy but the after-effects
    divine.
Poor Uncle Harry
Got a bit gay and longed to tarry.
This, Aunt Mary couldn't quite allow,
She lectured him severely on a number of church
    affairs
But when she'd gone to bed he made a get-away
    down the stairs,
For he longed to find the answer to a few of the
    maiden's prayers
Uncle Harry's not a missionary now.

Poor Uncle Harry
After a chat with dear Aunt Mary
Thought the time had come to make a row,
He lined up all the older girls in one of the local
    sheds
And while he was reviling them and tearing
    himself to shreds
They took their Mother Hubbards off and tied
    them around their heads
Uncle Harry's not a missionary now

212

He's awfully happy
But he's certainly not a missionary now!

VERSE 2

Now Uncle Harry was just a 'seeker',
A 'dreamer' sincerely blest,
Of this there couldn't be a shadow of doubt.
The fact that his flesh was weaker
Than even Aunt Mary guessed
Took even her some time to figure out.
In all those languid latitudes
The atmosphere's exotic,
To take up moral attitudes
Would be too idiotic,
Though nobody could be meeker
Than Uncle had been before
I bet today he's giving way
At practically every pore!

REFRAIN 2

Poor Uncle Harry
Having become a missionary
Found the natives' morals rather crude.
He and Aunt Mary
Quickly imposed an arbitrary
Ban upon them shopping in the nude.
They all considered this silly and they didn't take
    it well,
They burned his boots and several suits and
    wrecked the Mission Hotel,
They also burnt his mackintosh, which made a
    disgusting smell.

Poor Uncle Harry
After some words with dear Aunt Mary
Called upon the chiefs for a pow-wow.
They didn't brandish knives at him, they really
    were awfully sweet,
They made concerted dives at him and offered
    him things to eat,
But when they threw their wives at him he had to
    admit defeat.
Uncle Harry's not a missionary now.

Poor dear Aunt Mary
Though it was revolutionary
Thought her time had come to take a bow.
Poor Uncle Harry looked at her, in whom he had
    placed his trust,
His very last illusion broke and crumbled away to
    dust
For she'd placed a flower behind her ear and
    frankly exposed her bust.
Uncle Harry's not a missionary now.
He's left the island
But he's certainly not a missionary now

However, the original cast recording reveals certain variations. It was placed to follow immediately after a number ("If I Were a Man") sung by six girls. A dialogue segue sets up a link of sorts. One of the girls wishes their backgrounds weren't "quite so prim and correct. I wish we were descended from buccaneers instead of missionaries." One of the two young men interjects that there were missionaries and—*mission-*

aries. At which point all eight of them sing a celebration of "our beloved family skeleton, poor dear Uncle Harry" with a totally different first verse . . .

*Our family has traditions,
We've heard them a thousand times,
Our ancestors were unequivocally right,
They frequently went on missions
To very peculiar climes
To lead the wretched heathen to the light.
Though some of them got beaten up
And some of them stampeded
Though quite a lot were eaten up
A few of them succeeded.
On one of those expeditions
An uncle we'd thought a bore
Turned out to be more spirited than ever he'd
    been before!

Later in the second refrain there is a minor variation in the natives' reaction . . .

They all considered this silly and decided to rebel,
They burned his boots and several suits, which
    made a horrible smell,
The subtle implication was that Uncle could go
    to ——!

During his wartime incarnation Uncle Harry had to undergo other indignities . . .

They all considered it silly but they didn't give a
    hoot,
The older girls just tossed their curls and gave the
    Nazi salute,
And one remarked that Uncle was a dreary old
    bore to boot.

Fortunately, time took its toll of those particular references and by the time he made the journey to Las Vegas in 1955, he'd also shed references to "Chester Square" and families sending pheasants as presents. Instead, Noël introduced him with . . .

*My family has traditions,
I've heard them a thousand times
My relatives were not excessively bright.
They loved to go off on missions
To rather peculiar climes
And lead the wretched heathen to the light.
A few of them got beaten up
In course of these rampages,
My Great Aunt Maude got eaten up
While singing "Rock of Ages".

Noël, with his pianist, Norman Hackforth, in Arakan, entertaining the troops, 1944.

These family expeditions
Admittedly are a bore,
But there is just one uncle that I positively adore.

*   *   *

Although Noël performed solo, "accompanying me on many of these trips both corporeally and on the piano" was Norman Hackforth. "It was he who cherished and tuned the piano when we were able to travel a piano and he who coped valiantly with the noteless, tuneless horrors we were faced with in camps and messes when we were not able to travel a piano. Rain or shine, drought or monsoon, there was Norman bashing out my accompaniments on those monstrous instruments with as much careless insouciance as if he had been playing on a series of Steinway Grands."

While they were in Calcutta during that 1944 trip, they made five test recordings in one day. Hackforth kept a copy and the variations from the final and published lyrics make interesting reading.

In "I Wonder What Happened to Him?"—in addition to the occasional altered surname—there was an extra couplet—

Have they let out that chap Delavigne?
There was some beastly story about a golf caddie
In tears on the seventeenth green!

*   *   *

And, of course, there was "Nina" (from Argentina), who dropped in on a train journey in South Africa.

"On the night journey from Bloemfontein to Pretoria I was suddenly aware of a rather tiresome South American rhythm thumping in my head. This went on intermittently all night and emerged next morning as "Nina." Both Norman and I were delighted with it and, gaily ignoring the fact that both the lyric and the accompaniment were complicated, we decided to put it into the second half of our programme the following evening. Unfortunately, during the day I had to make a long speech at a public luncheon, open something or other in the afternoon and attend a reception in my honour at the Country Club, and so, apart from an hour or two in the morning, I had had no time to rehearse it. Experience should have warned me that to attempt to sing a new song when it was still hot from the oven was dangerous, but the voice of experience was silenced by over-confidence and it was only when I heard myself announcing it to a packed audience that black fear descended on me. I shot Norman a hunted look while he was bashing out the introductory chords,

started on the first verse and dried up dead. Norman, with misguided presence of mind, prompted me loudly with what I knew to be a phrase from the second verse. There was a dreadful moment of silence during which my heart pounded and my brain searched vainly for the right words, then, realising that the game was up, I laughed with agonised nonchalance, asked the audience to forgive me, and started again from the beginning, praying that when I came to the forgotten phrase it would drop automatically into my mind. This was a desperate risk, but it worked; I scampered through the whole number without a further hitch and the audience were delighted with it. I, on the other hand, was furious with myself . . ."

Over time the lady underwent a few changes. In the Calcutta recording the first refrain runs:

She said that frankly she got colic
From all their over-advertised romantic charms
And then she grew more vitriolic
And told them where to put their tropic palms.
And she could not refrain from saying
That the idiotic swaying
And those damned "guitarras" playing
Were an insult to her race
She said she really couldn't face
Such international disgrace.

However, in the original *Lyrics* (1965) appears a version of that refrain that went unrecorded by Noël:

NINA

Señorita Nina
From Argentina
Knew all the answers,
Although her relatives and friends were perfect
    dancers
She swore she'd never dance a step until she died.
She said, "I've seen too many Movies
And all they prove is
Too idiotic,
They all insist that South America's exotic
Whereas it couldn't be more boring if it tried."
She added firmly that she hated
The sound of soft guitars beside a still lagoon,
She also positively stated
That she could not abide a Southern Moon,

She said with most refreshing candour
That she thought Carmen Miranda
Was subversive propaganda
And should rapidly be shot,
She said she didn't care a jot
If people quoted her or not!

She refused to begin the Beguine
When they requested it
And she made an embarrassing scene
If anyone suggested it
For she detested it.
Though no one ever could be keener
Than little Nina
On quite a number
Of very eligible men who did the Rhumba
When they proposed to her she simply left them
    flat.
She said that love should be impulsive
But not convulsive
And syncopation
Has a discouraging effect on procreation
And that she'd rather read a book—and that was
    that!

REFRAIN 2
Señorita Nina
From Argentina
Despised the Tango
And though she never was a girl to let a man go
She wouldn't sacrifice her principles for sex.
She looked with scorn on the gyrations
Of her relations
Who danced the Conga
And swore that if she had to stand it any longer
She'd lose all dignity and wring their silly necks!
She said that frankly she was blinded
To all their over-advertised romantic charms
And then she got more bloody-minded
And told them where to put their Tropic Palms.

She said I hate to be pedantic
But it drives me nearly frantic
When I see that unromantic
Syncophantic
Lot of sluts
For ever wriggling their guts,
It drives me absolutely nuts!
She declined to begin the Beguine
Though they besought her to
And in language profane and obscene
She cursed the man who taught her to,
She cursed Cole Porter too!
From this it's fairly clear that Nina
In her demeanour

Was so offensive
That when the hatred of her friends grew too
    intensive
She thought she'd better beat it while she had the
    chance.
After some trial and tribulation
She reached the station
And met a sailor
Who had acquired a wooden leg in Venezuela
And so she married him because he couldn't dance!

CODA There surely never could have been a
More irritating girl than Nina,
They never speak in Argentina
Of this degenerate bambina
Who had the luck to find romance
But resolutely wouldn't dance!
She wouldn't dance!—Hola!!

Later singers have tended to reinstate the Carmen Miranda lines, probably as a reflection of the kitsch cult figure the Brazilian singer became with her distinctive headdress adorned with "an average day's output from the Covent Garden fruit market."

The song, to be fair, has never been an easy one to perform. Graham Payn, who starred in the 1945 revue, *Sigh No More*, which introduced "Nina" to the West End public, remembers Cyril Ritchard performing it with what Noël referred to as "raucous vulgarity.""There was this marvellously witty number, full of internal rhymes that needed pointing not pounding," Payn wrote in his autobiography, "but he (Cyril) couldn't control himself . . . He had invented his own version of choreography-by-numbers, a kind of syncopated St. Vitus' dance that totally detracted from the meaning of the song. Noël repeatedly tried to pull him down, 'Just do the number, Don't *over*do the number.' The only time the song really worked was when Cyril missed a few performances and Noël took over his part. Then audiences saw how the song should be sung—with the minimum of gesture and everything in the flick of a hand or a raised eyebrow. But when Cyril returned, so did the gesture-a-word routine."

*   *   *

So prolific did Noël become in this period that he might easily have lost track of some of the new material, if Norman had not been on hand to transcribe it. One song, composed in India, only survives because of his vigilance. Noël had talked about using it in something after the war and then seemed to forget about it. Luckily, Norman had committed it to paper around 1978 and Chappells eventually published it. . .

*THERE WILL ALWAYS BE

There will always be
Enough in the world for me—
Moonlight and stars and sea,
These there will always be.

I shall always find,
If Destiny's only kind,
Something that's new
And good and true
To calm my questing mind.

Though dark days may grieve me,
Though the fates deceive me,
I'll always know
Deep down inside me
Love will be there to guide me.

There will always be
This personal thing
To set my spirit free
This there will always be—
This there will always be.

*   *   *

All songwriters have their favourite devices and a comparison of Noël's "point" numbers reveals one of his. To begin with, the "narrative" form dictates a longer and more regular line, which discourages musical ingenuity; the wit is in the words. Several of the songs, in fact, have a fundamentally similar construction, particularly the "question" numbers—"Why Must the Show Go On?," "What's Going to Happen to the Children?," "Why Do the Wrong People Travel?" as well as "Uncle Harry" and "There Are Bad Times Just Around the Corner."

As the song built to its climax, Noël became fond of what might be called "milking the ending" by interpolating a throwaway line that called for the last line to be repeated, sometimes more than once.

In "Why Must the Show Go On?", for instance, he adds . . .

"I sometimes wonder"
"I'm merely asking"

. . . and finally . . .

"Oh, Mammy!"

When we leave Uncle Harry to vanish into the sunset . . .

"He's awfully happy"
"He's left the island"

In "Bad Times" waiting "until we drop down dead" is prefaced by . . .

"A likely story—
Land of Hope and Glory"

But he saves his best shots for the later "Why Do the Wrong People Travel (When the Right People Stay Back Home)?" . . .

"And mind their business"
"With Cinerama" (or "with Television")
"And eat hot donuts"

. . . then somewhat irrelevantly . . .

"And clip their coupons"
"With all that lettuce" (or "with all those
    benefits")

and in one of the many versions . . .

"With Dr. Brothers"

a reference to the well-known "lonely hearts" columnist . . .

. . . then, as if exhausted by all the possibilities . . .

"Won't someone *tell* me?"

Considering the alternative pursuits he attributes to them, it's a moot point whether the "right people" are all that "right" either, except as alternative figures of fun. Noël may have liked America but on the lyrical evidence, he didn't have a very high opinion of the average *American* . . .

*   *   *

Coward pastiche has always been popular. Asked to contribute a song to the 1939 Kaufman and Hart play, *The Man Who Came to Dinner*, Cole Porter came up with a number which Beverly Carlton, a Noël clone, performs for the incapacitated hero, Sheridan Whiteside . . .

WHAT AM I TO DO?

Off in the nightfall
I think I might fall
Down from my perilous height;
Deep in the heart of me,
Always a part of me,

Quivering, shivering light.
Run, little lady,
Ere the shady
Shafts of time
Barb you with their winged desire,
Singe you with their sultry fire.
Softly a fluid druid meets me,
Olden and golden the dawn greets me:
Cherishing, perishing,
Up to the stairs I climb.

What am I do do
Toward ending this madness,
This sadness,
That's rending me through?
The flowers of yesteryear
Are haunting me,
Taunting me,
Darling for wanting you.
What am I to say
To warnings of sorrow
When morning's tomorrow
Greets the dew?
Will I see the cosmic Ritz
Shattered and scattered to bits?
What not am I to do?

In recognition of his "borrowing," Cole attributed the song to "Noël Porter"!

In 1985 the song writing team of John Kander and Fred Ebb paid similar homage with this song that was included in the Broadway revival of *Hay Fever* . . .

NO, MY HEART

Love and I, you must be told,
Are not a felicitous meld.
So in me you now behold
A lass disinclined to be held
No, my heart!
Not again.
Please don't fall.
Count to ten.
Considering the last time,
How sordid it became.

Remember love's a pastime
Empty words, just a game.
No, my heart!
No, not now!

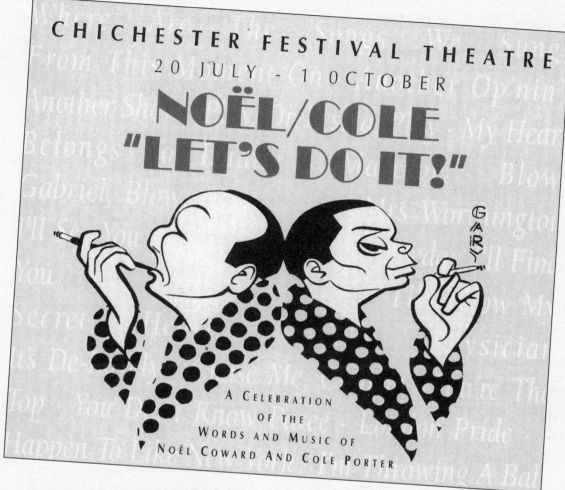

"Let's Do It!" agree Noël and Cole in this production of their music at the Chichester Festival Theatre, 1994.

Don't be kissed.
Resist
Somehow.
Let other fools be tempted
But no, *mon cher*, not I
No, my heart!
Once burned, twice shy
I'll soon be a victim,
No matter how I try
Oh, my heart,
Dear heart,
Goodbye

* * *

Pastiche, of course, can work both ways . . .

Coward students are inclined to associate "his" version of "Let's Do It" with his cabaret work and specifically with the Las Vegas season of 1955. In fact, it started during the war, prompted by his need "to acquire as large a repertoire as possible. I remember cabling to Cole Porter to ask his permission . . . He gave it generously. 'Let's Do It' was not only a great song as he originally wrote it but it happens to have a rhyming scheme which can be utilized indefinitely without destroying the basic metre."

On his travels Noël wrote versions for his different audiences: "I wrote special refrains for the Navy, the Army, the Air Force, hospital nurses, civic receptions, etc., etc." With suitable updating he was to use it as his "finisher" in almost all of his solo performances from then on.

We'll look at what he did to it for American consumption when we get to Las Vegas. (see p. 293) Meanwhile, here is a typical version . . .

LET'S DO IT

(With acknowledgements to Cole Porter)

VERSE 1   Mr. Irving Berlin
Often emphasises sin
In a charming way
Mr. Porter, we know

Wrote a song or two to show
Sex was here to stay.
Mother Nature, it seems,
Can provide a lot of themes
In a sly biological way.
We had better face facts
Every glad that overacts
Has an alibi.

REFRAIN I He said that Belgians and Dutch do it,
Even Hildegarde and Hutch do it,
Let's do it, let's fall in love.
Monkeys when ever you look do it,
Aly Khan and King Farouk do it,
Let's do it, let's fall in love.
The most *recherché* cocottes do it
In a luxury flat,
Locks, Dunns and Scotts do it
At the drop of a hat,
Excited spinsters in spas do it,
Duchesses when opening bazaars do it,
Let's do it, let's fall in love.

REFRAIN 2 Our leading writers in swarms do it,
Somerset and all the Maughams do it.,
Let's do it, let's fall in love.
The Brontes felt that they must do it,
Mrs. Humphrey Ward could *just* do it,
Let's do it, let's fall in love.
Anouilh and Sartre—God knows why—do it,
As a sort of a curse,
Eliot and Fry do it,
But they do it in verse.
Some mystics, as a routine do it,
Even Evelyn Waugh and Graham Greene do it
Let's do it, let's fall in love.

VERSE 2 In the Spring of the year
Inhibitions disappear
And our hearts beat high,
We had better face facts
Every gland that overacts
Has an alibi,
For each bird and each bee,
Each slap-happy sappy tree,
Each temptation that lures us along
Is just Nature *elle-même*
Merely singing us the same old song.

REFRAIN 3 Girls from the R.A.D.A. do it,
B.B.C. announcers may do it,
Let's do it, let's fall in love.
The Ballet Joos to a man do it,
Alfred Lunt and Lynn Fontanne do it,
Let's do it, let's fall in love.
My kith and kin, more or less, do it,

Every uncle and aunt,
But I confess to it,
I've one cousin who can't.
Critics as sour as quince do it,
Even Emile Littler and Prince do it,
Let's do it, let's fall in love.

REFRAIN 4 The House of Commons *en bloc* do it,
Civil Servants by the clock do it,
Let's do it, let's fall in love.
Deacons who've done it before do it,
Minor canons with a roar do it,
Let's do it, let's fall in love.
Some rather rorty old rips do it
When they get a bit tight,
Government Whips do it
If it takes them all night,
Old mountain goats in ravines do it,
Probably we'll live to see machines do it,
Let's do it, let's fall in love.

Nor was this to be the only Porter "borrowing." His repertoire also contained his version of Cole's 1930 song "Let's Fly Away" . . .

LET'S FLY AWAY

(Music by Cole Porter)

VERSE I I so despise civilized existence
Which is why I say
I long to take the line of least resistance
And break away.
The Twentieth Century Blues have got me,
This rat-race may appeal to you but not
    to me,
I'm fed up with reading in Sunday papers
The private lives of adolescent rapers,
I candidly confess my spirit reaches
At snaps of Tiny Tots with dogs on beaches,
There's only one solution, dear,
Let's firmly disappear.

REFRAIN I Let's fly away
To where no threats of war obsess us
And where the Press does not depress us
Every single day.
Let's fly away
From diplomatic, static missions

To where the feet of politicians
Are not of China clay.
Let's leave the milk-bar snacks,
'Perms' and breakfast foods
To those girls in plastic macs,
Slacks and pixie hoods.
Let's start today
For somewhere gayer, warmer, dryer,
England's too damp for us,
Let's fly away.

REFRAIN 2 Let's fly away
From photographs of battered boxers
And sex-besotted bobby-soxers
Assaulting Johnnie Ray.
Let's fly away
From all that roguish imprecision
Of Parlour Games on television
Which ends our Sabbath day.
Let's find a peaceful spot
Taking care to choose
Where Rita Hayworth's not
Always in the news.
Let's kneel and pray
To Mister Thomas Cook Esquire,
Let's pack our bags today
And fly away.

VERSE 2 If modern life must be democratic,
Be that as it may,
Without desiring to be too dogmatic
I frankly say
I tear up each paper that publicises
The rather uninspiring enterprises
Of truck-drivers' wives who win
    competitions
By photographing birds in odd positions
I don't care if a widow in Thames Ditton
Plunged into a well to save her kitten
And if three mothers swam Loch Ness
I just could not care less.

REFRAIN 3 Let's fly away
In any aeroplane or glider
Before the movie screens get wider,
We can't afford to stay.
Let's not delay,
For lots of larger, longer, duller
Biblical films in Technicolor
May be on the way,
We're sick of crimped and curled
Over-coloured sex,
Let's face the brave new world
Minus 3-D specs.

Let's firmly say
To Messrs Metro-Goldwyn-Mayer,
'You've had it chums. Okay! Let's fly away.'

REFRAIN 4 Let's fly away
Before they send us any more girls
Like those ubiquitous Gabor girls,
Alas alack-a-day,
Let's frankly say
We won't discuss the qualche-cosa
Possessed by Mr. Rubirosa,
We'd better not delay,
Let's plan to spend La Vie
In some Paradise
Where we're not asked to see
War and Peace on ice,
Let's see today
If helicopters are for hire
And gaily say, "Hey, hey, Let's fly away."

As with "Let's Do It," the notes indicate rhymes he discarded and variations he considered. "Rita Hayworth," for instance, was interchangeable—according to the audience—with "Diana Dors" . . .

　　*Let's fly away
　　And find a twenty-seventh heaven
　　Where no one cares what Mr. Bevan
　　Is inspired to say
　　Let's seek far latitudes
　　Where nobody hears
　　Stale moral platitudes
　　Voiced by ageing Peers.
　　Let's start today
　　And scramble out under the wire,
　　England's too pure for us—let's fly away.

　　*********

　　Let's fly away
　　From our archaic welfare state laws
　　To where they have more up to date laws
　　Which we can all obey.

　　*********

　　Let's find a gentler clime
　　Where we can be quite
　　Sure that sin and sex and crime
　　Still are black and white.

　　*　　　*　　　*

Once again, there were custom-tailored versions. There was the "Army Version" that did duty during the war tours . . .

*'ARMY' VERSION

VERSE 1.　Though Army life has its compensations
　　There are several 'buts'
　　It's all the bloody rules and regulations
　　That drive me 'nuts'.
　　I'm tired of those 'pep talks' to which we listen
　　In lousy little huts designed by Nissen
　　I'm tired of performances run by E.N.S.A.
　　I'd willingly castrate the Unit Censor
　　I'm fed up with those stews of spuds and gravy
　　I only wish to God I'd joined the Navy
　　When sweating in my Army bed
　　These thoughts run through my head.

REFRAIN 1　Let's fly away
　　Before we go completely 'daffy'
　　Where no one's ever heard of N.A.A.F.I.
　　And life is Sweet F.A.
　　Let's find a gal
　　Whom we can firmly requisition
　　Who has the technique and ambition
　　To keep up Morale.
　　Let's say 'good bye' for keeps
　　And explain with thanks
　　Where they can stick their Jeeps
　　Lorries, trucks and tanks.
　　God knows it's gay
　　This blood and thunder under fire
　　But be that as it may
　　Let's fly away.

REFRAIN 2　Let's fly away
　　To where we don't do things by numbers
　　Where no 'Reveille' wrecks our slumbers
　　Before the dawn is grey
　　Let's stake a claim
　　To some retreat of sweet perfection
　　Where there is no 'Short-Arm Inspection'
　　To make us blush with shame.
　　Let's find a cushy spot
　　Oh how grand it sounds!
　　Where each address we've got
　　Isn't out of bounds.
　　Let's sing 'Hey Hey'
　　And send the G.O.C. a wire
　　We've had it chum—Okay—Let's fly away!

. . . and then there was a version for the show business "in" crowd . . .

*'IVY' VERSION

REFRAIN 1　Let's fly away
　　And make our life one round of "Beanos"
　　Away from all those damned Lupinos
　　And also Sally Gray.
　　Let's fly away
　　Further than Maine or San Francisco
　　Where there's no fear of Arthur Riscoe
　　Acting with Francis Day
　　Let's find a 'camping' ground
　　Where there's sweet content
　　No agents stamping round
　　For their ten per cent
　　Let's disobey
　　Both Binkie B and Elsie Beyer
　　No matinée today
　　Let's fly away.

REFRAIN 2　Let's fly away
　　From Judy Kelly and Pat Kirkwood
　　To somewhere where Patricia Burke would
　　Not be asked to play
　　We must break free.
　　Let's do it now, this very minute
　　And leave O'Brien alone with Linnit
　　And possibly Dunfee.
　　Jack Hylton and Jack Payne
　　Bore us till we're sick
　　Let Oliver remain
　　London's oldest Vic.
　　Let's not delay
　　Till Dotty Dickson's kicks are higher
　　We haven't that much time—Let's fly away!

There were two more unknown Porter parodies. Neither appears to have been completed or, therefore, performed . . .

*YOU'RE THE TOP

REFRAIN 1　You're the top
　　You're a classy cloister
　　You're the top,
　　You're a prairie oyster,

You're the hottest note
Gershwin ever wrote
Or played,
You're the Himalayas
A tin of Player's
You're *Cavalcade*.
You're the cream
Any cat would lap up,
You're a dream
Dr. Freud would snap up,
I'm an all-time low,
A gigolo,
A wop,
But if, baby, I'm the bottom
You're the top.

VERSE 1   I hate explaining
My lack of training
In the art of the spoken word,
I'm like a creaky, discordant bird
That when it's heard
Sounds absurd.
You make me dumber
Than any plumber
When he's called in to mend a car!
Altho' it's boring,
This troubadouring
At least may convince you how grand
    you are . . .

REFRAIN 2   You're the top,
You're a suite symphonic,
You're the top,
You're a gin and tonic,
You're the star-lit sky
All the poets sigh
To see,
You're a Grieg sonata,
You're the Magna Carta
You're M & B.
You're the peak
Of my most complex life,
So to speak
You disturb my sex life.
I'm the undercut on
Last week's mutton
Chop,
But if, baby, I'm the bottom
You're the top.

A 1934 Porter song called "Thank You So Much, Mrs. Lowsborough-Goodby" written to amuse his friends, describes the weekend from Hell. The verse contains the lines . . .

When I left Mrs. Lowsborough-Goodby's
The letter I wrote was polite
But it would have been bliss
Had I dared write her this,
The letter I wanted to write . . .

Noël picks up the refrain with . . .

*MRS L-G

Thank you so much, Mrs. Lowsborough-Goodby,
Thank you so much.
Thank you so much for that miserable weekend
    with you.
I'm a wreck, Mrs. Lowsborough-Goodby, really a
    wreck.
If I were not, at this moment I would be wringing
    your neck!
I can clearly recall
Nursery tea in the hall,
The hideous noise
Of your dear little boys
And also your butler who, frankly, unnerved me
By hiccuping loudly each time that he served me.
The fourposter bed draped in mock *cinquecenta*,
The mattress of lead with a ridge down the
    centre,
For the bathroom I shared with your friend, Dr.
    Glazer,
Who ruined my sponge and blunted my razor. . . . .

*   *   *

Porter's catalogue songs clearly held a special fascination for him. Here he plays with a number from *Panama Hattie* (1940) . . .

*FRESH AS A DAISY (1943)

(Cole Porter)

I'm fresh as a daisy,
Bald as a coot,
Dead as a doornail,
Deaf as a mute,

Weak as a kitten,
Meek as a mouse,
Black as a Hottentot,
Safe as a house,
Proud as a peacock,
Fit as a fflea,
Smart as a whippet,
And busy as a bee,
Cold as an iceberg,
Hot as an 'ov.

I swear like a trooper,
Bark like a dog,
Puff like a grampus,
Eat like a hog,
Shake like an aspen,
Run like a deer,
Bleat like a nannygoat,
Kick like a steer,
Wail like a banshee,
Dive like a seal,
Shake like a jelly,
And wriggle like an eel,
Bray like a donkey,
Coo like a dove –
That means, mister, I'm in love.

Extra verse and refrains:

    I was an unfrocked curate,
A kindly light with no lead.
I was a joke that nobody saw,
I was a broken reed.
I was a job half finished,
A furrow without a plough
The Hi di Hi – from out of the sky
Came – well – just look at me now.

I'm fresh as a daisy,
Ripe as a plum,
Clean as a whistle,
Tight as a drum,
Red as a lobster,
Pale as a ghost,
Brown as a berry,
And warm as a toast.
Slow as a tortoise,
Fat as a pig,
Dead as an adder,
And merry as a grig,
Bright as the starlight shining above –
That means, mister, I'm in love.

*   *   *

There was to be a *quid* with the *pro quo* . . .

Above: White Cliffs at St. Margaret's Bay near Dover, Noël's headquarters while waiting to recover Goldenhurst from its wartime use by the Army. Right: friends Joyce Carey, John Mills and Mary Hayley Bell visit with Noël. Below, left and right: Graham Payn and Kay Thompson were frequent guests. New friends made during the war, Eric Ambler, Ian Fleming, Katharine Hepburn and Spencer Tracy enriched the weekends.

220

In 1954 Cole was preparing what was to be his last Broadway musical—*Silk Stockings*, based on the Lubitsch/Garbo film, *Ninotchka* (1939). He had a number for the three Russian commissars sent to the U.S. to shadow Ninotchka. In a song called "Siberia" they gloomily predict their likely fate. Cole confided to Noël that it was giving him trouble and in a letter from Jamaica, Noël replied:

"I have no illusions about the enclosed meagre little rhymes, but I really have been beating my brains out in a flustered and very flattered effort to help. I have done whole refrains each time because I couldn't get a swing on them unless I did, and not much then, I am afraid. However, there may be one or two bits that will be useful to you, so here they are with my love. I got carried away for a moment with:

'If the atmosphere gets cornier
We can all sing Ortchitchornia'

. . . only I can't spell Ortchitchornia, which puts me off, but probably you can—if not there's always Serge Obolensky or Natasha or Valentina."

*SIBERIA

When we're sent to dear Siberia
To Siberi—eri—a
We must hope they'll let us sign our bills
For there ain't much gold up in dem dar hills
If, from living in a Frigidaire,
We acquire a rather frigid air
Our *esprit de corps*
Will uphold us when we thaw
In dreary Siberia.

When we're sent to dear Siberia
To Siberi—eri—a
Every Christmas night we'll all produce
For our charming hostess a cold snow goose
We shall not hurl dirty words around
With those flocks of Arctic birds around
We'll just wring their necks
And incline our thoughts to sex
In dreary Siberia.

When we're sent to dear Siberia
To Siberi—eri—a
We can smear ourselves with ambergris
And at last have time to read *War and Peace*

If our comrades understood enough
We might put on *Boris Goudenuv*
Which would give those dolts
Some reactionary jolts
In dreary Siberia.

When we're sent to dear Siberia
To Siberi—eri—a
We shall have no change *comme autrement*
To digest pressed ducklings at the Tour D'Argent
If we're told in cold Siberia
That the cooking is inferior
We'll say 'Why the deuce
Don't you make a mousse of moose?'
In dreary Siberia

*   *   *

Porter wasn't the only source of borrowing in these war years. Another "list" song was derived from Harry Warren and Mack Gordon's "I Take To You," which appeared in the 1941 film, *The Great American Broadcast*.

I TAKE TO YOU

Like a cake takes to icing
Like a long boat to a crew
Like a P.O. takes to a main brace splicing
I take to you.
Like a cart takes to oxen
Like a 'chippy' takes to glue
Like a 'snottie' takes to an ageing coxswain
I take to you.
Like E.R.A's on tropic days
And sweat and swearing and tea
They all go together—and, honey, so do we.
Like a mast to a pennant
Like a tart to navy blue
Like an Admiral takes to a Flag Lieutenant
I take to you.

Like a pipe to a tanker
Like a churchman to a pew
Like a matelot takes to the Crown and
   Anchor
I take to you.
Like a bird takes to Spring song
Like the French to *Parlez-vous*
Like a Padre takes to a mess deck sing-song
I take to you.

Like 'Stern' and 'Stem' and 'T.G.M.'
And 'C.P.O.' and 'A.B.'
They all go together—and, honey, so do we.
Like a Scot to a Thistle
Like the 'Chief' to God knows who
Like a Bos'un takes to his bloody whistle
I take to you.

Like a windward to leeward
Like a stoker to tattoo
Like an 'M.O.' takes to a wardroom steward
I take to you.
Like a corn takes to plasters
Like a galley takes to stew
Like 'Hearts of Oak' to Marine bandmasters
I take to you.
Like spray and splash and scrounge and gash
And 'Nearer My God to Thee'
They all go together—and, honey, so do we
Like a babe takes to weaning
Like a flower takes to dew
Like the whole damn ship takes to boiler
   cleaning
I take to you
Baby—I take to you.

THE 1940s

"SAMOLAN OPERETTE"

EARLY 1940s

(A.K.A. SIGH NO MORE)

The musical that was to become *Pacific 1860* (see p. 234) had a complex genesis. Long before he wrote the libretto for *Scarlet Lady* (now lost), which was the direct antecedent of *Pacific*, Noël was plotting a "Samolan Operette" and had given it the working title of *Sigh No More*. Since he gave this title—and its title song—to his first post-war revue (1945), it seems reasonable to date this work somewhere in the early 1940s.

Set in the British Embassy in Samolo at an unspecified date, the background story concerns Sir William and Lady Orkney. Sir William is the Ambassador and he has five daughters—Margaret, Caroline, Georgina, Prudence and Ursula—who provide the incidental interest and (with the young ADCs) the chorus numbers. The Orkneys also have a son, Julian.

Enter Carlotta, the heroine who has just arrived on the island to meet her fiancé, Colin. It becomes clear that she and Julian were once lovers, although he, too, is now engaged to Liza. It is equally clear that they are not over each other. Off stage we hear the siren of an arriving ocean liner.

(To this point Noël's synopsis indicates the placing of songs to be written—e.g. "duet and dance" for Ursula and her fiancé, Edward; Carlotta's "Merry Widow-ish song with young people"; a "love duet of old days" ("Changing World"?) between Julian and Carlotta, and so on. Later he refers to specific songs which he had actually written for the intended show.)

Carlotta arrives with Colin, Julian with Liza. Amid the general introductions it becomes clear that Colin and Liza already know one another, since they both travelled on the same boat. There is also a slight strain which suggests another romance is developing here.

Left alone with the young people, Lady Orkney sings . . .

*THAT WAS BEFORE YOUR DAY

Pink malmaisons,
Courtly liaisons,
But that was before your day.
Afternoon teas
Neath shady trees
Seem to be far away.
Ascot races
Unlifted faces
Seem not to mind their age.
High born virgins
Pensively slumbered
And seldom encumbered
The stage.
Lunch at Henley
W.S. Penly.
Arthur Pinero's
Strong silent heroes
The waltz's romantic sway—
That was before your—hey, hey—
That was before your day.

Later in the Summer Room of the Embassy Carlotta and Julian run into each other and begin their usual bickering, which is interrupted by the sound of Colin and Liza arriving. From the safety of the terrace Carlotta and Julian witness a love scene between their respective fiancés. Colin and Liza admit their love for each other in "I Saw No Shadow" (see p. 247). Another general scene in the Embassy, ending with the girls and the ADCs singing "His Excellency Regrets" (see p. 239). Sir William arrives and joins in.

Later that night there is the Embassy Ball, which is followed by a cabaret. This allows an Admiral to sing a "naval song," Edward and Ursula to perform "a Samolan traditional number with dance"; and Carlotta to be persuaded to sing her "big number" ("Sigh No More") followed by a refrain from "Changing World" (see p. 244).

The Ball is over and the guests gone. Once again Carlotta and Julian are unseen witnesses to Colin and Liza in each other's arms.

Liza expresses her feelings in a song of which only the refrain exists . .

*HEAVENLY MOMENT

REFRAIN   This is the moment
The Heavenly moment
This is the hour and the day and the year
All my thoughts led to it
Every dream fled to it
This is the moment eternally, dear
Out of the twilight
And into the highlight
Out of the darkness
And into the dawn
This is the moment
The wonderful moment
The moment for which we were born.

In the next scene Carlotta brings things to a head. Colin and Liza are relieved and happy; Julian apparently less so. When she has despatched them all, Carlotta sadly reprises "Sigh No More".

Some time later and there has been a wedding— Colin and Liza. The guests speed them on their way. Julian's luggage is put outside on the terrace while he explains to Lady Orkney how he has never really got over Carlotta, irritating as she can be. She is "quizzically sympathetic". Julian leaves to say his goodbyes to the girls and Carlotta enters. Her luggage is also put on the terrace. As Julian returns, Lady Orkney makes an excuse to depart leaving them alone. They ruefully compare notes about the mistakes they've made and how they'll probably go on making them. The ship's siren sounds and they say goodbye and make for the terrace. The sight of the luggage tells them they are doomed to sail together and they burst out laughing.

Now the waltz—"Changing World"—starts. Still laughing, they dance. Unseen by them, the rest of the characters have entered and hidden behind the pillars. As the music swells and the couple dance off, they are pelted with rice and confetti.

From this it becomes clear that several of the numbers which eventually appeared in *Pacific 1860*— "Changing World," "I Saw No Shadow" and "His Excellency Regrets" at the very least—were originally intended for this "Samolan Operette." The traditional Samolan number may also have been "Ka Tahua" (see p. 237). Wasting and wanting not, Noël also transferred "Sigh No More" to his 1945 revue of that name.

224

First presented by John C. Wilson and H. M. Tennent at the Opera House, Manchester on July 11, 1945 and subsequently at the Piccadilly Theatre, London on August 22, 1945. (213 performances.)

Cast included Cyril Ritchard, Madge Elliott, Joyce Grenfell, Graham Payn.

Once the war was safely over, the professional Noël largely chose to treat it as though it had never happened.

On a personal level it had left an impression he had no desire to erase. "If I forget these feelings or allow them to be obscured because they are uncomfortable, I shall be lost," he wrote in the *Diaries*. "I must hang on to those moments or I shall not have survived the war."

Certainly, he had little taste for Austerity Britain—as many of his songs, as well as much of his other work—were to show. He dealt with it in the only way he knew—through mockery. In "The Burchells of Battersea Rise" he depicted the postwar world as an affront to the people who'd fought for their London Pride:

We're the Burchells of Battersea Rise
We believe every word that we read in the Press,
When encouraged to argue and stick out our chins
We go off half-cocked and Bureaucracy wins,
We resent and detest and despise
Being talked of as "This Happy Breed" in the Press
If the author we meet
We'd be happy to greet
Him with two lovely black eyes
From the Burchells of Battersea Rise

Apart from these side swipes, he personally proceeded to "rise above it" and pick up the threads of his prewar career. The first item on his agenda was to be a revue in the tradition of *Words and Music*, "written, composed and directed by Noël Coward."

Sigh No More contained several numbers Noël had composed during his wartime travels. "Indian Army Officer" ("I Wonder What Happened to Him?") and "Nina" were both sung by Cyril Ritchard, though Noël was never to be happy with the way Ritchard performed—or, rather overperformed them. Ritchard himself admitted how nervous Noël made him when they were rehearsing the material. Noël would start by running through the songs himself, then turn to Cyril and say—"Now you do it." Not surprisingly, his performance was anything but relaxed. After a few days of this Noël had had enough. Red in the face and finger raised, he bore down on the hapless Cyril, who had the presence of mind to explain away his deficiencies on the song in question—"I Wonder What Happened to Him." It made him *uncomfortable*, Cyril explained to have to sing the lines—

Whatever became of Lord Keeling?
I hear that he got back from France
And frightened three nuns in a train at Darjeeling
By stripping and waving his lance!

When asked why, he snatched at a lyrical straw. It was the line about the "three nuns in a train in Darjeeling." And *what*, Noël asked, was uncomfortable about that? "Well, you see," said Cyril, "I had an aunt who was a nun." There was a pause while Noël considered his verdict. "Oh, very well, then—make it *four* nuns . . ."

Graham Payn himself—playing in his first Coward show since his boy soprano days of *Words and Music*—opened it as Harlequin in the title number, which Noël described as "a devil to sing" . . . though the title of the song and show "turned out to be the best part."

SIGH NO MORE

Poor mournful ladies
Are you weeping for a dream
Once dreamed?
Are you still listening for some remembered
Theme
That seemed
To promise happiness and love and gentle years
Devoid of fears?
Sweet music starts again
Lift up your hearts again,
And dry, ah, dry those tears.

REFRAIN

Sigh no more, sigh no more.
Grey clouds of sorrow fill the sky no more.
Cry no more,
Die no more
Those little deaths at parting,
New life and new love are starting,
Sing again, sing again,
The winter's over and it's spring again.
Joy is your

225

Troubadour,

Sweet and beguiling ladies, sigh no more,

Sigh no more,

Sweet and beguiling ladies, sigh no more.

The files contain further material cut from the version finally performed.

*Where is love—where is joy—has laughter fled
   for ever from the glade?

Although in dreams

It seems

We hear the echo of a lover's serenade,

The echo's fading.

Even the trees

Shed tears in the breeze,

The willows weep in monotone.

Don't pass us by.

Dear love, we sigh

Leave us no longer—alone.

RHYTHMIC REFRAIN

Enough of creeping,

Time to be gay,

New brooms are sweeping your worries away.

No more disconsolate years,

No more disconsolate tears

That were betraying

And laying

You low;

For now the pendulum swings again,

Think of happy things again,

Spread your little wings again,

Fly,

If there's a cloud in the sky,

Forget it,

Forget it

And let

Mayhap

Evap-orate

Beneath entrancing

New and blue moons.

The stars are dancing

To elegant tunes.

You'd better change your regime,

Decide to wake up and dream.

It's time to get yourself set

And let

Go.

When all the men are done with fighting they'll

Be eager to stand

List'ning to the nightingale

And holding your hand.

There's love and joy in the air again,

Be debonair again,

All weeping willows are barred,

You needn't sob in your pillows and take it so
   hard.

To weep and roar

Becomes a bore,

Pretty ladies,

Sigh no more.

He had three other solo songs, as well as taking part in several ensemble routines. "Never Again" was taken from Noël's earlier Broadway revue *Set to Music* (1938). Then there was a homily on being patient in matters of the heart . . .

WAIT A BIT, JOE

VERSE   When I was quite a tiny lad

My nurse rehearsed me in a set routine

Of good and bad.

When I grew up my parents would

Unduly emphasize the gulf between

The bad and good.

Aware that Love can be a most destructive
   force

I try to steer a middle course.

REFRAIN 1   There's a right way—and a wrong way,

There's a weak way—and a strong way,

Take it easy,

Drive with caution when the road is greasy,

Wait a bit—wait a bit—Joe.

There's an old way—and a new way,

There's a false way—and a true way,

Keep your ears back

And you'll never have to fight the tears back,

Wait a bit—wait a bit—Joe.

Never trust your conscience as a method
   of defence

When 'Old Adam' bubbles up inside,

On mature reflection you will find that
   common sense

Is a far more serviceable guide.

There's the wrong life—and the right life,

There's the home life—and the night life,

But whichever direction you go

Wait a bit—wait a bit—Joe!

REFRAIN 2   There's a right way—and a wrong way,

There's a short way—and a long way,

Let your hair down

But before the thrill begins to wear down

Wait a bit—wait a bit—Joe.

There's a dull way—and a smart way,

There's a head way—and a heart way,

Love may fret you

But before you let the goblins get you

Wait a bit—wait a bit—Joe.

Try to keep your balance and endeavour to
   create

A design for living at your ease,

If you're ever eager and go snapping at the
   bait

You will end by giving at the knees.

There's a last love—and a first love,

There's a best love—and a worst love,

If you don't want to lose on the throw

Wait a bit—wait a bit—Joe!

But it was "Matelot" which made Payn's name and which, in Noël's opinion was "one of the best songs I ever wrote. The words are staunchly married to the music and the whole has charm and atmosphere. It was beautifully sung by Graham Payn and it has remained strongly embedded in my affections to this day."

It was also by way of being an after-thought. Payn's original solo in the second half had been a song (not by Noël) called "It Couldn't Matter Less"; trying to breathe some life into it, he was forced to agree. After a while, Noël exercised his prerogative as actor/director and tried the number himself:

226

"'You're quite right,' he conceded, 'it *isn't* strong enough. I'll write you another song.' 'Oh, yes, chum,' I thought, 'I've heard *that* one before.' Then Noël pulled a muscle in his leg and couldn't come to rehearsals for a few days, which turned out to be a lucky break for me. He called to say he'd written a new song. 'It's called "Matelot." Come round and I'll play it for you.' After the first eight bars, I knew we had a hit. Later Noël was to say that it was the only thing about the show he couldn't say goodbye to without a pang."

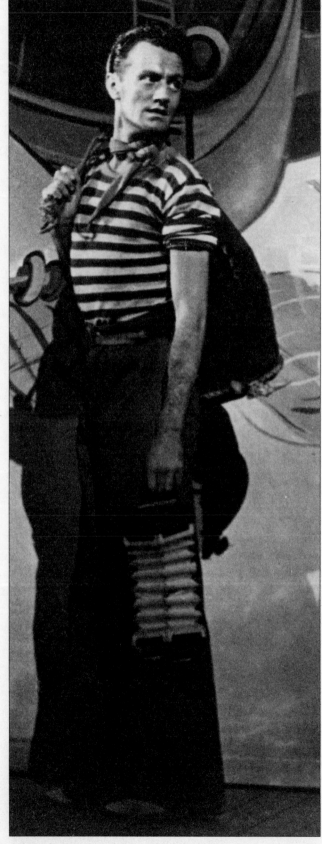

Graham Payn.

MATELOT

VERSE 1   Jean Louis Dominic Pierre Bouchon,
           True to the breed that bore him,
           Answered the call
           That held in thrall
           His father's heart before him.
           Jean Louis Dominic sailed away
           Further than love could find him
           Yet through the night
           He heard a light
           And gentle voice behind him say:

REFRAIN 1 Matelot, Matelot,
           Where you go
           My thoughts go with you,
           Matelot, Matelot,
           When you go down to the sea.
           As you gaze from afar
           On the evening star
           Wherever you may roam,
           You will remember the light
           Through the winter night
           That guides you safely home.
           Though you find
           Womenkind
           To be frail,
           One love cannot fail, my son,
           Till our days are done,
           Matelot, Matelot,
           Where you go
           My thoughts go with you,
           Matelot, Matelot,
           When you go down to the sea.

VERSE 2   Jean Louis Dominic Pierre Bouchon
           Journeyed the wide world over,
           Lips that he kissed
           Could not resist
           This loving roving rover.
           Jean Louis Dominic right or wrong
           Ever pursued a new love,

Till in his brain
There beat a strain
He knew
To be his true love
Song:

REFRAIN 2 Matelot, Matelot
           Where you go
           My heart goes with you,
           Matelot, Matelot,
           When you go down to the sea.
           For a year and a day
           You may sail away
           And have no thought of me,
           Yet through the wind and the spray,
           You will hear me say
           No love was ever free.
           You will sigh
           When horizons are clear,
           Something that is dear
           To me
           Cannot let me be,
           Matelot, Matelot
           Where you go
           My heart goes with you,
           Matelot, Matelot
           When you go down to the sea.

REFRAIN 3 Matelot, Matelot,
           Where you go
           My heart will follow,
           Matelot, Matelot,
           When you go down to the sea.
           When there's grief in the sky
           And the waves ride high
           My heart to yours will say
           You may be sure that I'm true
           To my love for you.
           Though half the world away,
           Never mind
           If you find other charms,
           Here within my arms
           You'll sleep,
           Sailor from the deep,
           Matelot, Matelot,
           Where you go
           My heart will follow,
           Matelot, Matelot,
           When you go down to the sea.

*   *   *

Another wartime composition was "That Is the End of the News" ("begun and completed in *H.M.S. Charybdis*, a light cruiser in which I was given passage to Gibraltar in 1943"). In putting the song into *Sigh No More* Noël had envisioned it as a trio, but somehow that didn't seem to be working. He assigned it to Joyce Grenfell as a solo number. Payn remembers that Joyce didn't exactly warm to the idea. At the time she was just achieving recognition for her radio monologues and thought the lyric was a bit strong for her:

"She said, 'Oh, no, it would upset my public.' 'And what public might *that* be?' Noël enquired. 'My radio public,' beamed Joyce proudly. 'Never mind about your radio public, dear. You just learn the lyrics and do the number.' Which, dressed in a schoolgirl's gym tunic and grinning toothily, she did—and stopped the show every night."

THAT IS THE END OF THE NEWS

Introduction:
For the past five years we have been told by everyone— on the wireless and in the newspapers—to keep our chins up and be BRIGHT. This is a story of an ordinary family who decided to obey and take their troubles gaily . . .

VERSE 1 We are told very loudly and often
  To lift up our hearts,
  We are told that good humour will soften
  Fate's cruellest darts
  So however bad our domestic troubles may be
  We just shake with amusement and sing with
   glee.

REFRAIN 1 Heigho, Mum's had those pains again,
  Granny's in bed with her varicose veins again,
  Everyone's gay because dear cousin Florrie
  Was run down on Saturday night by a lorry,
  We're so thrilled, Elsie's in trouble,
  That hernia she had has turned out to be
   double,
  When Albert fell down all
  The steps of the Town Hall
  He got three bad cuts and a bruise.
  We're delighted
  To be able to say
  We're unable to pay

Off our debts,
We're excited
Because Percy's got mange
And we've run up a bill at the vet's.
Three cheers! Ernie's got boils again,
Everything's covered in ointment and oils again,
Now he's had seven
So God's in His heaven
And that is the end of the news.

VERSE 2 We are told that it's dismal and dreary
  To air our despairs,
  We are told to be gallant and cheery
  And banish our cares
  So when fortune gives us a cup of hemlock
   to quaff
  We just give a slight hiccup and laugh, laugh,
   laugh.

REFRAIN 2 Heigho, everything's fearful.
  We do wish that Vi was a little more cheerful,
  The only result of her last operation
  Has been gales of wind at the least provocation.
  Now don't laugh, poor Mrs. Mason
  Was washing some smalls in the lavatory basin
  When that old corroded
  Gas-heater exploded
  And blew her smack into the news.
  We're in clover,
  Uncle George is in clink
  For refusing to work for the war,
  Now it's over
  Auntie Maud seems to think
  He'll be far better placed than before.
  What fun—dear little Sidney
  Produced a spectacular stone in his kidney,
  He's had eleven
  So God's in His heaven
  And that is the end of the news.

REFRAIN 3 Heigho, what a catastrophe,
  Grandfather's brain is beginning to atrophy,
  Last Sunday night after eating an apple
  He made a rude noise in the Methodist chapel.
  Good egg! Dear little Doris
  Has just been expelled for assaulting Miss
   Morris.
  Both of her sisters
  Are covered in blisters
  From standing about in the queues.
  We've been done in
  By that mortgage foreclosure
  And Father went out on a blind,
  He got run in

For indecent exposure
And ever so heavily fined.
Heigho hi-diddle-diddle,
Aunt Isabel's shingles have met in the middle,
She's buried in Devon

Joyce Grenfell.

So God's in His heaven
And that is the end of the news.

. . . and some unused material . . .

> *What fun, dear Uncle Alfie
> Has got an idea
> He's the Duchess of Malfi.
> We've been done in
> Because father took to liquor
> And went on a terrible blind,
> He got run in for assaulting the Vicar
> And ever so heavily fined!

> Good egg, kind little Mary
> God hold of a hat pin
> And stabbed a canary

*   *   *

The rest of the songs failed to survive the show . . .

THE PARTING OF THE WAYS

(Cyril Ritchard and Madge Elliott)

HE You're looking just as you used to look,
     Almost the same coloured dress,

Nothing is changed
And your hair's still arranged
With that light, unforgotten finesse.
Gay lady out of a story book,
I miss that flame-coloured scarf,
You left it behind
When we went out to find
All those bluebells—remember? Don't laugh!
Later we dined and saw a show,
That was a long time ago.

REFRAIN I

> We've reached the parting of the ways,
> That melancholy phrase is true,
> The days we knew
> Are ending.
> We know that though we may be hurt
> The only thing that's certain is
> The curtain is
> Descending.
> Stars have faded,
> Our hearts are jaded,
> Enchantment loses its glow,
> No use pleading
> When love lies bleeding
> And so heigho.
> We know now the ending of our song,
> Our love aflfair was horrid and it lasted far too
>   long.

SHE You haven't changed, not a little bit,
     Same old half-cynical smile,
     I see you now,
     Overdressed, in the prow
     Of that houseboat we hired on the Nile.
     Do you remember those exquisite
     Oysters we had in Peking?
     And the stale caviar
     That we ate in the bar
     Of the Station Hotel in King's Lynn?
     What a sophisticated pair
     And what a dull love affair!

REFRAIN 2

> We've reached the parting of the ways,
> One more depressing phase is through,
> I gaze at you dumbfounded,
> This is our final rendezvous
> My little love canoe, my dear,
> With you, my dear,
> Is grounded.
> While we bickered

**Madge Elliott and Cyril Ritchard in
"Parting of the Ways" as sketched by Tom Titt**

The love-light flickered
And burned unpleasantly low,
Cupid clocked out,
We've both been knocked out
And so heigho.
There's no sense in waiting for the gong,
Our love affair was horrid and it lasted *far* too long.

MOTHER AND DAUGHTER

(Gwen Bateman and Jay O'Neill)

*(The setting is a reproduction of a full page in the
Illustrated London News circa 1905. The* MOTHER
and DAUGHTER *are posed artistically in the manner of
the day. The whole scene is in different shades of
black and white and grey.)*

MOTHER: In the broad Edwardian era
         Forty years ago
         Virtue was undoubtedly dearer,
         Marriage had a clearer
         Status Quo

DAUGHTER: That was very long ago,
         That was very long ago.

MOTHER: Though young girls about to be mated
         Couldn't pick and choose
         In the *Illustrated*
         London News.

DAUGHTER: Though they couldn't pick and choose
         They were definitely news.
         Fond Mama
         Stiff with pride
         Basking firmly in reflected glory.

MOTHER: Fond Mama,
         Sweet young bride,
         What a thoroughly successful story,
         Marriage was the crowning glory
         Girls could choose.

DAUGHTER: No—no—no,
         No—no—no,
         Married bliss was always over-rated
         Even in the *Illustrated*
         London News

BOTH: Moments from life that you could never lose
         Framed in the *Illustrated London News.*

Mother and daughter both doing well,
Tralalalala—tralalalala—tralalalalalalalalalalala,
Elderly doe and timid gazelle,
Tralalalala—tralalalala—tralalalalalalalalala
    —la la la.

MOTHER: Just a mother

DAUGHTER: With her daughter

BOTH: In a pose triumphant and meek.
Has the mother
Taught her daughter
Any really useful technique?
Tralallalalalalalalala
Tralalalalalalalalalala
Tralalalalalalalalalala—lalalalalala—la la la.
Though the mother
Taught her daughter
How to look both modest and shy,
Then the camera
Fairly caught her
With that steely glint in her eye.
Tralala etc., etc.
A most resolute glint in her eye,
And a camera, like Washington, can't tell a lie.

BOTH: Mother and daughter both doing well,
Fully blown rose and bud.

MOTHER: Better to laugh
While quaffing Moselle
Than to stay gently mooing
And chewing
The cud.

DAUGHTER: When the heart is young
Sentimental songs are sung,
There are primroses on the ground.

MOTHER: But when youth is gone
You must base your dreams upon
Something more commercially sound.

BOTH: Two of a kind
Resolved and refined,
Binding an age-old spell,
Any observer could tell
Mother and daughter both doing well.

BOTH: Mother and daughter both doing well,
Ah, what a graceful phrase,
Amorous thrill
We're willing to sell
For a nice dividend
To the end
Of our days.
In another class
We should be as bold as brass,

But in High Society—no.
We should miss the bus
If we were promiscuous
It would overcome *comme-il-faut*,
Ladies who leer
Aren't likely to hear
Chimes of a wedding bell.
Though self-control can be hell,
Mother and daughter both doing well.

    *   *   *

"Willy" had a particular significance for Graham Payn, even though he didn't perform it himself in the show. In advising the hero on his course in life the First Good Angel sings the lines:

> Dear little lad unheeding.
> Pray give a thought to your immortal soul

Some time later, when Payn had joined the Coward "family," he interrupted a business conversation between Noël and Lornie, his protecting angel and secretary. To warn Graham that this was not quite the moment, she quoted the lines. To Noël and the rest of the family he was "Little Lad" from that moment on . . .

WILLY

(Tom Linden, Cyril Ritchard and Madge Elliott)

ANGELS' VOICES:
Willy—Willy—Willy,
Sweet boy secure in innocence,
Give an ear to the Angels' choir,
Steer clear of all incontinence,
Put a curb on all base desire.

Willy—Willy—Willy .

1ST GOOD ANGEL:
Dear little lad unheeding,
Pray give a thought to your immortal soul,
May the path you choose be right,
Let virtue's light become your goal.
    (spoken) Over to you.

1ST BAD ANGEL:
That's a dull book you're reading,
You're far too old to be so prim and staid,
I've some postcards here from France,

Just take a glance,
Don't be afraid.
I'll show you many delightful things
If you'll but meet me half way.
    (spoken) Over to you.

1ST GOOD ANGEL:
Pray pay no heed to the frightful things
That dreadful creature may say.
    (spoken) Excuse me.

1ST BAD ANGEL:
The really pure always do the spiteful things,
They can't endure gaiety and joy.
    (spoken) Over.

1ST GOOD ANGEL:
Turn a deaf ear,
Concentrate on rightful things,
You're such a dear
Pretty little Boy.

Willy—Willy—Willy.

Try to exert some self-control,
Try to be captain of your soul,
Virtue's path is hilly,
Never look—never look
Left or right,
Press on gallantly to the light,
Pitfalls lie in waiting,
Try to avoid them one by one
If you would be a man my son,
No procrastinating,
Think pure thoughts like a nice boy should
And try, oh try to be good.

1ST BAD ANGEL:
Willy—Willy—Willy.
Don't waste your time with wrongs and rights,
There can be more exciting lights,
Stroll down Piccadilly,
Never mind, never mind what they say,
Gather rosebuds while you may,
What are you afraid of,
Purity can be overdone,
Learn to be gay and have some fun,
That's what boys are made for,
There's no future in 'Good' my lad
So try, oh try to be bad.

2ND GOOD ANGEL:
Don't hover on the parapet
'Twixt the hills and the shifting sand.

3RD GOOD ANGEL:
Read Bunyan and Dean Farrar, pet,
They will help you to understand.

230

(They offer him a small gold halo. He turns it over carefully in his hands, scrutinizes it and hands it back disdainfully)

ALL GOOD ANGESL:
  Willy—Willy—Willy—Willy—

1ST BAD ANGEL: *(Producing a smart opera hat)*
  Suppose you took
  This entrancing opera hat
  Which has a sheen to match a raven's wing,
  You couldn't look
  Anything but smart in that,
  Imagine strolling down the Mall in Spring
  With, by your side,
  Some little lady-love
  Smirking with pride
  At everyone you meet,
  It's very sweet
  To have a shady love,
  A most discreet
  Rosie O'Grady love,
  Life's incomplete
  And, on the whole, extremely flat
  If you go marching down the years without an
        opera hat.

1ST GOOD ANGEL:
  The laws of Right
  Are quite immutable,
  A robe of white
  Would be more suitable,
  You'll look a sight
  And it will serve you right at that,
  Just fancy turning down a halo for an opera hat!

(Willy puts out his tongue at her, takes the hat, opens and shuts it once or twice, then puts it behind him on the chair. Three Bad Angels dance up to him)

BAD ANGELS:
  Don't throw up the sponge, Willy,
  Your youth will swiftly fly,
  Love's a thing to conjure with, Willy,
  You don't know till you try,
  Don't retire to a cloister, dear,
  All the world is your oyster, dear,
  Don't become a muff, Willy,
  Just learn to do your stuff, Willy,
  It's time to take the plunge,
  Don't throw up the sponge!

GOOD ANGELS: *(Chanting in counter melody)*
  All things bright and beautiful
  Will guide you to the light
  If you'll just be dutiful
  And keep the goal in sight.

  Turn aside from temptation, dear,
  Give a thought to salvation, dear,
  Get into your stride, my boy,
  Don't let down the side, my boy,
  Hark to the trumpet call
  And keep your eye on the ball.

(Six of the Bad Angels, who have been sitting round on the floor playing poker, spring to their feet and execute a brisk and saucy 'Can-Can'. Two Good Angels return with the halo to which is attached a packet of milk chocolate. Willy accepts it and places it on the chair with the opera hat)

ALL: Willy—Willy—Willy—
  You can be good or the reverse,
  There is one thing that's much much worse,
  That is to be silly,
  Keep that ever before your eyes
  And try, oh try to be wise!

(All the Angels Good and Bad circle round him until he is completely obscured from view. Finally he pushes through them. The music and singing stop abruptly)

WILLY: *(furiously)* With all these bloody Angels in the house a chap can't get a moment's peace.

(He takes a large bite of chocolate, rams the opera hat on to his head and stamps off)

———

THE MERRY WIVES OF WINDSOR

(Cyril Ritchard and Madge Elliott)

VERSE Here are ladies
  Set in tranquillity
  Living our lives
  In a haze of gentility,
  Charming ladies
  Secretly yearning
  To cherish a burning
  Desire.
  This decade is
  Fiercely Victorian,
  Though it has charm
  For the modern historian
  We despise it

  For in our eyes it
  Denies us the right to acquire
  Full completeness.
  In a life that is far too brief at best
  All the sweetness,
  As you've possibly guessed,
  Makes us very repressed.
  Though our trade is
  Wifely devotion
  We long for emotional thrill.
  Someone some day
  Might lead us astray
  But probably nobody will.

MRS MACADOO:
  Pity us—pity us—pity us, please,
  We are living in a tedious age.

ALL: Mrs Macadoo means
  We're might-have-beens
  Wilting in a gilded cage.

MRS MACADOO:
  Nobody—nobody—nobody sees
  How admirably bored we feel.

ALL: Mrs Macadoo means
  Our love routines
  Are far too damned genteel.

REFRAIN 1 We're The Merry Wives of Windsor,
  Of Windsor—of Windsor,
  In this grey town
  Of fabulous renown
  We all reside,
  Though our whist is rather pseudo
  We're adepts at ludo,
  We sit and sew
  And hardly ever go
  Outside.
  As so many men have written sonnets on
  Female charm and grace
  We've popped our latest shawls and bonnets on
  Just in case,
  When we watch the soldiers drilling
  It's thrilling—too thrilling,
  We all assert
  That virtue doesn't always pay,
  We say
  We're The Merry Wives of Windsor
  And if good luck comes our way
  We shall all be Merry Widows
  One fine day.

REFRAIN 2 We're The Merry Wives of Windsor,
  Of Windsor—of Windsor,
  Domestic pets

Whose conjugal duets
Are just off key,
If our better halves, who bore us,
Should pass on before us
We'd like to know exactly when it's going to be,
As we live enclosed by prunes and prudery,
Jaded, faded flowers,
We can't resist a little rudery
Out of hours,
We're extremely *comme-il-faut* here
But life is so slow here
That if we meet
A reasonably sweet—dragoon
We swoon,
We're The Merry Wives of Windsor
And we ask of Fate one boon
That we'll all be Merry Widows
Fairly soon.

JAPANESE SPIES

(Cyril Ritchard and Madge Elliott)

VERSE 1

Can you guess who we are?
It will take you some time to discover.
Can you guess what we do?
We're telling you.
We're fearfully secret agents who unwisely
    undertook
To continue our activities in Asia.
This simple explanation will account for why we
    look
Like a rather old production of *The Geisha*.
We're adepts at deciphering and learned a lot of
    tricks
From a sweet old couple in Spain.
We tried to take up sabotage in nineteen-thirty-six
But we had to drop it again.
We've mastered lots of secret codes and since
    the War began
We've been on a special training course in Eire
And now we're on our way to see the Emperor
    of Japan
With a note of introduction from Valera.

REFRAIN 1

Two little Japanese spies are we,
Eager to do some undermining,

Off on a gay subversive spree
Hoping the Rising Sun's still rising.
The language we have never known
But still we take no risks,
We practise with a Linguaphone
And twelve delightful discs,
We have been told by the C.I.D.
That the Mikado's simply pining
Just to utilize
Two little Japanese spies.

VERSE 2

Our training in the early days was really rather
    fun,
With our darling old professor in Geneva
We had to learn disguises and our repertoire
    would run
From the Sultan of Johore to Little Eva.
You have to be resourceful and you have to use
    your brains
When you're drugging somebody's drink
And you have to keep your temper when you're
    scrubbing out the stains
Of that damned invisible ink.
You're taught to swallow documents no matter
    where you are
And if you bring them up again they cane you.
One evening in a restaurant we went a bit too far
And ate two *Daily Workers* and the menu.

REFRAIN 2

Two little Japanese spies are we,
Wine in the wood and not quite mellowed,
Off for a voyage across the sea
Under-equipped but over-yellowed.
We said to the authorities
'An exit permit, please,'
But all the 'A' priorities
Were taken by M.P.s
One day an eminent C. in C.
Gave us a look and fairly bellowed,
'Pardon my surprise—pardon my surprise,
You're not Bulgarian,
Not Roumanian,
Not Bavarian,
Not Albanian,
Not Hungarian,
Not Ukrainian,
Far too alien
For Australian,
Suddenly it's struck me like a blow between the
    eyes
That's a great disguise,
You're two little Japanese spies.'

*EXTRA LINES

We've mastered loads of secret codes
And since the War we've been
In County Kerry brushing up our blarney,
We've learnt to sing in Japanese
'The Wearing of the Green',
'The Minstrel Boy' and 'Lily of Killarney'.

*   *   *

Several of Noël's songs failed to survive their era because they were too closely tied to it. This is particularly true of the comic songs. While references to Germany may still have a certain iconic resonance within a loosely-gathered European Union, "bren guns" require a visit to the dictionary for a contemporary audience. And as for the Burchells of Battersea Rise, we'd like to think that their plaintive cry of the post-war *petit bourgeoisie* was very much of then—but we wouldn't want to bet on it . . .

As the song ends, the Burchells are . . .

. . . faced with a dismal selection again,
We may find if we swallow the Socialist bait,
That a simple head cold is controlled by the State

Their words were prophetic. While the show was trying out in Manchester, Labour defeated Winston Churchill's Conservative party and became the first post-war government . . .

THE BURCHELLS OF BATTERSEA RISE

*(Cyril Ritchard, Madge Elliott, Joyce Grenfell
and Graham Payn)*

VERSE 1

We are those people who seldom make fusses,
You see us in tubes and in trams and in buses,
We couldn't be classed as 'Noblesse',
Nevertheless
We're not so humble,
Any observer who's really observant
Can see how we flinch at the phrase 'Civil Servant'.
The Government fools us,
Bureaucracy rules us,
But still we mustn't grumble,
We're the class that they take for a ride,
Still we say with commendable pride:

232

REFRAIN 1

We're the Burchells of Battersea Rise,
We're the backbone of England and proud of the
    fact,
Though in utter confusion we're frequently hurled
By political views from the *News of the World*
We're supposed to be solid and wise
Though we don't hold with boasting out loud of
    the fact.
If the workers unite
We'll be Left and quite Right
And cry, 'Oh what a surprise
For the Burchells of Battersea Rise!'

REFRAIN 2

We're the Burchells of Battersea Rise,
We believe every word that we read in the Press,
When encouraged to argue and stick out our
    chins
We go off at half-cock and Bureaucracy wins,
We resent and detest and despise
Being talked of as 'This Happy Breed' in the Press,
If the author we meet
We'd be happy to greet
Him with two lovely black eyes
From the Burchells of Battersea Rise.

VERSE 2

Though we're fed up with restrictions and
    strictures
We learn about life from the Press and the
    Pictures
So all our inaccurate views
You must excuse
And rise above them.
Having survived over five years of war
If the National government wants an encore
We shall pray that it warms up
And fill some more forms up
To prove how much we love them,
Though we're dead against rocking the boat
Still we hold the majority vote.

REFRAIN 3

We're the Burchells of Battersea Rise
And we see at least four Double-Features a week,
To American war films we'd rather not go
For we say, 'How by Golly would Hollywood know?'
If they have people to advise
We can only surmise that their teachers are weak,
Though we've seen many actors
Win through through Max Factor's
We can't hand them a prize
From the Burchells of Battersea Rise.

REFRAIN 4

We're the Burchells of Battersea Rise
And we've written and written and written again
To some local official who Dad seems to think
Might concede us a permit to build a new sink,
We've already had several tries,
It's as bad as the Battle of Britain again,
Though we've drawn up the plans
We shall sit on our cans
Till the old bastard replies
To the Burchells of Battersea Rise.

REFRAIN 5

We're the Burchells of Battersea Rise
And we all believed firmly in 'Peace-in-our-time',
We heard speeches from Germans and Eyeties
    and Frogs,
No one knew what they meant so we went to
    the dogs
And the Government told us such lies,
We've heard plenty of cackling old geese in our
    time,
We were mugs to agree
But in future we'll see
That they don't capitalize
On the Burchells of Battersea Rise.

EXTRA REFRAINS:

We're the Burchells of Battersea Rise
And when foreigners murmur, 'We hope you're
    all right,'
How we wish that they'd buzz off and leave us
    alone
For we live chock-a-block in an occupied zone
With the land full of alien spies.
Poor old England's a bleeding Utopia all right.
We've got Bishops and Peers
Who will burst into tears
If the Huns won't fraternize
With the Burchells of Battersea Rise

We're the Burchells of Battersea Rise
And we're faced with a dismal selection again,
We may find if we swallow the Socialist bait
That a simple head cold is controlled by the
    State,
Though we know Winston Churchill is wise
And we'd love him to win the election again,
If he's forced to say 'Yes'
To the Beaverbrook press
There'll be loud animal cries
From the Burchells of Battersea Rise.

And an extra unperformed verse:

*As we're told we're a power in the nation at
    last,
We shall sit on our fannys and patiently wait
Till a simple head cold is controlled by the State.
We'll be healthy and wealthy and wise.
Under Government regimentation at last
When they've cleared all the decks
There will only be sex
That they can't nationalise
For the Burchells of Battersea Rise.

*   *   *

The files contain one other song that was submitted to the Lord Chamberlain's Office for the original production but never used . . .

*WALTZING

1ST CHORUS:

Let's all go waltzing
The band has begun
Keep in rhythm with 'em, counting 1 2 3—1 2 3
It's as easy as the A B C—A B C
Let's all go dancing,
The day's work is done,
And there's lots of time
Before the midnight chime—
Swing together, everyone.

VERSE After dark in the evening,
    There's music for dancing
So how about taking a turn with me?
After dark in the evening the music's entrancing
As gay as can be.
There's a moon sailing over,
The tune is entrancing.
So come and see.

2ND CHORUS

Let's all go waltzing,
Let's all go waltzing,
Let's all go dancing
The day's work is done,
Hear the drum a-drumming with a rum tum
    tum—rum tumtum
Swing together, everyone with a rum tum tum—
    tum tumtum.

17 Gerald Road, Noël's London home until the early 50s. Note the chair that was to travel around the world with him before ending up in Switzerland.

234

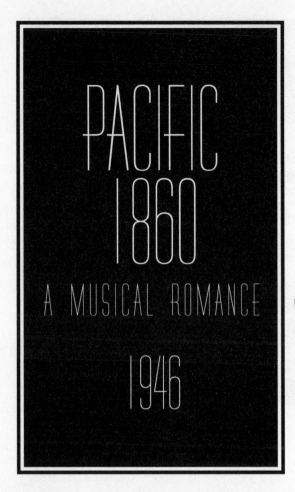

PACIFIC 1860

A MUSICAL ROMANCE

1946

*Right, Drury Lane
Theatre is restored
after bomb damage
from the war.*

*Below, Pacific 1860
was the first show to play
at the newly resetored
theatre.*

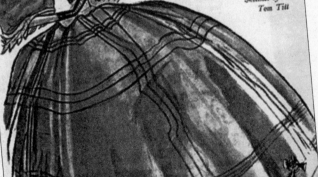

*Elena Salvador (Mary Martin)
and Kerry Stirling (Graham Payn) show
that it is not only the albatrosses of Samolo
who "indulge much in curious dances two
by two"*

THE TATLER AND BYSTANDER, JANUARY 1,

"Pacific 1860

DRURY LANE reopens not with a cavalcade
but with a charade, a pretty, pratling
tuneful charade. Mr. Noël Coward
always knows what he is after, and this time
it is a romantic escape to as far as possible
from the present in time and space.

He could not have made his points of contrast to London 1946 more decisively. Well
and truly aided and abetted by Mrs. Ca[...]
throp's invariably charming décor, by M[...]
Alick Johnstont's scene painting, and by co[...]
tumes in which the gentlemen look as litt[...]
cramped by coupons as the ladies, he keep[...]
the temperature throughout the evening a[...]
a nice warm tropical level.

THERE is a harmless little plot about a famou[...]
singer's toings and froings between he[...]
career and her heart. There is an incessan[...]
patter of easy sentimental music coming dow[...]
with more than once quite a downpour o[...]
vintage Coward melody. And there is rea[...]
lightness in the conversation pieces, breakin[...]
here and there into quite a jolly little ligh[...]
lyric.

Mr. Coward at his worst (which this is very
far from being) never lacks style, and here he
keeps it up by entrancing the eye with hi[...]
colours and movements and neat handling of
crowds, and by soothing the ear with bland[...]
polished words and music. But the tende[...]
scenes are never more than operetta at it[...]

*When the Crinoline sweps
all before it, literally as well as
figuratively. Mary Martin as the
enchanting singer lost in a mass
of misunderstandings*

*Sketches by
Tom Titt*

First presented by Prince Littler at the Theatre Royal,
Drury Lane, London on December 19, 1946. (129
performances.)

*Cast included Mary Martin, Graham Payn, Sylvia
Cecil, Tudor Evans, Daphne Anderson.*

The mythical South Sea island of Samolo haunted
Noël, even though he had invented it. With its
"equable temperature, abundant sunshine and,
except for the months of June and July, very few
tropical storms," it was the setting for *We Were
Dancing* and was to be for his only novel, *Pomp
and Circumstance* (1960). He invented a history
and a language for it and took it altogether too
seriously.

While *Pacific 1860* wasn't exactly operetta, it
had leanings in that direction. Noël's original story,
Samolo, became *Scarlet Lady*, written with Irene
Dunne in mind. When she turned out to be unavail-
able, he persuaded himself that Mary Martin had
the vocal range for the part of Elena Salvador, the
multi-lingual opera singer. Immediately, he ran into
problems. As Graham Payn, the intended co-star
recalls: "Mary wasn't a true soprano and lacked the
necessary range for operetta. Apart from which, she

was almost exactly my age, which altered the entire meaning of the book. Instead of a poignant story of love lost between the generations, it became a straightforward romance . . . Noël had to entirely rewrite the libretto." (In an early draft it was called *"Time Remembered: a Romantic Operetta in 3 Acts,"* using the title of a play Noël had written in 1941 but which had never been produced.)

The play opens with the Stirling family at breakfast. Mr. Stirling sings the family grace . . .

FAMILY GRACE

(Tudor Evans)

For what we have received
May the Lord fill our hearts with gratitude
And through the coming day
We humbly pray
With appetites relieved
In this remote, most eccentric latitude

That He, with tolerance of all small mistakes,
May walk beside us
And, in His understanding, guide us.
For what we have received
Accept, O Lord, in your serene beatitude
Today and all our days
Our thankful praise
For tropic fruits
And bamboo shoots,
For tender roots—incredible
And fortunately edible—
And also for the boon
Of most delicious fish from the lagoon.
This morning prayer
Represents our attitude
Please fill our hearts,
Instil our hearts
With gratitude.
Amen—amen.

After the meal the younger members of the family are left alone. The six Stirling daughters express their very different views of life . . .

IF I WERE A MAN

(Ann Martin, Islin Hall, Peggy Thompson, Jay O'Neill, Daphne Peretz and Ann Sullivan)

HENRIETTA: If I were a man I would marry a wife
 Who would help me to lead an exemplary life
 And the house that I'd build
 Would be pleasantly filled
 With children belonging to me.
 It would also command
 Several acres of land
 And an excellent view of the sea,
 A most excellent view of the sea.

CAROLINE: If I were a man I would sail away
 To the uttermost ends of the earth,
 And I would return a millionaire
 With jewels of fabulous worth.
 Diamonds and rubies beyond compare
 Ropes of pearls for my true love's hair
 And I'd guarantee on that happy day
 That, unlike us, she need never say
 That she hadn't a thing to wear!

LOUISE: If I were a man I would make up my mind
 To be wise, understanding and gentle and kind.
 I wouldn't catch fish and I wouldn't kill birds,
 I wouldn't shoot poor defenceless rabbits
 Nor would I use inelegant words
 And I'd try to control my annoying habits.
 I wouldn't play jokes and make apple-pie beds,
 Get drunk and stagger upstairs,
 Nor steal people's pencils and break off
 the leads,
 And leave grease on the backs of the chairs.
 I wouldn't be sly and get money from Mother,
 If I were a man,
 If I were a man,
 I would not be my brother!

CAROLINE: We can't all be noble and good, Louise,
 And I'm not at all sure that we should, Louise,
 For think of your miserable plight, Louise,
 If everyone else were as right, Louise,
 And true, Louise,
 As you, Louise.

GEORGINA: If I were a man I'd go out in the dawn
 And I'd gaze at the curve of the bay
 And I'd write in a book
 How the mountains look
 At the beginning of day.
 If I were a man
 I should wish to be bom
 With a dream that would set me apart
 And I'd search the world over
 To find my true lover
 And give her my passionate heart!

TWINS: If we were a man we'd be dashing and bold
 And exceedingly witty and cruel.
 Our hearts would be warm but our eyes
 would be cold,
 And the legend for hundreds of years would
 be told
 How we died for the honour we'd lived to
 uphold,
 In the Bois de Boulogne—

ALL: Why the Bois de Boulogne?

TWINS: In the Bois de Boulogne in a duel.

* * *

(After opening night it was felt that a comic song was needed to pick up the pace here and rather incongruously, we are introduced to Noel's wartime travelling companion, "Uncle Harry." The number had originally been placed in the second act and was cut before the production opened. Even here it

236

seems an obvious interpolation and its awkwardness is accentuated by being sung at breakneck speed by Kerry, Rollo and the girls to the detriment of the clarity of the lyrics. Noel had written it as a point number for himself and proceeded to return it to that status, where it became a mainstay of his cabaret repertoire.)

*   *   *

A family birthday party is imminent. Should they invite the mysterious Madame Salvador, a famous opera singer convalescing on the island? The family elders strongly disapprove. Who is this woman? The Stirlings' younger son, Kerry, decides to invite her anyway and composes an invitation in song . . .

DEAR MADAME SALVADOR (LETTER SONG)

(Graham Payn)

Dear Madame Salvador,
Although this note may seem absurd to you
I feel impelled to run the risk of your
    disdain.
In writing thus a warning word to you,
My one desire is but to spare you pain.
Poor Madame Salvador—
Poor Madame Salvador,
I do not know if you're aware or not
Of the malicious, foolish things that people
    say,
I gravely doubt whether you care or not,
But all the same—in a quite humble way,
Dear Madame Salvador.
Your name and reputation I am eager to
    defend,
So count on me, I beg of you, sincerely as your
    friend.

As he sings, without his realizing it, Elena enters and is charmed by what she hears. She is there by the kind of accident that operetta thrives on—her horse has cast a shoe. Kerry offers to drive her home . . .

MY HORSE HAS CAST A SHOE

(Mary Martin and Graham Payn)

ELENA: My horse has cast a shoe,
A careless thing to do.
Although he has apologized
And shown that he is most upset,
For conduct so uncivilized
I cannot quite forgive him—yet.

KERRY: Of course—of course.
There is nothing so incautious as a horse.

ELENA: My horse has cast a shoe
So I appeal to you,
I meet you by a happy chance
In this untimely circumstance,
Pray tell me what to do.

KERRY: To be able to assist Madame Salvador
Is an honour that I shan't forget,
I will drive you safely home
In my father's wagonette.

ELENA: You are so kind
I'll be ever in your debt
For your chivalry combined
With your father's wagonette.
Who could foretell
That a most obliging fate
Would arrange for what befell
To befall me just exactly by your gate?
Who knows
What magic power guides the hearts
Of those
Who drive about in little carts?

KERRY: Often in dreams
I have known about this meeting
And awakened to the beating
Of my too romantic heart,
Although it seems
Too ridiculous to mention
My intolerable tension
Has been lightened by a little horse and
    cart.
I know
My dreams are fated to come true,
And so
Your horse discreetly cast a shoe.

BOTH: Who knows—what magic power guides
    the hearts
Of those—who drive about in little carts?

Who could have known
We should feel this lovely glow?
We were strangers and alone
Such a little while ago.
Fate set the course
And decided to unbend
By arranging that my horse
Should have led me to the finding of a
    friend.
Who knows
What magic power guides the hearts
Of those
Who drive about in little carts?

Later she recounts the incident to Rosa, her duenna . . .

REPRISE

ELENA: My horse had cast a shoe,
A careless thing to do,
Then Kerry smiled and sympathized
And said that all could be arranged
And suddenly I realized
That everything in life had changed.

ROSA: Of course—of course
I could murder that annoying little
    horse!

ELENA: Then when Kerry whispered 'Dear Madame
    Salvador'
I discovered that my eyes were wet
And he drove me safely home in his
    father's
Wagonette.
How could I know
What incalculable force
Had impelled that rather slow
But beguiling little horse ?
How can I wait
Till the evening shadows fall
To go through that little gate
And to find, in him, the answer to it all?
That cart led me to him and now I know
My heart will never never let him go.

*   *   *

As they leave, the girls return with Penelope—a jolly rather plump girl. As they enthuse about a forthcoming picnic, only Penelope sees it from another point of view. . .

I WISH I WASN'T QUITE SUCH A BIG GIRL

(Daphne Anderson)

VERSE 1

PENELOPE: I was told
When not very old
That if my will were strong enough
And if I tried for long enough
The wish that I wished would come true.

GIRLS: Penny dear,
We're pining to hear
Just how and when and where you built
Those castles in the air you built
And whether or not they vanished—
or they grew.

PENELOPE: Sad to relate
A cruel fate
Disdained my plea
And mocked at me
For the only wish I ever made
Was doomed, biologically, to fade.

GIRLS: Tell us, please, we're all on fire
To hear of this frustrated heart's desire!

REFRAIN

PENELOPE: I wish I wasn't quite such a big girl,
It's not a very nice thing to be,
I've prayed to be more delicate and suffer
from migraines,
But even with a temperature my appetite
remains.
I wish I wasn't sturdy and healthy
To such an unromantic degree.
Nobody even in joke
Would ever lay down his cloak
For a big girl—like me.

VERSE 2

GIRLS: Penny dear,
No really sincere
True love would ever mind a bit
If you stuck out behind a bit
Provided your heart was for him.

PENELOPE: That, dear friends,
Entirely depends
On snatching opportunity
And in this small community
The chances of finding true love—are
rather dim.

GIRLS: That may be so
But still you know
You'll never win
If you give in.
The only thing for you to do
Is take a more optimistic view.

PENELOPE: I know you're right, but come what
may
I must continue wistfully to say:

REFRAIN 2 I wish I wasn't quite such a big girl!
It's such a very dull thing to be.
I fell into the water once when playing on
the brink,
But no one paid attention for they knew I
couldn't sink.
I never really eat all I want to,
But still I seem to grow like a tree.
Nobody quite understands
The strange irresolute glands
Of a big girl—like me.

REFRAIN 3 I wish I wasn't quite such a big girl!
I wish I could be more 'petite fille'—
I'm rather good at guessing games because
I'm not a dunce,
But if I'm playing hide-and-seek I'm always
found at once!
Papa used to come into the nursery,
He'd never let me sit on his knee—
Nobody, even a Truk,
Would give an amorous smirk
To a big girl like me.
The stars may blaze above
But no one ever makes love
To a big girl—like me.

As they leave, the Samolan servants enter to prepare the house for the evening. Naturally, they sing a traditional Samolan song . . .

KA TAHUA

Samolan	*English Translation*
AYANO AND SERVANTS:	
Ka tahua aoana una	Now Spring love brings,
Ka tuhua silo	Now Spring appears,
Tango mero ha anu anu	Life beautiful becomes,
Saalo-lala belo	Skies are blue,
Seu unyea	All the earth
Apra lalua	Has flowers,
Seu alani umpalo	All the stars ride,
Ka tahua aouna una	Now Spring love brings,
Ka tahua aouna una	Now Spring love brings,
Saalo-lai belo	Skies are blue,
Tahali belo.	Happy blue.
Lapuana a seu alani	The moon and all the stars
Jinga pralo tahali yani.	Dance with happy laughter.

Noël indulged his fondness for made-up languages with Samolo and fragments of Samolan turn up in two plays—*South Sea Bubble* (1956), known in America as *Island Fling*, and the unpublished *Volcano* (1957)—a novel, *Pomp and Circumstance* (1960) and a short story, "Solali." For *Pacific 1860* Noël and Coley went to great pains to invent the whole island, topography and all. In *Remembered Laughter* Coley recalls: "We compiled a dictionary of the language with enough verbs and vocabulary for Noël to write one of his songs ("Ka Tahua"). "Fumfumbolo" also contains some lines in this language in it. Just to give you an idea, a flower was *lalua*, thunder *bumbolo*, nuts *kraaki-kraaki* and to copulate was *klabonga*."

*   *   *

Later Kerry invites Elena to the party and they sing a duet . . .

238

BRIGHT WAS THE DAY

(Mary Martin and Graham Payn)

KERRY: This morning when I woke, the light was
              clear in the sky,
          A sweet wind murmured through the trees

A singing bird was singing very near in the sky,
And in the breeze
Which drove the clouds so gaily by
I thought I heard a different note—a little sigh
Which seemed to say
This is your day,
Be careful, please,
Be careful, please!
Don't let this light enchantment fade away,
This is your day.

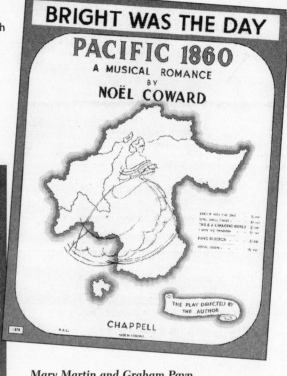

Mary Martin and Graham Payn,
"Bright Was the Day."

ELENA: This morning when I woke I seemed to
              know in my heart
          That some new happiness was near.
          I waited for this unexpected glow in my
              heart
          To disappear.
          But strange to say it would not go
          And as the moments hurried by it seemed
              to grow.
          If, as you say,
          This is your day,
          Kind cavalier,
          Kind cavalier,
          We'll try to let this brief enchantment stay
          Just for today—
          This is your day.

KERRY: Though we—may never meet again,
          There'll never be a day so sweet again.
          Deep in my heart, no matter what the
              troubled years may bring,
          A secret voice—will ever sing.

REPRISE   Bright was the day when you came to me,
          Someone had whispered your name to me.
          Someone had told me how fair you were,

Then at last—there you were!
Light was the music that played for me,
You were the song Destiny had made for me,
I heard the melody start
Delicately—delicately—in my heart.

ELENA: Here in the sunshine I came to you,
Someone had whispered my name to you,
Some potent magic impelled me here,
Touched my heart—held me here !
Dreams long forgotten revive again,
Suddenly life seems to be alive again,
I heard the melody too—
Beckoning me—beckoning me—here to you!

REPRISE Bright was the day when you came to me,
Shyly you whispered your name to me,
I knew the theme of your song before,
Far away—long before,
Sweet was the music that played for me
Part of a dream that can never fade for me,
I heard the melody start
Passionately—passionately—in my heart.

This was the show's principal waltz song of which Noël wrote: "It has a nice, melodic refrain but from the musical and lyrical point of view I prefer the verse."

At the party a double sextet—the Stirling girls and their partners—sing an "Invitation to the Waltz" . . .

INVITATION TO THE WALTZ

GIRLS: This is the high—
Light of the year for us,
Dressed to the nines
Up to our chins,
Stars in the sky,
Moonlight is clear for us,
Candlelight shines
And the music begins.

MEN: Social event
Reeking with quality,
Gentlemen bow,
Ladies advance,
We represent
Stately frivolity,
Youth's at the prow

And so on with the dance.
When we say, 'How good the floor is—
Providential
Circumstance,'

GIRLS: We shall blush
And reply,
'What a crush!
Really we'll swoon
If they play one more tune!'

MEN: 'Music,' we'll say, 'furthermore is
So essential
To romance!'

GIRLS: What seems a terrible bore is
That you'd far rather talk than dance!
This is the high—
Light of the year for us.

MEN: Gentlemen bow,
Ladies advance.

ALL: Stars in the sky,
Moonlight is clear for us,
Youth's at the prow
And so on with the dance.'

MEN: Ladies—dear ladies—beguiling and sweet—

GIRLS: Gentlemen—gentlemen—please try to be discreet.

MEN: Ladies—dear ladies—be kind to our—
Blind to our—
Faults.
One waltz
Need not sweep you off your feet,
Though we may gasp at your beauty
Sense of duty
Will prevail.
We represent
To a large extent
The purely domestic male.
Strong emotions and desires
Training has taught us to check.

GIRLS: What if you unbanked the fires?

MEN: God forbid. We'd get it in the neck!
Ladies—dear ladies—how charming you are.

GIRLS: Gentlemen—gentlemen—don't think us too bizarre,
Though we're prepared to be kind to your—
Blind to your
Faults,
One waltz
Will not get us very far!

The Girls discuss with the young men their duties at Government House in a number "performed with considerable verve by twelve attractive young people whose enthusiasm compensated, up to a point, for their lack of diction."

HIS EXCELLENCY REGRETS

GIRLS: Oh, tell us please
Entirely confidentially
How A.D.C.s
Are trained in social grace.
It's awfully brave
Daily to be called upon to save
His Excellency's face!

MEN: Any explanations
Of the duties of an A.D.C.
Prove the complications
That are rife at Government House.
Certain situations
We could never let a lady see,
There are strange vibrations
In the life at Government House.
Truth is often sacrificed for reasons of diplomacy.

GIRLS: That of course we understand
But all the same it must be grand
To be
So suave, so calm, so dignified!

MEN: If you knew what all that signified—we—
Who break the Ninth Commandment every day
Would hang our heads in shame and say
Forgive—we have to live
Officially on feet of clay.
Every minute
We're made to sin it
Is really very depraved,
But to Hell
With the lies we tell,
His Excellency's honour must be saved.

REPRISE I

His Excellency regrets
That owing to an attack of Gout
He really dare not venture out
On Saturday to dine.

His Excellency regrets
That owing to doctor's orders he
Cannot attend the Mission tea
And also must decline
Your kind invitation
For Wednesday week.
A slight operation
And poor circulation
Combined with a weedy physique
Has made him unable to speak.
All this in addition to what
The Doctors describe as a 'Clot'
Which may disappear
By the end of the year
But may, very possibly, not!
His Excellency regrets
That owing to his exalted state
He can no more associate
With amiable brunettes.
Walk up—walk up—we're willing to take
    your bets
That that's one of the principal things
    His Excellency regrets!

GIRLS: So now we know
About the Diplomatic Corps,
How it can so
Corrupt the soul of youth.
What happens if
Some day you give the waiting world a whiff
Of plain, unvarnished truth?

REFRAIN 2
MEN: His Excellency regrets
That, failing a better alibi,
He must admit he'd rather die
Than open your Bazaar.
His Excellency regrets
That, lacking enough official scope,
He can't disband the Band of Hope
No matter where they are.
He frankly despises
The people he rules,
His gorge also rises
When giving the prizes
At co-educational schools
To rows of illiterate fools.
And if you should write in the book
He'll give you a murderous look.
For it ruins his day
To be taken away
From his rod and his line and his hook!
His Excellency regrets
He hasn't enough to run the house

Or pay the staff—or feed a mouse
Upon the pay he gets.
Heigho—heigho—he's up to his ears in debts
But that's one of the least of the things
    His Excellency regrets!

As the party continues, Kerry and his elder brother, Rollo, sing a quartet with their respective partners . . .

THE PARTY'S GOING WITH A SWING

(Graham Payn, Pat McGrath, Celia Lamb, Daphne Anderson)

There's something about a family rout
That thrills us,
We like to observe our elders on the sly.
We have to repress the urge to laugh which
    nearly kills us
But nevertheless we try,
Observing every action
And recording every clue
We notice with satisfaction
What some claret cup can do.
The stately advance
Of uncles and aunts
In dozens
Is something to be remembered till we die.
It's often a strain to be polite to all our
    cousins
But nevertheless we try.
When gossiping and scandal has the party in its
    grip
The only way to handle it is just to let it rip.

REFRAIN 1
The party's going with a swing, with a swing,
Gay abandon seems to be the thing.
We can say sincerely
That it's really really really
Very pretty to see our elders have an adolescent
    fling.
Dear old Mrs Giles
Having driven thirty miles
Has an appetite that wouldn't shame a horse,
Having tucked away

Nearly all the cold buffet
She shows every inclination that she's going to
    stay the course.
We're all so glad that Cousin Maud,
Thank the Lord,
Hasn't yet been prevailed upon to sing.
Though dear Miss Scobie's principles forbid her
    to carouse
She's apt to get flirtatious when the atmosphere
    allows
But it's hard to be seductive when there's junket
    on your blouse.
The party's going with a swing.

REFRAIN 2
The party's going with a swing, with a swing.
Mrs Drew quite took away our breath,
She remarked with candour
Sitting out on the verandah
That as far as she knew old Mr Drew had drunk
    himself to death.
Pretty Mrs Bowles
Having had five sausage rolls
Was compelled to leave the ball room at a bound.
Also Colonel Blake,
Rather gay on tipsy cake,
Emitted first a hiccup then a more peculiar sound.
We can't say what the Vicar did,
God forbid,
But we can blame the moonlight and the Spring,
With hearty joviality he started playing 'Bears',
He pounced on Mrs Frobisher and took her
    unawares,
We had to cut her laces at the bottom of the
    stairs.
The party's going with a swing.

REFRAIN 3
The party's going with a swing, with a swing,
All the old folks hand in hand with youth.
Mrs John Macmallard
Bit an almond in the salad
Which completely removed the stopping from
    her one remaining tooth.
Dear old Mrs Spears
Who's been mad for several years
And believes she has the gift of second sight
Went into a trance
Just before the supper dance
And let loose a flood of language which was
    highly impolite.
We're glad Aunt May who's deaf and dumb
Couldn't come
For she does put a blight on everything.

When Mrs Edward Pratt arrived Papa was
   scandalized,
To dance in her condition is a little ill-advised,
If we get her through the Lancers we'll be very
   much surprised.
The party's going with a swing.
Mrs Rogers did some conjuring which held us all
   in thrall,
She cleverly produced a lot of rabbits from her
   shawl!
But after that the rabbits did the neatest trick of
   all.
The party's going with a swing.

In a scene involving the older people Mr. Stirling
welcomes them in song . . .

DEAR FRIENDS, FORGIVE ME, PRAY (BIRTHDAY TOAST)

(Tudor Evans)

MR. STIRLING: Dear friends, forgive me pray
         If as your host
         I should seem importunate,
         But my paternal pride
         Can't be denied,
         My daughters' natal day
         Demands a Toast,
         Which is very fortunate
         For though the lemonade and cup's all right
         No wine has flowed yet,
         I haven't heard a cork explode yet.

ALL: How charming—how appropriate—what
            perfect rectitude!
         Dear Mr Stirling never says a word that
            might be misconstrued.

MR. STIRLING: Allow me to express
         My cheerful mind
         In this refined community
         And say with what delight
         I see tonight
         Our friend the Dean
         And Mrs Green
         Accompanied by Oliver
         And dear Miss Ruxton-Bolliver.

I also must extend
To Canon Banks
My ardent thanks
For bringing Jane and Harriet
And also Mr Marryot,
Our ever faithful friend
Who never leaves a party till the end.

So now, my dearest Twins,
Pray make the most
Of this opportunity,
This evening you may frolic with impunity.
In Faith be strong
Refrain from wrong
And may your lives be both enjoyable and long.

Much to their surprise, Madame Salvador enters.
Her reception is chilly and only relieved by the
arrival of Their Excellencies, the Governor and his
wife, who turn out to be friends of hers . . .

MAKE WAY FOR THEIR EXCELLENCIES

(Company)

Make way for Their Excellencies,
Make way for Their Excellencies,
Make way for Their Excellencies,
Make way for Their Excellencies,
Kindly step aside,
They are a symbol representing
Sceptre and Crown and Mighty Race,
Gently but firmly ornamenting
This remote but pleasant place—
Over the ocean's far horizon
Proudly the Ruler of the State
Keeps her astute and watchful eyes on
Every wandering delegate.
Hail to this pair whose steely nerve is
Equal to tasks that others fear.
Hail to the Diplomatic Service
 Which, so discreetly, sent them here.
Make way for Their Excellencies,
Make way for Their Excellencies,
Make way for Their Excellencies.
 Welcome them with pride.

As part of the traditional entertainment at this annual
Stirling party, Kerry sings a Samolan song, accompanied by a native orchestra . . .

FUMFUMBOLO

(Graham Payn)

Ages ago when the world was dawning,
Early in Time—in the beautiful years,
Bolo—the water God of Samolo
Was dying
And on the sands were lying
A million weeping fishes
To hear his final wishes
And watch his soul depart.
Out on the reef there were turtles mourning,
Fumfum, the Goddess of fire, was in tears.
Bolo—the dying God of Samolo
Perceiving
His enemy was grieving
Put out the flames around her
And, though it nearly drowned her,
He took her to his heart.
Then a mountain rose from the sea
And its summit was wreathed in flame
And that is the fabulous history
Of how the volcano came.

Fumfumbolo—Fumfumbolo
Dua kopala—Dua kopala
Fumfumbolo—Fumfumbolo
Bumbumbala—Bumbumbala

When Fumfumbolo lights the sky
No monkeys chatter—no parrots fly,
No flying fishes skim the bay
And every sea-bird hides away.
The salamander leaves the sand,
Even the turtles understand
When God is angry, they move inland.
First the hills seem to crumble,
A deep rumble
Proclaims
That danger is nigh,
From the top of the mountain
A strange fountain
Of flames
Disfigures the sky,

242

Elena then contributes a polka song . . . (This song was a replacement) Mary Martin recalls: " . . . it went 'There is nothing so beguiling as a One, Two, Three, A One, Two, Three and a hop!' All very quick, clipped British. Noël could play it very well, in his own keys, and he did. Well, in the middle I was to sing all this in seven languages—French, Italian, Spanish, German and whatnot. It was hysterical. He kept asking, 'Do you like it?' and I kept saying 'Yes, yes' forgetting that I not only couldn't sing the words in all these other languages, I couldn't sing them in English eye-ther. But I was so enamoured of this man that if he'd said 'Sing the alphabet,' I would have done it.")

ONE, TWO, THREE

(Mary Martin)

Eagles take flight,
Little lizards and snakes
Creep away out of sight
When our Fire Mountain wakes.
And the surf on the reef
Sings of sorrow and grief
And the birds of the air
On the wings of a prayer
Cry to the sky through the smoke and the glare
Fumfumbolo!—Beware!
Crocodiles on sandy banks
Immediately break their ranks
And slide away in fear.
Kinkajous in sore distress
Refuse to venture out unless
A hideaway is near.
Tadpoles and toads
Obstruct the roads
Seeking for shelter.
Oysters retire
Into the mire
Down on the delta.
In the hills
All the whip-poor-wills
Are wailing—wailing.
From far and near
You only hear
The sounds of fear,
The sounds of fear,
The island quivers and quakes,
Shivers and shakes.

Whenever Fumfumbolo wakes!
When Fumfumbolo lights the sky
No monkeys chatter—no parrots fly
No parrots fly—no parrots fly
And that is why!

Samolan—English translation

NATIVES:

Jolan baliya a abu	The world bewares and hides away,
Keya Kopala lalilu	When Gods awake
Li saalo-lali tori foom	The sky rains fire
A twa alani abadum	And all the stars fall down,
Twa nawa juka pralo kwi	All little creatures with a shriek
Abu koanu tariki	Hide fearfully their faces,
Kopala toonga—Kopala kai	The Gods are angry—the Gods are athirst.
Doka jinga doka jinga	Devils dance, devils dance,
Upa bana upa bana	On the sands, on the sands,
Hola pui kriza	The milk turns sour,
O klabonga o klabonga	No love-making—no love-making,
Apu tali apu tali	Under the trees—under the trees,
Twadidi luma	Everything is sad,
Luma solali a luma solaba	Sad night and sad day,
Twa tali yololu a tola lalua	All trees weep and flowers die,
Twa luma solali a luma solaba	All sad night and sad days,
Ka Kopala toonga ka	Now the Gods are angry,
Kopala toonga	Now the Gods are athirst,
Ka Kopala toonga	Now the Gods are angry,
Ka Kopala kai. Haliya!	Now the Gods are athirst—
	Beware!

VERSE   A brand new dance
Invaded France
In April Eighteen Forty,
Through every street
The rhythm beat,
It swept beyond
The demi-monde
And though some people hissed it
They couldn't long resist it.
The Right bank fell,
The Left bank fell
And though the Court was haughty
They took the floor
When some old bore
Declared the dance was naughty.
Sur le pont d'Avignon
People cried, *'C'est bon,'*
As they twirled in the magic of the moon
All the world and his wife
Seemed to take a new life
From that absurd—hurdy-gurdy little tune.

REFRAIN I   There is nothing so beguiling as a One Two
Three,
A One Two Three and a hop,
The music sets you buzzing like a bumble bee,
Oh dear me,
You dance until you drop.
Old folks can't abide the One Two Three,
The reason's easy to see,
Every beat for them
Spells defeat for them,

One Two Three.
But of course for flaming youth
It's quite a different affair,
They maintain with perfect truth
That nothing can compare
With the fascinating rhythm of the One Two
    Three,
It makes them shining and free.
Point your toe,
Off you go,
One Two Three.

REFRAIN 2 There is nothing so exciting as a One Two
    Three,
A One Two Three and a hop,
It definitely *épaters* the bourgeoisie,
Oh dear me,
Their eyes begin to pop,
Missionaries frown upon the One Two
    Three,
Deacons dither with fear,
Grave anxiety
Racks society,
When they hear
Those scandalous audacious strains
They give a terrible cry,
They fear that such flirtatious strains
Are bound to lead to—My! My! My!
So when anybody shudders at the One Two
    Three
We just say 'Fiddlededee!'
Arms out straight,
Tête-à-tête,
One Two Three.

. . . which leads to all the young people joining in this daring new dance. Precisely the outrageous kind of behaviour everyone had been expecting from this dangerous woman of the world!

    A week or so later in Elena's house her companion, Rosa, is awaiting her return. Inspired by the evening, she sings with the cook and Elena's maid . . .

THIS IS A NIGHT FOR LOVERS

(Sylvia Cecil, Maria Perilli and
Winifride Ingham)

The clouds are following the moon,

The night will be over soon,
The silver pathway fades from sight,
Across the still lagoon
The mountains stand against the sky
Watching the little clouds pass by,
Watching the shadows grow,
Watching the shadows grow
On the sleeping world below.

This is a night for lovers,
A night to be set apart
For ever in somebody's heart,
This is a moment for ever and above,
This is a night for love.
Soon when the dawn discovers
Secrets the night conceals
There'll be bright new hills and a coloured sea
Instead of the delicate mystery
The moon only half reveals.
When dawn is lighting up the sky
The air will be shrill with birds,
The magic of love will gently die
Along with its foolish words.
The mountains stand against the sky.
Watching the little clouds pass by,
Watching the shadows grow,
Watching the shadows grow
On the sleeping world below.

This is a night for lovers
Set between yesterday's fears
And tomorrow's most probable tears,
This is a moment for ever and above,
This is a night for love.

*   *   *

When the song was used again—in the out of town US tryout of *Sail Away* in 1961—the first four lines were replaced with . . .

The clouds are following the moon
The dawn will be breaking soon
The stars are fading one by one
The night is nearly done

*   *   *

Rosa then sings a solo, "All My Life Ago," which was eventually cut and subsequently used in *After the Ball* (see p. 290).

Pacific 1860 *makes the cover of*
PICTURE POST. *Noël Coward, designer*
Gladys Caltrop *and Mary Martin.*

*ALL MY LIFE AGO

Why spoil the night with so much sentiment
What is so new, so wonderful, so strange?
Romantic hearts defy presentiment
But all the same we know the scene will change.

Once when I was young
A song was sung,
A song of love too passionate to last.
All my life ago
Among the echoes of the past.
Dawn is coming soon
But, with the moon
It's stange to find that half-remembered tune
Still can hurt me so,
Though it was all my life ago.
Waste no time regretting love,
The skies are clear—the sea is blue
There's more contentment in forgetting love
If once your love has proved untrue.

Live your life apart from it
Let high romance serenely pass you by
Help your mind—to shield your longing heart
      from it
And you'll be happier than I.

*   *   *

Elena and Kerry come in. They are too happy to
notice Rosa's disapproval. After Rosa leaves, Elena
confesses that she never knew "love could be so
sweet before" . . .

I NEVER KNEW

(Mary Martin and Graham Payn)

KERRY AND ELENA:
      I never knew
      That love could be so sweet before,
      I never knew
      That life was incomplete before,
      I never knew—this tremulous ecstasy
      That seems like a dream to me
      Could yet be true.
      How could I guess, dearest, that within my heart
      All other loves apart
      There would be you?
      How could I know
      That I should love you so,
      I never knew—I never knew.

KERRY:
The dearest love I ever knew
To hold for ever and for ever,
Though this moment sweet
May with its magic fade away,
It is complete for us
For ever and a day.
Our hearts will beat alone
No more—asleep or waking
This is our own,
This happiness we've known,
This lovely moment is our own,
All other loves forsaking.
I never knew,
I never knew you could love me,
I never knew.

ELENA:
Dear love, let this be true,
Dear love to last for ever,
Though the magic of tonight
May fade away
We'll remember it
For ever and a day.
No more asleep or waking,
This is our own,
This loveliness our hearts have
      Never known,
This is our own,
All other loves forsaking,
Dear love, I never knew
Love—could be so true,
Love—I never knew.

KERRY AND ELENA:
      I never knew
      Such happiness could be—before,
      I never knew
      Such colours in the sea—before,
      I never knew those mountains were dear to me
      Until you were near to me
      And made it true,
      I feel that now every bird sings to me,
      Will lend its wings to me
      To bear me through
      Each weary day
      That I'm away from you.
      I never knew.
      I never knew.

*   *   *

When the song was also revived for *Sail Away*, the
line—

      I never knew those mountains were dear to me

was replaced with . . .

      I never knew that life was so dear to me

and the duet became a solo number.

*   *   *

Rosa returns and warns Elena of the danger of sac-
rificing a career to an unwise love affair—something
she herself had done in the past. She advises her to
take love lightly . . .

THIS IS A CHANGING WORLD

(Sylvia Cecil)

The world was young
So many many years,
The passage of time must show
Some traces of change,
Love songs once sung,
Much laughter, many tears,
Have echoed down the years,
The past is old and strange.
Each waning moon,
All dawns that rise, all suns that set,
Change like the tides that flow across the sands,
Each little tune
That fills our hearts with vague regret,
Each little love duet

Fades in our hands,
Don't stray among the moments that have
      fled,
New days are just ahead,
New words are still unsaid.

REFRAIN 1   This is a changing world, my dear,
            New songs are sung—new stars appear,
            Though we grow older year by year
            Our hearts can still be gay,
            Young love at best is a passing phase,
            Charming and foolish and blind,
            There may be happier, wiser days
            When youth is far behind.
            Where are the snows of yesteryear?
            When Winter's done and Spring is here
            No regrets are worth a tear,
            We're living in a changing world, my dear.

REFRAIN 2   This is a changing world, my dear,
            New dreams are dreamed,
            New dawns appear,
            Passion's a feckless cavalier
            Who loves and rides away,
            Time will persuade you to laugh at grief,
            Time is your tenderest friend,
            Life may be lonely and joy be brief
            But everything must end.
            Love is a charming souvenir,
            When day is done and night draws near
            No regrets are worth a tear,
            We're living in a changing world, my dear.

REPRISE   This is a changing world, my dear,
            The clouds have gone—the skies are clear,
            What is there in the atmosphere
            That lifts my heart away ?
            Can you not hear it, that lovely tune,
            Urgent, entrancing and sweet,
            Telling me clearly how soon,
            How soon my love and I will meet?
            This that I feel will always be,
            This voice that calls is Destiny,
            Can't you hear it—can't you see
            That love has changed the changing world
                  for me?

Felix, Elena's manager, shares Rosa's concerns. He
tells Elena that arrangements have been made for
them all to leave on the boat the next day. She sends
Kerry a note but he arrives at the harbour just as the
ship has sailed.

COME BACK TO THE ISLAND

(Graham Payn & Company)

Come back to the island,
Please leave your heart behind you,
Heartache
Is a keepsake
That will haunt you and remind you,
Keep faith—and remember,
Keep faith—and we'll remind you,
Come back to the island,
Come back to your heart.
Soon—the shore will fade,
The pounding surf you will not hear,
The mountain tops will disappear
And be a memory
Beyond the empty sea,
Here—the sun and shade,
The green lagoons, the gleaming sand
Of this benign and loving land
Still will be
Your certainty.

Come back to the island,
Please leave your heart behind you,
Heartache Is a keepsake
That will haunt you and remind you,
Keep faith—and remember,
Keep faith—and we'll remind you,
Come back to the island,
Come back to your heart.

* * *

A year has passed. Elena arrives back in Samolo. Rosa, now accepting that her friend's feelings for Kerry are more than just a passing fancy, sings with the maids . . .

GIPSY MELODY

*(Sylvia Cecil, Maria Perilli and
Winifride Ingham)*

SOLANGE AND TRUDI:
Tell us pray what made you become so clinical?

Did your head persuade you to count the cost
Though your love betrayed you and made you cynical?

ROSA: I'll sing a song to you, both sad and true,
About a highly born Hungarian,
Although the husband she was married to
Was far removed from a barbarian
She loved a proletarian
In a valley far away,
A Gipsy minstrel came to play
A serenade,
Everyone from far and near
Collected in the woods to hear the tune he played.

Wild and free.
That haunting melody
Enchanted maid and man
Young and old
Believed the tales he told
And joined his caravan,
A most impulsive, foolish plan.

Their troubles then began.
The rain soon drove them home again
No longer wild and free,
Snow and hail had made that nightingale
Sound very much off-key,
A sorry tale you will agree.
What fools these mortals be.

But one poor lady left her heart behind
And from that moment life was sad for her,
Naught could bring comfort to her troubled mind
Which, on the whole, was very bad for her.

That is why
To any Gipsies passing by
She'll always sigh:

REFRAIN
ROSA: Play me
A Gipsy melody from far away,
An echo wild and gay
From some forgotten yesterday,
My lonely heart can still remember
Those magic nights beneath the open sky,
So Gipsy play for me
That song I'll love until the day I die.

SOLANGE AND TRUDI:
Play me
A Gipsy melody from far away,
An echo wild and gay
From some forgotten yesterday,
My lonely heart can still remember

Those magic nights beneath the open sky,
So Gipsy play for me
That song I'll love until the day I die.

* * *

(This number was added after the opening night and replaced another trio sung by the same artistes.)

*POOR LADY IN THE THROES OF LOVE

ROSA: Poor lady in the throes of love,
So heedless of the woes of love
Hold to the magic true,
Your story's old
And ever new.
Someday your heart will sigh no more.

TRUDI: Someday the glory and the passion and
the pain will fade away

DORA: Someday you'll wonder why no more
You wished to stay
Enclosed within a dream,
A gentle half forgotten dream.

ALL: Soon these troubled years will seem
No more important than a dream.

ROSA: Poor lady in the throes of love,
Wait a little while and see,
So heedless of the woes of love
Only time can set you free,
Free from all the pains of love,
The cruel chains of love
That hold and bind you
You'll know before your days are done
Sorrow must end
But although such love in your heart
The years will mend,
You will remember love
Until the end.

TRUDI: *(counterpoint)* Your story's old and ever new,
You'll know when these enraptured
And enchanted days are done, poor lady,
soon
You'll know that disenchantment
May already have begun
You'll know that each

Lovely, lovely day will end,
All that's sad or gay will one day end.

*   *   *

Elena enters, radiant at the prospect of seeing Kerry again—only to be told that the town is celebrating the wedding of "Young Master Stirling." Elena orders the servants to stop unpacking. They will soon be leaving again.

At the Stirlings' house the wedding guests are celebrating the joys of matrimony . . .

THIS IS THE NIGHT

(The Company)

This is a night
Made for posterity,
Here on this isle
Weddings are rare,
We can, with slight
Lack of sincerity,
Greet with a smile
This most fortunate pair.

Here without doubt
Nature can grin again,
Men can be slow,
Men can be sly,
Girls who come out
Have to go in again
Principally owing to lack of supply.

Please do not think we are jealous
Or disgruntled or aggrieved,
We can sigh,
We can coo,
We can cry,
'Really it's too—
Too too good to be true!'
All social instincts compel us
To be joyful and relieved,
Still we'd like someone to tell us
How this marriage has been achieved.

This sublime and Christian rite
Aims to replenish the stock,
But of course the bridal night
Frequently—is something of a shock!

Life we believe
Really requires some

Sine qua non
Neatly defined,
Owing to Eve
Having been tiresome
Man must go on
Reproducing mankind.

. . . as well as some of its minor sorrows . . .

MOTHER'S LAMENT

*(Maidie Andrews, Gwen Bateman,
Rose Hignell)*

Here in the twilight of our days
From all maternal bondage freed
We've earned this sweet repose no doubt
But still it's dull to sit about
And watch the sands of time run out
With such indecent speed.

Now, as our eyes begin to glaze,
We peer from our domestic cage,
Here in the sere and yellow leaf
Our task is done, our time is brief,
We know that we should feel relief
But all we feel is rage.

Being at last put out to graze
Like cows that are too old to breed
We know that by maternal pride
Our spirits should be fortified
But all the same we're mortified
And very cross indeed.

The six Stirling girls have their own views on all this dressing up . . .

PRETTY LITTLE BRIDESMAIDS

We humbly and devoutly pray
That some kind gentleman some fine day
Will fling all gnawing doubts away
And cordially invite us
To stroll along some shady path

And there to offer us home and hearth
Remarking, as an aftermath,
That the Church should first unite us.

We long to bear the heavy weight
Of the matrimonial halter,
We're tired of following friends we hate
Sedately to the altar.

We're sick of being pretty little bridesmaids,
We're weary of the fussing and the fume,
We dread the awful destiny that guides maids
Unwanted and unmarried to the tomb,
We long to lose our purity
And plump for the security
A wedding-ring undoubtedly provides,
We're sick to death of being pretty little
    bridesmaids
Instead of being pretty little brides.

We're bored with all those brooches made of
    seed pearls,
We hate each insignificant bouquet,
We'd like to feel that should we ever need
    pearls
We could earn them in a more attractive way.

We'd face with equanimity
The intimate proximity
Of someone snoring loudly by our sides,
For we're sick to death of being pretty little
    bridesmaids
Instead of being pretty little brides.

We shudder every time we see the vicar,
We shrink from orange blossom and
    champagne,
It's such a very acid-making liquor,
No sooner down than up it comes again.
There's nothing very nice about
Relations throwing rice about,
But that we'd bear and other things besides,
If just for once instead of pretty little
    bridesmaids
We might be being pretty little brides.

We can't enjoy those roguish implications
Concerning the approaching bridal night,
Nor share the strange, vicarious sensations
In which our elder relatives delight,
If ever we are married off
We pray that we'll be carried off
To where no eager family presides,
For we'd loathe to think of all our beastly little
    bridesmaids
Imagining us pretty little brides!

As all the guests go into the house the stage is empty until Elena enters. She wants one last look at Kerry . . .

I SAW NO SHADOW

(Mary Martin)

I saw no shadow on the sea,
No warning star appeared,
The skies were free,
No vagrant gipsy told me
Of a fascinating stranger,
Gave no hint of where the danger
Might be.

Then came that strange, disturbing day
That love that I so desired,
The sun and the moon conspired
Above me,
Now like a ghost I watch my happiness depart,
The light of love has cast a shadow on my heart.

All through my life I have wandered,
Ambition my compass and my chart,
Moments I heedlessly squandered
Now return to haunt me—mocking at my heart.
Love, with its lovely illusions,
I neatly, discreetly set aside,
Fear kept me safe from confusion
Leaving me with only
Loneliness and pride,
Cold was the starlight above me,
Time in its passing was slow,
I had no need of a lover to love me
But oh—
That was long ago.

I saw no shadow on the sea,
No voices called to me,
My life was free,
How could I open wide my arms
To the paradise around me
When no love had ever found me
The key?
And then I dreamed some foolish dreams
And, leaving my world behind,
I gaily set out to find
My lover.
Now, in a moment, all those dreams are torn
    apart,
The light of love has cast a shadow on my heart.

The guests emerge to see the happy couple depart. To her surprise she sees not Kerry and Melita but Rollo and Penelope. Kerry is the best man and toasts them . . .

WEDDING TOAST

(Graham Payn)

Your Excellencies—Ladies and Gentlemen—
Dear Friends—in this sweet circumstance
When all the air around us and above
Is charged with tenderness and early love
And that enchantment which is called Romance,
I beg of you to lift your glasses up
And drink to those we love—a loving cup.

No one can vouch for love—none can be sure
How long its ardent magic may endure,
No one can order love—all we can do
Is, in our deepest hearts, to keep it true.

To you we love—to you we hold so dear
I drink to here and now and ever after,
May every tear you shed dissolve in laughter,
May joy be yours through every changing year.
I drink to you with certainty and know
That Destiny could never never part
Two lovers when they love each other so.

And oh I envy you with all my heart.

As the couple leave, followed by the guests, Elena observes as Melita returns Kerry's ring to him. She knows his heart can never be hers. She leaves Kerry alone. Elena begins to sing softly "Bright Was the Day." Kerry sees her and the rest, as they say . . .

*   *   *

A number that was in the original script was intended for Elena's entrance in Act II. Because Mary Martin refused to perform it, it also had to wait for Noël and cabaret. In her autobiography, *My Heart Belongs*, Miss Martin recalls the incident:

> "The main song Noël had written for me was 'Alice Is At It Again.' Probably this was because he had heard me sing 'My Heart Belongs To Daddy,' which was naughty. A few years older and wiser when I read the lyrics to 'Alice,' I nearly dropped dead. Alice was really *at* it, with

---

the birds and bees and the beasts of the field. I thought it wasn't right for a gal from Texas to make her London debut with this scandalous song. I also didn't think it was right for Mme. Salvador, for her character. I knew it was funny, terribly funny, and now I know that I should have sung it. It would have stopped the show every night. But I refused. Noël was very sweet and said he would write me another. He later sang 'Alice' himself . . . and made it a tremendous number."

ALICE IS AT IT AGAIN (ORIGINALLY SWEET ALICE . . .)

VERSE 1   In a dear little village remote and obscure
A beautiful maiden resided,
As to whether or not her intentions were pure
Opinion was sharply divided.
She loved to lie out 'neath the darkening sky
And allow the soft breeze to entrance her,
She whispered her dreams to the birds flying by
But seldom received any answer.

REFRAIN 1   Over the field and along the lane
Gentle Alice would love to stray,
When it came to the end of the day,
She would wander away unheeding,
Dreaming her innocent dreams she strolled
Quite unaffected by heat or cold,
Frequently freckled or soaked with rain,
Alice was out in the lane.
Whom she met there
Every day there
Was a question answered by none,
But she'd get there
And she'd stay there
Till whatever she did was undoubtedly done.
Over the field and along the lane
When her parents had called in vain,
Sadly, sorrowfully, they'd complain,
'Alice is at it again.'

VERSE 2   Though that dear little village
Surrounded by trees
Had neither a school nor a college
Gentle Alice acquired from the birds and
    the bees

Some exceedingly practical knowledge.
The curious secrets that nature revealed
She refused to allow to upset her
But she thought when observing the beasts
    of the field
That things might have been organised better.

REFRAIN 2 Over the field and along the lane
Gentle Alice one summer's day
Met a man who was driving a dray
And he whisked her away to London.
Then, after many a year had passed,
Alice returned to her home at last
Wearing some pearls and a velvet train,
Bearing a case of champagne.
They received her
Fairly coldly
But when wine had lifted the blight
They believed her
When she boldly
Said the Salvation Army had shown her the
    light
When she had left by the evening train
Both her parents in grief and pain
Murmured brokenly, 'More champagne—
Alice is at it again!'

RHYTHM REFRAIN *(used in Las Vegas)*
Over the field and along the lane
Gentle Alice would make up
And take up—her stand.
The road was not exactly arterial
But it led to a town near by
Where quite a lot of masculine material
Caught her roving eye.
She was ready to hitchhike
Cadillac or motor-bike,
She wasn't proud or choosey,
All she
Was aiming to be
Was a prinked up,
Minked up
Fly-by-night Floosie.
When old Rajahs
Gave her pearls as large as
Nuts on a chestnut tree
All she said was, 'Fiddlededee,
The wages of sin will be the death of me!"
Over the field and along the lane
Gentle Alice's parents would wait hand in
    hand.
Her dear old white-headed mother, wistfully
    sipping champagne
Said, "We've spoiled our child—spared the rod,

Open up the caviar and say Thank God,
We've got no cause to complain,
Alice is at it,
Alice is at it,
Alice is at it again."

The archives reveal a further unused refrain . . .

*Over the field and along the lane
Gentle Alice had learned to wait
And, while waiting, to cogitate
On the foibles of man with maiden.
One day a curate with good intent
Told her that she should repent for Lent
She said she might but he'd have to guess
Just what she had to confess.
Her confession
Stunned the preacher—
Tho' the things he heard made him blush,
His concession
Was to teach her
That a bird in the hand was worth two in
    the bush.
When she took up her stand again,
Humming some little hymn refrain,
All the clergy with loud 'Amen'
Sang—"Alice is at it again!"

For him, Noël was eminently reasonable: "As I have never felt really right about it, we tried it a couple of times and then cut it from the show." At this point he still regarded Mary as "a dream girl, quick and knowledgeable; she has all the mercurial charm of Gertie at her best with a sweet voice and more taste."

It was a verdict he was to revise before opening night . . . He also had a jaundiced view of the theatre which housed his growing frustrations, rechristening it "Dreary Lane."

*   *   *

The archives reveal three other songs that were never used in the show. The first was presumably intended for Mme. Salvador to sing, having left the island.

---

*WAIT FOR ME

Wait for me,
Love me only

Tho' life is lonely
Around you.
Keep—within your tender heart
My memory apart
And never break the dream that bound you.
Wait for me,
Seek no new love,
Believe the true love
That found you
For—one little moment more
It may not be too late
If you will wait—for me.

For a year and a day
I have hidden my heart from you
Still I knew
Though I tried to be gay
Life was empty apart from you
That is true
All those desolate moments without you
All those dreams I dreamed about you
Made me know that my world could no longer
    be free
We—wherever we may be—are together.

Wait for me
Doubt me never
Be true whatever
Betide you.
Please—however much you grieve
I want you to believe
That you have still my love to guide you.
Wait for me
'Till our meeting
My heart is beating
Beside you
Though this love has hurt you so
Don't let me be too late
My dearest—wait—for me.

Alternative:

Tho' the flame is burning low,
It may not be too late
If you will wait—for me.

The next is more problematical, since it is by no means clear which of the characters might have sung it. It appears to be a draft for what eventually became "Josephine" in the later *Ace of Clubs* (see p. 263).

*URSULINE

Ursuline, Ursuline
Left the convent far behind.
She was sweet seventeen
But she certainly knew her mind.
If the men
Now and then
Looked at her in a peculiar way
And fluttered like moths around the flame,
Tho' able to handle
A possible scandal,
She just lit a candle
In case.
Ursuline, Ursuline
Always kept the party clean.
Her intentions were veiled
But the gentlemen failed
To coerce
Ursuline.

The third was intended for Penelope (the 'Big Girl').

*IF ONLY A GIRL COULD BE SURE

VERSE:　Life can be bleak
And fraught with anxiety
In, so to speak,
Victorian society.
Once you've come out
You can't gad about
With beaus,
God knows!
Girls go to war
On reaching maturity,
Fight tooth and claw
For ultimate security
And, in that fighting,
Snarling and biting,
Every illusion goes.
I've never been that kind of Amazon,
I'm not provocative to men
I stand aside when all the clamour's on,

But I get worried now and then.

REFRAIN 1　If only a girl could be sure
That the future was going to be rosy,
She could give up the fight
With a sigh of delight
Completely relax
And stop dead in her tracks
And take off her shoes and be cosy.
If only a girl could be sure
That no longer she'd have to endure
The perpetual dread
Of remaining unwed.
If only a girl could be sure,
Heigho
If only a girl could be sure.

REFRAIN 2　If only a girl could be sure,
If only there wasn't that 'Maybe'
All the fusses and frets
Of domestic upsets
She would gladly surmount
If she knew she could count
On a husband, a cook, and a baby!
If only a girl could be sure
That to be both genteel and demure
Was the adequate bait
For acquiring a mate
If only a girl could be sure
Heigho
If only a girl could be sure

REFRAIN 3　If only a girl could be sure,
If only a girl could be certain
Of some set guarantee
And forever be free
Of that sinister doubt
As to what might jump out
From behind Fate's implacable curtain.
If only a girl could be sure
That her prospects were not so obscure
She could throwup the sponge
And prepare for a plunge
If only a girl could be sure
Heigho
If only a girl could be sure!

Alternative:

　　If only a girl could be sure
That her future was really secure,
She could kick over traces,
And cut all her laces

An unproduced musical that began life as *Hoi Polloi* and was during the course of 1949—when Noël was more concerned with writing *South Sea Bubble* and filming *The Astonished Heart*—variously retitled *Over the Garden Wall* and *Come Out to Play*. It was to have been produced by Prince Littler whose detailed comments initially irritated Noël considerably. By November, however, the *Diaries* record that: "Beginning to realise that after all, Prince was right. The book is not good enough and doesn't only need strengthening. It needs bloody well rewriting."

*　　　*　　　*

The opening chorus sets the theme of a story of ordinary Londoners and how they had survived the war that "London Pride" had been about. In the lyric he acknowledges that the piece is, in one way, *This Happy Breed* revisited . . .

　　*Two houses—side by side—respectable
Near Clapham Common—in the present day
Provide our theme—perhaps a bit suspectable
Of being rather like an earlier play.
Here beneath neat, refined suburban trees
Our star-crossed lovers, shorn of deathless rhyme,
Owing to their cantankerous families

Have, on the whole, a fairly bloody time.
But happily the centuries have changed
Not human hearts but human circumstance.
And so our noble author has arranged
A less depressing seal to this romance.
And now if you will kindly concentrate,
We'll show you life and love S.W.8.

Had he followed this direction, he would have anticipated *West Side Story* (1957) by nearly a decade. Instead, he substituted for the "star-crossed lovers" a gentler tale of E.1. moving the setting from Clapham to bomb-damaged Stepney and other familiar parts of tourist London.

The story begins in Covent Garden market. Barmy Flo is sitting at her flower stall, Mr. Capper at his fruit and veg, while all around them market porters load and unload produce and sing about the lives they lead . . .

*WE LIVE OUR LIVES IN CITY STREETS

We live our lives in city streets.
Although we deal with country things,
Tomatoes, turnips, spuds and leeks,
We take them all for granted.
We seldom see a field or hedge
Or watch a swallow spread its wings,
We merely sell the fruit and veg
That other men have planted.
We never hear a country sound,
The rattle of the Underground
Is more familiar to us than the humming of the bees.
The London traffic's steady roar
Can stir our hearts a great deal more
Than listening uneasily to wind among the trees.
We don't like orchards, moors or fens
Or digging earth or pruning shrubs
And as for living duck and hens,
We have no patience with 'em.
We live our life in city streets.
In cinemas and local pubs.
In us the heart of London beats
A gay, undaunted rhythm.

Pinkie Macklin ("a well dressed, lively girl") enters with her younger brother, Alfie, who is pushing the family barrow, ready to fill it for the day. She is a manicurist on her day off and full of the joys of spring, which she proceeds to share with the world at large in "Top of the Morning"—one of several songs written for the show and then taken over into the one that grew out of it, *Ace of Clubs* (1950) *(Note: In these cases the lyrics will be found under the show in which they were actually performed.)*

Enter Harry Hornby, a sailor in London on a one day leave. He meets Pinkie and flirts with her outrageously. They are obviously attracted and express that in a "getting-to-know-you" number . . .

*SUNDAY AFTERNOONS

VERSE 1

HARRY: Meeting for the first time you and I
Feeling rather strange and rather shy,
How can we make our minds unfreeze
And put our hearts at ease?

PINKIE: Couldn't we discuss, to make things go,
What we have in common—who we know?
And if we agree about plays and books
And Ingrid Bergman's looks?

HARRY: Leaving aside the rest,
Tell me things you like the best.

VERSE 2

HARRY: On a first impression much depends,
I begin to feel we're really friends.
The things you like are true and sweet
But how can I compete?

PINKIE: Having trotted out my box of toys,
All the foolish things my heart enjoys,
You must admit it's only fair
That you should do your share!

HARRY: I shall be put to shame—
All that I like sounds awfully tame . . .

BOTH: Sunday afternoons,
Sunday afternoons,
Hearing music playing in the park

HARRY: Finding a girl who is friendly and flirtable,
Taking her out in a Daimler convertible.

PINKIE: Only for export!

BOTH: Walking through the streets
Sucking coloured sweets,
Going to the 'Pictures'

PINKIE: In the most expensive seats

HARRY: Donald Duck cartoons

PINKIE: Tin Pan Alley tunes

BOTH: With you on Sunday afternoons.

In his notes for the show you can see Noël experimenting with various combinations of couplets. . .

Listening to music in the park
Waiting in queues for the pit or the gallery,
Discussing Laurence Olivier's salary
(Also his love life)
Cigarettes in bed,
Toasted currant bread,
Getting to the zoo in time to see the sea-lions fed

* * * * * * * * * *

Sunday afternoons,
Watching rich tycoons
Driving Ford saloons,
Cadillacs, Rolls-Royces and MGs
Drinking beer in bars,
Smoking good cigars,
Dreaming of a world composed of garages
and cars.
Purchasing at Moon's
Several Ford saloons
For you—on Sunday afternoons

It's clear from the *Diaries* that he later had the song in mind for *Ace of Clubs* but it was never used in the show.

Pinkie and Alfie take Harry home to Stepney to meet their family—Fanny and Charlie Macklin and Doreen, Pinkie's younger sister. The neighborhood kids ask Harry what it's like to be in the Navy and Harry sings "Something About a Sailor" (see p.261).

Left alone with an inquisitive Doreen, Pinkie admits that maybe she is falling in love with Harry. The song, "I'd Never Never Know" was also transferred to *Ace of Clubs* (see p. 261) but, since the character of Pinkie was transformed from sweet Cockney girl to a slightly soiled cabaret performer, the sentiments in the song also went through a transformation. Here is how the song started . . .

*I'D NEVER NEVER KNOW

Why is the Springtime giving
London this lovely glow?
What is this joy of living?
Without him—I'd never never know
I'd never never know
Why am I so excited
Over a movie show?
Why do the streets seem lighted?
Without him—I'd never never know.
He called around on Sunday,
He said it was only by chance
But we've got a date next Monday
To go to the Palais de Dance.
When will the week be over?
Why is the time so slow?
I love him so,
Will he ever know?
Will he ever ever know?

The subplot concerns another young couple, Julian and Linda Curtis. They are newly married and we meet them when he, as an RAF Wing Commander, goes to the Palace to be decorated. They were supposed to sing the show's major waltz duet, "Happy For Ever After," which was never written.

The two couples meet in the crowds outside the Palace and exchange a few words.

Out of the Palace gates come three eminent theatrical ladies, "splendidly dressed"—the newly ennobled Dame Rosie, accompanied by Dame Laura and Dame Margaret. They pause on the kerb . . .

DAME LAURA: We could walk, really—it's only a little way.

DAME ROSIE: These shoes are giving me hell!

DAME MARGARET: Very well, dear—it's your day. (*In stentorian tones*) Taxi!

DAME LAURA: There's no need for *quite* such a noise, Margaret. Remember we're *outside* Buckingham Palace and not *inside* His Majesty's.

DAME MARGARET: I thought your curtesy was just right dear—Not too jerky and above all, not too low. When I came with poor Violet to get hers last year, she stayed on the floor for hours.

DAME ROSIE: She told me she'd caught her heel in her dress.

DAME MARGARET: Nonsense. She was over-rehearsed.

DAME LAURA: That's more than she was in that play with John last year. She didn't know a line—not a line.

DAME ROSIE: It was a terrible part, dear. All those oaths and that dreadful scene in the Crypt.

DAME MARGARET: Taxi!

DAME LAURA: If you go on making those ear-splitting sounds, Margaret, you'll never get through your matinée.

DAME MARGARET: Rubbish, dear. Correct breathing. Diaphragm muscles hard as nails. I could shout all day if I wanted to without even getting husky.

DAME LAURA: Well, for God's sake—don't!

THREE THEATRICAL DAMES

VERSE 1
DAME LAURA:
I started from scratch
In a house with a thatch
With two very unpleasant old ladies.
My parents were dead
So I finally fled
And appeared in a tent
Outside Burton-on-Trent
In a very small part in *Quo Vadis*
I toured in *East Lynne*
And *The Wages of Sin*
Till I couldn't tell one from the other,
Then I found a rich friend
And achieved the West End
In a farce called *She Did It For Mother.*

REFRAIN 1
ALL: Three theatrical Dames,
Eminent and respectable,
Our accents are undetectable
And though we've achieved our aims
If they knew what we'd done
In Eighteen Ninety-One
They certainly wouldn't have made us Dames

VERSE 2
DAME ROSIE:
My very first step

Was Shakespearian 'rep'
Where an awful old 'Ham' used to train us.
I'd nothing to do
In *The Dream* and *The Shrew*
But I carried a spear
In *King John* and *King Lear*
And a hatchet in *Coriolanus.*
I ranted for years
In pavilions on piers
Till my spirits were really at zero,
Then I got a small role
Of a Tart with a soul
In a play by Sir Arthur Pinero

REFRAIN 2
ALL: Three Theatrical Dames,
Models of prim propriety,
Accepted by High Society
Because of our famous names,
If they'd asked us to tea
In Eighteen Ninety-Three
They certainly wouldn't have made us Dames.

VERSE 3
DAME MARGARET:
I made my debut
In a canvas canoe
In a horrid American drama
It wasn't a hit
So I left the 'Legit!'
And got myself backed
In a musical act
Called "A Night in the Garden of Karma",
An agent called Klein
Said, "I'm willing to sign
Whoever that girl who unveils is"
So I got my first chance
With a Biblical dance
In a flop at the Old Prince of Wales's.

REFRAIN 3
ALL: Three theatrical Dames,
Each of our houses we adorn
With photographs of the highly-born
In elegant silver frames,
If they'd caught us in Crewe
In Eighteen Ninety-Two
They certainly wouldn't have made us Dames

REFRAIN 4
ALL: Three theatrical Dames,
Prominent high and mighty girls,
The fact that we once were flighty girls

Our manner today disclaims,
If they'd seen our high kicks
In Eighteen Ninety-Six
They certainly wouldn't have made us Dames

There was a half-hearted attempt to include it in the subsequent *Ace of Clubs*—where it appears in one draft as part of the Act 2 "Cabaret scene," featuring showgirls Baby, Yvonne and Mavis.

The song was eventually produced in a quite different context—on June 28th 1956 at the London Palladium it was an item in *The Night of 100 Stars*, a midnight matinée in aid of the Actors' Orphanage. Dame Rosie was played by Peter Ustinov, while Laurence Harvey was Dame Margaret and Paul Scofield was Dame Laura. *The Daily Telegraph* critic concluded "a more virile-looking trio is hard to imagine," while the trio themselves steadfastly insisted that any resemblance between the characters they portrayed and Dame E...h, Dame S...l or any other incumbent was purely coincidental.

*   *   *

The scene then moves to Hyde Park. The Curtises express their happiness in the song "In a Boat, On A Lake, With My Darling" (see p. 264). Once again, the two couples run into each other. Amused at the coincidence, the Curtises invite Pinkie and Harry to the fancy dress party they are holding that evening. Pinkie wants to go but Harry—anxious to keep Pinkie to himself for the whole of this precious day and feeling they would be socially ill at ease—wants to refuse. When the Curtises have gone, there is a row and Harry storms off. Left alone, Pinkie soon realises the quarrel is about nothing and sends a small boy off to try and find Harry. Determined that nothing will spoil her day, she sings a song which finally has everyone in the park joining in—"Chase Me, Charlie" (see p. 267).

*   *   *

Act 2 opens in Piccadilly Circus. General Trott and his wife—one of the several couples we met briefly outside Buckingham Palace—are regretting the passing of the old days of Empire.

GENERAL: Everything has changed—the upper classes have become vulgar and the lower classes pretentious.

MRS. TROTT: To which do we belong, my love? I get so muddled.

GENERAL: Upper middle—decayed gentry—bourgeoisie—and proud of it.

*LONG LIVE THE BOURGEOISIE

VERSE

SOLO: Since Tudor times and long before
        Our authors and musicians
        Have praised in song and praised in prose
        The English horse, the English rose,
        And other fine traditions.

CHORUS: And other fine traditions.

SOLO: Through every peace and every war
        Our patriotic fervour
        For English thought and English ways
        Must fairly frequently amaze
        The more detached observer.

CHORUS: To Hell with detached observers!

SOLO: From Chaucer on to Mr. Donne
        And further on to Milton
        We've praised our beer beyond belief
        We've praised our mutton, praised our beef
        And eulogized our Stilton!

CHORUS: We've raved about our Stilton!

SOLO: By Shakespeare's time restraint had gone
        Still more effusion flowed
        Since Kipling crowed and Byron brayed
        We've even sat through *Cavalcade*
        By Mr. Noël Coward.

CHORUS: God bless and speed him
          How we need him!

REFRAIN I

SOLO: Long live the Bourgeoisie
        We oil our bats
        And we clean our clubs
        We're democrats
        In the local pubs
        We like Britannia to rule the waves
        We don't believe that the waves are ruled by slaves.
        Let the "Workers" unite
        Let the classes fight
        We'll be glad to referee—
        (From our seat on the sidelines)
        Esprit de corps, lads
        Wins every war, lads
        Long live the Bourgeoisie.

REFRAIN 2

SOLO: Long live the Bourgeoisie
        We keep our heads
        And defend our rights
        Against the "Reds"
        And the so-called "Whites"
        We keep afloat on a stormy sea,
        Although the Communists say we're N.B.G.
        We contrive to relax
        Though the income-tax
        Robs us of our L.S.D.
        (We can give up the Austin)
        Workers despise us
        Cripps crucifies us
        Long live the Bourgeoisie.

Among his notes Noël had scribbled an alternative to the 'Britannia' couplet . . .

Only in church do we bend the knee
And treat the Lord like a rather bored Trustee.

The number was extremely topical, since the Chancellor of the Exchequer, Sir Stafford Cripps, had recently brought in a swingeing "austerity" Budget. It was time for the bourgeoisie to find its voice.

*   *   *

Harry enters and chats to Barmy Flo, who is now selling flowers under the statue of Eros. He confides to her his row with Pinkie and buys the rest of her roses as a peace offering. Even so, he's not optimistic about his chances of making up with her in the time he has left. In the 2nd draft of the script he contemplates going away in the song "Sail Away" (see p. 263) but decides to at least try. In the 1st draft he was to have sung the obligatory "London" number—"There's a Lot To Be Said for London"—which does not appear to have been written.

Meanwhile, Pinkie has gone home to Mum and Dad. She confides to Flo that she also regrets falling out with Harry and when Flo has gone, sings "Why Does Love Get in the Way So?" (see p. 266).

The next scene takes place in the Macklins' garden. Fanny sits in a deck chair and enjoys the evening air. She sings "Evening in Summer" (see p 266). Harry arrives and he and Pinkie fall into each other's arms. Of course, they'll go to the Curtis's party and they begin to choose Pinkie's costume from Fanny's old wardrobe from the days when she was "Florence Follette" ("Mum never got to the West End but she was a riot in the provinces").

While the girls are occupied, Charlie Macklin asks Harry about his travels. Harry sings "I Like America" (see p. 265).

In some early notes Noël had envisaged a scene

Noël as seen through the lens of Roddy McDowall.

in a pub in the Mile End Road. By the first full draft this had turned into a transitional scene that contained a short ballet but was otherwise without dialogue. Originally, we were to have been taken into the pub to meet a barmaid who, far from being the cheerful dispenser of drinks, turns out to be less than enamoured of her work . . .

*TIME, GENTLEMEN, PLEASE

Time, Gentlemen, Please—
You've had it—it's time to go.
The hour has struck,
You're out of luck,
You'd best run home to mother—
I will not serve you another.
Gin and lime, Gentlemen, please,
So take your change and stop stuttering.
Stop spluttering,
Stop chattering,
Stop nattering,
Be on your way.
You may all be plastered
And call me a bastard
But I'm gone at the knees—
Time, Gentlemen, Please!

Back now to a blitzed area in Stepney, Barmy Flo sits outside her house. Originally, she was also to have sung "There's A Lot To Be Said For London." Instead she reflects on the changes she's seen and what the war has done to her neighborhood . . .

*WE'VE GOT THE COUNTRY AT THE CORNER OF THE STREET

VERSE 1   Since the war
Mucked up our town a bit
We've been more
Lucky than we know.
Tho' before

Life got us down a bit,
Today we can share
A breath of fresh air
And watch things grow.
We're quite delighted with the transformation scene,
It's nice to know that grass is really green.
We've got the country at the corner of the street.

REFRAIN 1   We've got the country at the corner of the street,
Where rows of ugly little houses used to meet.
We let the kids go and play there,
The whole day they stay there
With fresh air and fun complete.
We were in trouble when our houses tumbled in,
Now in the rubble we can see the Spring begin.
We don't begrudge the highest in the land his country seat
We've got the corner of the street.

REFRAIN 2   We've got the country at the corner of the street,
And we can tell you here and now it's quite a treat
To see how green is our valley
That once was just an alley
Dingy with dirt and heat.
Altho' we shiver when we look back on the war,
We see the river, which we never could before.
Now if a girl and boy need a romantic place to meet,
They choose the corner of the street.

REFRAIN 3   We've got the country at the corner of the street,
We sometimes sit there in the dusk and rest our feet
And when we're ready for supper,
We bring out a 'cuppa'
And maybe a bite to eat
We lift our eys and watch the clouds go sailing by.
It's a surprise
To find there's such a lot of sky.
So when we want to rest our tired plates of meat,
We've got the corner of the street.

Once again, Noël's notes indicate some of his alternative thoughts . . .

Who'd have thought
When we were 'buying it'
All alone—
That was quite a year

****

We've got the country at the corner of the street,
Where once the pavements used to swelter in the heat,
It isn't tidy like a garden but it's sweet

*   *   *

The fancy dress party. In the 1st draft this was a set piece to showcase a variety of outrageous and amusing characters—a less frenetic version of that "marvellous party." By the 2nd draft the scene has acquired more of a "message," as the host, Julian Curtis, toasts his guests in a speech that has more than an echo of *Cavalcade* or *This Happy Breed* . . .

JULIAN: This party . . . is, in its small way, a gesture of defiance. We are sick to death of grim warnings, economic crises, austerity and social significance. We wish, for a few short hours to prove, not to anyone else in the world but to ourselves that London can still be gay. Tonight, at the back of our minds, we are worried about many things, but I hope that at least for a little while we have been able to forget them.

During the party Pinkie's costume is much admired. She is encouraged to sing about the character she represents, Napoleon's Empress Josephine . . . "Josephine" (see p. 263).

The story ends where it began in Covent Garden market with Barmy Flo arranging her flowers. Harry and Pinkie enter, Harry with his kit bag over his shoulder. As he leaves they agree to meet the next weekend. Flo, who has seen it all before, looks on as the curtain falls.

*   *   *

The folder has some other numbers, which may have been intended for the show at some point but which didn't survive into the running list Noël left. Titles under "Songs to be completed" . . .

"Morning, Noon and Night"

"The Country's Going to the Dogs"(possibly an alternative title for what became the "Bourgeoisie" number)

"Barmy Flo" (which probably indicates her solo number "Corner of the Street")

"Honeymoon in London"

"Spivs' Quartette" (which may have been the genesis of"Three Juvenile Delinquents")

"Fellow Travellers" (?) to be sung by the Prices, a dreary militant couple we meet in the Palace crowds.)

An alternative pub song to "Time, Gentlemen, Please" told the story of Maudie the Barmaid . . .

*MAUDIE (EVERYTHING'S CLOSING DOWN)

Maudie was a barmaid
Working in a 'local',
Serving every yokel
With a sneer.
When they tried to joke with her they all
    complained
Her smile was really more bitter than the beer.
Such a la-di-da maid
Made the clients nervous
All they got was service
With a frown
And they'd jump like startled rabbits when she
    shrieked—
"Thank God!
Drink up! Drink up!
Everything's closing down!"

Maudie's old papa made
Efforts to control her
But she flung his bowler
On the floor,
Flatly contradicted every word he said
And cursed the customers more and more and
    more.
This uncouth, bizarre maid
Hated every liquor,

Said it made her sicker
Than a pup
And when they had her psycho-analysed she'd
    only yell—
"Drink down! Drink down!
Everything's closing up!"

Another number seems to have been intended for the Buckingham Palace scene . . .

*DAMN GOOD SHOW

Everyone in London likes a damn good show,
A properly planned procession or parade.
It's not because we're snobs
But we like to be sure the Nobs
With all that kow-towing
And bobbing and bowing
Are bloody well doing their jobs.
Flags against the sky,
Horses galloping by,
Yards and yards of Guards
In their golden braid.
We'll stand in the sun,
We'll stand in the rain
Or fog or sleet or snow,
For Londoners like a damn good show.

By late 1949 Prince Littler's lack of enthusiasm for the project made Noël decide to move on to another and more contemporary subject . . . and one he knew rather less about than his "little London sparrows."

Noël as seen by the French in Joyeux Chagrins (Present Laughter), 1948

MISCELLANEOUS THE 1940s

ALWAYS BE NICE TO THE GENTLEMEN

VERSE 1   A mother and her daughter were strolling
                hand in hand,
           The primroses and violets were carpeting
                the land,
           A lark on high
           Caressed the sky
           With Spring's eternal lullaby,
           The young girl gave a little sigh
           And said, "By God, it's grand!"
           Her mother smiled benignly
           And wiped away a tear,
           "You put things so divinely,
           I'm proud of you, my dear!"
           The daughter sniffed the evening breeze,
           And gallantly controlled a sneeze,
           Then gave her mother's hand a squeeze
           And whispered in her ear:

REFRAIN 1   'Hey Momma, hey Momma,
             Now that I am twenty-one,
             The urge to have a bit of fun
             Is bubbling up inside.
             Say Momma, say Momma,
             I am awfully keen to know
             How far a nice young girl should go.'
             Her mother then replied:
             'My daughter, bear in mind
             That God has given you
             One remarkable gift;
             Although it's not refined

To talk too much about it,
Don't forget, my daughter, that the race is
     to the swift!'
'Hey Momma, hey Momma,
What am I to say
If one fine day
I find that I've been led astray?"
Her mother said, 'Oh pooh!
Always be nice to the gentlemen,
Consider them your whole life through;
For if you are nice to the gentlemen,
And kind,
You'll find
That if you keep them half as happy as your
     mother used to do
They'll probably be nice to you!'

VERSE 2   The mother and her daughter pursued their
                way along
           To where the village church bells were tolling
                evensong.
           Upon the green
           A local Dean
           Imparted glamour to the scene,
           The mother smiled, 'This might have been
           The place where I went wrong!'
           Her daughter roared with laughter,
           And looked at her askance,
           'Was that before or after
           You ran that house in France?'
           Her mother gave the girl a clout
           And said, 'All dirty cracks are out,
           You may do better, though I doubt
           You'll ever get the chance.'

REFRAIN 2   'Hey Momma, hey Momma,
             Is there any guarantee
             That pure unsullied girls like me
             Will never be beguiled?
             Say Momma, say Momma,
             Is to be a model wife
             The ultimate reward in life?'
             Her mother said, 'My child,
             Although a moral lapse
             Is reprehensible,
             Boys, you know, will be boys!
             You may amuse the chaps,
             But if you're sensible
             Whatever else you sacrifice hang on to
                  social poise!'
             'Hey Momma, hey Momma,
             Where can I apply
             If by and by,
             I find that I'm left high and dry?'

Her mother shouted, 'Whoops!
Always be nice to the gentlemen,
For that's the stuff to give the troops!
For if you are nice to the gentlemen,
And smart, sweetheart,
If you can hook 'em, and then rook 'em like
     your mother used to do,
They'll probably be nice to you!'

REFRAIN 3   'Hey Momma, hey Momma,
             Though I am so innocent,
             You've helped me to a large extent
             To formulate a creed.
             Say Momma, say Momma,
             What the hell am I to do
             If I should make a slip or two
             By following your lead?'
             Her mother said, 'Don't fuss,
             Just face realities,
             You're no longer at school.
             I really can't discuss
             Such trivialities,
             You'll have to face the music if you're such a
                  bloody fool!'
             'Hey Momma, hey Momma,
             What am I to think
             If some old gink
             Should really put me on the blink?'
             Her mother said, 'Oh nuts!
             Always be nice to the gentlemen,
             And never mind the "ifs" and "buts",
             For if you are nice to the gentlemen,
             And gay,
             Hey! Hey!
             If you can keep the bastards guessing like
                  your mother used to do,
             They'll probably be nice to you!'

Noël's notes include additional material . . .

*Her mother cried, "Three cheers!
Always be nice to the gentlemen,
And put some scent behind your ears
For if you are nice to the gentlemen,
What joy
Oh boy,
You'll find the gentlemen will last for years.

Her mother said, 'Hey, hey,
Always be nice to the gentlemen,
No matter what they say or do
For if you are nice to the gentlemen,
And gay,
Okay,
You'll find the gentlemen will pay, pay, pay!"

THE 1950s

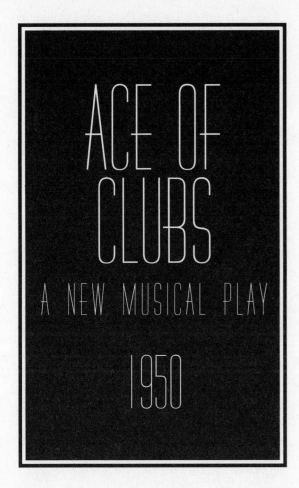

ACE OF CLUBS

A NEW MUSICAL PLAY

1950

First presented by Tom Arnold at the Palace Theatre, Manchester on May 16, 1950 and subsequently at the Cambridge Theatre, London on July 7, 1950. (211 performances.)

Cast included Pat Kirkwood, Graham Payn, Sylvia Cecil, Jean Carson.

"*Ace of Clubs* was a musical comedy written in an idiom entirely different from my other musical plays. The action was laid chiefly in a Soho night club, in which Pat Kirkwood was the star, Pinkie Leroy, and Graham Payn the sailor who fell in love with her. The story was full of gangsters, black marketeers, tough chorus girls, stolen jewellery, etc. There were no vocalized opening choruses or finales, no quartettes . . ."

In point of fact, Noël was never anywhere near his home ground with the show—starting with the title, which was variously *Over the Garden Wall, Hoi Polloi,* and *Come Out to Play.* None of his usual backers like Prince Littler and Binkie Beaumont were enthusiastic and in the end it was Tom Arnold, a producer associated with popular and spectacular shows, who picked it up. Arnold had produced several Ivor Novello shows and Noël warmed to him initially: ". . .he was practical and sensible and didn't

yawn in my face when I was singing." (Prince Littler apparently had.)

In his *Diary* for December 27, 1949 he records:

"Woke bright and early with a wonderful idea for the show. I am going to do the whole thing virtually in one set—the night club . . . This set-up will give perfect opportunities for all the numbers because those not in the story can be done in the floor show . . . In fact it really is a very good idea indeed. The title is *Ace of Clubs.*"

The opening number came from the club show, *London Frolic . . .*

TOP OF THE MORNING

(Jean Carson)

VERSE   On my way
Walking along the street,
Noticing the expressions
Of the people that I meet,
I seem to feel a sort of gay beginning
To a brand new lovely summer day beginning,

Come what may
Winter is on the wing,
I can't prevent myself from singing—

REFRAIN   Top of the morning to you!
Top of the morning to you!
The sun is high,
The summer sky
Is clear and gay
And I've just heard from the B.B.C.
There won't be rain today.
London is shining and free,
That is, as free as a Democracy can be.
Though your cares distract you,
Though your boss has sacked you,
Though your dad has cracked you
On the jaw—
Yesterday's
As hazy as a far-off shore,
Top of the morning
After the night before!

With the logic appropriate to floor show numbers, the Ace of Clubs Girls performed in "pearly brassières and trunks and large feathered hats, while the soubrette was dressed as a Covent Garden porter."

Pinkie, the star of the show, comes on for her solo, which she performs walking among the tables . . .

MY KIND OF MAN

(Pat Kirkwood)

VERSE In me you see a lonely girl
Though certainly not the only girl
Whose love-life is as cold as driven snow,
I can't explain why passion chills me so,
I only know—

REFRAIN 1 I want to find my kind of man,
My heart has designed my kind of man,
He may be—a gay hussar,
A movie star,
A gentleman of renown,
But when we meet I'll never let him down,
I want to find my kind of man
And I shall do the best I can
Not to meet or mate or marry
Tom, Dick or Harry,
Till I find my kind of man.

REFRAIN 2 I want to find my kind of man,
I've never designed my kind of man,
He may be—a copper's nark,
A City clerk,
Or even a gigolo—
But when we meet I'll never let him go.
I want to find my kind of man,
And I shall do the best I can
Not to fall for any stinker
Hook line and sinker
Till I find my kind of man.

REFRAIN 3 I want to find my kind of man,
My dreams have designed my kind of man,
He may be a country type
With tweeds and pipe
Or merely a London spiv—
But when we meet, I'll give and give and
give.
Until I find my kind of man,
I'll keep my heart so spick and span,
All decked out in love's apparel,
Lock stock and barrel,
When I find my kind of man.

When I find my kind of man,
We'll start a five year—jive year plan,
Maybe tinker—maybe tailor,
Soldier—or sailor,
But I'll find my kind of man

There is an incident involving a gangster in the audience who insults Pinkie and a young sailor (Harry Hornby) who comes to her rescue. In the confusion she now rescues him and they run out into Soho. As they sit on a park bench, an attraction is clearly developing . . .

THIS COULD BE TRUE

(Pat Kirkwood and Graham Payn)

VERSE Chance brought us both together
In a strange, unconventional way,
Here in the starlight with the night all round us
Destiny seems to have caught and bound us.

REFRAIN 1 This could be true,
This could be true,
Let's both be terribly careful
What we say or do
We may find—shadows on the stairway
When we try to climb too high,
We may find—hazards on the fairway,
Niggers in the woodpile,
Daring us to try—but—
This could be right,
Love at first sight,
Let's take particular pains
To keep the flame alight,
Let's face the fact
That wonderful—wonderful moments in
life are few,
Let's defy those niggers in the woodpile,
darling,
This could be true.

REFRAIN 2 This could be true,
This could be true.
Maybe the ultimate goal
Our lives were leading to,
Let's take care—people may resent us,
Laugh at us and call us fools,
Let's beware—time is only lent us,
Stick to regulations,
Follow all the rules—for
This could be sweet,
Gay and discreet,
If you will give me your hand

The future's at our feet.
This is the most—
Incredible, magical moment we ever knew,
So to Hell with rules and regulations, darling,
This must be true!

Pinkie agrees to see Harry again but warns him not to come back to the club, which is run by her boyfriend, Benny. She goes back to the club, where Benny is distraught at the loss of a mysterious package that happened to be in the pocket of the coat Pinkie had seized in her hurry—a package that Harry has innocently picked up. The row is stopped by Rita, the owner of the club. Telling Benny to go home and cool off, she reflects in the empty club . . .

NOTHING CAN LAST FOR EVER

(Sylvia Cecil)

VERSE Why should I mind?
Why should I weep for him?
Love as frail as ours could never last.
A little time will pass
And everything we've said and done
Will lie forgotten in the past.
Yesterday
Swiftly fades away,
Now it is over there's nothing to say,
Early or late,
Guided by Fate
Passion will lie to you,
Love say goodbye to you
And when that moment comes
It's wise to face the truth,
The best of it belongs to youth.
Why should I mind?
My heart will keep for him
Some of the love he left behind.

REFRAIN Nothing can last for ever,
Love is a lost endeavour,
Foolishly I
Would plan and scheme,
Foolishly try
To hold my dream,

Dreading the hour of waking,
Dreading the moment of breaking,
Now it is dead
And buried in the past,
Nothing can ever last.

Next day the Ace of Clubs Girls are rehearsing when
Harry enters, looking for Pinkie. They make a fuss of
him and he sings . . .

SOMETHING ABOUT A SAILOR

(Graham Payn)

VERSE 1 The songs they sing of the rollicking deep
Are rather out of key
But one thing you'll agree—is true,
That men who work for the women who weep
Acquire a roving eye
Nobody in their senses would deny.

REFRAIN 1 There's always something about a sailor,
Nobody's ever able to define,
There's a gay—salty sort of tang about
His devil-may-care,
His nautical air
Of brawn and brine,
When wives and sweethearts are told the
fleet's in
Most of them have a perm and tuck the
sheets in,
Girls in Gosport hit an all-time high,
Wives in Weymouth have a spree,
Brides in bridal veils
Will vault the altar rails
To follow—the fellow who follows the sea.

VERSE 2 The course is set for original sin
On every man-of-war
As everyone ashore—well knows.
Yo-ho my lads, and a bottle of gin
Inspires the happy thought
Of somebody else's wife in every port.

REFRAIN 2 There's always something about a sailor,
Every time he sets his foot ashore
All the pubs—do a roaring trade until
Each swaggering Jack

Goes staggering back
To sea once more.
So hang the flags out and throw confetti,
Liberty boats are heading for the jetty,
Tarts are tearful when the anchor's weighed,
Geishas grumble on the quay,
Every courtesan
From Tyne to Turkestan
Will follow—the fellow who follows the sea.

Harry and the girls leave and Pinkie arrives to find
the flowers he has left for her. Benny warns her
about the kind of life she'd have if she settled for
someone like Harry and leaves her with her flowers
to reflect . . .

I'D NEVER, NEVER KNOW

(Pat Kirkwood)

VERSE I met a boy—an ordinary character,
A little shy, a bit reserved,
Until that day—my heart had known no
trespasser,
I put my trust in Fate,
I knew my path was straight,
But now my path has swerved
And I'm alone in time and space,
Now the whole world is quite a different
place.

REFRAIN 1 Why is the summer giving
London this lovely glow?
What is this joy of loving?
Without him—I'd never, never know—
I'd never, never know.
Why do I feel excited
Each time he says 'Hallo'?
Why do the streets seem lighted?
Without him—I'd never, never know—
I'd never, never know.
He wouldn't please the highbrows
Or drive Alan Ladd from the screen,
But when he lifts his eyebrows
I blush like a girl of fifteen.
Soon it will all be over,
He'll say goodbye. and go—
I love him so—
But will he ever know?
Will he ever, ever know?

REFRAIN 2 Why do I like 'Torch numbers'
Crooned on the radio?

"The Ace Of Clubs."

Why do they haunt my slumbers?
Without him—I'd never, never know—
I'd never never know.
Why do I sing quite loudly
Hurrying through Soho?
Why do I walk so proudly?
Without him—I'd never, never know,
I'd never, never, know.
I'd never quite surrender,
I wasn't cut out for a slave,
But when his voice goes tender,
My heart has a permanent wave.
When he's 'in front' I tremble,
Can't hardly play the show,
I love him so—but will he ever know?
Will he ever, ever know?

*   *   *

One of the genuine hits of the show was an interpolated number, "Three Juvenile Delinquents," "which invariably brought the house down at every performance. It was brilliantly performed by John Warwick, Peter Tuddenham and Colin Kemball. "They looked degraded little brutes and were exceedingly funny. A very disgruntled old magistrate wrote a letter to a newspaper protesting that not only was the song vulgar but it was also an incentive to crime! I cannot help wondering whether or not he was one of those who missed the point of 'Don't Let's Be Beastly to the Germans' a few years ago. The tone of his letter was almost identically obtuse. I have suffered many slings and arrows in my life from enraged moralists. I do wish they'd shut up. As far as I am concerned their cause is a lost one from the outset."

THREE JUVENILE DELINQUENTS

VERSE 1
Three juvenile delinquents,
Juvenile delinquents,
Happy as can be—we
Waste no time
On the wherefores and whys of it;
We like crime
And that's about the size of it;
People say that films demoralise us,
Lead us to a life of shame,

Mental doctors try to civilise us,
Psycho-analyse us,
Blimey, what a game!
They don't know how to treat us,
For if they should beat us
That would never do,
When they say, 'Go steady!'
We've the answer ready:
And the same to you!

VERSE 2
Three juvenile delinquents,
Juvenile delinquents,
Happy as can be—we
Hit and run
For the thrill and the sport of it;
Nice clean fun
And that's the long and short of it.
Dear old ladies often get the vapours
When we meet them after dark—whoo!
Then next day we read about our capers
In the daily papers,
Blimey, what a lark!
We thrill the Sunday readers,
But the silly bleeders
Haven't got a clue
When the judge says 'Chokey'
We say 'Okey-dokey'
And the same to you!

VERSE 3
Three juvenile delinquents,
Juvenile delinquents,
Happy as can be—we
Lick our chops
When we read what they write of us
All the cops
Hate the bloody sight of us.
Once we pinched a Cadillac and drove her
From the Marble Arch to Kew;
Hit a fat old geezer in a Rover,

Fairly bowled her over,
Blimey, what a do!
We said,'You mustn't fuss, dear,
There's a lovely bus, dear,
Number twenty-two.
If we've bruised your bonnet,
Stick a plaster on it.'
And the same to you!

VERSE 4
Three juvenile delinquents,
Juvenile delinquents.
Every now and then—when
Kind old cranks
Mention angels of light to us
We say, 'Thanks,
Don't forget to write to us.'
Nowadays the younger generation
Never has to face brute force.
Some old judge, instead of flagellation,
Puts us on probation!
Blimey, what a sauce!
Last night we got an earful
From a rather tearful
Clergyman we knew.
When he turned the sobs on
We replied, "With knobs on'
And the same to you!

VERSE 5
Three juvenile delinquents,
Juvenile delinquents,
Happy as can be—we
Break our backs
To achieve popularity.
Three sharp whacks,
Faith and Hope and Charity.
Once we knocked a pair of silly sluts out
Just behind the 'Horse and Plough',
Dragged them round to where the railing
juts out,

"Three Juvenile Delinquents"
Peter Tuddenham, Norman
Warwick, Colin Kemball.

Bellowing their guts out,
Blimey, what a row!
We had to cosh 'em proper,
Then we saw a copper
Starting to pursue
Then we cried vibrato,
'How's your old tomato?'
And the same to you!

Predictably, the Delinquents attracted the scrutiny of the Lord Chamberlain's Office. The line "Stuff it up your jumper" was removed forthwith and the "number twenty-two bus" did not pass unscathed. Instead of the bruised bonnet that eventually appeared, the original couplet read—

If you can't drive better,
Flood your carburettor.

Three Juvenile Delinquents were allowed out on parole on two subsequent occasions. At a charity show in 1953 they were played by Laurence Olivier, John Gielgud and John Mills. When the number was repeated in 1955 Danny Kaye replaced John Gielgud.

*　　*　　*

Harry and Pinkie meet again. Pinkie remembers Harry still has the parcel. He promises to bring it to the next day's rehearsal and, even though she's worried about his safety, Pinkie agrees. After she leaves to return to the club, Harry sings . . .

SAIL AWAY

(Graham Payn)

VERSE 1　When a sailor goes to sea,
　　　　Though he leaves his love behind,
　　　　Time and tide will set him free
　　　　From the grief inside him.
　　　　Sea and sky will ease his heart,
　　　　Regulate his troubled mind,
　　　　Every sailor has a chart
　　　　And a star to guide him—home.

REFRAIN 1　When the storm clouds are riding through
　　　　　a winter sky,
　　　　Sail away—sail away.

When the love-light is fading in your
　　sweetheart's eye,
Sail away—sail away.
When you feel your song is orchestrated wrong,
Why should you prolong
Your stay?
When the wind and the weather blow your
　　dreams sky-high,
Sail away—sail away!

VERSE 2　Love is meant to make us glad,
　　　　Love can make the world go round,
　　　　Love can drive you raving mad,
　　　　Torment and upset you.
　　　　Love can give your heart a jolt
　　　　But philosophers have found
　　　　That it's wise to do a bolt
　　　　When it starts to get you—down.

REFRAIN 2　When your life seems too difficult to
　　　　　rise above,
　　　　Sail away—sail away.
　　　　When your heart feels as dreary as a
　　　　　worn-out glove,
　　　　Sail away—sail away.
　　　　But when soon or late
　　　　You recognize your fate,
　　　　That will be your great, great day,
　　　　On the wings of the morning with your
　　　　　own true love,
　　　　Sail away—sail away—sail away.

"'Sail Away' is good, I think," Noël wrote. "It has a nice swing to it and the tune is catchy." When *Ace of Clubs* failed to run to his satisfaction, he used the song a decade later as the theme song for a show of that name.

*　　*　　*

Back at the club, Pinkie is performing another of her solo numbers in the show. Descending a flight of stairs in a white Empire style dress, a long blue velvet cloak and a glittering crown, she sings . . .

JOSEPHINE

(Pat Kirkwood)

VERSE 1　The lady was beautiful
　　　　The lady was dark,

She wasn't too dutiful
But still left her mark
On volumes of history
And thousands of cheques
And all through the mystery
Of 'Ole Debbil Sex!'

REFRAIN 1　Josephine—Josephine
　　　　From the first was rather chic,
　　　　As a tot
　　　　She would trot
　　　　Through the island of Martinique,
　　　　Her fortune was told by an aged crone
　　　　Who prophesied fame and romance,
　　　　And who hissed in her ear
　　　　The outrageous idea
　　　　That she'd also be Empress of France!
　　　　Josephine—Josephine
　　　　Had, with men, a set routine
　　　　And the people who thought
　　　　Her technique was self-taught
　　　　Didn't know—Josephine.

VERSE 2　Whatever she nearly did
　　　　From five to fifteen
　　　　We know that she really did
　　　　Begin the Beguine.
　　　　On first meeting Bonaparte
　　　　She murmured, 'Hell's bells!
　　　　You let down the tone, apart
　　　　From anything else!'

REFRAIN 2　Josephine—Josephine
　　　　Very seldom lost control
　　　　Though her wit
　　　　Was a bit
　　　　Over-seasoned with 'Sauce Créole'.
　　　　She very soon married this short young man
　　　　Who talked about soldiers all day
　　　　But who wasn't above
　　　　Making passionate love
　　　　In a coarse, rather Corsican way.
　　　　Josephine—wasn't keen
　　　　And she made an ugly scene,
　　　　Until Bonaparte said,
　　　　'We must rumple the bed!
　　　　Just for show—Josephine!'

REFRAIN 3　Josephine—Josephine
　　　　Though a Queen remained at home
　　　　While her lord
　　　　Was abroad
　　　　Sending postcards, in code, from Rome.
　　　　He often appeared

With a three-day beard
From Austria, Poland or Spain,
And one dreadful night
He arrived, rather tight,
Having balled up the Russian campaign.
Josephine—turning green—
Cried, 'Whatever does this mean?'
Then Napoleon said, 'Whoops!
I have lost all my troops
In the snow, Josie—
Oh, Josie,
Snow—Josephine!'

Pat Kirkwood as Pinkie Leroy singing "Josephine."

The archives once again have notes for alternative
couplets . . .

    *If a hot blooded Corsican
    Has wedded a shrew,
    If he wants a divorce he can
    Of course put it through

    ****
    Historical mysteries no longer perplex
    For all the world's histories are based upon sex.

*   *   *

The Ace of Clubs Girls do their novelty number,
waving coloured balloons . . .

WOULD YOU LIKE TO STICK A PIN IN MY BALLOON?

Would you like to stick a pin in my balloon,
    Daddy?
Would you like to stick a pin in my balloon?
Just make a grab
When you hear the melody stop,
One little jab
And you'll hear a beautiful pop,
If you'll only suit the action to the tune, Daddy,
You'll be bound to get the hang of it soon,
All the boys I know can do the trick,
So, Daddy, Daddy, won't you stick
A pin in my balloon?

While the show continues, Harry has arrived and is
sitting at his usual table. As she starts her number,
Pinkie sees him but as she passes the table again, it
is empty. The gangsters, who badly want the mysterious parcel he's carrying, have hustled him outside
the club.

    Realising what must have happened, she finish-
es her number hurriedly and goes to find him. On
stage the juvenile leads go into their duet . . .

IN A BOAT, ON A LAKE, WITH MY DARLING

(Jean Carson and Myles Eason)

VERSE   In my dreams, I often get a
        Vision that's divine
        Of a very still lagoon
        With you in white
        And me in blue
        Alone in quite
        A safe canoe.
        Failing this what could be better
        Than the Serpentine
        On an afternoon
        In Love, in June?

REFRAIN In a boat, on a lake, with my darling
        In the heat of a sweet summer day,
        There's the sound of the breeze
        In the green willow trees
        And the noise of the town fades away
        Letting time flutter by like a starling
        As we gaze into
        The infinite blue
        Above
        Hand in hand,
        Heart to heart,
        Just a moment apart
        In a boat, on a lake, with my love.

Out in the street, Harry escapes after a scuffle and
sneaks back into the club. While he was away Rita
has received a visit from the police and now knows
that the parcel contains a stolen necklace. Pinkie is
distraught about Harry and, left alone, bursts into
tears. Harry finds her and reassures her: "It's all
right. The Navy's here."

    The Girls are rehearsing yet another number in
which they represent luxury brands of perfume . . .

BABY'S BOTTLE

REFRAIN 1   When it's time for Baby's bottle
Give her a bottle of scent.
Sweet perfume
Leads to love in bloom,
So that's—money well spent.
You can fill her Christmas stocking
Full of emeralds and pearls
But some Schiaparelli 'Shocking'
Is the way to get the girls.
When it's time for Baby's bottle
Give her a bottle of scent!

VERSE 1   My lady's boudoir, satin, silk
And foamy laces cast aside,
A pair of shoulders white as milk,
A woman's glory and her pride,
A tendril here, a dimple there,
The flutter of a painted fan
Can catch a fellow unaware,
Can make a fool of any man,
Yet, lovely ladies, if by chance
To challenge you I should presume
I vow the essence of romance
Lies in the magic of perfume.

REFRAIN 2   When it's time for Baby's bottle
Give her a bottle of scent,
Fragrant perfume
Leads to Love in bloom
And that's money well spent.
You can fill her Christmas stocking
With emeralds and pearls
But Schiaparelli 'Shocking'
Will always get the girls.
When it's time for Baby's bottle
Give her a bottle of scent.

REFRAIN 3   When it's time for Baby's bottle
Give her a bottle of scent,
Soir de Paris
Makes her say 'Oui oui'
Without Father's consent,
She may come a social cropper
And really go too far
If you'll just pull out the stopper
Of Chypre or Shalimar,
When it's time for Baby's bottle
Give her a bottle of scent.

INTERLUDE   At night to greet the Eastern Star
My Lady's drenched in Shalimar,

Another Spring has come to pass
Full of the fragrance of Blue Grass,

When Evening breeze the branches stir
My heart responds to Quelques Fleurs,

A Water nymph beside the Loire
Her melody is Narcisse Noir,

A shaded light, a Kiss unseen,
A night of love and Crêpe de Chine,

Two throbbing hearts neath passion's sway,
Ladies beware it's Indiscret,

The Seine, Montmartre and you, *chérie*,
Toujours, l'amour, Soir de Paris,

Two roguish eyes serenely mocking,
A whispered promise—that is Shocking.

VERSE 2   Any wolf who's any good
Pounces on Red Riding Hood
But today—he will not get away with it.
Modern maids are mellowed in the wood.
If you find that cheek to cheek
Dinner dances twice a week
Don't get quick results
You'll get slick results
With my new technique. . . .

Harry arrives with the parcel and, while waiting for Pinkie, chats to the girls, who ask him about his travels. He tells them about America . . .

I LIKE AMERICA

(Graham Payn)

GIRLS: Tell us, sailor,
Tell us, please,
For we're terribly keen to know
What it's like to be fancy free
Footloose on the rolling sea?
China girl chop-chop,
Gay Maltese,
Hot Mommas from Mexico—

HARRY: If you'll forgive a crude remark
And don't resent a rude remark
I'll let you into a secret—

GIRLS: Well?

HARRY: They're all alike in the dark!

GIRLS: There must have been
Some place you've seen
Superior to the rest?

HARRY: As a matter of fact
With political tact
I like America best.

GIRLS: There's a good time a-comin on de ole plantation
For a jolly Jack Tar
Has just confessed
That he likes America best!

VERSE 1
HARRY: I don't care for China,
Japan's far too small,
I've rumbled the Rio Grande,
I hate Asia Minor,
I can't bear Bengal
And I shudder to think
Of the awful stink
On the road to Samarkand.

GIRLS: The heat and smell
Must be sheer hell
On the road to Samarkand.

HARRY: I like America,
I have played around
Every slappy-happy hunting ground
But I find America—okay.
I've been about a bit
But I must admit
That I didn't know the half of it
Till I hit the U.S.A.
No likely lass
In Boston, Mass.
From passion will recoil.
In Dallas, Tex.
They talk of sex
But only think of oil.
New Jersey dames
Go up in flames
If someone mentions—bed.
In Chicago, Illinois
Any girl who meets a boy
Giggles and shoots him dead!
But I like America
Its Society
Offers infinite variety
And come what may
I shall return some day
To the good old U.S.A.

266

VERSE 2

HARRY: I've loathed every acre
From Cannes to Canton,
I also deplore Bombay,
I've jeered at Jamaica
And seen through Ceylon,
And exploded the myth
Of those Flying Fith
On the Road to Mandalay.

GIRLS: We'll never mith
Those blasted fith
On the road to Mandalay.

HARRY: But I like America,
I have travelled far
From Northumberland to Zanzibar
And I find America—okay.
I've roamed the Spanish Main
Eaten sugar-cane
But I never tasted cellophane
Till I struck the U.S.A.
All delegates
From Southern States
Are nervy and distraught.
In New Orleans
The wrought-iron screens
Are dreadfully overwrought.
Beneath each tree
In Tennessee
Erotic books are read.
And when alligators thud
Through the Mississipi mud
Sex rears its ugly head.
But—I like America,
Every scrap of it,
All the sentimental crap of it
And come what may
Give me a holiday
In the good old U.S.A.

In Graham Payn's recording the "New Jersey dames" were clearly felt to be a little too risqué in their pre-delictions and were replaced by—

In Tennessee
The BBC
Would blush to hear what's said

*   *   *

This was another song to survive the show. Noël felt that it had "an effective lyric, but unfortunately, owing to its musical structure, the last phrase is not sufficiently telling." Graham Payn, who introduced the number, was never entirely comfortable with it, either:

"'I Like America' was lyrically marvellous, but I worried about having to carry a comedy song . . . Noël agreed to end the number with the girls and me dancing our way off, which worked, but didn't ever stop the show. We were never sure what was wrong with the construction of that number; it just seemed to go on too long. A couple of years later Noël appeared at the Café de Paris. 'Do you want to hear how the song *should* be sung?' he challenged me. 'I'm putting it in the act.' I'd always been convinced it was my fault that it hadn't worked but after three performances in cabaret Noël knew it was wrong and he cut the number. He never rewrote it but he did sing it brilliantly on the *New York* albumn. Perhaps it was Peter Matz's clever arrangement that transformed it."

*   *   *

The crucial parcel has accidentally been switched for one belonging to one of the chorus girls, so Harry ends up returning the wrong one to Pinkie. She wants to give it to Benny. Harry believes they should give it to the police. They argue and he leaves. When Benny arrives, she throws it at him and tells him she is through with him and the club. Benny leaves with the parcel and Pinkie sings . . .

WHY DOES LOVE GET IN THE WAY?

(*Pat Kirkwood*)

VERSE 1 Suddenly my world has altered,
Suddenly my step has faltered,
Common sense has flown,
Here I am alone
Coping with these new sensations,
Dark despairs and wild elations,
Eros with his bow—has laid me low.

REFRAIN 1 Why does love get in the way so?
What have I done
That the son-of-a-gun
Should pick on me?
A little while ago my heart was serene
and bright,
Everything seemed all right,
Now I've been struck by a charge of dynamite,
Why does love lead one astray so?

Tell me why
I want to laugh,
I want to cry?
I was gay as a sparrow
Till Cupid's arrow
Punctured this perfect day,
Why does love—get in the way?

VERSE 2 Everything is blown to blazes,
Ordinary familiar phrases
Seem to mean much more
Than they did before.
Colours look a great deal brighter,
Black is blacker, white is whiter,
Every sight and sound.
Has changed around.

REFRAIN 2 Why does love get in the way so?
Why should it fret
And completely upset
My peace of mind?
A little while ago my heart was serene and gay,
Everything seemed okay,
And now I suddenly find—I've lost my way.
Why does love lead one astray so?
Why the hell
Should I be caught within its spell?
Life was quite un-enchanted,
All that I wanted,
Now it's a Passion Play!
Why does love get in the way?
Why does love get in the way?

Taking a quiet stroll through Soho Square, Rita sings about the joys of "Evening in Summer" . . .

EVENING IN SUMMER

(*Sylvia Cecil*)

VERSE After the heat of the day is done
Everyone
Who has a garden likes to sit in it and dream
Or read the paper—while the noises of the
distant traffic seem
Remote and gentle
Sentimental variations on a theme
That comes and goes,
Only London knows
This sweet repose.

REFRAIN Evening in summer,
London in June,
Sparrows from roof-tops calling,
Two streets away
You hear a barrel-organ tune,
Night will very very soon
Be falling,
Ships on the river
Londoners hear
Suddenly near,
Sweet to the ear,
Twilight is fading,
Stars shining down,
Evening in summer,
Evening in summer,
Summer in London town.

The chorus girls had given June, one of their number, as a joke birthday present a pair of "falsies." She, however, having received the "wrong" parcel, now has the jewels. She promises the girls she will wear their present in the show that evening—which puzzles them more than a little. To the police in the audience, however, it provides a fairly unmissable clue, when June proceeds to do just that. As they go backstage, Pinkie enters to sing her solo, dressed as a small girl and carrying a toy black cat . . .

CHASE ME, CHARLIE

(Pat Kirkwood)

VERSE I When it's late
And the world is sleeping
Our little black cat
No bigger than that
Has a date
Which she's keen on keeping,
No use dissuading her
She's serenading her—beau
In the garden below,
She sings, 'Oh, won't you—

REFRAIN I Chase me, Charlie,
Chase me, Charlie,
Over the garden wall?
I'd like to wander for miles and miles
Wreathed in smiles
Out on the tiles with you.

Chase me, Charlie,
Chase me, Charlie,
Don't be afraid to fall,
Love in the moonlight can be sublime,
Now's the time,
Charlie, I'm
Bound to give in if you'll only climb
Over the garden wall."

VESE 2 Every night
At about eleven
Our little black cat knows,
Our little black cat goes
Quick as light
To her private heaven,
No use restraining her,
She's set on gaining her—prize
With her amorous cries
Hypnotizing him.

REFRAIN 2 "Chase me, Charlie,
Chase me, Charlie,
Over the garden wall.
Who gives a damn if the neighbours yell?
Let's rebel
Just for the hell of it,
Chase me, Charlie,
Chase me, Charlie,
Maybe I'll give my all!
Won't you come out and be gay with me,
Play with me,
Stay with me?
Just try a roll in the hay with me
Over the garden wall.

REFRAIN 3 Chase me, Charlie,
Chase me, Charlie,
Over the garden wall.
Why not give in to the joys of Spring,
Have a fling,
Why are you lingering?
Chase me, Charlie,
Chase me, Charlie,
This is my final call.
Pussy-cat, pussy-cat don't be shy,
This is my
Alibi,
Nature intends us to multiply
Over the garden wall."

* * *

The number, Noël said, was based on the old music hall song, "Ompapa." "I always envisaged in my mind someone like Lottie Collins or Florrie Forde swing

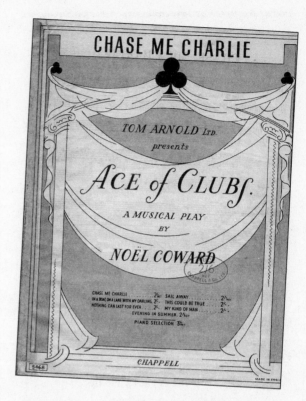

ing up and down the stage in sequins and belting it over. Pat Kirkwood could not be said to resemble either of these ladies, but she put it across in her own way very effectively."

Once again, Noël found himself running into the brick wall of the BBC's definition of good taste. When they insisted that the song could not be broadcast until the lyric "bound to give in" was replaced by "waiting for you," Noël could only comment: "Apparently, the BBC thinks the idea of a cat giving in is more likely to create immoral thoughts in the listeners' minds than the idea of a cat waiting to achieve its object."

* * *

Backstage the many loose ends of the plot are rapidly tied together, the jewels recovered, the gangsters arrested. On stage the show—as it must— has been going on. Pinkie, singing "My Kind of Man" sees Harry at his usual table. He hands her yet another bunch of roses. They embrace, as the audience applauds and they sing the final bars of "Sail Away":

On the wings of the morning
With your own true love,
Sail away—sail away—sail away.

* * *

The archive contains an additional song for Pinkie to sing (in Act 1 Scene 3) that was never used. A note suggests it later became "I Want To Find My Kind of Man."

*I WANT A MAN ABOUT THE HOUSE

VERSE   In me you see a lonely girl
         Though certainly not the only girl
         Whose instincts are domestically inclined.
         Won't some kind gentleman relieve my mind
         Because I find . . .

REFRAIN 1 I want a man about the house
           I crave for
           A man about the house
           To slave for
           I want to darn his socks for him
           And make him a cup of tea
           And rock myself to sleep upon his knee
           I want a man about the house
           I'll be as meek as Mickey Mouse
           Won't you help me with my plan about
           A great strong man about—the house?

REFRAIN 2 I want a man about the house
           To cook for
           A man about the house
           To look for.
           When I come home at night I find
           There's never enough to do,
           So here's an opportunity for you.
           I want a man about the house
           To share my iced champagne and grouse
           I'd be glad as Pollyanna
           With a nice strong man about —the house.

Extra Refrain:

         I want a male about the place
         To hold me tight in his embrace.
         I might settle for a sailor
         As a handy male about—the place.
         If I'd a chap about the flat,
         We'd have a cigarette and chat,
         Then my loving arms I'd wrap about
         That chap about the flat

*   *   *

By August it was clear that the run was coming to a close. Noël confided to his *Diary*: "I really am very, very angry. If the public don't want to see that easy entertainment and listen to those lyrics and that music and if they do want to pack out *King's Rhapsody* (Ivor Novello's latest and last production), then they can get on with it." It was one of the few touches of sour grapes he was ever to allow himself—and that only in private.

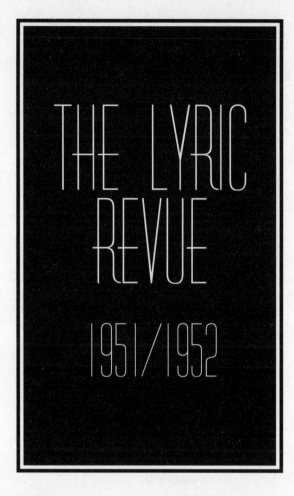

THE LYRIC REVUE 1951/1952

First presented by Tennent Productions on May 7, 1951 at the Pavilion, Bournemouth and subsequently at the Lyric Theatre, Hammersmith on May 24, 1951. (141 performances.) Later transferred to the Globe Theatre London.

Cast included Graham Payn, Dora Bryan, Ian Carmichael and Roberta Huby.

Noël was never to attempt another fully-fledged revue of his own after *Sigh No More* but he did contribute to two more in the early 1950s.

1951 was Festival of Britain Year—the government's rather heavy-handed attempt to persuade its citizens that if all was not for the best in this best of all possible post-war worlds, there was nonetheless a lot to celebrate. Noël had his own views on the subject, which he expressed in another satirical song. Having been misunderstood more than once in the past, he added the *post facto* proviso that "It is neither pro-German, pro-Russian nor particularly anti-British. I do not believe that it has been an incentive to crime and it is too much to hope that it could in any way be a deterrent to bureaucratic idiocy. It is a jolly number but, alas! too topical to live on in the hearts of men."

DON'T MAKE FUN OF THE FAIR

(*Graham Payn, Dora Bryan, Joan Heal, Ian Carmichael*)

VERSE 1 We're proud to say
         In every way
         We're ordinary folk,
         But please to observe
         We still preserve
         Our sturdy hearts of oak.
         Although as servants of the state
         We may have been coerced,
         As we've been told to celebrate
         We'll celebrate or burst.
         Though while we brag
         Our shoulders sag
         Beneath a heavy yoke
         We all get terribly heated
         If it's treated
         As a joke. So:

REFRAIN 1 Don't make fun of the festival,
           Don't make fun of the fair,
           We down-trodden British must learn to
               be skittish
           And give an impression of devil-may-care
           To the wide wide world,
           We'll sing 'God for Harry',
           And if it turns out all right
           Knight Gerald Barry,
           Clear the national decks, my lads,
           Every one of us counts,
           Grab the traveller's cheques, my lads,
           And pray that none of them bounce.
           Boys and Girls come out to play,
           Every day in every way
           Help the tourist to defray
           All that's underwritten.
           Sell your rations and overcharge,
           And don't let anyone sabotage
           Our own dear Festival of Britain.

VERSE 2 We've never been
         Exactly keen
         On showing off or swank
         But as they say
         That gay display
         Means money in the bank,

We'll make the dreadful welkin ring
From Penge to John O'Groats
And cheer and laugh and shout and sing
Before we cut our throats,
We know we're caught
And must support
This patriotric prank
And though we'd rather have shot ourselves
We've got ourselves
To thank. So:

REFRAIN 2 Don't make fun of the festival,
Don't make fun of the fair,
We must pull together in spite of the weather
That dampens our spirits and straightens
    our hair.
Let the people sing
Even though they shiver
Roses red and noses mauve
Over the river.
Though the area's fairly small,
Climb Discovery's Dome,
Take a snooze in the concert hall,
At least it's warmer than home.
March about in funny hats,
Show the foreign diplomats
That our proletariat's
Milder than a kitten.
We believe in the right to strike,
But now we've bloody well got to like
Our own dear Festival of Britain.

REFRAIN 3 Don't make fun of the festival,
Don't make fun of the fair,
We must have a look at a cookery book
To prevent us from spreading alarm and
    despair.
We can serve whale steaks
When the weather's hotter
And in place of entrecôtes,
What's wrong with otter?
Greet the gala with fervence, boys,
Learn to dance in the dark,
Build the Sunday observance boys
A shrine in Battersea Park.
Cross your fingers, hold your thumbs,
Blow your trumpets, roll your drums,
Even if nobody comes
Don't be conscience-smitten.
If no overseas trade appears
We'll have to work for a thousand years
To pay for the Festival of Britain.

REFRAIN 4 Don't make fun of the festival,
Don't make fun of the fair.

We mustn't look glum when the visitors come
And discover our cupboard is ever so bare.
We must cheer, boys, cheer,
Look as though we love it
And if it should be a bust
Just rise above it.
Take a nip from your brandy flask,
Scream and caper and shout,
Don't give anyone time to ask
What the Hell it's about.
Face the future undismayed,
Pray for further Marshall Aid,
Have the toast from *Cavalcade*
Drastically re-written.
Peace and dignity we may lack,
But wave a jolly Trades Union Jack,
Hurrah for the festival,
We'll pray for the festival,
Hurrah for the Festival of Britain!

REFRAIN 5 Don't make fun of the festival,
Don't make fun of the fair,
Our Government Bosses
Are counting their losses
And one of them's taken to brushing his hair.
We must all salute—those who double-
    crossed us,
Fire a round
For every pound
Ground-nuts have cost us,
Blow a kiss to the Board of Trade,
Learn to laugh like a drain
If a million has been mislaid,
Who are we to complain?
Join our civil servants' ball,
Cheer our near Decline and Fall,
Gibbon might have dreamed it all,
Also Bulwer-Lytton,
If our workers begin to slack
Let's get some enemy aliens back,
Hurrah for the Festival of Britain!

REFRAIN 6 Don't make fun of the festival,
Don't make fun of the fair,
We must have a look
At a cookery book
To prevent us from spreading alarm and
    despair.
You will find tinned Spam—much improved
    by mustard,
But when served Vanilla Shape
Scrape—off the custard.
Eat together or eat alone,
Order tea and a bun,
Break your teeth on a scone of stone

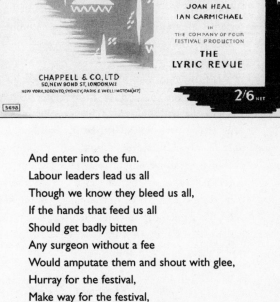

And enter into the fun.
Labour leaders lead us all
Though we know they bleed us all,
If the hands that feed us all
Should get badly bitten
Any surgeon without a fee
Would amputate them and shout with glee,
Hurray for the festival,
Make way for the festival,
Sing Hey for the Festival of Britain!

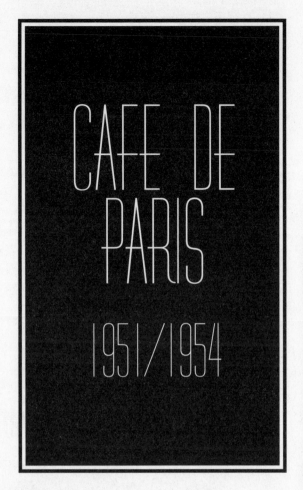

CAFÉ DE
PARIS

1951/1954

Noël made his debut at the Café on October 29, 1951 and played seasons there for the next three years.

Every June Noël was to be found energetically raising funds for charity at his favourite Theatrical Garden Party. June 1951 saw him try an experiment. Inside a tent with a placard NOËL COWARD AT HOME he and Norman Hackforth gave a series of half hour concerts. Up to this point Noël had never seriously attempted solo performances—numbers in shows, of course, but always with someone on stage to back him up.

He probably remembered all too well his less than auspicious debut at the Elysée some thirty-five years earlier with his young partner, Eileen Dennis. The sixteen year old Noël tried his hand at a solo, only to forget his words after the first chorus. His exit to a series of diminishing la-la-las was fortunately not repeated that day in the charity tent. In fact, the occasion gave him enough confidence to accept a booking that same October to appear in cabaret at the Café de Paris—as the old Elysée was now called. An omen, if ever there was one . . .

**Noël Coward at the Café de Paris, with
his accompanist Norman Hackforth.**

This time things turned out very differently. Noël—in one of his favourite phrases—"tore the place up." Kenneth Tynan likened his singing to the "cooing of a baritone dove," while "he displays his own two weapons, wit and sentimentality."

Noël himself was well-pleased at his performance:

"In the fifties I emerged, to my own and every-one else's astonishment, as a highly successful cabaret entertainer. True, when I first appeared at the Café de Paris, a captious journalist announced recklessly that I 'massacred' my own songs. If I did, I can only say that it was the most triumphantly successful massacre since Saint Bartholomew's Eve . . . My (four) seasons at the Café de Paris neccessitated renewal of my material as often as possible . . ."

It was here that songs such as "Uncle Harry," "Alice Is At It Again" and many of the other comedy numbers came into their own, divorced from "production values," each word benefiting from Noël's clear, clipped delivery and the controlled style of performance he had tried to impose on those he had directed over the years. One of them, Judy Campbell, remembers the advice:

"You walk out and look around at the assembled company, as though you were giving a party and you were delighted so many of your friends and acquaintances had managed to make it . . . Just look at them and say what you're going to sing. And when you have hush, nod to your accompanist and then start. If you're going to make a gesture, make it above the waist—never, never, *below*. And remember—*panache, panache, toujours panache*. If you believe you can do it, you'll make them listen. And that's the whole trick."

Among the songs he wrote specially for the act were a group of burlesque numbers under the heading "These I Have Loathed." In addition to "Devon" (p. 52), there was the "French Song" . . .

FRENCH SONG (PARIS EST TOI)

Paris ensorcelée, magique,
Dis que son nom et j'suis ému.
Quand j'me trouve loin d'son charme unique
Mon pauvre coeur est éperdu.
Je ne chercherai qu'une autre maîtresse,
Elle ne me fera jamais cocu,
Elle tiendra toujours ma tendresse,
Tous mes voeux, toutes mes caresses
Dans mes bras vers elle tendus.
Ah les belles nuits que nous passions ensemble!
Ah les beaux jours quand j'étais si malheureux!
Ces souv'nirs brisent mon âme et je tremble
Chaque fois j'regarde tes yeux.

Tu es Paris et Paris est toi
Pour moi—pour moi—pour moi.
Ville bien aimée,
Chacun sa vérité,
Pour moi la vérité est claire,

Si extraordinaire
Que j'me dis, 'Que faire?'
Si tu m'ignore
Moi j't'aimerai encore,
Pourquoi—pourquoi—pourquoi?
Maîtresse troublante,
Plume de ma tante,
Toujours je crie—Paris.

Notre Dame, La Madeleine,
P'tits bistros au bord d'la Seine,
Opéra, Boul' Mich' et Bals Musettes.
Champs-Élysées, Montparnasse,
Ceux qui restent et ceux qui passent,
Même Cécile Sorel et Mistinguette.
Tous les arbres dans les Bois,
Les marchands d'charcuteries,
Tous les pédicures Chinois
Si plein de nostalgie.
Toutes les filles d'la rue, narquoises,
Toutes les fraises et les framboises
Remplissent de joie mon âme fleuri,
De Montmartre a Père Lachaise
Paris est un doux malaise
Dont mon coeur ne sera jamais guéri,
Paris est un diable—Paris est un ange,
Tu es toujours tous les deux—quel affreux mélange.

Mystérieuse et vilaine blageuse,
Je bois—je bois—à toi
Bock, Fernet-Branca,
Hook, line et Sanka,
Toujours je crie—Paris!
. . . an "Irish Song" (Rosie O'Grady) . . .

IRISH SONG (ROSIE O'GRADY)

When first I was courtin' sweet Rosie O'Grady,
Sweet Rosie O'Grady she whispered to me
'Sure you shouldn't be after seducin' a lady
Before she's had time to sit down to her tea.'

With a Heigho—Top-o-the-morning-Begorrah and Fiddlededee

Her cheeks were so soft and her eyes were so trustin',
She tossed her bright curls at the dusk of the day,

She said to me 'Darlin', your breath is disgustin',
Which wasn't at all what I hoped she would say.
With a Heigho, maybe Begorrah, and possibly Fiddlededee

Our honeymoon started so blithely and gaily
But dreams I was dreaming were suddenly wrecked
For she broke my front tooth with her father's shillelagh
Which wasn't what I had been led to expect.

With a Heigho, maybe Begorrah, and certainly Fiddlededee.

In an earlier draft the heroine was called Sally O'Grady and she came to an even unhappier ending . . .

*When I married Sally from over the water
The dreams we'd been dreamin' were suddenly wrecked
For Sally gave birth to a two-headed daughter
Which wasn't what I had been led to expect

With a Heigho, Whist-Marajuana—and certainly Fiddlededee.

. . . an "Old Scottish Air" . . .

*OLD SCOTTISH AIR

Dinna show him your nutmeg, Alwyn,
Tho' bonnie and braw he be,
For he'll go his ways
Over lochs and braes
Wi' nary a thought of thee—
'Twere best to bide a wee.

Dinna give him your nutmeg, Alwyn,
Tho' his words be soft and sweet,
For many's the maid
Who has been laid
To rest in a winding sheet.
And we can't have the neighbours
Tossing their cabers
All over Arthur's Seat

. . . and a "Spinning Song" . . .

SPINNING SONG

Here at my spinning wheel I stay
While the robin sings 'Ho!' on the orchard bough,
Where is my love who rode away,
Where be he, be he now?
Where be he, be he, be he, be he, be he, be he, be
    he now?
Winter comes and then the Spring,
I weave and weave and weave and weave,
I've worked for a year
On a coat for my dear
And I've not yet finished the sleeve.
Here at my spinning wheel I stay,
My bobbin goes click-clack, click-clack,
I've got my warp right up my woof
And I can't get the bloody thing back.

It was at this time that we also first made the acquaintance of Mrs. Wentworth-Brewster . . . The idea came to him while staying on Capri and watching "hordes of middle-aged matrons pouring off every boat, all set to have themselves a ball." He is believed to have written it for Bea Lillie, who did later record it.

A BAR ON THE PICCOLA MARINA

(UK Lyric)

VERSE

In a 'bijou' abode
In St Barnabas Road
Not far from the Esher by-pass
Lived a mother and wife
Who, most of her life,
Let every adventure fly past.
She had two strapping daughters and a rather
    dull son
And a much duller husband who at sixty-one
Elected to retire
And, later on, expire,
Sing Hallelujah, Hey nonny-no, Hey nonny-no,
    Hey nonny-no !
He joined the feathered choir.
On a wet afternoon
In the middle of June

They all of them came home soaking
Having laid him to rest
By special request
In the family vault at Woking,
And then in the middle of the funeral wake
With her mouth full of excellent Madeira cake
His widow cried, 'That's done,
My life's at last begun,
Sing Hallelujah, Hey nonny-no, Hey nonny-no,
    Hey nonny-no,
It's time I had some fun,
Today, though hardly a jolly day,
At least has set me free,
We'll all have a lovely holiday
On the island of Capri!'

REFRAIN I

In a bar on the Piccola Marina
Life called to Mrs Wentworth-Brewster,
Fate beckoned her and introduced her
Into a rather queer
Unfamiliar atmosphere.
She'd just sit there, propping up the bar
Beside a fisherman who sang to a guitar.
When accused of having gone too far
She merely cried, 'Funiculi!'
Just fancy me!
Funicula!'
When he bellowed '*Che Bella Signorina!*'
Sheer ecstasy at once produced a
Wild shriek from Mrs Wentworth-Brewster,
Changing her whole demeanour.
When both her daughters and her son said,
'Please come home, Mama,'
She murmured rather bibulously, 'Who d'you
    think you are?
Nobody can afford to be so lahdy-bloody-da
In a bar on the Piccola Marina.'

INTERLUDE

Every fisherman cried.
'*Viva Viva*' and '*Che Ragazza*',
When she sat in the Grand Piazza
Everybody would rise,
Every fisherman sighed,
'*Viva Viva che bell' Inglesi*',
Someone even said, 'Whoops-adaisy!'
Which was quite a surprise.
Each night she'd make some gay excuse
And beaming with good will
She'd just slip into something loose
And totter down the hill.

REFRAIN 2

To the bar on the Piccola Marina

Where love came to Mrs Wentworth-Brewster,
Hot flushes of delight suffused her,
Right round the bend she went,
Picture her astonishment,
Day in, day out she would gad about
Because she felt she was no longer on the shelf,
Night out, night in, knocking back the gin
She'd cry, 'Hurrah!
Funicula
Funiculi
Funic yourself!'
Just for fun three young sailors from Messina
Bowed low to Mrs Wentworth-Brewster,
Said '*Scusi*' and politely goosed her.
Then there was quite a scena.
Her family, in floods of tears, cried,
'Leave these men, Mama.'
She said, 'They're just high-spirited, like all Italians
    are
And most of them have a great deal more to offer
    than Papa
In a bar on the Piccola Marina.'

Then there was the sad story of the lonely movie queen. . .

LOUISA

VERSE

Louisa was a movie queen.
Before she'd achieved the age of sweet sixteen,
Long before Cagney threw those girls about,
Little Louisa tossed her curls about.
Later when the talkies came
The whole world
Resounded with her fame,
Each time she married
Every daily paper carried
Headlines blazing her name.
Not only headlines
But photographs and interviews,
Everything she did was news
That held the world in thrall.

Some said she read lines
Better than Marlene could,
No other entertainer could
Compare with her at all.
But regardless of the fact
That she could sing and dance and act

And owned furniture that wasn't 'Little Rockery',
And regardless of her gems,
Which were hers, not M.G.M.'s,
Her life was one long mockery.

REFRAIN 1

Louisa was terribly lonely,
Success brought her naught but despair.
She derived little fun from the Oscars she'd won
And none from her home in Bel Air.
She declared she was weary of living
On a bestial terrestrial plane.
When friends came to visit their hands she would
    clutch
Crying, 'Tell me, why is it I suffer so much?
If only, if only, if only
My life wasn't quite such a strain.'
And soon after that she was terribly lonely,
All over again.

REFRAIN 2

Louisa was terribly lonely,
Louisa was terribly sad.
It appears that the cheers that had rung in her ears
For years had been driving her mad.
She sobbed when men offered her sables
And moaned when they gave her champagne.
She remarked to her groom on their honeymoon
    night
As he tenderly kissed her and turned out the
    light,
'If only, if only, if only
I'd thrown myself out of the plane. . . .'
The very next day she was terribly lonely,
All over again.

REFRAIN 3   (Rhythm)

Louisa was terribly lonely
(The girl had no fun),
Louisa was tired of it all
(Not a call from anyone),
She gazed like a dazed belated Sphinx
At her hundred and eight mutated minks
And she wrung her hands and she beat her breast
Crying, 'My, my, my, I'm so depressed.'
Nobody knew the trouble she'd seen,
Nobody knew but you know who
The tribulations of a movie queen.
So farewell to lovely Louisa
(Who just let life tease her),
Let's leave her seeking in vain
(To find someone to explain)
Why destiny should single her out to be only
    lonely,
Over and over again!

And in the intimacy of the company of several hundred close personal friends he allowed himself to ask the heretical show business question . . .

WHY MUST THE SHOW GO ON? (1954)

VERSE 1

The world for some years
Has been sodden with tears
On behalf of the Acting profession,
Each star playing a part
Seems to expect the 'Purple Heart',
It's unorthodox
To be born in a box
But it needn't become an obsession,
Let's hope we have no worse to plague us
Than two shows a night at Las Vegas.
When I think of physicians
And mathematicians
Who don't earn a quarter the dough,
When I look at the faces
Of people in Macy's
There's one thing I'm burning to know:

REFRAIN 1

Why must the show go on?
It can't be all that indispensable,
To me it really isn't sensible
On the whole
To play a leading role
While fighting those tears you can't control,
Why kick up your legs
When draining the dregs
Of sorrow's bitter cup?
Because you have read
Some idiot has said,
'The Curtain must go up'!
I'd like to know why a star takes bows
Having just returned from burying her spouse.
Brave boop-a-doopers,
Go home and dry your tears,
Gallant old troupers,
You've bored us all for years
And when you're so blue,
Wet through
And thoroughly woe-begone,
Why must the show go on?
Oh Mammy!
Why must the show go on?

VERSE 2

We're asked to condole
With each tremulous soul
Who steps out to be loudly applauded,
Stars on opening nights
Sob when they see their names in lights,
Though people who act
As a matter of fact
Are financially amply rewarded,
It seems, while pursuing their calling,
Their suffering's simply appalling!
But butchers and bakers
And candlestick makers
Get little applause for their pains
And when I think of miners
And waiters in 'Diners'
One query for ever remains:

REFRAIN 2

Why must the show go on?
The rule is surely not immutable,
It might be wiser and more suitable
Just to close
If you are in the throes
Of personal grief and private woes.
Why stifle a sob
While doing your job
When, if you use your head,
You'd go out and grab
A comfortable cab
And go right home to bed?
Because you're not giving us much fun,
This 'Laugh Clown Laugh' routine's been
    overdone,
Hats off to Show Folks
For smiling when they're blue

But more comme-il-faut folks
Are sick of smiling through,
And if you're out cold,
Too old
And most of your teeth have gone,
Why must the show go on?
I sometimes wonder
Why must the show go on?

REFRAIN 3 Why must the show go on?
Why not announce the closing night of it?
The public seem to hate the sight of it,
Dear, and so
Why you should undergo
This terrible strain we'll never know.
We know that you're sad,
We know that you've had
A lot of storm and strife
But is it quite fair
To ask us to share
Your dreary private life?
We know you're trapped in a gilded cage
But for Heaven's sake relax and be your age,
Stop being gallant
And don't be such a bore,
Pack up your talent,
There's always plenty more
And if you lose hope
Take dope
And lock yourself in the John,
Why must the show go on?
I'm merely asking
Why must the show go on?

*   *   *

All of these were naturally interspersed with his more romantic songs, including one new one, which he described as "wry on the rocks" . . .

TIME AND AGAIN

VERSE 1   Life is what you make it
As someone once observed,
A phrase that sounds a trifle glib,
But whoever thought it out
Had clearly never sorted out
The vexing problem of Adam's spare rib.
Chastity, I take it,
Is specially reserved

For those possessing moral fibres,
Mine fail me all the time
And maybe that's the reason I'm
A Baa Baa Black Sheep—calling all subscribers.

REFRAIN 1 Time and again
I make good resolutions
But somehow they don't seem to stay,
Just when I think I've got the whole thing
        sewn up
I must own up
Everything gets blown up.
Sex and Champagne
As social institutions
Stampede me and lead me astray,
I begin Beguine-ing
And my Spring cleaning
Is ditched—bitched—bundled away.
All my instincts respond
To an amiable blonde
Which is fatal.
And if some brisk brunette appears
Old Adam cheers,
Back go my ears,
Maybe it's all pre-natal.
How can I train
My hormone distributions
To be less aggressively male?
Time and again I try,
Time and again I fail.

VERSE 2   Moralists disparage
A variable heart
And say that it should be fenced in
But they never think about
Effective means of casting out
That dear old Die-Hard, Original Sin.
Table d'hôte is marriage,
Free love is *à la carte*,
And once you've crossed forbidden fruits off
You merely find that you've
Unwittingly set out to prove
The age-old saying,
'It's better with your boots off!'

REFRAIN 2 Time and again
I'm tortured by contrition
And swear that I'm sorry I've sinned,
Then when I've lashed myself with whips
        and scourges
Sex emerges,
Out pop all the urges.
Freud could explain
My curious condition

And Jung would have certainly grinned.
When I meet some sly dish
Who looks like my dish
I'm drunk—sunk—gone with the wind.
How can I start afresh
When the sins of the flesh
Override me?
Maybe some psycho-analyst
Might slap my wrist
And give a twist
To what goes on inside me.
If I could feign
The glandular transition
I'd settle for taking the Veil.
Time and again I try,
Time and again I fail.

REFRAIN 3 Time and again
I've tried to form a 'credo'
But somehow I don't seem to learn,
Just when I think my Guardian Angel's winning
I go spinning
Back to the beginning.
I can't refrain
From firing a torpedo
Abaft or ahead or astern,
If I hit my quarry
I can't feel sorry,
I'm hooked—cooked—done to a turn.
Though I frequently wish
I could curb my conditioned
Reflexes
I'll be damned if I'll sacrifice
Sugar and spice,
To be precise
Nothing's as nice as sex is.
I can't restrain
My lecherous libido
From slipping and tipping the scale.
Time and again I try,
Time and again I fail.

*   *   *

The Café de Paris was to be a home from home for him from 1951 to 1954. In that year, having broken his own professional ice, Noël was only too happy to help his old friend, Marlene Dietrich, when she made her own cabaret debut there. Introducing her on her opening night, he did so in rhyme . . .

We know God made trees
And the birds and the bees
And the seas for the fishes to swim in.
We are also aware
That he has quite a flair

Noël Coward and Marlene Dietrich rehearsing "Land, Sea and Air" (1954) for "Night of a Hundred Stars."

For creating exceptional women.
When Eve said to Adam,
"Start calling me Madam"
The world became far more exciting
Which turns to confusion
The modern delusion
That sex is a question of lighting.
For female allure
Whether pure or impure
Has seldom reported a failure
As I know and you know
From Venus to Juno
Right down to La Dame aux Camélias.
This glamour, it seems,
Is the substance of dreams
To the most imperceptive perceiver.
The Serpent of Nile
Could achieve with a smile
Far quicker results than Geneva.
Though we all might enjoy
Seeing Helen of Troy
As a gay, cabaret entertainer,
I doubt that she could
Be one quarter as good
As our legendary, lovely Marlene.

On one memorable occasion—at another theatrical charity event, *Night of a Hundred Stars,* June 24, 1954—the two exceptional people appeared together in a number Noël wrote specially for them . . . "a duet which neither of us knew" . . .

*LAND, SEA AND AIR

REFRAIN   Gonna travel by land, sea and air
Shovin' off by land, sea and air
Movin' out by takin' that train
To the boat, to the plane
And I hope we meet you there.
Ridin' out by land, sea and air
Glidin' out by land, sea and air
Slidin' out by takin' that train to the boat,
    to the plane
And I hope we'll greet you there.

VERSE 1
NOËL: We're just a couple who earn big dough
By using dulcet tones

MARLENE: Though one sings high and the other sings low
We can both use microphones.

NOËL: It's a well-known fact that we both inhale

BOTH: Champagne and caviar
And if we fail we can take the veil
And retire to Shangri-la

VERSE 2
MARLENE: We're just a couple who love to sing
If such it can be called

NOËL: If we go off key when we're in full swing
The "mike" gets overhauled.

MARLENE: We sleep till noon and stay up late
And we feel extremely well

BOTH: So when they state that we're ninety-eight
We can both say "What the Hell!"

VERSE 3
NOËL: We're just a couple who work our way
We love to rove and roam

MARLENE: And wherever we are we can always say
That it's lovely to be home

NOËL: And when our travelling days are through
And up to Heaven we spring

BOTH: Before St. Peter says "Howd'you do?"
We shall raise a mike and sing.

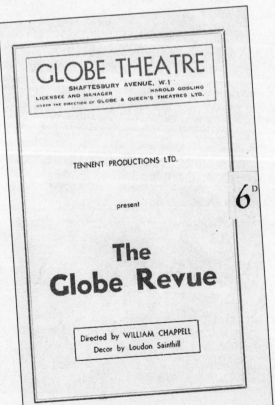

First presented by Tennent Productions at the Theatre Royal, Brighton on June 30, 1952 and subsequently at the Globe Theatre, London on July 10, 1953. (234 performances.)

Cast was the same as The Lyric Revue *with the exception of Joan Heal, who replaced Roberta Huby*

The Lyric Revue *evolved seamlessly into* The Globe Revue *and moved into the West End proper. This time there were two Coward numbers.*

"Give Me the Kingston By-Pass" was the wistful musing of a garage mechanic as he contemplates the kind of cars he handles daily but will never get to drive . . .

GIVE ME THE KINGSTON BY-PASS

(Graham Payn)

VERSE
Pity the souls
Cursed with a wanderlust,
Each man builds his castle in the air,
I've got a Rolls Daimler Lagonda lust,
Pity me and say a short prayer.
I'm well aware that my heart's desires
Cost a bloody sight too much dough,
Week-ends abroad I couldn't afford I know
And so—

REFRAIN
Give me the Kingston By-Pass
On a Saturday afternoon
In a bran' new Bugatti
Made for Cincinnati
Or a fairly flash Fraser Nash Town Saloon.
Watching the country fly past
In a carbon-monoxide swoon
Is to me more romantic
Than a South Atlantic
Cruise,
If I had to choose,
I'd tearfully, cheerfully wipe out
The sins that clutter my decks
To take a Humber Snipe out,
I'd even sacrifice Sex.
But in our pre-war Seven
That's the apple of Father's eye
All I can do
Is join the push-bike queue
And let the By-Pass pass by.

Give me the Kingston By-Pass
And a thoroughly 'posh' machine
Like a Healey three-litre
All complete with heater
Or a shiny grey Chevrolet Limousine.
Watching the summer sky pass
Through a blue haze of gasoline
Is to me more attractive
Than an over-active gland.
Try to understand I take my pleasure gently,
My moral lapses are few,
But for a drop-head Bentley
I'd be convertible too.
But in our pre-war Seven
I'm immune from the evil eye,
Jekyll or Hyde,
I hug the left-hand side
And let the By-Pass pass by.

In the second song Noël revisits the lugubrious glee the British seem to feel when spotting the dark cloud behind every silver lining. In many ways it was a companion piece to the earlier "That Is the End of the News."

THERE ARE BAD TIMES JUST AROUND THE CORNER

(Graham Payn, Dora Bryan, Joan Heal, Ian Carmichael)

VERSE 1
They're out of sorts in Sunderland
And terribly cross in Kent,
They're dull in Hull
And the Isle of Mull
Is seething with discontent,
They're nervous in Northumberland
And Devon is down the drain,
They're filled with wrath
On the Firth of Forth
And sullen on Salisbury Plain,
In Dublin they're depressed, lads,
Maybe because they're Celts
For Drake is going West, lads,
And so is everyone else.
Hurray—hurray—hurray!
Misery's here to stay.

REFRAIN 1
There are bad times just around the corner,
There are dark clouds hurtling through the
        sky
And it's no good whining
About a silver lining
For we know from experience that they won't
        roll by,
With a scowl and a frown
We'll keep our peckers down
And prepare for depression and doom and
        dread,
We're going to unpack our troubles from our old
        kit bag
And wait until we drop down dead.

VERSE 2
From Portland Bill to Scarborough
They're querulous and subdued

And Shropshire lads
Have behaved like cads
From Berwick-on-Tweed to Bude,
They're mad at Market Harborough
And livid at Leigh-on-Sea,
In Tunbridge Wells
You can hear the yells
Of woe-begone bourgeoisie.
We all get bitched about, lads,
Whoever our vote elects,
We know we're up the spout, lads,
And that's what England expects.
Hurray—hurray—hurray!
Trouble is on the way.

REFRAIN 2
There are bad times just around the corner,
The horizon's gloomy as can be,
There are black birds over
The greyish cliffs of Dover
And the rats are preparing to leave the B.B.C.
We're an unhappy breed
And very bored indeed
When reminded of something that Nelson said.
While the press and the politicians nag nag nag
We'll wait until we drop down dead.

VERSE 3
From Colwyn Bay to Kettering
They're sobbing themselves to sleep,
The shrieks and wails
In the Yorkshire dales
Have even depressed the sheep.
In rather vulgar lettering
A very disgruntled group
Have posted bills
On the Cotswold Hills
To prove that we're in the soup.
While begging Kipling's pardon
There's one thing we know for sure
If England is a garden
We ought to have more manure.
Hurray—hurray—hurray!
Suffering and dismay.

REFRAIN 3
There are bad times just around the corner
And the outlook's absolutely vile,
There are Home Fires smoking
From Windermere to Woking
And we're not going to tighten our belts and
        smile, smile, smile,
At the sound of a shot
We'd just as soon as not
Take a hot water bottle and go to bed,

Dora Bryan, Graham Payn, Joan Heal and Ian Carmichael as The Morris Dancers warning *"Don't Make Fun Of The Fair."*

We're going to untense our muscles till they
   sag sag sag
And wait until we drop down dead.

REFRAIN 4

There are bad times just around the corner,
We can all look forward to despair,
It's as clear as crystal
From Bridlington to Bristol
That we can't save democracy and we don't much
   care
If the Reds and the Pinks
Believe that England stinks
And that world revolution is bound to spread,
We'd better all learn the lyrics of the old 'Red
   Flag'
And wait until we drop down dead.
A likely story
Land of Hope and Glory,
Wait until we drop down dead.

*   *   *

Publishing this particular song brought Noël up against one of song writing's commercial realities in that every syllable and bar of music belongs to somebody. *En passant* he'd briefly "quoted" from several other songs, most notably "Drake Goes West," "Land of Hope and Glory" and "Pack Up Your Troubles." Francis Day and Hunter, the copyright owners of the last, were happy to give Chappells (Noël's publisher) their permission but suggested he contribute ½d. a copy on the sheet music and 10% of his mechanical and performing broadcast fees, because, as their director pointed out, "I happen to know that both the widows of the writers . . . could do with every little bit of money that is coming their way and I am sure Mr. Coward could afford to be generous . . . Incidentally, I think it is a brilliant piece of work." He need hardly have added the sweetner. Noël instructed the Performing Rights Society accordingly and immediately.

*   *   *

When Noël later used the number in his Las Vegas cabaret act, he adapted it to the American *milieu*, as he did with many of the topical numbers . . .

THERE ARE BAD TIMES JUST AROUND THE CORNER

(American Lyric)

VERSE 1

They're nervous in Nigeria
And terribly cross in Crete,
In Bucharest
They are so depressed
They're frightened to cross the street,
They're sullen in Siberia
And timid in Turkestan,
They're sick with fright
In the Isle of Wight
And jittery in Japan,
The Irish groan and shout, lads,
Maybe because they're Celts,
They know they're up the spout, lads,
And so is everyone else.
Hurray! Hurray! Hurray!
Trouble is on the way.

REFRAIN 1

There are bad times just around the corner,
There are dark clouds hurtling through the sky
And it's no use whining
About a silver lining
For we KNOW from experience that they won't
   roll by,
With a scowl and a frown
We'll keep our spirits down
And prepare for depression and doom and dread,
We're going to unpack our troubles from our old
   kit bag
And wait until we drop down dead.

REFRAIN 2

There are bad times just around the corner,
The horizon's gloomy as can be,
There are black birds over
The greyish cliffs of Dover
And the vultures are hovering round the
   Christmas tree
We're an unhappy breed
And ready to stampede
When we're asked to remember what Lincoln said,
We're going to untense our muscles till they
   sag sag sag
And wait until we drop down dead.

VERSE 2

They're morbid in Mongolia
And querulous in Quebec,
There's not a man
In Baluchistan
Who isn't a nervous wreck,
In Maine the melancholia
Is deeper than tongue can tell,
In Monaco
All the croupiers know
They haven't a hope in Hell.
In far away Australia
Each wallaby's well aware
The world's a total failure
Without any time to spare.
Hurray! Hurray! Hurray!
Suffering and dismay.

REFRAIN 3

There are bad times just around the corner,
We can all look forward to despair,
It's as clear as crystal
From Brooklyn Bridge to Bristol
That we CAN'T save Democracy
And we don't much care.
At the sound of a shot
We'd just as soon as not
Take a hot-water bag and retire to bed
And while the press and the politicians nag nag nag
We'll wait until we drop down dead.

REFRAIN 4

There are bad times just around the corner
And the outlook's absolutely vile,
You can take this from us
That when they Atom bomb us
We are NOT going to tighten our belts and
   smile smile smile,
We are in such a mess
It couldn't matter less
If a world revolution is just ahead,
We'd better all learn the lyrics of the old 'Red Flag'
And wait until we drop down dead.
A likely story
Land of Hope and Glory,
Wait until we drop down dead.

*   *   *

At one point during the reconstruction of *Sail Away* (1961) (See p. 329) he considered using "Bad Times" but presumably the task of significantly rewriting it, together with the fact that the show already had two "negative" numbers in "Useful Phrases" and "Why Do the Wrong People Travel?" dissuaded him.

280

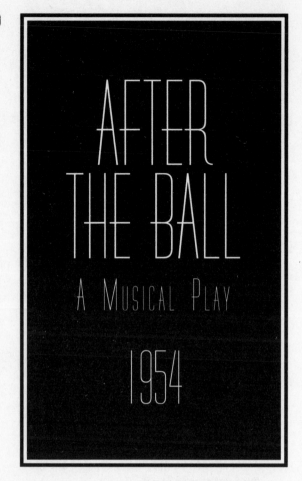

AFTER
THE BALL
A MUSICAL PLAY
1954

Based on Oscar Wilde's *Lady Windermere's Fan*

First presented by Tennent Productions at the Royal Court Theatre, Liverpool on March 1, 1954, followed by a twelve week tour. Subsequently presented at the Globe Theatre, London on June 10, 1954. (188 performances.)

Cast included Mary Ellis, Graham Payn, Vanessa Lee, Peter Graves, Irene Browne, Patricia Cree, Tom Gill, Shamus Locke, Dennis Bowen, Pam Marmont, Lois Green, Marion Grimaldi, Donald Scott.

The combination of Coward and Wilde should have been two and two adding up to five. In fact, it turned out to be less than the sum of its parts.

Despite the fact that for the Liverpool tryout he called it an "operette," Noël truly intended *After the Ball* to go beyond operetta and approach true opera. On the surface Wilde's somewhat melodramatic play provided the basis of a more serious "book" than most operettas enjoyed. While he found unexpected difficulties with the text, his real problem came with the casting of the lead role.

Mary Ellis had created a number of leading musical roles on both sides of the Atlantic, most notably *Rose Marie* and several Ivor Novello shows. As with Mary Martin in *Pacific 1860*, Noël made the mistake of casting her, assuming that she had the vocal range he required. While Mary Ellis in her prime could certainly have sung the role, her voice was no longer up to it. Several key numbers had to be cut and with them the musical stature of the show.

It began encouragingly enough. In an October 1953 *Diary* entry Noël wrote:

"The music is pouring out and I can scarcely go to the piano without a melody creeping from my fingers, usually in keys that I am not used to and can't play in; it is most extraordinary and never ceases to surprise me."

*   *   *

It's 1892. A number of elegant ladies and gentlemen are strolling through Hyde Park on a sunny afternoon. They sing a quartet:

OH, WHAT A CENTURY IT'S BEEN

Oh what a century it's been,
From George the Third to Queen Victoria
We've never had to sing 'Sic transit Gloria',
Oh what a century it's been.

Unhappy foreigners with jealous eyes
Can only gaze at us in awed surprise
For how indeed—ah how indeed
Could any lesser, lower breed
Be even vaguely guaranteed
To understand
This tomb of kings, this earth, this dear dear land,
This race so certain of its quality
And so convinced of its innate superiority.

Oh what a century it's been,
None can deny the upward trend of it
And though we've very nearly reached the end of
    it
What innovations we have seen,
A British transformation scene.

We've seen the birth of Queen Victoria
And the death of William Pitt
And then we won the battle of Waterloo

Which gave our island story a
Certain lift you must admit
And if you don't, we do.
We've seen the National Gallery open
And the Houses of Parliament burn
The introduction of Income Tax
Which gave us quite a turn,
We've seen the late Prince Consort on a magic-
    lantern screen.

What a happy and glorious,
Most meritorious
Century it has been.

We've read *The Daisy Chain* and *Romany Rye*
And passionately clung
To Walter Scott and Emily Brontë too,
We're rather cross that so many buy
The works of Charlotte Yonge
But none the less—they do,
We simply worship Christina Rossetti
And we're mad about Tennyson's 'Maud',
We love to be up an apple tree
With Mrs Humphry Ward,
From William Blake to Kipling,
With the Brownings in between.

What an unsupersedable,
Wonderfully readable,
Drinkable, feedable,
This happy breedable,
Follow my leaderable,
Oh yes indeedable
Century this has been.

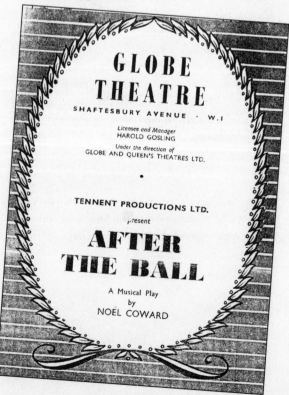

GLOBE
THEATRE
SHAFTESBURY AVENUE · W.1

Licensee and Manager
HAROLD GOSLING
Under the direction of
GLOBE AND QUEEN'S THEATRES LTD.

•

TENNENT PRODUCTIONS LTD.
present

AFTER
THE BALL
A Musical Play
by
NOËL COWARD

REPRISE

We've praised the works of Frederick Leighton
and hurled
Abuse at Holman Hunt
For he invites Pre-Raphaelites to tea
And if they hung 'The Light of the World'
Completely back to front
We shouldn't even see.
We only care to go shootin' and huntin'
On chestnuts and fillies and roans,
We're sick to death of Watts-Dunton
And we'd like to burn Burne-Jones.
We much prefer the pictures in a weekly magazine.

What a Royal Academy,
Too Alma-Tademy,
Practical, mystical,
Over-artistical,
Highly pictorial,
Albert Memorial
Century this has been.

We've made the most exhaustive scrutiny
Of the cause of England's might,
Convinced that every Britisher's born to boss,
We thought the Indian Mutiny
Was extremely impolite,
It made us feel quite cross,
We then embarked on a war in Crimea
With egos a little enlarged
And cheered the charge of the Light Brigade
No matter why they charged,
And then those swine in China made a most
disgusting scene,
What an uneconomical,
Tragical, comical
Century this has been.

What a quite irresistible,
Oliver Twistable,
Woman in White-able,
Wuthering Height-able,
Mill on the Flossible,
Frankly impossible
Century this has been.

We've been brought up on dear Kate Greenaway
And a little while ago
Amelia Bloomer came to promote her cause,
She threw her crinoline away
While the public cried, 'What Ho!'
And walked about in drawers.
We've had to hear Evangelical preachers
But we couldn't believe in them quite
For such hysterical creatures
Couldn't spread the slightest light,

Old William Booth has bawled at us and banged
his tambourine.

What a pompous, erroneous,
Too sanctimonious
Century this has been.

What a pompous, erroneous,
Too sanctimonious,
Praise-able, Laudable,
Madame Tussaudable,
Lovable, laughable,
Too good by halfable
Century this has been.

Lord and Lady Windermere appear, discussing the
ball they are about to hold to celebrate her birthday.
They are still very much in love . . .

I KNEW THAT YOU WOULD BE MY LOVE

(Vanessa Lee and Peter Graves)

VERSE 1
LORD WINDERMERRE

Summer sings its songs to me,
The lark pours rapture from the skies
And all the world belongs to me
As more and more I realize
That love was never blind to me,
He shot his arrow straight and true,
Destiny was kind to me
And led my heart to you.

REFRAIN

I knew that you would be my love
So long, so long ago,
Before we met
The moment was set
And the time drew near
Year by year,
I dreamed the same enchanted dream
That you were dreaming too,
I had no doubt of it, neither had you,
Deep in our hearts we knew.

VERSE 2
LADY WINDERMERE

In all the early years I wandered through
Each step I took was leading me to you
And then, and then, and then

There came the moment when
I found my vision had come true.
I dreamed a sweet enchanted dream
So long, so long ago.
Gone is that dream
That enchanted me so
Deep in my heart I know.

REFRAIN

I knew that you would be my love
So long, so long ago,
Before we met
The moment was set
And the time drew near
Year by year,
I dreamed the same enchanted dream
That you were dreaming too,
I had no doubt of it, neither had you,
Deep in our hearts we knew.

As they leave, Mr. Hopper, an Australian, enters with
two friends, who are teasing him about his affection
for Lady Agatha. Talk of his family and the country
of his birth leads them into a trio . . .

MR. HOPPER'S CHANTY

(Graham Payn, Tom Gill, Dennis Bowen)

MR HOPPER: My Grandpa landed from a convict ship
On the beach of Botany Bay.

OTHERS: Haul away; haul away; how peculiar people are,
Fancy landing Grandpapa
On the beach of Botany Bay.

MR HOPPER: He didn't strike oil and he didn't strike gold
But he lived to be very very very very old
In a rather disgusting way.

MR. GRAHAM: What a curious thing to say!

MR HOPPER: My Grandma's meeting with this gay young rip
Was achieved on the very first day.

OTHERS: Haul away; haul away; having travelled all that far
Fancy meeting Grandmama
On a beach on the very first day!

MR HOPPER: She happened to be, when he landed there,
Combing her fuzzy-wuzzy blue-black hair
And he sprang at her straight away.

MR DUMBY: Steady, old man, Fair Play!

MR HOPPER: They lay on the sand of that alien land
Where the wallabys gaily frisk

282

And plighted their troth, in a way that was both
Effective and fairly brisk.

MR GRAHAM: He ran an appalling risk!

MR HOPPER: And the net result of the whole affair
You can perfectly plainly see
By my coloured skin and kinky hair
That I'm half aboriginee.

MR DUMBY: What a socially regrettable, un-Debrettable,
Maddening thing to be!

MR HOPPER: It's a solemn thought for a son and heir
To know who his forebears really were
And whether or not you know or care
Before my Dad was a millionaire
We lived . . .

OTHERS: Where?

MR HOPPER: In our family tree!

OTHERS: Haul away; haul away;
My goodness gracious me!

MR HOPPER: I can see my brothers and sisters now
Swinging about from bough to bough
On the very, very top . . .

OTHERS: For heaven s sake stop!

MR HOPPER: The top of our family tree!

We now return to the Windermeres. He tells her he has a surprise for her but won't reveal it. She says she wants to enjoy every moment of her birthday.

SWEET DAY

(Vanessa Lee)

REFRAIN   Sweet day, remain for me
Clear in my memory,
When my heart's chilled by the snows of
   December,
Let me remember
Let me remember
Sweet day
That seems to be
Made up of dreams for me
But when they've faded away
Let me remember today.

VERSE   No melancholy dream,
No shadow on my heart,

No transitory gleam
Of danger in the sky,
Why should such happiness fill me today,
Why must such loveliness fade away,
Why must these magic moments fly
Just as the leaves of summer fall and die?
No melancholy dream,
No shadow on my heart
Excepting that I know perfection cannot stay,
This has not been in vain
This I will not betray
When summer comes again
I shall remember . . .

REFRAIN   Sweet day, remain for me
Clear in my memory,
When my heart's chilled by the snows of
   December,
Let me remember
Let me remember
Sweet day
That seems to be
Made up of dreams for me
But when they've faded away
Let me remember today.

REPRISE   This melancholy dream,
This shadow on my heart,
This bitter disillusion
That has blown away
All that I held so true,
Love that was here to stay,
All I believed I knew
Has now betrayed me.

Sweet day, how brief you were
Sweet day, what grief you bear
Never again shall I say
Let me remember today.

Sweet day, that seems to be
Made up of dreams for me
But when they've faded away
Let me remember today.

As she sings, Lord Windermere leaves and Lord Darlington enters. He is attracted to her but she warns him that she is happily married and, if they are to remain friends, he must behave with due courtesy. Lord Darlington then puts a hypothetical question to her. If a husband should become the friend of a woman of doubtful character, doesn't the wife have the right to console herself? Seeing that Lady Windermere does not see or perhaps chooses not to see the connection, Lord Darlington sings . . .

STAY ON THE SIDE OF THE ANGELS

(Shamus Locke)

Stay on the side of the angels,
Keep all your illusions enshrined,
But, Lady Windermere, dear Lady Windermere,
Do not forget to be kind.

The lilies and the languors of virtue,
Though rather oppressively 'nice',
As Swinburne implied,
Can be elbowed aside
By the roses and raptures of vice.

Stay on the side of the angels
But in the stern life that you live,
Lady Windermere, dear Lady Windermere,
Do not forget to forgive.

Those other less fortunate mortals
Who find to their infinite pain
That love, when unjust,
Is more cruel than lust,
Forgive me for quoting again.

Stay on the side of the angels,
Secure and remote and apart,
But, Lady Windermere, dear Lady Windermere,
Keep a compassionate heart.

Later the Duchess of Berwick (Agatha's mother) warns Lady Windermere that her husband has been seen with a mysterious widow, Mrs. Erlynne and may even be keeping her. Lady Windermere now sees the significance of Lord Darlington's remarks. When Lord Windermere returns with his surprise—a beautiful fan—she pours out all she has been told. He swears his undying love for her but refuses to explain the relationship with Mrs. Erlynne. He also insists she be invited to the ball. Lady Windermere threatens to strike the woman with her fan, if she should dare to appear. Insisting that he has a most particular reason for wishing Mrs. Erlynne to be present, Lord Windermere leaves his distraught wife to reflect on how quickly a "sweet day" can lose its sweetness . . .

*   *   *

The second act Prologue begins with the Society ladies and gentlemen praising themselves.

CRÈME DE LA CRÈME

Ladies and Gentlemen, pillars of London Society,
Never in doubt that our blood is impeccably blue,
Any summery afternoon
In the months of July and June
From the bridge on the Serpentine to Rotten Row
Backwards and forwards we go—so
Aristocratically free from financial anxiety,
Blandly aware we belong to the privileged few,
Though the Socialists fume and fight,
To our houses we don't invite
Anybody who dares to claim
The Crème de la Crème
Isn't quite, quite right.
Natural laws
Kindly provide for us
And set aside for us
All the top drawers.
Such metaphors,
Though they are fiction,
Uphold our conviction
That, born to applause,
True to the old routine,
Several gold spoons were seen
Clenched in our jaws
Which was because
Nature selected us,
Perfected us,
Expected us to be
Ladies and Gentlemen, born to eternal prosperity,
Firmly convinced our position is really unique,
We believe in the status quo
Because deep in our hearts we know
That though social reformers try to queer our pitch
God's on the side of the rich—which
Leads us to mention with more than a touch of
    asperity
Heaven can wait if it's only concerned with the
    meek,
If the angels are really bright
And decide on a plebiscite
They'll discover that, praise or blame,
The Crème de la Crème
Has been quite-quite-right.

We are now at the ball and all the leading characters
are assembled. Lady Windermere repeats her threat
to use her fan. Her husband is on the point of telling
her why he has insisted on Mrs. Erlynne's presence
when that lady is announced. Lady Windermere

drops the fan and goes out on the terrace with Lord
Darlington. Mrs. Erlynne makes an immediate
impact on the group and particularly on Lord
Augustus Lorton, the Duchess's brother. After flirting with him a little, she sings . . .

LIGHT IS THE HEART

(Mary Ellis)

Years of discretion strike a bargain with the past,
Ships that sailed the troubled seas find anchorage
    at last,
The far horizon clears
And all the ecstasies and all the tears
That in our youth we knew,
That in our youth we shed,
Die like the winds that blew
The clouds from overhead,
Years of discretion strike a bargain with the mind,
Middle age is chivalrous when youth has been
    unkind,
Seek in Autumn for the happiness that Spring has
    undermined
And you will find . . .

Light is the heart that has learned to surrender
Dreams that we dreamed in the Spring of the year,
Though we awoke from them
Time can evoke from them
Music that only our memories hear,
Gone are the visions of passionate splendour,
Calm are the waves of the turbulent sea,
Pity the rover
Whose journeys are over
But envy the heart that is free.

Light is the heart that discreetly remembers
Words that were spoken and far away tears,
Memory grieves for them,
Sentiment weaves for them
Colours and meanings that fade with the years,
Though we may still feel a glow from the embers,
Love cannot be what we hoped it would be,
Pity the lover
Who fails to discover
The peace of a heart that is free.

The notes contain an extra verse:

*Light is the heart of a woman of forty
Years of discretion are mellow and gay

Actions that once seemed impulsive and naughty
Take on a different complexion to-day.
Pity the lady whom love has defeated,
Pity the lady whom love has betrayed
But when the cycle of youth is completed
None of it matters—the price has been paid.
Now in the autumn the sunlight is golden,
Wisdom assuages the passionate heart
No more enslaved and no longer beholden
Nature's designs are perfected by art.
Muted by time are the songs she recaptures,
Calm are the waves of the turbulent sea,
Gone are the tears and the roses and raptures
Light is the heart that has learned to be free.

*   *   *

Mrs. Erlynne proceeds to win over many of her former critics before she takes her leave. The Duchess
returns with her daughter, Lady Agatha, and Mr.
Hopper claims her for a dance . . .

MAY I HAVE THE PLEASURE

(Graham Payn, Irene Browne, Patricia Cree)

MR HOPPER: May I have the pleasure of a dance,
        Lady Agatha,
    Are you free by any chance, Lady Agatha,
    To oblige me with a One, two, three,
        One, two, three,
    One, two, three-fold miracle.
    Magical, lyrical
    Waltz, Lady Agatha.
    I may have faults, Lady Agatha,
    But I can dance all night and never tire,
    Every note of music sets my heart on fire
    To go, Lady Agatha,
    Please don't say No.

DUCHESS OF BERWICK:
    Really, Mr Hopper,
    This is really most improper,
    You must learn to be more discreet.
    Frankly, Mr Hopper,
    You will come a social cropper
    If you try to sweep debutantes off their feet.

*Following page: Mary Ellis as Mrs. Erlynne
sings "Light Is The Heart."*

MR HOPPER: I can't look at other debutantes,
      Lady Agatha,
You're the heart of my romance, Lady
Agatha,
      For to me you're more than One, two, three,
        One, two, three,
One, two, three times prettier,
Lovelier, wittier,
So, Lady Agatha,
Come weal, come woe, Lady Agatha,
Let's let the music of the violins
Hold us both together till the dawn begins
To glow, Lady Agatha,
Please don't say No.

DUCHESS OF BERWICK:
    Really, Mr Hopper,
    This is really most improper,
    Your Colonial ways are quaint.
    Frankly, Mr Hopper,

You will come a social cropper
If you cannot learn, candidly, self-restraint.

MR HOPPER: None the less I beg you for a dance,
      Lady Agatha,
    I am truly in a trance, Lady Agatha,
    Please don't say No.

Lady Windermere tells Lord Darlington how her husband has insisted on inviting Mrs. Erlynne into her house. She is upset and asks for his friendship. He tells her he cannot offer her friendship—only love.

As he sings of his love, she joins in a duet, begging him to go away. . .

Letter from Stephen Tennant to Noël Coward critiquing "After The Ball" during its twelve week tour before arriving in the West End.

I OFFER YOU MY HEART?

(Shamus Locke)

LORD DARLINGTON:
    I offer you my heart
    And everything I own,
    I offer you my life
    And yet you spurn it.

LADY WINDERMERE:
    What can you hope to gain
    By offering your love
    To someone else's wife
    Who can't return it?

LORD DARLINGTON:
    Are you so sure, so sure that this is true
    .And not an empty phrase, a barricade
    Built to prevent the world from hurting you,
    Built to prevent my arms from holding you,
    Because you are afraid ?

LADY WINDERMERE:
    Leave me alone, I beg of you, and go;
    Speak not the words your passion bids you say;
    For if you truly love me you must know
    Why I must say goodbye to you—and so
    I beg you to go away.

LORD DARLINGTON/LADY WINDERMERE:
    I offer you my heart
    You offer me your heart

LORD DARLINGTON/LADY WINDERMERE:
    And everything I own,
    And everything you own,

LORD DARLINGTON:
    I offer you my love,

LORD DARLINGTON/LADY WINDERMERE:
    Don t turn my love away.
    I beg you go away.

As the guests depart, Lady Windermere overhears a conversation between her husband and Mrs. Erlynne which, in her distraught state, she misinterprets. She now determines to follow Lord Darlington and writes a letter to Lord Windermere to tell him she is leaving. The letter is intercepted by Mrs. Erlynne, who reads it: "The same words that I wrote to her father twenty years ago!" The secret Lord Windermere had to tell his wife was that Mrs. Erlynne is, in fact, her mother. Mrs. Erlynne goes off to find her daughter and bring her back.

*   *   *

An interlude. A trio of society ladies ask . . .

WHY IS IT THE WOMAN WHO PAYS?

(Pam Marmont, Lois Green, Marion Grimaldi)

Pity three wives in the world of fashion,
Pity three lambs into the slaughter led,
Tied for their lives to their husband's passion
Not for themselves, but for others instead,
What disillusion,
Shame and confusion
Goes with the marriage bed.

REFRAIN I

Why are men permitted to sin and sin again,
Say they're sorry and then begin again?
Have they certain glands that automatically combust?
Why is it accepted that they just must lust?
It isn't fair to their relations,
Kind to wife or child,
Though it gives dramatic situations
And a cynical glaze
To the plays
Of Oscar Wilde.
When a girl has gritted her teeth and tried to be
All a husband expects a bride to be
Why, to coin a phrase,
Must it be the woman who pays and pays
And pays and pays and pays
To the end of her days?

She quickly learns what utter hell it is
To face the fact that men are hunters,
She hears her husband's infidelities
Served up with strawberries at Gunter's.
If she complains, there'll be a scene, of course.
So she remains niminy-piminy
Though she's aware that really he has been of course
Down to Brighton with Miss Thingummy.
But when she is old and grey and full of sleep
What harvest will she reap?
The answer's—none,
There she'll sit, depressed and weary,
Thumping out a rather dreary
Chopin Polonaise—
Proving it's the woman who pays and pays
And pays and pays and pays
To the end of her days.

REFRAIN 2

Why are men permitted to smile and smirk
again,
Say they're sorry, and go berserk again?
We can guess, when they are clasping pearls
around our necks,
All they've been indulging in is sex—sex—sex!
It isn't right, it isn't moral,
We'd agree to be
Hung with beads of imitation coral
If it weren't a bribe
To our tribal loyalty,
Why are men acquitted of social treachery
When we women, with one light lechery,
Set our world ablaze?
Why is it the woman who pays and pays
And pays and pays and pays
To the end of her days?

She will be treated with contumely,
She'll have to live on the Riviera,
She will be seen parading gloomily
Along the front at Bordighera.
She will be hounded from society
And, growing daffier and daffier,
She may achieve some local notoriety
By wearing sandals made of raffia.
Maybe she'll have one dull German maid with
her,
Old friends who've played with her
Will cut her dead.
She will murmur, *Faites attention*
As she sadly eats the pension
Salmon Mayonnaise.
Portrait of a woman who pays and pays
And pays and pays and pays
To the end of her days.

In his *Diary* Noël recalls the origin of the song. He had been reading *Blessed Girl*, the letters of Lady Emily Lutyens, in which he came across the passage: "'Why should men be allowed to sin as much as they like without incurring more than the slightest criticism, whereas if a woman makes one slip she is socially damned for ever?'

"This was not the exact phrase but it gave me the idea, and yesterday I worked like a beaver and completed the number, music and words."

*   *   *

In Lord Darlington's room Lady Windermere sings an aria expressing her lonely state of mind . . .

LADY WINDERMERE'S ARIA

(Vanessa Lee)

I feel so terribly alone,
He should be here
To calm the beating of my heart
And still the fear,
The anguish tearing me apart,
He should have known
That, by this folly, I have thrown away,
Renounced for ever,
Home and honour and the pride of living,
This I know to be beyond forgiving,
Shall we walk in shadows until we die
My love and I?
What hope for future years,
What gifts have I to tender to him?
Chill hands and bitter tears,
These only I surrender to him,.
What have I left to repay him,
How can I honour, love and obey him?
My lifeless heart will betray him,
This I know,
Too late I know.

I feel so terribly alone and so afraid,
A love that cannot be repaid
Must swiftly fade,
Too soon, too soon, when eager passion dies away,
High romance flies away
And disenchanted, we shall stare
Into the future that the wrong we've done
Forces us to share.
How can I bear,
How can I bear
Such dark despair?
I must return to where my duty lies
And leave him free,
This ardent lover who would compromise
His life for me,
How could I ever repay him,
How could I honour, love and obey him?
My lifeless heart would betray him,
This I know,
At last—I know.

I feel so terribly alone.
Lost, and alone.

Mrs. Erlynne enters and tries to persuade Lady Windermere to return to her husband . . .

288

GO, I BEG YOU, GO

(Mary Ellis)

MRS ERLYNNE:: Go, I beg you go,
For you must never know
The tears, the sorrow and the blame
That lie in wait for you,
It's not too late for you
To fly from the shame
That threatens your name.

LADY WINDERMERE:
What can it mean to you
That I should remain or go
And would you dare to say
To me, his wife,
What he has been to you,
The husband I trusted so,
It's you who led his love away
And broke my life.

MRS ERLYNNE:: The only love he bears, he bears for you,
In heaven's name believe that this is true.

Mrs. Erlynne (Mary Ellis) begs Lady Windermere (Vanessa Lee) to return to her husband.

LADY WINDERMERE::
His traitor's love means nothing to me,
I'm not so blind that I cannot recognize
All this implies,
Why should you think that I could not see
The truth behind all your lies?

MRS ERLYNNE:: Once long ago
A woman innocent as you
Decided to throw
Her happiness away,
You cannot know
What misery it led her to,
I swear this is so,
I swear that this is true.

LADY WINDERMERE::	MRS ERLYNNE::
Why should you think I'd undergo	Once long ago
The same dishonour?	A woman innocent as you
What has this woman that	Decided to throw
you know	
To do with me?	Her happiness away,
Why should her degradation be	You cannot know
Quoted thus to show	The dark despair it led
	her to,
What price is paid?	I swear this is so,
Why should I care?	I swear that this is true.
My choice is made.	

MRS ERLYNNE:: If you take this foolish step you
contemplate
No love will compensate
For all you lose.

LADY WINDERMERE:
Say no more,
Say no more,
Leave me, for
My heart alone must choose.

MRS ERLYNNE::	LADY WINDERMERE:
Go, I beg you go,	Now I know that I must go
For life can hurt you so	For if life should hurt me so
As once it hurt me long ago,	As it hurt you long ago
To realize one day	I'd realize one day
You've thrown true love away,	I'd thrown true love away,
That ultimate woe	That ultimate woe
You never must know.	I never must know.

There were some unused lyrics:

*MRS ERLYNNE::
Demand no pity when that heart's betrayed,
Expect no mercy from the world that you
knew,
The price of sin and folly can be only paid
In terms of suffering and sorrow.
Seek no compassion if you break the rules.
Do not misunderstand these words that I say,

Humiliation is the bitter cup of fools,
Is the reward for those who throw their
lives away.
I'll ask no pity for a heart betrayed,
I'll claim no mercy from a world I'll leave
behind me.

LADY WINDERMERE:
No compromise with pride
Will make me stand aside
And see my life and honour overthrown,
Nothing can change the bitter choice I've
made,
No more illusions, no more tears will ever
blind me.
My sorrow is my own
I'll deal with it alone—alone.

MRS ERLYNNE:: Go, I beg you, go!
For you must never know
The tears, the sorrow and the blame
That lies in wait for you.
It's not too late
To fly from the shame
That threatens your name!
Dishonour must not stain
Your young immaturity.
Let me not plead in vain,
Forget your pride
And try to realise that virtue and purity
Need all the sweet security
Love can provide.

Mrs. Erlynne finally makes her see sense. She may have ruined her own life but she will not stand by and see her daughter do the same. They are about to depart when they hear Lord Darlington and his group of male friends (which includes both Lord Windermere and Lord Augustus, Mrs. Erlynne's admirer) arrive. Lady Windermere is told to hide behind the curtains and Mrs. Erlynne goes into a back room.

The young men sing a sextet . . .

LONDON AT NIGHT

(Peter Graves, Shamus Locke, Graham Payn, Tom Gill)

VERSE   When summer twilight fades away
And darkness falls and night begins
There ends another dusty day

With all its dreary disciplines
That have tied us to
The work we do
Until the evening gives us ease
To wander for an hour or two
Beneath our London trees.

REFRAIN 1 London at night
With the gas lamps alight
Is a wonderful sight
For the eye to see
With its clubs and pubs and bars
And the sleepy
Thames reflecting the stars,
London at night
Whether sober or tight
Is a sight
That Americans die to see,
From the naptha flares that glow
In the markets of Soho
To the far less exotic
And more patriotic
Restraint of Pimlico,
London's a place
That your heart can embrace
If your heart is free
And prone to be
Receptive to delight,
Rome was once gay
In a decadent way
But we're sure that it never was quite
Like London at night.

REFRAIN 2 London at night
With the gas lamps alight
Has an air of sublime unreality
When the moon has thrown
Her grace
On the shadowed stone
Of Hamilton Place,
Though Shepherd Market
Looks nice in the dark it
Is rather a vulgar locality,
On an even lower scale
Are the streets of Maida Vale
Where nocturnal behaviour
Compared with Belgravia
Is quite beyond the pale,
Blue blood we know
Is entitled to flow
In between Mayfair
And Onslow Square,
But by some oversight
Low class and high class

Contrive to defy class
And brightly, politely unite
In London at night.

REPRISE London at night
With the gas lamps alight
Is renowned for its moral fragility
From ornate, sedate Pall Mall
To the dark romance of Regent's Canal.
Girls in large hats
Outside Boodle's and Pratt's
Lie in wait for the younger nobility
And they frequently compel
Some inebriated swell
To hop into a hansom
And shout through the transom,
'Drive home—drive home like hell!'
Men who survive
Piccadilly alive
And can take the air
In Leicester Square
And not be put to flight
Earnestly say
That Port Said and Bombay
Are a great deal more prim and upright
Than London at night.

London at night
With the gas lamps alight,
Though it wasn't laid out continentally,
Read the words that Wordsworth wrote
And you can't avoid a lump in your throat,
Creaking four-wheelers
And certainly 'Peelers'
If only they're viewed sentimentally
Have a reassuring charm
Quite unlike the French Gendarme
Who, by shrieking such graphic
Instructions to traffic,
Inspires profound alarm.
Here in our city
We're all of us pretty
Well sure that vice
Will in a trice
Be bundled out of sight,
Old men in lobbies
With dubious hobbies
Can still get the deuce of a fright
In London at night.

As they begin to exchange confidences about their respective love lives, they notice the fan Lady Windermere has left. The others are amused to think Darlington has a woman hidden in his rooms, except Lord Windermere, who instantly recognises it. Mrs.

Erlynne saves the situation by appearing and claiming that she took Lady Windermere's fan in mistake for her own. While their attention is diverted, Lady Windermere makes her escape. Lord Windermere, not believing Mrs. Erlynne's story for a moment, silently hands her the fan.

*　　*　　*

Back home the next day Lady Windermere reflects on the new light in which she now sees things . . .

CLEAR, BRIGHT MORNING

(*Vanessa Lee*)

Now in the clear bright morning
When the shadows of night
Are dispelled by the light
I can see at last
How my youth and my pride
Swept me away on the tide.

Now in the clear bright morning
With my pride in the dust
I must win back the trust
And the tender love I so nearly betrayed.
How can such love be repaid?

Now in the clear bright morning
When the fear and the dread
And the darkness have fled
I can see at last
How my pride and my youth
Led me so far from the truth.

Lord Windermere suggests they should go to the country. He forbids his wife to see Mrs. Erlynne after the events (as he sees them) of the previous evening. At which point the fan is returned, together with a note from Mrs. Erlynne, asking to see Lady Windermere, who agrees. Mrs. Erlynne announces that she is going abroad at once and asks for a photograph of Lady Windermere and her child. While she is out of the room, Mrs. Erlynne has a straight talk with Lord Windermere, who asks her not to see his wife again. "My daughter, you mean," Mrs. Erlynne replies. Lady Windermere returns with the photo, which she gives to Mrs. Erlynne who sings her farewell in a song originally intended for *Pacific 1860* . . .

ALL MY LIFE AGO

(Mary Ellis)

Once when I was young
A song was sung,
A song of love too passionate to last,
All my life ago,
Among the shadows of the past,
Now I try in vain
To hear again
The echo of that far away refrain,
Once it hurt me so
But that was all my life ago.

Now the future's clear to me,
I cannot say, I can't explain
Why you will be for ever near to me,
Though we may never meet again,
Time has paid its debt to me
And though I know that I must say goodbye,
Oh, my dear, if only you'll remember me
I shall be grateful till I die.

In a garden the Society ladies sing . . .

OH, WHAT A SEASON THIS HAS BEEN

Oh what a season this has been,
We find our nerves are simply worn to shreds,
We've not a thing to wear that isn't torn to
        shreds,
Our gloves are smelling of benzine.

The social world has whirled us off our feet,
Too much to drink and far too much to eat,
We feel the lure—we feel the lure
To give up 'Beurre' and 'Petits Pains'
And take our aches to Aix-le-Bains
And do a cure,
We're sick of other people's recipes,
We're not surprised by *Soufflés en surprise*,
We'd loathe to pay a single call again
And rather die than be invited to a ball again.

Oh what a season this has been,

We just despise the very thought of it
And if you want to know the long and short of it
Rather than start the same routine
We'd gladly face the guillotine,
Oh what a season this has been.

Lord Augustus still wants to marry Mrs. Erlynne who sadly refuses him. He sings a farewell song before they both leave . . .

FAREWELL SONG

(Donald Scott)

MRS ERLYNNE:: Don't ever think me ungrateful,
        What you have said has made me very proud.

LORD AGUSTUS: Farewells and partings are hateful,
        'Goodbye' for us must never be allowed,
        Ah, promise me,
        Ah, promise me
        That somewhere in the future there may be
        A distant day,
        A distant day
        When you and I can meet again and say
        Although no tears between us flowed,
        Our eyes were dry, our words discreet,
        This foolish little episode
        Was really very sweet.
        Though I may not claim your hand and heart,
            my dear,
        And we must part, my dear.
        It's not the end,
        Where you are,
        Near or far,
        Count on me for ever as your friend.

The Duchess enters with Lady Agatha and several friends. She confides that she is quite glad the season is over. Now she can relax and have . . .

SOMETHING ON A TRAY

(Irene Browne)

Advancing years may bring about
A rather sweet nostalgia
In spite of rheumatism and gout

And, certainly, neuralgia.
And so, when we have churned our way
Through luncheon and a matinée,
We gratefully to bed retire
Obsessed with an acute desire
To rest our aching, creaking vertebrae
And have a little something on a tray.

Some ageing ladies with a groan
Renounce all beauty lotions,
They dab their brows with eau-de-Cologne
And turn to their devotions,
We face the process of decay
Attired in a négligé
And with hot bottles at our toes
We cosily in bed repose
Enjoying, in a rather languid way,
A little eggy something on a tray.

Advancing years that many dread
Still have their compensations,
We turn when youth and passion have fled
To more sedate sensations,
And when we've fought our weary way
Through some exhausting social day
We thankfully to bed retire
With pleasant book and crackling fire
And, like Salomé in a bygone day,
Enjoy a little something on a tray.

When weary from the fray
Something on a tray
Sends weariness away,
Something on a tray,
Thank God, thank God we say,
For something on a tray.

Lady Agatha meets Mr. Hopper, who talks to her about the beauties of his homeland . . .

FARAWAY LAND

(Graham Payn)

REFRAIN 1 I come from a far away land
        Beyond the rim of the sea
        Where the North is hot and the South is cold
        And nothing is more than a few years old
        Except the mountains and desert sand
        And the eucalyptus tree.
        I come from a far away land
        Beyond the rim of the sea.

VERSE 1 have seen your country in the gentle
English light,
Hedges and farms and cornsheaves in a row,
I have seen your quiet woods and meadows
under white
Counterpanes of snow.
I have smelt the tang of wood-smoke in the
Autumn air,
Listened to a barrel-organ in a London
square,
There is so much of England that I know
Almost as though I'd lived here long ago.

REFRAIN 2 I come from a far away land
Below the arc of the sky,
A land where Englishmen blazed the trails
From Nullarbor Plain to New South Wales,
And conifer trees like sentries stand
On the road to Gundagai.
I come from a far away land
Below the arc of the sky.

REFRAIN 3 I come from a far away land
On the other side of the world,
A land that's primitive, crude and brave,
Where no one's master and no one's slave,
Yet one and all of us primly stand
When the English flag's unfurled.
I come from a far away land
On the other side of the world.
The journey's long and the seas are wide
But it's sweet to know that there's English
pride
On the other side of the world.

He proposes and is accepted. Mrs. Erlynne now has a last talk to Lady Windermere, who still does not know of the relationship between them. She wants to confess everything to her husband but Mrs. Erlynne dissuades her: "Don't spoil the one good thing I have done in my life by telling anyone about it." Lady Windermere offers to give her the fan, except it has her own name on it. "Margaret is my name, too," says Mrs. Erlynne, as she accepts it.

The play ends with reconciliations all around and suitable reprises of the key songs.

*   *   *

There were three songs London audiences did not get to hear. Mary Ellis's voice proved to be unsuitable for Mrs. Erlynne's two arias . . .

The first came in Act I to introduce Mrs. Erlynne . . .

---

*GOOD EVENING, LADY WINDERMERE (MRS. ERLYNNE'S ENTRANCE)

MRS ERLYNNE:: Good evening, Lady Windermere,
How gracious of you to receive a stranger
Who for many a year
Has been away.
It's really so delightful here,
Forgive me if I sound naive
But having been abroad so much
And, frankly being bored so much
With foreign ways and alien skies
I find to my immense surprise,
The London that I used to despise
Is really gay.

ALL: What there was in London that she used
to despise,
She is really not prepared to say.

MRS ERLYNNE:: This city really can't compare
With any other that I know
From Lincoln's Inn to Grosvenor Square
It's quite unique.
Saint Petersburg, of course, has flair
But can be dull without the snow,
Berlin is much too polyglot
And Rome in Summer is dreadfully hot,
Vienna makes one ill at ease
With all those vocal Viennese,
And Athens with its ruins and fleas,
Is far too Greek.

ALL: Though we know that Athens
Has a great many fleas,
It is certainly a Greek antique.
Who is the fabulous lady
Who lives abroad
And makes no secret of the fact,
That she is bored
With half the cities of the world?
Can she afford
To be so blasé and selective
And to take up such a tone?
It would perhaps be more effective
To be rather less high-flown.
We disagree
With such excessive *jeu d'esprit* . . .

Can there be anything shady
About her past?

MRS ERLYNNE:: It's such a pleasure to be
Home again at last
Your wife looks radiant tonight.
I'm quite aghast
And all these formidable glances.
Worse than croupiers at Nice,
Their eyes are piercing me like lances
And they're cackling like geese.
Don't turn away
And leave me utterly at bay

ALL: Who can she be?
Lord Windermere looks thoroughly at sea
Her gown is bold,
Her eyes are cold,
Her manner seems a trifle too controlled.

MRS ERLYNNE:: Ah, Lord Augustus, how d'you do?
How shamefully you've neglected me!
I haven't heard a word from you
Since yesterday at three.

LORD AGUSTUS: Missis Erlynne, pray let me explain to you.

MRS ERLYNNE:: No, that I cannot do
It's such a bore.
I simply loathe explanations,
I cannot bear expressions of regret.

292

They upset all my vibrations.
And my vibrations mustn't be upset.

LORD AGUSTUS: Forgive me, please,

Forgive me, please

And set my heart a little bit at ease.

MRS ERLYNNE::   Just hold my fan, you foolish man.

I promise to forgive you if I can.

But do not speak of hearts to me,

For hearts are only for the young

And songs of love, at forty-three,

Have long ago been sung.

SEGUE: "Light is the Heart"

And as the finale of Act I Noël wrote an aria for Mrs. Erlynne . . .

---

*WHAT CAN IT MEAN? (MRS. ERLYNNE'S ARIA)

MRS. ERLYNNE:

What can it mean, this desolate sense of dread?
I who have been so sure that the past was dead
Why, when at last I thought I had paid in full
With suffering and shame
Should life defeat me, cheat me?
How much can one mad moment of passion cost?
How little joy is gained and how much is lost?
How can I save my child from the same despair,
The same humiliating fate
Before it is too late?
I cannot ever let her know
The lonely anguish that
The sight of her awakes in me
For I renounced long ago
The right to hold her close to me,
Lovingly and tenderly.
She must not hear the secret words
My empty heart is sighing, crying
Now I must plead with her alone
This is the punishment that Destiny had held for
me
This is my chance to atone
For all those bitter years ago
When my love failed her so
No matter what the Gods decide,
I shall at least, at least, have tried.

The third song was sung by Lord Darlington . . .

LETTER SONG

Accept, dear Lady Windermere,
This letter from a libertine
Whose love for you for many a year
Will still be true,
Regard this as a souvenir,
An echo of what might have been,
For now I know all hope has gone,
That all my dreams were based upon
The shifting sands of make-believe,
The fabric that all lovers weave,
And though my heart for ever will grieve
I'll love you still.

Beloved, do not blame me for adoring you,
Forgive me with your all-forgiving smile,
Also forgive me, dearest, for imploring you
To hold me in your memory awhile,
This letter is the last I'll ever write to you,
My heart is bleaker than a winter sky,
And so, dear love, I write the words 'Good night'
to you,
And so, dear love, I write the words 'Good night'
to you,
Because I cannot bear to say 'Goodbye'.

It was the omission of the first two in particular that unbalanced the show musically and reduced its operatic potential.

Production had been a war of attrition—not least on Noël's nerves. In April he watched a performance during the pre-London tour and recorded: "Mary Ellis acted well but sang so badly that I could hardly bear it." Numbers were cut or rearranged with rewriting necessary to cover the gaps. Looking back later in a fair degree of anger he complained to Cole Lesley that he had had to cut almost a third of his original score—which included "seven minutes of my best music and most charming lyrics sacrificed."

All of which was true but if—as Noël frequently maintained—the success of a musical depended on its "book," he had to bear some of the blame himself.

From the outset he was competing with Wilde. In his *Diary* he notes:

"I am forced to admit that the more Coward we can get into the script and the more Wilde we can eliminate, the happier we shall be."

As the show's director, Robert Helpmann concluded:

"There was no way it could ever work . . . Everything that Noël sent up, Wilde was sentimental about and everything Wilde sent up, Noël was sentimental about. It was like having *two* funny people at a dinner party."

*   *   *

Noël's file on the show contains an unused lyric which would have been placed in the opening scene of Act 1. Two boys in the uniforms of the Church Lads' Brigade were to have sung:

---

*ALL THINGS BRIGHT AND BEAUTIFUL

All things bright and beautiful
Inevitably come from Britain
Though we're supposed to muddle along
We're sturdy and strong
And right or wrong
When other nations criticise
Our Anglo-Saxon attitude,
We just dismiss with pained surprise
Such vulgar, sordid, base ingratitude
For we've won our assured position
By our tact and intuition.
Al things wise and wonderful
That anybody's said or written
We're bred to believe
And led to believe
Indubitably came from Britain.

All things bright and beautiful
Unquestioningly come from Britain.
We journey from the womb to the tomb
And rightly assume
That we've no room
To entertain the slightest doubt
Of our infallibility.
Britannia rules the waves without
Admitting their intractability.
We don't brag and when foreigners say we're
priggish,
We dismiss the remark as piggish
And a wee bit infra-diggish.
All things wise and wonderful
Including every Persian kitten
Can loudly protest
That only the best
Monotonously comes from Britain.

WILBUR
CLARK'S
DESERT INN

LAS VEGAS
JUNE/JULY 1955

In November 1954 Noël received a visit from Joe Glaser, an American agent, making him an offer for "a rather excessive salary" ($35,000 a week) to appear in cabaret for a month. The booking turned out to be at the Desert Inn in Las Vegas. "The prospect of this engagement filled me with misgivings because, although I had proved that my sophisticated songs and apparently even more sophisticated personality could go down all right with the *crème de la crème* of London Café Society, I doubted that the less urbane cross-section of Americans who frequented Las Vegas with the main object of gambling would understand and appreciate the essential 'Englishness' of my material and my performance. My fears, however, were unfounded. From the first 'dinner show' onwards, when I made my entrance with brisk outward assurance and inward panic, the audiences in that strange desert playground received me twice nightly with the utmost generosity, attention and enthusiasm."

The four seasons at the Café de Paris had obviously helped, as had "the invaluable apprenticeship of performing during the war years to the troops . . . they taught me some sharp lessons, the most important of which was never to betray irritation, temper or dismay, and to press on firmly with my program for so long as they allowed me to do so."

One thing Noël did change for the transatlantic trip were his arrangements. Marlene Dietrich pointed him firmly in the direction of arranger/accompanist, Peter Matz.

Graham Payn recalls:

"In truth Noël hadn't given much thought to adapting the Café de Paris act. He supposed that he and Norman Hackforth would take it lock, stock and barrel, but it transpired that Norman couldn't obtain an American work visa. Enter Pete . . . He took one look at Noël's orchestrations and said—'You're not going to use these, are you?' Noël was quick enough to say—'Oh no, I want you to re-orchestrate all the songs,' which he did. The songs Noël performed at the Café de Paris are unrecognisable on the Las Vegas album. Pete modernized the material, changing tempos, making the sound fuller without drowning Noël out. By comparison, the Café de Paris arrangements sounded like an English tea-lounge trio, complete with a singer whose high notes might break at any time."

Matz found working with Noël a professional challenge:

". . . he was very comfortable working in front of people. He was extremely prolific, he was just natural . . . he loved the language. He would just sit down, take out a pen, cross his legs and away he would go. Musically, he was not as literate as he was verbally . . . He would play the piano—he played OK, didn't play any wrong notes—but he was limited harmonically and, since he didn't read or write music, he'd have to get someone to transcribe what he composed . . . If something was needed, he'd sit down and compose a few bars and say—'Did you get that, did somebody write that down, that'll do for the transition?' He was quite comfortable doing that."

Once again, there was the need for more material. Alice, Nina, Mrs. Wentworth-Brewster and Uncle Harry made the trip, along with the other expected favorites.

Several of them needed a lyrical brush up. "Nescafé Society"—as Noel dubbed his new audience—couldn't be expected to struggle through layers of English introductions to get to the song proper.

Mrs. Wentworth-Brewster had to undergo a little cosmetic surgery. Out went the "bijou abode in St. Barnabas Road," "the family vault at Woking" and—rather more regrettably—the "excellent Madeira cake." Instead. . .

> I'll sing you a song,
> It's not very long,
> Its moral may disconcert you,
> Of a mother and wife
> Who most of her life
> Was famed for domestic virtue.
> She had two strapping daughters and a rather
>   dull son
> And a much duller husband, who at sixty-one
> Elected to retire
> And, later on, expire.
> Sing Hallelujah, Hey nonny-no, Hey nonny-no,
>   Hey nonny-no.
> He joined the feathered choir.
> Having laid him to rest
> By special request
> In the family mausoleum,
> As his widow repaired
> To the home they had shared,
> Her heart sang a gay *Te Deum.*
> And then in the middle of the funeral wake
> While adding some liquor to the Tipsy Cake
> She briskly cried, 'That's done.
> My life's at last begun.
> Sing Hallelujah, Hey nonny-no, Hey nonny-no,
>   Hey nonny-no
> It's time I had some fun.
> Today, though hardly a jolly day,

> At least has set me free,
> We'll all have a lovely holiday
> On the island of Capri!'

"Mad Dogs" was obviously a must but by this time Noël was so tired of singing it that he had to do *something* to keep his own interest alive. He decided to speed up his delivery and instructed Peter Matz accordingly. The result was he sang it so quickly that he caused Cole Porter to remark that it was the only time in his life that he'd ever heard an entire song sung straight through in one breath! Cole also had the opportunity to hear what Noël was now doing with "their" song . . .

---

*LET'S DO IT
(LAS VEGAS VERSION)

VERSE 1 Mr. Irving Berlin
Often emphasizes sin
In a charming way.
Mr. Coward we know
Wrote a song or two to show
Sex was here to stay.
Richard Rodgers it's true
Took a more romantic view
Of this sly biological urge.
But it really was Cole
Who contrived to make the whole
Thing merge.

REFRAIN 1 He said the Belgians and Greeks do it
Nice young men who sell antiques do it,
Let's do it, let's fall in love.
Monkeys whenever you look do it,
Aly Khan and King Farouk do it,
Let's do it, let's fall in love.
Louella Parsons can't *quite* do it,
For she's so highly strung,
Marlene *might* do it,
But she looks far too young.
Each man out there shooting crap does it,
Davy Crockett in that dreadful cap does it,
Let's do it, let's fall in love.

REFRAIN 2 Our famous writers in swarms do it,
Somerset and all the Maughams do it,
Let's do it, let's fall in love.
The Brontës felt that they *must* do it,

Ernest Hemingway could—*just*—do it,
Let's do it, let's fall in love.
E. Allan Poe—ho! ho! ho!—did it,
But he did it in verse.
H. Beecher Stowe did it,
But she had to rehearse.
Tennessee Williams self-taught does it,
Kinsey with a deafening report does it.
Let's do it, let's fall in love.

VERSE 2   In the Spring of the year
Inhibitions disappear
And our hearts beat high,
We had better face facts
Every gland that overacts
Has an alibi
For each bird and each bee,
Each slap-happy sappy tree,
Each temptation that lures us along
Is just Nature *elle-même*
Merely singing us the same
Old song.

REFRAIN 3 In Texas some of the men do it,
Others drill a hole—and then do it,
Let's do it, let's fall in love.
West Point cadets forming fours do it,
People say all those Gabors do it,
Let's do it, let's fall in love.
My kith and kin, more or less, do it,
Every uncle and aunt,
But I confess to it—
I've one cousin that *can't*.
Teenagers squeezed into jeans do it,
Probably we'll live to see machines do it,
Let's do it, let's fall in love.

REFRAIN 4 Each baby bat after dark does it,
In the desert Wilbur Clark does it
Let's do it, let's fall in love.
We're told that every hormone does it,
Victor Borge all alone does it,
Let's do it, let's fall in love.
Each tiny clam you consume does it,
Even Liberace—we assume—does it,
Let's do it, let's fall in love!

As he left Las Vegas in triumph, (*"Las Vegas Flipping, Shouts For More As Noël Coward Wows 'Em In Cabaret Turn"*—VARIETY) Noël confided to his *Diary*:

"It has been an extraordinary experience and one of the most reverberant successes I have ever had. I am really proud and pleased that I succeeded in doing what no one suspected I could, and that is please the ordinary audiences."

*   *   *

One of the undoubted hits of his act—as it had been for some years now—was his version of "Let's Do It." Or rather, *versions*. Noël would adapt the material endlessly to suit the specific occasion, maintaining the verse but playing games with the refrain.

Sometimes it would be the "Belgians and Dutch" who would "do" it, if he needed to rhyme with "Hildegarde and Hutch"; the "Greeks" would be dragged into it when "nice young men who sell antiques" were the object of his scrutiny. Over time he turned the poor Belgians into the possessors of Europe's largest libidos . . .

Other than that, it was mix-and-match with lines that played in any context sitting cheek by jowl with references that wouldn't survive the moment and the particular audience but which brought the house down when the audience realised that Noël had prepared material specially for them. At this date some of those references require explanatory footnotes. Even Noël scribbled in the margin of an "extra couplet (unused)" that "This will need explaining" . . .

Well-made young actors in tights do it
Without mentioning names,
Glamorous knights do it
With theatrical dames.

His handwritten notes include many such variations. Some of them are minor . . . "the Brontës" were sometimes "the Brownings" . . . "our leading writers" were "the literati" (presumably in front of a literate audience) . . . Since most of the versions were written in the 1950s, for reasons of space and sanity you'll have to take my word for it that the other references that "need explaining" were topical at the time.

Teenagers, mainly self-taught, do it
Readers of the Wolfenden Report do it . . .
****
French poets when they're sure do it,
Prousts *à la recherche du temps perdu* do it.
****
Tommy Steele will do it
With the aid of a mike
****
Gangsters by hook or by crook do it,
Exiled monarchs like Farouk do it
****

Some rather sly younger sons do it
In a luxury flat
****
The Dockers out on strike do it,
Even Mamie Eisenhower and Ike do it
****
When the little brown coot
Doesn't really give a hoot
If its feet get wet,
When the little ewe lamb
Is too old to give a damn
If its ma's upset,
When the little tom cat
Wants a bit of this or that
And gives vent to a fervent 'Miaow',
That is nature sublime
Slyly hinting that the time is now . . .

*   *   *

There were versions for "Animals" . . .

The chimpanzees in the Zoos do it,
Have you heard the news Gnus do it?
Let's do it—let's fall in love,
Hyenas just for some laughs do it,
After necking, the Giraffes do it,
Let's do it—let's fall in love.

Old Sloths who hang down from twigs do it,
Tho' the effort is great,
Sweet guinea-pigs do it,
Buy a couple and wait.
I know that bears in their pits do it,
Even pekineses at the Ritz do it,
Let's do it—let's fall in love.

. . . and even a "Fishy" version . . .

Cold salmon, just when they wish do it,
Even lazy jellyfish do it,
Let's do it—let's fall in love.
Sedate old skate swimming by do it,
Even eager octopi do it,
Let's do it—let's fall in love.

The most select schools of cod do it,
Tho' it shocks them, I fear,
Sturgeon—thank God—do it
(Have some caviar, dear)
In shallow shoals Dover soles do it,
Goldfish in the privacy of bowls do it,
Let's do it—let's fall in love.

*   *   *

Three other specific examples . . . On June 24, 1954 at the *Night of 100 Stars* charity show . . .

1

He said that Belgians and Dutch do it
Even Hildegarde and Hutch do it
Let's do it, let's fall in love.
Monkeys whenever you look do it
Aly Khan and King Farouk do it
Let's do it, let's fall in love.
Most of the stars cannot quite do it
Being so highly strung
Marlene might do it
But she looks far too young.
Visiting statesmen "incog" do it
All the cast who acted in *The Frog* do it
Let's do it, let's fall in love.

2

Our leading writers in swarms do it
Somerset and all the Maughams do it
Let's do it, let's fall in love.
The Brontes felt that they must do it
Mrs. Humphrey Ward could *just* do it
Let's do it, let's fall in love.
Both T.S. Eliot and Fry do it
But they do it in verse
Priestley and I do it
But we have to rehearse.
Most mystics as a routine do it
Even Evelyn Waugh and Graham Greene do it
Let's do it, let's fall in love.

3

Girls from the R.A.D.A. do it
Some T.V. announcers may do it
Let's do it, let's fall in love.
Trippers on day trips to town do it
Bureaucrats on Crichel Down do it
Let's do it, let's fall in love.
My kith and kin, more or less, do it
Every Uncle and Aunt
But, I confess to it,
I've one cousin that *can't*.
The BBC personnel do it
Both the brothers Littler and Parnell do it
Let's do it, let's fall in love.

4

The House of Commons en bloc do it
Civil Servants by the clock do it

Let's do it, let's fall in love.
Food cranks who only eat roots do it
Teddy Boys in horrid suits do it
Let's do it, let's fall in love.
We know that both of the Lunts did it
And they're still in their prime
McCarthy once did it
But it took a long time.
Those girls who change into chaps do it
Doctors say Roberta can perhaps do it
Let's do it, let's fall in love.

Four years later on July 24th at the same event the evolutionary process had taken another turn. The Belgians had been "rested" in favour of the Norwegians and some of the best of the Las Vegas lines had been incorporated . . .

*LET'S DO IT

He said Norwegians and Danes do it
Strange old gentlemen in trains do it
Let's do it, let's fall in love
Lollobrigida—My! My! does it
Alec Guinness on the Kwai does it
Let's do it, let's fall in love
The House of Lords, to a man, do it
If you know what I mean
Jayne Mansfield *can* do it
On a very wide screen
Every sardine you consume does it
Even Liberace we assume does it
Let's do it, let's fall in love.

In Texas some of the men do it
Others drill a hole and then do it
Let's do it, let's fall in love.
Each of those charming Gabors does it
Elvis Presley, forming fours, does it
Let's do it, let's fall in love.
We're *fairly* sure Kenneth Clark does it
When he isn't upset
All Regents Park does it
Under cover if wet
Teenagers, mostly self-taught do it
Readers of the Wolfenden Report do it
Let's do it, let's fall in love.
We have been told Evelyn Waugh does it
Willie Maugham at eight-four does it
Let's do it, let's fall in love.

We know that every hormone does it
Victor Borge, all alone, does it
Let's do it, let's fall in love.
Poor Lady Huggins, nonplussed, does it
In publicity's glare
Yul Brynner just does it
Without turning a hair
Mr. Onassis, in Greek, does it
Madame Callas with a piercing shriek, does it
Let's do it, let's fall in love.

Angry Young Men in Sloane Square do it
Both the Dockers, if you care, do it
Let's do it, let's fall in love
Margot Fonteyn, whirling round, does it
Michael Wilding, wired for sound, does it
Let's do it, let's fall in love.
Miss Nancy Spain cannot quite do it
When she's wearing those slacks
Even I might do it
But I'd have to pay tax
Each Sputnik, whizzing through space, does it
Rex, though he's accustomed to her face, does it
Let's do it, let's fall in love.

And finally, a more "local" version written for his Jamaican neighbours . . .

Roundhill investors, God knows, do it
Most De Lissers I suppose do it
Let's do it, let's fall in love.
Shareholders paying high rates do it
Everard and Stella Gates do it
Let's do it, let's fall in love.
The Wilsons, up on the hill do it
As an open air sport
Adèle can still do it
Read the "Kinsey " Report
Some barracudas and sharks do it
When they see that Joan and Henry Tiarks do it
Let's do it, let's fall in love.

Harper's Bazaar, Life and *Look* do it
Even Clive and Milly Brook do it
Let's do it, let's fall in love.
We know the dear Macadoos do it
Press reporters, if it's news, do it
Let's do it, let's fall in love
Bettina Ballard and Bill do it
In this tropical clime
Both Higgs and Hill do it
Though they take a *long* time.
Investors, when in a frizz do it
Though they're quite exhausted John and Liz do it
Let's do it—let's fall in love.

There are many more variant versions and you'll hear them in any Coward anthology show. The only trouble is that the performers—in their search for the topicality that permeated the original—have a habit of adding their own (uncredited) embellishments. Some lack scansion, most lack wit and, rather than stray accidentally off—Noël, let's not do it any further . . .

Top: *Noël's painting of workmen building the pool at Blue Harbor, Jamaica.* Bottom: *with Vivien Leigh on the beach in Jamaica.*
Following page: *Noël on porch at Blue Harbor.*

Noël and Beatrice Lillie, 1954

Noël, Elsa Maxwell and Cole Porter
partying in the '50s.

Charlie Chaplin, Mary Martin and
Noël, in the '50s.

Alfred Lunt, Lynn Fontanne, Cecil
Beaton and Noël, 1952.

TOGEHER
WITH
MUSIC

OCTOBER 1955

A 90 minute entertainment presented by "Ford Star Jubilee" on CBS TV network live and in colour from New York on October 22, 1955. Written and directed by Noël Coward for himself and Mary Martin, it contained some items written specially for the occasion.

Together With Music was to be Noël's TV debut as a performer, as opposed to a guest on an interview or chat show—part of a three show contract with CBS. The concept was a bold one—just the two of them with no supporting cast, minimal props and without the safety net of having the show filmed, as it would be today. Fresh from Las Vegas, his only insurance policy was to be the continuity of having Peter Matz take care of the orchestrations.

Noël invited Matz to join him and the Hallidays (Mary and her husband, Richard) in Jamaica to start preparation of their material:

"... by then I was a little more experienced ... and I remember being just in awe of the work that was going on, the quality of the rehearsal and the feeling—a dangerous feeling in terms of your ego—that something rather historical was happening here ... We would work separately in the mornings. I was doing the orchestrations and Noël was doing what he did, then we would meet at lunch, swim, and then rehearse all afternoon, have dinner and then rehearse a little bit more in the evening ..."

By the time the Hallidays arrived, Noël had written their two opening numbers—"Ninety Minutes is a Long, Long Time" and "Together With Music," which he played for them on their first evening:

"To my horror Mary took against 'Together With Music' very firmly indeed. I admired her honesty but it was dreadfully irritating and disappointing. Actually, I am afraid she is right, so I am now in the throes of rewriting and making it more romantic."

*TOGETHER WITH MUSIC

(First Version)

VERSE   Bear with us, bear with us, please.
We are both of us slightly over-wrought
For we're dreaming a dream we always thought
Would never quite come true for us.
Share with us, share with us, please
The excitement of standing hand in hand
While this very select, exclusive Band
Plays a personal Tattoo for us.
For many a year and many a day
We've laid our plans away
For many a day and many a year
We've prayed that somewhere, sometime
   we'd appear.

REFRAIN 1   Together with music,
Together with music
For us it is magic to walk
Out here, right near that orchestra
We're re-united and over-excited
For we're all set to lose our inhibitions
Just we two and a few musicians
Give us some light, Wire us for sound
And our personal world goes round and round
And our personal dreams will all come right
So don't turn your sets off
When we tear duets off
For we're together with music to-night.

REFRAIN 2   Together with music,
Together with music,
Forgive us for having a ball
But this is bliss enthralling us
We're highly paid for the one thing we're
   made for
Which is following through our true vocations
Just we two and some orchestrations.
Give us some brass, Give us some strings
And our personal world with rapture sings
And our personal skies are shining bright
You may long to choke us
But keep us in focus
For we're together with music to-night.

The second version, he felt, was "...better than the first, really, but it was bloody hell to do. However, now it is done and Mary's delighted and everybody's delighted."

TOGETHER WITH MUSIC

REFRAIN 1
BOTH: Together with music,
Together with music,
We planned this moment long ago,
Many a year we've sighed in vain
For both of us knew
Many a moon would wax and wane
Before this dream came true.
Together with music,
Together with music,
The thought of it enchants us so,
When those first chords crash out

NOËL: We know beyond a doubt
That everything's going to be divine

MARY: Watch us rise and shine
Riding as high as a kite

BOTH: Our hearts are fancy free
Because at long long last we happen to be
Together with music tonight,

VERSE   Bear with us, bear with us, please,
If we look a bit wild and overwrought,
But we're dreaming a dream we never thought
Would ever quite come true for us,
Share with us, share with us, please
The excitement of standing hand-in-hand
While this very select exclusive Band
Plays a personal Tattoo for us.
For many a year and many a day
We've laid our plans away
For many a day and many a year
We've prayed that somewhere, sometime
   we'd appear ...

REFRAIN 2
BOTH: Together with music,
Together with music,
Now suddenly our hearts feel gay,
Ever since that first day we met
We both of us guessed
Many a sun would rise and set
Before we coalesced
Together with music
Together with music
At last the Gods have said Okay,
When those first notes we hear
A million stars appear,

NOËL: Our personal world goes round and round

MARY: Gaily wired for sound

BOTH: Everything's shining and bright
This is our jubilee
Because at long long last we happen to be
Together with music tonight.

*REFRAIN 3
BOTH: Together with music
Together with music ...
And shadows seem to fade away.

Many a vanished moon and June
Enchant us again,
Many a long forgotten tune
Brings back its old refrain.

Together with music,
Together with music . . .
An orchestrated holiday,
We hear the beat of wings
When those romantic strings

NOËL: Play something remembered long ago,

MARY: Then, of course, we know

BOTH: Everything's bound to be right,
Because at long, long last we happen to be
Together with music tonight!

Noël scribbled alternatives . . .

Our hearts are riding high
We can't explain just why (And we can testify)
Our personal world goes round and round

NINETY MINUTES IS A LONG, LONG TIME

MARY: *(speaking to music)*
Noël dear,
Let's get things clear,
It's rather too late for bickering,
The warning lights are flickering,
We mustn't fool about.

NOËL: *(speaking to music)*
That's OK
But let me say
Before we go any farther, dear,
I'd really so much rather, dear,
You cut that number out.

(Singing) Apart from slowing up the pace
It truly isn't strong enough.

MARY: *(singing)*   Without that number in that place
Our programme won't be long enough.

BOTH: Ninety minutes is a long, long time,
A long, long time,
A long, long time,
To make people laugh
For an hour and a half
In this very exacting medium
Is a lot to expect
And the final effect
May be nothing but tears and tedium,
Don't imagine that we've not rehearsed
We did that first.
But fear the worst
We hope to amuse the customers with
    music and
With rhyme
But ninety minutes is a long, long time,
Ninety minutes is a long, long time.

FIRST REPRISE

> Ninety minutes is a long, long time,
> A long, long time,
> A long, long time,

MARY:
> We need the Rockettes
> And some marionettes
> And a handful of stars supporting us

NOËL:
> When we visualize
> All those millions of eyes,
> All those millions of screens distorting us,

BOTH:
> Don't imagine it's a bagatelle
> To cast a spell,
> We know darned well
> Whenever a song
> Goes on too long
> It isn't worth a dime
> And ninety minutes is a long, long time,
> Ninety minutes is a long, long time.

*SECOND REPRISE

BOTH:
> Ninety minutes is a long, long time,
> A long, long time,
> A long, long time,

MARY:
> We hope for success
> But we have to confess
> Our sponsors have spent a lot on us.

NOËL:
> Tho' talented fleas
> On a flying trapeze
> Might be certainly less monotonous.
> Don't imagine that we've lost our nerve

BOTH:
> But please observe
> We planned to serve.
> Our musical feast
> That should at least
> Appear to be sublime
> And ninety minutes is a long, long time—
> Ninety minutes is a long, long time.

An alternative unused couplet . . .

> We yearn for Bob Hope
> Danny Kaye or The Pope

Much of the show was devoted to medlies of the songs each of them had made famous but Noël did find time to squeeze in his version of "Deep In the Heart of Texas" (Mary's home state) . . . After singing the first few bars more or less straight, he segued into the Coward version of swing . . .

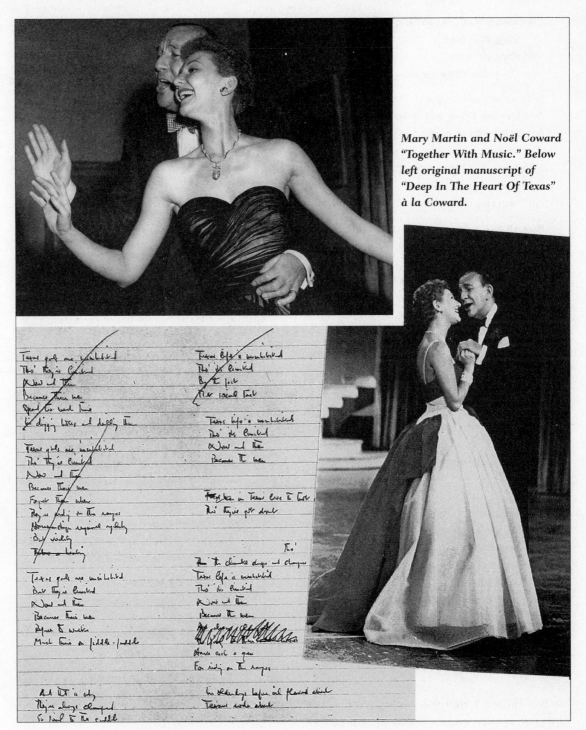

Mary Martin and Noël Coward "Together With Music." Below left original manuscript of "Deep In The Heart Of Texas" à la Coward.

*DEEP IN THE HEART OF TEXAS

(Hershey and Swander)

The husbands roam, no stopping them,
The wives go shopping,
Year after year the program never changes.

Though Texans can become stinking.
Every man without thinking,
Just gallivants out,
Wearing his pants out,
Ridin' on dem ranges.

Watch 'em comin' 'round the mountain,
Always comin' 'round that mountain,
And it couldn't be a greater bore.

When they yell loud 'n' strong—"Yip-ee!"—
Some cowboy song,
And whatever high notes they aim to hit,

They always, inevitably, end with: "Git
    along little dogie"
"Git along, git along,"
"Git along little dogie, get along."

In Texas they've only got the Brazos River,
And they like a tune with wow and zip in it,
Something with some vim and yip in it.
Rhythm has 'em rolling on the floor.
When they first heard some blue notes,
Somebody played a few notes,
No Texan asks for any more.

How I'd love a chart of
How they brought the art of
Be-bop to the Heart of Texas
Be-bop, Mambo, Samba, Conga too,
Day by day the urge is stronger to
Give those guys who don't like fun around
One big Texan rhythmic run-around.

Give them something to collapse about
When those cowboys flap their chaps about
Deep, deep, deep,
In the sleepy heart of TEXAS!

Noël's notes indicate that he went to a great effort to master the strange idiom. Among the many unused jottings . . .

    Texas girls are uninhibited
    But they're limited
    Now and then
    Because their men
    Don't spend
    Much time on fiddle-faddle
    And that is why
    They're always clamped
    So long to the saddle

*   *   *

He took further license with his introduction to a medley of nostalgic songs, when he adapted Carmen Lombardo and John Jacob Loeb's "Get Out Those Old Records" . . .

*GET OUT THOSE OLD RECORDS

(Lombardo and Loeb)

BOTH::   Get out those old records,
    Those old phonograph records,
    The ones we used to play so long ago.
    What if they sound scratchy,
    The tunes really were catchy.
    Remember how we used to love them so.
    They bring the past right into the present
    And they make the future shine
    For every one of them
    Each single one of them's
    A vocal Valentine
    Get out those old records,
    Those old phonograph records,
    The ones we used to play so long ago.

NOËL: I remember them all,
    I can also recall
    How you turned down every laddie
    With "My Heart Belongs to Daddy"

MARY: I've a memory too
    Of "A Room With A View"
    And that rather obsolete waltz
    Could I mean the *Bitter Sweet* waltz

NOËL: Mary, how the melodies vary
    When our memories capture
    The rapture
    Of all those gentle,
    Sentimental old records,

BOTH::   Those old phonograph records,
    The ones we used to play so long ago.

*   *   *

Another "novelty" number that was not used in the televised show was "Tit Willow" from *The Mikado*— Gilbert and Sullivan amended by Coward . . .

*TIT WILLOW

MARY: On a tree by a river
    A little tom tit
    Sang—"Willow, tit willow, tit willow"

NOËL: And I said to him—
    "Dickie Bird,
    Why do you sit
    Singing—"Willow, tit willow, tit willow"?"

MARY: "Is it weakness
    Of intellect,
    Birdie?" I cried
    "Or a rather tough worm
    In your little inside?"

NOËL: With a shake of his head
    He replied—

BOTH: "Tit, tit, tit, tit, tit, tit willow"

MARY: "Tit, tit, tit, tit, tit, tit willow"

BOTH::   We could not believe that the
    Song that we heard

MARY: "Tit, tit, tit, tit willow"

NOËL: "Tit, tit, tit, tit willow

BOTH::   Came from the throat of this
    Dear little bird

MARY: "Tit, tit willow"

NOËL: "Tit, tit willow"

MARY: "Is it weakness
    Of intellect
    Birdie?" I cried
    "Or a rather tough worm in your little inside?"

NOËL: Or the moment when Gilbert
    And Sullivan died?

MARY: Tit, tit, tit willow.

*   *   *

During one of the rehearsals Noël enjoyed the rare experience of having one of his lyrics criticised. An executive from Ford, who was sponsoring the show, asked him to cut some of the words of "Nina." "Why?" asked Noël in a dangerously icy tone. "You sing about her 'forever wriggling her guts,' the man from Ford said 'and we consider that vulgar.'" "Well," replied Noël, "you ought to know about vulgarity because I've just seen the commercial for your new model." Exit Ford party, pursued by inscrutable Coward smile. Señorita Nina continued to wriggle.

Ninety minutes was indeed a long time to fill in those primitive days of TV but fill it they did to the satisfaction of the important newspaper reviewers. "Channel 2 Rings Out With Song, Talent" enthused the *New York Times*, while the *New York Journal-American* rated "Coward's Debut Stylishly Magnificent." Noël wrote to his secretary, Lornie: "Compared to this, Las Vegas was like a bad matinée at Dundee."

LATER THAN SPRING

1956–1959

Reading the *Diaries*, it's easy to assume that *Sail Away* (1961) always existed in its own right and the show simply changed its name before it reached the stage. In fact, it had a much more complex genesis.

In early 1956 Noël was in Jamaica and "decided to use my peaceful mornings by writing a film script . . . a brittle, stylized, sophisticated, insignificant comedy with music and called *Later Than Spring* . . . from the suspense point of view it will be as unexpected as *Cosi Fan Tutte*." In his mind it would be a vehicle for himself and Marlene of Mozartian subtlety.

Two years later the film is forgotten and he has written two numbers for the stage musical that it has become—a waltz, "Time Will Tell" (later cut, transferred to *The Girl Who Came to Supper* and eventually cut from that, too) . . . "and a rattling good point number called 'Why Do the Wrong People Travel?'"

By this time Mozart was out and Mrs. Wentworth-Brewster (she of the Bar on the Piccola Marina) had taken over. Ethel Merman would, of course, play the part. We would follow the adventures of the lady who had so lately discovered that "life was for living," as she embarked on a cruise.

Naturally, there would be some changes. The implicitly overage and overweight matron of the song would be not only significantly glamourised—she would be "Americanized," too. His ideal casting was now Rosalind Russell, fresh from her success in Leonard Bernstein's *Wonderful Town*. After his recent disappointments in the West End, Noël was determined to have "a big fat hit" on Broadway instead.

While he waited to hear from Miss Russell, he mused in his *Diary* about the problem that would dog the show:

"The book . . . is causing me trouble . . . books for musicals invariably cause trouble . . . In a straight play you have time to develop your characters and lead up to and away from moments of crisis. In a musical you hardly have any time at all. The music and lyrics, on which the show really depends, interrupt all flow and sequence . . . I am sure the only thing to do is to finish the whole thing roughly and then go back and see what has to be pointed up, filled out, cut or re-done. I have no worries about the score or lyrics."

Rosalind Russell finally said no—so, having briefly considered Irene Dunne, he looked elsewhere: "I can make it fit Judy Holliday with some judicious alterations, and as there is a whole act virtually complete it would be stupid to rack my brains for something entirely different."

In the event he had to, since Judy Holliday didn't see herself in the role either. Why this surprised Noël is not quite clear. Few "mature" Broadway leading ladies have ever wanted to play the ugly duckling, even when the swan was waiting in the wings.

The first act and the songs it contained is all that remains of the original show. By December 1960 "I have decided to change the title . . . to *Sail Away*, which is a gayer title and more appropriate. I wrote yesterday a wonderful opening number for Kay Thompson . . ." Mrs. Wentworth-Brewster never got to take her reincarnatory cruise. Nor, as it happened, did Kay Thompson take the revised role . . .

Later Than Spring moved Polly Wentworth-Brewster from her "bijou abode in St. Barnabus Road, not far from the Esher by-pass" to "a small town in Massachusetts" and turned her into an American. As the play opens the various family members are gathered there to mourn her recently deceased husband, Calvin, whom they have just laid to rest. No one is happy with the will and the various uncles and aunts make their feelings known.

*FAMILY DIRGE

ALL: Hand of implacable destiny
Has lopped a bough from our family tree
And though our hearts unquestionably ache
We're afraid there's been some hideous mistake
Not in the fact of being bereft
But because of the will our loved one left,
The irritating will our loved one left.

AUNT CALLY: I who gave him a rocking horse

UNCLE HILARY: I who encouraged him to play the game

UNCLE PAWNIE: I who set his mathe-e-matic course
Have not been left so much as a photograph frame

UNCLE HILARY: I who gave him a pocket knife

AUNT CALLY: I who brought him all that butter-scotch

AUNT SARAH: I who taught him the facts of life
Have not been left so much as an Ingersoll watch

ALL: Ingratitude, ingratitude
The sin of age,
The curse of youth
Ingratitude, ingratitude
More bitter than a serpent's tooth

AUNT SARAH: I who nursed him and watched him grow

UNCLE HILARY: I his voluntary football coach

AUNT CALLY: I who read him Edgar Allan Poe
Have not been left so much as a cameo brooch

AUNT SARAH: I who taught him his childish prayers

UNCLE HILARY: I who saved him from that ghastly blonde

UNCLE PAWNIE: I who advised him on stocks and shares
Have not been left so much as a government bond

ALL: A blind implacable whim of fate
Has whisked our darling through heaven's gates
Before he'd time to turn around and pause
Just to add one small subsidiary clause
Which might have eased our heart's discontent
On reading his will and testament,
His *idiotic* will and testament

Polly enters, "a pleasant looking woman in her early forties . . . she looks a trifle older than she really is, because she has never devoted much time to her appearance. Her figure, however, is passable, although her nondescript hair is turning grey." None of which could be expected to survive the first act. She shocks the assembled family by telling them that she is leaving within days on a Mediterranean cruise, taking Aunt Cally with her. "I'm independent and free for the first time in my life."

*NOW I'M A WIDOW

Now I'm a widow
And free from restrictions
I placidly bow to my fate
No more a slave to those fusses and frictions
That daily disfigure the conjugal state
All the swot of it
I'm well shot of it
And I'm glad of this chance to explain
Losing or winning
Excuse me for grinning
My life is beginning again

Now I'm a widow
Alone and foresaken,
A middle aged mother and wife,
Left with no husband to bring home the bacon,
I'm firmly determined to start a new life.
If I'm crazy,
Whoops-a-daisy!
And the hell with what people may say.
Dressed in my beautiful
Mourn - ing -
Everything's coming my way!

*   *   *

In Scene 2 we are on the cruise ship. The Chief Steward briefs the stewards on what is expected of them in a number that was transferred intact to *Sail Away* . . . "The Passenger's Always Right" (See p. 322).

(See p. 322).

Now the rest of the principal characters arrive.

There's Max (Prince Maximilian McCropolis Vulponi), described as a "handsome, distinguished man in his mid-40s, impeccably dressed and becomingly suntanned." He introduces himself in song . . .

*HOME

VERSE 1

I'm Prince Maximilian McCropolis Vulponi
My forebears were French
And Italian and Greek
My accent is sometimes a tiny bit phoney
Depending of course on which language I speak
My mother's mama was of Russian extraction
My father's papa was a Spanish grandee
So always I have the supreme satisfaction
Of knowing wherever I happen to be
That I'm . . .

REFRAIN 1

Home,
Home,
Home like the hunter
I'm home like the sailor returned from the sea
I'm at home
Home.
Home like the swallow who east, north or west
Finds some sort of nest
I've an uncle in Chile
And two rather silly
Old aunts on the outskirts of Rome
So wherever I go
It's delightful to know
That I'm home, home, home.

REFRAIN 2

I'm at home,
Home,
Home in the Andes
I'm home in Hong Kong
And the streets of Jahore
I'm at home
Home,
Home sipping brandies in drab English clubs
With my brothers-in-law.
I've a bachelor flat just beyond Ancorevat
And a fairly big igloo in Nome
So wherever I stray
I can truthfully say
That I'm home, home, home
Wherever I stray
I can truthfully say
That I'm home, home, home.

VERSE 2

To explain my unique cosmopolitan demeanour
It's simpler I think to go back to my birth
Which occurred on a yacht in the Straits of
        Messina
En route from Shanghai to the City of Perth
This caused all my Scottish relations to ponder
My mother, of course, was a trifle upset
From that moment onwards
I started to wander
And frankly I haven't stopped wandering yet . . .

REFRAIN 3

Home,
Home,
Home, dancing tangos
With dubious ladies in Argentine bars
I'm at home
Home,
Home munching mangoes beneath
Those monotonous tropical stars
In my bijou pink villa
Due north of Manila
I keep an old toothbrush and comb
So wherever I move
I can certainly prove
That I'm home, home, home

REFRAIN 4

I'm at home
Home,
Home on the Pampas
I'm home on Mont Blanc
Or the green Sussex Downs
I'm at home
Home
Home on the campus
Of some of those strange university towns
I've dozens and dozens
Of charming white cousins
And some that are candidly chrome
So in any old nation despite segregation
I'm home, home, home
In any old nation despite segregation
I'm home, home home

Had the show ever come to the stage, Noël might well have found that particular song a problem, since it bears a marked resemblance to Cole Porter's "I've a Shooting Box in Scotland," down to one virtually identical line. Porter writes: "I've an igloo up at Nome," while nearly fifty years later Noël's Prince sings of "a fairly big igloo in Nome." He then goes on to confide . . .

So wherever I go
It's delightful to know
That I'm home, home, home.

. . . just as Porter had previously concluded . . .

Yes, in travelling
It's really quite a comfort to know
That you're never far from home.

This would by no means be the first time one song writer had "absorbed" another's work and then forgotten he'd heard it. The Porter song (from *See America First* 1916) had, after all, not been played in many years. Sooner or later Noël would have realised what he'd done.

*   *   *   *

Also on the cruise is Tamarinda Bruce (in an earlier draft, Malina Drury), "a platinum, double-breasted movie star," clearly based on Marilyn Monroe. She has recently been divorced from Max and is taking the cruise to get away from it all—in apparent ignorance of who else is on board. In the synopsis she is supposed to have a solo number, "I'm Tired of Being Me," which Noël didn't get around to writing.

Max and Polly soon find themselves attracted to each other. She fights the feeling. How can this be happening to a middle-aged woman? Max reassures her . . .

"Don't have doubts about 'leaving things too late.' Doubts about the years hurrying by—it's a waste of time. Spring is all right in its way, so is high Summer, but Autumn can sometimes be the best of all . . ."

LATER THAN SPRING

(*Max*)

Have no fears for future years
For sweet compensation you may find,
Make your bow
To the moment that is now
And always bear in mind:

REFRAIN 1 Later than Spring

The warmth of Summer comes,
The charm of Autumn comes,
The leaves are gold.
Poets say
That the blossoms of May
Fade away
And die.
Yet, don't forget
That we met
When the sun was high.

Later than Spring
Words that were said before,
Tears that were shed before
Can be consoled.
Realize that it's wise to remember
Though Time is on the wing,
Song birds still sing
Later than Spring.

REFRAIN 2 Later than Spring
Though careless rapture's past
No need to gaze aghast
At days gone by,
You can still if you will
Feel the thrill
Of a new desire,
Still
Feel that glow
When you know
That your world's on fire.
Later than Spring
Remembered April showers
May bring our present hours
A clearer sky.
We pretend and pretend it's the end
But the pendulum must swing,
Nightingales sing
Later than Spring

REPRISE
POLLY: Later than Spring
Much disillusion comes,
Sometimes confusion comes,
You lose your way.
Need it be such unbearable sadness
To face the truth?
Love, with its passionate madness
Belongs to youth.
Later than Spring
Our values change, my dear,
It would be strange, my dear,
If they should stay.
Waste no tears

On the hurrying years,
For whatever they may bring
Song birds still sing
Later than Spring.

*   *   *

The notes contain an extra verse the title suggested to Noël in a less romantic vein . . .

*"Have no fears
For future years"
May sound very brave and true
But I hold
With regard to growing old
A less romantic view.

Later than Spring
The first Bursitis comes
The first Arthritis comes
And that's not all.
No reprieve—when the arteries harden
You've run your race
Even Elizabeth Arden
Can't save your face.
Later than Spring
Enamelled skin appears,
Chin after chin appears,
The arches fall.
With regard to the nightingales singing
I don't care if they 'swing'
Every damned thing
Later than Spring.

*   *   *

Later, when Polly and Aunt Cally leave the cruise to tour Europe, Max follows her. In fact, not surprisingly, all the leading characters happen to find themselves in the same small hotel in Paris, where Max serenades her.

*I WANTED TO SHOW YOU PARIS

(*Max*)

I wanted to show you Paris
In the spring of the year
When all the blossoms are flaming gaily

Proclaiming high romance is near.
I wanted to walk beside you
On the banks of the Seine
And to recapture that by-gone day
When I first saw those barges drifting by.
Along the boulevards and down the Champs-Élysées
There's music in the air
The lilting melodies of Offenbach and Bizet
Are still echoing there.
This beautiful day for me will stay forever sublime
If I can show you this world I know
For the very first time.

VERSE

Many of the dreams we dream
Are doomed to disappoint in reality,
Many of the schemes we scheme
Have little to redeem them from banality
But in this enchanted minute
Share my dream for you are in it
Making true all I've looked forward to.

I wanted to show you Paris
In the spring of the year
For when this ever beguiling city is smiling
Troubles disappear
I wanted to walk beside you
Through the trees of the Bois
And to remember that day that once I knew
When I was gay and young like you

With implications we'll refuse all invitations
The world considers chic
We'd rather plan on seeing *Manon*
At the Opéra Comique three times a week
This wonderful day for me will stay forever sublime
If you will share it, my love, with me
For the very first time.

. . . a song which Polly is later to reprise . . .

*PARIS (REPRISE)

(Polly)

How lovely to be in Paris
In the spring of the year
For when this ever beguiling city Is smiling
Troubles disappear.
How lovely to watch the dancing world

Go hurrying by
And to remember this warm enchanted glow
Stars above and lights below.
Although I cannot understand
A word they're saying, until my dying day
I'll call to mind the kind
Of music they are playing
And feel suddenly gay
This wonderful day for me
Will stay forever sublime
Because I'm feeling
That life's worthwhile
For the very first time.

Another character, destined as the comic lead, is Skid Cabot, "oppressively handsome and his clothes are Beverley Hills to the last stitch." Not surprisingly, he and Tamarinda fall in love and share a love song of sorts.

*LET'S BE SINCERE

SKID: Let's be sincere
Every day of every year
Let's stay true
Me and you

TAMARINDA: You and me, dear

SKID: Let's you and I

TAMARINDA: You and me

SKID: Together try
Just to prove
How sincere
Life can be, dear.

TAMARINDA: Let's keep searching for that Bluebird
And however blue we feel
Let's be absolutely genuine
And absolutely real

SKID: Let's be co-starred
On Life's Sunset Boulevard
Let's we two

TAMARINDA: Let's us two

BOTH: Be sincere.

TAMARINDA: Let's be sincere
Every day of every year
Let's be true

To ourselves
And to others

SKID: Let's never sneer
At those prayers
We used to hear
At the knee
Of our white-headed mothers

TAMARINDA: Let's keep looking for that Rainbow
To which poets have referred

SKID: Let us prove that true "Togetherness"
Is more than just a word

TAMARINDA: Let's I and you

SKID: You and I

TAMARINDA: Remain true blue
Through and through
Let's us two
Be sincere

*   *   *

After the first few scenes the plot becomes sketchy, as Noël found himself running into the kind of troubles he had foreseen. The notes indicate other intended songs. For instance, Polly, Aunt Cally and Calvin Jr. (who also got to make the trip after all) would sing about "There Are Good Times Coming."

*THERE ARE GOOD TIMES COMING

ALL: There are good times coming for the three of us,
There's adventure knocking at the door.

POLLY: We shall know, we shall see
Just how wonderful life can be

CALVIN: If we open wide our arms to it and take it on the jaw.

AUNT CALLY: Although nobody back home does
When in Rome we'll do as Rome does

ALL: And we'll definitely have ourselves a ball.

POLLY: We may run into trouble and receive some nasty shocks,

AUNT CALLY: Our ships of dreams may founder and be stranded on the Rocks

Above: Label for record demo of songs from Later Than Spring. Left: Noël in the recording studio.

CALVIN: But as long as mother loves you and she
              holds a lot of Stocks—

ALL: There are good times coming for us all

AUNT CALLY: And should my arteries harden
                 I'll rush to Baden-Baden

POLLY: And when I'm well
              I'll run pell mell
              To the arms of Elizabeth Arden

There was another duet, presumably intended for Polly and Max . . .

*YOU AND I

You and I have wandered through a lovely day
And come what may
It belongs to us
We'll remember it when we are far away
And sirens sing other songs to us

We have moved together through a private
    dream
And even though we wake from it
Nothing can ever take from it
This memory we hold
It is ours alone,
It is ours alone.
Let our future be consoled
By the sweetest dream that we have ever known.
You and I have wandered through a lovely day
And come what may it belongs to us.

The sea is silver grey
And one by one
Down the pathway of the setting sun
Fishing boats steer
Far out across the bay
The shadows creep
Soon the vivid day will fall asleep
Night will be here
Why must the sunlight fade away
Hiding the sea and the shore?
Couldn't the dark have stayed away
One minute more,
One minute more?

. . . another (early) solo for Polly to express her loneliness . . .

*WHY AM I ALWAYS ALONE?

Why am I always alone?
Why am I longing for only
Somebody tender and gentle beside me
Someone to lead me, love me, guide me?
Winter makes way for the Spring
Why is my heart doomed to linger
In an unoccupied zone?
Why am I always alone?

. . . and another duet, which may have been for the
principals but could easily have been for another
secondary couple of passengers never developed in
the synopsis. In the subsequent book for *Sail Away*
Noël was to follow this structure and it seems reasonable to infer something similar was intended
here—but his notes leave no further clues.

*WHEN THE JOURNEY'S OVER

REFRAIN 1 When the journey's over and we're home again
We'll remember every single day
All the thrills, all the joys.
Already part of the past
Fading so fast
Away.
If we never have the chance to roam again
We'll have learned a lot we never knew before
Like a dream
These wonderful weeks will seem
When we are home once more.

REFRAIN 2 When the journey's over and we're home again
In the old, monotonous routines
Shall we feel gay or sad
When we remember the strange
Pattern of changing
Scenes?
Will our restless hearts desire to roam again?
Shall we long for some remote, enchanted
    shore?
Gay or sad
We'll nevertheless be glad
To be at home once more.

REFRAIN 3 When the journey's over and we're home
    again
On the porch each evening we will sit
While we stare at "Transparencies"
And albums of "Prints"
Maybe we'll wince
A bit
We'll re-live each day in Kodachrome again
Though the neighbours may consider us a bore
How our folks
Will dread all our travel jokes
When we are home once more.

*   *   *

In Act 2 Noël went so far as to write a disembodied
scene in "Tamarinda's Suite." Tamarinda is surrounded by her entourage. Also present is a
Freud-type "Professor." The entourage serenade
Tamarinda, who is lying on her couch.

SCENE IN TAMARINDA'S SUITE

(TAMARINDA *is lying on a couch surrounded by* MONTY, AMY, PIPI, GREFF *and* DELIA. *Behind her the* PROFESSOR *is seated on a chair with a note-book in his hand.*)

ALL: (*Singing*)
    Little Princess with golden hair,
    What are you thinking of, lying there?
    Knights in armour from old Castile?

TAMARINDA: I'm thinking of Skid—the lousy heel.

ALL: Beautiful girl by Nature blest,
    What are you thinking of—there at rest
    Like the Lily-Lady of Astolat?

TAMARINDA: I'm thinking of Skid—the two-faced rat.

ALL: Skid—Skid—Skid!
    Nobody else but Skid
    Morning till night
    It's always the same.
    Sober or tight
    She bellows his name.
    Rockabye Baby, the cradle will rock
    Brother, has she got a mental block!
    And whatever the bastard said or did
    It's Skid—Skid Skid.

PROFESSOR: (*Speaking*) You'd better leave her to me.
    She should never have been allowed to see that
    copy of *Photoplay* anyway.

MONTY: She got it at a newstand when we weren't
    looking. How were we to know there'd be a
    picture of him in it with that Swedish broad at
    the Stork Club?

PROFESSOR: Go away all of you. I'll deal with this.

TAMARINDA: (*Sitting up*) I don't want them to go away.
    I want to play 'Gin' with Monty.

MONTY: Hush, Honey. Do what the Professor says.

TAMARINDA: It's the only thing that takes my mind off
    my broken heart.

PROFESSOR: (*With authority*) Out! (*They file out. To*
    TAMARINDA) Lie down again dear. I want you to
    answer some nice easy questions.

TAMARINDA: I'm sick of nice easy questions. What good
    are they supposed to do? I've told you about my
    brother and the rabbits, and how Momma got

stung by a bee when she was pregnant. What more d'you want to know?

PROFESSOR: Lie back and relax.

TAMARINDA: And so I relax—and so I answer your God-damned questions and you put what I say down in a book and what happens? Does my mental block get any smaller? Like Hell it does!—It just gets bigger and bigger and bigger with every breath I take.

PROFESSOR: Quiet Honey—Close your eyes.
(TAMARINDA *sulkily does so. He sings*)
Can you remember, as a tot,
Lying alone in your tiny cot
Waiting for Mummy's loving hand
To waft her darling to slumberland?

TAMARINDA: *(Spoken)*
If I'd waited for Mummy's loving call
I'd never have got any sleep at all.

PROFESSOR: *(Singing)*
Can you remember the Candy Store
And the games in the yard with the boy next door?

TAMARINDA: *(Spoken)*
You don't have a yard or a boy next door
In a cold-water flat on the sixteenth floor.

PROFESSOR: *(Singing)*
Can you remember, for instance, when
You first became interested in men?

TAMARINDA: *(Spoken)*
I knew damn well since the age of three
That men were interested in me.

PROFESSOR: *(Singing)*
But there must have been a moment when you tossed your childish curls
And realised you weren't quite the same as other girls?

---

*WHEN DID YOU FIRST DISCOVER YOU WERE DIFFERENT?

REFRAIN 1 When did you first discover you were different?

When, Oh, when did you first become aware
That a psychosomatic tendency was lurking
And some rather important glands were over-working?
When you dreamed improper
Dreams about your Poppa
Did you resort to penitence and prayer?
Whether you did or not, my dear,
It's all too clear
That you are not—quite—square.

REFRAIN 2 When did you first discover you were different?
When, oh, when could you accurately tell
That the rather bizarre formation of your bust meant
You were suffering from some basic maladjustment?
Did some crisis throw you?
Did your brother show you
Anything that your instincts might repel?
Whether he did or not, my dear,
It's all too clear
That you are not—quite—well.

REFRAIN 3 When did you first discover you were different?
When, Oh, when did your clock begin to tick?
Was the moment you lost belief in your Creator
When they told you about the birds and bees—or later?
Did your nurse ill-treat you?
Did your mother beat you
Regularly with slipper, hand, or stick?
Whether she did or not, my dear,
It's all too clear
That you are sick—sick—sick.

*   *   *

During their stay in Paris—in a fragmentary scene not indicated in the full script—Polly and Aunt Cally inevitably visit a French restaurant and inevitably have trouble with the language. Polly takes out her phrasebook and to Aunt Cally's embarrassment tries to order. Noël appears not to have completed the song—or, at least, not until he transformed it into "Useless Useful Phrases" in *Sail Away* (See p. 323).

POLLY: *(With phrase book)*
Waiter!
*Apportez-moi deux tasses de thé . . .
trois de thé, deux*
Consommés.

---

*Fonds d'artichaut.
Deux têtes de veau.*

AUNT CALLY: Don't, darling, you'll confuse him so.

POLLY: *Trois soles meunières.
Une bonne grillade*

AUNT CALLY: This poor man thinks you're raving mad.

POLLY: I'd like one fork, two forks, three forks
And a knife and a strawberry flan
And I wouldn't say *Non*
To a *saucisson*
And a small pot roast
With some melba toast

AUNT CALLY: Don't torture the poor young man

POLLY: I don't care for this table.
This is a very nice table.
Bring me a serviette.
I have three serviettes . . .

*   *   *

By this time, Noël had obviously realised this particular cruise was going nowhere and it was time to sail away . . .

The Master takes tea in Jamaica . . .

MISCELLANEOUS THE 1950s

Most of the "miscellaneous" songs Noël wrote in the 1950s finally found a home in one or other of his cabaret acts. One that didn't—perhaps because it was neither romantic nor acerbic enough was:

A RIBBON IN HER HAIR (1955)

VERSE:

In an album filled with daguerrotypes
A youthful face
Full of grace
Shines among the prim straight and narrow types
On every yellowing page,
Great Aunt Millicent Gertrude May
Photographed on a winter's day
Tripping home from a bygone school
In a very, very bygone age.

REFRAIN

With her books and her satchel and a ribbon in
    her hair
And a neat winter coat discreetly braided,
You can see from the picture she was exquisitely
    fair,
Although the background's slightly faded,
She was like a day in spring,
Eyes rather wide apart,
Head held a little bit high,
Something worth remembering,
If you had seen her pass by,

Nobody could deny
She was gay and enchanting as a fairy tale retold
As she strolled every evening through the square
With her books, pencil box and school satchel
And a bright blue ribbon in her hair.

The archive contains an extra refrain which casts a slightly more jaundiced light on Great Aunt Millicent's eventual fate . . .

With her gloves and her bouquet and a veil upon
    her hair
She was led by her father to the altar,
Having coaxed rather cleverly a multi-Millionaire
To share the matrimonial halter.

(The song was originally sung by Graham Payn in his own cabaret debut at the Café de Paris.)

*   *   *

Words were a reflex action with Noël. To amuse or cheer up a member of the "family" who might appear to be flagging, he would dash off a few lines of light verse but it might just as easily be a song lyric, which expressed the momentary thought but which he had no intention of producing or performing.

One such occasion followed a lively debate he and Cole Lesley had been having about Mary Baker Eddy, the well-known faith healer and founder of Christian Science, about whom Noël had strong and negative views. When Coley was confined to bed a little later, Noël sent him medicine and then appeared to render the following song, "sung with gusto to a racy tune." The lines later appeared in the *Collected Verse* but began life as a lyric . . .

*WHAT A SAUCY GIRL

Steady, steady, Mary Baker Eddy,
You've got to play the final scene.
Admit that it's distasteful
To say that pain ain't painful
What about some more morphine?
In your great fight with sin, come
Admit you made an income
Far greater than your friend the Nazarene,
Steady, steady, Mary Baker Eddy,
What a saucy girl you've been!

Ian Fleming.

*   *   *

In Jamaica, he wrote another "private" song to celebrate the long awaited wedding in 1952 of his friend and neighbour, writer Ian Fleming to Ann, the former Lady Rothermere. For years their affair had been a well kept secret as the lady found occasion to leave Lord Rothermere to run his Kemsley Press and *The Daily Mail*, while she ran off to her paramour's Jamaican retreat, Goldeneye. Hence the title.

Goldeneye appears to have been a house of surpassing discomfort—at least to Noël, who once borrowed it and claimed it reminded him of a hospital. He christened it "Goldeneye, Nose, Throat and Ear."

*GOLDENEYE CALYPSO

Mongoose dig about sunken garden
Mongoose murmur "Oh my—Oh my!
No more frig about—beg your pardon
Things are changing at Goldeneye!

Mongoose say to Annee
Mongoose say to Annee
Your man shady as mango tree

**Painting by Noël Coward
of the sunken garden at Ian
Fleming's house Goldeneye
at Oracabessa in Jamaica.**

Sweet as honey from bee.

Hey for the Alka-Seltzer
Ho for the Aspirin
Hey for the saltfish, ackee, ganja, Booby's
    eggs, Gordon's gin.

Mongoose listen to white folks wailin'
Mongoose giggle, say, "Me no deaf.
No more waffle and Daily Mailin'
Annie Rothermere's Madame F."

Mongoose say to Annee
Carlyle Mansions N.G.
Goldeneye a catastrophee
White Cliffs too near the sea.

Hey for the blowfish, blowfish.
Ho for the wedding ring
Hey for the Dry Martinis, old goat fricassee,
    Old Man's Thing.

Mongoose love human sacrifices
Mongoose snigger at Human Race
Can't have wedding without the Bryces,
Both the Stephensons, Margaret Case.

Mongoose say to Annee
Now you get your decree
Once you lady of high decree
Now you common as me.

Hey for the piggly-wiggly
Ho for the wedding dress
Hey for the Earl of Dudley, Loelia
    Westminster, Kemsley Press.

There were many other offerings that had the recipients too busy laughing to write them down.

There were one or two odd songs written during the 50s—one of them very odd indeed. The song is entirely in Spanish and is accompanied by a so-called "translation." The likeliest explanation is that Noël was attempting a revue sketch which satirised the way the most romantic songs in foreign languages can be brought to nought when rendered into our literal unromantic prose . . .

*MATADOR

I dream of past triumphs
My dreams are blood stained

I remember in all bull fights
The joy in my heart—
Hurray, Hurray!
The joy in my heart,
The hours so entertaining.

He had infinitely more success with the Italian language and a Venetian setting . . .

*LAST WEDNESDAY ON THE PIAZZA

Last Wednesday on the Piazza
Near San Marco's rococo *Duomo*
I observed *una grassa ragazza*
With a thin, middle Western *uomo*.

He was swatting a *piccola mosca*
She was eating a chocolate *gelato*
While an orchestra played (from *La Tosca*)
A flat violin *obligato*.

They stared at a dusty *piccione*
They spoke not a single *pârole*
She ordered some *té con limone*
He ordered an iced Coca-Cola.

And while the *tramonto del sole*
Set fire to the *Grande Canale*
She scribbled haphazard *postale*.

Alternative version:

Last Wednesday on the Piazza
In the shade of that bulbous *Duomo*
I was eating a chocolate *gelato*
While a stupid untalented *uomo*
Was playing a flat *obligato*
To a rather self-conscious *ragazza*

The fluttering, dusty *piccione*
Lethargic from guzzling *pane*
Were circling round the *Triniti*

Allora, un poco piu tardi
He gave an enormous *stradiglio*

*   *   *

There are several other typed lyrics, which date the

---

material as post-war. From the content they may have been first drafts of material originally intended for shows and then discarded. Until and unless further evidence comes to light that assigns them elsewhere . . .

*LONG AGO

Long ago
Joy seemed unending.
We were slow
To know the things we'd miss.
We could dine and dance
And follow romance.
Ah what pains we took
There were fat cigars
And restaurant cars
On the trains we took.
Did we know
Night was descending
On this Oh,
So ignorant bliss?
We could laugh and play
And gamble away
The gains we took
That was so
Long ago.

*YOU AND YOU ALONE

You and you alone
Have brought me all the joy I've ever
    known
You've taught me to forget the tears
Of other years
Now my fears have flown
All my love I'll show to you
All my heart must go to you
All I have in life I owe to you
You and you alone.

THE 1960s

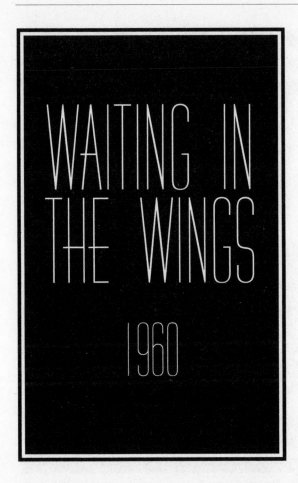

WAITING IN THE WINGS

1960

Presented by F. E. S. Plays in association with Michael Redgrave Productions at the Duke of York's Theatre, London on September 7, 1960.

Cast included Dame Sybil Thorndike, Marie Lohr, Mary Clare, Graham Payn, Una Venning, Maidie Andrews, Betty Hare, Norah Blaney, Edith Day, Maureen Delany, Lewis Casson, Margot Boyd, William Hutt.

The action of the play takes place in the lounge of "The Wings," a charity home for retired actresses.

In their various ways all the ladies are living in their past, some more contentedly than others. References to their past successes, real or imagined, abound:

MAUD: I was in *Miss Mouse* at the Adelphi and I had a number in the last act called "Don't Play the Fool with a Schoolgirl." It used to stop the show.

CORA: So far as I can remember it was the notices that stopped the show.

At one point a well-meaning journalist writes an article about "These old faithful servants of the public, wearily playing out the last act of their lives, all passion spent, all glamour gone, unwanted and forgotten, just waiting—waiting in "The Wings."

BONITA: That would make a wonderful number.

MAUD: I've got it (*She plays a few chords on the piano and sings*)

*WAITING IN THE WINGS

MAUD: Waiting in the Wings,
  Older than God,
  On we plod,
  Waiting in the Wings.

BONITA: (*Joining in*)
  Hopping about the garden
  Like a lot of Douglas Byngs,

MAUD AND BONITA:
  Waiting, waiting, waiting in the Wings.

Later, at their Christmas party, several of the ladies go into their party pieces:

*CHAMPAGNE

MAUD: Champagne—Champagne—Champagne,
  So sublime, so divine, so profane
  It fizzes and bubbles,
  And banishes troubles,
  Champagne, Champagne, Champagne.

BONITA: That's a common little lyric if ever I heard one.

MAUD: It's the waltz from *Miss Mouse*. Poor Dolly Drexell sang it at the end of the second act; she had a big head-dress of ostrich feathers and they kept getting in her mouth.

LOTTIE: Play the other one, Maudie, the one I like, about little bits of cheese.

MAUD: Oh, dear—I can't remember much of it—wait a minute.

*MISS MOUSE

MAUD: Won't you come and live in my house—
  Miss Mouse?

ALL: Miss Mouse

MAUD: It's as sweet as any apple-pie house, Miss Mouse

ALL: Miss Mouse

MAUD: I will give you honey from the bees,
  Bread and milk and lovely bits of cheese
  Please, please, please, please, please, please, please
  Come and live in my house—

ALL: Come and live in my house—

MAUD: Come and live in my house—

ALL: Miss Mouse

MAUD: (*Laughing*) That really is the most idiotic song I Ever heard.

MAUD: Come on, Bonita—"Over the Hill I'll Find You"

BONITA: Good God, no—it's too long ago—I couldn't.

MAUD: Come on—I'll prompt you.

*OVER THE HILL

(Music by Norah Blaney)

BONITA: Over the hill I'll find you
  There by the murmuring stream
  And the birds in the woods behind you
  Will echo our secret dream
  There in the twilight waiting,
  Gentle, serene and still,
  All the cares of the day
  Will be banished away
  When I find you over the hill,
  When I find you over the hill.

DEIDRE: Sentimental poppycock!

MAUD: The words are a little sugary but it's a very pretty tune.

BONITA: That'll go better second house

MAUD: What was that number you did in *Two's a Crowd*, Perry?

COME THE WILD, WILD WEATHER

(Graham Payn)

Time may hold in store for us
Glory or defeat,
Maybe never more for us
Life will seem so sweet
Time will change so many things,
Tides will ebb and flow,
But wherever fate may lead us
Always we shall know—

Come the wild, wild weather,
Come the wind and the rain,
Come the little white flakes of snow,
Come the joy, come the pain,
We shall still be together
When our life's journey ends,
For wherever we chance to go
We shall always be friends.
We may find while we're travelling through the years
Moments of joy and love and happiness,
Reason for grief, reason for tears.
Come the wild, wild weather,
If we've lost or we've won,
We'll remember these words we say
Till our story is done.

* * *

In the final scene, the "guests" are awaiting the latest arrival—Topsy Baskerville. Several of them knew her in "the old days."

BONITA: I was with her at the Hippodrome during the first war, in Nineteen-fifteen. She sang "Oh, Mr. Kaiser."

*OH, MR. KAISER

MAUD: Oh, Mr. Kaiser,
See your legal advier
You've bitten off much more than you can chew
For when Mr. Tommy Atkins comes a-marching

Left to right, Graham Payn, Sybil Thorndike, Una Venning and Mary Clare, "Waiting in the Wings."

To Berlin
You'll be gibbering like a monkey in the Zoo
Have a banana!

MAUD AND BONITA:
Oh, Mr. Kaiser,
When you're older and wiser
You'll learn some things you never learnt
at school.
When we've wound up the watch on your
dear old Rhine,
You're going to look a Potsdam fool.

The play ends with Topsy arriving as they play her song . . .

* * *

Noël was particularly fond of period pastiche and used it frequently in his early revues. In *Cavalcade*, in addition to the real songs of turn of the century Victoriana and World War I patriotism, he employed once again the show-within-the-show device to add a few of his own. In *Waiting In the Wings* the age of the ladies provided him with the opportunity to pay affectionate tribute to the songs from the music hall and operetta of his youth. Yes, they were "idiotic" and "sentimental poppycock" but they evoked a pace and grace of living and he still regretted its passing.

In *Ace of Clubs* he had done the same—though with less affection—for the cheerful emptiness of third rate 1940s night club floor shows and he was to attempt it one more time, when he summoned up Cockney cockiness in the "London" sequence of *The Girl Who Came to Supper.*

"Cheap music" remained strangely, extraordinarily potent to the end . . .

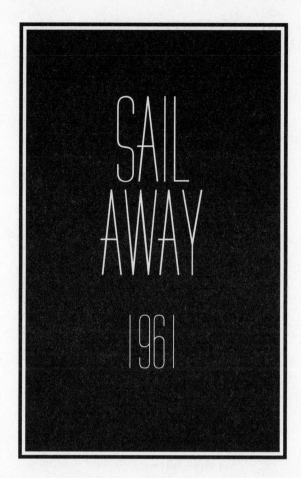

First presented by Bonnard Productions at the Colonial Theatre, Boston on August 9, 1961 and subsequently at the Broadhurst Theatre, New York on October 3, 1961. (167 performances.)

Cast included Elaine Stritch, James Hurst, Grover Dale, Patricia Harty, Charles Braswell. Jean Fenn and William Hutt were in the original cast but their parts were cut before the show reached New York.

The change of title was more than symbolic; it brought out Noël the surgeon. He determined that the reason he couldn't cast the main role was that she was essentially unattractive. Mrs. Wentworth-Brewster would have to go. In early 1961 he records: "Last night I decided to perform a major operation and cut Max and Polly out entirely. They are neither of them real and never were . . . they are hangovers from that abortive enterprise and have been worrying me ever since . . ."

The setting switched to a British cruise liner, the S.S.Coronia with the heroine, Mimi Paragon, a cruise director who has seen the horrors of tours and tourists more than once before and whose patience is beginning to wear a little thin—just as Noël's was as a professional traveller in a world increasingly populated by amateurs. But who should play Mimi?

Then he remembered being impressed in an unimpressive 1958 show (Goldilocks) by a girl who had something of an Ethel Merman quality, a combination of the streetwise and the soft hearted. He called her and Elaine Stritch was hired.

He records in the Diary that the show came to him easily. "The opening number," he felt "is exactly right and my talent for lyrics obviously hasn't abandoned me. I had begun the tune before but now three refrains are complete and the verses will be easy. Verses always are."

Joe Layton, who choreographed the show, remembers Noël's distinctive work habits from that period. Layton paid a visit to Chalet Coward:

"He never got out of bed in the morning, so that you would have the meetings upstairs. He only got up for lunch, though he would get up very early and read. When you went into his suite of rooms up on top—he lived right on top of his Chalet—there must have been five to six hundred books, either being read or having been read or going to be read and they were all over the bed and the tables and such. He went to sleep reading and he woke up reading, and then he'd go to work.

"He'd sit and write in his minuscule handwriting, which bespoke him, because he wrote like he looked and behaved. But it's sometimes very hard to read. And he'd sit and he'd write the lyric, and then hand the lyric or read it to me like a piece of poetry, which would be quite hysterical. And it was none of my business, I was only the choreographer, but since he was directing and writing, a lot of the staging and the big stuff he was just throwing all over to me. . . He would give me all the problems. And then the next thing you knew, you'd hear the piano going, and then he'd sing a verse or something, that he was in the middle of.

"And he loved to pull from his trunk, too, you know. What I mean is that he wrote so many songs that he never used, he would keep pulling, 'How about this . . . how about that . . .?' And I'd say, 'Well . . . I don't know . . .' but he'd manage to squeeze in one or two of the old songs."

*   *   *

The show begins with the passengers boarding the cruise ship, shepherded by Mimi. Once she's got them settled, she explains her job to the members of the crew . . .

COME TO ME

(Elaine Stritch)

STEWARDS: Thank the Lord,
Mimi Paragon's on board,
She can organize the horde
Of morons—we said morons—
That we take abroad,
She will see that they're occupied every
        moment of the day,
Keep the fatheads out of the way,
Hurray! Hurray! Hurray!
Give a cheer,
Mimi Paragon is here,
She will firmly commandeer
The dumb-clucks—we said dumb-clucks—
Till they're on their ear,
She will ride 'em till they qualify for the
        psychopathic ward,
Hallelujah—thank the Lord,
Mimi Paragon's on board.

MIMI: They christened me Mimi,
My tiny hand is frozen
But heaven forbid that I should shirk
The work that I have chosen,

To be a professional pepper-upper
Isn't everyone's cuppa tea
But I've wit and guile
And a big false smile
And the tourists rely on me.

BOYS: That's quite, quite true,
They always do,
They're crazy about Mimi.

MIMI: On the very first dreadful day
I stand them in line,

BOYS: She stands them in line,

MIMI: I keep them in line,

BOYS: She keeps them in line,

MIMI: I stand them in line and say:
'If you're mad keen to be cultural
I'm the gal

"Thank the Lord, Mimi Paragon's on board."

With whom you should roam,
I can show you every ruin from Jerusalem to
Greece,
Also quite a few between Antibes and Nice,
If you can't live without antique pots
I'll find lots for you to take home,
If you long to take bad photographs of
classical débris
Come to me—come to me,
If you want to crouch in churches till you've
water on the knee
Come to me, poor fools—come to me.'

BOYS: She's terribly energetic,
She's so full of vim and zip,
If we hit a gale
And the turbines fail
She can easily drive the ship.

MIMI: 'And if to play games is what you call fun
I'm the one
To keep you in form,
I can organize a treasure hunt or even
clockwork trains,
Anything to occupy your poor dim brains.
We've some fine backgammon boards on
board
If the Lord should send us a storm,
If Canasta, Bridge or Bingo are your kind of
Jamboree
Come to me—come to me.
But if you want to play strip poker with
the girls in Cabin B
Come to me—dear boys—come to me—
dear boys.'
(spoken)
We will now have one fast chorus of
'Beyond the Blue Horizon'.
(resumes singing)
'Come to me!
And if you feel lonely and need a pal
I'm the gal
To take you in tow.
If you're pining for affection and a
sympathetic friend
I've a large collection I can recommend.
If you want something discreetly planned
On this grand
And gracious bateau,
If you're basically frustrated and a martyr to
ennui
Come to me—come to me.
Or if you need a marijuana or a quiet cup
of tea
Come to me—lost lamb—
Come to me—lost lamb—come to me!'

One of the passengers, Johnny van Mier (James Hurst) is taking the trip to try and forget a romance that hasn't worked out. He sings the show's title song, rescued from *Ace of Clubs* but significantly changed in the sentiment of its verse in the intervening decade . . .

SAIL AWAY

(James Hurst)

VERSE   A different sky,
New worlds to gaze upon,
The strange excitement of an unfamiliar shore
One more goodbye,
One more illusion gone,
Just cut your losses and begin once more.

REFRAIN 1   When the storm clouds are riding through
a winter sky,
Sail away—sail away.
When the love-light is fading in your
sweetheart's eye,
Sail away—sail away.
When you feel your song is orchestrated wrong,
Why should you prolong your stay?
When the wind and the weather blow your
dreams sky high,
Sail away—sail away!

REFRAIN 2   When you can't bear the clamour of the
noisy town,
Sail away—sail away.
When the friend that you counted on has
let you down,
Sail away—sail away.
But when soon or late,
You recognise your fate,
That will be your great, great day.
On the wings of the morning with your
own true love,
Sail away—sail away.

Another passenger has come hoping to find love. Nancy Foyle (Patricia Harty) a timid young woman, is acting as secretary/companion to her aunt, the famous novelist, Elinor Spencer-Bollard. She is anxious to let go but . . .

WHERE SHALL I FIND HIM?

(Patricia Harty)

NANCY: *(Singing)*
Oh, darling mother, this
Was a mistake. I can never do the job
I never should have come
I'm far too dumb.
I know she's going to miss
That other girl, for at least she knew the
    job.
Can you imagine how she'd rage at me
Should she discover
I'm really searching for a lover?

(Speaking)
I mustn't think of that—I really mustn't. It's
disloyal to Aunt Elinor. She's paying all my
expenses. I must do all I can to help her.
I can touch-type. My shorthand's all right,
as long as I don't get into a fluster and lose
my head. I must keep calm.

(Singing)
It won't be long before
She'll realise
That I'm going to screw the job!!!
(Spoken) Damn!

(Singing)
I'll lose her notes
And misquote "quotes"
She's bound to take a hate to me
And if she should dictate to me
I'll either turn and flee
Or fling myself, head first, into the sea!

VERSE   I just can't keep out of my mind
What my heart is longing to find
All I do is wait and hope
And wait just a little bit more.
Shall I find my personal dream
On some distant shore?
Or will he appear
Suddenly—right here?

REFRAIN   Where shall I find him?
Where will he be?
Where shall I find him
The one for me?
Suddenly—suddenly—maybe we'll meet

On an ordinary day—on some ordinary street.
How shall I know him?
What will he wear?
How shall I show him
How tenderly I care?
How shall I prove to him
Make him clearly see
That he's the only love for me?

As this is a musical, of course she finds him almost
immediately in the person of Barnaby Slade (Grover
Dale), who tempts her with the prospect of a . . .

BEATNIK LOVE AFFAIR

(Grover Dale)

VERSE   Why suffer from moral convictions?
Social restrictions?
Let's thumb our noses at
Cold wars and atomic predictions
They're merely a waste of time.
Let's make a romantic decision
Follow a vision
Now is the moment to—see clearly
And realise that really
We are on the brink of it
Come to think of it.

REFRAIN I   You and I could have an upright, downright,
        watertight, dynamite
Love affair.
We could either play it up-beat, down-beat,
        off-beat, on-the-beat
Fair or Square
Hey—for those flip Calypsos
Ho—for that rhythmic din
Heigho—for those Dopes and Dipsos
Rum Punch—Coconuts—Gordon's Gin
Think if we tried out
Some little hide-out
On some tropical isle
Naked and warm
From dawn to moonrise
Somerset Maugham-wise
Blue Lagoon-wise
Every time we saw an evening star show
We could wonder if the same Jack Paar
    show

*Grover Dale (Barnaby) and Patricia Harty (Nancy)
rehearsing "Beatnik Love Affair."*

Still was on the air
While we carried on with our on-beat, off-beat,
    Beatnik love affair

REFRAIN 2   You and I could have an in-board, out-board,
        bed-and-board, overbnoard
Love affair
All we need's a little off-key, on-key, sweet-jazz,
Rasmataz
Time to spare
There—by the Caribbean
We'll—cross the Rubicon
We'll have—by the deep blue sea an
All-out, roustabout—carry-on
We'll get a "Man-Tan"

322

Gargantuan tan
On those shimmering sands
Nothing to do but read and rest dear
We could get through *By Love Possessed,*
	dear
While we have a little good-night kiss I'll
Quite forget our last misguided missile
Just missed Gracie Square
And we'll carry on with our sweet-jazz,
	rasmataz, Beatnik love affair.

(By the time the show finally settled, certain lines had changed. "Sweet-jazz, rasmataz" had become "king-sized, organised" and . . .)

We could lie upon the beach at nights,
	dear,
Watching all those Russian satellites, dear,
Whizzing through the air.

Every time we hear a seagull whistle
We'll forget our last misguided missile
Just destroyed Times Square

Noël had also decided *Times* Square made a more recognizable landmark than *Gracie* Square!

Later, when the romantic ice had been broken, Barnaby—again, in true musical tradition—reprises her song in his own words . . .

WHERE SHALL I FIND HER? (REPRISE)

Maybe I've found her,
Can this be she?
Maybe I've found her,
The one for me.
Suddenly, suddenly I wonder why
Such a lot of extra stars
Seem to shimmer in the sky.
Can this be my girl
Do you suppose?
This rather shy girl
With freckles on her nose?
How can I prove to her,
Make her clearly see
That she's the only love for me?

Johnny by now has become attracted to Mimi, who refuses to take him seriously. After all, she tells him, she is older than he is. Johnny, however, is already in love.

What do the years matter! What matters is the way two people feel. He woos her with "Later Than Spring" (p. 307).

*   *   *

In a quieter moment when the passengers have all departed to pursue their various interests, Joe, the ship's purser, reminds the crew of the pecking order on board a ship like the *Coronia*. . .

THE PASSENGER'S ALWAYS RIGHT

(Charles Braswell)

CARRINGTON: The woman in cabin forty-nine has lost
	her diamond brooch.

JOE: Calm her, Carrington,
	Charm her, Carrington,
	That's the correct approach.

HOSKINS: A gentleman on the Promenade Deck just
	called me a lazy slob.

JOE: Smile at him, Hoskins,
	Smile at him, Hoskins,
	That is part of your job.

STEWARDS: The three fat children in B Deck 3
	Have thrown their bathmat in the sea.

SHUTTLEWORTH:
	The silly old broad in Main Deck 2
	Has dropped her dentures down the loo.

JOE: Passengers since the world began
	Have been querulous, rude and snooty.
	England expects that every man
	This day should do his duty.

	Weatherby?

WEATHERBY: Here.

JOE: Hoskins?

HOSKINS: Here.

JOE: Green, Blake, Richardson?

GREEN/BLAKE/RICHARDSON:
	Here. Here. Here.

JOE: Crawford?

CRAWFORD: Here.

JOE: Shuttleworth?

SHUTTLEWORTH: Here.

JOE: Smith, Brown, Parkinson?

SMITH/BROWN/PARKINSON:
	Here. Here. Here.

JOE: Where the devil are Bruce and Frome?

HOSKINS: One's got shingles and the other's gone home.

JOE: Where's O'Reilley and Jock McBride?

GREEN/BLAKE/RICHARDSON:
	One got married, the other got fried.

JOE: Carrington?

CARRINGTON: Here.

JOE: Brewster?

BREWSTER: Here.

JOE: Where's young Fawcett and Windermere?

WEATHERBY: Fawcett stayed at home in bed.

STEWARDS: Poor old Windermere dropped down dead.

JOE: In the course of each cruise
	I always choose
	To lecture each subordinate.
	You're not damned fools
	And you know the rules,
	So see you all co-ordinate.

STEWARDS: We've heard all this before.

HOSKINS: I can't stand any more.

JOE: Bow, smile, charm, tact,
	Never forget one vital fact:

	The passenger's always right, my boys,
	The passenger's always right.
	Although he's a drip
	He's paid for his trip,
	So greet him with delight.
	Agree to his suggestions.
	However coarse or crude,
	Reply to all his questions,
	Ply him with drink—stuff him with food.
	The passenger may be sober, boys,
	The passenger may be tight,
	The passenger may be foe or friend

Or absolutely round the bend,
But calm him,
Charm him,
Even though he's higher than a kite
The passenger's always right.

The passenger's always right, my boys,
The passenger's always right.
Those dreary old wrecks
Who litter the decks
Demand that you're polite.
Don't count on any free time,
Be kind to all the jerks,
And every day at teatime
Stuff 'em with cake . . . give 'em the works.
The passenger may be dull, my boys,
The passenger may be bright,
The passenger may be quite serene
Or gibbering with Benzedrine,
But nurse him,
Curse him
Only when the bastard's out of sight.
Remember, boys,
The goddamned passenger's always right.

*　　*　　*

In an earlier version of the song—intended for *Later Than Spring*—Noël used some of the couplets that later appeared in "The Customer's Always Right." There were also two that were dropped. "Young Fawcett and Windermere" suffered different fates:

Fawcett's found some new young chick,
Poor old Windermere's sick, sick, sick

and . . .

The passengers may tell anecdotes
Until you want to cut their throats

*　　*　　*

Alone in her cabin, Mimi forces herself to do some homework by studying an Italian phrase book.

USELESS USEFUL PHRASES

(Elaine Stritch)

When the tower of Babel fell
It caused a lot of unnecessary Hell.
Personal "rapport"
Became a complicated bore

And a lot more difficult than it had been
　　before,
When the tower of Babel fell.

The Chinks and the Japs
And the Finns and Lapps
Were reduced to a helpless stammer,
And the ancient Greeks
Took at least six weeks
To learn their Latin grammar.
The guttural wheeze
Of the Portuguese
Filled the brains of the Danes
With horror,
And verbs, not lust,
Caused the final bust
In Sodom and Gomorrah.

If it hadn't been for that
Bloody building falling flat
I would not have had to learn Italiano
And keep muttering "*Si, si*"
And "*Mi Chiamano Mimi*"
Like an ageing Metropolitan soprano!
I should not have had to look
At that ghastly little book
Till my brain becomes as soft as mayonnaise
　　is,
Messrs. Hugo and Berlitz
Must have torn themselves to bits
Dreaming up so many useless useful
　　phrases.

REFRAIN 1　Pray tell me the time,
　　It is six,
　　It is seven,
　　It's half past eleven,
　　It's twenty to two,
　　I want thirteen stamps,
　　Does your child have convulsions?
　　Please bring me some rhubarb,
　　I need a shampoo,
　　How much is that hat?
　　I desire some red stockings,
　　My mother is married.
　　These boots are too small,
　　My Aunt has a cold,
　　Shall we go to the opera?
　　This meat is disgusting.
　　Is this the town hall?

REFRAIN 2　*How much is this ribbon?*
　　It's cheap
　　It's expensive
　　What very fine linen!

What pretty cretonne
What time is the train?
It is late,
It is early,
It's running on schedule,
It's here,
It has gone,
I've written six letters,
I've written no letters,
Pray fetch me a horse,
I have need of a groom,
This isn't my passport,
This isn't my hatbox,
Please show me the way
To Napoleon's Tomb.

REFRAIN 3　The weather is cooler,
　　The weather is hotter,
　　Pray fasten my corsets,
　　Please bring me my cloak,
　　I've lost my umbrella,
　　I'm in a great hurry,
　　I'm going,
　　I'm staying,
　　D'you mind if I smoke?
　　This man is the Purser
　　This isn't my cabin
　　This egg is delicious,
　　The soup is too thick,
　　Please bring me a trout,
　　What an excellent pudding,
　　Pray hand me my gloves,
　　I'm going to be sick!

Again, certain lines would change as the show took shape and Noël was able to see what played and what didn't. The italicized lines were replaced with:

My cousin is deaf,
Kindly bring me a hatchet,
Pray pass me the pepper
*　　*　　*
To the Gentlemen's Room
*　　*　　*
This mutton is tough
There's a mouse in my bedroom

*　　*　　*

Later, on deck she tells the passengers that they will soon be in the glamorous Mediterranean . . .

324

YOU'RE A LONG, LONG WAY FROM AMERICA

(Elaine Stritch)

MIMI: Hail Pioneers! Hail Pioneers! Hail Pioneers!
You have survived
The mighty ocean's turbulence,
The sudden tempest's fearful roar,
The fury of the elements
Until at last the welcome shore
Rises against a star-filled sky
To crown your glorious Odyssey.

ALL: We have arrived! We have arrived!
      We have arrived!

MIMI: Give thanks to him, this blessed day,
To one above, who set the course,
I am referring, need I say,
To Captain Wilberforce.

ALL: All praise to him,
All praise to him,
We heartily endorse
Your most appropriate salute
To Captain Wilberforce.

MIMI: You are about to land
Tomorrow morning,
Upon an alien strand
Your feet will tread,
Accept from me I pray
A final warning,
Remember what I say,
Remember what I say,
Remember what I've said . . .

REFRAIN 1 You're a long long way from America,
You're a long long way from home,
Let the standard guide books
Be your bedside books
And don't read snide books
Like *The Lays of Ancient Rome.*
If you're not put off
By the continental coffee
That arrives on your breakfast tray
You'll find you've learned a little from the
    bad old world
When you're back in the U.S.A.

REFRAIN 2 You're a long long way from America,
Be prepared to face the worst,
While guitars are strumming
'The Yanks Are Coming',
You'll find the plumbing
Rather frightening at first.
Do not be surprised
If the milk's not pasteurized
And appears just a wee bit grey,
You'll have learned a little something from
    the bad old world
When you're back in the U.S.A.

COUNTERMELODY

ALL: Get out the greenbacks,
Get out the greenbacks,
They will extricate us
If we should go astray,
In ancient nations
The populations
Have learned to count upon
American donations,
Travellers' cheques can
Do more than sex can
To consolidate us,
Don't let the status quo go,
Hand out those dollar bills,
Be loyal, brave and true
To the traditions of the U.S.A.

REFRAIN 3 You're a long long way from America,
Be prepared for stress and strain,
Don't expect hot showers
Or search for hours
To find fresh flowers
That are wrapped in cellophane,
You need not suspect
If you've had enough injections
Every fish dish that comes your way,
You'll have learned some hints on cooking
    in the bad old world
When you're back in the U.S.A.

*   *   *

By the beginning of Act 2 the ship has reached Tangier. A merchant reminds his fellow vendors waiting to fleece the tourists that even they have a code . . .

THE CUSTOMER'S ALWAYS RIGHT

(Charles Braswell)

VERSE

ALI: Ibrahim?

IBRAHIM: Here.

ALI: Stefanos?

STEFANOS: Here.

ALI: Scarface Molyneux?

SCARFACE: Here, Boss. Here.

ALI: Heinrich?

HEINRICH: Ya.

ALI: Stanislas?

STANISLAS: Da.

ALI: Levi Finkelstein?

LEVI: Rah Rah Rah

ALI: Where is Pedro the Portuguese?

IBRAHIM: In Gibraltar with a touch of D.T.'s.

ALI: Where the devil is Wang-Hi-Chung?

IBRAHIM: He's deported and his brother got hung.

ALI: Ismail?

ISHMAIL: Here.

ALI: Abdul?

ABDUL: Here.

ALI: Where's Mohammed Ben Al Kazir?

IBRAHIM: He was caught forging cheques
Got religion, and changed his sex.

ALI: When a cruise ship comes
I expect you Bums
To make your own deductions
Inspired by greed
You will all proceed
According to instructions

ALI: The suckers land to-day
Hurray—Hurray—Hurray!
Cringe—beg—steal—whine
Never forget the famous line . . .

A merchant (Charles Braswell) reminds his fellow vendors waiting to fleece the tourists that even they have a code.

REFRAIN

ALI: The customer's always right, my dears
The customer's always right.
The son-of-a-bitch
Is probably rich
So smile with all your might
Be wiser than a monkey
Be on to all the tricks
If one of them's a Junky
Give him a break—Give him a Fix.
The customer may be black, my dears
Or yellow or brown or white
He may have a yen for raw recruits
Or mountain goats or football boots
But smooth him
Soothe him
Pander to him morning, noon and night
The customer's always right.

REFRAIN 2 The customer's always right, my dears
The customer's always right
They may pay a price
For curious vice
Or merely want a fight.
They may have inhibitions,
And yearn for secret joys,
Obey your intuitions,
Offer them girls . . . offer them boys.
The customer may be dumb, my dears
Or terribly erudite,
Perhaps you can satisfy his needs

With strings of rather nasty beads,
Compel him,
Sell him
Anything from sex to dynamite.
Remember, dears
The God-damned customer's always right.

Mimi has taken yet another party through the Casbah and, to her surprise with a moment to herself she finds herself thinking about Johnny . . .

SOMETHING VERY STRANGE

(Elaine Stritch)

VERSE   This is not a day like any other day,
This is something special and apart.
Something to remember
When the coldness of December
Chills my heart.

REFRAIN 1 Something very strange
Is happening to me,
Every face I see
Seems to be smiling.
All the sounds I hear,
The buses changing gear,

Suddenly appear
To be beguiling.
Nobody is melancholy,
Nobody is sad,
Not a single shadow on the sea.
Some Magician's spell
Has made this magic start
And I feel I want to hold each shining
    moment in my heart.
Something strange and gay
On this romantic day
Seems to be
Happening to me.

REFRAIN 2 Something very strange
Is happening to me,
Every cat I see
Seems to be purring.
I can clearly tell
In every clanging bell
Some forgotten melody
Recurring.
Tinker, tailor, soldier, sailor,
Beggar-man or thief,
Every single leaf
On every tree
Seems to be aware
Of something in the air.
And if only I were younger I'd put ribbons
    in my hair.
Something strange and gay
On this romantic day
Seems to be
Happening to me!

*   *   *

In later years Noël was in the habit of recording the scores of his own shows, assuming with some justification that he was the best performer of his own material. In this song he had trouble with the "ribbons" in his hair. Having sung the original line in the audition demo tape, when he came to record for Capitol, he changed the line to—

And I know that tired old nightingale still sings
    in Berkely Square.

*   *   *

Johnny is also feeling something he can't explain. He tells himself to proceed with caution . . . "Wait A Bit, Joe" becomes . . .

Mimi tries to organize the smaller children in the nursery with a conspicuous lack of success.

GO SLOW, JOHNNY

(James Hurst)

Go slow, Johnny,
Maybe she'll come to her senses
If you'll give her a chance.
People's feelings are sensitive plants,
Try not to trample the soil and spoil
    romance.
Go slow, Johnny,
No sense in rushing your fences,
Till you know that you know
Your stars are bright for you,
Right for you,
Mark their courses,
Hold your horses,
Speak low, Johnny,
Tip toe, Johnny,
Go slow, Johnny,
Go slow.

Go slow, Johnny,
Slow goes it,
Wait a bit, Johnny,
There's no need to stampede.
Don't forget if you wish to succeed
One truth had better be faced,
More Haste less Speed.
Watch those road signs,
They'll indicate a bit, Johnny,
Which direction to go,
Rely on time and tact,
Face the fact
You're no Brando,
Rallentando,
Speak low, Johnny,
Tip toe, Johnny,
Go slow, Johnny,
Go slow,
Go slow, Johnny,
Go slow!

Luckily for Mimi, she isn't given time to think too much about the state of her heart. She tries to organize the smaller children in the nursery with a conspicuous lack of success . . .

THE LITTLE ONES' ABC

(Elaine Stritch)

VERSE

MIMI: A. B. C. D. E. F. G.
H. I. J. K. L. M. N. O.
Oh what a jolly little jocular
Group we are.

ALVIN: Bla—Bla—Bla!

MIMI: Vocalize and harmonize
When mother cries
One, two, three—go.
Try, if it's possible to keep on key,
Sing the letters after me.

CHILDREN: Just how corny can you be?

MIMI: If you sing when you are blue
You find you
Never have to care a rap,
When the skies are dark and grey,
You just say—

CHILDREN: What a lot of crap!

MIMI: P. Q. R. S. T. U. V.
And W. X. Y. Z. or Zee.
This is my personal recipe
For the little ones' A.B.C.

REFRAIN 1   A. Stands for Absolutely Anything,
B. Stands for Big Brass Bands,
C. Stands for Chlorophyll,
D. Stands for Dexamil,
E. Stands for Endocrine Glands,
F. and G. Don't suggest a thing to me.
Nor do H. I. J. K. L.
But after L. comes M. for Mother
And Mother's going to give you Hell.

REFRAIN 2

MIMI: A. Stands for Artichokes and Adenoids,
B. Stands for Bolts and Belts,
C. Stands for Cottage Cheese,
D. Stands for Dungarees,
E. Stands for Everything Else,
G. Of Course
Stands for Getting a Divorce
And F. Sometimes stands for Fridge,
But if I really were your mother
I'd throw myself from Brooklyn Bridge.

A. Stands for Romeo and Juliet,
B. Stands for Ku Klux Klan,
C. Stands for Bethlehem,
D. Stands for M.G.M.,
E. Stands for 'So's Your Old Man',
F. and G. Stand for Home in Tennessee
And we know H. Stands for Stoats,
But after L. comes M. for Mother
And Mother'd like to slit your throats!

*   *   *

Johnny's mother clearly disapproves of his feelings towards Mimi, which only makes him more determined. When they're finally alone, he explains his conviction that you must follow your own feelings . . .

DON'T TURN AWAY FROM LOVE

(James Hurst)

Don't turn away from love
Because you know there'll be an end to it.
No lyric lover's song
Has ever lasted long,
Why not be tender to it ?
Let your heart surrender to it.
Don't turn away from love,
Don't play it false or condescend to it,
Here in the moonlight with the eager stars
      above
Don't turn away from love.

Don't turn away from love
No matter what it holds in store for you,
Don't fear the pain it brings
If once again it brings
That sweetness every lover
In his heart can re-discover.
Don't turn away from love,
Please let the music play once more for you,
Here in the moonlight with the eager stars
      above,
Don't turn away from love,
Don't run away from love!

Meanwhile the young lovers have no doubts about the way they feel . . .

WHEN YOU WANT ME

(Grover Dale and Patricia Harty)

VERSE
BARNABY: I'll have to get the bees and birds to tell you
That I've loved you from the start,
I simply haven't got the words to tell you
What is truly in my heart,
Joking apart.

REFRAIN

When you want me—if you want me
Call me—call me—if you care.
When you need me—if you need me
Say so—say so—I'll be there.
I've nothing but my heart to bring to you,
No money but a questing mind,
But if this little song I sing to you
Means a thing to you
Please be kind.
When you're lonely—if you're lonely
Call me—call me—anyhow.
If you want me—need me—love me
Tell me,
Tell me,
Tell me now!

NANCY: I'll love you longer than *The Forsyte Saga*
And I'll tremble at your frown.

BARNABY: I'd like to cable to Balenciaga
To prepare your wedding gown,
Don't let me down.

NANCY:	When you	BARNABY:	When you
	Want me,		Want me,
	If you		If you
	Want me,		Want me,
	Call me,		Call me,
	Call me.		Call me.

NANCY AND BARNABY: If you care.

BARNABY: I've got an answer service.

BARNABY:	When you	NANCY:	When you
	Need me,		Need me,
	If you		If you
	Need me,		Need me,
	Say so,		Say so,
	Say so.		Say so.

NANCY AND BARNABY: I'll be there.

NANCY: I want to make my feelings clear to you,
I've never felt like this before.

BARNABY: I'd sacrifice my whole career to you
To be near to you
Evermore.

NANCY AND BARNABY: When you're lonely—
      if you're lonely
Call me—call me—anyhow.

NANCY: You can reverse the charges.

NANCY AND BARNABY: If you want me—need me—
      love me
Tell me—tell me—here and now!

BARNABY: I really haven't any goods and chattels
But a beat-up Chevrolet.

NANCY: I only know I've got a heart that rattles
Every time you look my way.

NANCY AND BARNABY: There's really nothing more to say
Except that I should like to stay
With you for ever and a day,
Olé!

On the last night of the cruise, as the ship nears New York, Mimi decides she must follow her head and not her heart. She tells Johnny their relationship just won't work. The ship docks and Mimi is overwhelmed by neurotic passengers. Her patience finally snaps and she sings what Noël regarded as "a rattling good point number with a complicated but very funny lyric" . . .

WHY DO THE WRONG PEOPLE TRAVEL?

(Elaine Stritch)

VERSE I   Travel they say improves the mind,
An irritating platitude
Which frankly, *entre nous*,
Is very far from true.
Personally I've yet to find
That longitude and latitude
Can educate those scores
Of monumental bores
Who travel in groups and herds and troupes

328

Of various breeds and sexes,
Till the whole world reels
To shouts and squeals
And the clicking of Rolleiflexes.

REFRAIN I Why do the wrong people travel, travel, travel,
When the right people stay back home?
What compulsion compels them
And who the hell tells them
To drag their cans to Zanzibar
Instead of staying quietly in Omaha?
The Taj Mahal
And the Grand Canal
And the sunny French Riviera
Would be less oppressed
If the Middle West
Would settle for somewhere rather nearer.
Please do not think that I criticize or cavil
At a genuine urge to roam,
But why oh why do the wrong people travel
When the right people stay back home
And mind their business,
When the right people stay back home
With Cinerama,
When the right people stay back home,
I'm merely asking
Why the right people stay back home?

VERSE 2 Just when you think romance is ripe
It rather sharply dawns on you
That each sweet serenade
Is for the Tourist Trade.
Any attractive native type

Who resolutely fawns on you
Will give as his address
American Express.
There isn't a rock
Between Bangkok
And the beaches of Hispaniola,
That does not recoil
From suntan oil
And the gurgle of Coca-Cola.

REFRAIN 2 Why do the wrong people travel, travel, travel,
When the right people stay back home?
What explains this mass mania
To leave Pennsylvania
And clack around like flocks of geese,
Demanding dry martinis on the Isles of
    Greece?
In the smallest street
Where the gourmets meet
They invariably fetch up
And it's hard to make
Them accept a steak
That isn't served rare and smeared with
    ketchup.
Millions of tourists are churning up the gravel
While they gaze at St Peter's dome,
But why oh why do the wrong people travel
When the right people stay back home
And eat hot doughnuts,
When the right people stay back home
With all those benefits,
When the right people stay back home?
I sometimes wonder
Why the right people stay back home!

REFRAIN 3 Why do the wrong people travel, travel, travel,
When the right people stay back home?
What peculiar obsessions
Inspire those processions
Of families from Houston, Tex,
With all those cameras around their necks?
They will take a train
Or an aeroplane
For an hour on the Costa Brava,
And they'll see Pompeii
On the only day
That it's up to its ass in molten lava.
It would take years to unravel—ravel—ravel
Every impulse that makes them roam
But why oh why do the wrong people travel
When the right people stay back home
With all that Kleenex,
When the right people stay back home
With all that lettuce,

When the right people stay back home
With all those Kennedys?
Won't someone tell me
Why the right,
I say the right people stay back home?

    *   *   *

Although Noël appeared in several ads during his career—most notably for Phosferine, Gillette blades and Rheingold beer—*Sail Away* was the only show of his to feature what has come to be called "product placement." Morton Gottlieb, the production's general manager persuaded Cunard and American Express between them to pay $100,000 (a quarter of the production's costs). In exchange the cruise ship was christened the *Coronia* (close to Cunard's *Caronia*)—having been the *Carolinia* to begin with—and the crew's uniforms said Cunard. In addition, Noël was persuaded to change a lyric line to include American Express and there is even a minor character called "Man from American Express." Clearly, his attitude had mellowed since the Ford sponsorship days of his 1950s TV shows. Now he "loved the idea of . . . saving a hundred thousand dollars on the show." Other lyrics also included references to Chevrolet, Gordon's Gin, Coca-Cola, R. J. Reynolds Tobacco, Kleenex, Rolleiflex, Canada Dry and Kodak. There is no evidence that any of them put their hand in their corporate pocket but the theatre program does credit sixty-six companies with "contributions."

    *   *   *

The ship has arrived and the passengers are leaving with vociferous vows to keep up the instant friendships they have made on board—promises most of them will have forgotten before they leave the dock . . .

WHEN YOU WANT ME (REPRISE)

REPRISE
NANCY/PAT/ANN:

    When you want me
    Phone me, phone me.

ANN: MU Six Two
    Nine Four Three.

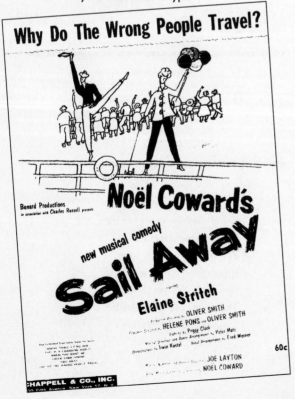

RAWLINGS: We'll have a drink or something.

CANDIJACKS: If I'm not in
Try Algonquin
Four three thousand
When you're free.

MRS LUSH: All Saturdays are quite all right with us.

ELINOR: Drop by and see my bulldog pup.

ALL: Maybe you'll stop and have a bite with us,
Spend the night with us,
Just call up.

NANCY: Dial TE two
Four one three two,
That will get us
Up to ten.

BARNABY: You must come to the wedding .

ALVIN: Try Filmore two
Six five four two.

ALL: That will find me
Up to noon.

ALVIN: If not just leave a message.

ALL: It's been swell, pal,
Give a yell, pal!
What the hell, pal,
See you soon!

Nonetheless, as she watches them leave, Mimi can't help but reflect that many of them—like Nancy and Barnaby—seem happier than when they came aboard. To that number she can soon add two more, when Johnny reappears to brush her objections aside and carry her off.

*   *   *

That was the show New York audiences saw. In Boston they would have seen something substantially different.

The main love story dealt not with Mimi but with an unhappy wife, Verity Craig (opera star Jean Fenn) taking the cruise while contemplating divorce. Sea air being what it is, she finds herself attracted to Johnny. Their romance was supposed to give the show "its tender lyrical moments." In Boston it became clear that, although both of the principals sang their parts well enough, the dialogue Noël had written for them was beyond them. Consciously or not, he had written Noël and Gertie.

When the audience reaction in Philadelphia mirrored Boston, he did the only thing he could do—

he cut the whole sub-plot and with it the role of Verity and her husband (William Hutt). Instead, he had Johnny fall in love with Mimi. Elaine Stritch now had to carry the comic *and* romantic lead. With Verity went the songs "This is a Changing World," "I Never Knew" and "This is a Night For Lovers"—all from *Pacific 1860* and thus never heard in the U.S. Also cut was another romantic song—"I Am No Good At Love." When Jean Fenn's character left the plot, so did the song.

True to his tradition of recycling songs, there is evidence that at one point in the show's development Noël had it in mind to have Nancy and Elinor sing "There Are Bad Times Just Around the Corner," which had originally appeared in *The Globe Revue* (1952) (See p. 277) and been "adapted" for American audiences in his Las Vegas act.

*   *   *

The lyrical variants of "I Am No Good At Love" that survive show how a lyric might be played with over a period of time. In a version he recorded in 1961, the year of the show, it ran . . .

*I AM NO GOOD AT LOVE

I am no good at Love
I try and I try in vain
To capture the magic I know is there
But never quite attain
For something within me breaks the spell
And I am alone again.

I cannot ever quite believe
That Love can be
Really happening to me
My jealous mind seems to keep my heart
From being free
A strange uncertainty
Destroys the dream for me
Will I never, never know?
Will I never discover why
The dream must die?
I am no good at Love
I betray it with little sins
I see the unhappiness of the end
The moment it begins
And the bitterness of the last good-bye,
The bitterness of the last good-bye

Is the bitterness that wins
Is the bitterness that wins.

In the sheet music, however, the first verse has been reworked . . .

I am no good at love
My heart should be wise and free
I kill the unfortunate golden goose
Whoever he may be
With over articulate tenderness
And too much intensity.

Today most people recall it as a poem in the *Collected Verse* (1967), when it read . . .

I am no good at love
My heart should be wise and free
I kill the unfortunate golden goose
Whoever it may be
With over-articulate tenderness
And too much intensity.

I am no good at love
I batter it out of shape
Suspicion tears at my sleepless mind
And, gibbering like an ape,
I lie alone in the endless dark
Knowing there's no escape.

I am no good at love
When my easy heart I yield
Wild words come tumbling from my mouth
Which should have stayed concealed;
And my jealousy turns a bed of bliss
Into a battlefield.

I am no good at love
I betray it with little sins
For I feel the misery of the end
In the moment that it begins
And the bitterness of the last good-bye
Is the bitterness that wins.

By this time "the unfortunate golden goose" was no longer a "he" but an "It"! Interestingly, it is this version that survives in the show's file of "Unused Lyrics."

Stritch was also given "Something Very Strange" and to begin with Noël was nervous about how she would interpret it, having conceived it for a "classical" romantic leading lady. Of one of the preview performances he noted in his *Diary* that—"Stritch's performance was nothing short of miraculous and she did 'Something Very Strange' so movingly that I almost cried."

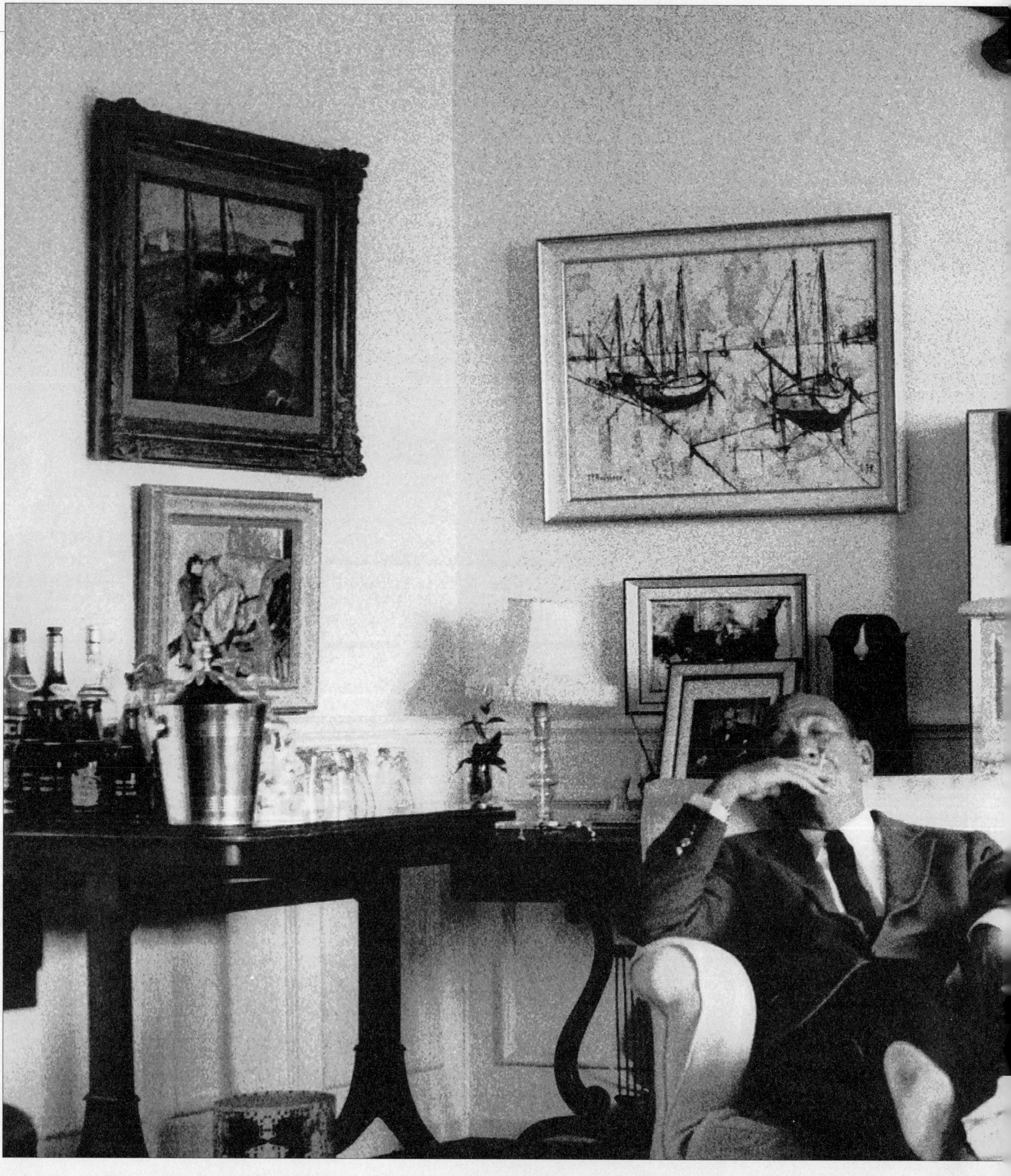

332

In rehearsal two of the minor characters, elderly passengers Mr. And Mrs. Sweeny, had a number which was cut before performances began. Although American audiences never saw it, the song was included in the London production.

BRONXVILLE DARBY AND JOAN (DEAR OLD COUPLE)

VERSE 1

We do not fear the verdict of posterity
Our lives have been too humdrum and mundane
In the twilight of our days
Having reached the final phase
In all sincerity
We must explain

REFRAIN 1

We're a dear old couple and we HATE one another
And we've hated one another for a long, long time
Since the day that we were wed, up to the present
Our lives, we must confess
Have been progressively more unpleasant
We're just sweet old darlings who despise one
     another
With a thoroughness approaching the sublime
But through all our years
We've been affectionately known
As the Bronxville Darby and Joan.

VERSE 2

Our Golden Wedding passed with all our family
An orgy of remembrance and rue
In acknowledgement of this
We exchanged a loving kiss
A trifle clammily
Because we knew

REFRAIN 2

We're a dear old couple who DETEST one another
We've detested one another since our Bridal night
Which was squalid, unattractive and convulsive
And proved, beyond dispute
That we were mutually repulsive

Preceding page: relaxing at Les Avants, Switzerland.

We're just sweet old darlings who torment one
     another
With the utmost maliciousness and spite
And through all our years
We've been inaccurately known
As the Bronxville Darby and Joan

REFRAIN 2

We're a dear old couple and we LOATHE one
     another
With a loathing that engulfs us like a tidal wave,
With our deep sub-conscious minds we seldom
     dabble
But something *must impel*
The words we spell
When we're playing "Scrabble'.
We're just sweet old darlings who abhor one
     another
And we'll bore each other firmly to the grave,
But through all our years we've been referred to
     more or less
As the Bronxville Porgy and Bess.

*　　　*　　　*

There were other songs that fell by the out-of-town wayside—some of them, such as the "imports" from *Pacific 1860*, because there were no longer suitable characters left to sing them. The same fate befell "You and I" from *Later Than Spring*. But there were others.

The problem with such extensive plot surgery is that it's easy to get your characters confused. Skid Cabot belongs to *Later Than Spring* (as the errant swain of Tamarinda Bruce), yet he turns up mysteriously in one of the interim drafts of *Sail Away* when—not having been introduced in the opening cast list—he exits with Mimi at the end. The only explanation is that at one point there was intended to be a love interest for Mimi in the original version and that Skid was brought in to be it. An unfinished love duet (of sorts) would seem to prove it, though several of the references in the lyric seem more suitable to Skid and Tamarinda.

*LET'S HAVE ONE MORE TRY

REFRAIN 1

SKID:　　Let's you and I get reunited—Baby
　　　　Let's me and you have one more try

Though our lovelight may have flickered a bit
Treating it in the way we did
And although we have bickered a bit . . .

MIMI:　　*Bickered* a bit?
　　　　I'll say we did!

SKID:　　Let's keep searching for that Bluebird
　　　　And however blue we feel,
　　　　Let's be absolutely genuine and absolutely
　　　　　　real
　　　　Though, in the past, our hopes were blighted
　　　　　　—Baby
　　　　Let's have one more try.

REFRAIN 2

SKID:　　Let's you and I get reunited—Baby
　　　　And not regret the days gone by
　　　　When we climbed on board our honeymoon
　　　　　　plane
　　　　I can recall how swell it was
　　　　All that caviar and vintage champagne . . .

MIMI:　　Vintage *champagne*?
　　　　Like Hell it was!

SKID:　　Let's keep looking for that rainbow
　　　　To which poets have referred
　　　　Let us prove that true 'Togetherness' is more
　　　　　　than just a word.
　　　　Let's have our love-song copyrighted—Baby
　　　　Let's have one more try.

REFRAIN 3

SKID:　　Let's you and I get reunited—Baby
　　　　Forget I ever made you cry
　　　　Though I did go round with some of the
　　　　　　gals
　　　　I never overstepped with them
　　　　They were nothing more than casual pals . . .

MIMI:　　Casual *pals*?
　　　　You slept with them!

SKID:　　Let us cleave to one another
　　　　For forever and a day,
　　　　Let our marriage be a sacrament arranged
　　　　　　by M.C.A.
　　　　Time Magazine will be delighted—Baby
　　　　Let's have one more try.

*　　　*　　　*

Another duet between Verity and Johnny didn't even reach rehearsal of the first version:

*IF WE'D MET

VERSE   Life is just a chain of circumstances
        Always with an unexpected twist
        I don't mind the state of my finances
        When the hazards and the chances
        Of romance still exist.
        When the gods decide on lovers meeting
        Ordinary logic's overthrown.
        Let's go,
        We know
        And we'd always have known.

REFRAIN 1   If we'd first met in France,
            Venezuela or Brazil
            If we'd run across each other accidentally
            Strolling down Richmond Hill
            If we'd met just by chance
            (It would still have been okay)
            In a scruffy, rather stuffy little road-house
            On the road to Mandalay.
            If we'd met in Samarkand it
            Still would have been plain enough
            That our Guardian Angels planned it
            Guardian Angels know their stuff.
            We'd have seen at a glance
            In the snows of the Ukraine
            Behind the Iron Curtain
            That one thing was certain
            We were going to meet again.

REFRAIN 2   If we'd met in Bangor
            Or the wind-swept Hebrides
            Or perhaps on some unpleasant little schooner
            Rolling through the China seas.
            If, on some far off shore
            We had just said 'How d'you do',
            We have realized exactly what the score was
            You for me and me for you.
            Time and Tide will wait for no love,
            Fate is nearly always right
            Let's accept the *quid pro quo* love,
            Grab your hat and hold on tight.
            If in San Salvador,
            Amsterdam or Portland, Maine
            Our destiny had beckoned,
            We'd know in a second
            We were going to meet again.

*   *   *

The other two numbers would have been lost through sheer lack of stage space, being variants on the theme of the wrong people travelling.

*PATTERSON, PENNSYLVANIA

When we're home in Patterson, Pennsylvania
How we'll bore the folks to tears
With our lengthy dissertations
On the places we have seen
'Til our neighbours and our relations
Wish to God we'd never been.
We'll produce a terrible miscellanea
Of profuse and useless souvenirs,
We'll bring them stringy table mats and hats of
    plaited wheat
We won't forget that loose Burnous we bought
    for Uncle Pete
And yellow Arabian slippers that play hell with
    Grandma's feet
When we're home in Patterson, Pennsylvania.

When we're home in Otterville, Oklahoma
We'll produce unending shoals
Of the snaps we took in colour
Of a man we hardly knew
And some others a trifle duller,
Of a donkey in Corfu
We'll reduce our family to a coma
By projecting rolls and rolls and rolls
Of Kodachrome transparencies with insufficient
    light,
Which look as though we'd taken them at twelve
    o'clock at night.
No one will catch the drift without the gift of
    second sight
When we're home in Otterville, Oklahoma.

*DON'T LET FATHER SEE THE FRESCOES

Don't let father see the Frescoes
For they really might
Excite
The beast in him.
Elderly gentlemen often stray
When they
Are past their prime.
Don't let father see the Frescoes

For unworthy thoughts
Might be
Released in him
Hurry him, hurry him
Swiftly by
Get him back
Home and dry.
Give him the standard guide books,
Force him to stay at home,
Don't let him read those 'snide' books
Like *The Lays Of Ancient Rome*
Though he's not an immature man,
Quite a pure man
He'll remain
But if you let father see the Frescoes,
He may never be the same again.

*   *   *

On reflection the critical consensus was that in 1936 it would have been the best musical of the year. In 1961 it was merely a respectable five-month success in New York and slightly more so in London but it was never the "great big fat hit" Noël was hoping for that would provide him with his old-age pension. In the *Diary* he tried to analyse why:

"Perhaps the book was not strong enough, perhaps Stritch, with all her talent and vitality, hasn't enough star sex appeal, perhaps some of the lyrics are just a bit too clever."

But then he told himself:

"I have deliberately kept the 'book' down to the minimum, in the belief that the public would be relieved at not having to sit through acres of dialogue between numbers. In fact I have used a revue formula with a mere thread of story running through it. Presumably I was wrong . . . I planned a light musical entertainment with neither undertones nor overtones of solemnity, and this, so help me, is exactly what I have achieved. It will have to succeed or fail on its own merits, there is nothing more to be done with it."

Like *Pacific 1860* and *After the Ball* before it, the show suffered the fate of anything that starts life being tailormade and then ends up being publicly turned into something "off the peg." He may have put too much Noël Coward into *After the Ball*; the general view was that he put too little into *Sail Away*.

THE GIRL
WHO CAME
TO SUPPER

1963

THE BROADWAY THEATRE

PLAYBILL

the magazine for theatregoers

The Girl Who Came To Supper

A MUSICAL BASED ON TERENCE RATTIGAN'S 1953 PLAY, *The Sleeping Prince.*

First presented at the Colonial Theatre, Boston on September 28, 1963 and subsequently at the Broadway Theatre, New York on December 8, 1963. (112 performances.)

Cast included José Ferrer, Florence Henderson, Tessie O'Shea, Irene Browne, Roderick Cook, Sean Scully, Carey Nairnes.

In April 1962 Noël received a call from Broadway producer, Herman Levin. Levin's credits included *My Fair Lady* and no producer needed more than that to command serious attention. Noël had been his original choice to play Professor Higgins and Levin was determined to work with him in some capacity.

The offer was to write the score and lyrics for a musical version of Terence Rattigan's 1953 play *The Sleeping Prince.* Hollywood screenwriter Harry Kurnitz had been signed to do the book.

"I feel rather torn about this. At the moment (after the disappointment of *Sail Away*) I naturally feel that I don't want to have anything to do with an American musical ever in my life again, but this, of course, will pass and I have always

loved *The Sleeping Prince.* Also it is period and a perfect period, what's more, for my music and lyrics. I have given an evasive answer."

The answer was not to remain evasive for long. By July "I have already roughed out three numbers for *The Sleeping Prince* and I find that the talent is still there waiting to drip off my fingers. It is a comfort."

Joe Layton (who had choreographed *Sail Away*) was brought in to direct, the title was changed to *The Girl Who Came to Supper* and after Rex Harrison and Christopher Plummer had turned down the role, José Ferrer was engaged to play the Prince. By which time Noël was experiencing "a curious feeling being concerned with a big endeavour . . . and yet not being concerned with it. I find it a trifle frustrating."

*   *   *

1911. The night before the Coronation of George V and the whole of London is celebrating. At the Majestic Theatre we see the finale of the first act of a period musical, *The Coconut Girl.* Backstage there is a visitor—the Grand Duke Charles, Prince Regent of Carpathia (José Ferrer). The company pay their respects by singing the Carpathian national anthem . . .

*YASNI KOZKOLAI

Kraz-na klieg spling az-ka do
Praz-lik narn bal-a-chu vu
Zveg-al az-ga bloot nyez kaz-ka bliek-la vai
Probst quas-ka-la-ka yaz-ni yaz-ni ko-zko-lai.

Klieg klieg plach-a-vitz
Klieg klieg plach-a-vitz
Nyez nyez zla-ba-cai
Zla-ba-cai vai! Hey!

Klieg klieg plach-a-vitz
Klieg klieg plach-a-vitz
Nyez nyez zla-ba-chai
Zla-ba-cai vai! Hey!

The Prince explains his somewhat unusual background . . .

*MY (SHADY) FAMILY TREE

(José Ferrer)

REGENT: My father was Hungarian,
My mother came from Spain
I've several aunts
In the South of France
And a grandmamma
Maternal grandmamma
In the Ukraine

NORTHBROOK: She went too far,
Your grandmamma
For it's cold in the old Ukraine!

REGENT: My uncle was Bavarian
I've learnt some tricks of his
So if I'm not a polyglot
I should like to know who is!

NORTHBROOK: Sir, if you're not
A polyglot
I should like to know who is!

REGENT: I was born in the shade of my family tree
And I'm bound to admit
That it
Was pretty shady
The dynasty
In 1033
Was founded by Queen Eulalie
Who never exactly acted like a lady.
Many a gaudy night she'd spend
With a troupe of strolling players
If her lovers were laid out end to end,
They'd stretch to the Himalayas.
She gave birth to such scads
Of Illegitimate lads
With results that you can all too clearly see
And one of those ultimate results was me
And my shady family tree.

My grandpapa on mother's side
Was far more East than West
He spent his life
With a Chinese wife
In a mental home,
Half-Oriental home,
In Bucharest

NORTHBROOK: What a cruel fate,
I'd simply hate
To be batty in Bucharest!

336

REGENT: My grandma on the other side
Was Russian to the core
She danced in Kief
And came to grief
In a brawl in Singapore!

NORTHBROOK: Oh what a blow,
To sink so low
As a brawl in Singapore!

REGENT: I was born in the shade of my family tree
And believe it or not
It's got
A lot of branches.
My Uncle Fritz
Took leave of his wits
And walked into the Hotel Ritz
Attired in an evening dress of Cousin
Blanche's.
One of my forebears took a bride
But because of inter-breeding
He tried and tried and tried and tried
Without ever quite succeeding.
I've a grandmother who
Went mad in 1882
And drove, naked, to her Diamond Jubilee
Proving beyond all doubt, you will agree,
That I've a very shady,
Julia O'Grady,
And the Colonel's Lady,
Shady Family Tree.

(The song was a late addition to the show and was a reworking of "Countess Mitzi" from *Operette*. The original number Ferrer was given was "Long Live the King (If He Can)."

LONG LIVE THE KING (IF HE CAN)

(José Ferrer)

VERSE 1

PRINCE: As regent of a Balkan state
I have to be realistic,
My loving people cultivate
An impulse to assassinate
That is positively sadistic.

POLICE: But nevertheless artistic.

PRINCE: My uncle, the Grand Duke Stanislas,
Slept tight—in a bullet-proof nightshirt
Until one fatal Michaelmas
His valet, like a stupid ass,
Forgot to lay out the right shirt.

POLICE: Believe it or not,
The naive little clot
Forgot—to lay out the right shirt!

PRINCE: Everything went according to plan
And that, my friend,
Was the end
Of Uncle Stan.

REFRAIN 1 Long live the King—if he can,
And if he can, it takes a most remarkable man
To remain undismayed
When a hand-made grenade
Makes a loud explosion every time the
national anthem's played.
When launching a ship
With a stiff upper lip
Or opening a Church bazaar
He longs for the calm
And the gracious charm
Of a heavily armoured car.
Every procession of state
May, or may not, be lightly shot at as it
leaves the palace gate,
If the Monarch's bodyguard is twenty
seconds late,
He'll be as dead as Queen Anne,
Long live the King—if he can.

VERSE 2

PRINCE: The ruler of a Balkan state
Must always be closely guarded,
No oil magnate, or potentate,
No nun, or undergraduate
Though he's mentally retarded

POLICE: Must ever be disregarded.

PRINCE: My uncle, the Grand Duke Vladimir,
Was brave, but they never forgave him
For every morning of the year
Throughout his brief, but gay career
No one but his wife could shave him.

POLICE: Believe it or nay,
It grieves us to say
That even this didn't save him!

PRINCE: They finally mined his hot-water pad
And that, my friend,
Was the end
Of Uncle Vlad.

REFRAIN 2 Long live the King—if he can,
And if he can he'll be a very fortunate man.
From the womb to the tomb
He must always assume
That he might be strangled every time he
enters the drawing-room,
He's wise, on the whole,
To refrain from a stroll
Down any little country lane,
It's a hundred to five
That he'll never arrive
Alive, on his private train.
Each Monarch learns when a boy
That Christmas parties, by and large, are not
unmitigated joy,
On the tree there's apt to be
A dynamited toy
(Probably made in Japan),
Long live the King—if he can.

The song was pulled from the show in Philadelphia in November but not because it was poorly received. It happened to be the week that President Kennedy was shot . . .

*   *   *

During his visit the Regent has been attracted to one of the chorus girls, Mary Morgan (Florence Henderson). Northbrook (Roderick Cook), the British diplomat assigned by the Government to attend the Regent, brings her an invitation to supper with the Regent after the show. Thinking about it, she can just see herself as the belle of the ball—or at least the supper party . . .

I'VE BEEN INVITED TO A PARTY

(Florence Henderson)

I've been invited
To a party.
Everyone will say,
'Who's that pretty girl?'
As they see me swirl
Round the floor
And before
The night is through
I'll be drinking champagne out of

everyone's shoe.
People will murmur,
'But she's charming!
What a lovely smile!
What a sense of style!'
Nobody will guess
That my dress
Is the one that I wear in Scene Three
And the whole Royal Court will agree
That the Belle of the Ball—is me.

The most entrancing waltz will be
The waltz the Prince
Will dance with me
And as we're floating
Cheek to cheek
The pressure of his hand
Will make me understand
There's really no necessity to speak.
Guests will cheer
And cry 'Bravo!'
As round and round and round we go
And when the music comes to an end
He'll say—'Hey,
You've found a friend!'

I've been invited
To a party
And when they've at last
Played the final dance
Someone will advance
And I'll wait
Till a stately
Limousine
Drives me back through the sunrise to
    Camberwell Green
And when I write home
To Milwaukee
Mom will have a fit
When she reads the bit
Saying that I danced with a Prince
And that since
I've been asked round to tea.
Then she'll tell all the neighbours with glee
That the Belle of the Ball—was me!

REPRISE   I was invited
To a party,
Though it wasn't quite
What I had in mind
I must be resigned
To the fact
That it lacked
That magic touch,
That I over-romantically

Wanted so much
And when I get back
To the Theatre
It will be a strain
Having to explain
How my pretty song
Went all wrong
And insisted on changing its key

The Carpathian Embassy is at sixes and sevens. It isn't every day, fortunately, that they receive a royal visitor.

WHEN FOREIGN PRINCES COME TO VISIT US

(Carey Nairnes)

When foreign Princes come to visit us
Usually from the Balkans
We spend our time looking helpful and solicitous
And hovering about like falcons.
If one of them wants a—tra la la la la
We have to set the stage for a seduction
And what with the lighting, champagne and caviar
It's certainly the hell of a production.
For Emperors and Czars
Fresh flowers in every vase
And we introduce some spruce loose-covers,
We also burn some scent,
In a spoon that's rather bent,
Essential for potential royal lovers,
Arch-Dukes—Grand Dukes
And rather out-of-hand Dukes
Whose countries can't be found on any map,
To inflame their tepid blood
We release a gurgling flood
Of Cordon Rouge and Chateauneuf du Pape.
When foreign Princes come to visit us
Life is an exhausting strain,
We long and pray
For that happy happy day
When they bugger off home again.

*   *   *

The Regent arrives, worried by reports of civil insurrection at home. Northbrook arrives with Mary, who is naturally nervous. How should she behave?

What should she say? Northbrook gives her a lesson in protocol.

SIR OR MA'AM

(Roderick Cook)

NORTHBROOK:
The privilege of supping with a Royal Prince
Is granted to very few,
Allow me to give you one or two hints
As to what you may say or do,
Maintain a dignified demeanour,
Be relaxed but not too expectant
And always remember protocol . . .

MARY: It sounds like a disinfectant.

NORTHBROOK:
Protocol, my dear,
Is just a set of simple rules
Designed to lubricate Pro-Consular machinery,
For example it is wiser
When you talk with King or Kaiser
To confine your conversation to the scenery.
But I digress,
The very first thing you must master is the
    method of address . . .

REFRAIN 1   Sir or Ma'am,
Ma'am or Sir,
One's addressed to him of course,
The other's addressed to her,
Majesty or Highness
Can once a while be used
But you'll notice a certain dryness
If you get the terms confused.
Ma'am or Sir,
Sir or Ma'am,
Accompanied by a simple bob,
Not a profound salaam.
Don't have a stroke
If a casual joke
Is received with funereal gloom,
Smother a curse
And in quick reverse
Back right out of the room.

REFRAIN 2   Sir or Ma'am,
Ma'am or Sir,
The mumbling of this simple phrase

Betrays the amateur.
Royal condescension
May murmur a Christian Name
But you'll notice a certain tension
If you try to do the same.
Ma'am or Sir,
Sir or Ma'am
Makes every royal personage as happy as a clam.
If some remark
Should go wide of the mark
And you're suddenly conscious of doom
Sink to the ground
And in one swift bound
Back right out of the room.

The sight of a table laid for only two makes Mary suspicious but Northbrook persuades her that important issues are at stake, relationships between their two countries, etc., etc. Mary agrees to stay—but only for forty-five minutes.

Alone together, Mary and the Prince Regent get along fine and we share their private thoughts . . .

Mary and the Regent share a drink and their private thoughts in "Soliloquies."

SOLILOQUIES

(José Ferrer and Florence Henderson)

REGENT: She looks quite sweet,
Perhaps a little young for me,
But still that youthful charm will be
A change.
I must arrange
For Northbrook to receive
Some sort of minor decoration,
He's really done exceedingly well
And shows—in fact
Much tact
Combined with shrewd discrimination.

MARY: He looks quite nice,
I'm not a bit afraid of him,
The image that I made of him
Was wrong,
His face is strong
But I can see
Some tired little lines of dissipation,
His eyes are kind and just a bit sad
I think—I'm glad
That I'm the girl who had the invitation.

The vodka flows and the interruptions pile up. The Queen Mother pleads with the Prince to be lenient with his young son, King Nicholas, who has sided with the rebels . . . Nicholas himself arrives. When he has dealt with them all, the Regent tells Mary that underneath it all he is a lonely man . . .

LONELY

(José Ferrer)

Imagine if you can
A solitary man
Eternally surrounded—yet alone.
A royal prince
Who ever since
He first began to dream
Has lived within the shadow of a throne,
Pity him and think of him
Weighed down by cares of state,
Hearing happy lovers laughing by
Weary and oppressed
But maybe you have guessed
The sad unhappy prince I am referring to
Is I.

Lonely—lonely,
A pawn of destiny,
A sawdust puppet on a string,
No one near to me to know or even care
That the heart behind this royal mask I wear
Beats out its melancholy days
Proving the falseness of the phrase
"To be as happy as a king".

Only—only
Swift moments here and there,
A brief illusion that I'm free,
I know too well true happiness
Can never ever be
For a solitary soul like me.

Only—only
I hold deep in my heart
The foolish dream that there may be
Just one last blossom flowering
On true love's eternal tree
For a solitary soul like me.

This is the version of the lyric that appeared in the *Lyrics*—even though the song was cut from the Broadway production. However, it's interesting to compare the published version with the one Noël used and performed when the score was looking for backers and record companies. Although they share similar titles, they were really two separate songs in their own right.

*I'M A LONELY MAN

VERSE

Imagine, if you can,
A solitary man.
Eternally surrounded—yet alone.
A royal prince
Who ever since
He first began to dream
Had lived within the shadow of a throne.
Pity him and think of him
Weighed down by cares of state,
Hearing happy lovers laughing by,
Weary and oppressed,
But maybe you have guessed
The sad, unhappy prince I am referring to
Is I.

REFRAIN 1

I'm a lonely man,
A victim of my destiny,
A sawdust puppet on a string.
I just turn away
When I hear some idiot say ñ
"He's happy as a king".
With no one to share
The burden that I bear,
Nobody to care or even dream
That the heart behind
This royal mask I wear
Is beating out a melancholy theme.
I can only plan
A fleeting moment here and there,
A brief illusion that I'm free,
But I know true happiness can never be
For a solitary soul like me.

REFRAIN 2

I'm a lonely man,
A victim of the ancient blood
That courses sadly through my veins.
I dream secretly
That true love might find the key
To free me from my chains.
But as time goes by
Impatiently I sigh
Must I wait 'til I
Am old and grey
Before I hear someone
Passionately sigh

"I am yours for ever and a day!"?
I can only plan
And hope and pray
And wonder if such joy could ever, ever be.
Is there one last blossom
On the flowering tree
For a solitary soul like me?

Having bared his soul—not for the first time—he
finds the lady has passed out . . .

*   *   *

The disconsolate Nicholas wanders through the
London streets, where he meets the quintessential
Cockney, Ada Cockle (Tessie O'Shea), the larger
than life—in every way—fish-and-chips seller, who
introduces him to some Coward pastiches of
Cockney songs . . .

LONDON SEQUENCE

(Tessie O'Shea)

VERSE: I was born and bred in London,
           It's the only city I know,
           Though it's foggy and cold and wet
           I'd be willing to take a bet
           That there ain't no other place I'd want to go

LONDON IS A LITTLE BIT OF ALL RIGHT

REFRAIN 1

London—is a little bit of all right,
Nobody can deny that's true,
Bow Bells—Big Ben,
Up to the heath and down again
And if you should visit the monkeys in the zoo
Bring a banana,
Feed the ducks in Battersea Park
Or take a trip to Kew,
It only costs a tanner there and back,

Watch our lads in the Palace Yard
Troop the Colour and Change the Guard
And don't forget your brolly and your mack:
And I'd like to mention
London—is a place where you can call right
Round and have a cosy cup of tea,
If you're fed right up and got your tail right down
London town
Is a wonderful place to be.

What Ho, Mrs Brisket

What ho, Mrs Brisket,
Why not take a plunge and risk it?
The water's warm,
There ain't no crabs
And you'll have a lot of fun among the shrimps
     and dabs,
If for a lark
Some saucy old shark
Takes a nibble at your chocolate biscuit
Swim for the shore
And the crowd will roar,
What ho, Mrs Brisket!

Don't Take Our Charlie For The Army

Don't take our Charlie for the Army,
He's a sensitive lad
And like his dad
His heart is far from strong,
He couldn't do route marches
On account of his fallen arches
And his asthma's something terrible
When the winter comes along,
He's a nice boy—one of the best
But when he gets a cold on his chest
He coughs until he nearly drives us barmy,
So nightie-night—close the door,
Go back to the barracks and think some more
Before you take our Charlie for the Army.

SATURDAY NIGHT AT THE ROSE AND CROWN

Saturday night at the Rose and Crown,
That's just the place to be,
Tinkers and Tailors
And Soldiers and Sailors
All out for a bit of a spree,
If you find that you're
Weary of life
With your trouble and strife
And the kids have got you down
It will all come right
On Saturday night
At the Rose and Crown.

LONDON IS A LITTLE BIT OF ALL RIGHT

REFRAIN 2

London—is a little bit of all right,
Nobody can deny that's so,
Big Ben—Bow Bells,
Have a good laugh and watch the swells
Treating themselves to a trot in Rotten Row
Sitting on horses,
Grosvenor Square or Petticoat Lane,
Belgravia, Peckham Rye,
You can stray through any neighbourhood,
If you haven't a swanky club
Just pop into the nearest pub,
A little of what you fancy does you good,
And I'd like to mention

London—is a place where you can call right
Round and have a cosy cup of tea,
If you use your loaf a bit and know what's what
This old spot
Is a bloody good place to be.

*　　*　　*

Next morning Mary emerges, happily convinced that she and the Regent are now lovers. She sings of her love.

HERE AND NOW

(Florence Henderson)

VERSE

Here on this gay,
Glorious day
How can I keep my feet from dancing?
Some entrancing tune
Makes me want to fly

Tessie O'Shea as the quintessential Cockney, the larger-than-life Ada Cockle, introduces "London."

Higher than the moon
In the sky.
Who can I tell?
What can I say?
How can I breathe and not betray
To every soul I see
What today
Means to me?

REFRAIN

Here and now
I've a wonderful secret that nobody knows,
Here and now
I've got rings on my fingers and bells on my toes,
When I woke as today was dawning
All the world seemed to glow
On this marvellous, magic morning,
Suddenly I know
I'm in love,
I adore every moment that's hurrying by,
Up above
There's a lovely new light in the sky,
When my prince appears
I'll burst into tears
And curtsy three times and bow,
Who could foresee
That such happiness could happen to me
Here and now?

REPRISE

Here and now
I've a wonderful secret that nobody knows,
Here and now
I've got rings on my fingers and bells on my toes,
Though it ought to be quite alarming
I'm not nervous at all,
Arm in arm with my young Prince Charming
Going to the ball.

She can't understand why he doesn't appear to feel the same. As Northbrook is in the process of smuggling the puzzled Mary from the Embassy, they run into the royal retinue on their way to the Coronation. When her personal lady-in-waiting is suddenly taken ill, the Queen Mother co-opts Mary, who is soon dressed like royalty. To his disgust the Regent even has to bestow on her a token honour—the Order of Perseverance, "for personal service to the head of state"!

REPRISE

REGENT: It s too absurd,
           I can't protest—my hands are tied,
           I'm trapped in this undignified
           Charade,
           I find it hard,
           On top of having
           Passed a night of amorous frustration
           To give this girl—for passing out cold
           An old
           Pure gold
           And really quite expensive decoration.

MARY: He looks so cross,
           His mouth is set—his eyes are grim
           But still I'm not afraid of him
           At all.
           I knew I'd fall
           In love with him
           Which obviously wasn't very smart of me,
           But even though I see him this way
           I know
           He'll stay
           For ever in my heart a special part of me.

*   *   *

Act 2 opens in Westminster Abbey. The Carpathian delegation—with the exception of Mary—are bored to tears.

CORONATION CHORALE (IT'S ALL SO WONDERFUL)

(Florence Henderson and José Ferrer)

ALL: A Coronation is spectacular
       And though, as pageantry, not easy to improve on,
       To coin a phrase in the vernacular,
       We wish to God they'd get a move on.
       We hate the weight
       Of our robes of state
       And our jewellery weighs a ton
       And we'd sell our souls
       For some nice hot rolls
       Or the smell of a Chelsea bun.
       We rise at dawn and put our ermine on
       And then we squeeze into a freezing open landau,
       To lift our trains with all this vermin on
       Requires the muscles of a Sandow,
       With stays too tight
       We sit bolt upright
       In a rigidly unyielding pew,
       Even British oak
       Gets beyond a joke
       When you've sat on it from nine till two.
       Part of a royal education is
       To be resigned
       To your behind
       Becoming numb.
       The worst of every coronation is
       We always wish we hadn't come.
       Here we sit—exquisitely bored,
       Hear our stomachs rumble
       As we watch late-comers stumble
       Up the nave.
       Good Lord!
       Look at Cousin Maud,
       Someone should have given her a shave.
       Here we all elegantly squat
       Praying that Aunt Xenia
       Won't give way to Schizophrenia
       Again.
       Great Scott!
       Look at what she's got
       Dragging from the bottom of her train.

MARY: It's all so wonderful—wonderful—wonderful,
       It's like the most entrancing fairy tale I ever
            knew,

Florence Henderson as the showgirl getting carried away by José Ferrer as the Prince.

Diamonds, rubies and pearls,
As I can't quite believe it's true
How can I explain it to the girls,
They'll think that having got into some awful
        scrape
I'm trying—just by lying—to forget
And when I start to tell about this sable cape
They'll gape,
You bet.

ALL: Here we sit—dummies in a row,
Heaven knows how many
Of us long to spend a penny
But we're stuck
And so
Though it's touch and go
We shall simply have to trust to luck.

MARY: It's all so wonderful—wonderful—wonderful,
It's the most lovely lovely lovely sight I'll ever see,
All this glitter and gold,
In my heart this will always be
Something to remember when I'm old,
I'll think of it each time I see a summer sky
However sad and weary I may grow,
And every year another lovely June goes by
I'll sigh

Heighho,
It was so wonderful—wonderful—wonderful
But it was long—long ago.

Mary returns to the Embassy to return the borrowed finery. Nicholas asks her to help him place a political phone call but they are discovered by the Regent, who places his son under house arrest. Mary lectures the Regent on being a proper parent before he dismisses her. Left alone, the Regent has to admit to himself that he is no longer in control of the situation.

HOW DO YOU DO, MIDDLE AGE?

(José Ferrer)

What's wrong?—What's wrong?
I'm behaving like an utter fool,

I've always hitherto
Seen clearly what to do
And remained—restrained
And cool,
But since this idiotic girl appeared
With her sentimental ignorance and youth,
Though I merely asked her to sup with me,
She's made me feel the years are catching
        up with me
And that now I must compromise slightly
And politely
Face the truth

How do you do, middle age?
How do you do, middle age?
If you're planning to upset
And fret
And ultimately diminish me
Let—this wet
Soubrette—set to and finish me,
Knowing that I'm
In my prime
And mellow season
Must I permit her
To twitter
Pure high treason?
Give me one reason.
Can I still love now and then?
Shall I be sweet or gentle,
Sane or mental?
Must I spend my days in a blazing rage?
Give me a clue,
Over to you,
Middle age.

Comment ça va, middle age?
Qu'est ce que tu as, middle age?
Autumn winds begin to blow
And so
I'd better unbend my mind to you
Though—you know
I'm not quite yet resigned to you,
More relaxation,
More ease,
More time for snoozing,
What consolation
Are these
For those amusing
Pleasures I'm losing?
Shall I survive this decade
Or shall I merely fade out,
Done for—played out?
What are your designs for the final page?
It's too absurd
To let myself become morose,

Disconsolate and lachrymose

And dull

Because a nattering, chattering ingénue

Is making me feel I'm ninety-two

Instead of a muscular forty-five.

I've still got teeth—I'm still alive,

My legs still take me where I want to go

And so

I'm damned if I'll let this little whipper-

snapper lay me low.

A feather-brained, garrulous small-part minx

Who never draws breath and seldom thinks,

Who teases my amorous appetites

And then recites the Bill of Rights

And lectures me about my son and heir,

I swear

I'll not let this dizzy little busybody see I care.

Why should I so upset myself?

Let myself

Get myself

In a state of acute dismay

Because some years have passed away?

Why should I crucify myself?

Sigh myself

By myself?

When I still feel bright of eye,

Clear of brain

And ready to start from scratch all over

again.

Don't jump the gun,

Middle age,

Life is still fun,

Middle-age,

I'm not ready to kow-tow

Just now

And impotently unbend for you,

Stay

Away

And wait until I send for you,

Must taxes paid on the past be retroactive?

Waves of self-pity

Are pretty

Unattractive

When you're still active,

Don't be so dumb,

Middle-age,

Spare me that glum recital.

I'm still vital.

I've enough bombast

For one last

Rampage.

Just wait and see,

Leave it to me

Fiddle-de-dee,

Middle-age.

The Regent agrees to let Nicholas attend the Foreign Office Ball and the Queen Mother insists Mary accompany him. Meanwhile the Regent has invited the elegant and available Lady Sunningdale to be his supper guest. He and Northbook contemplate the evening ahead.

CURT, CLEAR AND CONCISE

(José Ferrer and Roderick Cook)

REFRAIN 1

REGENT: Curt, Clear and Concise

Is the way that a lady should be.

I am not a perfectionist who seeks the sublime,

All I ask is a woman who won't waste my time.

I'm frankly sick to death of females who

procrastinate,

Who guard their virtue like a sort of holy

grail,

I much prefer the type who's willing to

co-operate,

Concentrate,

Smack on the nose,

Bang on the nail.

Coy maidens who shed

Bitter tears at the thought that they might

be misled

And who faint dead away at the sight of a bed

Soon find out that my parting advice

Can be curt, clear and concise.

You must forgive me, Northbrook, if I should

philosophize,

At moments such as these

I find myself at ease,

In matters of the heart I'm sure our points

of view indubitably harmonize,

You're quite a connoisseur.

NORTHBROOK:

You're flattering me, Sir.

REGENT: I feel that really

You look on sex clearly

And factually

Which saves you quite a lot of time and

tears,

You have an air,

Libertine—debonair.

NORTHBROOK:

Well, Sir—actually

I've been engaged for nearly seven years.

REGENT: You must excuse me, Northbrook, if I seem

to minimize

The prevalent idea

That sex should be austere,

I've always had a notion

Sensual emotion

Was a cracking bore

And as I mentioned before,

REFRAIN 2   Curt, Clear and Concise

Is the way that a lady should be,

She should not sentimentalize the physical

act

And believe she can dodge biological fact,

I think it is behaving really indefensibly

To take exception to an amorous advance,

Give me the kind of girl who mutters

comprehensibly,

Sensibly,

Off with the lights.

On with the dance.

Though moralists say

That it's better to honour and love and obey

I have found that a casual roll in the hay

Without bridesmaids, confetti or rice

Is more curt, clear and concise.

*   *   *

Strolling back after the ball, Mary tries to tell Nicholas the somewhat complex plot of *The Coconut Girl*:

NICHOLAS: Why is it called *The Coconut Girl?*

MARY: Because she's a great heiress, the daughter of Pootzie Van Doyle and Pootzie has this coconut plantation in Florida from this Indian chief who he was kind to when he was a little boy and he makes a fortune out of coconut oil and that's why she's an heiress and that's why everyone calls her "The Coconut Girl", because of the coconut oil. And he brings her to Europe and has her presented in Court and she becomes the rage of the Continent. And the first scene is in the garden of his gorgeous villa he's rented for her in Monte Carlo and it begins with us all singing the Opening Chorus.

344

OPENING CHORUS: WELCOME TO POOTZIE VAN DOYLE

Welcome to Pootzie Van Doyle
Who's made millions and millions from coconut oil,
He's travelled by train
And he's travelled by ship
And the dear little coconuts paid for his trip
A man of the people,
A man of the soil,
All welcome to Pootzie Van Doyle

There are lots more verses and they both come on and we all cheer.

NICHOLAS: What's her name?

MARY: Her name's Tina. She makes her first entry down the terrace steps with her maid, he secretary, her hairdresser and her butler, her cook and several footmen and she sings her "opener" . . .

NICHOLAS: Her "opener"?

MARY: In the theatre we always call someone's first number their "opener". Anyway, the orchestra strikes up the intro and off she goes with the verse. It's rather a long verse, all about how it feels to be a great heiress . . . So I'll just do the chorus . . .

THE COCONUT GIRL

I am known as the Coconut Girl
Though my intimate friends call me Tina
I'd be more contented
If dad hadn't rented
Quite such a grand place as the Villa Marina,
The style is ornate
There's lots of gold plate
And my bathroom is mother of pearl,
But beneath all this show
I should like you to know
That I'm simply—just simply—The Coconut Girl.

And everyone cheers again and she goes off and we

all follow her. Then there's the comedy theme and Cy Mortimer and his room mate, Bob Garfield, come on in this terrible old automobile. Cy Mortimer is a Yale baseball player who Tina is secretly in love with and has had to say goodbye to in Jacksonville. Anyway, they do the automobile number and we all come on in dustcoats wearing motoring hats and veils. This is the refrain:

PADDY MacNEIL AND HIS AUTOMOBILE

Paddy MacNeil
Bought an automobile
And invited his girlie for a spin
Everything was fine and dandy for the first few miles
Until he let the clutch right out
And couldn't let it in.
As they drove at full speed
Paddy tried to proceed
With a little original sin
But he found he couldn't cuddle her with both
    hands on the wheel (crash!),
That's why Paddy had to buy another automobile

NICHOLAS: That's wonderful

MARY: It stopped the show on the opening night.

NICHOLAS: Oh, what a shame. I hope it went on again?

MARY: That's just another theatrical expression. Anyway, Tina (played by Jessie Maynard) comes on in a pink dress and sits in a swing, because she's always had a swing in every show she's ever been in since "Swinging to Happiness" in *May Blossom*—she tore the place up! Anyway, there she is in the swing and the music plays softly and Count Alexis comes on to pay his respects to her. That's Tony Morelli— good baritone but on the short side. This Count Alexis has a very bad reputation but he's a terrific gambler and adventurer and although she's been warned against him by Monsieur Dupont, the local mayor (who I forgot to tell you about), she can't help finding him attractive. Anyway, he gives her a bouquet of gardenias and sings . . .

SWING SONG

VERSE

TINA: My foolish heart may yet discover
That all the dreams I have been dreaming
    are in vain.

GIRLS:: She has the air of one who's waiting
    for a lover
And who she's dreaming of we'll ascertain

TINA: No matter what the end may be,
Here in my golden reverie
As I swing to and fro,
High and low—high and low,
All my cares drift away
Like a cold winter's snow.

Enter Alexis

GIRLS:: Would you permit Alexis for a while to stay
    with you?

TINA: Maybe

GIRLS:: To share this beautiful day with you?

TINA: We'll see

ALEXIS:: Forgive me please for thus intruding
Upon a lady who is fairer than the day.

TINA: Kind sir, if it should be
To me you are alluding
I must beseech you pray
To go away.

ALEXIS:: Be not unkind,
Be not unfair,
Moments so sweet
Are all too rare.

TINA: Not a cloud in the sky
And a lark singing high
And the sound of the sea far below.

ALEXIS:: Would you permit this fellow who has
    nothing
But a lonely heart to bring
Just to kiss you as you swing
To and fro?

TINA AND ALEXIS::
As we swing to and fro
High and low—high and low
All our cares melt away
Like the cold winter snow.

Right: The Master reflects . . .

After that they do an encore and she does a lot of trills and finishes on her B flat and that's the end of the first scene …Then at the end of the third scene of the first act, that's when I come and say my line—"Count Alexis, you are a cad and a bounder!" And then she turns on him and says she never wants to see him again and flings herself into the arms of the nearest waiter who turns out, of course, to be Cy Mortimer, whom she at last recognises. And she faints dead away and that's the curtain.

NICHOLAS: What happens in the next act?

MARY: Count Alexis goes away heart broken, because he really loves her and isn't an adventurer at all. He comes from a very noble Hungarian family. Anyway, he goes to the Casino to gamble with his last 100 francs. That's when he sings his big number, "Play the Game" (which I'll do for you in a minute). In the meantime, there's a sextette, which I do with five other girls. We're all dressed in sequinned evening dresses, each one in a different colour Mine's mauve—and we carry fans to match.

LILIES OF THE VALLEY

We're six lilies of the valley,
Rose, Maud, Kate, Jane, Marybelle and Sally,
We toil not neither do we spin much,
But we find, in the Casino, that we win much
More
By being gentle with the gentlemen
Playing at the tables
Often sentimental men
Give emeralds and sables
To Rose, Maud, Kate, Jane, Marybelle and Sally,
Six pretty fillies,
Far from being silly billies,
Six little lilies of the valley.

Then, when Count Alexis comes to the roulette table, we all crowd round him and he sings—

Lady Luck, come to my aid,
This is a game that must be played
And won …

And we all sing—"What fun! What fun! What

fun!"Then it goes on—I can't remember all the lyrics and there's a big vocal arrangement for him and all the croupiers but I can't do that, on account of it being in harmony and I only have one pair of tonsils. Anyhow, the chorus goes like this …

*PLAY THE GAME

Play the game—play the game—play the game!
Win or lose
Pick or choose
It's your fate
Wait until the wheel begins
And spins and spins and spins
Is it seven
Or eleven
Or sixteen or twenty-eight?
Throw your plaque
Red or Black
Low or high
The Gods are on the side of those who try
I pledge my heart and fortune and the honour of
    my name
Play the game—play the game, play the game!

Then he wins and wins and wins. And the last scene is when this party's being given in her honour and the hotel terrace is being decorated with coconut palms and we all wear grass skirts. He drives over the terrace wall—just as she's about to elope with Cy Mortimer—and throws all the money he's won at her feet and she at last realises he loves her for herself alone and they sing …

*TIME WILL TELL

Time will tell,
Time will show
Whether we shall ever know
Which jealous gods have decided our fate
What joys and sorrows are lying in wait.
Here we stand,
You and I,
Hand in hand

Beneath the sky
Will the dawn break the spell?
Time alone will tell.

(This song had originally been written for *Later Than Spring*. Unlike several other numbers, it did not make the transition to *Sail Away*. Nor did it survive in this show.)

NICHOLAS: What happened to Cy Mortimer?

MARY: He behaves beautifully. He wishes them both happiness and goes back to Yale with his room-mate. Then we all do the "Walla Walla Boola."

NICHOLAS: What on earth's that?

MARY: It's the dance hit of the show and this is the chorus …

THE WALLA WALLA BOOLA

When you dance the Walla Walla Boola,
Walla Walla Boola,
You will find it more exciting
Than the Honolulu Hula.
First you swing to the left,
Swing to the right,
It's got a kick that makes you want to dance all night
Your hips start to wiggle
You give a little giggle
And begin to wish the temperature was cooler,
So stand up and holler,
Throw away your collar,
Come on and dance the Walla Walla Boola,
Walla Walla Boola,
Walla Walla Walla Walla Boola!

Or—for those with good memories—"The Baseball Rag" or "The Saggie Boo.")
     By the time the show reached Broadway, "Play the Game" and "Time Will Tell" had been cut.

*   *   *

Back at the Embassy Mary patches up the situation between father and son and brings peace to Carpathia. Relieved to be offered a way out, the Regent happily admits . . . .

THIS TIME IT'S TRUE LOVE

(José Ferrer and Florence Henderson)

MARY: There's nothing more to say
Because at least your heart has beckoned
In this brief fleeting second
I know
You really are a lonely man
The one and only man
I dreamed of all my life ago.

This time it's true love
This time it's real
Last night I knew love
Now I can feel
A lovely certainty at last has come true
I know you care for me as I care for you.
This is no light love
No passing phase
This is the right love
For all my days
I need no violins

PRINCE REGENT AND MARY:
No moon, nor stars above . . .
You are my own true love

MARY: *(Spoken)* I'll sure be glad to get out of this
dress!

MARY: This time it's true love
All else apart
Out of the blue love
Has touched my heart

PRINCE REGENT:
Dare I believe that from our brief rendezvous
You've grown to care for me as I care for
you?
This is no light love
Too well I know
No fly-by-night love
Could move me so.

PRINCE REGENT AND MARY:
We need no violins, no moon nor stars above

PRINCE REGENT: You are my own true love.

Once again, the final version was somewhat different from Noël's audition lyric. After an identical opening verse, the refrain ran . . .

*COME BE MY TRUE LOVE

I should adore to say
Enchanted words to sing your praises
But all those easy phrases
I know
Would not ring true tonight
I look at you tonight
And see that suddenly, at last
A miracle is happening to me.

Come be my true love,
Come be my dear
Maybe a moment,
Maybe a year.
Now at long last the secret magic begins,
Set to the music of discreet violins.
Come be my true love,
Time will not stay,
Old love and new love
Both fade away.
We need no moonlight
Or romantic stars above
Come be my own true love.

*   *   *

In the morning the Regent is full of plans to take Mary back with him to Carpathia but she is the realist. They have had their special moment but it's a moment, not a life. Perhaps somewhere, some day . . . who knows? They say their goodbyes. The Regent is left to reflect on what might have been.

I'LL REMEMBER HER

(José Ferrer)

I'll remember her,
How incredibly naive she was,
I couldn't quite believe she was
Sincere,
So alert,
So impertinent
And yet so sweet.
My defeat
Was clear.
I'll remember her,

Her absurd exaggerating
And her utterly deflating
Repartee
And the only thing that worries me at all
Is whether she'll remember me.

I'll remember her
In the evenings when I'm lonely
And imagining if only
She were there.
I'll relive,
Oh, so vividly,
Our sad and sweet,
Incomplete
Affair.
I'll remember her
Heavy-hearted when we parted,
With her eyes so full of tears she couldn't see
And I'll feel inside a foolish sort of pride
To think that she remembers me.

*   *   *

Once again, the show Broadway audiences saw differed significantly from the version that previewed in Boston, then Toronto and Philadelphia.

Apart from the obvious need to drop "Long Live the King," a number of other songs were cut for more conventional "artistic" reasons. While Tessie O'Shea's "London" sequence was the guaranteed show stopper, Noël found it too long and complicated in the out-of-town performances and cut one of the pastiche Cockney songs . . .

*WHAT'S THE MATTER WITH A NICE BEEF STEW?

(Tessie O'Shea)

What's the matter with a nice beef stew
With greens and mashed potatoes?
It fills the crevices and makes you grow
And it's the bit of ballast to your Darby Joe.
When you've had a little grouse
At Lyons' Corner House
Or a steak and kidney pud at Slater's
You'll appreciate a chew,
At a nice beef stew
With greens and mashed potatoes.
When you've been upon a trip
And fairly got the pip

With the kids and perambulators,
You'll appreciate a chew
At a nice beef stew
With greens and mashed potatoes.

*   *   *

In Boston early in Act 1 there was a scene in the drawing room at the Embassy in which the Queen Mother, King Nicholas and Princess Louisa—a character subsequently dropped—discuss the relative merits of traditional English and German music . . .

*HEY, NONNY NO

(Irene Browne, Tracy Rogers, Sean Scully)

LOUISA: Hand in hand through the forest straying
          Birds on the branches sing—nonny nonny no
          Dragonflies o'er the water lilies playing
          Hey nonny nonny nonny—nonny nonny no.

          Lads and lasses so merrily dancing
          Summer's a cummin in—nonny nonny no
          Dappled shade where the butterflies are glancing
          Hey nonny nonny nonny—nonny nonny no.
          La La La La La . . .

QUEEN MOTHER:
          How delightfully she plays
          So definite!
          She's such a clever little soul
          To have such musical control

NICHOLAS: Every time you reach that phrase
          With F in it
          Why must you play a G instead?

LOUISA: Will you be quiet and go to bed!

QUEEN MOTHER:
          Having been deafened by Wagnerian bassoons
          I much prefer these ultra-British
          Rather skittish
          Little tunes
          Hey ho, hey nonny nonny no
          Hey ho, hey nonny nonny no
          Hey ho, hey nonny nonny no
          Hey ho, hey nonny no

LOUISA: No. No, hey nonny nonny no,
          Hand in hand through the forest straying
          Birds on the branches sing—nonny nonny no.

NICHOLAS: What a lot of wrong harmonies you're playing

LOUISA: Why won't you please shut up and say
          goodnight and go!

QUEEN MOTHER:
          What a very charming theme
          So chirrupy
          It's early English, I suppose
          With all those nonny nonny no's
          Though to others it may seem
          Too syrupy,
          I must admit I like it better
          Than all that *sturm* and *donnerwetter*
          That Mr. Wagner so relentlessly employs
          I much prefer a more harmonic
          Less Teutonic
          Kind of noise
          Hey ho, hey nonny nonny no

*In rehearsal,
left to right:
Director Joe Layton,
José Ferrer,
Florence Henderson
and Noël Corward.*

Hey ho, hey nonny no.

*   *   *

There were other songs which didn't survive rehearsal. In one, Mary attempts to explain to the Prince the nuances of New World culture and free speech in particular. The number was originally called "Free Speech" but—presumably feeling such a title to be a little demagogic, Noël changed it for the rest of its brief life to . . .

*IF ONLY MRS. APPLEJOHN WERE HERE

(Florence Henderson and José Ferrer)

MARY: If only Mrs. Applejohn were here
          She'd explain a lot of things that I'm unable to
          And I'd get your views on America right
          Before tomorrow night
          If only I had her home address to cable to
          For instance—Thomas Jefferson
          Free speech—free religion—free press
          And what about President Lincoln and the
             Gettysburg Address?
          And I'll bet your own damn politics wouldn't
             be in such a mess
          If only Mrs. Applejohn were here,
          If only Mrs. Applejohn were here.

PRINCE: Let's drink a toast to Mrs. Applejohn
          For Mrs. Applejohn had knowledge, sense
            and vision

MARY: *(Spoken)* You're jeering at me.

PRINCE: Let's pour one more for Mrs. Applejohn
          Who hit the nail upon
          The head with such precision

MARY: *(Spoken)* You're sneering at me.

PRINCE: *(Furious)* Mrs. Applejohn's words may sound
            like truth
          To every gangling, gawky,
          Pubescent, adolescent youth
          Residing in Milwaukee
          But however admired she was in school
          She sounds like a bigoted, damned old fool
          And whatever she taught each snarling little
            pup—

MARY: (Shouted)

Mrs. Applejohn was a darling

So shut up!

(Sung)

If only Mrs. Applejohn were here

She'd say crowned heads were renowned for
their hypocrisy

She'd explain why George the Third was a cad

And very likely add

Hurray—for the swift decay—of aristocracy!

She'd speak to you of liberty

Free press—free religion—free speech

And all about all for one and one for all and
each for each

And you'd learn about all those Indians and
those pilgrims on that beach!

If only Mrs. Applejohn were here,

If only Mrs. Applejohn were here.

FREE SPEECH

(In the earlier version)

MARY: Free Press—Free Religion—Free Speech

Is what Mister Thomas Jefferson used to preach,

And what Mister Thomas Jefferson said
sounds just as true today

To ev'ry single citizen of the USA

The ultimate good of Mankind

Is what Mister Jefferson had in mind.

He said—"Boys, just for the hell of it, let
the people steer the boat

Freedom, once they get the smell of it, will
encourage them to vote

One for all, all for one; and possibly each for
each.

Free Press—Free Religion—Free Speech."

PRINCE: Let's drink a toast to Mister Jefferson,

For Mister Jefferson had knowledge, sense
and vision.

MARY: (Spoken) You're jeering at me!

PRINCE: Let's pour one more for Mister Jefferson,

Who hit the nail upon

The head with such precision.

MARY: (Spoken) You're sneering at me!

PRINCE: Mister Jefferson's words may sound like truth

To every gangling, gawky,

Pubescent, adolescent youth

Residing in Milwaukee.

But Jefferson, bless his greying hairs,

Had a slippery grip on world affairs

And whatever he taught each snarling little
pup . . .

MARY: (Furious)

Mister Jefferson was a darling—so shut up!

Free Speech—Free Religion—Free Press

Form the basis of our policy—more or less.

And when Mister Thomas Jefferson said that
mean had equal rights

He certainly got his name up in electric lights.

When Britain said, "This cannot work",

Darling Mr. Thomas Jefferson went berserk.

He said—"Down with aristocracy, all that
royal bally-hoo.

We'll establish a democracy, and you know
what you can do

With your throne and your crown and
possibly Good Queen Bess!"

Free Speech—Free Religion—Free Press!

*   *   *

The young King Nicholas was given his own love
song, sung to Princess Louisa. Like the Prince, he
can foresee a future of pomp, circumstance and
precious little privacy.

---

*JUST PEOPLE

(Sean Scully and Tracy Rogers)

VERSE   Face the future brightly

Though we know there's something missing,

We can live politely

Without making love and kissing.

No nightingales for us,

No symbols of high romance,

No fairy tales for us,

We'll learn to deny romance.

But if only we'd been born beneath some
distant star,

If only we were just not who we are.

REFRAIN 1   If we could only be just people

Just people,

Just us.

If we could only find a house and live there,

No fanfare,

No fuss.

If we could just employ an ordinary day

Furbishing up our own front parlour

If we could just enjoy an ordinary play

Rather than an all star gala.

If we could roam the streets together,

Bright weather

Or grey,

Life would be right as a trivet

If only they'd let us live it

In a straightforward ordinary way,

In our own sweet way.

REFRAIN 2   If we could only be just people,

Just people,

Just us.

If we could find a sweet humdrum home

And come home

By bus.

If we could spend a Sunday strolling through
the park,

Smiling at strangers when we meet them,

If we could one day merely for a lark

Cook ourselves some eggs and eat them.

Though we shall have our ermine gowns on

And crowns on one day,

We're prepared to grin and bear them,

If only they'd let us wear them

In a straightforward ordinary way,

In our own sweet way.

*   *   *

When Mary receives her invitation to join the Prince
for supper after the show, the other girls in the
Chorus are quick to share their wealth of experience
with her . . .

---

*PUT NOT YOUR TRUST IN PRINCES

(Florence Henderson and Chorus Girls)

GIRLS: Mary dear, you must

For a moment—just

For a moment

Think a little, think a little

Why should a blue-blooded, bloody
grand Prince

Suddenly pick on you?

You can bet this quaint

Little revel—ain't

On the level
Wait a little, wait a little
Nobody's fallen for this lark since
Fifteen forty-two.

MARY:: He may be sweet and kind
A man of refined and cultured mind
Whose only desire is just to find
How simple people live.

GIRLS:: That may be
But when you see
He's getting more primitive
No matter what
He's got on the spot
Whatever you've got—
Don't give!

Put not your trust in Princes, baby
Though they may be
Gay and glamorous
But the moment that they start becoming
    amorous
Run like a hare, dear
Take care, dear
Ordinary citizens are amiable and pliable
But loyalty in royalty is frankly unreliable
A "regal romance" in fact
Is a classy little farce
With a weak last act
There are loads of other men keen and adept
Willing to accept your heart
But you won't hear that organ playing
    "Here Comes The Bride"
If you've got yourself disqualified.
Apart from the suave punctilio
A royal beau evinces,
If you're hoping for a little more lassitude
    and lust,
Put not your trust in princes.

Put not your trust in Princes, baby
Princes may be
Tough and treacherous
And the moment that they start becoming
    lecherous
Don't ask for rape, dear
Escape, dear
Don't expect a gentleman so regally luxurious
To let you say "Goodnight, sweet Prince"
    without becoming furious
You'd much better save your breath
And anticipate a fate
That is worse than death
There are loads of other men modest and shy
Eager to supply romance

But you won't hear that organ playing
    "Here Comes The Bride"
If the union isn't sanctified
A Prince may be bright and most polite
But never quite convinces
If you want more than a garnet brooch to
    fasten on your bust
Put not your trust in princes.

*　　*　　*

The Prince Regent at one point had another song to express the isolation of high birth. Presumably it was felt that its sentiment was too close to "Lonely Man" and even that was eventually cut. The lonely man was becoming too lugubrious to be lovable.

*LIFE WITHOUT LOVE

(José Ferrer)

Life without love
Is an all too familiar royal state
Too melancholy to contemplate
Without a wistful sigh,
Picture the ghastly desolation,
The biological frustration
Life without love
Is a desert of unrequited dreams,
A nightmare of bleak and blighted dreams
With nobody nearby
Each picture's colourless
Each song has a dying fall
Life without love
Is no kind of love at all.

No joy in the springtime
In winter nothing but grief
Imagine summer without a single rose
And autumn without a falling leaf.
Nobody to hear you
If you should cry,
No one to help you count those sheep at night
To get to sleep at night
No one to croon you a lullaby
Nobody to run to
No one you know you can trust
You're all alone in a vacuum with just
No one to
Stand beside you,
Gently guide you

Through every day you live,
Giving the way you live
Purpose and charm and style
Don't ever doubt it
Without it
Nothing's worth while

Life without love
Is a twopenny halfpenny episode
A journey along an empty road
Beneath a sunless sky
No hopeful gleam on the horizon
No lyric theme to improvise on
Life without love
Is a melody played in monotone
A forest from which all birds have flown
A river running dry
No treasured memories,
No ecstasy to recall
Life without love
Is no life at all

*　　*　　*

Though he was disappointed by the *Girl's* short run—and the fact that the hoped—for London production never came to fruition—he remained pleased with what he'd achieved:

"No one in their sane senses could say the lyrics and music . . . were not good. They are good. Very good indeed. As a matter of fact, this is the first time I have had—on the whole—enthusiastic notices for my music for years, if ever."

Nonetheless, a later *Diary* entry comes to terms with the fact that it will not be a "real block-buster" and he speculates on what it lacked. "If Harry had written it with more 'heart.' If Joe had directed it with more 'heart,' and if Jo Ferrer and Florence could have emanated more 'heart' . . ." But in all of this rationalization he was either unable or unwilling to see the real reason why the show ultimately failed.

The Girl Who Came to Supper was altogether too close to *My Fair Lady*. The chorus girl and the Regent were the flower girl and the Professor without the charm, while one Cockney character (O'Shea) stood in for another, the dustman Doolittle. Instead of Ascot we had the Coronation and one society ball looks very much like another.

Apart from which, the show could hardly have been unluckier with its timing. If it hadn't had to face the competition of *Hello Dolly!* and *Funny Girl* in the same season, perhaps the Girl would have been invited to stay for breakfast.

HIGH SPIRITS

1964

AN IMPROBABLE MUSICAL COMEDY

Based on *Blithe Spirit*

First presented at the Alvin Theatre, New York on April 7, 1964. (375 performances.)

Music, Book and Lyrics by Hugh Martin and Timothy Gray.

Cast included Beatrice Lillie, Tammy Grimes, Edward Woodward. Directed by Noël Coward (later Gower Champion).

Over the years there had been several suggestions that one or other of the straight plays might be turned into a musical by other writers. In 1958 Noël noted that Leonard Bernstein had planned a version of *Brief Encounter* and Hugh Martin of *Hay Fever* but that neither had come to anything. He was understandably sceptical, therefore, when Hugh Martin and his partner, lyricist and liberettist Timothy Gray wanted to tackle *Blithe Spirit*.

However, since he had liked the team's earlier collaboration, *Love From Judy* (1952), he gave them permission to develop their approach.

In February 1963 Martin and Gray called upon him in his 55th Street, New York apartment—ready

to present not merely an approach but the complete score for the musical plus an outline of the book provisionally entitled *Faster Than Sound*.

> "I was all set to turn it down, because it really has been going on far too long and I was sick of the frigging about. Coley and I sat with our mouths open. It is quite brilliant. The music is melodious and delightful, the lyrics really witty . . ."

He later complimented them on the way they had remained faithful to the original text but managed to "open up" the book. He confessed he'd toyed more than once with the idea of adapting the play into a musical himself but found that he was too close to it. "I could never get the bloody thing out of the living room!"

*   *   *

One number that invariably stopped the show was possibly the most Cowardesque song ever written—and one which Noël would surely have been proud to have written himself—"Home Sweet Heaven." Timothy Gray recalls that the inspiration came from the exchange in the play between Charles and a by now disenchanted Elvira who wants to go home.

ELVIRA: You were talking about me before dinner that evening.

CHARLES: I might just as well have been talking about Joan of Arc. But that wouldn't necessarily mean that I wanted her to come and live with me.

ELVIRA: As a matter of fact she's rather fun.

In Gray's hands the "home" Elvira wants to go back to soon became "Home Sweet Heaven," a catalogue song of the people who did live there. Strangely, the number didn't appeal to Tammy Grimes (Elvira) and she had to be literally pushed on the stage for her first performance of it. Her genuinely sulky delivery provided just the counterpoint to set off the extravagance of the lines and Miss Grimes—knowing a hit when she heard one—continued to perform it just so.

As the out of town tour continued, Noël began to play with the verse structure himself, though none of his lyrics were used in the American or British productions. By the time the show reached London, however, and the local cast recording was made, several Coward contributions are to be found (italicized) in the version he himself recorded.

In rehearsal, Noël Coward directs Tammy Grimes as Elvira and a prone Beatrice Lillie as Madame Arcati.

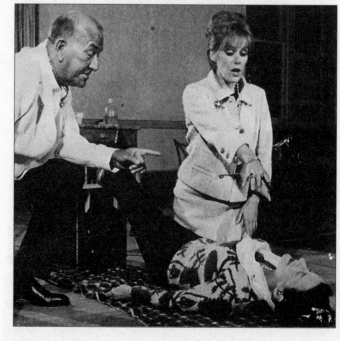

Tammy Grimes

HOME SWEET HEAVEN

Music and lyrics by Hugh Martin and Timothy Gray
(As Recorded By Noël Coward)

It's very simple, no angel choirs
But we have stereo and merry open fires
Caruso sings there
Salomé swings there
In my Home Sweet Heaven.

My house is modest, it's by Bernini
And I've a feeling that the ceiling's by Cellini
Old Tetrazzini bellows Puccini,
In my Home Sweet Heaven.

We all sit 'round King Arthur's table,
Freud and Cain and Abel,
Barnum and Bailey, Oscar Wilde and me
And it's such fun when Julius Caesar,
Proust and St. Theresa
Drop in for a cup of tea.

Disraeli's *witty* and Homer's hearty,
And Joan of Arc's the type who sparks the
    dullest party.
We crack a bottle with Aristotle
In my Home Sweet Heaven.

The King of Prussia, I call him Freddie,
Is living by mistake with Mary Baker Eddy.
And Aimée Semple, Aimée Semple has built a
    temple,
In my Home Sweet Heaven.
There's Dr. Crippen, he's fairly chummy
With Lizzie Borden
And her daddy and mummy.
They split a kipper with Jack the Ripper
In my Home Sweet Heaven.

After I've lunched with Keats and Shelley,
Brahms and Botticelli,
Martin Luther asks me out to dine
And it would really bowl you over,
Watching Casanova
Try to flirt with Gertrude Stein.
She's a gas, is a gas, is a gas.

Delilah's dreary but Samson's handsome,
And with his good looks,
Robin Hood looks
Fit for ransom.
Jane Austen giggles, Houdini wiggles
Then it's seventh heaven, eleventh heaven.

I miss the love, the laughter rippling and the
    tippling.
And Emily Bronte doing the twist with Kipling.
Oh, I'm homesick for my Home Sweet Heaven.

There's Mussolini, draped in a sari,
Mad as a hatter, like a fatter Mata Hari.
He's even ruder
Than Mary Tudor,
In my Home Sweet Heaven.

King Charles's spaniel, a golden cocker,
Jumps up and knocks poor Whistler's Mother off her
    rocker.

Though Cromwell's crummy,
We play gin rummy,
In my Home Sweet Heaven

Thomas-à-Becket loves absurd games,
Blind Man's Bluff and word games.
Boswell plays Bézique for hours on end.
And Horace Walpole's weekly whist drive
Handel, Bach and Liszt arrive
And drive everybody round the bend.

Lady Godiva is going steady
With old King Ethelred,
Who's hardly ever ready.
They share a chalet
With Walter Raleigh and his good Queen Bessie,
It's rather messy.

I miss the thrill of seeing Milton on a bender,
With Bonnie Prince Charlie,
And that old Pretender.
Ho-ho, I'm homesick for my
Home Sweet—one—two—Heaven.
It's a gas, it's a gas, it's a gas.
Oh, I'm homesick for my
Home Sweet Heaven.

In the archives a folder contains some extra variations under the heading "Extra Couplets by Noël Coward." In his own miniscule handwriting are his additional musings, many of them with emendations . . . Those that didn't survive to his own recording . . .

Poor old Cassandra,
The Fortune Teller,
Lives close at hand
With Ferdinand and Isabella.

Sometimes dear Goya,   (Lola Montez)
Castenets clicking,
Does a pavane
With good Queen Anne,
Alive and kicking.

A Doge in Venice   He's quite a menace
Beat me at tennis   At table tennis

And dear old Giotto
Coughed up a grotto   (Designed a grotto)

She carried on so
With King Alfonso

Houdini wriggles,
While Gladstone giggles
In my Home Sweet Heaven
It's pretty snappy,
The conversation

Between Voltaire
And Dumas Père
And Carrie Nation.
It's quite a sight to look at Chaucer
Launch a flying saucer,
Milton getting absolutely blind.
I miss the sight of Theda Bara
Dripping with mascara,
Whistler's Mother and the Brothers
　　Grimm.
And picture Garibaldi
Chasing Nita Naldi
As Nellie Melba chases him.

The little club we drink and dine in
Run by Texas Guinan
Where Carrie Nation drinks until she's
　　squiffed.

And when I tango
With Vincent Van Gogh
I feel artistic,
Impressionistic.

From which it would be easy to deduce that Noël had a certain rhyming fixation on Whistler's Mother.

In the margin, waiting to be suitably rhymed, were . . .

Mahatma Gandhi, Amos & Andy, Pontius Pilate, Mohammed, Queen Matilda, Monet, Manet, Debussy, Verlaine, Baudelaire, Robert Burns, Fanny Burney, Ben Franklin, Isadora Duncan, Sun Yat Sen, Sitting Bull, General Custer, Lenin, Stalin, Jenny Lind, Tom Thumb, Emile Zola, Marco Polo, Buffalo Bill, Beau Brummell, Nefertiti and Mrs. Beeton.

Gray recalls how helpful Noël was to him as a young lyricist—so much so that in the proposed revival of the show he paid him the ultimate compliment of including him in his personal pantheon of the more recent immortals . . .

I miss Tallulah dramatizing,
Judy vocalizing.
Joan Crawford and her motherly advice.
And when I waltz with Leslie Howard
Or laugh with Noël Coward
Then it's really paradise.

*　　　*　　　*

The handwritten notes contain other fragments.

Two look as though they might have been intended for Madame Arcati (Beatrice Lillie). The first is to do with riding a bike, although in both the Broadway and London versions of the show there is a full number by Martin and Gray called "The Bicycle Song." Noël's version runs . . .

Careering across Devil's Dyke
The crowds on the promenade get quite a shock,
The kiddies stop sucking their peppermint rock,
The cops on the corner cry—"Go it, old cock"
When they see me whizz by on my bike.

In the margin—as with many of the earlier songs—he lists possible rhyme words (strike/like/tyke/Mike/pike), leaves a few lines to be filled in later and then ends defiantly . . .

Can do what they bloody well like.

Then under "High Spirits (Unused)" is an untitled song about "The Society," again much amended. Records of the show indicate a Martin and Gray number of the same name that was used in New Haven and then cut.

Once again—if only from the wings—Noël felt the urge to contribute, if not compete. His own version of the same subject (never used) runs . . .

*THE SOCIETY

We were known as THE SOCIETY,
The Society of Psychical Research.
We achieved great notoriety
But the March of Time has knocked us off our
　　perch.
Though we were once expert at organising f
　　lights
Of disembodied spirits
Who whipped about like kites,
We're now mute with acute anxiety,
For the Spirit World has left us in the lurch,
Rah-rah,
For the Spirit World has left us in the lurch.

Our seances used to be a riot,
We'd sit in the dark completely quiet
Materializing trumpets by the score.
We once conjured up a psychic force
Which looked like an ectoplasmic horse
And left a nasty stain upon the floor.
I clearly recall how we enticed

*Coward-san was also popular in Japan.
(Drawing by Makoto Wada)*

A rather destructive poltergeist
Which stayed a month before we got it back.
But now, these creatures so dear to us
No longer seem to appear to us,
Which makes us think perhaps we've lost the
　　knack.

*　　　*　　　*

One Coward song did become part of the American production—for one performance only. As Charles learns to live with a first wife who is visible only to him, not surprisingly his friends and neighbours begin to notice—and comment on his behaviour. In a scene set outside a Hampstead Heath pub on a typical Hampstead Sunday morning they indulge in a typical Hampstead preoccupation—gossip . . .

*WHAT HAS HAPPENED TO CHARLES?

VERSE

BRADMANS AND DANCERS:

A suburban Sunday morning is an English institution,
It's as clearly defined
In the national mind
As the British Constitution.
A suburban Sunday morning is more or less unique,
Because the local pub
Is the focal hub
Of the scandal of the week that was.

JERRY: Some go to church if they like it—

MIRIAM: Some prefer to do a crossword puzzle—

JACK: Others stay indoors
And cope with household chores,

KATHY: While some instead
Remain in bed
For a routine amorous nuzzle.

BILL: Some take a golf ball and strike it—

BOB: Others puff and blow and mow the lawn;

ALL: But the one thing that brings unity,
To a limited community,
Is to gossip, gossip, gossip on a sunny Sabbath morn.

CHORUS

LARRY: What has happened to Charles?

MEG: He's different.

JACK: What has happened to Charles?

MEG: He's peculiar.

LARRY: He's jittery and nervousHis eyes can barely focus.

MEG: I saw him only yesterday
Arguing with a crocus.

LARRY: A crocus?

MEG: A crocus.

LARRY: A perfectly ordinary crocus?

MEG: He was all by himself in the garden
And I chanced to glance over the wall—
He was ranting and roaring with all his might

I looked to the left and I looked to the right.
It's the sober truth, if I drop down dead,
I'm prepared to swear on my mother's head
There was nobody there at all.

ALL: Nobody there at all!

2ND CHORUS

MEG: What has happened to Charles?

JACK: Perhaps he's drinking.

LARRY: What has happened to Charles?

JACK: He's schizophrenic.

ANGEL: He must be going mental
He's certainly hysterical.

JACK: A muttered curse he made in church
Was quite the reverse of clerical.

ANGEL: I saw him at the Grove Chester
His reason must have flown
He was capering about
Like a mad boy scout
And dancing all alone—

PATTER

LARRY: Really, they're both to be pitied
It's very hard to know just what to say—
Such a charming fellow,
A most enchanting host.
And now looks daffodil yellow.
And you'd think he'd seen a ghost.

MEG: Maybe she'll have him committed
Certainly he must be sent away.

ALL: Tho' we sit about or walk about,
We've at least got Charles to talk about.
So excuse us being spiteful on this most delightful day—
Please forgive us being bitches
On our witches' Sabbath day
Witches' Sabbath day
Witches' Sabbath day.

One performance was all it took to convince everyone, including Noël that the number was "too English." The audience just didn't "get it." Subsequent audiences, therefore, weren't even given the chance.

* * *

Although the show, which ran almost a year, was considered a Broadway success, largely due to the pulling power of Bea Lillie, it was not a happy experience for Noël and he was relieved to hand the directorial reins over to Gower Champion. His dis-

enchantment was compounded by the arbitrary closing of *The Girl Who Came to Supper*. He confided to his *Diary*: "After plodding through these two musicals I am really very tired indeed. I took on far too much . . . At any rate, I have done all I can do."

* * *

There were to be no more songs.

In 1963 a modest revival of *Private Lives* at the Hampstead Theatre Club—followed by an all star National Theatre production of *Hay Fever* the following year—marked the beginning of a major rediscovery of Coward the playwright that has continued to this day. Noël enjoyed every moment of "Dad's Renaissance," as he gleefully dubbed it.

The last years were dogged by steadily deteriorating health and the long-delayed knighthood in the 1970 New Year's Honours List wrote an effective *finis* to his career some three years before his death in Jamaica on March 26th, 1973.

In those years there were to be a series of celebrations of his musical work. On September 29, 1968 a revue, *Noël Coward's Sweet Potato*, devised by Roderick Cook, was staged at the Ethel Barrymore Theater in New York. Four years later in 1972 Wendy Toye put on an English equivalent at London's Mermaid Theatre with *Cowardy Custard*, while later that same year

Cook came back with a revised version of his revue, *Oh Coward!*—presumably a pun on the apparently endlessly-running *Oh! Calcutta*—at New York's New Theater.

Just before leaving for what was to be his last trip to Jamaica, Noël paid his final visit to the theatre. Accompanied by Marlene, he fittingly attended a gala performance of *Oh Coward!*. Asked his verdict later, he replied: "I went out humming the songs."

* * *

A great while ago the world begun
With hey-ho, the wind and the rain:
But that's all one, our play is done,
And we'll strive to please you every day.

CLOWN
Twelfth Night

Noël Coward escorts Marlene Dietrich to a gala performance of "Oh Coward!" In the background, Graham Payn and Cole Lesley

THE FRUSTRATION OF COMPILING ANYONE'S "COMPLETE LYRICS" IS THAT THEY CAN NEVER BE *complete*. The day after publication a fragment surfaces in some album or attic and, hopefully, the same thing will happen this time. There are various references—mostly in Mander & Mitchenson's *Theatrical Companion to Coward* (1957) to songs that were cut from the early shows which, although they occasionally show up in the publishers' files, are no longer extant. Many of the original firms were swallowed up and their inventory mislaid in the move. If the following list should inspire a visit to an old piano stool, it will have served its purpose. New discoveries will be included in future editions.

London Calling! (1923): There is reference to another song called "Little Baggy Maggy" but the program mentions no artiste. In the 2nd Edition of the show (December 1, 1923) Joyce Barbour had a number called "I Prefer To Be On the Safe Side."

On With The Dance (1925): Alice Delysia playing a character called "Vanoni" has a song called "Georgie."

This Year of Grace (1928): In the Manchester production—where the show was called *Charles B. Cochran's 1928 Revue*—there was a "Grand Production number" called "Jewels and Perfumes," featuring Maisie Gay and Mr. Cochran's Young Ladies. The by-line ("First performed in Lou Nadle's *Daggles* at the Theatre Royal, Puddleton") is a pretty clear indication of a rather broad parody of the genre . . .

When the show opened in New York there was another number called "Velasquez," which had greater pretensions. *The New Yorker* review refers to "a long song introduced a pretty but tedious dance: (arranged by Tilly Losch). The program indicates a Singer (Rita Mackay) and a pair of Dancers.

There are also two pieces of sheet music—which appear to date from the late 1930s or early 40s—which carry titles ("Malta" and "Why Do You Pass Me By?") but lack lyrics. "Malta" has a jaunty, almost music hall soud to it, while "Why Do You Pass Me By?" turns out to be a 1936 Charles Trenet melody. Did Noël intend to render an English version of it? He was to adapt the songs of other songwriters in later years, so why not Trenet? But now it's unlikely we shall ever know.

Sail Away (1961) has more cut numbers than any other Coward show, necessitated by his decision to abandon the sub-plot, reallocate key material and generally tighten. Most of the discarded items were carefully kept, with the exception of one with the working title of "Somethin' You Gotta Find Out Yourself."

I have seen references *en passant* to various other song titles without being able to trace the lyrics themselves. It's perfectly possible that some of them fall into the category of "Songs I Mean to Write" but undoubtedly a few were committed to paper, if not to music. It's also perfectly possible that a few appeared under alternative titles. Any help in unearthing them—or any others—would be greatly appreciated. I'd be particularly interested in "Strolling the 'Dilly'."

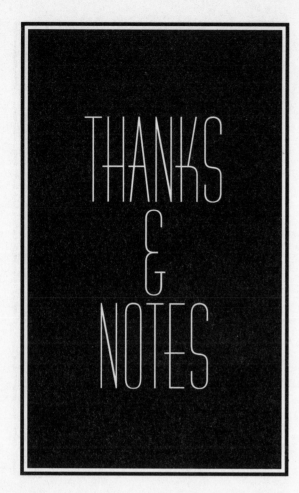

ACKNOWLEDGMENTS

It takes a lot of people to make a compilation like this possible. Here are just a few of the special people I'd like to thank. They know what they did . . .

Marianne Chach (The Shubert Archive); Alan Farley (the ultimate Coward fan); Rosalind Fayne; Timothy Gray; Peter Greenwell; Joan Hirst; Mark Horowitz (Library of Congress—Music Dept.); Marty Jacobs (Museum of the City of New York); Geoffrey Johnson; Kathryn Johnson (British Library); Robert Kimball; John McGlinn; Richard Mangan (Mander & Mitchenson Collection); Hugh Martin; Emma Profitt; Steve Ross; Caroline Underwood (Warner Chappell-UK); Dominic Vlasto.

I am grateful to the following organisations and individuals for permission to quote from or reproduce material in their possession: The estates of Ira Gershwin, Jerome Kern, Johnny Mercer and Cole Porter; John Kander and Fred Ebb.

PHOTO CREDITS

The Mander and Mitchenson Collection: pp. 37, 48, 53, 66, 89, 90, 97, 109, 115, 119, 134, 135, 157, 189, 227, 238, 264, 278, 288, 300, 302, 340; Corbis-Bettmann Archive: 33, 177, 275, 309; Museum of the City of New York: 71, 84, 85, 101, 102, 103; Roddy McDowall: 253; Horst Tappe: 356; PLAYBILL® covers printed by permission of PLAYBILL® Incorporated. (PLAYBILL® is a registered trademark of PLAYBILL® Incorporated, New York, NY). All other photographs and visuals are from the Archive of the Coward Estate. While we have made every effort to trace individual photo credits, the lapse of time has made this impractical in some cases. Should additional information come to light, we shall be pleased to include it in future editions.

Detailed credits are to be found against specific numbers in the INDEX OF SONGS.

A special *Noël Coward Centenary Songbook* will be released in 1999. The following publications are also available: *Noël Coward—Words & Music 1* PVC (Ref: 02078); *Noël Coward—Songs To Amuse* PVC (Ref: 02079); *Bitter Sweet—Vocal Selection* (Ref: 21626); *London Pride* (Ref: 03968). Available from all good music shops through International Music Publications Limited. for more details, telephone Music Mall on 0800 3769100.

NOTES ON SOURCES

The Lyrics of Noël Coward, published in 1965 contains 276 songs. *The Complete Lyrics* has unearthed over 200 more (They are marked * in text.). Some but by no means all of the new material was in the Coward Estate Archives in Switzerland. Joan Hirst, secretary to the Estate and successor to the legendary Lorn Loraine, was able to fill in some of the gaps, as were Norman Hackforth and Peter Greenwell, two of Noel's accompanists. Other missing pieces seemed to arrive by happy happenstance, like the song added to a 1934 American revival of *Bitter Sweet* for one out of town performance that turned up in the dusty recesses of the Shubert Archive in New York. As for the missing items we think we know about, if the combined might of the Estate, Warner/Chappell and the Internet can't flush them out and they do still exist somewhere, perhaps the fact of this book will do the trick—in which case we'll most certainly include them in the next edition.

Carefully preserved as the Archives are—with much of the material in Noël's own hand—many of the lyrics are undated. The teenage Noël was meticulous and copied out his material in notebooks until around 1920, after which he clearly had less time to catalogue.

The 1920s was a prolific song writing period for him but in some cases there is no way of dating a song specifically. Consequently, the material has been grouped under "1920s Miscellaneous" and so on—at least for now. Where the period is uncertain, I have "best guessed" its decade by stylistic and handwriting clues. Should later evidence indicate otherwise, corrected attribution will be published in subsequent editions.

SELECT BIBLIOGRAPHY

Bordman, Gerald
Jerome Kern: his life and music. Oxford, 1980

Castle, Charles
Noël. W. H. Allen, 1972

Citron, Stephen
Noël and Cole: the Sophisticates. Sinclair-Stevenson, 1992

Cochran, Charles B.
—*Showman Looks On.* Guild Books, 1941
—*Cock-A-Doodle-Do.* J. M. Dent, 1941

Coward, Noël
—*Present Indicative.* Heinemann, 1937
—*Future Indefinite.* Heinemann, 1954
—*Autobiography* (also includes *Past Conditional*) Methuen, 1986
—*The Noël Coward Diaries.* Edited by Graham Payn & Sheridan Morley). Weidenfeld & Nicolson, 1982
—*The Noël Coward Song Book.* Methuen, 1984
—*The Lyrics of Noël Coward.* Overlook Press, 1983

Davis, Lee
Bolton and Wodehouse and Kern: The Men Who Made Musical Comedy. James H. Heineman, Inc., 1993

Dean, Basil
The Theatre At War : the story of ENSA. Harrap, 1956

Dietz, Howard
Dancing In the Dark: Words by Howard Dietz. Quadrangle/N.Y. Times Books, 1974

Freeland, Michael
Jerome Kern a biography. Robson Books, 1978

Green, Benny
Let's Face the Music: the Golden Age of Popular Song. Pavilion Books, 1989

Hoare, Philip
Noël Coward: a biography. Sinclair-Stevenson, 1995

Kimball, Robert (Ed.)
—*Cole.* Holt, Rinehart & Winston, 1971
—*The Gershwins* (with Alfred Simon). Atheneum, 1973
—*The Complete Lyrics of Cole Porter.* Knopf, 1983
—*The Complete Lyrics of Lorenz Hart* (with Dorothy Hart). Knopf. 1986
—*The Complete Lyrics of Ira Gershwin.* Knopf, 1993

Lawrence, Gertrude
A Star Danced. W. H. Allen, 1945

Lesley, Cole
Remembered Laughter : the Life of Noël Coward Knopf, 1976

Lesley, Cole, Payn, Graham & Morley, Sheridan
Noël Coward and His Friends. Weidenfeld & Nicolson, 1979

Lillie, Beatrice
Every Other Inch A Lady. Doubleday, 1972

Mander, Raymond & Mitchenson, Joe
—*Theatrical Companion to Coward.* Rockliff, 1957
—*Revue.* Taplinger N.Y. 1971; Peter Davies, 1971

Matthews, Jessie
Over My Shoulder. W. H. Allen, 1974

Morley, Sheridan
A Talent To Amuse. Pavilion Books, 1985

Payn, Graham (with Day, Barry)
My Life With Noël Coward. Applause Books, 1994

Schwartz, Charles
Cole Porter: a biography. The Dial Press, 1977

Sterne, A & de Bear, Archie
The Comic History of the Co-Optimists. London, 1926

INDEX

INDEX OF SONG TITLES

*Indicates previously unpublished.

(Except where explicitly stated, all lyrics are the sole copyright of the Noël Coward Estate)